PRAISE FOR *BONES*

"With the flair of a mystery writer, Dewar explores the conflicting theories as they are influenced by academic and personal jealousies, government interference, ethnic concern, mishandled artifacts—all the human and bureaucratic folly that have gotten in the way of the science. A revealing and informative look not only at the archaeology in question but at the convoluted, intricate, and very human difficulties in 'doing science.'" —*Library Journal*

"Hard, synoptic . . . [Dewar] exposes the rivalries, political agendas, gossip, turf wars, threats, thefts, and outright lies among researchers that still cripple honest investigation of American antiquity." —*Baltimore Sun*

"A well-written and researched book." —*Choice*

"*Bones* not only pulls together the latest insights into the ancient mysteries clouding the origins of the 'First Americans,' [Dewar] does so in clear and lucid prose . . . and adds valuable original thinking. *Bones* lets you enjoy while you learn." —Tony Hillerman, author of *Skinwalkers*

"Sharp writing and strong reporting make *Bones* a compelling . . . take on the controversies inspired by the first Americans." —*Archaeology*

"Elaine Dewar [has] an excellent eye for hidden stories. . . . A fascinating exploration of the political and academic implications of unburied skeletons and the potential information they contain." —Robert McGhee (Curator of Archaeology at the Canadian Museum of Civilization), in the *Toronto Globe and Mail*

"Smoothly written . . . This is all fascinating stuff, and Dewar writes it up with the flair of a good mystery—yet what haunts the reader long after all the new theories have been posited are Dewar's condemnations of the field of archaeological study." —*Kirkus Reviews*

"A compelling account . . . the peopling of the Americas is one of the epic chapters in the human story." —*Maclean's*

"Anyone wanting to know the real state of archaeology and anthropology in the Americas needs to read this book. . . . Dewar peels away fallacy, uncovers hypocrisy, points out spurious logic and faulty reasoning. . . ." —*Ancient American*

"Controversial . . . Dewar's narrative, written with the zest of a travel account, will intrigue amateur archaeologists and readers interested in American Indians." —*Booklist*

# Bones

## DISCOVERING THE FIRST AMERICANS

## Elaine Dewar

CARROLL & GRAF PUBLISHERS
NEW YORK

BONES
*Discovering the First Americans*

Carroll & Graf Publishers
An Imprint of Avalon Publishing Group Inc.
245 West 17th Street
11th Floor
New York, NY 10011

AVALON
publishing group incorporated

Printed in the United States of America
Distributed by Publishers Group West

IN THE STUDY OF LITERATURE, *much usually depends on direct confrontation with a work. Who would dare to approach* A Farewell to Arms *by a synopsis? It is only natural to distrust a literary experience if we have been guided too carefully through it, for the act of reading must provide by itself that literary experience upon which our senses will later work.*

*But the study of science is different. Much like the study of history, it begins with legends and oversimplifications. Then the same ground is revisited, details are added, complexities are engaged, unanswerable questions begin to be posed. A scientific account is a story which can always be retold, for the line of the narrative in scientific writing is to be found in the deepening of the concept.*

— NORMAN MAILER, *Of a Fire on the Moon*

# Contents

Siberia

Bering Strait

Alaska

Arctic Ocean

N

Pacific
Ocean

•Blue Fish Caves

Great Bear
Lake

Greenland

Prince of Wales Island•

Mackenzie R.

Great Slave
Lake

Peace R.

Athabasca R.

Gore Creek•

•Fort McMurray

Okanogan R.

Columbia R.

•Kennewick

Snake R.

•Buhl

•Wanuskewin

•Wizards Beach
•Spirit Cave

C   a   n   a   d   a

United   States

L'Anse-Amour Mound•

Pendejo Cave•   •Clovis

Milton-Thomazi•

•Coteau-du-Lac

Mississippi R.

Mexico

Atlantic   Ocean

# Introduction

T HIS BOOK BEGINS with a simple question. Where did Native Americans come from? I know I was given an answer when I was just a child, before I had learned enough about the world, and enough about how we learn about the world, to even ask the question for myself. This answer was a comfort to immigrants and the children of immigrants as they broke ground, built towns and cities from one end of the hemisphere to the other, and muscled aside the descendants of people who were in the Americas before them. It often popped up before the question could be formed, particularly in those scarce moments of moral hesitation when new immigrants came face to face with those they had displaced, and recognized that Native Americans were suffering and dying even as they, the newcomers, prospered. For more than a century this answer was ready for anyone who needed it: Native Americans came from somewhere else—from Asia. All are descendants of the same immigrant people.

I was born in the middle of the twentieth century on the Great Plains—in the city of Saskatoon, Saskatchewan. I am the grandchild of immigrants from Eastern Europe who arrived there when it was still a frontier called the Northwest Territories. The government of Canada promised free land if my grandparents would go to the Prairies and bust the sod. And so they left the wars and racism and religious hatreds of Russia and Romania, migrating halfway around the globe to the New World. They helped to colonize the beautiful and frigid prairies. Their first homes were sod houses, built of thick squares of turf they cut out of the ground. They were known as pioneers, as if no one had ever been there before them.

If they had regrets about being part of a process that ended the ancient and complex relationship between Native peoples and their lands, I never heard them discuss it. By the time I came along, they were city folk with their own businesses (although my mother's father held fast to his northern farm for many years, not letting go even after his tractor fell on him, when he was eighty-five). Native people had been pushed so far to the margins of society that my contact with them came mainly at fairs and parades and multicultural festivals where ethnics of all sorts came forward, in costume, to sing their foreign songs and dance their foreign dances. We were all immigrants together in the New World and therefore in my mind we were equivalent: we came from Eastern Europe, they came from Asia. I did the hora, they had their powwows, their drums and their fancy dancing. We came on boats and built the railroads. Exactly how they came was a matter to be determined by science because they had no written histories, just stories about their origins, encased in languages that no one but the old people spoke anymore. Governments and church schools tried to wipe those languages away because they interfered with the process of making Native Americans just like everybody else. If the Native peoples were unhappy about that we didn't hear of it. (How could they complain? Status Indians in Canada only got the right to vote in 1960.) It was up to science to dig up the Truth—and teach it to them.

As I grew older, as the wail of Native songs and the beat of Native drums became as familiar to me as the whine of the bag-pipes and the thump of a tambour, as I acquired bits and pieces of Native clothing in my wardrobe, the stock answer to my simple question morphed from a single word ("Asia") into a complex story, rich with significant detail. Native Americans originated in northern Asia; they did not even represent their own particular category of the Races of Man as I had once been taught, they were just another Mongoloid people, like the Chinese or the Japanese except less culturally developed. (Well, yes, it was acknowledged that there had been great urban civilizations in Mexico and Central America and Peru, but weren't they fairly recent and anyway, hadn't they crumbled under the onslaught of European civilization?) The issue of when they came was tied to the issue of how they came. The first of these Mongoloid people came to the Americas over the Bering Strait, we were told, at the end of the last ice age. They migrated across the land bridge up there, just before it disappeared under rising oceans, and made their way down into the continent through what was called the "Ice-Free Corridor"—those areas of the Yukon, Northwest Territories, Alberta and Saskatchewan where the two great ice sheets that covered Canada at the height of the glaciation had never met. And how did they get here? They walked.

I know I rebelled briefly when this story was first revealed to me. It was on a class trip to Regina, where we were introduced to the newly built provincial Museum of Natural History. There was a diorama at the museum with representations of the first human beings in Saskatchewan. It was set up to look like a kind of cave or shelter. The Paleo-Indians, a man and a woman dressed in raggedy furs, their arms and legs bare, stood with their backs to the cave hearth and looked out on a broad, dreary plain. They were dark, their hair gross and black and their foreheads low and rugged, as if to signify that while these were people, they weren't really like us, they were a primitive version of us. The world outside their cave was terrifying, populated by gigantic buffalo and great prowling cats. These primitives had somehow made their way from the top of the world to southern Saskatchewan, carving out an existence with nothing to help them but some great stone spear points tied to heavy sticks.

Oh sure, I thought, with their arms bare like that they'd have lasted about ten minutes in a January blizzard, and where on the Prairies would they have found a cave?

I didn't think this diorama could be right, but its images stuck with me anyway. I stashed them in that niche in my mind where admiration and fascination had begun to grow: these people had lived a free life, a different life from mine. Some part of these images must surely have come from evidence provided by science, or it would never have been shown to the public in a museum. The story also had a certain power. It intrigued me almost as much as the stories I was reading about ancient Greece and Rome. It echoed what I saw on television westerns, stories about dangerous and devilish or noble Native Americans. One could imagine that these were Tonto's larger-than-life ancestors, who had fought their way across Arctic wastes, mountain glaciers, and frigid Prairies, killing gigantic Ice Age animals like saber-toothed tigers as they went. This voyage made my grandparents' trek from Eastern Europe seem small by comparison. Their way had been smoothed, after all, by European technologies. My father's father was a blacksmith who helped build the Grand Trunk Railway and who, before he was done with life, built as a hobby Saskatoon's first electric car. I used to ride around in it in parades. The disciplined control of metallurgy, electricity, nuclear power, science defined us: tenacity, brute strength, stoicism defined them.

This answer was complex enough to shape and frame and limit my questions for many years. It never occurred to me that it had been steeped in the dark, bitter tea of racism. I accepted it before I understood the first thing about how frames of reference create the vector of inquiry. I forgot there was a question.

The process of making this book began when the question returned—many years after I first learned these answers. I had long since left Saskatchewan and taken up my adult life in Toronto. I had become a journalist, a person who pokes into things for a living, sorting and sifting and trying to make patterns out of various phenomena. I had been battle-tested in the course of various investigations: I had learned well how one can be trapped by a question, hobbled in one's understanding of another's circumstance by unnoticed assumptions. I had a lifelong interest in archaeology, but had never written about it—there just never seemed to be a story I needed to tell, or an editor who wanted to hear it, and besides, who had ever heard anything of interest about the less-than-monumental archaeology of Southern Ontario? But I had travelled widely and done a book on Brazilian Native Americans and their impact on North American environmentalists, so I knew enough of the anthropological literature from South America to be deeply interested in the prehistory of the Americas. I had followed the debate on climate change and knew something of what scientists were discovering about how the last ice age ended. Little by little, and following one trail after another, I had gathered up the pieces of a puzzle without really understanding that there *was* one, until one morning in my garden I found a very odd, very large bone.

In the process of poking into things, I had left behind the awe I once felt for the authority of scientists. I had learned that scientific investigation is a very human enterprise. Science is a method of inquiry, it is also a framework to hang queries and answers on, it is as mutable as any substance at the right temperature and pressure, and it is carried out by men and women who make mistakes. They are motivated by the same demons and dreams that goad the rest of us. There is good science and bad, just as there is good journalism, bad fiction, wretched law. Good scientists ask nice, tight questions that produce precise predictions, which can then be tested and disproved. Poor scientists pile inference on inference and create amorphous theories that may arouse interest and attract money, but in the end merely confuse. Great scientists intuit and test their way to a framework unimagined before, and they always make a good story.

Many, many stories opened up for me as I pursued this question: where did Native Americans come from? I read widely and traveled far. I became uncomfortably familiar with the remains of the dead, and the fears of the living. I went from Fort McMurray in northern Alberta to the arid plains of the Brazilian state of Piaui, from skull-and-bones-lined offices in the Smithsonian Institution to the basement lab of an archaeologist in Washington State who wondered if the FBI was going to come for him. I spent too many hours in airplanes, jounced over back roads from Minas Gerais to Nevada, slept on too many buses across North America. I learned that archaeological science and physical anthropology were invented by adventurers digging for treasure in ancient graves. The current practitioners are fractious and litigious. They are hampered in their outlook by their acceptance of authority, by national boundaries, by possessiveness about finds, by conservative gatekeepers who control the flow of research money, by their fear of stepping one inch beyond their expertise onto someone else's turf, and by the organized outrage of Native Americans. They are enlivened by new physical, geological, biological and genetic technologies and computer models, which are teaching them undreamed of things about the human journey. Everywhere, these practitioners are growing more specialized, and as they do so, less able to read one another's work and make use of it.

So why, you might ask, should a journalist investigate a question that has bedeviled scientists for 150 years? Journalists are willing to go anywhere, to be passionate fools, to ask innocent questions, to ignore barriers, to look for patterns that connect disciplines and solitudes, and to have no vested interest in anybody's intellectual capital. Science must be public and transparent or it loses all meaning, and journalists bring evidence out of the lab and spread it before the general public. Journalists are the last of the generalists. We are also a little like bees. We dip into everybody's business and carry the news along. We cross-pollinate. We fertilize. Sometimes, we sting.

The experience of researching this book has stripped me of many answers. I learned how the old belief about the path used by the First Americans to enter the continent has been disproved. In the place of answers, I learned new questions about who we are, how we are made, why we change, and the impact our communities have on each one of us. Those of you who read this account will find yourselves asking questions I have not thought of, but here are some I know you will ask. What if Native Americans are right in their belief that they have always been in the Americas and did not migrate to the New World at the end of the Ice Age? What if the New World's human story is as long and complicated as that of the Old? What if the New World and the Old World have always been one?

The new answers will be found where we should have looked first—in ancient parables, in the damp old earth, and written in the bones of our departed elders—if we have the wit and the courage to read them.

# Part One

*T*he hand of the lord was upon me, and the Lord carried me out in a spirit, and set me down in the midst of the valley, and it was full of bones; and He caused me to pass by them round about, and, behold, there were very many in the open valley; and, lo, they were very dry. And He said unto me: "Son of man, can these bones live?" And I answered: "O Lord God, Thou knowest." Then He said unto me: "Prophesy over these bones, and say unto them: O ye dry bones, hear the word of the Lord. Thus saith the Lord God unto these bones: Behold, I will cause breath to enter into you, and ye shall live. And I will lay sinews upon you, and will bring up flesh upon you, and cover you with skin, and put breath in you, and ye shall live; and ye shall know that I am the Lord."

So I prophesied as I was commanded; and as I prophesied, there was a noise, and behold, a commotion, and the bones came together, bone to its bone. And I beheld, and, lo, there were sinews upon them, and flesh came up, and skin covered them above; but there was no breath in them. Then said He unto me, "Prophesy unto the breath, prophesy, son of man, and say to the breath: Thus saith the Lord God: Come from the four winds,

*O breath, and breathe upon these slain, that they may live." So I prophesied as He commanded me, and the breath came into them, and they lived, and stood up upon their feet, an exceeding great host. Then He said unto me, "Son of man, these bones are the whole house of Israel; behold, they say: Our bones are dried up, and our hope is lost; we are clean cut off. Therefore prophesy, and say unto them: Thus saith the Lord God: Behold, I will open your graves, and cause you to come up out of your graves, O My people; and I will bring you into the land of Israel. And ye shall know that I am the Lord, when I have opened your graves, and caused you to come up out of your graves, O My people. And I will put My spirit in you, and ye shall live, and I will place you in your own land; and ye shall know that I the Lord have spoken, and performed it, saith the Lord."*

— EZEKIEL 37: 1–14

# 1

# Asian Origins?

## Clovis First Across the Bering Strait

O NE SATURDAY MORNING in the spring of 1995 I was out in front of my house, grovelling in the dirt, trying to wrench beauty and order out of nothing. Moving this bush, cutting out that hunk of sod, I sliced my hands on coal clinkers and broken glass, pieces of sharp pottery and bits of metal. The earth belched up an old bone near the roots of the forsythia. It was dark, dank, redolent of mildew and rot and it rolled lasciviously among the lilies of the valley. Human or animal? It was very large, very heavy. Its ends had been cut neatly, and they were smooth, as if they'd been polished. No one would do that to a human bone. It must be animal, but what kind of animal had bones so dense? I tossed it toward the porch. It landed in a hill of mouldy leaves and vanished from sight, but I couldn't stop thinking about it. It was odd to find such a large bone in the middle of a city garden, odder still that it had been worked like that.

The recognition that I had no knowledge of the prehistory of where I live, no idea who was here before me, came up out of the ground with the bone. I live in a First World War-era house on a quiet street at the top of a high ridge that runs across the center of Toronto. Davenport Road follows its curve down below: I'd read the heritage plaque near the bus stop down the hill that said this ridge was once the beach of Glacial Lake

Iroquois, and the road had once been a major Native trail. That was all I knew.

As the maple trees unfurled their acid-green leaves from their hairy pouches, the bone reappeared, as if to say "Remember me?" I buried it deep, and deeper still. But with each grunt over my spade, there it was again, like a reproof. Eventually I asked around among the neighbors. Had anyone found anything like it? I learned that a mastodon or mammoth's bone, a relic of the first warming at the end of the Ice Age, had been found straight down the hill from my house.[1] Maybe my bone was a piece of some ancient Ice Age animal. But someone had cut it, someone had polished its ends. So when, I wondered, did men and women get to Southern Ontario? One Native treaty discussed on the front pages of the newspapers said that these particular Native people had been in their homeland "since time immemorial."[2] But this obviously had a limit, defined by the glacial ice.

The former Native trail below the hill runs out toward the Niagara Escarpment, a huge limestone spine connecting the western edge of Lake Ontario and the eastern lobe of Lake Huron. I had become interested in that escarpment, which bore on its cliff faces long-lived trees that were a biological record of past shifts in temperature. When I wasn't sweating over my garden, I was working on a project about climate change.[3] What evidence is there that man is actually changing the climate of the planet? How can science separate the signature of the hand of man from natural processes? What caused the last ice age to start and stop? Surely the earth had its own powerful rhythms independent of human behavior?

These questions led me to experts on the ebb and flow of climates past, who told me about the many ice ages that have occurred over millions of years—the ice age state has long been the dominant climate pattern for the planet. Each period of glaciation has lasted up to 100,000 years: warm periods, such as the one we are now enjoying, have been brief interregnums of about ten to fifteen thousand years' duration. These fluctuations between warmth and ice are like an extremely long form of seasonality, possibly brought on by eccentricities in the earth's orbit and spin. As in all things related to climate, no ice age has been exactly like any other. The last one was the worst. The Laurentide ice sheet, which formed on the northeast side of North America, waxed and waned repeatedly (as did the Cordilleran ice sheet over the Rocky Mountains) but just before the last ice age came to an end, the Laurentide sheet stretched farther than the ice ever had before. There was a carapace about two kilometers thick all the way from the high Arctic to New York City, from east of Newfoundland to the foothills of the Rocky Mountains. When it melted away, about 12,000 years ago, it left behind a flattened-out landscape covered by vast, ice-dammed lakes. Utterly empty, ice-scourged and ground up, Southern Ontario was rapidly colonized by insects, grasses, trees, mammoths, mastodons, horses, giant bison and caribou. Then, within a short span of time, these Ice Age animals all vanished. The landscape has been reshaping itself ever since, climbing higher in a process known as isostatic rebound.[4] These changes at the end of the Pleistocene (as the last cool period was called) were sudden. Ice cores taken from the Greenland glaciers, which never melted through millions of years of climate fluctuation, showed that temperatures rose sharply, then fell, then rose steeply again, and that the carbon dioxide in the atmosphere fluctuated very quickly too.[5] No one knows why.

I visited a biologist, Doug Larson, who reads the patterns of climate change in the growth rings of the ancient trees cloaking the escarpment's face. What about people? I asked him. What does the archaeological record show? When did people first come to Southern Ontario, the very center of the North American continent? Larson sent me to Dr. William Finlayson, then the director of the London Museum of Archaeology.

Finlayson laid out the chronology of culture change.[6] Archaeologists had worked back from the historical record left by the Jesuits, the first Europeans to study and write about the

Iroquoians they found in Southern Ontario. The Iroquoians were living in villages of up to 2,000 people when the French explorers arrived around 1615. The Iroquoians grew corn, beans, squash, sunflowers and tobacco. Their precursors had been pottery makers, who hunted, fished and gathered. These Woodland people (as they were called) had replaced the Archaic hunter-gatherers, who had themselves replaced the Paleo-Indians who were the First Americans, the first people to populate this New World. The time span between the Iroquoians and the Paleo-Indians was about 11,000 years. Only spear points and other tools, along with the occasional fragment of burned bone, marked the Paleo-Indians' passage in Ontario. There was nothing like the rich archaeological record found in Europe and Asia, which dated far back into the Pleistocene.[7]

But how could these people have made their way so far south and east of Alaska, almost as quickly as the ice withdrew? Archaeologists knew much more about later people than about the Paleo-Indians, Finlayson told me. They could draw inferences about the Iroquoians and their ancestors from what they found in abandoned middens, from the shadows of postholes and sweat lodges left in the soil. Finlayson described their longhouses, their crenelated pottery and their 1,500-year-old methods of agriculture.[8] He showed me fragments of ceramic pots, bone hair combs, flexible bone armbands. He showed me tobacco pipes with bowls like heads, with great, noble-nosed faces carved in profile. The French Jesuits recorded minor and major events of the complex societies they encountered, and also something of the politics, the beliefs, the division of labor and ownership by gender. Finlayson and his colleagues had traced these societies back in time. Women farmed and owned the houses. Men lived with their wives' families: they hunted and built the villages and made war. At periodic festivals held for the dead, individual burials were dug up and carried to a newly excavated pit and the commingled bones reburied all at once. It was believed that this mixture of the bones of the dead promoted harmony among the living. Villages moved every ten to fifteen years—the villagers regularly burned new areas of the forest to open them for farming.

Finlayson's description of the way of life in Ontario a thousand years ago matched in many details accounts by modern anthropologists of life among tribes in the Amazon rain forest. It was all so familiar—farming corn (in the rain forest they also grow manioc and potatoes), using fire to clear and fertilize the land, households run by women farmers, decorative styles of pottery passed mother to daughter.[9] How could there be such similarities between cultures a thousand years and eight thousand kilometers apart?

Finlayson wasn't familiar with Amazonian anthropology. He spoke more comfortably of North American trade networks, of ancient Viking silver found on a dig near Toronto, of the drilled conch shells that came all the way from the Gulf of Mexico found in local burials, and the ear spools modeled on those worn by the mound builders of the lower Mississippi River, who in turn took their inspiration from Mexico. Copper was used all over Southern Ontario to make tools; it came from mines dug north of Superior and from Cobalt.

This isn't common knowledge, Finlayson explained, because the practice of archaeology in Ontario has become a disgrace. There are laws and rules, similar to laws and rules found throughout the rest of Canada and the United States, which have turned archaeology into a kind of handmaiden of industrial development. All archaeology has to be done under license, and is supposed to be documented in reports to preserve the knowledge of the past for the future[10] but the whole system is a sham. Very little archaeology is published in peer-reviewed journals. Most of it is done by contract archaeologists who "salvage" sites about to be destroyed by development, which means they dig them, remove what they find and write up their findings. But then their reports languish in a provincial archive closed to the public, unavailable even to academics like Finlayson without the express permission of the reports' authors. Permission to see artifacts or to read and cite the reports is regularly withheld. Thousands of digs have been done under these rules in the last twenty years. There is no way to know exactly what has been found. Finlayson calculated that he'd pulled 1.5 million artifacts out of the ground himself. He has a well designed storage system in his museum[11] but other archaeologists keep these artifacts in basements, lockers, maybe worse. Things keep going missing. Little information from the thousands of digs done under license since the 1970s has found its way to the public domain.

I dug into it and, sure enough, Finlayson was right. The archive was full of reports, marked confidential, that had never seen the light of day in peer-reviewed journals—the normal method for communicating new finds in any scientific discipline. Important reports were missing, artifacts could not be found. Artifacts dug in the archaeologically rich Toronto area by the province's own bureaucrats had been stored in an unprotected, unheated, vermin-ridden public storage facility—as if they were no more important than old furniture being stashed between moves.[12]

Private consultants, developers, looters, provincial universities and foreign museums all have pieces of Ontario's prehistory scattered among their collections. The Royal Ontario Museum (ROM) is one of the largest and best maintained. The ROM is one of the great institutions in the Americas created to be the public's memory, on a par with the Peabody Museum at Harvard and New York's American Museum of Natural History. The ROM's American materials come from the whole hemisphere. The head of anthropology, Mima Kapches, took me into the labs of the main building and opened drawers for me. The riches she showed were spectacular, but rarely seen by the public and lately, due to budget cuts, available only with difficulty to academics. The permanent exhibit on Native Americans languished in a small room in the basement.

That basement room was a revelation to me. It had the same sort of diorama I remembered from my childhood in Saskatchewan—a group of buckskin-clad people, life size, butchering a large animal took up one whole wall of the exhibit. But the other displays clearly showed that my unexamined notions about the simplicity of ancient Native cultures in the Americas were wrong. This room provided evidence of striking technological ingenuity and ancient mastery of the continent. A gigantic quarry north of Thunder Bay had been used by Paleo-Indians from all over the Great Lakes region. Copper from mines in the north had also been found in the Rockies, southern Mississippi and the St. Lawrence. The ROM's display of copper tools said they were from the Archaic period, and therefore about 5,000 years old. They had been made by the annealing process, cold hammered. They were strikingly sophisticated, beautifully crafted. A provincial archaeologist later told me of an Archaic copper woodworking tool in his care that a Native woman had found on a beach at the western tip of Lake Superior. He'd been amazed to see there was a piece of wood still attached to it. The wood fragment had been radiocarbon dated and turned out to be about 6,800 radiocarbon years old.[13] The copper tool had been made almost 3,000 years *before* metal tools were forged in Europe, only about 1,500 years after Paleo-Indians were supposed to have faded from the scene. The Americas, I'd always assumed, lagged way behind the timelines of African and European development. The history of metalworking in Ontario turned those notions upside down.

Why, I asked the archaeologist, wasn't the fantastic antiquity of metalworking in North America widely known?

Well, he replied sardonically, do you read a journal called *Radiocarbon?*

Archaeologists find only a tiny fraction of the things human beings have made over the millennia, mainly stone fragments and sometimes bits of metal or burned wood and bones that, by some fluke of nature, have been preserved. The earth usually eats its dead—organic remains rarely survive for long—and so our picture of the lives of those who went before us has accumulated in a biased way.[14] Scientists have inferred most of what we think we know about the first people who lived and died in the Americas from the stones they worked, the charcoal remains of their camp fires and the graves we've stumbled on.

And yet, from this scant evidence, a story of who came first to the New World had been crafted. With some refinements, it was the same story I had heard as a young student. Most archaeologists I spoke to, both academics and those in private business, could recite it, often prefacing their comments with the word "accepted." It is accepted that no hominids ancestral to modern humans entered the Americas.[15] While skeletons of *Homo erectus*, the primate from whom we are supposedly descended, have been found in Africa and Asia, no *erectus* remains have ever showed up in the Western Hemisphere. Modern humans date back only 200,000 years—about two ice-age cycles.[16] The oldest modern human bones discovered outside Africa were excavated at a place called Qafzeh in Israel: they are about 100,000 years old.[17] Archaeologists believe that modern people arrived in Australia at least 50,000 years ago, crossing a short stretch of open ocean to get there.[18] Modern human artifacts of the same antiquity have been found in Indonesia and other parts of East Asia. Modern people first made their way into Europe between 45,000 and 35,000 years ago.[19] According to the story, none of these early modern travelers found their way to the Bering Strait, the Secret Gate to the West, until thousands more years had passed.

It is still accepted that the First Americans came on foot from Siberia, over the Bering Strait when it was dry land during the last ice age.[20] At glacial maximum, which was thought to be around 18,000 years ago in Europe, the water level of the oceans was lower than it is now by 120 meters—the water was locked up on land as ice.[21] Asia was then connected to America by a ribbon of tundra 1,500 kilometers wide. It is accepted that the first North Asians to enter the Americas simply followed herds of buffalo, caribou or mammoths over the dry strait into Alaska. Eventually they worked their way down through an ice-free corridor along the Mackenzie River Valley into what is now Alberta and Saskatchewan. Then they fanned out over the entire Americas, including Southern Ontario. The ROM's basement room had a big map that laid this story out, with arrows illustrating the movement of people into the continent.

These Paleo-Indians came equipped with the knowledge of how to sew fur clothing to protect themselves from the vicious, scouring winds of the Arctic tundra; otherwise, they could never have survived a winter at the top of the world.[22] Further, it is accepted that when these modern North Asians finally burst into Alaska, they found themselves in the Garden of Eden. The huge Ice Age animals in the Americas had no fear of human predators because they had no knowledge of them: they allowed themselves to be slaughtered wholesale. The First Americans had a brand new hemisphere full of wildlife all to themselves, and they soon spread from one end of it to the other. The Bering Strait acted as a kind of disease filter, letting in man and beast but keeping out almost all of the tropical parasitical diseases that preyed upon them.[23]

Oddly enough, most of the sites with the oldest dates had been found in the lower United States, not Alaska. In New Mexico, near the town of Clovis, sites with distinctive stone spearheads (later called Clovis points) were found, early in the century. The Paleo-Indians had crafted these large, beautiful, fluted stone tools, which they tied onto a weighted throwing device called an atlatl. No one had been able to locate the place where this technology was invented; it seemed to have spread across the continent all at once. Like Pallas Athene popping from the forehead of Zeus, Clovis culture was suddenly everywhere—at 11,500 Before Present. (Before Present, or BP, is the term used to refer to radiocarbon years, which differ from and only approximate actual calendar years. All dates in this book are radiocarbon dates unless otherwise noted.) The ROM's exhibit said the First Ontarians,

Clovis people, had worked their way around the ice and moved into the province from the south.

Stranger still, no Clovis tools had ever been found in archaeological sites in Siberia or anywhere else in Asia. Nor had they been found in Alaska: the crafting of spear points there was similar to Folsom technology, which came after Clovis.[24] (Folsom spear points were also named for the place they were first found— Folsom, New Mexico—in 1926.) Folsom spear points, fixed in the bones of a now extinct bison, were long ago accepted as clear evidence that the First Americans got their living by killing animals that died off at the end of the Ice Age. In fact, it was this find that provoked the first big revolution in American archaeology. Previously, it had been accepted that people first came to the New World only about 4,000 years before Columbus (in other words, at about the time when, according to creationists, God created humans).[25] The Folsom find pushed the earliest accepted date for man coming to America back to about 10,000 BC. Folsom-like points have been found in Southern Ontario, just as they have all over the southern United States.

Paleo-Indian experts mainly concerned themselves with arguments over how many migrations of North Asians had made it to the Americas. Some said one wave, others said up to four. One single-wave theorist, the American scholar Paul Martin, calculated that people could easily have reached the very tip of Tierra del Fuego within about a thousand years of their entry into Alaska. He also argued that human beings were responsible for the swift demise of all the large Ice Age fauna throughout the hemisphere. In Martin's view, men hunted these animals to extinction within a matter of a few thousand years, which explained their sudden, almost catastrophic disappearance from the paleontological record.

Most of the archaeologists I spoke to still believe that the First Americans walked into the New World. They acknowledge that some scholars, long ago, proposed ocean crossings between Europe and the New World, but this idea has never been accepted. It is by contrast widely accepted that no Europeans reached the Americas until the Vikings arrived in Newfoundland. I asked various archaeologists their opinion of Thor Heyerdahl's theory of ocean voyages by Sumerians in reed boats, and of the Harvard biologist and epigrapher Barry Fell's claim to have found ancient Celtic runes carved into rocks in eastern North America. The mere mention of Fell or Heyerdahl's names quickly raised a red flag. There is no evidence, I was firmly told, of reed boats crossing from Sumer, let alone boat travel in the Americas at the end of the Ice Age. Science rules in archaeology, I was reminded, and science requires physical evidence sufficient that inferences can be safely drawn.

Science is a house undergoing constant renovation, a narrative constantly turning, and yet this story of the First Americans had held its shape for more than forty years. "Accepted" should mean that results have been replicated so often that the basic conclusions are unassailable. Yet there was not much evidence offered to support claims made about the First Americans.

Science is supposed to be about evidence; it is organized observation of the world. A construct or theory or narrative is built up from the public labors of those who've gone before and made records of their findings. Their work, once successfully tested, is believed—until it's overturned. Science is a competition to be the first to get it right, but the interpretation of evidence keeps shifting. Evidence accumulates, and the new ideas it spawns lead scientists to look down new pathways. Eventually someone comes along who puts the new evidence together with the old in a clever way, and the framework is recrafted again. The resulting construct is not the Truth: it's just the best one can do with what one has. Science is therefore both conservative and radical.

The ideology implicit in science is that there is virtue in open and free inquiry. This belief also supports much of what we do in law and politics in the West. I have learned to wear this ideology like a good suit: it permits me entry everywhere and allows me to question everything, but I am expected to work within its rules of argument. Those rules can be stated this way: a heap of instances may lead to an inference, but they can never be proof; association is not the same as causation; lack of evidence cannot be construed as proof of absence; a good investigator knows she is biased and borrows or invents experimental methods to take that into account; all methods and all results, no matter how contradictory or disappointing, must be publicly reported so that theories can be disproved or supported, and new evidence woven into the larger construct.

This is not the only way to experience and report on the world. Most of us rely on intuition as much as orderly observation. Intuition is the sudden recognition of innate patterns, linking seemingly disconnected items or events into unexpected and often fruitful configurations. We also put our faith in luck. Luck is a form of chance that works in our favor if we happen to be in the right place at the right time. It is not a factor in the ideology of science (although it is very much a factor in the practice of journalism), yet every scientist (like every journalist) hopes to be lucky, to hit upon the right question or the right technique early, and get answers that lift the shroud of ambiguity. Not that ambiguity is a bad thing; it points to the place where discontinuous domains layer over each other, or where two narratives run close to each other but can't be merged.

Given these rules, if archaeology is a science, why had so much of it languished unpublished in government archives and private basements? Without publication and independent evaluation, what use are these reports? Similarly, why had the story of the First Americans been built on such a small base of evidence? And, given that the evidence base was small, why wasn't there more dissent?

This story of the First Americans turned out to be deeply mired in politics of the worst sort—land politics, religious politics, academic politics. For one thing, many Native people consider the Beringian Walk to be a ridiculous theory. According to their oral histories and beliefs, they have been in the Americas for time immemorial. They are not just another group of immigrants. Further, they see this story as something invented to undermine their land claims.

A small number of archaeologists also quarrel with the story. Few of these dissenters directly question the Beringian Walk, although some wonder whether there really was an ice-free corridor and suggest instead that people might have made their way down the Pacific coast. Most are concerned that the timing attributed to the first entry is wrong. They are critical of the idea that the Clovis culture was the earliest in the Americas. They believe there is evidence that other cultures arrived first. The ROM, in a corner of its Native American room, has small maps showing the locations of two dissenters' finds. One deals with the evidence found on Lake Huron's Manitoulin Island by the now deceased archaeologist Tom Lee, at a site called Sheguiandah, in the early 1950s. Lee recovered ancient tools at a depth suggesting they were more than 70,000 years old. The ROM's display makes it quite clear that this claim is not accepted. Beside it, there is a map showing a discovery at a rock shelter in Pennsylvania called Meadowcroft. Various artifacts found there have been dated to about 14,000 years BP, but these findings too, according to the ROM, are not accepted.

Several of the dissenters I spoke to work in Canada; they knew of other archaeological finds in the Americas that had radiocarbon dates older than 11,500 BP, and of sites with ancient dates that had no Clovis tools. Two of these sites are in northern Canada, and one is in southern Chile. In 1966 a team of scientists from the University of Toronto and the National Museum of Canada (now the Canadian Museum of Civilization) found artifacts made out of ancient animal bones in the gravel beds of the

Old Crow River in the Yukon. Four critical artifacts were found.
One was a flesher, a tool used for stripping meat, made of caribou
bone. The others had been made of the flaked bones of a mammoth. The flesher looked suspiciously like an artifact from a
relatively recent period, but all these bones had been directly
radiocarbon dated at about 27,000 BP.[26] A few years later, at
Blue Fish Caves in the Yukon Territory, other researchers with
the National Museum found the bones of many Ice Age mammals, some of which had also been made into tools. The
researcher who dug Blue Fish Caves, Jacques Cinq-Mars, also
found tiny pieces of stone that he claimed were part of an extremely ancient toolmaking tradition found at around 10,500 BP
in Alaska and at 18,000 BP in Siberia. Other artifact dates on this
site went back to 25,000 BP.[27]

Then there was Tom Dillehay's discovery. Dillehay, a professor at the University of Kentucky, had worked a site known as
Monte Verde in southern Chile back in the late 1970s and early
1980s. He claimed to have proof of an extremely ancient human
settlement. The evidence he pulled out of the ground included
fragments of wooden tools, clay-lined braziers, all kinds of floral
remains, twists of cordage, a human footprint, and even a human
bone. The carbonized material on the site had been radiocarbon
dated to around 12,500 BP, a thousand years earlier than the oldest Clovis sites in North America.[28]

The two Canadian discoveries were in an area far to the north
that had never been covered by the big ice sheets. Their proponents suggested that early man had come to the Americas from
Asia and holed up in these ice-free places until the glaciers parted,
opening the way south. Monte Verde, on the other hand, was
near the southern tip of South America, just twenty kilometers up
a river from the Pacific coast. No explanation was offered as to
how the First Americans might have got there.

These finds were all disputed. Old Crow's flesher and three
other worked bone artifacts had since been redated by newer and
more reliable techniques: they turned out to be between 3,000

and 1,350 years old.[29] Cinq-Mars has still not published all his findings in peer-reviewed journals more than twenty years after completing the dig. Tom Dillehay's work stood at the center of a heated debate. One enormous volume of his evidence, titled *Monte Verde: A Late Pleistocene Settlement in Chile*, was published in 1989 through the Smithsonian Institution and another was on the way.[30] Some said Dillehay's interpretations of his data were questionable. His supporters claimed he'd broken open the dead hand strangling American archaeology, blowing away a settled orthodoxy that was incapable of explaining the facts in the ground and pulling down the artificially conservative house erected on the back of Clovis, over seventy years ago.

Dissenting Canadian researchers thrummed the themes of suppression and arrogance as an explanation of why their alternative claims are not accepted. The Americans are obsessed with their own material, I was told. They pay no attention to anything outside their own borders, they're ignorant of what is being found and published in Canada or South America because they don't trust anything published outside their own learned journals; besides, most of them only read English. It was lucky for Dillehay that he was an American, I was told—otherwise he never would have got to first base. And what about American researcher Anna Roosevelt's site in the Amazon? If I was looking for old, they said, I should investigate Scotty MacNeish's site at Pendejo Cave in New Mexico. And if I was really interested in who got here first, I should talk to a researcher in Brazil, Niéde Guidon, who insists she has dates going back 50,000 years.

But not all Canadians were dissenters. Check out the Smithsonian's Web site, said one senior researcher at the Museum of Civilization in Ottawa. I could tell from his voice that he found the dissenters' views ridiculous. The Smithsonian's Web site, he said, argued that Clovis technology was similar to a stone technology found in southern France and Spain on sites more than 25,000 years old. Dennis Stanford, a Smithsonian scientist who had encouraged Dillehay, was daring to suggest this Solutrean culture was actually the precursor of the American Clovis technology, that somehow Solutreans had come to America across the North Atlantic, that Europeans, in other words, were the First Americans. The researcher said it was all a great circle: this Solutrean connection had been raised more than sixty years ago by an archaeologist named Emerson Greenman and had been talked about fifty years before that, too.[31]

It was about this point that I began to think (naively) that this whole issue could best be resolved by the study and dating of human bones. Surely dating human remains would be the only certain way to settle the matters of timing of entry and place of origin.

There are no human remains in the Americas that date back more than 10,000 years, I was told. This absence of finds confirmed the majority in their view that people didn't arrive in the Americas until after the Ice Age. If they'd been here, their remains would have been found by now. Those remains that have been found are clearly North Asian, Mongoloid, in their form.

I'd just put my finger on the flaw in this argument (absence of evidence cannot be used as evidence of absence) when I heard about the ancient Caucasoid skeleton found at Kennewick, Washington.

# Bones 101

## A Sordid History Begets a Compromised Science

O NE WARM JULY night in 1996, a young man named William Thomas waded with his buddy into the shallow, murky waters of the Columbia River in the city of Kennewick, Washington. He was trying to get a better vantage point from which to watch the annual boat races at Columbia Park. Looking down, he saw a white rock shaped like a human skull in the muddy river bottom. He thought he'd use it to scare the crap out of his friend. He reached down, grabbed, pulled, heard the sucking sound of the river muck as it came loose. As he was brandishing it over his head, he realized that it actually *was* a skull. He also saw a long bone sticking up from the mud. He and his friend stashed the remains on the riverbank, went off for a few drinks, then did their civic duty and called the police.

These bones, and some others the police later found floating along the edge of the park's beach, were taken by the Benton County coroner, Floyd Johnson, to a local archaeological contractor and physical anthropologist, James Chatters. Chatters' task was to examine the bones and determine whether the man had died recently, and if so whether from natural causes, by misadventure, or means more foul. Chatters laid the bones out on his worktable and quickly decided they were the remains of a gracile (meaning slim), long-headed white male of more than fifty years of age. But certain aspects of the skeleton were puzzling. For one thing, the teeth were worn, which could mean he had been a nineteenth-century settler who ate a lot of stone-ground grains. And there was something lodged in the pelvic bone that had healed over. Chatters took the bone to the local hospital and had it X-rayed. Whatever was stuck in the pelvis, the X-rays showed nothing; they went right through it as they would through stone. He had the bone CT scanned, which revealed a stone arrowhead that the bone had grown over. Chatters recognized it as a Cascade point, a style found in the Pacific Northwest and tentatively dated between 8000 and 7000 BP. None of this made any sense.

With the coroner's authorization, Chatters sent a sample of bone to the University of California, Riverside, for radiocarbon dating. In August, a month after the bones had been brought to him, word came back from University of California—this Caucasoid-like man, as Chatters had begun to characterize him, had died about 8400 BP in the interior of Washington State.

The mayor of Kennewick and the coroner held a news conference. The press swarmed. To those uninitiated in the arcana of physical anthropology, putting "Euro-American" features together with such an ancient date was the virtual equivalent of saying Caucasians discovered America 8,000 years before Columbus. The skeleton got a name—the Ancient One, or Kennewick Man. The United States Army Corps of Engineers, near whose land some of these remains were found and who had given Chatters an archaeological permit to hunt for more of the bones in their jurisdiction, quickly came to attention. Local Native Americans demanded the return of these remains to them, citing the Native American Graves Protection and Repatriation Act (NAGPRA). Under this 1990 U.S. federal law, Native American remains found on federal lands must be turned over to the closest culturally affiliated tribe recognized by the United States.[1] Within days of the press conference, the bones were abruptly removed from Chatters' lab and locked up by the U.S. Army at the Pacific Northwest National Laboratory in Richland, Washington. The army then published its intent to immediately repatriate these remains (along with some others) to the Native American tribes of the area.[2] The leadership of the interested tribes—the Confederated Tribes of the Umatilla Reservation, the Confederated Tribes of the Colville Reservation, the Wanapum Band, the Confederated Tribes and Band of the Yakama Nation, and the Nez Percé Tribe—announced they had formed a coalition and intended to rebury the remains as soon as they were returned without any study by anthropologists, which they considered desecration of the dead.[3]

This horrified two physical anthropologists—Doug Owsley of the Smithsonian Institution and his colleague Richard Jantz of the University of Tennessee. They had just studied a mummy long stored in a museum in Carson City, Nevada, which had been believed to be only a few thousand years old, but had recently (along with several other remains stored at the museum, including the bones of a man from an area called Wizards Beach) been discovered to be a thousand years older than Kennewick Man.[4] Like Kennewick Man, the mummy looked quite different from modern Native Americans. The skeleton was gracile, which was how Chatters had described Kennewick. It was similarly long-headed, as opposed to wide-headed, like modern Native Americans (and other Mongoloids). Owsley, Jantz and several of their colleagues had lately begun to think that there might be more remains like these, of similar antiquity, forgotten in museums in the U.S., and they were forming the opinion that contrary to the accepted story, these Paleo-Americans were not the ancestors of modern Native Americans. But just as Owsley and Jantz realized there were new questions to ask about who discovered America, the bones that could answer them were going back in the ground under the provisions of NAGPRA and state laws like it. The remains at Carson City were also being actively sought by Native groups.

Owsley and Jantz later estimated that the number of human skeletons known to be older than 8,000 years in the United States could be counted on two hands. Kennewick Man was certainly a "rare discovery of national and international significance," a treasure for anthropological science of incalculable value.[5] Owsley pleaded by mail and phone with the army to be allowed to study the remains. The Corps didn't respond. Other eminent scholars also wrote and phoned. Nothing. In October, just before the bones were to be repatriated, Owsley and his colleagues contacted Alan Schneider, a Portland lawyer who had a lifelong interest in archaeology. Schneider thought the army should be prevented from turning the remains over to the Native tribes. He thought the army had failed to establish that Kennewick Man was a Native American under the NAGPRA, because it had made its decision capriciously and without the proper study or due procedure required by the law. He also thought that the army was interfering with scientists' First Amendment rights by denying them the opportunity for study, and had violated their rights to equal protection under the law on the grounds of their race, religion and national origin. He and a Portland litigator named Paula Barran took the case on a pro bono basis. Owsley, Jantz, Dennis Stanford of the Smithsonian and five other scientists, a Who's Who of American anthropology, launched a suit against the United States Army.[6]

Chatters was not among them, but he'd already had a chance to study the remains, and he'd made the most of it. Just before the Kennewick bones were removed from his care he had had the presence of mind to make a cast of the skull. Then he and an artist friend made a forensic reconstruction of Kennewick Man's head. Building up strings of clay, crisscrossed and layered like real muscle and sinew and flesh on top of bone, they created their version of what Kennewick Man had looked like. A photograph of this head was published in *The New Yorker* in February of 1998.[7]

"Wouldn't stand out walking down a Stockholm street," Chatters had previously told *The New Yorker*.[8]

This was the equivalent of throwing a torch into a tinder-dry boreal forest.

On a weirdly warm morning in March 1998, I sat staring up at the high ceiling in the white-painted auditorium of the Native Canadian Centre of Toronto. The brick walls stepped in at the top, as if to form the curved ceiling of a barrow. The air was dry and dusty, and caught at my throat.

I was thinking about the accepted narrative about who first populated the Americas. The Kennewick find and the remains in Carson City suggested that the most ancient human skeletons in North America were not all Mongoloids, as I'd been told. And all that accepted wisdom about there being no remains older than 10,000 BP was based mainly on dating by association. Few of the bones left lying on museums' and universities' and private collectors' shelves for years had been radiocarbon dated directly. Nor were they likely to be. As the Kennewick affair had made clear, some Native people were very upset about their ancestors' bones being studied.

I had come to this center to attend a meeting of the authorities in charge of dealing with the Native dead inadvertently found in Toronto. The previous fall, Frances Sanderson, the executive director of a Native organization called Nishnawbe Homes, had heard a radio newscast about the discovery of a Native ossuary under Moatfield soccer park in suburban Toronto. Canada has no federal law like the NAGPRA regarding the discovery of Native burials. Until the early 1990s Ontario law didn't really cover such issues either. In 1992, after the NAGPRA was passed in the U.S., Ontario passed amendments to its Cemeteries Act that set out how Native burials are to be treated.[9] Until then, there were no rules specifically protecting them, other than common law, which was only a little better than useless. A series of early cases in England in the seventeenth century had established that there is no such thing as ownership or property right in a dead body, but that the land, clothes, winding sheets and coffins belong to the deceased's estate. Since human bodies are not property, they fell under the protection of the ecclesiastical courts, which had no enforcement arm. Only the land and grave goods were under the authority of the state. These rules effectively gave carte blanche to grave robbers looking for human remains for dissection, so long as they left the clothes and other grave goods in the ground. This situation was eventually remedied and, in many jurisdictions, graves are considered sacred ground. It is a criminal offense to disturb or disinter such remains.[10] Nevertheless, the law did not stop the despoiling of Native graves anywhere in either the U.S. or Canada. In the nineteenth century, Native remains were considered fascinating collectibles. There had been expeditions to dig them up, donations of remains to museums, and private trade in bones.

The idea of treating human bones like hockey cards is barbaric. But that was surely different from the careful modern study of remains by qualified scientists, which can yield information for the common good. The NAGPRA and the rules in Ontario were designed to recognize that Native Americans have deeply held views on human remains. These rules seemed to me fair and considerate: if a body is found, the landowner must contact authorities who in turn must determine if the person died as the result of foul play. If it is obvious the person was a Native Canadian, the landowner must contact the nearest band likely to be culturally affiliated with the remains. The only scientific study permitted under Ontario's Cemeteries Act is the minimum amount necessary to determine who the closest affiliated band is. Permission for the method of reburial may be given by that Native band only. There are provisions for negotiations between band and landowner. If remains are to be reburied on the spot, the owner of the land must establish a portion of his property as a cemetery and pay for its upkeep forever. Similar rules are in place for public land. The point of these amendments is to treat inadvertent finds of Native remains as disturbances to the dead and to make certain the dead are treated as they would have liked to be by their own.

The difficulty, as usual, was in the details, and in the conflict between science and sentiment. The ossuary under the soccer park was on land owned by the municipality, and yet, as Sanderson complained to this roomful of officials, no one had called the Native Canadian Centre to inform them of the find. Were they not the closest Native people? The radio newscast had reported that the bones had been dated by an archaeologist to the early fourteenth century. The whole thing bothered her. Why were archaeologists studying a burial site at all? Who was taking care of the bones? Who was reburying them? She had spoken to her colleagues, and the community liaison of Aboriginal Legal Services of Toronto had called the coroner's office. There had been confusion about where exactly the bones were (in fact, the coroner's office had mislaid the first bag of bones taken off the site). Reburial had not taken place until five months after the find.[11] Why, she wanted to know, had it taken five months to get these people back in the ground, when Native beliefs require immediate reburial of exposed remains? She put herself in the place of the dead. All she wanted, she said, once she went in the ground, was to stay there. Was that too much to ask? This was a meeting to call people to account.

I had heard about this meeting from Mima Kapches of the Royal Ontario Museum. She had been invited herself but was too busy to attend, and said she thought it might give me insight into the Native point of view on the study of ancestral remains, something I certainly needed help with: I couldn't understand why the Native communities in Washington State were trying to prevent study of the Kennewick remains. The dead are dead, my rational mind said. They feel no pain, no humiliation. In the Kennewick case, the man had been dead for eight millennia, so there could be no proof of cultural affiliation to any living Native Americans without study. How else could affiliation be established? It seemed obvious to me the needs of science and law should prevail over religious views: North Americans are democrats, after all, not theocrats.

On the other hand, I was bothered by what I'd learned about the way in which some Native American remains had been handled. I had been asking around about the methods of recording and storing bones and had found that human remains were sometimes treated in the same slipshod way as archaeological artifacts in Ontario. One archaeologist recounted, in disgust, the practical impact of the revised Cemeteries Act. He described bones left on a site for weeks in a brown paper bag until the province finally got around to doing something about it. He explained that when ancient remains were found, developers often looked the other way while their workers covered them up and built on top of them, so as to avoid costly delays and the possible expense of maintaining a cemetery in perpetuity. I was told of an amateur archaeologist who kept human remains under the glass top of a coffee table in a living room. I was told of U.S. archaeologists who'd dug and removed human bones from Ontario more than twenty years earlier. When I'd phoned one of these scholars to ask where the bones were now, he couldn't say, and neither could the institution that was supposed to be housing them. The archaeologist had not published on what he'd found.

I also read some reports issued by David Boyle, Ontario's first provincial archaeologist, whose collections were eventually merged into the Royal Ontario Museum's. He described, in his "14th Ontario Archaeological Report to the Minister of Education," what had happened when a burial mound was discovered in Clinton Township in 1901. The burial was estimated to be fifteen feet in diameter and contain the remains of 250 people:

> This is only a guess, based on statements made by those who took part in the wild resurrection mania that seemed to take possession of the neighbours when it became known that an Indian grave had been discovered. Mr. Moyer of Campden informed me that he saw fully thirty vehicles of various kinds

tied up along the fence of the field where the grave was, and that as many as seventy persons were engaged in digging at one time...the result was deplorable. What should have proved an excellent opportunity to examine carefully an undisturbed ossuary in a part of the country where such places of burial are rare, has been lost, and all that is left is a few skulls most of which are held by those who procured them in the scramble.[12]

I had gone again to see Kapches after realizing that many museums in Canada and the U.S. had human remains "collections," and that a tug-of-war had erupted in the United States over the control of such remains. I asked how many skeletal human beings the ROM held. I was told an answer would be extremely difficult to get. I later heard from others that Kapches was just then embroiled in negotiations over a demand for the reburial of the most famous ossuary found in Ontario, the one called Ossassané, which had been described in its making by Jean de Brébeuf in 1636 when he lived among the Huron. The bones of what Kenneth E. Kidd thought were as many as a thousand individuals (actually around five hundred), tumbled together into this burial pit, had been part of the ROM's human remains collections since 1948 and used for study at the University of Toronto for forty years.[13] The ROM had decided to return the Ossassané remains to the descendants of the Huron, which outraged some physical anthropologists who believed this ossuary was far too valuable to science to be reburied. But none of this had yet been made public: anything to do with the human remains in its care was kept as quiet as possible by the ROM.

At lunch in the basement cafeteria at the Native Canadian Centre, I sat with several of the Native people who had opened the meeting that morning. One was a man with a long gray braid, who had been introduced as a pipe-carrier, a person who upholds the traditional spiritual practices of his band. Before the meeting began, he and his colleagues had washed us all in the sharp, sweet scent of burning sage and had offered us tobacco and a few moments of meditation. At the meeting they had explained that the exposure and study of human bones offended Native spiritual views. Over rice and chicken I asked him to explain the basic beliefs of his people about death and the proper treatment of the dead.

There is a dualism involved, he said. Human beings have two souls, two spirits. There is a higher soul, which at death moves out through what he called the western door on its perpetual journey. But there is another soul, the dangerous, violent warrior soul, which resides in the bones forever. When bones are unearthed, this dangerous half of the duality, unchecked by the kinder social impulses of the higher soul, is set free to wreak havoc. He believed that these ideas were common to all Native persons, or at least all Native persons in Ontario. But only the traditionalists in Native communities, not the elected officials, really knew the nature of the important spiritual concerns surrounding human remains. The elected officials could not be trusted, he said. They would sell out the spiritual welfare of their communities without batting an eye. "These guys just don't know what they're letting loose," he said to me.

Surely not all Native cultures at all times had these same beliefs about the dead, I argued. It didn't matter, he replied, all Native remains had to be treated the same way. It made no difference whether they were pulled from an extremely ancient burial in some Ice Age gravel pit or from a historic ossuary: both sets of bones had to go back in the ground right away, without any study at all. His beliefs were absolute.

The more he talked, the more perplexed I became. He kept putting the needs of restless spirits ahead of science, ahead of democracy, ahead of fairness. He talked about the danger these wayward bones represented to both Native people and those who studied them. I tried to keep an open mind about his point of view, but it was hard. According to the archaeologists I'd read, human remains have been treated in as many ways as there are cultures in the Americas. These different methods suggest different beliefs about death and the afterlife of the soul. Some have been cremated, some buried as individuals in mounds, some buried sitting upright in pits, some laid out and tied down under water, some buried twice—once to remove the flesh, the second time mixed up with others' bones. Some remains had been exposed on platforms above ground or just covered over with rocks. Who was to say that Archaic people in Ontario 5,000 years ago had the same beliefs about souls in bones as fourteenth-century Iroquoians? The pipe-keeper's warnings about danger sounded like the equivalent of the curse of Tutankhamen's tomb.

The meeting soon wandered from the particular case of what had gone wrong with the reburial of the bones in the ossuary off Moatfield Road to the way in which Canadian museums deal with demands for repatriation. Kapches had sent a representative to this meeting to lay out the ROM's brand new human remains policy, committed to paper only about a month earlier (three months after a request for the return of the Ossassané bones).[14] The ROM would not provide a general list of the human remains on their shelves, he explained, but if Canadian Native persons came and asked for particular remains, they would consider the request very respectfully. The museum was committed to returning Canadian remains, but not committed to returning the remains of Native persons brought to the ROM from other jurisdictions. The ROM had human remains from Africa, the U.S. and South America, some received in trade with other museums.

There is no law to compel the ROM to do anything more. This situation is very different in the United States, where all federally funded institutions are required by the NAGPRA to prepare inventories of the dead for publication in the federal register and for return to their descendants. Once a museum or university has established which tribe is the most closely related to the persons in their care, they are required to notify the tribe and begin the process of returning both the bones and any grave goods associated with them. In other words, it's up to the museum to inform the tribes about what they have; the tribes are not asked to become detectives and ferret out the remains of their relatives.[15] After the NAGPRA passed, various Canadian Native people pounded on the doors of Canadian institutions demanding similar treatment. At an Ottawa conference organized by the major museums, a compromise was reached. Museums could keep the goods they had acquired by purchase, fair and square, but everything else had to be given back if they were asked for it.

The sticking point in both jurisdictions was this: how do you prove cultural affiliation, and what happens when two tribes disagree? How could one show that the bones in a museum box were culturally affiliated to any tribe now living, especially if they were thousands of years old and looked "Caucasoid" to qualified physical anthropologists? How did physical anthropologists determine group affiliations through the study of bones in any case? The Kennewick find, and the outraged U.S. scholars suing for the right to study in the open, were like ghosts at this meeting—not on the agenda but hovering over the coffee.

An official of the center said that there were some 20,000 Native American remains residing in boxes in a museum in Scotland (a number I was unable to verify) and similarly high numbers squirreled away in universities, museums, private collections and federal institutions in the U.S., largely unstudied by anyone. No one could be sure how many there were in Canada (although the Museum of Civilization later confirmed it alone had about 6,000). No lists of these remains were available, so how would even scholars know who had what?

None of the bureaucrats or professional archaeologists in the room denied this. In fact, none of them even stood up and made a case for what they did. I kept waiting for them to speak out about the ways in which their work served the public good. I expected them to argue about the value of knowledge for its own sake. They were silent. "Aren't any of you guys going to stand up for science?" I hissed at one of them during a break. But that other part of me, the intuitive part, was beginning to feel extremely uneasy. I was unable to swallow what had not been denied—that there were still private collectors of human bone, that museums retained collections of human remains they'd bought in the past. Somehow this was not how I'd thought physical anthropology went about its business.

A young woman stood up to speak. The sound of her voice made it clear she was on the verge of tears. She had dark curly hair falling to her shoulders, a slight build, limpid black eyes, an oval face. She said she was a university student and her first degree was in physical anthropology. "I'm ashamed of it," she said softly. "It was forensic anthropology. I had to practice on skeletons brought from Holland Landing…." These remains were part of the University of Toronto's teaching collection and had been found in or around 1965 in the course of construction. The graves were dug by students at the U of T under the direction of professor Norman Emerson. There were many different people's bones, European, Métis, African and Native Canadian mixed together. She had quickly realized that some were her ancestors. "I saw how the bodies were treated, some of them with flesh on their bones," she said in a choking voice. "They would fall apart, people would be joking around with skulls in their hands." It had especially disturbed her that there seemed to be no pressing need to violate human dignity in this way. No urgent studies were being made on these remains. Many of these skeletons had lain in their boxes in the lab, untouched, for years. They were a population of the undead, the unburied.

"I have to wonder about the whole field of physical anthropology," she said. "What are we learning?" She ticked off the kinds of studies done on bones—studies to determine prehistoric diet, the origin of diseases, the marks of famine and other forms of stress that could speak of environmental crises past. And as in all studies of human variation, the more bones studied, the more likelihood that they actually represented a population. Studies of whole cemeteries were the best: they showed the ratios of men to women, average ages at death, the proportions of young children to the general population of the dead, the average number of dental cavities, how widespread or anomalous was any particular disease. She had no problem with any of that, so long as the studies were done on bodies donated to the university and not on the bones of people who'd been jacked up, unwilling, out of the ground.

She paused and took a breath of air and began to cry. "I've seen bones dropped on the ground. There's no respect . . . for our ancestors, no respect for nations today. It's got to stop."

The hair rose on the back of my neck. It wasn't her words, but something about her softness, her hopelessness. She spoke with the slow rhythms of the afflicted, of someone who knew what was right but was totally without power to bring it about. This was, in fact, a tone I'd heard to a lesser degree in the voices of all the Native persons who'd spoken, a mix between pleading and utter disgust with those to whom pleas must be made. I found myself muttering the little phrase I had been taught to say for my own dead since childhood—*Rest in peace*. And then I remembered all the footage I'd seen over the years of Jewish men in Orthodox garb scurrying on the streets of Tel Aviv or Jerusalem after yet another bombing incident. They ran to scoop the tiniest shreds of the flesh and bone of the newly dead into plastic bags. Some practicing Orthodox Jews believe that bodies must be buried whole, because when the Messiah comes the Good will be called to God and the bones will rise, clothed in flesh again. Who would want to be redeemed in pieces? Hitler wasn't content with ordering pain, suffering and death for the living: by burning the remains of the dead in crematoria he crushed even the faintest hope of redemption.

"Find out what turd taught her," one of the more distinguished archaeologists in the room commanded me at the break.

Plunging into the history of physical anthropology (to find out what turd had taught her) was akin to leaping into a river in a spring flood. Just under the cool surface, there were such horrors. Physical anthropologists study human bodies as botanists study plants. They are interested in how bodies work, in the relationships between human groups and human precursors, in the changes of the human form over time, in the natural history of human beings. They ask marvelous questions. How did we become as we are now? What does pathology or injury write on the human skeleton? Why don't our skulls all look alike? Why are some people's teeth shovel-shaped, and others not? Why do some have molars with three roots, and others only two? Why do some faces slant forward from the jaw to the nose, while others are flat? Why have hominid foreheads changed over the last million years? What are the forces that cause human features to morph, and how many generations does it take? What are the specific influences of gene flow (which is what physical anthropologists are pleased to call fruitful sex), adaptation to the environment or genetic accident to the human form?

They had mainly tried to answer these questions, to my bemusement, by measuring human skulls and bones and comparing their findings. Like botany, physical anthropology started as a descriptive science about three hundred years ago. Physical anthropology arose alongside archaeology, which had its roots in the robbing of graves in Europe in the seventeenth century. When European kings rifled their ancient predecessors' tombs for gold and treasure, they found stone tools and arrows remarkably like those used by the people they'd just discovered in the New World. And they found human bones. Physical anthropologists pried loose from tombs and graves the story of human descent and transformation.[16]

American anthropologist Aleš Hrdlička had presided like a colossus over the development of modern American anthropology. He was curator of the Division of Physical Anthropology at the United States National Museum in Washington, D.C., when he founded the *American Journal of Physical Anthropology* in 1918. In the first issue of the first volume, he defined physical anthropology as "the study of racial anatomy, physiology and pathology."[17] Hrdlička credited the French scholar Paul Broca as the true founder of the field. Broca, he told his readers, had described it as "the natural history of the genus Homo," or as "the study of man's variation." He believed the impetus to the whole field was "the discovery of America, with its new race of people, no mention of which occurred in any of the old accounts or traditions. This most sensational event was followed by discoveries of other lands and peoples in the Pacific and this was succeeded by rapidly increasing knowledge of organized beings in general, including the anthropoid apes. All this led irresistibly to new lines of thought by scientific men as well as to a general doubt as to the correctness of the old theories of creation...."[18]

It was precisely in this description of human differences, of variation, that physical anthropology separated itself from archaeology and its scholars began their long walk down bizarre and dangerous paths. It was anthropologists who refined the concept of race, who insisted on hierarchies between and among different sorts of people. Many of the nineteenth and early twentieth-century physical anthropologists were virulent racists. They believed that there was such a thing as a pure racial type, and that measurement of the living and the dead could define the racial box into which each individual fitted. Some believed that the genetic mixing of racially pure types would lead to the degradation of the whole of humanity. Hrdlička believed that. "In the United States," he wrote, "we are confronted on the one side with the grave problem of mixture of white and negro, and on the other with that of white and Indian. We know something of the general results of such miscegenations, but in both cases, the subject calls urgently for more thorough investigation."[19] In other words, scientists' measurements and the outrageous inferences they drew from them supported the wretched Jim Crow laws in the United States, apartheid in South Africa, the vicious treatment of Native Americans throughout the Americas, and the Nazi attempts to exterminate Jews, Gypsies, the intellectually blighted and the homosexually inclined.

In 1918, in the first number of his brand new journal, Hrdlička provided a brief history of the field to that point. The first book on physical anthropology was published in 1655. In 1699, Tyson published the comparative anatomy of man and monkey, and in 1735, thanks to the great natural scientist Linnaeus, man "for the first time was placed within the line of living beings in general, and...his close organic relations with the first of the primates was authoritatively expressed."[20] Around the time Charles Darwin was finishing his great work on the origin of species, Paul Broca and his colleagues in Paris in 1859 created the Société d'Anthropologie. According to Hrdlička they had to plead with higher authorities to be allowed to meet: it was believed their work might be subversive to the state and religion. Their success led to other societies being founded in Germany, Britain and the U.S. Various expeditions were mounted in North America to examine Native people. Broca and his colleagues standardized measurement of the human form and devised instruments to do it with, thus making comparison of results possible. Finally, "collections were begun"—meaning human bones were gathered, by fair means or foul.

The first physical anthropologist in North America, according to Hrdlička, was Samuel G. Morton, M.D., of Philadelphia. In the 1840s, Morton had become interested in paleontology, phrenology (the study of human character by feeling out the bumps on the skull), comparative anatomy and "questions relating to the origin, types and racial affiliations of the American

Indians." Morton backed into these issues when teaching a class in anatomy. He wanted to show the races of men (Caucasoid, Mongoloid, Negroid, South Asian, Native American) by holding up a skull from each group to his class. He realized he did not have examples of Mongoloids or Malays so he set about to collect some. By the time he died he had put together a personal collection of almost a thousand skulls. He measured them most intelligently, according to Hrdlička, somehow devising for himself many of the same measurements of the important features of the skull that two international conventions of anthropologists couldn't agree on until 1912. In spite of using his own methods and working basically on his own, Morton had shown, in Hrdlička's estimation, that all Native Americans, with the exception of the Eskimo, were one people divided into two families. Morton's main error, wrote Hrdlička, was his failure to see that Native Americans and Mongoloids were also one people.[21]

By the 1860s, Morton's practice of collecting human skulls had spread to many institutions of higher learning in North America. David Boyle in Ontario dug many graves and grave mounds, collecting and describing the skulls he found. University of Toronto history professor Sir Daniel Wilson collected crania, measurements and opinions on whether or not there was one distinctive cranial type exhibited by all Native Americans. Professor J.W. Dawson, principal of McGill University for many years, did the same. Hrdlička liked Dawson's work, which he quoted approvingly: "Our primitive American men," Dawson had written, "seem to fall short in interest of those pre-historic races in Europe with which we have been comparing them, and which are by many believed to reach backward to a time enormously exceeding that to which any history, sacred or secular, extends."[22]

By the time he founded his anthropological journal, Hrdlička had also examined and measured countless bodies, starting with living orphaned children, moving on through the institutionalized insane, and culminating with thousands of living and dead Native Americans.[23] He had come early to the conclusion that all

Native Americans were basically similar, and all fitted into the Mongoloid racial box: broad-headed, large-nosed variants of a North Asian stock, he said. In the first number of his new journal, Hrdlička made it clear that by 1918 his view of Native Americans had triumphed utterly over all opposing theories when he introduced the work of Dr. Herman ten Kate by saying he was the last "living physical anthropologist of note who defends the theory of the multiplicity of races on the American continent, though that is largely if not entirely due to his interpretation of the term 'race.'"[24]

He bemoaned the fact that most collectors and collections focused on the skull and ignored the rest of the skeleton. He believed the skeleton told as much of the story of human descent and variety as the skull. The goal of physical anthropology was to study all human remains "... to determine the complete range of variation in these parts in at least the most significant groups of mankind. The requirements in this direction will appear more clearly when it is appreciated that, to determine the total range of variation in a single long bone such as the humerus, in any group to be studied, there are needed the remains of hundreds of adult individuals of each sex from that group."[25]

He also explained the difficulties that prevented his colleagues from meeting these goals: "Religious beliefs, sentimentality and superstitions, as well as love, nearly everywhere invest the bodies of the dead with sacredness or awe which no stranger is willingly permitted to disturb. It is seldom appreciated that the remains would be dealt with and guarded with the utmost care, and be used only for the most worthy ends, including the benefit of the living.... Even old remains are sometimes difficult to acquire. Such conditions, with occasional exceptions, are common among the civilized and savage alike, hence to collect large supplies of material indispensable to Physical Anthropology is often arduous and unsatisfactory."[26]

By 1918, thanks to Hrdlička and his colleagues, institutions in Washington, New York and Chicago were full of skulls brought back from various archaeological and anthropological expeditions to the Native communities (whose members had no civil rights and so could not stop these scientists from looting graves). The National Museum had become a part of the Smithsonian Institution, which had already received the collections of Native American remains ordered gathered by the Surgeon General of the U.S. Army immediately after the Civil War. The Surgeon General had instructed the troops battling Indians on the Great Plains to cut off the heads of the Native dead on the battlefield and ship them back to Washington for study. This study was to be used to prove by measurement that Native people were inferior to Caucasians.[27] By Hrdlička's day there were 10,000 skulls and other remains stashed in various offices and bureaus and government departments in Washington. But even as he attested in one part of his journal to the great care with which these remains were treated, he acknowledged in another that some inventories could not be trusted.[28] The bones were slipping away.

Although there were a few dissenting physical anthropologists who found wide variation among Native Americans, Hrdlička's views dominated the field, not only because he edited a journal, but also because he was a careful and patient observer, always looking for more data to confirm or disprove theories. His views also seemed to fit well with some archaeologists' ideas of how primitive First Americans might have entered the New World— over the Bering Strait from North Asia, on foot. There was a nice convergence of different sorts of evidence.

Some of the North Asian evidence came from Hrdlička's contemporary, an anthropologist who made vital contributions to the study of the cultures of the Pacific Northwest, Franz Boas. Boas had measured thousands of living Native persons in the 1880s and '90s.[29] At the turn of the century he suggested the formation of an expedition to test the notion (in which he already firmly believed) that Native Americans were descendants of ancient North Asian migrants to the New World who eventually spilled back into eastern Siberia; Boas relied on the assumption that measurement could determine both relatedness and descent.[30]

He accompanied the Jesup expedition, which studied the cultures of the tribes of Washington, British Columbia, Alaska and the Siberian peninsula in an attempt to prove or disprove their relatedness. Boas was a great ethnographer who recorded everything he could, from songs to recipes, of the native cultures he encountered, even as they were being brutally forced into the European mode of living by both the U.S. and Canadian governments.[31] Museums were to act as the public keepers of the memory of these cultures that were being destroyed. Knowing the abhorrence Native persons had for disturbance of their dead, Boas nevertheless bought and paid for skulls and bones and burials. He brought them back to New York's American Museum of Natural History, and to the Field Museum in Chicago.[32]

Boas preferred the word *type* to the word *race*.[33] He worked on the principle that every individual conformed to a type, but that impossibly large numbers of study subjects would be necessary to establish each and every deviation from the pure type. He applied statistics and probability analysis to his data, to show that measurements taken from small numbers of subjects could at least identify whether certain changes were significant.

In 1912, Boas was hired by the U.S. government to measure and determine whether there were any differences between immigrants from Europe and their American-born children. What he learned was that the skull shapes of the American-born children of immigrants from Sicily, from Calabria, and of people he identified as "Hebrew" (Jews from Eastern Europe), all became more like each other than like their parents. While each ethnic group's parents exhibited particular cranial shapes that identified them as members of a particular type, the longer their children had been in America, the more the children of these different types resembled each other. As Boas described it, "the east European Hebrew, who has a very round head, becomes more long-headed; the south Sicilian who in Italy has an exceedingly long head, becomes more short-headed; so that both approach a uniform type in this country as far as the roundness of the head is concerned."[34]

This observation caused a sensation. It was picked up by American magazines as evidence of the creation of an American type, something that Boas tried to disclaim.[35] It was still being debated many years later. For some, these observations discredited the basic notions of physical anthropology, the principles Boas had relied upon when he went off to establish or disprove that Native Americans were descended from North Asians. How, these critics asked, could one use skull and facial measurements, which Boas had so clearly shown can change so quickly, to draw any conclusions about human relationships and descent? If human skull shapes could change from long-headed to more round-headed in one generation, what was the point of measurement at all? Boas and other physical anthropologists answered that change needed to be investigated as much as stability, and it needed to be explained.[36]

By the end of World War II, after the exposure of the crematoria at places like Auschwitz, and the release of the living dead from various other camps in Europe and Asia, the word *race* had the flavor of ashes. Physical anthropologists began to concern themselves with the characteristics of populations, instead of how individuals varied from some arbitrary concept of a type or a race. Their problem had become obvious—what does the word *race* actually mean? Is a short, stocky, olive-skinned, black-haired, brown-eyed person from Lebanon the same "race" as a tall, slim, pale-skinned, blue-eyed, blond-haired person from Sweden? If so, how is this category of any use to anyone? What meaningful distinctions does it draw attention to? Is race a synonym for species? Obviously not: human beings of all head shapes, colors and body sizes mate and have offspring. Human beings are much more alike than they are different. But physical anthropologists still wanted to explain the differences found between groups; they wanted to account for and explain the variation that shows itself in human bones. Measurements of skulls and faces and long bones continued to be taken, the shape and traits of teeth continued to be examined.

Scholars now realized that one couldn't base sweeping generalizations about populations on a small number of individuals. Boas had understood that any changes or differences identified had to be statistically significant. Anthropologists came to see that significance needed to be considered in a wide, representative context. The work of gathering representative data began in the 1950s. With the advent of computers, data gathered by many researchers could be entered into databases and widely shared. Any researcher using the same measures could pool his few samples with the larger number of population samples offered in various databases, and gain greater certainty about the meaningfulness of his results. W.W. Howells at Harvard spent much of his career creating one large database of measurements of individuals' skulls and faces, sampled from all the known ethnic groups of the world, which he thought reflected evolutionary change. C. Loring Brace of the University of Michigan, Howells' student, created another database of more than eight thousand individuals, trying at first to get measurements that reflected the action of selection. He eventually realized that craniofacial traits have almost nothing to do with survival. Such "trivial traits" (as Brace calls them) as the size and shape of the nasal opening speak eloquently and precisely about family relationships and distinctions—and nothing else.[37]

By the late 1980s, physical anthropology was undergoing constant reconstruction. Population studies had completely replaced anthropologists' early attempts to find the perfect individual expression of a racial category. Anthropologists had become extremely reluctant to study and draw conclusions from single skeletons or skulls, because a single example could not be shown to be representative of a population. They also began to borrow the biological sciences' new technologies, particularly those that shed light on genetic variation. The field began to divide between those who measured the outside of bones and made careful note and comparison of their shapes, and those who applied techniques from molecular biology and genetics to the human story, hoping to tease out patterns of relationship and descent as expressed in blood types and genetic patterns of disease. Nuclear, mitochondrial DNA and Y-chromosome studies began to add new information about kinship. Dating of the bone protein collagen collected from old skeletons was also discovered to be a much more reliable method of figuring out how old a bone is than previous methods of dating the inorganic portions of bone.

Through all these changes, right up to the early 1990s, Hrdlička's dictum that Native Americans are one people, descendants of North Asians, remained unshaken. It was the main support, still, for the story of the First Americans. And oddly enough, in spite of the fact that the use of the categories of race was considered virtually scandalous by most cultural anthropologists,[38] racial designations developed in the previous century continued to be used by physical anthropologists doing forensic work. Why? Because nobody but anthropologists seemed to be aware that the concept of race had been discredited (only to be replaced by a much vaguer catch-all category—ethnicity). Governments and police still asked the same old questions: What is the person's stature, age, sex, and race? Forensic anthropologists responded in the old, familiar categories: Caucasian, Negroid, Mongoloid. And newspapers repeated these words as if they meant something.

# 3

# Found and Lost

The Misplaced Remains of
the Accepted Path

IN SPITE OF THE MURKY history of the study of human
remains, it still seemed to me that the only way to
resolve the question of the origin of the First Americans was through examination of their bones. While the U.S. had
legislation that made such study difficult, Canada did not. And
if the Bering Strait entry theory was correct, the most ancient
human remains in the Americas ought to be in the Canadian
Northwest, not the U.S. Southeast. I also imagined that in light
of the Kennewick find, many physical anthropologists would be
thinking again about old bones in Canadian museums, and looking at them with new eyes. I started asking around. How many
ancient human remains had been found in Canada and what had
been published about them? Had anyone gone back and looked
at them again?

Certainly some scholars had been remeasuring bones in
American museums. Physical anthropologists Gentry Steele and
Joseph Powell, in an important paper published in the journal
*Human Biology* in 1992, had determined that the tiny U.S. Paleo-
Indian population (which they defined as any human remain
in North America older than 8500 BP) is subtly different from
modern Native Americans. Living Native Americans' teeth are
similar to those of North Asians. Both groups share a bundle of

traits catalogued by Christy Turner of the University of Arizona and characterized as sinodonty (these traits include shovel-shaped incisors, three-rooted molars, and other such arcana). Turner distinguished North Asian, or sinodont, traits from those associated with South Asians, which he referred to as sundadont. In 1992 Powell and Steele looked at eight Paleo-Indian crania and teeth previously sampled by Turner and others. They compared them not only to modern Native Americans and Asians, as Turner and others had done, but to ancient North Asian remains found at Minotawaga in Okinawa, and near a place called Zhoukoudien in China. In other words, they compared ancient remains to ancient remains—or apples to apples.[1]

There had been many arguments about whether these very ancient remains found in Asian caves looked like modern Mongoloids. Some physical anthropologists believed that skeletons found in 1934 in the upper part of an ancient cave system near Zhoukoudien represented the way Asian people looked before the specialization called Mongoloidism developed. Those found in the Upper Cave were thought to be extremely ancient, dating back into the Ice Age. Others looking at the same bones or their casts argued that one of the skulls at Zhoukoudien was like a Caucasian, another Melanesian and another like the Eskimo, and that they represented the bones of a family displaying the actual variety of worldwide populations. Powell and Steele indirectly declared themselves in favor of the first theory: in their view, modern humans had been morphing over the last 10,000 years.[2]

This dispute was part of a larger argument about modern human origins, also being carried on hammer and tongs by physical anthropologists. The out-of-Africa hypothesis holds that modern humans developed in Africa and spread out from there over the last 100,000 years.[3] The counter theory, multiregionalism, holds that microevolution has been going on at different rates in different places at different times around the world.[4] Modern human beings, who share a distant common ancestor, have developed various characteristics in various pockets around the world, then shared most of them through gene flow (sex).

When Steele and Powell compared their ancient American to ancient Asian skulls, a large crack opened in the Hrdličkan pillar of American physical anthropology. They found the ancient American and Asian remains had characteristics more "proto-caucasoid" than "protomongoloid," with teeth more sundadont than sinodont. Their paper challenged Hrdlička's view that all living and dead Native Americans were descendants of the same Mongoloid population. Even so, Steele and Powell accepted that Beringia was the point of entry to America and that Asia was the point of origin of Americans. They set their findings in the context of the dominant archaeological view of who peopled the Americas. They cited the Clovis First proponents, who argued that the First Americans entered Beringia around 13,000 years ago, and by 11,000 BP entered the rest of the continent. They also presented the arguments of the few dissenters, such as Ruth Gruhn of the University of Alberta and Knut Fladmark of Simon Fraser University, who had suggested that the first migrants made their way down from Beringia along the B.C. coast anywhere from 20,000 to 40,000 years ago. Powell and Steele offered no opinion on that, but made it clear that the first Paleo-Indians did not look like modern Native Americans.

Interestingly, the oldest of the North American remains they listed had been found in Texas, and in Florida at Warm Mineral Springs. This was not the sort of distribution one would expect if the Bering Strait was the point of entry. And while they said their paper dealt with North American Paleo-Indians, Canada was a blank, a place through which it was assumed the First Americans must have passed, but from which no evidence was offered up.

One American scholar who had looked north of the border to see what had been found in Canada was the person who presented Kennewick Man to the world, James Chatters. He told me of at least one ancient skeleton, about the same age as Kennewick Man, found in British Columbia in the late 1970s at a place called

Gore Creek. He said he'd been meaning to call up the lead author of the paper that described it, Jerome Cybulski. A glance at the map explained why. Gore Creek drains into the South Thompson River close to lakes that lead to the Okanogan River. The Okanogan meets the Yakima, the Snake and the Columbia rivers right at Kennewick. The modern populations of the Pacific Northwest are interrelated. The ancient Kennewick and Gore Creek remains could have been part of a related population too.

In 1975 Morley Eldridge, then an archaeology student living in Kamloops, British Columbia, went out on an expedition to Gore Creek. He was looking for volcanic ash for his mother, a potter, who wanted it for a glaze. He knew of a place where the eroded creek bank revealed two ash layers. The lowest had been laid down about 6,000 years ago when Mount Mazama in Washington State blew its top spectacularly. The ash settled like a thick blanket all over the Pacific Northwest, and now provides a handy chronological reference point to archaeologists. Eldridge found human long bones sticking out of the wall of a gully that crossed the creek, well below the Mazama ash. He didn't think many human remains of such antiquity had ever been found before in Canada. He was right. By 1975 only two remains thought to be really old had been reported—fragments of an infant found at Taber, Alberta (which were later dated to less than 1,500 years old) and a piece of a mandible found near Old Crow.[5]

Eldridge reported his find, as the law required, to the provincial government archaeologists, who hired two students to remove the bones. The students used a backhoe to push off the thick layers of soil lying on top of the remains. They found more bones in a flexed position oriented towards the south, one meter below the ash. The skeleton was complete except for the skull, which was nowhere to be found. They put the bones in a box. No more work was done. Eldridge called provincial officials from time to time to find out what they had learned, but no one could tell him anything, because the bones were still lying unstudied in the box at the Royal British Columbia Museum in Victoria. There they stayed, until Jerome Cybulski came along in 1979.

Cybulski was by then doing physical anthropology at the National Museum. He was an American who had followed a teacher to Canada. He had spent a good deal of his professional life measuring Northwest populations, following in Boas's footsteps. He was looking at other remains at the museum in Victoria when a curator mentioned to him the bones found at Gore Creek. These were the first really old bones Cybulski had ever seen. The tag on the box said they'd been found by Eldridge, who by then was working as a contract archaeologist out of Vancouver.

Cybulski contacted Eldridge and together with two other scientists, Donald Howes and James Haggarty, they went back to find the site. They did the study of the stratigraphy and geology that should have been done when the remains were first found and learned what they could. They concluded that deglaciation in this area had not been complete until about 10,000 BP and that the way the rivers currently run wasn't established until 8900 BP. Cybulski sent samples of the bone for radiocarbon dating to Simon Fraser University's radiocarbon lab. They also used a then new technique, nitrogen isotope analysis, to see if they could learn what this man had eaten. The initial date of 8250 plus or minus 115 years, was corrected to 8340 plus or minus 150 BP.[6]

Since the skull was missing and no artifacts were found, Cybulski and his colleagues believed the death was an accident, that the man had likely been killed and buried by one of a number of sudden mudslides that had raced down the narrow valley. Cybulski concluded the skeleton was of a man who was twenty-three to thirty-nine when he died, depending on whose method of analyzing pubic bones was relied on. He assumed the man was Mongoloid, since all Native Americans were believed to be

Mongoloid, and he applied a formula devised by physical anthropologists to estimate the stature of a Mongoloid skeleton (which
he estimated at 167.96 centimeters). But when Cybulski compared these remains to those he'd studied a few years earlier from
a prehistoric cemetery at Prince Rupert harbor (on the B.C.
coast), of people who lived between 4000 and 1500 BP, he found
the Gore Creek skeleton to be considerably different. The Prince
Rupert population was stocky, broad, short. They had the size,
shape, and marks on their bones one would expect of people who
made their living fishing in canoes. The Gore Creek skeleton, by
contrast, was tall and slender, with development lines on the leg
and foot bones suggestive of large muscles for leg and foot flexion.
That was what one would expect of a man who ran long distances
while traveling and hunting. Cybulski believed the Gore Creek
man had hunted the big game foraging on the new grasslands
that opened up as the great Cordilleran ice sheet melted away.
The isotope analysis said he was a meat eater, not a fish eater.

At that time there was no truly ancient population to compare
Gore Creek to, other than some fragmentary bones discovered at
the Marmes site in southeastern Washington (not far from where
Kennewick Man was found).[7] Aside from the missing skull, the
Gore Creek man was the only fairly complete human skeleton of
such antiquity unearthed in the whole Pacific Northwest until
Kennewick Man was pulled out of the Columbia River twenty-
one years later.

Cybulski's study, published in 1981, had gone as far as the
technology then available could take it. A lot more could be
learned now through the new technology of mitochondrial DNA
(mtDNA) analysis or Y-chromosome analysis. I called Cybulski
up and asked if he knew where the remains were now. He didn't,
but suggested I get in touch with the curator at the Royal British
Columbia Museum, Grant Keddie.

Keddie explained what had happened to the Gore Creek remains. For years, he said, Native people had been asking for the
return of their ancestors' remains, which they knew were in the

museum. Some had been given back, but others had never been formally requested by band councils and so they remained in trust at the museum. Finally, in the summer of 1995, the museum launched a major exhibit, which attracted tourists from abroad. One Native person, acting as an individual, organized a sit-in. Within days, the museum handed over forty-five boxes of human remains to three bands from the Shuswap Lake and Adams Lake areas. The Gore Creek remains were included and returned to the Nesconlith band (who had been asked for, and had given, their permission for archaeologists to excavate and study the remains). If I wanted to know where they were exactly, the curator suggested I speak to the bands involved.

The Nesconlith office referred me to a man who could remember bringing the boxes back, but not much more. Each band had taken a few. He had no idea where each of the remains had been interred, other than that they were in an extremely old burial ground; nor did he have any knowledge of the Gore Creek remains in particular. An official with another band remembered there had been a list of remains handed over with the boxes. But nothing on that list made it clear that any of the remains were more than 8,500 years old. He was astonished to hear of it. He was also furious. He was very interested in archaeology. He often spoke to archaeology classes and explained that one day the archaeologists would find out that what his people had always said was true—they'd been there forever. There were active land claims in the area. It would have been an important thing for the band to know about Gore Creek's age.

This was the equivalent of reburying King Tutankhamen without marking the site.

The Gore Creek bones were still the oldest human remains ever found in British Columbia, and they came from the interior. No more ancient remains had been found along the British Columbia coast. But surely other remains of equal antiquity had been found farther east in Canada: if the First American story was correct, the most ancient bones should have been found along the ice-free corridor, since that was supposed to have been the route of entry to the rest of the hemisphere. There was no Canadian database listing such remains (although Cybulski's colleague Richard Morlan was preparing a database of all radiocarbon dates for just this sort of inquiry). I checked with several scholars. None knew of any human remains of any great antiquity that had been found in the area of the ice-free corridor.

On the other hand, a colleague of Cybulski's did know of quite ancient remains that had been found in the eastern half of the country. A find of partially cremated bones at the huge Archaic quarry north of Thunder Bay on Lake Superior had been dated to around 8480, plus or minus 390, BP. These were still listed as being in the Museum of Civilization, but the drawer supposedly containing them was empty; the few shards of bone found had been consumed by the process of dating. When graves were inadvertently destroyed in the construction of an airfield 600 kilometers north of Thunder Bay, human bones were found that gave dates between 6300 and 7080 BP, but they had been reburied with little study.[8] Another skeleton had been excavated at Coteau-du-Lac in southwestern Quebec. This was one of several intentional burials, but the only one covered with red ocher—something seen in many Ice Age burials around the world, and also seen on less ancient burials throughout the Americas. The museum still held those remains.[9] They had dated to around 6600 years BP.

The oldest complete skeleton ever found in Canada had been discovered on the east coast of Labrador. It was unearthed from the oldest burial mound ever found in North America. The site was called L'Anse-Amour, the name of the nearest village. This mound had been dug in 1974 by Jim Tuck of Memorial University in Newfoundland and Robert McGhee (then at Memorial, later the National Museum in Ottawa). The museum had published a thin but beautiful book showing the mound and the human being inside. Archaic-period artifacts were found at the head and feet of the skeleton. The bones had not been dated directly. Instead, a piece of charcoal "from apparent grave-fire on same level as skeleton and one to two meters south of skeleton" had produced a date of 7530 BP, with a range of error on either side of about 140 years. The archaeologists simply inferred that the skeleton was the same age as the charcoal.

At first the archaeologists thought the burial mound was just another dune on a beach covered with them. But when they cleared off the trees on top, they found a roughly circular pile of boulders about eight to ten meters in diameter. Underneath they found a second and then a third layer of boulders. Beneath the third layer, rocks had been set on edge to form a cist made of two parallel lines of upright boulders. Below that was sand. They dug half a meter into the sand and found the skeleton. The body had been laid out in a prone position. The head was turned to the west. The sand all around it was stained red with ocher, the first indication of its great antiquity. A flat rock rested on the skeleton's back. There were grave goods—chipped stone and polished bone spear points, a pile of ocher and graphite stones, a pestle for grinding them to make paint. A walrus tusk. A bone pendant, and a flute made of a hollow bird bone. A carved ivory crescent lay under the chest.

Nothing like this had been found in the region before. A prone burial in a mound was extremely rare anywhere. Archaeologists had found about one hundred pit burials (the body inserted in a sitting position into a hole) in Newfoundland at Port au Choix, but they were only 4,000 years old. The way this skeleton was laid out, chest down in the sand, reminded Tuck and McGhee of ancient bog burials in Denmark. "As far as we know at present," wrote McGhee, "no peoples on earth were taking such pains in disposing of their dead in this manner at that time— a period that preceded the building of the Egyptian pyramids by more than 2,000 years."[10]

Although there were fine photographs of the artifacts and remains, the book said almost nothing about what the physical anthropologists had found. Sonja Jerkic of Memorial University still had the remains in her care. She faxed me all she had ever published about them—a two-page sheet prepared for the National Museum.

The best preserved parts of the remains, her report said, were the skull and lower jaw. The teeth told her this was a young person of between eleven and thirteen years of age, but the teeth were odd. The left incisor was missing, but reconstruction showed there would have been no room for the missing tooth. She wasn't certain about sex or group affiliation and nothing much could be said about the shape of the skull because it "was reconstructed and therefore unreliable in shape and proportion," and because this person was so young (significant craniofacial changes continue throughout adolescence). "However," Jerkic wrote, "from a limited number of traits present the individual seems to be more Indian than Eskimo."[11]

No measurements could be made of the rest of the skeleton; it was too fragmentary. The height of the person could be inferred only from the site itself, at around 150 centimeters. "Consequently," she wrote, "we can presently conclude only that the individual interred beneath the mound at L'Anse-Amour was young, approximately 12 years of age, and was apparently an American Indian."

More than twenty years had gone by since she had produced that slender report—on the second oldest individual ever found in Canada, under the oldest burial mound ever found in North America. That was all she had managed to write about it.

I thought that since L'Anse-Amour was of a similar antiquity to Kennewick, and since the population of known Paleo-Indians was so small, it should be looked at again and possibly compared to Kennewick. Jerkic's paper said the youth's teeth had been recovered. I called and asked if anyone else was doing studies on the remains. She said a graduate student from the Netherlands had recently tried to do something with mtDNA but she had no results. Well, I asked, would she consider looking again at the teeth in light of Joe Powell and Gentry Steele's findings? She advised me that she was much too busy to take the time to get out her notes.

A provincial archaeologist told me about the Milton-Thomazi skeleton, the oldest complete remains ever found in Ontario. In fact it seemed to be one of the oldest skeletons found in the whole of northeastern America, with the exception of the youth in the burial mound at L'Anse-Amour and the remains at Coteau-du-Lac. The bones had been found in the loose, sandy soil of a farmer's field on the south side of a small slope in Peel County, just north of Toronto, in the spring of 1977. A small hill was being mined for gravel when a mandible and teeth popped out. The farmer called the police, the police called Dr. Margaret Milton, then the coroner, a legendary figure given to large hats and strong opinions.[12] Coroner Milton took one look at the teeth, which had no cavities, and after issuing a coroner's warrant took the remains to the University of Toronto to get confirmation of her belief that they were very ancient. They were examined by the departments of anatomy and anthropology, but all she was told was that the remains were probably Indian; no more positive statement could be made. Then she asked the zooarchaeologist Howard Savage to examine the remains. The rest of the burial was eventually uncovered by Savage and four of his students and described in a short paper written by M. Anne Katzenberg and Norman C. Sullivan, published in *Ontario Archaeology* in 1979.[13]

They identified the remains as that of a middle-aged man of about fifty, who had died about 6000 BP. The skeleton had been radiocarbon dated by a good commercial lab, which properly dated the bone protein. The skeleton was essentially complete.

The face had been broken off, and there had been enough distortion from the weight of soil and gravel that it was impossible to put the total skull back together. Some bones were missing. Nevertheless, certain facts emerged. First, the head was fairly large but it was at the extreme lower end of the round-headed category, making it almost long-headed in shape, and therefore a little like Kennewick. The vault (the distance between the top of the eye sockets and the top of the skull) was not high in relation to the breadth of the skull. The skull fitted into the parameters of the Paleo population described by Steele and Powell in the U.S., who had made it clear that most of the Paleo remains they studied were also at the extreme lower end of the round-headed category.

These authors, like Cybulski with Gore Creek, assumed the skeleton was Mongoloid and estimated the person's stature according to the formula worked out by other scholars for Mongoloid populations. They believed the man had stood about 168 centimeters tall. His bones showed marks consistent with arthritis. The teeth he still had at death were free of cavities, but he had suffered from periodontal disease. There were few attempts made to compare this remain with remains of other populations. "The analysis presented is of a preliminary nature since more detailed examination of a single individual is not justifiable at this time."

Now, things had changed. I had already told Chatters that Gore Creek had been reburied. I thought I'd call him about this one, but I wanted to find the skeleton first. I called the anthropology department at the University of Toronto. No one in archaeology knew where these remains could be. I was handed off to Max Friesen in the zooarchaeology lab who could check the database of the university's collections. No, said Friesen, he didn't know of any such remains. Nothing of that sort was listed.

Well, I thought, maybe the coroner still had them. I called the coroner's office: Where might they be now? No idea, they said, call Margaret Milton (by then retired).

She had a story to tell, which was not reflected in the paper published in *Ontario Archaeology*. She faxed me over what she had in her files. She had the original report from the Geochron Laboratory on the skeleton's age: her husband had paid for the dating since no one at the University of Toronto had the budget for it. There was also a 1982 newspaper clipping from *The Toronto Star*, which showed a man identified as Howard Savage standing in a room in front of what looked like racks of rib bones hung in a window. He was holding the Milton-Thomazi skull playfully in his hand.[14]

Milton explained that as soon as she saw the skull, she realized that it was extremely old. Technically the bones were still in her control although she didn't have them in her possession. She'd placed the warrant on the remains because she did not want to send them down to the coroner's morgue in Toronto, which would probably have consigned them to a pauper's burial. She had called her friend Howard Savage. She'd come to know Savage when he was still practicing medicine down the hall from her. She'd sent him cases. Then she learned he was fascinated by zoological archaeology and, since she had a farm, she sent him the bones of any of the animals that died. He compared them to fragments of animal remains pulled off sites as aids in identification. He had amassed a vast collection of bones and become a world-recognized expert on identifying ancient species. He left medicine in the 1970s after he got a chance to go on the archaeological expedition to Old Crow. He had phoned his wife and told her to close up his medical office, that he was going to go into archaeology full time. The University of Toronto gave him a lab, and he taught until he had a severe stroke at the age of eighty-two. His students loved him so much that the university had never retired him. He died in 1996.

When the Milton-Thomazi remains were found, Milton and Savage were both very aware that Native people were upset about the digging of Native graves and were demanding that bones be reburied without study. The two of them were determined to save these remains for science. Howard Savage had kept the remains in his lab at the university all those years.

But Friesen can't find them in the database, I said.

Of course not, Milton replied. Savage never entered them into the university database. Deliberately. That way the Native groups would not hear of them and ask for them back.

I called Friesen and told him Milton's story. He explained that when he took over Savage's lab he had seen no such bones there. But that didn't mean Savage didn't have them. Savage had been a brilliant teacher and a wonderful scientist, but a notorious pack rat. Friesen had spent months trying to straighten out the paperwork regarding all the animal bones Savage had borrowed or loaned to others. Savage had also maintained a huge collection of bones at his home, which had been donated to the university after his death. No one had sorted through those boxes. Possibly the human bones had been mixed in.

Milton suggested I try another of Savage's friends—the secretary of a scientific society he had organized. The friend said she had cleaned out Savage's house herself. It had taken her three months to work her way from the front door all the way through to the back. The remains had been boxed and trucked to the University of Toronto. She had not seen anything remotely like a human bone or skull.

So I called Anne Katzenberg, now a professor at the University of Calgary and one of the authors of the paper on the Milton-Thomazi skeleton. Did she know where the bones were? No, but she knew where she'd last seen them. They had always been on a particular shelf by the door in Savage's lab, underneath the mummified heads.

How could a 6,000-year-old human skeleton have vanished? Remains of this age are so rare, each one had to be important. The Milton-Thomazi bones could help determine whether or not the story of the First Americans, as told for the last hundred years, was too simple. I thought the least I could do was make certain no stone was left unturned. I walked down to the University of Toronto's Borden Building and knocked at the door of Savage's former lab. I knew I was in the right place right away. There by the window stood a rack of animal rib bones, just as they had appeared in the *Toronto Star* photograph of 1982. Friesen was sitting at his computer. He was not at all pleased to see me. I offered to help him search the shelves. No, he said. No thank you.

There seemed to be no physical evidence of the First Americans trekking through Canada on their way south from Beringia. Most of the oldest Canadian remains had been discovered on the eastern half of the continent, not the western side. One had to wonder if evidence had been found, but had then been misdated, or lost, or forgotten on museum shelves. How could archaeologists say it was "accepted" that human beings had migrated down through an ice-free corridor when no dated human remains of the right age had ever been found in the right places?

The bad habit of making up one's mind about what things mean before investigating seemed to be a plague in archaeology. The Carson City, Nevada, story was particularly telling. In the late 1940s, before radiocarbon dating became broadly available, two archaeologists associated with Carson City's Nevada State Museum dug in an extremely dry rock shelter in the desert and came upon some human remains wrapped in mats and textiles. To them, the textiles looked just like others that had been found on other digs in the area, which they had dated by stratigraphy to 1500 BP. In Spirit Cave they found burial bags containing some cremated bone and ash. They also found one complete mummy with flesh and hair. Other skeletons were found later by others in separate locations and taken to the museum, which put them in boxes. Many years went by. In 1994, Ervin Taylor of the University of California at Riverside (the same person who dated Kennewick Man) told the Nevada State Museum curators that he was testing a new method of dating and was looking for bone and hair samples. He told them he'd do the dating for nothing. Curators Donald Touhy and Amy Dansie decided to send him some pieces of bone and hair from the Spirit Cave Mummy, which everyone believed was about 1,500 years old, and later, bone from a site called Wizards Beach.

The Spirit Cave Mummy turned out to have died 9500 years BP. The Wizards Beach skeleton was only slightly younger. Only then, after fifty years in the museum, were the woven textile bags holding cremated remains and the outer and inner wraps surrounding the mummy recognized as revolutionary finds. They pushed back the date for the first known woven textiles in the Americas by many thousands of years. The curators realized when they looked at them more carefully that these textiles were not like other materials in the museum as they had once thought. These textiles were distinctive—they were extremely tightly woven in a twill pattern they called diamond plaiting.[15]

The Augustine Mound in New Brunswick was supposed to be only about 2,000 years old—nothing much, compared to the antiquity of Milton-Thomazi or Gore Creek or L'Anse-Amour. But I found myself wondering if prejudice had interfered with its investigation, too. If scientists at the University of Toronto could lose track of a 6,000-year-old human skeleton while trying to save it for science, if Old Crow artifacts could become 25,000 years younger by dating another fraction of bone, anything was possible. The Augustine Mound, like the Spirit Cave Mummy and its textile wrap, might be much older than believed.

Chris Turnbull, the archaeologist for the province of New Brunswick, had dug the mound in the 1970s. Turnbull had found twenty bodies inside, a really good population. He had published one article in *Archaeology of Eastern North America*[16] and there was also one very extensive unpublished report languishing in the provincial archive. The physical anthropologist at Memorial University, Sonja Jerkic (the same person who studied the L'Anse-Amour burial), had studied the remains but her report still wasn't finished. Turnbull hadn't actually finished the dig either.

Why not?

"We've entered into a new relationship with the Native community," Turnbull said. "It has to do with the awakening of the Native voice in archaeology."

The mound is located on the Red Bank Reserve and had been found by a Native elder. There was an oral tradition that this particular round site was very important. This elder had read about Native American burial mounds and become concerned about preserving it when he heard about a plan to allow the mound to be dug as a gravel pit. The elder dug into it to save it. He found human remains and artifacts. He got hold of one of his kids at St. Thomas University in Fredericton, who passed this information along to his professor, who passed it along to Turnbull in 1972. Turnbull went out to see the site. "It's an important find and a puzzling one," Turnbull said. "It didn't look like things in the local sequence. There were quite different large-stemmed points and there was lots of copper made into beads." In other words, the spear points and the copper beads were unlike other artifacts found around New Brunswick.

After three years of delicate negotiation between the province, the Red Bank Band, and the federal government, the federal Department of Indian and Northern Affairs issued the first permit ever to allow the province to do an archaeological dig on First Nations land. All of this was made more complicated by the fact that the Natives of the Maritimes had never surrendered their lands to the Crown; they had only signed peace and friendship treaties.

In 1975 Turnbull began to dig, but under severe restrictions. The province had to recognize that all the materials found belonged to the Red Bank community. The second condition was that the human remains found had to be reburied. "We report to the band council on this," Turnbull said. "The control rests with the community."

The dig took place over the next three summers. The grave materials found with the human remains looked an awful lot like Adena cultural materials to him. The Adena were mound builders who created a complex society centered around the Ohio valley about 3,000 years ago.[17] He had believed until the Augustine Mound dig that the Adena culture was mainly confined there. Yet this mound suggested to him that this culture had left its mark 1,500 miles to the northeast of the Ohio Valley, at the confluence of two branches of one of the great salmon and sturgeon rivers of the world, the Miramichi, only thirty miles from the ocean. The Augustine Mound was just as old as the oldest Ohio Valley sites. Turnbull also dug a big stratified site nearby that went back 3,000 years. The burial-mound remains were well preserved and were of several types: there were a dozen individual pit graves, one cremation, several secondary and one or two primary burials. He found fly pupae on the bodies, which meant they were quite fresh when interred. He also found red ocher. And textiles.

The textiles were both baskets and wraps made of something that looked remarkably like hair twined around something like gut. Their excellent state of preservation was due to the huge quantity of copper beads found in the graves. Copper is antibacterial and prevents decay. The origin of the copper was unknown. The complete analysis of the textiles hadn't been done either. He gave me the name of a woman working on the textiles at the Nova Scotia Museum. Some of the materials found in the mound were local and some were not, but he wanted to emphasize that it wasn't just the material goods that had travelled up from Ohio, it was the whole cultural style. The goods in the graves in the Augustine Mound were very much like the things found in Adena graves in the Ohio Valley. But it made no geographic sense. The Ohio River was so far away.

The dates were done on charcoal "taken from the grave fill," he said. This is not exactly the gold standard for radiocarbon dating. He hadn't dated the bone. He hadn't dared to suggest it to the Native community. And it was too late now. "We have returned all Native remains in New Brunswick," he said. "All."

I phoned Sonja Jerkic again with a heavy heart. What had she published on the twenty bodies pulled from the mound and put back in the ground? (The twenty angry souls disturbed at their rest, was how the man with the long gray braid would have put it.) She had gathered data on them, she said, but had never written it up.

Why not? I asked.

"I'm slow," she said. "I haven't thought about them in twenty years."

Was the date reliable? I asked. Was it not possible that these remains were of the same vintage as the skeleton found under a mound up the Labrador coast? She agreed it was only an assumption that the charcoal had burned at the same time the bodies were interred and that the charcoal and the bodies were therefore about the same age. But she didn't doubt the date. "The artifacts show Adena-like characteristics."

Since the bones were gone, I turned my attention to the textiles that had wrapped them. Ruth Holmes Whitehead of the Nova Scotia Museum and her volunteer research associate Joleen Gordon had studied them. Whitehead was planning a book, but what she could say was that the textile work was so rich that nothing had been made in the Maritimes to match it until four hundred years ago. For example, there were pieces of thirty-strand finger-woven cloth, and there were samples of material spun out of hair dyed in two different colors. The RCMP forensic lab in Halifax had only been able to establish that these hairs were mammalian, but Whitehead speculated that these textiles could have been made from dog, woodland buffalo or muskox hair. Whitehead hadn't tried to compare these fabrics with other samples of the same period elsewhere: she did know that most of what she saw was not like what Native people were doing in New Brunswick at the time of European contact.

Two pictures of the textile fragments appeared in a booklet published through the museum. Whoever they were, the people who made these materials really moved around, Whitehead offered. The burial goods included what seemed to be a remnant of a two-sided woven carrying bag that would have fitted more easily into a canoe than a hard basket.

Was she aware of the textiles at the Carson City Museum? I asked—long shot of long shots.

She certainly was. "I'd love to go see that." She sent me a copy of the publication. In amongst the samples of nineteenth-century Mi'kmaq weaving and basketry there was a small picture of a twined fabric made of moose hair, and a large photograph of a rougher textile made of cat-tail interwoven with rush. It looked just like the outer mat used to wrap Nevada's Spirit Cave Mummy.[18]

# The Battle for Monte Verde

## Rewriting the First American Story—by Committee

THE TONGUE-TWISTING phrase "absence of evidence is not evidence of absence" soon became a kind of mantra for me. I kept having to use it to explain why, in spite of the fact that there was no direct evidence of human beings entering the hemisphere through Canada, the old story of the First Americans was broadly accepted. But in the summer of 1998, stiff winds of change whipped through its rickety framework. *National Geographic* featured a long story about the finds made in southern Chile by Tom Dillehay at a site called Monte Verde. The National Geographic Society's reporter described an extraordinary meeting of twelve senior American archaeologists who'd made the journey down to Chile to evaluate Monte Verde. Dillehay's second book of evidence (*Monte Verde: A Late Pleistocene Settlement in Chile*, vol. 2) had been published in 1997. With copies of this weighty tome in hand, U.S. Paleo experts including David Meltzer, C. Vance Haynes, Dennis Stanford and Alex Barker went to look at the artifacts stored in Dillehay's Kentucky lab, and then traveled to Chile to visit a museum and take a look at what remained of the site itself. They then declared they were satisfied that Dillehay was right. Monte

Verde was a human site, without Clovis technology, a thousand years older than the oldest accepted Clovis dates in North America. Clovis, these arbiters declared, was no longer first. Monte Verde was.[1]

The *National Geographic* article also presented a somewhat fanciful reconstruction of the life lived by a small group of people in the southern part of the Chilean rain forest at Monte Verde more than 12,500 years ago. Dillehay had found evidence of a large structure, which consisted of a grouping of little huts tied together and covered over with the skin of a mastodon. It was described as an early form of a longhouse. Nearby, Dillehay had found the foundation of a wishbone-shaped hut. The article suggested that Monte Verdeans had gone there to chew a mix of seaweed and *boldo*, a hallucinogenic plant. There were pictures of some of the wooden tools, round bola stones and the twists of cordage Dillehay had found, plus an illustration of a human footprint that had been preserved in ancient clay. The amount of effort invested in this site had convinced Dillehay that these were settled people, not the wide-roaming hunters and gatherers all Paleo-Indians were believed to be.

The *National Geographic*'s few pictures and illustrations couldn't begin to do justice to the enormous volume of evidence Dillehay had recovered from the site. It had been studied and interpreted by a host of specialists, who published their findings in Dillehay's two-volumed *Monte Verde*.[2] I had taken both out of the library and gone through them. *Monte Verde* 1 opened with an introduction by Alan Bryan, an emeritus archaeology professor at the University of Alberta, who, in the 1960s, had put forward the thesis that there were many good pre-Clovis sites all over the Americas that were ignored by the Clovis First proponents. (For his pains, he'd been unable to attract graduate students.) Bryan's rousing, never-again-should-we-let-good-work-be-suppressed-by-bigots essay was matched in its fervent tone by Dillehay's own account of how his early work at the site had been denigrated and almost derailed by the late scholar Junius Bird. Dillehay had just won the Society for American Archaeology's National Book Award for these works.

Jack Rossen had been Dillehay's ethnobotanist at Monte Verde. I went to see him first because the plant remains pulled off the site were utterly entrancing. The Monte Verdeans apparently exploited the natural world around them as if it was a garden. Their knowledge of plants and their uses was so extensive that it suggested they had been in southern America for a very long time.

Rossen lives in Ithaca, New York, a college town strung out along a road that runs through a valley between limestone cliffs. Ithaca houses two schools of higher learning. One is Cornell University—the former home of Tom Lynch, a Clovis First proponent who had recently moved on to a natural history museum in Brasos, Texas. Lynch had fought off most claims for sites older than Clovis with a wonderful eye for the telling weakness in the way a site was dug and reported. For years Lynch had argued that Monte Verde should not be accepted as a pre-Clovis site, although he had never actually gone to evaluate it himself. Ithaca College is the other major school in town. Jack Rossen taught there then on a year-to-year appointment. (He is now in a tenure-track position.) While it is a very expensive private school ("It costs $27,000 a year to study with Jack," as Rossen put it) it is not the kind of place where people bent on a major research career hope to find themselves. But Rossen considered himself lucky— his work on Monte Verde had branded him a dissenter. He'd been threatened, he'd been accosted, he'd been accused of helping Dillehay plant evidence and mislead the world. The vituperation he endured was more than he could ever have imagined in his wildest dreams.

Rossen was a curly-headed, soft-eyed, soft-voiced man in his early forties with a sense of time passing him by ("Oh God, look how old I'm getting, my slides are fading," he said as he pulled his Monte Verde material off a shelf). He had started university as an English major but decided he didn't want to be like his dad, an optometrist who stayed in his office all day, every day. He wanted to be outside, doing something fun, like archaeology. The fun really started for him in 1982, when he was an MA student focusing on archaeological ethnobotany at the University of Kentucky. He'd gotten ten digs under his belt by his MA year, a vast range of experience. He bugged Professor Dillehay to take him on a dig in South America. He'd been there on his own in 1979—he'd worked and travelled in Peru and fallen in love with it. Dillehay was known then as an urban archaeologist, a man who specialized in large pre-Columbian city sites. But one day he called Rossen and asked if he'd like to work on a site called Monte Verde in Chile.

Rossen arrived in time for the big field season of 1983. By then, Dillehay had managed to get around the major roadblocks strewn in his path by the leading lights in South American archaeology. After applying and being rejected, he'd finally gotten a grant from the National Science Foundation to do a major excavation. He was taking extraordinary things out of the ground, particularly evidence of a very wide and interesting use of plants. Everything had been beautifully preserved by the peat bogs that covered the site. The wood was not fossilized. The feces looked as if they'd been laid down yesterday. "This is not an ephemeral site," Rossen said, "which is why it is so strange, this questioning of the site."

Monte Verde is south of the Chilean city of Valdivia, at about 40 degrees south latitude. Dillehay had thirty other students and workers housed in a tent city in the middle of a farmer's field just at the edge of woods. The site is affected by the South Pacific; it rains 250 days a year and there is ice at night even in the summer. But Rossen soon realized that in terms of ecological diversity it was a Garden of Eden. Some fifty kilometers west and twenty kilometers south at the coast were sand dunes and salt marshes. There was a high-canopy forest, a low swampy forest, an open meadow and true peat bogs. With help from local farmers and Chilean colleagues who knew the plants, their seasons and properties, he gathered in the evidence.

The geologists' studies showed that the climate at Monte Verde had swung as the Ice Age ended. At 11,500 BP the plant life was almost identical to current conditions. The site, dated to around 12,500 BP, produced remains of the pollen of seventy-two species of plants that are still growing in the area. They also found remains of eleven or twelve other plants that must have been brought from other locations by the people who used them.

Dillehay had told him that the site had dates older than Clovis, but never really emphasized it. Dillehay, in Rossen's recollection, had been more interested in the meaning of the site. What Dillehay wanted to understand was who these people were. The site suggested quite a sophisticated mode of living for people who seemed to rely so heavily on gathering. They lived together but had separate cubicles, which suggested a kind of social structure. "It's a hamlet, there's a separation of public and private space, a well-developed commerce and exchange system," Rossen explained. "This is not a simple culture.... The way they dealt with plants in some ways almost approximates the way agriculturalists deal with plants."

He meant by this that the people who lived at Monte Verde didn't just wander and gather fruits as they found them. They took maximum advantage of all kinds of plant properties that would take very careful observation to understand. All of this fascinated Rossen, whose area of specialization is understanding how people made the transition from gathering to agriculture. He experimented at Monte Verde and in the lab at the University of Kentucky trying to figure out how Monte Verdeans had used these plants, and whether it might have been possible to sustain a year-round community at this site by gathering. Using copies of the various split pebble tools Dillehay had found, to see how they would be most efficiently used, he harvested the local plants and processed them.

These tools had bothered the first experts who examined Dillehay's artifacts. They weren't carefully made spear points or scrapers like those one would find on a Clovis site. They were just hand-sized rocks, split to produce sharp working edges. Clovis First proponents did not believe they were tools at all. But Dillehay argued that their edges had been artfully shaped, and polished by use. Rossen bagged the junco weed, which grew everywhere, winnowed it in the air and pounded the seeds into a mush. He discovered that stone mortars didn't work well, but that a wooden mortar worked fine. And that's what was found on the site: wooden mortars with junco seed in the cracks. The mush he made was edible. "It's not that bad," he said, making a face.

As Rossen showed me his slides in one of Ithaca College's classrooms, he got angry about the critics all over again. He showed pictures of the artifacts found under the peat—including cordage tied into knots, wooden beams that had clearly been made square with a sharp plane tool, and pegs used to tie mastodon skin down tight to the ground, all obvious products of human ingenuity. But the better the artifacts, the worse the accusations had become. "I was accused," he said, "of helping Tom plant artifacts at the site."

He would not say by whom. "No one would go official, [but the rumors] would circulate around at meetings. These logs were squared and planed with stone tools. The wishbone structure has a vise with a tool still in place. They cut the logs, they'd burn and cut a little, burn and cut, so there's a stepped effect.... There's a mastodon tusk shovel...there's a broad sheen on the edge from use. It's absurd to question the site."

Rossen had been asked by Dillehay to dig the wishbone structure himself because he was very experienced and Dillehay wanted it done to the highest possible standard. What Rossen unearthed was a foundation made of a cement that he thought was made of animal fats mixed with soil, and inside, around this foundation's rim, a number of wads of the hallucinogenic boldo plant, all mixed in with four different seaweeds. These wads of chewed plant material still carried the imprint of human teeth. Rossen didn't think the structure could have been a sweat lodge because there were no hearths inside, but there were a great many hearths around the outside. He thought it was a medicine hut, a place where hallucinogens were used. He'd also found in the site the remains of a wide variety of plants, all entirely edible. There were seeds of fruiting trees that still grow in the area, which were delicious and available pretty much year round. And then there were the remains he found of a weird plant called a sundew.

"It's a carnivorous plant," he explained. "It has tentacles with gel and it envelops flies and insects and digests them.... It is saxifragous—it grows in rocks. There are some in the local area, but not at the creek. They brought it to the site." The researchers found these plant remains in the places where people lived, where flies gather. "They can eat a colony of fruit flies in a week." These plants, though inedible, have one other useful property. The gel that attacts flies also kills bacteria. The Mapuche Indians still use it as a medicinal agent.

More slides went by. He stopped at another plant. "Ah, club moss, lycopodium," he said. "This is from the mountains, at least fifty kilometers to the east. This stuff is most common on the site." Spores of this moss were found in all the places where people had made fires. Each cubicle space in the house structure had its own little clay-covered area that appeared to have been used as a brazier. "I discovered it was used in Shakespearean theater to make flash lightning ... it's really flammable.... A Chilean botanist put it in the water and wrung it out and this stuff lit. It's your fire starter." What, he asked, could be a more valuable thing to have in a rainforest than something that will always catch fire? But the moss didn't grow near the site: it came from the grasslands some distance away. "It needs open areas ... and high elevations.... Its [presence] suggests commerce and some movement." In fact, they'd found materials brought to the site from everywhere but the south.

Rossen learned that the junco weed and wild potatoes were available all year. They would have provided Monte Verdeans with a stable source of carbohydrates and proteins. The potatoes showed that there was some kind of selection going on. But in Rossen's view the most vital thing he learned was that the Monte Verdeans had been settled on this site. He'd carefully plotted the fruiting seasons of all the plant remains found in the living area. In order for all these varieties to find their way into the human living spaces at Monte Verde, the people would have had to be there all year.

It took Rossen four months in the field, then about a year of lab work, to reach these conclusions. He wanted to rush it into print. Dillehay wouldn't let him. "Tom's a smart guy. Probably a genius.... Partly he's a control freak.... He knew it had to be perfect.... When I went back to Chile on a Fulbright I...learned new stuff which made it a lot better.... I looked at seaweed hills on the coast. I was down there eight months and spent two months on seaweed ecology. It's very complex, like a jungle. I learned [the] ones we found [on the site] were seasonally specific."

Dillehay wanted to delay and win acceptance for the site before Rossen published anything about it. He was worried about Rossen's reputation. "He was protecting me as well as himself. I was still a graduate student." Dillehay knew that graduate students who published work challenging an orthodoxy as entrenched as the Clovis First story were going to find themselves in big trouble. So they kept Rossen's information about Monte Verde close to the vest. They were careful, they were conservative, they waited till they had all their ducks in a row. But it didn't do them any good. "The fraud thing circulated before we published a thing," Rossen said.

The consequences are still with him. Until 1998, he'd never had an interview for a tenure-track job, Rossen said. "I'm associated with Monte Verde, a pariah project for years...."

He found the atmosphere at learned meetings was often poisonous. Dillehay told him to "get an edge, Jack. When you're right and you know you are, snap right back, 'You're wrong.'" Of course, Rossen said sardonically, he found it hard to snap back when someone was shouting at him, which had happened to him at one academic meeting the previous year. No, he would not say exactly who did it—well, yes he would, but it was off the record.

Threading through stories of the consequences of a radical revision, we finally arrived at the troubling problem of career fear: it had hobbled Clovis First dissenters, and important facts had been suppressed because of it. It was a short jump from such fear to all the other real and imaginary problems archaeologists encounter when they work with human bones.

Rossen told me a story. Some time after he worked on Monte Verde, he had dug a whole cemetery in Peru. He was looking at the burial practices that seemed to be associated with the cultural transition from hunting and gathering to agriculture. He found that most of the skeletons in this particular cemetery had been smashed into tiny pieces, a common practice associated with the transition. He had no difficulty getting local workers to help him with these bone fragments. But then, one morning, they came across the skeleton of a huge man lying stretched out with a boulder on his chest as if to hold him down. Almost all of his bones were intact. The workers were terrified. The belief, Rossen explained, is that one breaks bones to set powerful spirits free—but this skeleton was not broken, ergo, the powerful spirit was still in there. His workers took off.

At the time, Rossen was suffering a bout of malaria. He was exhausted and dizzy. He went to his little field hut, stretched out on his cot and fell into a dream in which the man from the grave walked into his hut, sat down on the stool beside him, and said, Leave my bones alone. In his dream, Rossen argued and reasoned with him. He explained to the man the virtues of the work he was doing, how important his skeleton was to science. The man said, Leave my bones alone, or else. Rossen woke up covered with sweat, the "or else" hanging in the air. He knew what he had to do. He was in Peru on a grant. It was "Get on with the data or die right here." So he pulled the bones out of the ground, put them in a box, and took them into town to the office he used at a local university—his home base in Peru. He put the box on a high shelf behind his desk.

One night, the scholar in the office next door heard moaning and screaming coming from Rossen's locked room. He called the police. The police broke down the door. They found the room empty but the box of bones sitting on Rossen's desk. His terrified students begged him to rebury the bones. He ignored them.

He returned to the U.S. in 1987. He arrived home to find that his girlfriend had left him for his best friend. While he was trying to recover from that blow, he got a call from another friend asking him to work as a volunteer on a job. Land with Native graves owned by a Kentucky farmer named Slack had been leased out to a bunch of looters. They had torn the Native American burials found there to pieces—scattering human bones everywhere in their haste to get at the goods buried with them. Rossen helped put the mess back together. The American Indian Movement heard about it and set up a symbolic occupation. This drew camera crews, whose newscasts were seen by certain powerful politicians in Washington. The vicious greed at Slack Farm moved some U.S. legislators to cobble together an early version of the Native American Graves Protection and Repatriation Act.

So what are you telling me? I asked Rossen. Are you saying that pulling that man's bones out of the ground put a blight on your life?

He rolled his eyes, as if to acknowledge the absurdity of such a notion, but there were certain objective facts. He was forty-two, still unmarried; he had no permanent academic home, no tenure as of yet. His wonderful work on Monte Verde was more than a decade behind him, but it was still giving him trouble. It had taken twenty years for Dillehay, and, by extension, for him, to have this work accepted. At the annual meeting of the Society for American Archaeology he'd watched Dillehay accept the book award with tears in his eyes.

Tom Dillehay, professor of archaeology at the University of Kentucky, really did not look like a hero of science. He sat slouched in his black leather jacket in an empty restaurant near the University of Chicago. He had a scarf knotted at his neck, which did not look rakish. He was all legs and arms, with a ski-jump nose and an RCMP corporal's mustache. He stared out through the plate glass at the February fog, which merged with the gray snow. He was in Chicago starting a temporary appointment, and his girlfriend had flown in that afternoon. He was just back from Chile, where it was summer, so there was a certain tinge of browny pink to his skin—but he didn't look rested. He was still simmering over questions I had asked him earlier. What exactly did I want? Why was I asking these questions? Why did everyone ask him why certain things had *not* been found at Monte Verde, instead of talking to him about what he did find there? This was the kind of thing that had been driving him crazy, this was what he absolutely could not take anymore. He was sick to death of defending Monte Verde from questions like mine.

I had thought Monte Verde no longer needed defending. And I thought my question was reasonable enough. While he had found evidence of psychotropic plants brought to the site from the mountains and hunks of seaweed brought in from the ocean, he had found no evidence that the people of Monte Verde ate fish from the creek on their doorstep. There were no hooks, no fish-bones of any sort. Why not? I'd asked. And where was the human bone he'd found, but which had not been dated? A dated human bone would have put to rest all the controversy over the site. He had thought it important enough to put a picture of it in volume two of *Monte Verde*, but the information accompanying the picture was very vague.

I didn't press him. Alan Bryan had warned me that Dillehay's sense of humor had dwindled. Bryan, who had found and published on what he thought was an ancient, premodern calotte (the top of the skull) he'd found in Brazil, only to have it vanish in mysterious circumstances, knew all about the importance of a sense of humor. But one would not have thought that finding the first accepted archaeological site in the Americas older than Clovis would require a sense of humor.

Dillehay was born in Texas, did his BA in political science, then got his doctorate at one of the great schools in U.S. archaeology, the University of Texas at Austin. He'd been interested in archaeology since he was eleven or twelve, when he'd started hunting for arrowheads. He'd studied, dug, lectured and had academic appointments all over South America since 1972—in Uruguay, Peru and Chile, but mostly Chile. Doing contract work in Texas, Louisiana and New Mexico, he'd seen his share of Clovis and Folsom sites, but in his early years he wasn't interested in the whole debate about who got to the Americas first. He was interested in politics.

It was the Pinochet coup, overthrowing the elected government of Salvador Allende, that took him to Chile. Pinochet, like the other military dictators running Latin American governments in the 1970s, did not like social scientists, who were assumed to be dangerous leftists. Chilean social scientists were thrown in jail or out of the country, or both. The InterAmerican Development Bank, in association with the Vatican, wanted to restore some social science and humanities instruction in Chilean universities. Dillehay was hired by the Development Bank and the Universidade Catolica de Chile in Temuco as a professor of anthropology in 1975, before he officially had his doctorate. The next year the Universidade Austral de Chile at Valdivia in southern Chile asked him to found a department of anthropology. Southern Chile was unknown archaeologically—there was some information on late cultures, but no real survey work had ever been done. He sent out word that if anybody found anything of interest, they should let him know.

One day in 1977 a student came to see him. The student had been out in the country when people cutting down trees near a creek came upon some bones they thought were large cow teeth. The student brought them to the university for identification. They turned out to be the teeth of a mastodon. Dillehay went out and did some test pits. Certain indications made him suspect there might be a human site there. He went to the National Museum in Santiago to tell them about it, hoping they'd take it on. No one there wanted to pursue it. "They were used to working in the climate of central and northern Chile—warm and dry. I tried to give it away. When we got the radiocarbon dates, no one wanted to touch it, knowing it was older than 11,000 years. They knew they'd get burned by advocating an early site."

Research money in Latin America in those days came mostly from the U.S. Chilean students applied to agencies like the New York–based Wenner-Gren Foundation or the National Geographic Society, or their American colleagues shared their National Science Foundation grants. "If you were advocating pre-Clovis," Dillehay said, "you were putting your career in difficulty." This was utterly ridiculous, in his view, since no Clovis technology has ever been found in South America.

"It was imposed on South America," Dillehay said bitterly, "by Junius Bird of the American Museum of Natural History. He found flutes down there in the 1970s. Cornell's Tom Lynch picked up on that theme. There are one or two of these people in each generation, the experts on this topic. Everyone listens to them.... If the data doesn't fit, throw [the data] out. If the dates don't fit, something's wrong with the site."

Yet in spite of the fact that his first dates were early, the National Geographic Society gave Dillehay a grant of $5,000 to have a closer look at Monte Verde.[3] This gave the Society the right to "hang their logo on the research project," said Dillehay. In those days, five thousand dollars went a long way, and he was grateful because it helped launch the work, but in other respects it was disastrous. The Society sent down its watchdog, Junius Bird, to make certain its money was being properly spent. Bird had planned a yacht trip with a wealthy Chilean family for January 1979. Dillehay was told Bird would come by to investigate. Dillehay had found choppers, some flakes (pieces of stone left by the chipping of a stone tool), hearths, single-faced tools, some cut wood, bola stones and burned mastodon bones. But he had found no spear points like those used by ancient North American hunters. He gathered these artifacts, photos of hearths, his geologist colleague Mario Pina and twenty students at his lab to greet the great man.

"He spent about forty minutes," said Dillehay. "Most of it was focused on stories about his work at Tierra del Fuego.... The remaining few minutes [he] looked at the artifacts. He'd [also] found bola stones at Tierra del Fuego. He said he wasn't a bone specialist. He said, where are the projectile points? Got to have [them] if [this is] a kill site." At the time, Dillehay was nonplussed, but he wasn't worried because he thought he'd have a chance to show Bird the site later. "We went to set up the excavation of the site. Bird was supposed to come a week later. He came several days earlier and we were just removing the overburden. He stayed two nights and two days and left. He didn't see the excavation of artifacts in situ. If he'd come one week later he would have seen projectile points associated with a mastodon."

By March, Dillehay got the first bad news. Colleagues in Santiago said that Bird had come through and told people that Monte Verde was not an archaeological site. "He wrote a letter to the Chilean Archeological Society and the National Geographic Society putting the site in question," said Dillehay. "The suggestion was, maybe Tom should have stayed with pre-Hispanic, and not this stuff—he made mistakes.

"Junius fibbed," said Dillehay. "He did not see the dig or the excavation. He was at the site when we were taking off the overburden. He told people he had, by saying, 'I was at the dig and didn't see this.'... That set the stage for doubts on everything."

In 1980 Dillehay's National Geographic Society money was cut off. He called up to find out why. He was told Junius Bird thought it wasn't an archaeological site. Then he was turned down by the National Science Foundation, the chief funder of academic work in the United States. According to John Yellen, then head of archaeological grants at the foundation, the number of people who were qualified to peer-review grant applications on Paleo-Indian sites in South America was very small in the late 1970s and 1980s. The foundation was hard pressed to find the six North American experts required by its rules. The list of peers would certainly have included Tom Lynch, C. Vance Haynes and Junius Bird. Yellen, according to Dillehay, finally helped him to rebut his reviewers' objections in order to get his grant application accepted. By 1983, the National Science Foundation had begun to support Dillehay's work.

But doubts still clung to important Monte Verde finds. In the 1983 field season (the one attended by Jack Rossen), Dillehay and his students excavated human footprints in clay. There were fifty or sixty witnesses there at the time. Nevertheless, he later heard from critics that there were only a few there to observe the event, and those with doubts were "overwhelmed by Tom." Then he heard that critics were saying the footprints had actually been made by students who were drinking themselves silly at night and staggering through the exposed site barefoot. "We covered it every night, it was fenced, no drinks and it was thirty-five degrees Fahrenheit at night...it was totally absurd stuff."

By the time of this big field season, Dillehay had long since quit his job in Chile and taken up his academic appointment at the University of Kentucky. He came home because his wife had divorced him and he just couldn't take living full time in Chile anymore. It was hard to live on a local salary and also make child-support payments, but the politics were worse: the hard years in Chile were from 1976 to 1985. All the time he was there, either at a Chilean institution or working as a foreigner on his dig, he was under close scrutiny by the military, who thought he and his students were leftists. The Chilean leftists, on the other hand, thought he was working for the CIA. The military were trying to put down the Native American population and push them off their land. As the head of an anthropology department, he felt it was his duty to defend them. He wrote a book on Mapuche ethnicity and how their identification with their land long predated the Chilean state. The government allowed it to be printed, but as soon as the new books were stacked in the print shop, the shop and the books were burned to the ground. At one point he met with Augusto Pinochet to explain what he was doing down at Monte Verde. It wasn't that Pinochet gave a damn, but the people next to him were listening, and they could deny or give access to the countryside. The secret police liked to visit the wives of his American colleagues while they were away and tell them that their husbands had been killed. When the wives got hysterical and phoned the U.S. Embassy (which in its early days approved the Pinochet coup), they were treated with bland disinterest. His Chilean colleagues were picked up and beaten and jailed. As a senior university official and an American, it had fallen to him to escort their wives to jail to look for them: the wives often had to bed the jailers before they could see their husbands.

As early as 1979 he'd known he would need the help of specific science experts to really learn what the Monte Verde site had to offer. "We had pits, hearths, twine, footprints, timber foundations." They also found on the site stones from the ocean beach, rock from the Andes, plant remains, pollens and phy-toliths (tiny crystallized pieces of plant tissue) of nonlocal plants. The timbers were from saltwater estuaries. The boldo, which today is only found in central Chile, was not in the pollen record for Monte Verde either, meaning it was probably imported then, too. They found grasses and tubers that grow only in the high-lands and only at certain elevations, and they found only the usable portions. He had people look at the wild potatoes' chro-mosome structure and it turned out it was slightly different from current forms. "I thought it was too speculative to say they were semi-domesticated since all others were wild."

Instead of being persuaded by all these signs of the hands of humanity, Clovis proponents were bothered by this profusion of plant evidence. Most Clovis sites had been dug early on in the development of American archaeology when most archaeologists sifted the dirt on their sites through quarter-inch-mesh screens; the only things pulled from such sites were big worked stones, leftover flakes from the making of stone tools, and animal bones. Everything smaller just disappeared through the mesh. But by the 1980s, sophisticated archaeologists were using all the technologies the life sciences had to offer. Dillehay, using water flotation and tiny screens, captured minute grains of pollen, which could identify plant species, from which one could infer climate; he could recover feces, phytoliths, and human and animal hair, which is very slow to decay and can be dated. His experts tried to identify proteins left behind on stones or wood from the crushing of plants or the cutting of flesh or hide. Monte Verde was a spectacular piece of luck. The peat bogs that covered the site had sucked out all the oxygen that in the normal course would have hastened the chemical destruction of the organic remains. Dillehay was amazed at the preservation of the organic material under the peat. He found chunks of mastodon meat and thousands of flecks of animal hide. The pathologists could see clearly the cellular structure of a now extinct species of camel. "I thought, Jesus. The research team kept expanding. By 1985 the winds were swinging in favor of Monte Verde."

But some specialists wanted reassurance that Monte Verde really was an archaeological site—that is, a place used by human beings. They didn't want to waste their time and resources studying pollen grains from a site visited only by mastodons. They told him that they were hearing concerns about the archaeology, that this site could not possibly be as old as he claimed. The refusal by his peers to entertain the idea of a pre-Clovis site could have become a self-fulfilling prophecy. He had to prove this work was worth their time.

Which brought us to the issue of the dates. His early dates came in two groups, one cluster of dates around 12,500 BP and another group around 33,000 BP. He had done very little work on the section of the site that had produced the extremely ancient dates. He had found clay-lined pits containing charcoal, which gave the distinct impression that these pits had been used by people, and he had described them in his reports, but he spent little effort explaining what those features and dates meant. I asked him why he had just reported the second group of dates, and left it at that.

He'd come across the clay-lined pits in 1979, the same year Junius Bird gave him the thumbs down. He had cut a number of test pits and trenches around the site. One long trench had produced the more ancient material. Eventually, he found twenty-six stones in three clay-lined features (areas of the soil rather like hearths); burned and unburned charcoal lay on this lining in the depression at the same level as the stones. The radiocarbon dates came back 16,000, 18,000, and 30,000 to 45,000 BP (the outer limit that radiocarbon techniques can date). The stratigraphy was consistent with those dates.

So, I asked, what did they mean?

"Not much interested in it," he said with a flip of his hand. "I do become interested in the dating game when people say that if the dates are older than 12,000 there must be something wrong. I do have problems with that deeper component. Could geological processes form that, or natural fires? ... I have a hard time accepting human presence as far back as 40,000 years ago, to get people to Monte Verde by 33,000."

I was surprised by his reluctance to pursue this other find at Monte Verde. There were scholars working in linguistics and genetics who were beginning to say that their results could only be explained by human presence in the Americas at least 35,000 years ago. One linguist at the University of California had recently argued that the great language diversity found in the Americas must have taken at least 35,000 years to develop.[4] Those calculating the time it takes for particular genetic mutations to arise believed that certain peculiarly American genetic features would also have taken that long to appear. Dillehay knew of this work. But he couldn't imagine a Bering Strait entry that early, and he couldn't imagine oceanic contact at all. Yes, he knew that it was now accepted that man made his way across open ocean to Australia 50,000 years ago, but to think of prehistoric man traveling to the New World by way of the ocean required a large chunk of faith, which he didn't have.

"I don't think they came in any fashion other than the Bering Strait," he said. "Here's where I get hung up: What is the possibility of people having boat technology to traverse those seas?"

This resistance was built on the assumption that it would have been easier for primitive people to slowly follow herds across Alaskan mountains, down through the Northwest Territories, Alberta and Saskatchewan over hundreds of years (and therefore hundreds of winters) than to get into boats and drift on ocean currents around the Pacific or Atlantic rims. Yet Dillehay had evidence that the people who lived at Monte Verde 12,500 years ago were able to do sophisticated woodworking, tie complex knots, live together in a complicated fashion and bring in timbers and exotic plants from a 200-kilometer radius around their home. Why wouldn't people apply those same skills to making boats or rafts and using them to get around?

It wasn't just that, he said. It was also that one had to have boats big enough to bring a population of sufficient size to sustain itself.

I stared at him hard. His eyes were bland, blank. In my view, this was a sillier argument than the one before. If people could build one boat, or seaworthy raft, they could build twenty. Why this sudden failure of the imagination?

We began to talk again of the peer scrutiny of Monte Verde, which he felt was extreme. "Instead of looking at the positive information, they looked at one single blemish. One guy stood up at a meeting and said, That one timber on your tent has two stakes, not four. But how do you know what the criteria [for tent staking] are? ... People said, hey, three footprints. Clay [was] brought to the site, muddy clay was used to refurbish the pits and hearths. Some [pits were] walked across and where [the clay] tapers, the third [footprint] is smeared. Instead of focusing on the first two, someone will focus on the toe prints that are missing.... We found some feces; some were inconclusive as to whether they were human. Then there were the dung-eating beetles. There are beetles specifically adapted to eat human dung, but these were not that species." In other words, defending his conclusions about the part of the site that produced dates of 12,500 BP was hard enough. He didn't need the aggravation of trying to explain the far more ancient dates.

I wanted to know what he'd learned from the human bone. When I spoke to him to arrange our meeting, I mentioned that important remains had gone missing, or been reburied, in Canada. He found that fascinating.

"So what about the human bone?"

"Well, it's in the book," he said. "It's part of the piece. And while I was down there [in Chile] I mentioned about the remains disappearing to other colleagues and I heard of two more. That is what I find so fascinating... the way these things keep slipping away, how science loses its memory.

"In 1978," he went on, "we found bones eroded [out of the creek bank]. One was very distinct, with an old, weakened look. It looked different. I took it to the National Museum of Natural History in Santiago. The paleontologist said, 'I don't think this is an animal bone. Show it to Juan Munizaga.'" Munizaga was a Chilean physical anthropologist. "Juan said, 'It looks like human bone. Take it back to the museum and leave it there.'"

Munizaga thought someone at the museum could arrange for the careful examination of the bone. Dillehay took it to the museum and that was the last he ever saw of it. So nothing has been learned from the bone. Juan Munizaga, the only specialist who saw it, had offered the opinion that the bone was probably human, but he has since died.

I hung my head in frustration, thinking of what could be done with it now. It might have had enough collagen to get an accurate date. Its mitochondrial DNA could have been studied and possibly compared to current Native American and world populations. Most of all, a dated human bone would have spared Dillehay twenty years of struggle to get the site accepted as a place of human occupation older than any Clovis sites in North America.

"It was in a box marked Monte Verde," he mumbled, staring out the restaurant window. "I got a photo of it. I published it in the second volume at page 664. I was there [at the museum in Santiago] last month, and I asked them to please send it to me if it shows up. It's an old museum, not a very good catalogue system. There are bones everywhere. I think they put it in small box among tens of thousands of items.... I think if the box had said Clovis, human bone, it would never have been lost."

This was a variation of the disappearance of the calotte found by Alan Bryan, the man who wrote the introduction to Dillehay's first volume. In 1970 Bryan had been visiting at the Natural History Museum of the Federal University of Minas Gerais in Brazil. He had been looking at various Ice Age animal bones pulled out of caves and rock shelters in the area known as Lagoa Santa. He spotted what he thought was a premodern human calotte, the top of a skull, including the ridges over the eye sockets. He called his wife, the distinguished archaeologist Ruth Gruhn, to come into the room and witness it. He took a photo, and then brought the calotte to the attention of the director of the museum, telling him how important it might be for the understanding of Brazilian prehistory. The shape of it was such that it could have lain in the ground for perhaps as long as 100,000 years or just been an extreme example of a local population with heavy brow ridges. Bryan's visa had run out the day he found it: he couldn't stay to investigate further. The museum director put it in a special box and promised to take care of it till Bryan could return. When Bryan came back to Brazil, the director had been replaced. The new director had no idea what Bryan was talking about. Yet others at the museum confirmed the calotte had been kept in a special box in the drawer of the previous director's desk. In 1978 Bryan published a manuscript that included the photos along with illustrations and a discussion of this calotte. Some Brazilians argued that it was most likely a fake. But in 1984 Bryan and his colleague Owen Beattie published a short description of it in *Current Anthropology*.

Dillehay also had bad luck with some of the other direct evidence of human presence at Monte Verde, such as the coprolites (dried feces) found on the site. They had either yielded ambiguous results when tested, or had gone missing. In some cases, work assigned simply wasn't done. Dillehay asked for thermoluminescence studies on the rocks found in the most ancient pits— these would have shown whether the charcoal had found its way there because of a forest fire or because a fire had been built inside the pit, with the heat leaching out. The work was never completed.

Despite these setbacks the Smithsonian Institution supported him in a big way. He was invited to give a talk there in the mid-1980s. Dennis Stanford, one of the Smithsonian's Paleo-Indian experts, told him that the work looked first-rate, and if he needed any help he should apply to the Smithsonian for a fellowship— which he did. The Smithsonian offered to publish his material in book form.

The result was the huge, two-volume *Monte Verde: A Late Pleistocene Settlement in Chile*. It was so expensive to produce that the Smithsonian's managing editor said he would be embarrassed to see the figure referred to in print, but he admitted it fell somewhere between $100,000 and $500,000. The Smithsonian decided to publish all the data gathered by Dillehay and his colleagues because they thought it was vital that the most important find in the last fifty years be thoroughly documented. But only 750 copies were printed. It was far too costly for most libraries to afford to stock, and no one in his right mind would assign it as a course book for a university class. Thus, even with the publication of his books, Dillehay didn't believe the critics had finally been silenced or that his work had been accepted as part of the story of the peopling of the Americas. He told David Meltzer, a Paleo expert at Southern Methodist University, that he didn't think his critics would bother to read it.[5] "Meltzer said, 'Let's force 'em to look at it. Let's get some money.'"

Meltzer rounded up Dillehay's top critics and supporters in the U.S., people whose opinions could be counted on to sway others. The Dallas Museum got some donors to put up money. Doubters and supporters both went out to Dillehay's lab in Kentucky to look at the artifacts he had there, carrying with them their prepublication copies of volume 2. "They said, 'This is marvellous.' They looked at the data, and said they didn't need to go to Chile." But the group did go to Chile. They spent time looking at such artifacts as the footprints and went to the site as well. "C. Vance Haynes said that the 'stratigraphy looks good to me,' and signed off on it. It came off very well," Dillehay said.

Dillehay was pleased, but also irked. The real site had long since been covered over by a bulldozer, and the stratigraphy C. Vance Haynes looked at was not the actual site, but the creek bank nearby. Some of the organic remains were not available to these experts. Why couldn't they have come the first time he'd asked them? Why did they have to wait until all the work was done? During the digging, he'd invited skeptics to come and see the site. Specifically, he'd invited Tom Lynch and a senior Chilean archaeologist. "None of them came in the sixteen months of digging at the site.... I offered to pay their way."

His ire built again as he talked. He was tired of bigots who refused to question the Clovis First theory, but he ran into them everywhere, along with those who didn't bother to evaluate things for themselves, but just followed the leader. Lynch was the leader.

Lynch, Dillehay said, had gathered about him what amounted to a Clovis cult, people essentially blind to new evidence. The worst of it is that he and Tom Lynch were once good friends. He had consulted Lynch on Monte Verde. But he split with him for good in 1991. "I found out he was cutting me down behind my back, writing negative reviews of grants. He was in his difficulties at Cornell.... He was asked to resign. He was a full professor and he did."

I called archaeologist Anna Roosevelt, who recently published on a site in the eastern Brazilian Amazon that was contemporaneous with, but unlike, Clovis occupations in North America, to find out what she thought of Monte Verde. I wanted to know if Dillehay was correct, that in spite of the Smithsonian publications, the Society for American Archaeology's Book Award and the official acceptance organized by Meltzer, Monte Verde is still not widely believed by his colleagues. I also wondered if she had experienced the same difficulties as Dillehay in getting her own work taken seriously. She had published in 1996 in *Science* the results of her dig at Caverna Pedra Pintada, which had dates back to 11,000 BP. She had found ceramics dating back to 7000 BP. And she had found rock art too.[6]

She, like Dillehay, was very critical of the Clovis First proponents. She thinks all of the Clovis radiocarbon dates, with one or two exceptions, should be done again, that they all have problems.[7] Most were done on pooled flecks of carbon and therefore give averaged and possibly wrong dates. Some were done on associated bones that may not actually have been associated with the Clovis spearheads in life. The margins of error in the old dates are ridiculously large. And then there is the whole problem of precursor cultures in Siberia: there are none.

But just because she doesn't buy the Clovis First theory doesn't mean she supports Monte Verde. Far from it. She has read Dillehay's entire two-volume work. She was disturbed by the span of dates, which are inconsistent with Dillehay's claims that this was a brief occupation. And she was bothered by the failure to date the potatoes. "I would date those right away. Then there is the stratigraphy. It was not sealed in. Stuff could have been displaced, younger material could have mixed with the lower and older finds.

"Try to find a drawing of the house," she said. "I don't see the house in pictures.... When you make a [stone] point, you get a huge amount of debitage. We had only twenty-four points and 30,000 flakes [at Pedra Pintada]." Where were the corresponding flakes at Monte Verde? Then there was the problem of the really old dates. When they were submitted to the lab, they were sent in as if they were from the later occupation. She worried that in fact there was a problem with these dates. Archaeologists, she said, don't understand the difficulties with dating. She reminded me that bitumen was found on the site, and it is a hydrocarbon. In a wet site this could have produced an error in the count of carbon in other materials. In sum, regardless of what her colleagues think, she believes there are flaws in the brilliance of Monte Verde.

And how was I to judge between competing interpretations from two such knowledgeable authorities as herself and Dillehay?

"There are no authorities," she said. "You are going to have to be the authority."

I phoned Tom Lynch with reluctance. Dillehay had taken the trouble to send me an excerpt from a book arguing that argument can distort meaning by forcing people to take opposing sides. The book's thesis is that an argument culture is ruining public discourse in important ways.[8] I knew Dillehay would feel that I was just furthering the argument culture by putting his claims to Lynch, the lead critic, but I saw no way around it. I knew that Dillehay was angry at Lynch, so I didn't think it would be fair to let Dillehay characterize Lynch's views. (I would have phoned Junius Bird, too, but he's dead.)

Lynch insisted that, contrary to Dillehay's assertions, he had not been asked to leave Cornell; he had retired with full benefits.

And he hadn't worked to cut Dillehay down or refuse him grants. On the contrary, he had refused to review his grant applications when he realized that he and Dillehay had irreconcilable differences. Lynch sent me a mound of materials on his own archaeology, and on the history of archaeology as a discipline, that were models of clarity. He was not happy with the official acceptance of Monte Verde or the sudden return of interest in the possible connections between American Clovis and European Solutrean technologies. ("Have you seen *The New Yorker*?"[9] he bellowed. The magazine had given credence to proponents of the view that the European Solutrean culture might have been a precursor to the Clovis culture.)

As an undergraduate at Cornell and as a graduate student at the University of Chicago, Lynch studied Paleo-American cultures in relation to finds in Europe and Asia. He understood that the Ice Age was a worldwide phenomenon. He went south himself to the Atacama Desert in Chile and to Peru to look for something earlier than Clovis, and he found evidence of very old cultures.[10] Lynch was amused by the current fuss over Kennewick Man and the popular notion that possibly, just possibly, Caucasoids from Europe had gotten to America first. He thought this idea had been laid to rest many years ago when Emerson Greenman, at the University of Michigan, last proposed it. "It's Greenman revisited," he crowed. "He thought Solutreans came across the Atlantic. Greenman was a serious scholar at Ann Arbor who said the first inhabitants of America came across the North Atlantic in skin boats. The Upper Paleolithic people in Europe hunted reindeer and salmon. He proposed an expansion across the Atlantic [of] a derivative of the French Solutrean culture."[11] Lynch still prefers the view that the Upper Paleolithic people who lived on the open, unglaciated steppes of Eurasia mastered the art of tailored clothing and spilled into the New World through Beringia. "They did this between 15,000 and 11,000 years Before Present," he told me, stating it as a fact.

He laid into the dissenters' claims. Frank C. Hibben, for one, put forward the notion that there was material older than Clovis and Folsom to be found in the Americas. In the 1940s, Hibben had found, *under* the Clovis layer at a site, spear points that were unlike Clovis or Folsom points: they had only one shoulder. Hibben had dubbed their makers the "Sandia culture."[12] "Now we know they are unfinished preforms," Lynch said, meaning stones worked into the general shape of a spear point, but never finished completely. And then, warming to his task, Lynch went further. "Frank C. Hibben was the original tin man."

"What's that?"

"That's what we called aluminum siding salesmen after the war.... Aluminum siding cures all ills. We have them again now."

Lynch has all kinds of problems with Monte Verde. He thinks it looks like a "concatenation" of different things. He believes it is possible that Archaic materials found their way into a place where, coincidentally, ancient animals had died. "I'm not convinced by the photos. Junius Bird had the same problem. I knew Junius Bird quite well.... I'm tired of hearing Junius Bird badmouthed," he said. "[He was] a good man and an expert in Paleo-Indians. He was open to the idea [of man in the Americas before Clovis]."

Lynch said he had personally looked at Dillehay's work with an open mind. He corresponded with Dillehay when he was in Chile, and Dillehay had described the site to him as a swamp, which Lynch considered to be an unlikely location for Paleo-Indians. He'd invited him to speak to his colleagues and students at Cornell. "Dillehay lectured on the site uses when I was at Cornell. I provided him a platform."

That was when Lynch saw some of the Monte Verde artifacts, specifically the wooden ones. He also saw some that Dillehay had brought with him to show to colleagues at meetings. He was not impressed. And he hadn't deliberately avoided going to the site. "He talks of inviting me. I got invited at the last moment through my membership in the Chilean Association of Archaeology. Before that he had invited me when he knew I was in the field.

[He] expected I would agree. When I disagree, he reacts in anger. I can't take that from a colleague. All of us need to accept criticism or doubts about sites. Most of us can get along."

Most telling, in his mind, was that all the preserved plant remains at the site seemed to have been used or modified. Dillehay even had "Lucy's footprint."

"You mean the site's too good to be true?"

"Yes," he said.

"Aw, c'mon. What about the cordage, the knots he found? No animal made them."

"The first people we know of in South America are using cordage and nets and bagging game," he said. "These are dated directly. In *Science*, in 1985. Lynch is the first author." Lynch's site at Guitarrero Cave had a radiocarbon date of 12,560 (among dozens of other post-Clovis dates that he accepts).[13] He had another site with other old dates, which he also threw out because they were geologically impossible—the site having been under ice at the time. At a third site he reported, and questioned, another pre-Clovis date. He stressed that radiocarbon dates can be contaminated by dead carbon. Dillehay had bitumen on his site, a substance that is full of dead carbon.

I pulled out my trump card. "What about Juan Munizaga and the bone?"

"What about him? He was an all-around scientist, in paleontology, anthropology and archaeology. He worked with Tom. Quit...."

And on it went. He is convinced that evidence will be found of people moving through Beringia and into Canada at around 13,000 BP either along the coast or through the ice-free corridor. Lack of evidence is not evidence of absence, he reminded me. The fact that so far no bones of that age have been found means nothing.

In one paper published in *American Antiquity* in 1990,[14] Lynch did a round-up of all the evidence for and against early people in the Americas. He looked first for the human bones, just as I was doing. He concluded that there weren't any earlier than Clovis that stood up to scrutiny:

> Direct dating, by reliable means, would be a very convincing demonstration of the pre-Clovis thesis, as would be archaic morphological features, at least if they were found repeatedly. The scarcity of skeletal remains might be due to a lack of interest in underground burial, or perhaps a preference for cremation or exposure [platform] burial, both of which are found sporadically in later cultures. Still, the total lack of accidental entrapments or fossilization, and the absence of teeth or charred human bones in the supposed sites, is striking. The first Americans almost certainly passed through high latitudes and cold climates. They surely would have used fire regularly and would have made occasional shelter in caves where bone and tooth enamel should be preserved. Early man was probably not a cannibal, and he may not have buried, but he surely lost teeth.

Lynch then discussed the ancient human remains found in South America. He mentioned that although they were rare, they had been found in association with extinct Ice Age animals, particularly in Brazil at a place called Lagoa Santa. But there were no dates on those bones and they were dug by amateurs, so he dismissed them. Alan Bryan's calotte he put into a twilight category. He pointed out that the pictures Bryan published did not look Neanderthal, but like an ancient premodern human from southeast Asia called Solo Man. He put this find in the context of the theories of a French scholar, Paul Rivet, who had argued for many years that the First Americans found their way to South America by way of Australia. "If relocated, authenticated and dated, this specimen alone might force us to reconsider Rivet's long-abandoned [1926] theory of a non-Beringian initial population."[15]

However, the calotte was missing. And some Brazilian scholars did believe Bryan had been fooled by a fake. Without actually saying he didn't trust Bryan and Gruhn (which would have been an outrage), Lynch still moved the calotte out of the category of real science. It didn't matter to him that it had been seen, witnessed, photographed, drawn and discussed by two senior authorities and by various colleagues in Brazil. The study of human bones is not like chemistry, in which experiments can be replicated by anyone at any time. Bones are what they are and they must be available for others to see, so that opinions about them can be verified and new tests run when new technologies become available. The calotte, like Dillehay's bone, was gone: it might as well have never been found.

Lynch turned to the evidence of stones. One by one, he went through the known North and South American sites with claims to antiquity greater than 11,000 years, and found them all wanting. He saved Monte Verde for last, like a man savoring at the back of his mouth a particularly interesting sour candy.

"Dillehay and I have discussed the site many times, but in the end we have to agree to disagree," he wrote. "Perhaps with the publication of better photographs than have so far been available, he will convince [me] of his point of view. For the present, however, our arguments remind me of those between the priest and the agnostic, who disagree over the existence of God, in that they are not subject to proof. Our disagreements are not over the stratigraphy, chronology, paleontology and reconstruction of environment but instead, primarily, over the presence of 'the hand of man' at the crucial periods. In my opinion there are very few artifacts at Monte Verde, and they may not be in true association with the materials dated."

He congratulated Dillehay for making few claims for the 33,000-year-old dates also found at Monte Verde. "Most of all I find it improbable that 13,000 and 33,000-year-old sites would be found, one nearly on top of the other ... at a rather poor camping place along a minor creek. ... As I look back on 100 years of promotion and often passionate defence of improbable cases, I increasingly despair that the sure demonstration lies just around the corner."[16]

Nine years later, he hadn't altered his general conclusions: there wasn't much evidence out there, and he found what there was unpersuasive. He doubted everything, relied on nothing. He was no longer comfortable with the most basic methods of archaeology. He no longer believed that careful sifting of the layers of soil over a site was sufficient to allow one to reconstruct its general antiquity and history. Everything from rodents to earthworms to water perturbed these layers and left a trail of confusion no archaeologist could hope to untangle. Radiocarbon dates were unreliable. He cited an article by Stuart Fiedel in *American Antiquity* that explored the physical chemistry problems of all radiocarbon dates from the end of the Ice Age.[17] Meteorologists and chemists had studied the ancient atmospheric gases trapped in Greenland ice cores, corals in Barbados and ocean sediments off the Pacific and Atlantic coasts; they had learned that as the glaciers melted, there was a period of rapid fluctuation in the carbon dioxide content of the atmosphere. This would have had an impact on the carbon content of anything alive between 12000 and 9000 BP. Radiocarbon dating is done by counting the carbon decaying in an organic remain. From this count one can infer when the organism last absorbed carbon (when it died). Dates of around 11000 BP were, according to Fiedel, about 2,000 years too young.

And if that wasn't enough, there was outright fraud. Lynch told me he knew of a person at one western university who was being sued by the National Science Foundation for falsifying pre-Clovis dates. No, the world could accept Monte Verde as a pre-Clovis site if it wanted to: Lynch wasn't buying.

# 5

# The Founding Mothers

The Spectral Trail of Mitochondrial DNA

T OM LYNCH, the lead critic, has said it himself—
the proof of who came to the Americas first, and
when, will emerge from the human remains, not
from the sticks and stones and animal bones left behind in abandoned camps. But he is not willing to accept the reports of others:
the remains will have to exist in a place where they can be seen
and measured and dated by anyone, in perpetuity. Following this
reasoning to its conclusion, it seemed clear the reburial of ancient
remains under the NAGPRA in the U.S. would remove what had
already been learned about them from the scientific record. Even
though Kennewick Man was not as old as the most ancient remains studied in the Americas, the need to keep him above
ground for reference seemed perfectly obvious. If the skeleton
was reburied without study it would be treated by critics the way
the Israeli security establishment deals with unfortunate erup-
tions of secrets into the public domain—as things that never
were. This context made the U.S. Army Corps of Engineers'
behavior in the Kennewick affair more than a little interesting.

Since 1996 the story had been slowly unfolding in the popular
press through reports of the court battles between the group of
eight scientists and the U.S. Army Corps of Engineers. Then

there were the occasional human interest stories on the other parties claiming the bones. The tug-of-war over who would control Kennewick Man, and for what purpose, jerked back and forth between heavy politics and farce.

A religious/ethnic group called the Asatru Folk Assembly claimed to be the descendants of Kennewick Man because he had been characterized in *The New York Times* as Caucasoid. They argued the bones represented proof that their ancestors came to the Americas before the people we now call Native Americans. They wanted to have the bones studied, and then to take charge of the proper rites when the time came to put them back in the ground. They practiced their religion, involving worship at dawn with horns and mead, in a sacred grove near the house of the group's founder, Stephen McNallen. He lived in the small town of Nevada City, California. A former soldier, McNallen had acquired an interest in a "native European" religion, which he described as the worship of "the old Teutonic Gods" (Thor, Odin, Freja, etc.). Yes, he said blandly, there certainly were ethnic aspects to his religion. He was himself a man with an Irish father and an English and German mother, raised a Catholic. When he read a novel about Vikings as a teenager growing up in a Texas oil town, he had suddenly felt religiously comfortable for the first time. In the 1970s he had published a journal called the *Rhine Stone*. In his college days, he had belonged to a group called the Brotherhood (rumored to have Aryan Nation connections). Later it all sort of matured and transmogrified into the Asatru Folk Assembly, which he ran as a nonprofit, with the support of his wife, "who has a nice job." A lawyer in Portland had taken on the task of claiming their ancestor for him and his thirty-five regular adherents—pro bono.[1]

Then there was the man who called himself Thorz Hammer, who made a similar but more oddly spelled claim for the remains ("on behalf of all white people"). He appealed to the army, but not the courts.[2]

William Thomas, who had pulled the skull out of the muck,

together with his parents, Richard and Rosemary Thomas, claimed the bones from the army so they could hand them on for study.[3]

Meanwhile the local tribes involved—the Umatilla, Yakama, Nez Percé, Wanapum and Colville—eventually made a coalition claim for Kennewick Man's return. Some also made individual tribal claims.[4]

After hearing the evidence put forward by the plaintiff scientists and the army's defence, on June 27, 1997, U.S. Magistrate John Jelderks hammered the Corps for failing to follow appropriate procedures under the NAGPRA to determine the cultural affiliation of the Kennewick remains. The judge stayed the case, which forced the army to redo its decision-making procedure in order to arrive at some objective method of establishing who, if anyone, had a reasonable claim to the remains. The judge ordered the army and the plaintiffs to make quarterly progress reports to the court.[5] The army did report to the court but, as the plaintiffs later complained, continued to act as a kind of advocate for the tribes while doing a less than adequate job of figuring out who (if anyone) was culturally affiliated to Kennewick Man. The plaintiffs alleged that the army had allowed Native groups to send their representatives into the closed room at the lab in Richland where Kennewick Man's remains were stored, and that they had held ceremonies over the bones. Cedar boughs were placed on the remains, possibly contaminating the bones with new carbon and making further dating studies dicey. In addition, some of the bones had been kept in a separate box with other finds, a box that had been given to the Umatilla for reburial.[6]

Armand Minthorn, the man charged with oversight of these matters for the Umatilla, seemed to be a spokesperson for the Native American spiritual point of view, but he was not to happy to speak about it with me. I chased him and chased him, and when I finally got him on the telephone he interviewed me as to my state of mind and found it wanting. He asked me to describe how I was thinking about all the competing views in this matter. When I said I was skeptical, meaning open-minded, he said in that case he would not be able to speak to me. The same unskeptical Minthorn had just been appointed by the U.S. Secretary of the Interior to the NAGPRA review committee (and would later become its chairperson), which is charged in law with the exquisitely political task of resolving disputes over the disposition of remains for which Native American groups have made competing claims. The review committee consists of government-appointed scientists, museum officials and Native Americans.[7] It had been in a state of stalemate over how to deal with unaffiliated remains since it was created in 1995. Minthorn's appointment demonstrated the high political interest in Washington in the outcome of the Kennewick case. The U.S. Justice Department was vigorously defending the army in the legal combat over the study of the remains. Since several Native groups had put in claims, it could easily end up at the review committee.

Why would the U.S. government want to shape things in this way? *The Wall Street Journal* said it had proof that the U.S. government's interest in the case was guided from the White House. In 1996, the Army Corps began to discuss burying the riverbank where most of the remains had been found. It put together a plan to cover it up with tons of rock, riprap, trees and shrubs. To do this the army required, and sought, permission from state and federal agencies responsible for protecting heritage sites. When the plaintiffs were finally informed, in December 1997, they protested to the court that there were still applications before the army to study that land, to learn something of the archaeological and geological context. They protested that burying the site would destroy any possibility of future study. The army explained that it was only trying to protect the site, which was eroding into the river.[8] *The Wall Street Journal* argued that this whole harebrained idea to protect the site by destroying it had originated in an advisory committee called into existence by the White House.

The White House, the *Journal* sneered, was "exquisitely attuned to issues of multiculturalism."[9]

This didn't seem a good explanation for either the White House's interest or the army's determination to bury the site.

By 1998, the plaintiffs and the science community could see the way the wind was blowing: they decided to fight fire with fire, and politics with a nonprofit organization. Cleone Hawkinson, who lives in Portland and is a former colleague of one of the plaintiffs, volunteered to assist the lawyer Alan Schneider. She also put together an organization with a Web site that laid out the story according to the plaintiffs and discussed other incidents involving repatriation of remains. This Web site was the electronic face of Friends of America's Past, an organization created to raise money for the cause and keep an eye on Congress. There was some interest there: a congressman from Washington and a senator from Oregon had already floated bills to amend the NAGPRA, which passed the House and the Senate. An amendment was hastily tacked onto a money bill to block the reburial of the site. By March, it was almost ready to be passed on to the White House for signing.[10]

As if to rub the sticky Kennewick problem off its hands, the army signed an agreement with the Department of the Interior's park service on March 24, 1998.[11] This gave the park service the duty of determining, for the army, which studies should be done to determine Kennewick's cultural affiliation. Yet the army never really let go of its control of the science process, and kept up unrelenting pressure on the University of California, both at Riverside and at Davis, to return all samples of Kennewick bone that Chatters had sent. At Davis, a doctoral student named Frederika Kaestle had been trying to extract mitochondrial DNA (mtDNA) from a Kennewick bone sample. As if to divert attention from itself as it prepared to bury the site, in spite of the money bill amendment to prevent it, the army issued a report March 10, and a press release the same day, saying that some of Kennewick Man's bones were missing, that sections of the femurs (thigh bones) seen in James Chatters' photographs of the remains were gone.[12] Washington Congressman Richard "Doc" Hastings' amendment to an emergency supplemental appropriations bill was still in committee when the army wrote him on March 31 saying it would not go ahead as planned with burial of the site. The next day the army wrote Hastings to say it had changed its mind, and it used a minority contractor to bury the site on April 6, 1998.[13]

As a result of complaints from the plaintiffs, Judge Jelderks, at a hearing in May, ordered the army to move the Kennewick remains to the Burke Museum in Seattle, where they could be properly inventoried and conserved.[14] On October 29, to ceremonial accompaniment provided by Native Americans, the Asatru Folk Assembly and the whirring cameras of journalists, the remains were driven to Seattle.[15] Then the maneuvering began over who exactly would get to do an inventory of the bones, and which scientists the Department of the Interior's park service would favor with the assignment of studying the remains to determine cultural affiliation.

So: what was the army so anxious to cover up? Why did it want to be seen to let go of the Kennewick affair, while making the soil that might have originally contained the remains inaccessible for study? Why was it so important that every cell of uncontaminated Kennewick bone be gathered back into the army's hands? And in particular, what was so critical about what Frederika Kaestle had learned about Kennewick Man's mitochondrial DNA?

Frederika Kaestle sat munching on a sandwich off in the corner of Andy Merriwether's laboratory at the University of Michigan, Ann Arbor. She is a round woman, with a sharp pointy nose, short brown hair and the pale skin of a person who spends a lot of time indoors. She listened quietly as Merriwether talked to me about the ins and outs of mtDNA research, and then he called her over to join us. I didn't catch her last name at first, so I didn't realize who she was. I'd been there for more than an hour before the penny dropped. Merriwether's name was on the laboratory door, not hers. I had come to see him. She was an unexpected bonus.

Merriwether is one of the stars in the exploding new field of mtDNA analysis. He is only eight years older than Kaestle, but he carried a truckload of authority, the kind that comes from being responsible for many graduate students and hundreds of thousands of dollars in NSF grants. He is a large, broad-shouldered, square-headed man in his mid-thirties, who wears his hair roughly parted in the middle and tied back in a stringy blond/ brown/ gray ponytail. He has a blondish beard, a large beaky nose and big gray eyes.

I'd come to him for a briefing on mtDNA studies because I was having a great deal of difficulty figuring out what I thought about this work. I had been reading papers by Merriwether and his colleagues for weeks. I had grappled unhappily with the peculiar nomenclature they use—which arose out of the massive research effort to define each kink and twist in the strings of human DNA, to account for the billions of matched base pairs of nucleotides that carry the messages that produce human beings. Like the measurement of bones by physical anthropologists at the turn of the century, this is descriptive science in its purest form. One day we will be able to link some of these DNA configurations to particular human behaviors and diseases, but not yet. Meanwhile, every base pair is being noted and its position mapped. Each configuration, or site, as they are called, is referred to by a series of letters and numbers. The language of the whole field is less compelling than the label on the average drug prescription. The analysis of the DNA messages in the mitochondria of human cells is a subbranch of this larger study. In the papers I was reading, the meaning was buried under strings of numbers and letters and so-called "parsimonious trees" drawn to show relationships and the evolutionary history of certain configurations of nucleotides.

In spite of their peculiar and opaque language, the sheer number of these publications made it quite clear that many geneticists and physical anthropologists see mtDNA analysis as a whole new way of tracing human prehistory. The field is only about fifteen years old: breakthroughs and setbacks are coming fast. The first researchers who ventured into this work are still hard at it: their graduate students are moving out into laboratories of their own, stepping up the pace. Merriwether is part of the second wave and pushing forward its leading edge. He is sharp as an obsidian blade. Frederika Kaestle is only one short step behind him.

It was invigorating just to watch them struggle to remain patient with my ignorance. Their intellectual energy, sharply restrained, seeped through the strangely flat way in which they answered my questions. Most of all, Merriwether and Kaestle exuded the confidence that comes from adding a whole new wing to the house that contains the human story: there was nothing like this energy in any archaeology lab I had visited.

I thought I understood the basics. Mitochondrial DNA resides outside the nucleus of the cell and plays a role in the cell's metabolic processes, or energy exchanges. At fertilization, the contribution of mtDNA from sperm to egg is apparently not incorporated into the fetus. While nuclear DNA contains recombined information from both parents, the information in everyone's mtDNA, according to Merriwether, comes only from their mother. As a paper by some of the field's early leaders—Henry Harpending, Stephen Sherry, Alan Rogers and Mark Stoneking of Pennsylvania State University—put it in *Current Anthropology* in 1993:

> Since mtDNA sequences are not broken and reformed by recombination, they are tips of a tree of descent. There are several approaches to using mtDNA sequences to infer properties of the tree of descent and relate those properties to the history of the population in which the tree is embedded.
>
> The direct approach to inferring properties of the tree is to compute a reconstruction of it using one of a number of algorithms [a mathematical model] that make trees from differences among objects. Cann, Stoneking and Wilson (1987)

used a maximum parsimony algorithm to reconstruct the tree
of descent of a sample of mtDNA from many different human
groups and they were led to suggest that our mtDNAs all
descend from an African who lived approximately 200,000
years ago.[16]

Later, the authors explained, after refinements of the mathematics by critics, it was suggested that the idea of tracing back our
heritage to a single individual mother was too simple. There was
rather a small population who bred, and spread, and eventually
became us. The notion that all modern humans descend from
one ancient African population that later spread round the world
became known as the strong Garden of Eden hypothesis (now
referred to as the Mitochondrial Eve hypothesis). A competing
theory, the multiregional hypothesis, suggests a different view of
descent. Multiregionalists hold that we are the distillation of the
entire gene pool of modern humans, the result of constant sexual
interchange following the worldwide distribution of our prede-
cessor, *Homo erectus*.

In a paper published in *Science* in March 1988, one of the principal theorists working on genetic clues to human origins, C.B.
Stringer, with his colleague P. Andrews, laid out the basics of
using mtDNA information to create a kind of human family tree.
They pointed specifically to the differences between the range of
variation in the external shape of our bones, and the inner organization of the genetic material in our bone cells:

> The human species shows great morphological variation.
> However, in contrast to this, genetic variation between human
> populations is low overall. Genetic distances based on electro-
> phoretic analysis ... are small in comparison with those found
> in other hominoids. There is also relatively little protein vari-
> ation between human populations. As much as 84% of protein
> polymorphisms in human populations results from variation
> among individuals within populations, a further 6% repre-

sents genetic divergence associated with nationality, and only 10% varies between human 'racial groups.' Thus differences between populations are small when compared with differences within populations.

Analyses of mtDNA show similarly low variation between geographically distinct human populations. The mean pairwise difference between human populations based on mapping of mitochondrial DNA by restriction nucleases [a particular technique for mapping] is .3%. The nearest approach to this low figure in any other hominoid yet studied is a single subspecies of gorilla in which the mean mitochondrial sequence difference is about twice this figure.... The two most divergent humans differ by only two sites.[17]

In other words, there is so little variation, even among human populations that are widely separated from each other, that it is relatively straightforward to spot what variation there is, chart it, and work out by mathematical means who is the descendant of whom and who is more closely related to whom. Since mtDNA is not supposed to be involved in the sexual recombination of genes from both parents, but is passed directly from generation to generation by mothers, changes in mtDNA are caused by mutation. The rate of mutation of mtDNA is believed to be fairly rapid. Assuming a standard rate of mutation, researchers calculate back how many generations must have lived since the first time a particular mtDNA quirk appeared in a common ancestor. It is also fairly easy to describe these changes in mtDNA arrangements and note where these differences occur in bundles of shared mutations. It is assumed these markers will be found in those who share mothers, grandmothers and great-grandmothers. They will not be found in those who don't. These shared peculiarities are therefore called lineages. In other words, mtDNA is a kind of DNA record of who mothered whom back in time to the first mothers of us all. It allows us to make a maternity test on a population. Those interested in addressing the question of who the First Americans were, where they came from and when they got here have tried to use this maternity test in many ways, including tracing population movements through Beringia.

Merriwether worked as a student in two of the major labs in the U.S. where this work was first carried on—at Emory University, where Douglas Wallace has maintained an active research facility for about fifteen years, and at Penn State, where Mark Stoneking had a lab. Merriwether has been interested in who first populated the Americas since he was in high school. He was an anthropology undergraduate at Penn State when the earliest mtDNA work came out. "The first time I got excited about Beringia was in 1985," he said. "The Wallace lab [at Emory] published a paper on mtDNA and the peopling of the New World.... Molecular data was a new way to look at these questions that was not available before. I realized I was getting a liberal arts education. So I added biology with genetics as an option to get the background. It cost me an extra year as an undergrad."

That first paper from the Wallace lab was followed quickly by others: the thrust of all of them was that human beings are genetically so very much alike that the few differences can be identified. Mitochondrial DNA, Merriwether explained, has already been completely sequenced (meaning the order of the molecules coding for the mitochondria of the cell has been completely identified) in over one hundred individuals, as well as one gorilla and one orangutan, and several other species. It has been fairly well established that the rate of mutation of mtDNA is about six to twenty times greater than that of nuclear DNA. The way this is reported, he explained, is generally as a mutation rate per base pair per year.

All of this work was made possible by the invention of the polymerase chain reaction, a system for copying specific DNA regions and making an almost infinite number of clones, which can then be studied. DNA is a sequence of four nucleotide bases laid out like a series of pearls on a two-stranded, twisted choker. The polymerase chain reaction reads the order of the nucleotide sequence, the DNA's message, by chemically pulling the strands apart and copying first one strand then the other, producing a record of the order in which the nucleotides are laid down. These sequences form a kind of a three-dimensional Morse code.

Merriwether walked me through the copying techniques. "If you want to copy a region [of DNA] you use primers that are exactly complementary to the top and bottom strand of the DNA flanking the region to be copied. The polymerase only binds and copies when it's double-stranded, followed by a single strand of DNA.... It fills in the complementary base, it makes the single strand double. On the other side [of the pair] you have the reverse primer. You can force [the DNA] to do this [separation and copying] by changing temperature. You heat [the DNA] to ninety-four degrees centigrade—it makes two single strands of DNA. You lower it to fifty-five degrees and that's low enough for the primers to bind to the DNA, but only where they match. Then you run it up to seventy-two degrees to make copies. You change the temperature three times, and you get two copies of what you started with. You heat it again, copies are made, then back to the beginning. Now there's eight. After forty cycles, you have a billion copies of what you started with."

The 1985 Wallace paper on the origins of Native Americans showed that a group of subsets of Asian lineages were also found in Native Americans, but in drastically different proportions within populations. "One rare in Asia," he explained, "and [found] nowhere else, was at high frequency in the New World." Wallace thought this meant the original mother came to the New World with a small number of migrants.

As far as I was concerned, this sort of reasoning was the first problem I had with the assumptions underlying these studies. Why would a marker rarely found in Asians but found often in North American Native people say anything at all about the location of the mother? Why couldn't one just as easily assume that there had been a little contact between Asia and North America, but that the original mother had been a North American, some of whose descendants found their way to Asia? Why, in other words, was the assumption of gene flow in the papers I was reading always in one direction, from Asia to America and not the reverse? Were there one-way signs up there in Beringia? And come to think of it, why was the entry point assumed to be Beringia?

These basic assumptions, Merriwether explained, were just taken from what was accepted among archaeologists about how the Americas were peopled. "If people were here," he agreed, "they could have gone back."

The Wallace group's first paper did not say how many lineages from Beringia had entered the New World. In 1990, another graduate student at Wallace's lab, Tadd Schurr, published a paper saying that from the samples of living Native Americans that had been studied, including an isolated group in South America and the Maya who were known to have occupied the same region for at least five thousand years, it could be said that almost all Native American populations derived from four primary mtDNA patterns or lineages that originated in Asia and crossed over the Bering land bridge, becoming isolated and then mutating in the New World about 12,000 to 20,000 years ago.[18]

Only three percent of those studied didn't carry these lineages. "Wallace's lab has found others since," Merriwether said. The list of others that didn't fit was expanding. In an isolated population of Yanomami in Venezuela, the portion of the population that had these other lineages was as high as thirty percent.

We had now arrived at a second set of assumptions in these studies. How many individuals did it take to know one had a representative sample of a population? None of the studies I had read addressed that issue. Many of the studies had looked at the mtDNA of only a few hundred individuals, and yet they drew from them sweeping conclusions. Physical anthropologists had been asking for forty years if measurements of the skulls and faces of a few members of any ethnic group really captured the scope of human diversity. Wouldn't the same criticism apply here? Wouldn't one have to survey almost all Native Americans to be certain that they all derived from only a few basic mitochondrial lineages?

Merriwether agreed that most researchers based their studies on close examination of a few sites in samples taken from only twenty to forty individuals. He agreed that it was not safe to make sweeping statements based on such small numbers, but he argued it was necessary to recognize that there were two ways of working—one could survey many individuals by looking at one or two markers or sites, or one could study a few representative individuals and look at a large number of markers, a lot of which would turn out to be identical.

"There's a finite amount of money in the end," he shrugged. The Wallace lab's early work was done by looking at a few sites in a large number of people, which produced a low-resolution picture of a broad population. The lab then switched to examining many more of the sites carried by a small number of individuals per population. This work was done by "cutting people's DNA with restriction enzymes," said Merriwether.

To explain this technique he drew a diagram labelled A, G, C, T, the letters standing for the first initials of the four nucleotides, which, arrayed in various combinations, constitute all the message groups on any strand of DNA. Each restriction enzyme is known to recognize only one particular order of these four. Alu I, the name for one of these enzymes, only recognizes the order A, G, C, T. It always "cuts" (or breaks) the link between G and C. Thus, said Merriwether, writing on his plastic demonstration board, if you have the pattern CTAATC AGCT ATCCCAT, the enzyme can only make its cut at one place in the sequence. Researchers have figured out a method of reading the sequences from where the enzymes cut. They put the DNA in a gel, in a liquid buffer that will carry a charge, and run an electric charge through it, a process called electrophoresis. "DNA," Merriwether explained, "has a weak negative charge. When you run a current across it, it gets pulled to the positive electrode."

A sample of treated DNA extract is suspended in a dense liquid and put into a well within an agarose or polyachriminide gel on a tray. The tray is then put into a liquid buffer that acts almost like a car battery. A low 100-volt current is run across the gel. The DNA in the little wells begins to inch toward the positive electrode. Speed of movement is dependent on size: larger DNA fragments move more slowly than small ones. If the DNA has a different pattern from the one recognized by the enzyme, there will be no cut and the DNA strands will be left intact, moving more slowly up the well than cut ones. After about half an hour, "you end up with a pattern."

At this point, ethidium bromide is added, which binds to the DNA. Under ultraviolet light it glows, creating a series of bright orange bands. The tray is then examined. The DNA that didn't get cut by the enzyme shows up higher in the gel. In those that did get cut, two smaller bands appear instead of one large one. "We say there was a cut at the recognition site," said Merriwether. "The evolution hypothesis would be that the individuals with two bands shared a common ancestor." In other words, two individuals whose DNA was cut in the same place by the same enzyme have their DNA organized in the same way, and therefore probably shared a mother back in time.

But there could be another reason why two individuals would produce the same band pattern. They might both have the same mutation independently. Certain mutations happen in nature much more easily than others. Merriwether and his colleagues observed that it is much easier to lose a particular grouping of bases, or experience a site deletion as they call it, than to gain a site by mutation. "The likelihood of that is the mutation rate.... Site losses are much more frequent than site gains and site losses are more likely by chance. We look at two hundred to four hundred sites. We count the numbers that are shared and the numbers that differ. Here is where we are likely to make a mistake. The more data you have, the more sites per individual, the less likely you are to make mistakes."

Merriwether stayed at Penn State until his senior undergraduate year, 1988. Douglas Wallace allowed him to come to his lab at Emory and learn as a lab volunteer. "He taught me how to do mitochondrial genetics. I learned it on drosophila [fruit flies]." Merriwether stayed on with Wallace and worked on pulling together a worldwide data set, which he put together from all human mtDNA sites described in all papers published to that date on the subject, together with all the unpublished data he could gather directly from researchers. Mark Stoneking had by then settled in at Penn State, so Merriwether went back and got his master's in population genetics from there. Merriwether had by then become very interested in applying these techniques to the question of the origins of Native Americans. "After 1990 I turned my attention fully to the New World problem," said Merriwether.

That year, Tadd Schurr published a paper declaring there were four major Native American lineages. Merriwether wasn't convinced that there were only four to be found in the entire hemisphere, as Schurr's paper (which Merriwether had a hand in) suggested. Schurr had sampled few South American Native people. Bob Ferrell at Pittsburgh University's Department of Human Genetics had a large collection of South American blood samples. "I concentrated on South American and Alaskan Eskimo samples," Merriwether said, "which were not in the early papers. The ones I did were from Chile—Wallace's were from northern Brazil."

But he thought there were real problems with the North American samples too. He was concerned that the samples available to researchers did not reflect the real complexities of tribal movements across the Americas after the arrival of Europeans. "Most of the groups were not where they had been. They were on reservations or they had admixed with Europeans and others on reservations next door. It was harder to get samples that were reflective of tribal history. And the politics were hard. Many Native American groups are politically active and skeptical of scientists in general. They have their own oral history. Many mythologies say, 'We always lived here,' in situ, and they may not want outsiders to say they came from Asia." Tribes active in politics were much less likely to give blood samples to researchers.

He went to Ferrell's Pittsburgh lab, where they were working on samples collected from Chilean Native people and from Canadian Mohawks. These samples had been gathered for the study of the genetic linkages to high rates of diabetes in Native communities. The Pittsburgh lab also had samples of Dogrib, Alaskan Eskimo and Aleuts. None of these people and the areas where they lived had been surveyed for mitochondrial variation before. "We knew the four major clusters of Native Americans. We wanted to know their distribution in the New World.... We screened for markers that defined clusters."

He screened two thousand individuals. It took him until 1993 to finish and get his doctorate.[19] He also sequenced samples of four hundred individuals for a small control region of mtDNA known as the D-loop. This is a complex region where more than 30 percent of the variation found in individuals occurs. It doesn't appear to code for any particular function, so D-loop mutations happen that would be immediately selected against if they had occurred in a region coding for a vital function. Changes in the D-loop region therefore accumulate fast. How fast? That was another area of current argument.

"In 1993 we found, after pooling our data with the Wallace lab and others, that all Native Americans had [some or all of] all four haplotypes—the lineages previously identified and labeled by the Wallace group as A, B, C, or D." Most had three types. Many had all four. The variations among these groups also corresponded to what had been previously identified as the basic linguistic groups known in the Americas. Joseph H. Greenberg had identified a number of shared language traits to arrive at three basic language groups—the so-called Amerinds, the Na Dene (which included the Athabascans and Haida) and the Eskimo/ Aleuts. In 1986 Greenberg had published, with dental expert Christy Turner and genetics expert Stephen J. Zegura, a paper that said that all three lines of study came to the same conclusion: these language groups corresponded with three separate waves of immigration into the New World through Beringia after the end of the Ice Age. According to Greenberg, the Amerinds had come in around 12,000 years ago. The Na Dene came next, about 9,000 years ago—then the Eskimo/Aleut came, probably by boat.[20] Merriwether and his colleagues argued that the first wave of migrants carried the A, C and D mtDNA lineages and spread all over the New World. The second wave of migrants only carried the A lineage. Lineage B came last and was much more often found on the West Coast. But when they calculated the time frame necessary to produce the mutations seen only in the New World, the time for first entry came out at around 25,000 years ago. They did not compare this "divergence time" to the archaeological evidence, but it argued for a pre-Clovis entry into the New World, a finding with which Merriwether agreed fully. "The archaeology leans that way now," he said.

From 1995 to 1996 Merriwether worked away at identifying other haplotypes among Native Americans. He noticed that there was more than one version of each type in Asia and the New World. The most "parsimonious," or direct, path to explain this was to assume that there had been separate developments of an early, shared common type in Asia and the New World, which meant there had been possibly only one migration to the New World, not three.

As he laid out for me the way questions had been raised and answered, questions of my own boiled up. If it was difficult to get Native American samples for study, where and how were they getting Asian samples? How many had been used? Since Beringia was under water, and the former Soviet Union was not too amenable to allowing people into certain parts of Siberia, how had it been established that Asian and Native Americans had different versions of the same haplotypes and haplogroups?

There had not been much study of Asian samples, Merriwether replied. His own work was often done on samples of around forty-five individuals. Nevertheless, not only had he and many of his colleagues come to the conclusion that Native Americans were descendants of Asians, by 1996 he believed he knew where in Asia they had came from. He had published his conclusions in a paper asserting that Native Americans shared a common ancestor with a population now found in or around Ulan Bator, Mongolia. Or, as he put it, "We believe the current Mongolian population descended from the population that peopled the New World. For the populations that have been studied, they share eight of the nine subgroups found in the New World."[21]

Frederika Kaestle had been very quiet throughout this whole discussion. But at this point she began to heckle, ever so softly. "What about B, Andy," she prompted softly. "And X."

The Wallace lab, Merriwether explained, had found the Na Dene–speaking populations were mostly lineage A. Although they also found some C and D in these groups, they thought those findings were due to admixture. They thought mothers with those lineages had married into Na Dene tribes and had offspring. The Eskimo/Aleut populations studied seemed to be mostly lineages A and D. The Dogrib he studied—some thirty-two samples—were all lineage A. "We found A and C and another group called X at lower frequencies in other parts of the New World too ... in every group I found A, B, C and D."

He published those findings in several papers between 1994 and 1996. He had concluded that just one migration peopled the Americas, not three or four. He believed the Eskimo didn't come late as many archaeologists had proposed—they had just been separated by the Ice Age glaciers from those who moved south early, so there was no way for gene sharing with those who went south. Those who made it south, the Amerinds, slowly found their way back up north again after the glaciers melted. Merriwether believed he could predict with accuracy the frequency of the four haplotypes one would find in any Native American population simply by reference to the latitude where they lived.

"If it's northern North America, it will be lineage A...central America is a high frequency of B....It's a better predictor than language.... A is high frequency in the North and decreases in frequency as you go south....But all four make it to South America."

Frederika Kaestle snorted very softly. "What about B?" she said again.

I thought he'd answered, but obviously there was something here I didn't understand. So what about B? I asked Merriwether.

"It's nonexistent in Siberia," he said. "As you go south (in the Americas) it reaches higher and higher frequencies. In some it's 100 percent. In Aymara villages in Chile sixty-five percent was the average for B. There were two villages where they all had it. There were some where it was zero. The most common pattern was three of the four types and most often A was missing."

I didn't know what to make of this. How could B be the most common lineage in the south but nonexistent in the populations in Siberia, which should have had it if there was a common ancestor on that side of the Beringian bridge? And what was this X Kaestle kept raising?

A small percentage of people surveyed had been found to carry a marker Merriwether called X. At first the researchers thought this marker was just due to European admixture (meaning a European woman had married into a tribe and all her descendants carried that marker). They had tried to avoid taking samples from those who had mixed ancestry by making certain that samples were given by people with Native American surnames back at least two generations. They still came up with some who didn't have the A, B, C or D markers but did show this X marker. They then screened these samples for Asian-specific markers, markers never seen in the Europeans or Africans they had studied. Most of the samples turned out to also have these Asian-specific markers. The X marker had showed up in a Yanomami population that had been isolated from European contact, deep in the Amazon rain forest, until 1965. It also showed up in extremely low frequencies in Chilean Native people, among

Canadian Mohawks, and in Alaskan Eskimos. In Merriwether's view (not shared by all his colleagues), this was a separate founding lineage in the Americas.

It is important to note that none of this work was done on ancient mtDNA. The major labs making sweeping generalizations about the peopling of the Americas were working with samples taken from living Native Americans and Asians. They simply inferred that ancient peoples must have carried the same mtDNA markers as their descendants. But one couldn't be certain that living Native Americans were descendants of the most ancient Americans without looking at ancient DNA. Populations of women could have been replaced, leaving no descendants behind. The difficulty was extracting viable mtDNA from ancient remains.

Merriwether had recently set up a lab for that purpose. The work is infinitely trickier than extracting mtDNA from relatively fresh blood samples. In the first place, it's harder to create a population to work with when dealing with the extremely scarce ancient remains. In addition, the information content of DNA degrades over time. While the message remains in the bone for a very long time, the signal gets scrambled as it begins to break up at death.

"You have enzymes and liquids breaking open cells, the DNA is exposed and eventually damaged. You get missing base pairs. The way we read it requires that it be intact," said Merriwether. In ancient DNA it's hard to get more than two hundred base pairs still intact. One has to try to put together the whole signal by laying out a kind of jigsaw puzzle of pairs. But the probability of doing this well is low and the work must be verified repeatedly before one can be certain a signal has been read, and not invented by the process. Amplification—copying of the separated strands of DNA—is very difficult. If modern DNA gets mixed in the sample in the process of handling the material, the polymerase chain re-action tends to copy the modern and not the ancient DNA. Frederika Kaestle was trying to get mtDNA out of fifteen Paleo-Indian remains. She was in a hurry to get it done, but it was going very slowly.

Around the time Merriwether was identifying this other X lineage, but had not yet published on it, he had got a call from Bill Hauswirth of the University of Florida at Gainesville. Hauswirth was in charge of the Windover remains, a whole group of ancient humans pulled out of an old cemetery found on a private farm in central Florida. These individuals had undergone a very rare form of burial. Their bodies had been tied down beneath the sur-face of a small pool that had eventually turned into a peat bog. Because their bodies had not been exposed to oxygen, they were in such a perfect state of preservation when found that many of them still had intact brain tissue. The individuals had died between 8000 and 6900 BP. Hauswirth told Merriwether that he'd been trying to extract mtDNA from their tissues, which should have been easier with these than with other ancient remains, but he was getting weird results. "None of them were A, B, C or D," said Merriwether. "All of them were X-6 or X-7, two variants of this X type," he said.

"He says, 'I'm really worried,'" Merriwether recounted. "He was worried that since none of his material was A, B, C or D, no one would believe his data.... I told him the markers to screen for, and if they're there, it's not likely contaminated. It turned out they all had the Asian-specific marker."

Where had this been published?

Merriwether thought it was in a journal called *Experientia*. Frederika Kaestle went to look for a copy of it, but couldn't find it. In any case, Merriwether believed that the personal communi-cation of this data from Hauswirth was a form of confirmation that the X he'd found in modern samples was not the result of contamination, or European admixture either. If X or a variant of X was found in the ancient mtDNA extracted from the 8,000-

year-old Windover remains in Florida, it could not possibly be the result of European admixture.

The picture regarding this lineage called X became more complicated still. In November 1998, Michael D. Brown and colleagues at the Wallace lab published a new paper in the *American Journal of Human Genetics*, reporting the discovery of a fifth founding haplogroup among modern Native Americans.[22] They called this haplogroup X, although they were referring to a different set of markers than Merriwether's X-6 or X-7. In fact, their X was critically different from Merriwether's versions: it was also found at low frequencies in Europeans.

Brown and colleagues had compared twenty-two Native American samples with their haplogroup X to fourteen European samples with haplogroup X. Their X had mainly showed up in northern Native Americans, specifically the Ojibwa, the Nuu-Cha-Nulth, the Sioux and the Yakama. Brown and his colleagues also learned that while there were differences between the European and North American versions of X, there was a consensus of sorts between them that indicated they were distantly related to each other. "Time estimates for the arrival of X in North America," they wrote," are 12,000 to 36,000 years ago…thus supporting the conclusion that the peoples harboring haplogroup X were among the original founders of Native American populations."

They saved the most sensational observation to the end of the abstract: "To date, haplogroup X has not been unambiguously identified in Asia, raising the possibility that some Native American founders were of Caucasian ancestry."

The discussion section of the paper was even more intriguing. "Our analysis confirmed that haplogroup X is present in both modern Native Americans and European populations…. Recent European genetic admixture cannot explain the presence of haplogroup X in the Amerindians. First, if the occurrence of haplogroup X were the result of female gene flow from Europeans, then other more common European mtDNA haplogroups should also be present in the northern Native Americans and they are not. Second, the Native American and European mtDNAS are very different and are connected only through an ancient common ancestor. Hence Native American and European haplogroup X mtDNAS diverged long ago. Finally, Native American haplogroup X mtDNAS encompass substantial continent-specific diversity, implying an ancient arrival in America. Thus haplogroup X constitutes a fifth founding mtDNA haplogroup for the Native Americans...."

The authors went on to say that something like X had also been found in pre-Columbian samples—the 8,000-year-old Windover remains found in Florida were cited as well as remains studied in Brazil in 1996, but the results were not definitive. Americans Anne Stone and Mark Stoneking had found two samples of this X in ancient remains taken from a 600-year-old cemetery on the Illinois River, "demonstrating the presence of haplogroup X," they said, "in the Americas prior to European introgression." (They had obviously forgotten the Vikings, who were in Newfoundland a thousand years ago.) Surveying all the Asian samples studied, this haplogroup had not been "unambiguously" identified in Asians—a situation similar to the absence in North Asian groups of haplogroup B (which had been found in South Asians, such as Tibetans, Koreans, Japanese and Mongolians, but not in any of the tribes currently inhabiting the northeastern Siberian peninsula.) The authors calculated that the European X might have originated between 30,000 and 40,000 years ago. This was compatible with a Near Eastern "origin of haplogroup X and its subsequent spread, probably at a low frequency, into Europe, and Asia. If this is the case, then it is possible that this mtDNA was brought to Beringia/America by the eastward migration of an ancestral Caucasian population of which no trace has so far been found in the mtDNA gene pool of modern Siberian/eastern Asian populations."

This was a tortured way of saying that this X, like B, was not found in living Siberian populations either. It was also a way of shoehorning these curious facts into the accepted story of the origins of the First Americans. It was easier to publish that Native Americans and Caucasians shared a distant ancestor in people who'd moved east into Asia and eventually to America through Beringia, leaving no genetic trace of their passage behind, than to say they might have come direct from Europe to America. Or that Native Americans bearing this haplogroup might have carried it, 30,000 years ago, to Europe.

I wondered if Kennewick Man's mtDNA had this particular X marker.

"How do you explain the absence of B in [North] Asians?" Kaestle was asking Merriwether.

"Why should all who went back have all the types of all that went through?" Merriwether countered.

"They have Andy's X," she said sardonically to me, "but they don't have [the other] X."

"There's B on St. Lawrence Island," said Merriwether defensively. "There's almost no B in North America."

It was around this point in the conversation that he formally introduced Kaestle by her full name.

"Are you *that* Frederika Kaestle?" I asked, to which she nodded a doleful yes.

"So what did you find?" I asked with excitement.

Merriwether intervened right away: "She's under a gag order regarding Kennewick."

"From who?" I asked. The court had certainly not issued any such order.

Merriwether was referring to the U.S. Army. "They told her to cease and desist work before the evidence was confident enough," Merriwether said as Kaestle looked up at the wall, the ceiling, anywhere but at me.

I talked to Kaestle later on the phone. She was very young to be in the middle of such a hot controversy, just twenty-nine. She grew up in Madison, Wisconsin, where her father was a history professor. Her parents were friends with two anthropologists who encouraged her interest in human behavior and evolution. She went to Yale, then took up an internship to study prosimians at the Duke Primate Center. She was sitting on a log one day watching them when a group of yellow jackets began to buzz around her. She was stung and almost died. Such a strong allergy to insect bites made it impossible for her to do field work. She took several courses with Jonathan Marks, who was studying the relationships between the DNA of chimps, gorillas and humans, trying to establish who was related more closely to whom. He advised her to investigate hominid origins and kinship through the lens of genetics rather than behavior.

She moved to University of California at Davis, to study with David Glenn Smith. As a graduate student in a science program she had to work up a three-year research project that would be worthy of a grant from the National Science Foundation, which would then pay her fees and a stipend. "I was interested in the hybrid zones between primate species," she said. By which she meant the moving line that is supposed to define where one species begins and another leaves off. In a minority of primates, this boundary is fuzzy. (For example, some baboons that are definitely different species can still manage to interbreed and produce fertile offspring.) When it came time to get the blood samples she needed to do her study, she couldn't get access in time to complete her project in the allotted three years. She had to pick another subject, one based on blood samples already available in the lab. The materials available included human bone samples taken from ancient remains exposed by a flood at the Stillwater Marsh in the Nevada desert.

It was 1992, only ten years after the invention of the polymerase chain reaction. Kaestle decided to see if she could extract mtDNA from these ancient bones and see if what she found jibed with the archaeologists' theories about the early populations of Nevada. Amy Dansie at the Nevada State Museum helped her get permission to work on the Stillwater Marsh materials, and also on samples from nearby Pyramid Lake.

She was still working on this doctoral study when she got a call from Jim Chatters asking for help with the Kennewick remains. He asked her to try and extract mtDNA from a sample of bone.

I mentioned I had been told Chatters had compromised the remains, by using solvent on them. (In fact, as Chatters would later explain, he had used solvent on some of the skull bones but not on the portions of bone sent for radiocarbon and mtDNA tests.)

"The DNA I got out suggests not," said Kaestle.

Oh, ho, I thought. How interesting. She did get some results.

She had agreed to look at Kennewick Man's mtDNA, she explained, but she already had a trip planned to Panama. She didn't start work on the sample Chatters had Riverside send on to her until late August 1996. She divided the sample in two, and she had just extracted the first run of DNA when all hell broke loose. Even after they had the remains removed from Chatters' lab, the army had no idea he had ordered any genetic studies. When they found out Kaestle had samples of Kennewick bone and was working on them, they sent her supervisor, David Glenn Smith, a cease-and-desist letter, suggesting the lab was in violation of the federal Archaeological Resources Protection Act of 1973 (ARPA), which gives the U.S. government control over all remains or artifacts excavated under license, on land controlled by the United States. They demanded the bone back and any and all notes or papers regarding tests they had run, immediately.

"They threatened us with invading our lab and seizing our notebooks," she said, outraged. "We had phone conversations where they said the same. These lab books had my dissertation notes in them so I freaked out. We said, 'We'll stop.'" But she and David Glenn Smith refused to turn over the samples to the army. They argued they had obtained their bone from the people doing the dating at the University of California, Riverside, under the auspices of the coroner's investigation. Two sets of lawyers argued back and forth.

"C'mon, Frederika," I asked, "what did you find out?"

The truth was, she said primly, she really couldn't tell me anything about Kennewick Man's mtDNA—whether he shared a common ancestor with Europeans, or was himself an ancestor of the Yakama and Umatilla in the neighborhood. She'd only had time to do the one mtDNA extraction. And with ancient mtDNA, that just wasn't enough to know anything about anything.

# 6

# Virtual Bones

## Are Reburied Remains Hard Evidence?

THE BIGGEST STORM of the new year, 1999, hovered on the outskirts of Washington the January morning I made my way to the Smithsonian Institution. It was gathering itself over the Atlantic, glowering and grumbling like the Lord's cloud over the Israelites' tent of meeting. At the Capitol, a political blizzard was already in full howl. The first trial of a U.S. president in 130 years had just started in the Senate. The Smithsonian's lobby was frigid but tranquil, half in the realm of these Washington realities, half in the world of disinterested academia. It is not a federal agency but a federal trust, created by Congress according to the terms of a bequest left to the people of the United States by a British man named Smithson, who never set foot in America. Its board of regents includes the vice president of the United States, the chief justice, three members of the Senate, three members of the House of Representatives and nine citizen members, and it is supported by Congressional appropriations but free from direct governmental interference. But that doesn't mean it's immune to political pressure. Some of its employees are civil servants, some are not. There is a tradition of academic freedom at the Smithsonian; there is also a tradition of trying to make its curators knuckle under.

The Smithsonian Institution exists to increase and diffuse

knowledge "among men."[1] Native American activists see it in a different light. For them it is a charnel house stuffed with the bones of their fallen leaders and the spoils of their destroyed cultures, the embodiment of their defeat and oppression.[2] The Smithsonian is exempt from the NAGPRA but under the National Museum of the American Indian Act passed in 1989, it too must turn over its native American collections to the Museum of the American Indian, and it must repatriate human remains and grave goods to known descendants.[3] By 1999, a number of Native bones had already been sent back,[4] and some of the skulls had been molded and cast and stored away upstairs for future reference. If one couldn't have the real bones, one settled for a cast.

Upstairs in the anthropology department were the offices of Dennis Stanford and Douglas Owsley. They were both trying to rewrite the First American story and had also helped organize the lawsuit against the U.S. Army over the Kennewick remains. Downstairs in the paleobiology department, museum specialist Frederick Grady worked away making the plaster cast of a large walrus skull. He had watched as the bones of a man who died on an Alaskan island a thousand years before Kennewick Man was born (about 9800 BP) were pulled from a cave. Those remains were being quietly studied in Denver, without objection from Native Americans, while the Kennewick bones caused no end of strife. Upstairs it was the Sturm und Drang of science as politics. Downstairs it was the serenity of science for its own sake.

Dennis Stanford, chair of anthropology at the Smithsonian, is a round-cheeked, bearded, barrel-chested, suspendered man. He reminded me of that icon of plainspoken American virtue who sells oatmeal on television. He looked like just the kind of guy you'd like to have at your back in a bureaucratic war, or in any war. He has been shaking things up in American anthropology ever since he threw the Smithsonian's weight behind Tom

Dillehay's find at Monte Verde. When he vouched for Dillehay's integrity, only a nutcake could have any doubts. When he slashed, ever so softly, at Dillehay's detractors, one quaked for them. On the Kennewick matter he has put his considerable shoulder to the wheel alongside Douglas Owsley, a curator of human remains at the Smithsonian, a forensic anthropologist on a mission to save his subject from politics.

Stanford spoke in a voice so soft I could hardly hear him. Over his shoulder, across the street, hulked the massive square headquarters of the U.S. Department of Justice, which was vigorously defending the army from the Kennewick plaintiffs' suit. Every day, Stanford and Owsley came to work knowing that many good brains over there were working very hard to cut them off at the knees. Stanford and Owsley don't see science as something separated from the world. They see it as practical, useful and fundamental to modern life, and they believe that their right to practice it unhindered by the state is guaranteed by the U.S. constitution, the same as religion. They were suing the U.S. Army Corps of Engineers on behalf of all those lowly graduate students who wouldn't get to first base with a government bureaucrat in any future dispute over the study of human remains if they allowed Kennewick Man to be reburied without a fight. The essence of their suit was the government's failure to follow a proper process.

Owsley arrived in Stanford's office about half an hour late. He is a small, blocky man with curly sandy hair, a nose that curves at the tip like the top of a violin, and a smooth and boyish face unmarked by the stress of his profession. He had been out examining historic-period human remains uncovered by a developer's bulldozer in Fairfax County. He perched on the edge of an armchair, ready to spring to his feet, anxious to keep things moving right along. In fact, he and Stanford both seemed more than a little anxious about the Kennewick affair. The dirty water of ethnic politics lapped around their ankles: it would either pull them under or they would learn to swim in it.

Stanford has for some time been certain that the Clovis First/Bering Strait theory is wrong. He thinks that the Solutrean culture in Europe was the precursor of what became known as Clovis technology in America. There was no single find that clinched the matter for him: it was the pattern of evidence, and missing evidence. Clovis spear points have not been found in Alaska, have not been found in Siberia. They have, on the other hand, been found in large numbers in the southeastern United States and in decreasing numbers through the west and up into Canada. The simplest explanation for this distribution is an entry into the Americas from Europe on the Atlantic side. He considers it possible that early people, using some kind of watercraft, exploited the rich ecosystem along the sea ice margin that stretched across the Atlantic from the now submerged continental shelves of Ireland to the Grand Banks. Because he works for the Smithsonian, he can explore such ideas knowing that he will not lose his job. It was this position of privilege that allowed him to stand up for science in the Kennewick matter.

Neither he nor Owsley ever expected to have to sue their government over the right to study human remains. They worried about the NAGPRA before it passed, but Stanford had believed that the NAGPRA would mainly apply to historic-period remains in museums and universities where a clear line of cultural affiliation could be shown. The U.S. Army's behavior over Kennewick Man had blown that notion completely out of the water. Now they had to fight, to save what they could.

Owsley walked me down a long hall to his office. The walls on both sides were lined floor to ceiling with boxes full of collections. I could tell we were getting close to the physical anthropology section when we passed ten-foot-high artifact cabinets with a large number of what I took to be forensically reconstructed heads stored on their tops. Actually, they were sculptures made more than a hundred years ago. The heads were utterly artless. They were painted a peculiar browny flesh tone, they had eyes that stared at nothing, they had thick black hair. They were also swathed in clear, thick plastic, as if this was the warehouse where post-Christmas leftovers were held for the liquidation to come.

Owsley's office is in an unrenovated part of the building, painted white, with very high ceilings. Peculiar posters and photographs were scattered here and there, most of them having to do with mummies and skeletons. It was stifling hot. There was a work table, and a stone sink against one wall. There were wood and glass cases filled with human bones. There were bones on a side table, there were bones on the worktable. There were skulls, long bones, vertebrae, all in different shades. Where had I got the idea that human bone is a uniform white? Some of these bones were a mottled gray, some were a more uniform buttery yellow; none were white. I settled in the visitor's chair. There was a tray right beside me with a skull and all sorts of other bones mixed together.

As he told me about himself and his work, I found myself staring at the bones and the images of bones. The ones on my left belonged to a Civil War–era soldier. On my right there was a picture of Owsley in an attic room, full of hills of bones pouring out of dark plastic garbage bags. Sunlight sliced through slatted windows and a broken roof. The photo had been taken in Vukovar, he informed me. He had been in Croatia doing forensic anthropology: he could now diagnose the signs of death by AK-47 from across a room. High velocity weapons shatter the skull in a manner distinct from low velocity weapons. The bones in the garbage bags were not Serbs but Ustache, killed by Tito's partisans at the end of the Second World War and buried in mass graves. He'd examined them and learned how they'd died. Tito's partisans had forced them to dig the grave, wired their wrists behind their backs, forced them to kneel, then shot them in the back of the head. He'd learned more about the impact of gunshots on the body in Croatia than anywhere else. Not that he hadn't done forensic work in other places. There were shelves outside his office marked "Guatemala"; he'd done the Branch Davidian mess at Waco; he'd worked on the remains of soldiers in Desert Storm.

I kept waiting for some sort of emotion to be kindled in me as he talked. Each of these bones carried the information that had made up a human being. My heart was silent. The bones were too. They did not cry to me, they did not sing, they did not threaten or warn, they simply were. I tried to think how these people must have looked when they were alive. I tried to imagine the bones layered with flesh. Nothing doing. I found it hard to summon up a suitable mood. Mima Kapches of the ROM had suggested one needed a certain respectful reverence to give such remains their due. I failed utterly to achieve it—I was far too interested in hearing what this man could tell me. This bothered me more than I can say. After all, a woman had moved me almost to tears by crying in a public place about studying her ancestors' remains in a room just like this. Yet here, in a room full of ancestors, my eyes stayed quite dry. I felt I was lacking in the right kind of fellow feeling.

Owsley talked a blue streak, as if he had to stuff me with all the information he had gathered before it was too late. As of his last count, five months previously, 3,400 skeletons from the Smithsonian's collections had been returned for reburial. These bones and the grave goods returned with them were now lost to science. As Tom Lynch had made clear, whatever had been learned from them would now be unlearned. Since the early work done could no longer be repeated and checked for error, it would be almost as if they had never been studied, never measured. As Dennis Stanford had said, the next generation would regret this.

Owsley had no assistant, so the phone kept ringing as he lectured, and he kept having to break off to answer it. He'd been promised an aide when he took this job but the funding was cut in the latest round of budget whittlings: he stubbornly protested against the budget gnomes by never checking his voice mail. In between phone calls, he made it clear he was talking to me because he thought I was a fellow partisan, a supporter, a believer in the value of his science. Was I or wasn't I? How could a doctor's daughter have doubts about this? I had eaten my daily bread as a child because my father had learned from the study of cadavers. Owsley would find it difficult to understand how anyone in my position could be skeptical about his right to study and learn from human remains. But in spite of the fact I lacked fellow feeling about the human bones around me, I still wasn't at all sure what I thought about physical anthropology as a science.

His passion, his obsession, his fiery belief in the importance of what he did here—his determination to tell the story at all costs—reminded me of every great journalist I'd ever met. His computer technician came in, a retired military specialist who volunteers for him twice a week. There was nothing for it but we had to go to the next room so Owsley could show me some of his life's work. He is recording every measurement of every human bone ever found and stored in the western half of America that is more than one hundred years old. He has created a vast database of information about all western Native American remains found and studied ranging in age from 10,000 BP to 100 BP. The database records skeletal pathology, every datum one could want about each remain ever found, as measured by his staff of trained volunteers. His computer technician has worked out a program that allows comparisons between and among all the data stored. If one wanted to know about arthritic joints in all equestrian cultures of the Great Plains, Owsley could call up data about any joint ever examined. He has been to every museum and school that would have him. (The University of Nebraska has made its collection off limits to scholars not on its staff.) He has trained a group of eight physical anthropologists around the country to work to exactly the same measurement standard. The problem with measurement as a science is the inevitable error of investigators: it was vital that all members of this team measure and score in exactly the same way. Since the NAGPRA repatriations began, his pace had become frantic. Trans World Airlines gave the Smithsonian free tickets and he had used a large number of them for travel to museums, universities, and public or private institutions where Native American bones have been stored—at last count, eighty-seven flights. He had 7,000 individuals in the database.

Owsley flashed through different items of interest on the computer screen, calling data up at will. He was talking about trauma. Many of the ancient remains he'd studied exhibited broken arms, skulls, ribs; violence and traumatic death were ordinary. Owsley's measuring and studying had also shown him evidence of cannibalism, a practice not observed by ethnologists who'd studied Native American cultures. The human bones from one site in particular showed evidence of splintering, chopping, burning, defleshing and boiling, and also of using bones to stir—there was pot polish on the ends. Christy Turner had written about such cannibalism in the Southwest, and Owsley had picked up evidence of the same behavior in the Plains. This was a virtual rebuttal of the political theorists of the eighteenth century who had imagined tribal cultures as more simple, benign and peaceful than contemporary societies.

Owsley believes his is the last generation of scholars who will actually be able to see and measure these bones for themselves, to correct the mistakes of their predecessors. From now on, study of these repatriated remains will be entirely virtual—out of reach of new science technologies still to come. "Look at what DNA can tell us now," Stanford had said, "that no one even dreamed about even five years ago. What we'll do with it in twenty years will blow you away."

I thought Owsley and Stanford had to be concerned with something more fundamental than the lost opportunities of the future. Physical anthropology is descriptive: with the bones that make up this database repatriated and reburied and therefore unavailable to other scholars, Owsley's measurements might no longer form part of the trusted structure of science. One had only to look at how Lynch regarded Alan Bryan's published work on the calotte he'd found and lost in Brazil. Could virtual physical anthropology of reburied remains ever be entirely believable? Didn't people use the other databases available because they were made from the measurements of populations that could still be checked against reality? The other problem I saw with his data-base was that he calls it North American, but western Canada and Mexico are not well represented.

Owsley argued that he had some Canadian remains in the data-base. He'd gathered measurements on the nineteenth-century Blackfoot people from Canada whose remains were still in the Field Museum in Chicago. So, he asserted, his database was a powerful instrument. But he had none of the ancient material from Canada. I'd told him about Gore Creek before coming to Washington—he hadn't heard of it, even though it was relevant to his work. He'd asked for Jerome Cybulski's paper so I faxed it to him.

It was as if, in the view of this serious scholar, western North America consisted mainly of Alaska and the western half of the lower forty-eight states, as if Mexico and Canada's populations of ancient Native people could be assumed to be the same. Yet Jerome Melbye, a well-known physical anthropologist at the University of Toronto, had explained to me that this is not so. He is often called upon by the coroner to identify remains. He had found that Native Canadian remains do not fit the computer software categories derived from representative samples of U.S. Native populations. There are differences between the living populations on both sides of the border that are significant and meaningful. As with the living, so with the dead.

Like Dennis Stanford and several others involved in the Kenne-wick case, Owsley is from a small town in the West. His father worked for the Wyoming Fish and Game Service. When Owsley entered the University of Wyoming, he studied physical anthro-pology with George Gill, a man who became his mentor. "When

I needed help on Kennewick," Owsley said, "I called George to help."

Gill took him on forensic cases in Wyoming, took him to see thousand-year-old shell middens, introduced him to Bill Bass of the University of Tennessee who, according to Owsley, trained more forensic anthropologists than anyone in the country. He'd trained Gill. He'd trained his colleague Richard Jantz, who is still at Tennessee. "And he trained me," Owsley said.

Owsley worked on his doctorate in the 1970s, the decade in which the American Indian Movement found its voice and began to yell loudly about mistreatment of their ancestors' bones by American museums. He began his professional career explaining to Department of the Interior officials by letter why remains need to be studied.

Owsley also learned about the need to measure fast under pressure of losing study materials when he was at Tennessee. The university had borrowed a large collection of human remains from the Plains from the State of South Dakota. A Native organization insisted that the remains had to be returned and reburied and South Dakota agreed. When Tennessee was faced with demands to return the remains of 530 individuals, Owsley and his colleagues developed a systematic method to document the remains before they were lost. He got an NSF grant and pulled together a team of researchers to measure and describe the bones. They worked eight hours a day, seven days a week over ten weeks to get the job done. A book came out of it in 1994, called *Skeletal Biology in the Great Plains*.

But it wasn't until the early 1990s, after the passage of NAGPRA, that he and Richard Jantz began to understand how vital the old collections in American museums might be to a proper understanding of the origins of Native Americans. A paper by Brazilians Walter Neves and Hector Pucciarelli (1991) and a similar one by U.S. scholars Gentry Steele and Joe Powell (1992) argued that some of the earliest remains in the Americas were quite unlike modern Native Americans.[5,6] In the course of documenting remains at the Nevada State Museum, which had discovered that several of the human remains in its care were extremely ancient, Owsley and Jantz measured them. Owsley had the Wizards Beach skeleton and the Spirit Cave Mummy in his database.

He called up Spirit Cave on the screen. He showed me photos of the forensic reconstruction made of the Spirit Cave Mummy's head. Owsley's general codes revealed the various anomalies noted when they measured and examined the remains. The mummy was between forty and forty-four at death. It had a spinal anomaly. Its teeth were very interesting and unlike the Wizards Beach remains, only a few hundred years younger and found not too far away. The wear patterns suggested they had different diets. Some of Spirit Cave's teeth were worn right through to the pulp and abscessed. There were signs of arthritis. It also had marks of trauma, something it shared with Kennewick. The Spirit Cave skull had a round fracture that had already partially healed by time of death from other causes.[7]

Owsley and Jantz had compared their measurements of the cranium of Spirit Cave with the database created by W.W. Howells of populations around the world. Unfortunately, the Howells database included few Native American populations so they added to his database their own measurements from various collections. The final population they grouped to compare to Spirit Cave included samples from Blackfoot, Cheyenne, Crow, Sioux, Pawnee, Historic Arikara and some Numic speakers (peoples of the American Great Basin, which is the area where Spirit Cave was found). Howells had made sixty-one measurements on each skull he sampled. Jantz and Owsley measured Spirit Cave using most of these same measurements, and then joined some of them into complexes or sets of dimensions. "These smaller analyses," they later wrote, "allow us to focus on relationships reflected by these cranial complexes, and to provide a metric description of the Spirit Cave male stated in terms of the patterns of variability seen in modern crania."[8]

Spirit Cave's skeleton was described as gracile (no mention was made of any sign of the runner's muscles the Gore Creek bones had shown). The skull was narrow, with a long, moderately high vault. The face was short, the palate small and elongated. When these various features were compared to other modern populations in the database, most interesting things were observed. In the group of measurements having to do with the profile of the vault, the group most like Spirit Cave turned out to be the Ainu of Japan. The Ainu are an ethnic group who are the descendants of an early people, the Jomon, who populated Japan before the arrival of a Mongoloid population. The Ainu's non-Mongoloid features are echoed in the human remains recovered from Jomon sites in the Japanese islands, sites that date back to the end of the Ice Age, and the same features can be found, according to C. Loring Brace, in the skeletons from the Upper Cave at Zhoukoudien (in China).[9] The closest living populations to Spirit Cave, when evaluating this group of measurements, are Asian/Pacific, but also include the Zulu of Africa. The most distant population, the population least like Spirit Cave, is Bushman, but three Native American groups are also very different from Spirit Cave. "The Spirit Cave male would be an atypical member of any of these populations," Jantz and Owsley concluded.

They looked at projection of the middle face and prognathism of the upper jaw. When these measurements were compared to the populations in Howells' database, Spirit Cave turned out to be more like some European populations than any other groups. "The two closest are both European, but Norse has a much higher posterior probability than any other group." Their conclusion: if Spirit Cave was close to any living groups, it would be the Ainu, Norse and Zalavar (Hungarian) populations—in other words, to European or European-like populations—but Spirit Cave really fell outside the range of all modern populations.

These findings were quite unlike Hrdlička's claims that all Native Americans came from the same North Asian population. They weren't published in the *Nevada Historical Society Quarterly* until spring 1997, but Owsley and Jantz's findings were well known in the physical anthropology community before they published. They were already well launched on the task of trying to describe the rest of the suddenly important Paleo-Indian population still in museums when Owsley got a call from Jim Chatters in August of 1996. "Chatters...said he was working on a case for the coroner," said Owsley. "He thought it was a fur trader or a European explorer, but there was a point, he called it Cascade, in the right hip that was 4,000 to 9,000 years old. He sent a bone sample and got the date back. He said, 'I need help to interpret it.' I'd looked at Spirit Cave and Wizards Beach. I'd seen as many [ancient remains] as any. It did not sound strange that [Kennewick Man] had a different morphology [from present-day Native people]. I went to the assistant director for science, the liaison to the director, and said, I've got an opportunity to examine an exceptional skeleton. I want to bring it in."

The Smithsonian arranged to buy a plane ticket for Chatters, who would bring the remains to Washington. Richard Jantz agreed to come in from Tennessee to help examine it.

"One evening, I got...a frantic and anxious call from Chatters saying 'they seized it.'" Owsley became concerned that he'd never get to see these remains. He called the Army Corps of Engineers' archaeologist, who was in charge of the Corps's human remains, and he called the head archaeologist in Washington; he explained to both that this skeleton was very important and why. He felt he wasn't getting anywhere with them so he talked to the head of the Corps in Washington State, who listened to him carefully but that was all. Richard Jantz had one of his students put up a notice on the Internet about what was going on, asking any scientists who read it to write to the U.S. Army and explain why these remains had to be studied. Letters were sent from all over. Owsley consulted with Dennis Stanford and together they decided to appeal directly to the Umatilla. As it happened, they knew a young man named Minthorn (a relative of Armand Minthorn) who was working at the Smithsonian downstairs in the repatriation department. "He told me to send [a letter] to Armand Minthorn and Donald Sampson [of the Umatilla]," said Owsley. This also went nowhere.

"It was very clear we were not getting anywhere. I talked to Robson Bonnichsen [head of the Center for the Study of the First Americans at Oregon State University in Corvallis, Oregon]... Rob gave me [the lawyer] Alan Schneider's number and told me to point out to him how NAGPRA should be interpreted. Time was running out. I called Alan and asked if we could block it, what do we have to do. Neither one of us thought it would go on for years.... Jantz was with me. I called George Gill who came on board. Dennis was supportive but real hesitant and concerned."

When they decided to launch the lawsuit they had to answer to the Smithsonian Institution's attorneys. They were concerned about the spectacle of civil servants suing the government. They weren't even sure it was legal. "The Smithsonian attorneys sent me a harshly worded letter saying you can't be in that. I was ducking and dodging. I shared the letter with Alan. Alan helped craft a three-page response," said Owsley. In the end the attorneys agreed that he and Stanford were free to launch a suit, but only after their director backed them to the hilt.

In the end, eight plaintiffs joined together to sue the U.S. Army Corps of Engineers for the right to study the Kennewick remains. They were all well known to each other. "I am the youngest," said Owsley. "But altogether we have 200 years between us."

The lead plaintiff was Robson Bonnichsen. Alan Schneider had been on the Center for the Study of the First Americans' board, but resigned when he took the case. The other plaintiffs were: C. Vance Haynes, a recently retired geophysicist from the University of Arizona who has spent many years examining Paleo-Indian sites; C. Loring Brace, a leading physical anthropologist at the University of Michigan at Ann Arbor; D. Gentry Steele, a physical anthropologist at Texas A & M; George Gill, a physical anthropologist and forensic expert at the University of Wyoming; Richard Jantz, a physical anthropologist at the University of Tennessee, Dennis Stanford and Doug Owsley of the Smithsonian Institution. The plaintiffs were almost as numerous as the Paleo skeletons still remaining above ground in the United States.

When I visited Owsley, Judge Jelderks had already ordered the army to let the plaintiffs inventory the Kennewick remains. Owsley had flown to the Burke Museum in Seattle and worked for seventeen straight hours. He had filed a forty-six-page single-spaced description of what he found. Pieces of the femurs, which were clearly visible in the photographs and video Chatters made of the remains before they were taken from his lab, were definitely not among the bones Owsley saw. Even though the court had ordered that he be allowed to do this inventory, the Justice Department lawyers had played hardball. At the last moment, they denied him what had been previously agreed, which was that his former colleague Cleone Hawkinson could come into the room to assist him by recording his findings on a laptop computer. Instead, he'd had to talk his inventory into a tape recorder (and he had inadvertently recorded over some of the material, wiping it out). The one fight he did win was that Jim Chatters was allowed to go in with him. Owsley had insisted that Chatters be allowed to attend. Chatters had seen the remains first and was the only one who would know if they had deteriorated while in the army's control.

And what did he think of Chatters?

"He knew he needed help and tried to get it," said Owsley. But he thought Chatters was bang on when he said there was no way that Kennewick Man had a typical Native American face and head shape.

Well, I asked, could one actually see the differences between European and Native American bones just by looking?

He reached into a box on his work table and pulled out a skull. It was one of the so-called Giant population from the Nevada desert. It was only about eight hundred years old. He placed it in front of me like an offering. He pointed out that the nasal opening was heart-shaped, and there were the wide and very prominent cheekbones one expected to see on a Native American skull. It was, he said, a North Asian face.

He pulled another skull from the box beside me. This one was from one of Custer's men at the Battle of the Little Big Horn. This face was not at all like the Giant's. The whole skull was smaller, narrower, more delicate. To illustrate the most obvious differences, he pointed to the narrow cheek bones and the small nasal bone that turned up at the end like a little ski jump. The whole configuration was European.

Even I could see that these were clearly not the same. While race is a useless category to capture these differences, it was clear these people's bones were different from each other.

In the main floor paleobiology lab, Frederick Grady was peacefully, calmly at work among heaps of animal bones. Plaster casts he'd made were laid out around him. A walrus skull sat on his work table and plaster dust covered his jeans. He was a thin, pale-faced man with a very large square head that seemed to wobble above his narrow shoulders. His eyes swam myopically behind his glasses as he described his summer vacations spent on archaeological caving expeditions. That was how he came to be on Prince of Wales Island, just south of Juno, Alaska, in July 1996. Just three weeks before Kennewick Man was pulled out of the Columbia River, Timothy Heaton, the paleontologist Grady was working with, found a mud-encrusted human mandible on the floor of the cave, followed by a chewed piece of a human pelvis. Analysis suggested these were one man's bones, and radiocarbon tests said he had died between 9880 and 9730 BP, making these remains a thousand years older than Gore Creek and Kennewick Man.[10]

The contrast in the handling of the Kennewick and Prince Wales Island sets of bones couldn't have been more stark. There were yards of press clippings about Kennewick Man. The Native American community was up in arms. There was a court battle to control him. Every tiny piece of information about him had been snatched at as if it were vital to the well-being of humanity. Yet the human bones found up at the top of Prince of Wales Island had evoked barely a flicker of public interest. I'd only heard about them by chance. Richard Morlan, a paleontologist at the Museum of Civilization in Ottawa, had pulled out for me one of the few papers that mentioned the remains. The paper was mainly about the animal bones found in the cave. Two species of bear, long believed to have been mutually exclusive, had coexisted on the island during the Ice Age. The radiocarbon dates on the bear bones ran back to 41,600 and 35,365 BP. The paper made only a brief reference to the human bones found.[11]

Frederick Grady was one of the authors of the paper, along with Tim Heaton of the University of South Dakota and James Dixon from the Denver Museum of Natural History. Grady has only a BA in biology and described himself as incredibly lucky to have landed this job making casts of bones at the Smithsonian twenty-four years ago. In the summer of 1991 he went on the first of many expeditions to Prince of Wales Island.

The limestone caves of the region had been discovered years earlier by the couple who organized these summer expeditions. Kevin and Carlene Allred explored the caves, eventually with funding from the United States Forest Service, which was interested in having them mapped. The caves are long and narrow, with temperatures hovering around fifty degrees Fahrenheit. They are dangerous: one had a straight drop of almost six hundred feet. Regardless of such dangers, early people might have found shelter in them, a refuge from excessive heat or cold. At the end of the Ice Age, with the glacier front not far away, the temperature outside would have been frigid. Nowadays the caves are surrounded by a towering temperate rain forest, and the slick-wet limestone is overgrown with myriad creepers, vines, mosses, leaves and lichens. Grady and the other cavers camped on the beach. Getting up to the caves involved a slippery, dangerous forty-minute hike.

In the summer of 1991, Grady and his friends were shown bear bones—from a grizzly and a black bear found the previous year by Kevin Allred. These bones also attracted the interest of paleontologist Timothy Heaton, who got an NSF grant with Grady in the summer of 1992 to excavate. At this cave and others, he found remains of grizzly bears with dates going back to about 12,295 BP. He also found the bones of small rodents, shrews and red foxes.[12]

It was the 1996 trip that produced the first remains of human beings. "I found the first evidence of humans, the big biface," Grady explained. A biface is a two-sided worked stone tool, in the shape of a spearhead. This particular biface was almost like a Clovis spear point, but not exactly. It had the same general shape, but not the flutes characteristic of Clovis spearheads. "As soon as I found it I knew it was Paleo-Indian. It's a gray chert."

Grady didn't think there was any chert to be found on the island, which meant that whoever brought it here had come in some kind of boat. They also found microblades of obsidian that didn't come from the island either. So they had evidence that Paleo-Indians used boats. "When we found [the biface], we called Terry Fifield of the U.S. Forest Service. He said, yeah, eight to ten thousand years old, Paleo-Indian. He said keep on going. We found the human bones the last day."

In fact, the bones were found in the last hour of the last day of the season, on the fourth of July, 1996. Timothy Heaton reached his arm under a ledge and out came some mud-encrusted pieces of bone. He didn't realize what they were until he took them down to the beach and washed the dirt off them.

The differences between the Kennewick case and this one began at the moment of the discovery that these bones were human. Because this was a paleontological dig that had produced an inadvertent find of human bone, the procedures for notifying the Native bands in the area were followed right away. Terry Fifield, the forest service's archaeologist, lived on Prince of Wales Island. He called the Alaska state troopers and the coroner, but when they heard the context they had no interest in the remains. Fifield knew most of the members of the local Native communities well. There were four bands that had to be notified. They were uncomfortable with the fact of human bone having been dug up, but they decided to allow further excavation and study.

In 1997 Grady and Heaton returned to the site with James Dixon, a Paleo-Indian specialist from the Denver Museum of Natural History. Slide shows and talks were given for the community so they could know the scope of the work. The age of the remains was established at about 9200 BP. They were put in the care of the Denver Museum, which made a cast of the jaw. It was heavy, or robust. Grady thought it was of a man in his twenties. "There was not much wear on the teeth," he said. "The wisdom teeth were barely worn. All the teeth were intact except for the incisors."

All of this was great news. According to Frederika Kaestle, it is preferable to extract mtDNA from ancient teeth: the process does minimal damage and teeth protect DNA longer than bones. The fact that the teeth showed little wear would allow experts like Christy Turner to examine them for the traits associated with North Asians (sinodonts) or South Asians (sundadonts). I asked whether that work had been done. Grady assumed so, but he had heard no results.

Was there any particularly important thing that would come out of such analysis? Grady, refreshingly, didn't think so. He thought maybe DNA studies might be pertinent to improving the human condition, but not much else. "We do science because we like to," he said calmly. "Supporting science is like supporting the arts ... for its own sake."

Timothy Heaton, reached at the University of South Dakota, did not think mtDNA extraction had been attempted yet. (Later, he would report that one lab's attempt failed.) But carbon isotope ratios had established that Prince of Wales Man ate marine creatures exclusively. Heaton commended the behavior of the U.S. Forest Service in this matter, in sharp contrast to the U.S. Army Corps of Engineers. The forest service, he said, were totally supportive. He and the other researchers were given "helicopter support, funds for dating, ground and boat transport." Heaton was appalled that the Kennewick site had been reburied under boulders. "They should be court-martialled," he said of the U.S. Army. "It didn't have to go this way. And it shouldn't have."

His memory of the discovery was a little different from Grady's. He had put his hand under a ledge in the cave and pulled out a long bone, which he later understood had been used as a tool, and then the jaw, and part of a pelvis and some vertebrae. "I didn't know they were human till I got to the ocean. They were so caked in mud. [And then] it was, oh boy, what kind of trouble have we got here." Clearly, from the position the bones were in, they were ancient. Bear bones also found in the cave dated back to 42,000 BP, right in the middle of the last interglacial interval. As Heaton explained it, the last cool period had two distinct episodes of widespread glaciation. There was a time in between when the climate warmed and the ice withdrew. He had dates on animal bone from the island that clearly showed there had been animals living there during the period when the ice had retracted.

In many ways this find was a surprise. It had been assumed by just about everyone that the Ice Age glaciers covered everything on the West Coast of Alaska and Canada right down to the sea. Only a few dissenters (like Knut Fladmark, an archaeologist at Simon Fraser University, and the geologist Calvin Heusser) had argued that there might have been a way for human beings to move down the coast earlier.[13] Now Heaton had a record of bones showing that at least on this portion of this island there had not been continuous ice cover. At certain times, large mammals and small ones had been able to eke out a living in the area.

"My work and the work of others," Heaton said, "changed all that thinking. It makes the West Coast the logical route for humans entering the Americas.... We demonstrate that this was ice free and [used by] large mammals. We got ringed seals—they live on the ice only—they nest above the ice and drop down to the water to feed. It's too warm there now [for ringed seals]. The arctic fox predates the ringed seal. We also got caribou. The sea changes, the habitat changes. It got cold enough to freeze sea water. It must have been tundra. We don't have bears in the Ice Age, just before and after.... We found black and brown bear coexisting on the island. Black bear prefer forest, brown prefer the open."

But the only absolute proof of a human presence was the few bones found in the summer of 1996, one of which was a bone made into a tool. In the summer of 1997 Heaton went back with James Dixon. Dixon dug an archaeological trench in front of the cave mouth. "He found fire-cracked rocks, charcoal, and points outside. Tool scraps. Clearly they were correlated. They were in the 9,000-year-old range. The bone tool is even older— just over 10,000."

Heaton confirmed that they had found obsidian and other rocks that must have been traded into the area of the cave from other places. And since Prince of Wales is an island, whoever made the campsite in front of the cave "must have had water crafts before."

Had they found enough of the skull and teeth to be able to establish whether these remains looked like modern Native Americans?

"It's more Caucasoid," he said. "Talk to Dixon about that... the chin is quite prominent on the lower jaw."

In fact, I had already called Dixon, but he had been very, very cautious. He'd said he couldn't really say much about what had been found from the examination of the human remains. He'd explained that he was a party to an agreement that required him to inform the Native American groups on the island of his findings before making any information more widely available. This was not an attempt to control his work, he hastened to say, but just so we can "all be on the same page."

Well, I said, had the teeth been examined by Christy Turner to establish whether they had sinodont or sundadont characteristics?

The incisors were missing, he said. (Two were later found.) Shovel-shaped incisors are a tooth trait common among Native Americans and not often found in other groups. "We looked" was all he would admit. He'd said he'd call back after checking in with the tribes. But he didn't.

The U.S. Forest Service archaeologist, Terry Fifield, didn't exactly know what Dixon had meant about an agreement with the tribes not to make public any findings without telling them about it first. There was an agreement not to publish on the human remains without allowing the tribal councils to review the work first, but on the other hand, he was not aware of much that had been committed to paper. Very little about the human remains had been published, except that three more bones had been found in the summer of 1997. The tribes, mainly Tlingit, were told about them right away.

Fifield did know that a sample of bone had been submitted to David Glenn Smith at University of California, Davis, for mtDNA analysis. He hadn't heard of any results. He knew that Christy Turner had been contacted by Dixon to examine the teeth but he hadn't actually done it yet. In short, almost nothing had been published on the physical anthropology of the remains.

But he described what had been learned from the examination of the teeth of Prince of Wales Man. Last year, he said, he went to the Sealaska Corporation regional meeting, which was in the throes of working out a historic-sites management plan for the region. "I talked," he said, "on early Caucasoid populations. The organizers gritted their teeth, but there wasn't much of a reaction."

So, I said, just to be sure, the teeth were evaluated with Christy Turner's traits in mind?

"They were X-rayed," he said. "And there were two roots, not three. They were not Aleut/Eskimo."

Months later, when I called again, Fifield had become less decisive. Yes, some of the traits were suggestively Caucasoid—the chin was large and triangular, he said—but there were also traits that fell on the other side. If he had made any allusion to racial characteristics, such as the word "Caucasoid," in our previous conversation, which he did recall, "I was out of line."

7

# The Kennewick
# Chronicles

Science, History, Politics, Religion...
and the United States Army

I
N THE READING I had done about Kennewick Man
and the various activities of Jim Chatters, I had
formed a mental image of Kennewick as a small town
huddled in the middle of a forest, a wet sort of forest. The plane
set me down at the Tri-City airport (serving the sister cities of
Kennewick, Richland and Pasco) at midnight. The place was
almost empty. Three of us waited together at the curb for a taxi
for half an hour (the others were a nuclear engineer back from a
week of R and R in Chicago and a shaky old gambler poured off
the last flight from Reno). I was surprised to find myself staring at
the sere hills and low mountains of a high desert plateau.

The three cities are spread out along the Columbia River and
that night their lights twinkled far into the distance, as if this was
some sort of big-time urban center. Daylight revealed the illu-
sion: this was the middle of nowhere. To the north and south of
the river there are huge irrigated farms. Agribusiness is a main-
stay of the economy—built on irrigation made possible by the
U.S. Army Corp of Engineers' big dams, which discipline the
river all the way up to the Canadian border. The taxi driver told
me there are plans afoot to tear the dams down because they've

destroyed the salmon fishery, and the salmon fishery is Native
American business by treaty.[1] The Native Americans want the
dams gone, the farmers want the dams to stay: this is the new
political conflict dividing the region. Until the 1990s, the troubles here stemmed from the arms business. The Tri-City area is
close to the Hanford Nuclear Reservation, built during World
War II to make the plutonium used for the bomb dropped on
Nagasaki in 1945. Then it churned out warheads for the Cold
War. By the 1980s, Hanford had attained the dubious distinction
of being among the dirtiest nuclear facilities in the United States.
Its radioactive drums oozing poison and its location, right beside
the Columbia River, made it into a major environmental issue in
1986 when the Department of Energy revealed the extent of the
contamination to the public. Four separate sites on the Hanford
Reservation are listed on the EPA's national priorities list. In 1989
a tri-party clean-up agreement was signed between the Department of Energy, the Environmental Protection Agency and the
State of Washington. For the last ten years, the nuclear engineers
had mainly concerned themselves with containing and deconta-
minating the mess. This was supposed to have been done by now.
The engineer I shared my taxi with couldn't imagine what he was
still doing here, years after he took his clean-up job. The taxi driver told me of a friend who witnessed a recent spill of highly
radioactive material.

Native American names are all over the map. There is a county
called Umatilla, and one of the rivers that joins the Columbia
farther upstream is the Yakima. In 1885, the Umatilla and the
Yakama sat down with representatives of the U.S. government
and made treaties. They were peaceful. They got screwed. The
Hanford nuclear facility was built in 1943, close to or on lands
ceded by treaty for the use of the Umatilla, the Yakama and the
Nez Percé: it was a top secret facility safe not only from prying
enemy eyes but also from people who might complain to their
congressman. In 1940 the U.S. Army had built the Umatilla
chemical depot between the Umatilla and the Yakama reserva-

tions. It is a vast acreage where armaments are stored, including chemical weapons such as the neurotoxin sarin. Like the Hanford facility's nuclear mess, these chemicals are also leaking. The Environmental Protection Agency had put that site too on the National Priorities List of uncontrolled hazardous waste sites.[2]

But I get ahead of myself.

By the time I got to Kennewick enough people had said unkind words about James Chatters that I really wanted to like him. A high-placed official in Washington familiar with the Kennewick case insisted that Chatters had used a solvent that damaged the Kennewick skull. There had been public hints from the U.S. government that Chatters might also have knowledge of the missing chunks of Kennewick Man's femurs. There had been snide remarks even from the plaintiffs' side of the fence. I thought the government was after him because he'd been resourceful and nimble. But I'd arrived at his house as arranged, first thing in the morning, only to be told he wanted to go for coffee at a Starbucks and get some answers from me first. If my answers weren't right, there'd be no interview. I'd flown a long way to see Jim Chatters. I sat there as he ate a sticky bun, trying very hard to appreciate him. He made it tough.

He grilled me like a chicken. Round and round I turned, getting hotter under the collar. What exactly was my book about? he wanted to know. I told him about my book. He asked for more. I told him more. Why was he so concerned? I asked. Because he figured we were in competition, he said. He was working on a book himself. Only after he'd satisfied himself that our books were not in conflict, that I wasn't the enemy, did we get back into his dusty four-wheel-drive vehicle and roll back through the dead flat streets to his house so he could tell me his story.

It was February. The light played funny tricks. It was bright, but somehow somber. It was warm in the sun, but the wind had a bitter chill. There was a dry, dusty haze over everything. It all reminded me of Saskatchewan in the fall, especially the big sky over the big Columbia River.

Chatters was telling me that he didn't like it here. He'd bought a piece of land up in the hills. He was going to build on it and escape. I watched him as he drove: he is quite small, with heavily muscled forearms. He has a Western European face, with a narrow, short, upturned nose, ears flat to his head, thin lips, a small pointed chin hidden by his trimmed beard. If you pulled the flesh away to expose the bone, he'd be a dead ringer for that soldier of Custer's in Owsley's lab at the Smithsonian. Chatters had a nice gold hoop earring through one ear, a type of jewellery not often seen on a male scientist, and when he walked across the shopping mall's parking lot he moved with an aggressive little bop. His house was a split-level, painted green, with an untidy front yard and driveway, which looked to me like rebellion in a neighborhood that was seriously well groomed. He let me in the door and right away started with the sarcastic remarks. Some other hapless reporter had written of him that he had an unsophisticated home office in an ordinary tract house. Well, he said, pointing at his various microscopes and light boxes, computers, and measuring equipment, this is state-of-the-art.

His laboratory was in a former recreation room, with a walk-out to the back yard on the basement level of the split—not exactly the kind of place where one expects to find fine science done, and possibly not the kind of place where a Mima Kapches–like appropriate mood could be easily maintained in the presence of the dead. The front window was high enough that you couldn't see in from the street. The back sliding doors were curtained. There was a blocked-off fireplace, a number of large worktables, one with bags of mussels draped across the surface (Chatters is an expert in identifying mussel species). He showed me several microscopes, some very new and complex and one an antique that his father had collected, which came to him at his father's death. In spite of its location, this was a working lab—with the usual piles of academic papers on the floor, a large number of file cabinets and, beside the sliding doors, shelves with a number of casts of human skulls. Among them sat the cast of the skull of

Kennewick. It was bright toothpaste white. It had a jaw so large and sharp it looked like the prow of an icebreaker.

It was into this room that the Kennewick bones had been brought on July 28, 1996. Why to Chatters, I wondered? I'd already checked to see if he was listed as a member of the forensic anthropology society—he was not.

He sat with one leg thrown over the other knee, his short forearms pillowing the back of his head, his face turned away from me and aimed at his big window. His narrow European nose tilted up at the dubious sun struggling to cut through the gray. This dark three-week period in February was always his worst time of year, he said. He began to lay out his story.

Raymond Chandler would have loved Jim Chatters: he is a man of many pieces, of contrariness mixed with genuine curiosity and kindness. He is also very smart—too smart. His confidence in his abilities gave him the sort of edge Dillehay's former student Jack Rossen had been told to acquire, and he wrapped that edge in a layer of bluster or collegiality, depending on his mood. The son of an academic who changed jobs as often as most of us change cars, Chatters was a small man from a small town with a good education; thus, he developed a visceral hatred for bullies. At the time of his birth his father was a chemist in a mental hospital in Sioux City, Iowa. Then the family—Chatters, his father, mother, older sister and brother—moved to Oklahoma. They lived on five acres while his father taught botany at Oklahoma State University. "There was science in the house," Chatters declared, almost the way a fundamentalist would explain how he'd grown up steeped in Christian values.

His mother was a doctor's daughter. His father was the son of a Canadian—born in some town outside of Toronto: he couldn't remember the name. There wasn't much money. His father never had a new car in his life. But Chatters could remember actively exploring the world with his dad, getting water out of the cistern to look at its microbes under a microscope, having his artistic talent supported by his mother. He played a flute. "A Native American flute," he said. "I haven't touched it since this fiasco began."

He went to Washington State University in Pullman, where he did his degree in three and a half years to save money. Early on he'd wanted to be a paleontologist, but when his family moved to Idaho he kept finding artifacts all over the ground. He picked up arrowheads, collected them, and took them to professors, who persuaded him that he should help them find archaeological sites instead. From the time he was thirteen he spent his summers working on archaeological digs.

He pulled out an ancient coin to show me why archaeology had caught him in its toils. On one side there was a profile of Alexander the Great. "This passed from one hand to another, direct from Phoenician traders," he said. "In working with archaeology you have contact with that ancient time. I think there's a tendency for anthropologists not to be happy with the culture they are part of. They seek solace elsewhere."

He believes that the first Americans walked here over the Bering Strait, not that Clovis was first. He thinks the first entry to the Americas might have been earlier, perhaps about 40,000 years ago. He was influenced in this by Alan Bryan of the University of Alberta (the same Alan Bryan who wrote the introduction to Dillehay's book on Monte Verde). Bryan came to Idaho as a graduate student and Chatters took him and one other student around the countryside, pointing out likely sites. Robson Bonnichsen, the lead Kennewick plaintiff, was another archaeologist Chatters had met as a teenager, whom he remembered as being particularly patient with him. Chatters also knew Bryan's wife Ruth Gruhn. In those Idaho days, he explained, his dad was working as a radioisotope engineer.

So Chatters started university knowing what he wanted to be. He did a year as an undergrad at New Mexico. He got a National

Science Foundation grant to do graduate work at Cornell, but joined a University of Connecticut project on the Aleuts instead. He was drawn by the idea of going to an exotic place—he'd never been anywhere exotic. The project was to study the adaptation of Aleuts over the 8,000 years they were assumed to have been on the Aleutian Islands. But Chatters hated it: the project leader seemed to think that the Aleuts were somehow superior to other Native Americans, an idea that Chatters found repugnant. When he quit it was too late to take up Cornell's offer, so he went instead to the University of Washington to do his doctorate. His interest was in the complex relationships between people and their environments, and in the impact of climate change on human behavior—he'd seen patterns in the sites he worked in southern Idaho as a boy that he wanted to explain. He was still working on this kind of research. Skeletons kept showing up in the archaeological sites he was working on in Washington State. Contrary to the strong belief that people of the Columbia plateau were pacifists, he said, the bones often show signs of violence.

These skeletons had generally been found during irrigation projects. The first such remains he was involved with were found when he was working on a federal project at the Colville reservation. That particular skeleton was of the historical period, about 1750, but the artifacts found with it were not local. "He was a kid," Chatters said. "He was riddled with arrows." It was clear from the muscle marks on his bones that the "kid" had been a horse rider. Chatters believed he was a Blackfoot, raiding for salmon and women.

"They turned up over the next five years. Eighteen cases, of which twelve were homicides," said Chatters. "I took an interest in the issue of interpersonal violence." He was trying to work out its prevalence and its relation to patterns of climate change.

He got his doctorate in anthropology in 1982. But he'd also worked as a contract archaeologist—he got married in 1969 and, though the marriage broke up after nine years, he had a son to support, and after he remarried, a daughter. He wanted to teach, but there were no teaching jobs close to his family. He was on unemployment when a friend of his in the U.S. Army Corp of Engineers told him about a contract he could bid for—a program that was to run out of the university. He won it, and over the next six years he worked in salvage archaeology, then was offered a job at Batelle Memorial Institute, a huge private corporation that does contract research, mainly for governments. At Batelle, he developed a cultural resource program for the Hanford Nuclear Reservation. The job turned out to be 10 percent research and 90 percent paperwork.

It was obvious from his body language that he did not like to talk about his years at Batelle. (His wife, a mental health counselor, has working relationships there still, he said.) "When I parted company with Batelle, I felt I'd been released from jail."

Chatters has run his own archaeology and human osteology business (called Applied Paleoscience) since 1993. "I've been here twelve years, yecch," he said, to himself, looking out the window at suburban Richland. "My god, I never lived anywhere more than seven. I don't like it. It's flat, in a metaphysical sense...." It isn't that the place lacks culture, he explained. It has a symphony orchestra, it has a film society, it has an educated population. "But if you're in a place with a lot of people you'll notice that no one's laughing.... It's government work. It's all on the government tab. You never know when the job will end; the sword of Damocles is over everyone's head."

He felt he had developed pretty good working relationships with the tribes. He'd worked with the Wanapum, Yakama, Colville and Umatilla and helped to prevent the desecration of more than one sacred site. "I have a lifelong sympathy with the Indians, and an interest in the cultures, but the revisionism is shocking," said Chatters. "The real history is being replaced by fiat, the we've-always-been-here-so-go-away political position. The richness is draining away."

As he laid out his present circumstances, and pointed out for me the various ironies in his situation, I began to put aside my contrarian determination to like Jim Chatters. He was much too complex a person to just *like*. He was by turns helpful, defensive and aggressive; he was layered and he had a whole bag of motives for his various behaviors. One senior scholar and Kennewick plaintiff said he was glad Chatters had used the provocative phrase "Caucasoid-like" because that had got the press stirred up, and that was a Good Thing: the press was now reporting on these issues to a public that didn't have any idea what was going on in North American archaeology. I could almost feel Chatters rummaging in his mental files for tidbits of irony that he thought a journalist might like to use.

For instance, he has always been a supporter of the NAGPRA. His first big contract regarding human remains came as a direct result of it. In 1993 he was hired to resolve issues the Colville tribe had with five different institutions holding their ancestors' remains. In the rush to meet the NAGPRA's 1995 deadline to notify the tribes of the skeletons in their closets, these institutions had made some mistakes. A serious mistake had been made by the Burke Museum of Seattle, where, ironically, the Kennewick remains were now being curated: some Colville remains had been repatriated to the Wanapum tribe in error.

When Chatters was studying the remains at the Burke Museum on their behalf, the Colville permitted him to do whatever study he required, including analyses that involved the destruction of bone. These remains are from six hundred to a thousand years old, which means it's likely that they are the remains of the direct ancestors of the Colville. This is the same Colville tribe that in the Kennewick matter now insists that all studies of human remains are a desecration. "Their historian asked me for radiocarbon, radioisotope studies—if we could get the money, we'd do it," he fumed. "This thing of 'science can't be done' is definitely not [the tradition]." He was still working on that contract when the Kennewick thing broke. (He called *The New York Times* himself, but wasn't pleased with what the Associated Press reporter did to the story.)

"They demanded all the skeletons back," he said. The Colville also tried to make certain that he got no work in the future from one of his major clients. They tried to interfere with his contract, and he could prove it to me. He reached into a drawer, his hands trembling. He pulled out a letter dated September 13, 1996, just after the U.S. Army Corp of Engineers had grabbed back the Kennewick remains, and just before they announced their intent to immediately repatriate them for reburial. The letter had been sent out under the letterhead of the Colville Reservation–Colville Business Council to his client, whose name he showed me but asked me not to print. The letter said that if the client wanted to continue in a positive relationship with the Colville, the client's contract with Jim Chatters should be terminated. Other people had made certain that his contract was not terminated, but it wasn't because the Colville weren't trying.

Similarly, he said, the Nez Percé had passed a resolution saying that they were opposed to any contracts with Chatters. The Native tribes, he said, were taking over and doing for themselves the sort of work he did, hiring their own archaeologists, pushing competitors like him out of the business. And then came the implicit dare: he'd told other journalists about these letters, he said, and they'd all written about it, but their editors had pulled the mentions out of the stories. In his opinion, this was suppression of anything negative about Native Americans. It was all a result of political correctness.

While he did do some forensic work when he was at Batelle, Chatters' first private case for the Benton County coroner was in 1991. The police had a report of a body buried in an old barbecue pit that had been covered up and could no longer be seen from the surface. They called in Chatters as an archaeologist to find the pit, exhume the bones and identify the dead. Chatters' findings "motivated the accused to plead guilty to a lesser charge."

After that, he got frequent calls. By 1993 he had also seen a couple of hundred skeletons in the course of his work as a contract archaeologist. "I wasn't a leading expert," he said, "but I was real good with bones. I can recognize when something is wrong. When the professor tricked us in the osteology class, I'd always get it."

Kennewick Man came to him as a standard forensic case. The Benton County coroner, a former policeman named Floyd Johnson, called him at home and asked if he could bring some bones over. "It was a weekend, about ten o'clock, dark.... He has a skull in a bucket—the brain case and the upper jaw. I saw a long head, a prominent nose, brow, probably European, and I didn't think old.... It was this yellowish sandy color, a young bone color. It looked like it was not in the ground a long time.... There were concretions of cemented soil on it."

Later in the day, he walked to the back of his laboratory to get down the cast he'd made of Kennewick's skull, to show me the characteristics that made him think it was an early settler. He brought it back to his desk, holding it in the palm of his hand like a basketball. He pointed to the upper portion of the jaw, the maxilla. "It's very obvious this is not a wide face. It's narrow and the canine fossae are prominent. It's a small face. You find it in Western Eurasian people, the ones referred to as Caucasoids."

There it was, he'd said it, the C word. He'd used it when he wrote about the Kennewick find in the *American Anthropological Association Newsletter* in January 1997, as the affair exploded into a major *cause célèbre* for physical anthropologists. He wrote that the "presence of caucasoid traits, lack of definitive Native American characteristics and the association with an early homestead led me to suspect that the bones represented a European settler." After listing several characteristics of the skull and face, he declared that "many of these characteristics are definitive of modern-day Caucasoid peoples...." In the October 1997 edition of the *Newsletter*, the cultural anthropologist Alan Goodman had scolded Chatters for referring to "Caucasoid" traits, a word from the grim typological past of physical anthropology. Goodman also derided racial identification through the study of cranial morphology. "Let us suppose for a moment that races are real," Goodman had written. "Playing by the rules of racial science, just how often does a case come up in forensic work in which a skeleton is put into the wrong racial box? More specifically, how often is a Native American cranium misclassified? And should Chatters have been perplexed that a skeleton found in a context that unambiguously suggests Native American might not look exactly like the racial type?"

Ignoring the fact that the remains when found had little context at all except the river, Goodman referred to two studies on the accuracy of racial identification, which he claimed showed that erroneous classification of Native American crania as white or "Caucasian" was not uncommon.

"Chatters should not have been perplexed," wrote Goodman. "He probably made a mistake in racial classification, a common one.... What is uncommon is the subsequent effort to scientifically justify this likely, little mistake. Chatters ... [does] not hint at how easy it is to wrongly think that a Native American cranium might be 'Caucasian,' especially when it is old, not cradleboarded and only visually examined; they [Chatters and the journalists who wrote about Kennewick Man] do not even hint at this. Rather they unambigious [sic] accept the science of racial classification and the racial designation of 'Caucasian' which leads them to promote a new theory of how the Americas were peopled. A small mistake leads to more."

Goodman reminded his readers of the pre-1492 cemetery excavated long ago at Pecos Pueblo by Alfred Kidder. The one thousand human remains found were studied at the Peabody and written about by E.A. Hooten in 1930. Hooten, he said, identified eight different types. He found a hybrid group within his Mongoloid classification, and a significant residual group that didn't fit anywhere. According to Goodman, Hooten documented a "long, narrow-faced, un-Indian looking type" that Hooten called "long-faced European" and another he called "pseudo-Alpine." He also found a small, slender, long-headed group that closely resembled the "brown-skinned group often called the Mediterranean race." Similarly, there was a group that Hooten called Pseudo-Australoid. And another group he termed Negroid. Goodman said he used Hooten's work "not to suggest that Hooten actually found peoples of the 'Caucasoid,' 'Negroid' or 'Australoid' races at Pecos Pueblo.... The point is not that the different 'races' colonized or were overrun by North Americans. The point is that Kennewick Man's biology is not unique or unusual because within a group, local variation is great: in nearly any large population there is lots and lots of shape variation."

Finally, Goodman pointed to the uses made of the word "Caucasoid" in reference to the Kennewick remains, referring to "white supremacists, who are now finding support for their 'Caucasian genes-equals-civilization' scenarios in the interpretation of Kennewick Man as a 'Caucasian.'... I hope this mention is sufficient to raise the issue of what might be at stake and the need to set the record straight."[3]

Chatters responded to this article with one of his own in February 1998. "I regret," he wrote, "that because our language currently lacks an uncharged adjective encompassing the skeleton's characteristics, it was necessary to use a term with such incendiary connotations. It is unfortunate that scientific terms can be misused by extremists of all types. It is more unfortunate that reaction to the term Caucasoid has drawn attention away from the scientific meaning of Kennewick Man and other Paleo-american skeletons."[4] (In the April 2000 issue of *American Antiquity*, he defended himself further. He said that "in the forensic venue" he had suggested "an affiliation with modern Euro-americans. Once the skeleton's age was known, however, I referred to the remains as 'Caucasoid-like.'... I did not state, nor did I intend to imply, once the skeleton's age became known, that he was a member of some European group.") In the *Newsletter*, Chatters also pointed out that principal component analysis, not discriminant function analysis, had established the fact of a Paleo-Indian population different from modern Native Americans before Kennewick was found. He mentioned the possibility that there had been many migrations into the Americas, not just one. He referred to the remains found at Spirit Cave and Wizards Beach. He argued that the dominant theory of who peopled the Americas was way too simple, that the relationship between Paleo-Americans and modern Native Americans might not be straightforward descent.

Owsley's teacher and fellow Kennewick plaintiff George Gill was much more aggressive in response to Goodman. He had no problem with the use of race as a category for identifying populations and membership in populations. He wrote twice in the *Newsletter* in rebuttal, first in a letter in January,[5] and then in an article in March, 1998.[6] He chided Goodman for selectively quoting from Gill's own text to give the impression forensic scientists had no faith in using measurement of bones to identify populations. In his article, Gill claimed that in real court cases where a number of traits are taken into consideration, particularly nose, mouth, cranium and femur, the success rate of racial identification, determined after the individual was finally identified, was close to 100 percent. He defended the concept of race to distinguish differing populations, and the study of bones to determine race. Gill said he believed in the beauty of human diversity and made it clear that he believed skeletal identification of race is more accurate than trying to identify the race of a living person. Gill also deplored the fact that since 1990 (the year the NAGPRA was passed into law) any discussion of variation that used the word "race" had become taboo among U.S. anthropologists, a situation that he argued was as dangerous as the use of racial characteristics to support arguments about racial supremacy.

Why did you use the "Caucasoid" word? I asked Chatters.

"The police want to know what race it is," he said, "in order to narrow down whose remain it is. They want age, stature, gender, race. They need that fourth leg of the table or the table falls over."

The way he said this suggested he thought the police were wrong to ask about such characteristics. So, I said, there's no such thing as race, right? He answered me. I wrote down his answer. He was not satisfied with how I wrote it down, so he later gave me a corrected version of his answer, which I reproduce here:

"Right, there are no biological races. But anthropologists are fond of saying there's no variation among human beings, but when we say that, people are baffled. They can watch people walking down the street and clearly distinguish an Asian from a European from an African. They think we're lying to them. Then, when we tell them correctly that there's no difference in mental abilities between peoples, they are liable to think we're lying again. It is better to be up front and say 'there is geographic variation in people's physical forms, but it exists for these histori-cal reasons.... There is, however, no difference in their capabili-ties.' It's better to be honest with people from the outset."

He turned over the Kennewick cast in his hands so I could look inside the skull to see what he had first seen. "He's got...you see a parabolic dental arch.... Indians in this area have an ellipti-cal arch. It has to do with, as Loring Brace puts it, kinship writ large. Well, that shape says Western Eurasian. But the teeth are worn flat. That's not typical. The back of the skull, it's an old man, all the sutures [the lines showing where the skull remains soft until growth is complete] are obliterated, so it's fifty years plus.... He could be significantly older."

The matter of the teeth interested me greatly. In the January 1997 *Anthropology Newsletter*, Chatters had described the wear on the teeth as "light."[7] I asked Chatters when I first contacted him if the teeth on Kennewick Man had sinodont (North Asian) or sundadont (South Asian) characteristics. He'd said they were sundadont and he'd published that. I'd then asked C. Loring Brace if it was possible, given the wear on Kennewick's teeth, to say whether the teeth were sinodont or sundadont. Of course you couldn't say, Brace had said sharply. The teeth were worn flat.

Yet Chatters, when he first looked at the teeth, was certain he was looking at a European. Why?

"Stone-ground flour in the nineteenth century could wear 'em down. A fifty-year-old Indian here would have no teeth—there'd be dental abscesses, the teeth would fall out. It's the wrong wear pattern for a Northwest Indian. I told Floyd it's either a European or more than 5,000 years old. I hadn't seen the pattern before. The oldest one [I'd seen] in recent years was 5,000 years old. I said, let's say it's more likely it's modern."

The first European settlers came to the area around 1870. There was a Catholic mission in that year at the mouth of the Yakima River. These remains could have washed out of an unmarked grave by the river and fetched up in the mud of the Columbia. Chatters and the coroner went back to the river to search for more clues. In the light of day, Chatters had found more bones scattered over a thirty-foot area, bobbing in the eddies at the river's edge.

"Nothing was in a primary context at all," he said. "We found historic artifacts scattered. Horseshoes, square nails, china…. So I told [the coroner] it's probably a pioneer of the area, one of the first traders here in the first decade of the nineteenth century…. We gathered what was visible."

He brought the rest of the bones back to his workroom to drain, and then put them into plastic bags so they'd dry slowly and not crack. The measurements he made were consistent with his first assessment of the skull. He explained that the malars (the bones of the cheek) recede in Europeans: one can lay a pencil across the bone above where the lip would be. This cannot normally be done with later Native American remains. Chatters demonstrated this point to me on the upright Kennewick cast and the pencil did stay in its place. The rest of the skeleton also seemed consistent with the European designation, particularly and significantly the shape of the femurs. Native American femurs are strongly flattened. Kennewick's femurs were not like modern Native Americans'. "It's closer to round," said Chatters, "like Europeans and Aborigines from Australia."

He had carefully, carefully cleaned the bones so he could see them better. It wasn't until the third day that he noticed there was an object in the pelvis. Contrary to Goodman's assertion, he was always conscious that even though it seemed obvious this was a European, it might be a Native American and he might have to answer for how he treated it. He wanted to minimize the chance of being accused of desecration. He wasn't worried about the Colville or the Nez Percé. He was worried about some people he knew who were members of the Umatilla tribe. "I didn't want to break it in the process of cleaning it. I see something hard and gray in there. But it was not possible to see what it is without scraping."

Kennewick General Hospital does the coroner's tests for free, so he took the pelvis and had it X-rayed. But he still couldn't see what was stuck in the bone since an X-ray goes right through stone. He cleaned the pelvis some more and saw flake patterns on the stone's surface. He took it for a CT scan. "It's got the shape of a broken spear point."

"That raised a conundrum," Chatters said. "A stone point and it's healed in the pelvis, he'd carried it for months to years.... He had to have had a major limp. So it was not inconsistent, but it was exciting—an early trader in trouble with Indian people.... That point is unique...it has earmarks of 10,000 to 8500 BP, but the serrated edge of a later period. I know that now, but that's hindsight. I called a friend over for an opinion. He came over to help me and see if we could recover more of the skeleton...." (In his *American Antiquity* article of April 2000, Chatters said it was typical of a local Cascade phase, which dates between 5000 and 8000 BP.)

The U.S. Army Corps of Engineers had been informed of Chatters' work right from the beginning. In fact, as soon as a story about the find appeared in the newspaper, the Corps had called him. He'd had to apply for a backdated archaeological permit from the Corps on the Tuesday morning after the bones were brought to him, to legally cover the fact that he had picked up bones and artifacts on Corps land at Columbia Park after July 28. His request for an archaeological permit, written on July 30, referred to the fact that he had already conferred with Ray Tracy, one of the Corps's archaeologists. He thought the Corps had an interest because Columbia Park, where the remains were found, is Army Corps land. The Corps had bought private land alongside the river from citizens when they built nearby McNary Dam. Because the land belonged to a department of the U.S. federal government, the rules under ARPA applied. The law says no one can do archaeological surveying or remove any remain or artifact from federal land without a permit, and all such finds belong to the U.S. government.

What with an ancient stone spear point in the skeleton's hip, Chatters couldn't be sure if his initial characterization of the skeleton as Caucasian, male, was right. When the newspapers asked, he told them he thought it might be a settler, but he wasn't certain. "I needed a second opinion." He decided to get it from a physical anthropologist at Central Washington University in Ellensburg, where he'd tried to get a job over the years. "I wanted to use their equipment to do the analysis."

He was also hearing from people he knew in the Corps that the Umatilla had begun to say that any and every skeleton found along the Columbia River was theirs and they wanted to rebury this one. He couldn't understand why they were taking such an extreme position. He didn't want to turn over a European settler to them. Besides, this skeleton had not been found on Umatilla land, and in his view the government didn't have any statutory means to just turn it over to them without first showing cultural affiliation of the remains. He took the bones to a physical anthropologist at the university, Caty MacMillan.[8]

Chatters had another motive for taking it to her. He wanted the protection of a second opinion from someone who'd criticized him in the past. MacMillan had her own anthropology company, which competed with his. He'd heard she was upset about him doing forensic work. "I thought, who better for a second opinion? She looked for one half hour. She said it's obvious, it's Caucasoid, male."

He realized he would have to get a radiocarbon date done to resolve the question: settler?—or something else? "I agonized over it," he said. "If I hadn't run it he would have been an early pioneer and that's how the story would have ended. I talked to the coroner about getting a date. He concurred. And the Army Corps concurred."

He sent samples of bone to the University of California at Riverside. It took three weeks for the dating to be done. All the while, the bones lay on his worktable. They were a puzzle that he couldn't leave alone. This man, according to Chatters, had "been through the wringer.... He had a busted chest, damaged arm, a spear point festering in his hip, an old wound from long before he died. His ribs are shattered, he had multiple fractures of the ribs. He had ongoing infection ... depressed skull fracture long healed." Chatters got a preliminary phone call on a Friday at the end of August. The University of California told him that what he had was the remains of a man who'd died about 8400 BP. He didn't call anyone with this shocking news, other than the coroner, until the university faxed confirmation of this preliminary date to him on the Monday morning.

"I told the Corps. They told the Indians. Jeff Van Pelt [of the Umatilla] calls me and accuses me of violating the NAGPRA.... The day after the call on the radiocarbon date, I get a call at home about bones showing up a mile and a half away," said Chatters. "The Indians say it's a cemetery. It's skeletal parts. He [Floyd Johnson] brought me a body bag full—none of these were diagnostic. I went to the site."

He found more fragments in the mud, but this time, the skull fragments in his opinion were clearly Native American and less than two thousand years old. "We stopped picking up the bones," he said. "It's gonna be politically sensitive, you stop. Couldn't reach the Corps. Floyd tried next day. Couldn't get them till Monday. They already knew."

This second find was not widely reported in the press at the time. These bones turned out to be the remains of four or five individuals who had likely been buried in a mound that got washed out in the spring floods. As far as Chatters could tell from the state of the bones, they'd been in the water a long time.

Van Pelt dressed him down again. How dare you dig up the bones of five tribal members? he'd yelled at Chatters.

"'Excuse me,'" Chatters said he thought to himself at the time, "'they weren't carrying cards.'... He's gonna get us in jail, charge us with violation of the NAGPRA. I say, step back. He says, '[You] step back. You excavated the bones of five tribal members and you want me to step back?' I just hung up. I have been bullied my whole life and I hate it."

And this was the point where all of Jim Chatters' pieces folded in upon each other. Was he going to stand up for science or lie down for a bully? He was going to study the incredibly ancient Kennewick remains while he still had them in his control, that's what he was going to do. He knew he had very little time, only a few days or a week at most, before he got a final confirmed date from the lab at University of California, Riverside, which he would have to report.

"I want to make sure we get to know this person before it disappears," he said. "I know where it's headed. The Corps will turn it over to the nearest [interested] party...."

He didn't know what to do first, he didn't have the necessary equipment and he knew he needed help. "Gentry Steele was the first one I called. I'd seen his work."

It was significant that he turned to Steele. Following in the wake of the work of Neves and Pucciarelli in Brazil, Steele and Powell had been the first in the U.S. to assert that the Paleo remains they had studied were a different population from modern Native Americans. Chatters had heard about Steele's work from a colleague who'd worked with a remain of great antiquity in southern Idaho, which came to be called Buhl Woman. When his colleague had finally got back a radiocarbon date, it said she died 10,675 BP. There'd been little time to photograph and measure her before she was reburied by the Shoshone-Bannock tribes of Idaho.[9]

Chatters called Steele. "Turned out to be a wonderful, warm human being. He says, 'Get a cast.' We were already doing that—the coroner wanted a facial reconstruction. It was neat: there was no forensic reason to do it. If I do it, it costs nothing. I am a sculptor for fun. We did it. I borrowed material from a friend. He helped. It took three days. I got a final mold off it just before the press conference organized by the coroner and the mayor of Kennewick."

When University of California at Riverside confirmed by fax the date they'd given him by phone, the mayor and the coroner announced Kennewick Man's age to the world. Chatters had called the Colville tribe himself and told them the date on the Monday or Tuesday before the press conference. By then, he'd also taken the standard measurements of the skeleton as outlined in Bill Bass's forensic handbook. Steele had suggested some other measurements he should take, but Chatters didn't have the necessary equipment. It arrived the day after the bones were taken away.

Chatters also wanted a study made of the mitochondrial DNA. He had taken a sample of the fifth metacarpal of the left hand to get the radiocarbon date. "It was not mineralized on the surface. It promised to be relatively uncontaminated," he said. The University of California told him about Frederika Kaestle's work on extracting ancient mtDNA—they were doing radiocarbon dates for her too.

"I called her and she arranged to do it for free as part of her grant work," he said. "Floyd gave the go-ahead. I told Riverside to send [a sample] to Davis. Because she didn't get on it right away, it didn't get done."

Gentry Steele also suggested he get someone else to examine

the remains and recommended Doug Owsley. "I called Owsley. I'd met him once before. He was very interested. My idea was to get this recorded by someone other than myself. No scientific discovery is real until someone else sees it. He could have done it in two days at the expense of tickets to D.C...."

By this point, I had learned enough about some Native American activists' views of the Smithsonian to form a theory about why the U.S. Army had so suddenly taken the Kennewick remains out of Chatters' hands. I had worked out the chronology of events the previous day in Portland while looking through the clipping files maintained by the plaintiffs' lawyer, Alan Schneider. It was right after the army learned that Chatters was taking the bones to the Smithsonian that all hell had broken loose.[10]

So, I said to Chatters, you turned to the Smithsonian. How did the Corps hear about your plan to fly the remains to Washington?

Chatters explained that the coroner, Floyd Johnson, had told Linda Kirts, the Corps of Engineers' counsel. "The Corps's attorney got it out of Floyd Johnson. He's a former policeman, he couldn't lie if you put a gun to his head. If asked, he'd tell."

Well, I said, why did you tell Johnson about it?

"I was working for him," he said. "That's the authority I'm working under. He said, great, I'll deputize you so you can take the bones with you. I am now a deputy coroner."

He was supposed to fly to Washington on September 8, a Sunday. On Friday, August 30, at about five in the afternoon, Chatters got a call from Floyd Johnson saying the sheriff was coming to take the remains away from him within the hour. The coroner was very upset. He told Chatters that Kirts had just spoken with him and had been rude. With only moments to get the skeleton recorded for science, Chatters called a friend to come and videotape the bones still laid out on his worktable. The videotape clearly showed all the bones and their condition when they were last in Chatters' hands. Then the sheriff came, and the bones were removed to the lockup until Benton County could decide whether or not to hand them over to the Army.

A tense meeting was held the day after the Labor Day weekend. It was convened by the Benton County prosecuting attorney, Andrew Miller. The Corps's counsel, Linda Kirts, demanded back the remains under the terms of the ARPA permits issued to Chatters, which gave the Corps complete control of all the remains collected under the permit, and the NAGPRA.[11] Johnson was livid, according to Chatters: "Until the coroner makes his determination, no one is supposed to interfere."

That was not entirely the recollection of the Benton County prosecuting attorney. In Miller's memory, Linda Kirts had called him on Friday night, August 30, after calling Floyd Johnson and wheedling out of him that the remains were to be flown to Washington. "I would classify her as rude and abrupt," he said. He didn't agree to turn over the remains to her right away, only to put them in the sheriff's secure facility until he'd had a chance to meet with the interested parties on the matter the following week. The day after Labor Day, representatives of the Corps, the local Indian bands, the coroner and Chatters came to Miller's office. They demanded the remains be taken to Batelle until jurisdiction could be sorted out. Miller and his deputy prosecuting attorney Ryan Brown met outside with Chatters and Johnson for advice about what to do: neither, in Miller's recollection, advocated that the bones should be retained by the sheriff. The Corps insisted they had rights and duties under the NAGPRA and ARPA. After the meeting Brown reviewed the law. On his advice, Floyd Johnson agreed that all the remains—Kennewick Man and the five other individuals found later—should go back to the control of the army. The feeling was the army had the right to demand them back under the terms of Chatters' ARPA permits.

"Linda continued her rude demeanor," Miller said. "It was interesting. She was definitely that way. The Indian tribal representatives, one was there on a conference call, I was expecting more [trouble] from them. I found the tension was from the Corps of Engineers."

As I later learned after a freedom-of-information application, Kennewick Man's skull and the long bone first picked up by William Thomas about twenty feet out from shore,[12] and stuck in the mud of the river's bottom, were not included in the permit issued by the army.[13] The ARPA permit covering the period from July 28 to August 3 was "to conduct exploratory excavations to resolve the issues of age and racial affiliation of the remains discovered on July 28, 1996," according to the cover letter signed by Richard Carlton, chief of the real estate division of the Corps.[14] The permit was in the name of James Chatters: it allowed only Dr. Chatters to "conduct work upon public lands owned or controlled by the Department of the Army under the Archaeological Resources Protection Act." The bottom of the Columbia River is owned by the state of Washington, not the Department of the Army. In effect, Chatters' first ARPA permit applied only to the bones he had picked up himself on the beach or at its edge from July 28 until August 3. This original permit to conduct exploratory excavations was extended "due to low water levels" until August 18.[15] It was extended again on August 19, to September 2—two days after all the remains were abruptly removed from Chatters' lab. Neither the original permit nor these extensions covered the remains found by others in the river bottom or floating out in the water. But the Benton County prosecuting attorney never thought to challenge the army on its claims of jurisdiction over all the remains, even though the skull and the long bone arguably belonged to the state of Washington.

During the weekend before the final meeting, Chatters had called Alan Schneider to find out if the coroner's jurisdiction superseded the army's rights under ARPA and NAGPRA. Schneider is well known in the archaeological community. He is a member of the state archaeological society and is an expert on laws pertaining to archaeological resources. He'd prepared handbooks on these subjects for employees of the U.S. Forest Service.

Yes, he said, the army's rights take precedence over any coroner's investigation.

"Why was the army so determined to get the remains back instantly?" I asked Chatters.

"The Corps's thing was to stop the studies," he said.

But why? I asked. Other federal government agencies didn't act that way.

"The Indians wanted it stopped because the press had got the idea that it was a European," he said. At the press conference the first question put by a reporter was, what was a European doing here eight thousand years ago? The press, said Chatters, couldn't get enough of this story. "It does open a Pandora's box that needs to be opened. It is important to look at this stuff anew.... It's how science is supposed to work."

This still didn't answer my question. Why did the army rush to do the Native American community's bidding? The U.S. Army had rarely rushed to do their bidding before. There was nothing in the document record I got in response to my freedom-of-information applications that showed the Umatilla or a coalition of tribes had even put in a claim for these remains at the time they were snatched from Chatters' lab. The U.S. Army was acting on its own behalf when its counsel learned that Chatters was going to take the remains to the Smithsonian, that the Smithsonian would get physical control of the remains. By the time the Nez Percé tribal executive committee chairman, Samuel Penney, wrote a letter to the army on September 3, the day of the meeting in the prosecuting attorney's office, the remains were already out of Chatters' hands. Penney's letter made no NAGPRA claim to the remains; instead, it referred to the problems the U.S. Army was encountering with recovery and reinterment of all the remains found—Kennewick Man and the five other individuals, whose remains Chatters thought were about two thousand years old. Penney called for the NAGPRA to be followed in deciding what to do, and mildly suggested the remains should be reburied at the site of discovery.

"We request you take all actions needed to obtain possession of the remains that were recovered from land owned by the United States," said Penney's letter. "... We believe with the information available, it should be determined that the remains are not the result of a crime and therefore the Coroner's office should release the remains to the care of the USACOE at the earliest opportunity and the processes within the Native American Graves Protection Act (*sic*) should be the terms guiding the disposition of the remains. We would like to especially stress that we do not feel the remains of any or all of the individuals should be shipped anywhere for further research or subjected to further testing of any kind."[16]

This letter was copied to Andy Miller, the Benton County prosecuting attorney, Linda Kirts and John Leier of the U.S. Army Corps of Engineers, and Armand Minthorn.

What got the army so fired up? I asked Chatters.

Chatters thought he had an answer (and as I later learned, he did indeed have part of the answer). It all had to do with the Umatilla chemical depot. The army is under orders to destroy the thousands of tons of chemical weapons stored there due to an international treaty. Its plan was to burn these weapons in a massive incinerator to be built at the depot. The Umatilla wanted things in return for giving permission to proceed. One of the Umatilla's negotiators on the chemical depot issue was the same man who spoke for the Umatilla on the Kennewick matter, the same man appointed in 1998 by the Secretary of the Interior to the NAGPRA review committee—Armand Minthorn, relative of the Smithsonian employee Doug Owsley had asked for advice.

The government, Chatters suggested, was currying favor among Native Americans for the usual reasons: money and votes. The Umatilla had gone into the gambling business and there was money available. There had been donations: "Most of it went to Democrats," he said. (The Umatilla later explained that they gave to those who asked, and both parties asked.)

Had he checked these allegations himself, I asked? Was he politically active?

A group in Salt Lake City had sent him some material, he said. They had also asked him to be on their board. Their main concern was the intrusion of religion into the political arena. He'd turned them down.

I had allegations to put to Chatters. He reached into his desk and pulled out his tape recorder. "Mind," he asked? I didn't mind.

I told him that someone close to the defense had alleged that his treatment of the skull with a solvent had damaged it.

"I treated it with a water-based polymer," he said, and explained that the bone was shrinking as it dried, and was developing fine cracks. He used the polymer to stop the shrinking process. "It held up just fine."

What about the matter of the missing pieces of the femurs? Had he kept them?

All of them were with the skeleton when he handed the bones over to the sheriff. "I recorded it," he said. He pulled out slides he'd taken while his friend videotaped the remains as they lay on the table in this room. Both of the femurs were broken, but all the pieces were there. "That would be the last thing I would consider doing," he said, "taking the most obvious bone in the body. It's absurd. They've been accusing me of everything all along. The government wants to distract from their own screw-ups."

He pulled from his shelves a cast of another skull he'd made on a recent visit to central Texas. He wanted to show me that Kennewick really was like other Paleo-Indian remains, and they really did not look like modern Native Americans. The Texas skull was thought to be about 10,000 BP. It was in the possession of a private collector who'd let him study it and make this cast. He pointed to the shape of the eyes, nose and mouth, and the prominent chin on both casts. This group of features "is European," he said, but he did not mean that they actually had European ancestors. "This population has no modern representatives. It was replaced or genetically swamped. Both are possible. But we don't have people who look like that anymore."

The Kennewick lawsuit, he later explained, was an attempt to protect the right to use science methods in the pursuit of knowledge. "We are in a real sense protecting our culture," he said. "We have a culture too."

Chatters drove me over to see Columbia River Park. It was a big open space, a terrace beneath some low hills covered with winter-seared grass, bent, yellow and brittle. There were gopher holes everywhere, and drooping willows and locusts, the same kind of short, stubby, spreading trees one finds by the South Saskatchewan River. From a distance, the Columbia was a wonderful azure. Close up it was as murky as a mud puddle. A gang of teenagers moved purposefully across the grass, then down a path that led to a copse of thick bushes. He snorted knowingly: they were here to score dope, he said.

We got out of his Jeep, slid down a steep but low bank to the water's edge. He walked along looking for artifacts, not that he would pick them up if he found them. He said he was afraid of the consequences. He showed me where the bones had drifted along the beach. One could see that the water had been eating out this shoreline for years. There had been Clovis remains found about a hundred miles up the river at Wanatchee, but they were uncommon. The oldest artifacts found around here dated from about 10,500 years ago.

So where did this man come from? I asked.

"I say you can say European. Who could prove you wrong?" he said.

By the same reasoning I could just as easily say that Kennewick Man had floated in a dislodged clump of cemented soil from somewhere on the Canadian side of the border, up near Kamloops, say, where Gore Creek was found. I could say he was an ancient Canadian and no one could prove me wrong. There was no proof that he had lived and died right here.

Chatters pointed to the little peninsula jutting out into the water on our right. That was the place where most assumed Kennewick Man had been buried. The theory was that higher water levels after the heavy spring flooding in 1996 cut into the bank until a big chunk of soil holding the remains calved into the water. But no bones were ever found eroding out of that part of the riverbank. No one had thoroughly tested the soil that the remains were supposed to have come from. The army had sent its own experts to do a very preliminary and restricted investigation of the soil in the area, but had not granted the ARPA permit request filed by soil expert Dr. Gary Huckleberry in July 1997, instead only permitting him to work under the army's expert during her limited investigation in December 1997.[17] At the same time, the army had rushed through various regulatory offices to get approval of their plan to bury the area Chatters had identified as the probable source of the remains. This site was downriver from the Hanford plant and the Umatilla chemical depot. I wondered whether the army was afraid the soil was contaminated and that's why they covered it up.

The bones had probably been in the river for six months, Chatters was saying. They had to have come from an adjacent bank during the flood event. However "had to have come" is not the same statement as "did come." The army had covered the point with five hundred tons of rock dropped by helicopter, and with fiber matting and coconut fiber logs. They'd planted trees and bushes on top whose roots would disturb the stratigraphy of any archaeological site that had not been destroyed by the rocks. The army said they did this to protect the site from erosion. Chatters said the whole 180-foot-long structure had cost $160,000.

The teenagers traipsed slowly back from the sanctuary of the dogwood bushes. He watched them for a while with a brooding look on his face. He said he'd been thinking about my questions about the Smithsonian. The whole thing had blown up after he'd arranged to take the bones to Doug Owsley. I elaborated on what I'd been thinking: as long as the army had possession of the Kennewick remains, they had a bargaining chip in their negotiations over the Umatilla chemical depot. They would have lost the chip if the remains went to the Smithsonian, which isn't actually a government department at all.

"I'm not cynical enough," he said. "I knew they were frightened about the Smithsonian."

We began to talk again about who could have taken pieces of Kennewick Man's femurs and why. Chatters had first heard about the missing bones in February of 1998. The army had made no inventory of the remains when they first took them from the sheriff's lockup to Batelle labs. An archaeologist married to a member of the Umatilla tribe had done an informal list of the bones just after the army took them into custody, but there was only a cursory mention of the femurs in her handwritten list. The fact that pieces of the femurs were gone did not surface until the army's archaeologist realized that some remains he saw in Chatters' video, which had also been turned over to the army, were not in the boxes. But in the eighteen-month period during which the remains had been under the army's control at Batelle, forty-seven people had entered the room where they were kept, including members of the tribes.

"I wonder if they listen to my phone," Chatters mused. "The FBI is in this already because of the missing bones. I'm accused. I've got witnesses and videotape to prove I'm not the person [who stole the bones]. They don't shut up about it." He thought the Justice Department had been after him from the beginning. The Justice Department had asked to question him two years earlier to gather evidence for the army's defense against the plaintiffs' lawsuit. The Justice Department lawyers had deposed Floyd Johnson first. From the tenor of their questions, Johnson believed they were somehow going after Chatters. "Floyd called and said, 'They're after your butt. All the questions have to do with what you did and when.'"

Chatters called an attorney he'd worked with before on foren-sic matters, a criminal lawyer, and decided he would bring him along to his deposition. "I asked him to help. They jump on the fact I have a criminal attorney.

"The Justice Department sent a letter to my attorney saying there's bones missing, where are they. They [the Corps of Engi-neers] did a press release and said they had asked Jim Chatters where they were. They accused me through a very thin veil.... I had had to send them the video of the bones and one of the casts I made. They had this, they promised to return them within the month. That was two years ago. So I wonder what their plans are on that. I have wondered whether they will lay a criminal charge...."

We sat in his Jeep and stared out at the water. Chatters was living under a cloud. Yet the notion that Chatters might have held on to chunks of the femurs struck me as absurd. Their rounded shape was the best proof there was, other than the shape of the skull, that Kennewick Man was different from mod-ern Native Americans. If he'd taken these pieces of bone, what good would it do him? He'd never be able to publish on them, never be able to show them to other scientists who could repli-cate or disprove his work. They were of no scientific value to anyone outside the context of the whole skeleton. And it was the science that mattered to Chatters.

I wondered aloud if someone in the Native community thought that their shape disproved Kennewick Man's affinity with living Native American populations and removed them. Or maybe someone had wanted these bones for spiritual purposes.

Chatters began to tick off on his hands the misfortunes that had befallen some in "Indian country" since Kennewick was pulled out of the muck. There was the young man who'd com-mitted suicide. "And the Nez Percé with the loudest voice," Chatters said, "had a stroke. Jeff Van Pelt's brother died a few months into the beginning of it. There's others too. It's an inter-esting pattern."

He turned this around and around, examining it from all sides. The more he toyed with it, the more he liked the way this speculation, that Native Americans might have taken the bones, fitted the facts. "For those few who believe, it's terrifying to have the dangerous dead out there, especially if it's an enemy's dead. They want him buried in a secret place."

## 8

# Excavating the Museum Shelves

## Weaving a New Image of Ancient Americans

S O WHERE HAD Kennewick Man's ancestors come from? Did they make their slow way down from the north through the interior of the continent, following the rivers that cut south along the mountains until they fetched up at the high plateau around Kennewick? Did they paddle their way up the Columbia River from the Pacific coast? Or did they walk up from Texas, where that other skull that looked like Kennewick Man's was found? The chronologies of the bones found were contradictory. On the one hand, those discovered at Prince of Wales Island were a thousand years older than Kennewick Man's. But still older remains had been discovered hundreds of miles to the southeast, in Nebraska. The closest place where significant remains of greater antiquity had been found was due south, at Carson City, Nevada.

To get from Kennewick to Reno, and then to Carson City, I had to fly first to Seattle, hundreds of miles to the northwest. The plane shuttled back and forth over complex and conflicting eco-zones, soaring and then bumping its way from the high plains desert of the eastern interior, over the terrifying dark hummocks of the Olympics, to the sopping wet, lichen-encrusted, deep, dark green of the Pacific coast. The mountains are a huge barrier between the desert and the Pacific. The ranges all have names: the Olympics, the Cascades, the Sierra Nevadas. We give place names to orient ourselves, but also as a mark of respect. These mountains deserve respect. They run north and south, rank on rank right through California all the way up to the Richardson Mountains at the edge of the Arctic's Beaufort Sea.

As I flew through the pink of morning, Mount Hood shot right through the cloud ceiling like some dark sea monster coming up for air, and Mount St. Helens and the other brooding peaks were all white, all sharp. The sun was harsh. I could see nothing but the cheese-curd softness below, but I imagined the rivers at the very bottom of this atmospheric soup, cutting their cold way out of the deserts. The Snake is south and east of Kennewick cutting down through Hell's Canyon from southern Idaho till it joins the Columbia. The Humboldt ripples across the Nevada desert not far from the Truckee. The Truckee was named for the Native American guide who helped John Fremont, the U.S. geological surveyor, find his way between desert and mountain. The Truckee runs close to dry Lake Winnemucca and into Pyramid Lake, beginning in the tiny perfect emerald beauty of Lake Tahoe.

While the Spirit Cave and Wizards Beach remains were found in a rock shelter and on a former beach so dry they were preserved for nine millennia, Nevada was not always a great desert. Once this area was covered by a giant lake known as Lahonton. At the end of the Ice Age, as the glaciers melted and slumped back, their released water vapor rose up into the atmosphere, condensed, and came down as rain, swelling vast new melt rivers that cut deep new corridors. There were floods everywhere. The sea level in some places rose 400 feet. Glacial lakes like Lahonton first ballooned and shrank at around 11,000 BP. They filled and shrank again around 9000 BP, leaving their former beaches to mark them.

Reno and Carson City are set in the valley between brown desert hills on the edge of the Sierra Nevada Mountains, the very definition of ponderosa country. Archaeologists refer to this area as the Great Basin. The towns seem small and sketchy in comparison with nature. In winter, when the snow lies on the Sierras at glacier thickness, the desert foothills are rumpled, and bare-assed, and mean. When the winds roar down, the sand and grit fly hard enough to score paint. The Shoshone and the Paiute, like the Umatilla, the Colville, the Yakama and the Nez Percé, are embroiled in fights with these burgeoning gambling towns over scarce water. In this place, Native American nations are trying to recapture their cultures, their histories and their various languages. In the town of Sparks just outside Reno, the Shoshone Cultural Center offers Shoshone language training. At Nixon on Pyramid Lake, the Paiute had just opened their new cultural center. Kinship and Native American politics tie the Shoshone and Paiute to the Umatilla and the Colville. Science ties Kennewick Man to the remains at Carson City.

The Nevada State Museum is on the main street, near the new state legislature building and the nice old Greek-styled offices of the state's attorney general. The next street back is full of little cottages, remnants of the days when this was the center of the mining industry, when the ponderosa pines were cleared off to make power and shore up mine shafts, in the decade after the California Gold Rush of 1849. This is the heartland of the Western: the movie and television stories made in these hills have long since layered over the real history. The real Virginia City is just down the road and there is a theme park there called Bonanza. In front of the museum a stone monument commemorates one last Pony Express ride made in 1961, when Dwight Eisenhower still presided over the board of the company.

The museum is small, two-storied, with an anteroom decorated like a nineteenth-century frontier office. This part of the building was formerly a branch of the U.S. Mint, where the gold and silver from these hills was smelted into eagles and dollars. There is a scale reproduction of the townscape of pioneer Carson City. There are rooms set out to look as they once did in the saloons, hotels and homes of the suddenly rich and no longer famous of 140 years ago. There are many displays having to do with law and order, crime and punishment, including balls and chains worn by labor gangs and a black-and-white photograph of the last lynching—a man hanged from a telegraph pole like a broken-winged bird. There is a display case with physical anthropologists' measuring devices. A fellow named Bentillon created a method of identifying prisoners by recording their head lengths and widths, their ear lengths, and the length of their left middle fingers. Measured runaways could never hide from justice.

The anthropology section is in the new wing. A map showed the entry of the First Americans into the New World, implying they came over the Bering land bridge. But the rest of the story was different from that told in other museums I'd visited. The display said:

> Probably about 40,000 years ago, when the land bridge was a broad plain, some 1,300 miles wide, comparable to the distance from San Diego, California, to Seattle, Asiatic Man entered the New World along now submerged coastal plains. Certainly by 11,000 to 13,000 years ago when an interior corridor opened up between the Cordilleran ice sheet and the Laurentide ice sheet, we know the Paleo-Indian was firmly established in the New World, actively hunting big game animals. Shortly thereafter, Paleo-Indian groups reached to the tip of South America and the slow process of cultural development we see among the Indians began.

The map marked the place in Texas where the skull of Midland Man was found right on the surface. Tom Lynch had dismissed this skull from consideration because it has never been directly dated. According to this museum, however, it is the oldest in the New World, from 10,000 to 18,000 years old. On the chart of human development, Sandia spear points—also dismissed by Lynch as a recognized mistake in American archaeology—were shown as part of the American chronology, earlier than Clovis. At the bottom of the display were the words: "20,000 B.C., the Discovery of the Americas by the Indians."

I moved through the rooms, both irritated and fascinated. There were Anasazi and Pueblo pots—beautiful shapes, wonderful colors—but I was looking for the Pyramid Lake display. I wanted to see how the curators explained the Spirit Cave and Wizards Beach finds. The information on the wall said that early man was "definitely in the Truckee basin 11,000 years ago and probably earlier." Both Pyramid Lake and Lake Winnemucca, said the display, are remnants of Glacial Lake Lahonton. Pyramid Lake was named in 1844 by John Fremont for the tufa, or calcium carbonate formations, that rise out of its waters. One of them reminded him of the Great Pyramid of Cheops. There were cases showing finds from a place called Chimney Cave, rope made by early fishermen, fragments of a fur blanket. There was a huge, crescent-shaped obsidian ceremonial blade, and there were woven duck decoys more than two thousand years old, shaped so beautifully they could have been mistaken at a few paces for the real thing. There were stone balls that reminded me of Monte Verde's bola stones. There were displays of shells found on sites here that had come from California and Oregon. There were displays of the techniques of toolmaking and weaving. There were relatively modern Paiute winter dresses made of sage and a reed called tule, which reminded me of the Haida clothing shown at the Museum of Civilization in Ottawa, which in turn reminded me of samurai armor from Japan. There were baskets of all shapes and sizes with paintings on them, tightly woven of willow (including some from British Columbia, which clearly showed far greater figurative sophistication than the Paiute material). The local ancient pots, however, were absolutely spectacular. The Paiute and their predecessors had not made ceramics. They wove their pots. One in a display case was curved and handled just like a Greek wine vessel, but made of willow woven so tightly it had been used for carrying water.

I came to a full stop in front of a case that held a boat. It was made of bundles of thick reeds the way the ancient Sumerians made boats, the same way Native people at Lake Titicaca in Peru made them and were still making them when Thor Heyerdahl needed help with his ocean-going reed boat. This boat looked something like a small version of Heyerdahl's early experiments. Instead of the ends being tied to each other to make a U shape, this boat lay dead flat. The card beside the display explained that Native people had used boats like this as platforms for fishing: after a couple of hours they became waterlogged and had to be dried out.

But there was not a single word about the most important treasures the museum holds: the approximately 9,500-year-old Spirit Cave Mummy or the remains of the slightly younger man found at Wizards Beach.

Amy Dansie, then anthropologist of the Nevada State Museum, guided me down the stairs to her basement work area. She was a big, tall woman, with a graying ponytail and bangs, round glasses and a sweet face. She was careful about smiling—there were odd gaps between her teeth—but when she forgot herself, her face glowed like a beautiful moon. She was in a leather jacket, baggy pants. A large cross hung around her neck.

The curation and storage area was not impressive for a museum so blessed with wonders. The floors were cement; there were no windows. Dansie had a little desk, a chair and a computer underneath the stairs. The walls were lined with plywood storage lockers, floor to ceiling. There were bones in there, all the Grimes Point burials, which included Spirit Cave. All were being sought under the NAGPRA by the Paiute who say they are the bones of their ancestors. This claim was driving Amy Dansie nuts. As far as she was concerned, the archaeology showed the Paiute culture was just a thin veneer on top of a lot of other cultures that had moved in and out of this great desert basin over the millennia. She had spent the last twenty years trying to tie climate change, as measured by the rise and fall of Glacial Lake Lahonton, to the archaeological record found in the dry caves and shelters. There was a pattern emerging: Lake Lahonton had filled right up at the end of the Ice Age, then suddenly and sharply dropped at around 11,000 BP to a tiny remnant of itself. Then it filled again, and around 9,000 years ago it suddenly dropped to its lowest level ever. There had been no archaeological finds around here that dated between about 9000 and 6500 BP: the region had been so desiccated no one could live in it. After 6500 BP, the archaeological record begins again.

One wall held shelves, upon which sat three forensically reconstructed, painted busts. On the far left was the reconstruction of the head of the Spirit Cave Mummy. In the middle was the head of Wizards Beach Man. On the right was Island Man, from a much more recent culture. I sat opposite the shelf so I had a good view of them. I couldn't decide for the life of me if they looked like each other, or if they looked like Kennewick Man, or if they only looked like themselves. No matter which way I turned my head, I couldn't see Spirit Cave as Doug Owsley and Richard Jantz do.

While Dansie didn't think it was right to show me the actual bones, which were the subject of Native claims, she showed me the textiles (although under the NAGPRA some of these were grave goods and are sought along with the remains). She and her assistant Sue Anne Montoleone opened large boxes set out on the worktable. The most ancient textiles ever found in the Americas were stored in these cardboard boxes, wrapped in tissue paper. The lids came off. I was handed gloves to wear. I couldn't square the immense antiquity of these things with this easygoing handling: it was as if they were pulling out old wedding dresses saved by their grandmothers.

The first box held the rough outer wrapping that was laid on top of the 9430 BP Spirit Cave Mummy. It was as yellow as old teeth, and whispery and dry as last year's corn husks. It was made of tule, Dansie said, that is "ubiquitous and [whose use is] ancient." In fact, there was no difference between this mat and those found historically in the area except for the direction of the twist of the weft that holds the rushes together. The historic-period mats were twisted up, the ancient textiles were twisted down. According to Dansie, Peg Wheat, a geologist turned ethnographer working for the U.S. Geological Survey, had recorded how the modern Paiute made their mats and how they used the techniques of weaving to make so many of their household wares. "She said that Nevada Indians tied their world together," said Dansie.

I had brought with me the publication of the Nova Scotia Museum; I opened it to the pages showing the Augustine Mound textile fragments.[1] I looked, in awe, at this 9500 BP mat and then at the photograph of the fragment from the Augustine Mound. They appeared to be the same. It seemed to me that the ancient Native Americans who put the Spirit Cave Mummy to rest may have tied together a much larger world than just Nevada. The two mats were made of the same materials: cattails twined with tule. Cattails are brittle when green, and tule is flexible. But when they dry this is reversed: the tule becomes dry, the cattails bendable. There is nothing obvious about making even such a simple mat, as any textile maker can attest. It involves thinking through a number of spatial and material problems. One must select a material that can be worked, but will not fall apart from use; one must gather and store materials in different seasons, spring and fall; one must design the twists and the knots for strength and flexibility, and create a selvedge that will keep the mat whole. Cattail was used to make the warps, rush was used to make the wefts, at the Augustine Mound and here. And both of these textiles, from Nova Scotia and Nevada, were buried with the dead.

The next box contained the fragments of the Spirit Cave Mummy's moccasins, which Dansie thought might have been made out of marmot hide. These moccasins, so small and turned on their sides as if they still covered the feet of a man at rest, made Spirit Cave more real than his bones could have. Someone had hunted and skinned and worked and patched these hides to cover his feet. They were made with the fur turned out on the sole, not turned inward as they are now made in the north. These were crafted in three pieces, stitched together with hemp cordage instead of sinew. One of the three pieces was wrapped around the ankle and sewn down.

Fused to the moccasins were the twined remnants of the mummy's fur blanket. Dansie believes this may have been made in the same way the Paiute were making these things many millennia later. A whole rabbit was skinned in one piece, starting at the mouth. This skin was then cut in a continuous spiral. This produced one long strip of hide with its fur still attached. One end was tied to a twirling stick, and spun. Spinning turned the fur to the outside of the resulting rope, which was then twined into a blanket.

This fur blanket was the product of a genius for making do. There were no large game or fur-bearing animals around, so there was not very much sinew for sewing and no large furs to be used as throws. But it gets cold in winter. Someone, more than 10,000 years ago, had figured out how to merge two dissimilar technologies—twining and skinning—to produce a facsimile of a large furred skin taken off a bear or a caribou. There was a brilliance to this solution that put all those clever little spear points in the museum utterly to shame. And the time it would have taken to do this! Someone had hunted for enough rabbits to make a whole set of such fur ropes, which were dried and treated and spun, and then twined together into a blanket to cover up Spirit Cave. There was nothing primitive in any of this: these textile skills were of a high order and this broken man had been treated with love at his death.

But it wasn't the rough mat or even this blanket that was most surprising. Twining, after all, is the oldest known form of textile making. What was shocking about Spirit Cave was the inner mat wrapping him. This had been plain-woven. In the Old World, according to archaeological textile experts Olga Soffer and James Adovasio, impressions of fragments of twined or finger-woven material that are 27,000 and 25,000 years old have been found at sites in central Europe.[2] So far as Dansie knew, no weaving of such antiquity had been identified anywhere else in the so-called New World; it seemed to be unique to the Lahonton basin.

Dansie and Montoleone pulled out a tightly woven piece of mat and put in front of me. It was brown and thick, but flexible. It looked as if it had been made last month. It was woven more tightly than the sisal grass rugs sold nowadays: it was a richer color, and it was softer. They pulled out two bags with fringed sides about two feet long by eighteen inches high. These were cremation bags, both twined, in which were found remains more than 9,400 years old. They were almost machine-perfect, better finished than most of the crafts stuff found in student ghettos around North America. Finally there was a larger bag without fringe. It was two-toned in red and yellow ocher, and plain-woven in a diamond pattern—which reminded me of a seventeenth-century diamond twill mat woven of cedar strips that was found at Red Bank, the same reserve on which the Augustine Mound was found. I pulled out the Nova Scotia book again and showed them.

"That's really neat," said Dansie, though she wouldn't say they were the same: we sat and pondered how this technique could have found its way across a continent and 9,000 years.

Dansie said she'd seen poster displays at learned conferences that suggested a movement of early people from the southwest to the northeast. "Things that occur now only in the northeast are in the southwest seven thousand years ago," said Dansie. "It's the same with the craniofacial measurements. The long faces and heads are more common in the east than in the west.... We might be able to link where the earlier people from the southwest went ... but only if [we're] allowed to study them."

Actually, the museum had had almost fifty years to study these particular remains. They were found in 1940 by Sydney and Georgia Wheeler, avocational archaeologists who worked for the Nevada State Parks Commission.[3] The dry cave sites around the Lahonton basin were then being destroyed by guano miners and private collectors. The state of Nevada set out to salvage what it could. The Wheelers had stumbled on these Grimes Point burials by accident. In a deep depression in the rock shelter's wall they found one set of well-preserved bones, and when they dug beneath it they found another, carefully wrapped and buried even deeper. This second skeleton came to be called the Spirit Cave Mummy. Close to these two burials, Georgia Wheeler also found two fine bags placed one on top of the other, one with a second bag inside: both contained the ashes of cremated people. They published an estimated age for these finds of about 1,500 to 2,000 years. They displayed the mummy, which still had a lock of hair attached to its skull, at the nearby town of Fallon, near a Paiute reservation. Then it was put into storage in a wooden box. "Someone put in mothballs," Dansie said with a sardonic snort. "Probably a good thing. If not, there'd be no hair left."

Mothballs protect textiles and hair from moths and other insects, but they also contaminate the radiocarbon dating process—not that anyone even tried to date any of this material until 1994. R.E. (Erv) Taylor of the University of California at Riverside had developed a new method for dating the total amino acid constituents of proteins, as a way of dating hair and bone and teeth more precisely. Scotty MacNeish had found hairs on his dig at Pendejo Cave in New Mexico, at a level that suggested they were older than Clovis. "Hair was becoming critical," said Dansie. Taylor "wanted to calibrate his radiocarbon system to resolve problems of dating bone. He found if he extracted amino acids and dated the acids he got good dates." But the dates they got from the Spirit Cave bone were so very old that there was an immediate concern that they might be wrong. Worse, some fragments of the textiles produced dates within the last fifty years. "The lab manager could smell mothballs . . . so the lab person said treat the tule as bone—take out the amino acids. And we got a date [on the acids] absolutely consistent with the other dates."

In 1995, after getting back the first set of dates from Riverside and realizing how old the woven material was, Dansie went on a frenzied hunt through her own museum. She was the first to recognize that the textiles inside the Spirit Cave box were not all twined, as the Wheelers had stated when they wrote up the find, but some had been made with a plain weave. Another piece of this diamond twill woven matting had been on public display for years: no one had seen it for what it was. She read the literature published about these mats. She found that in 1974 a textile expert named Charles Rozaire had referred to this type of weave as "plaiting" when he looked at a similar piece taken from Crypt Cave. She found that another scholar, Stacy Goodman, had noted the same thing about a tiny piece of mat found at Hidden Cave in the same area as the Spirit Cave shelter. But the stratigraphy and the chronology produced at these sites said these materials had been made within the last two thousand years, so no one cared that they'd been woven. Guano miners had found another burial covered in matting in 1939. This matting too went unrecognized as being woven in the distinctive plain-weave pattern. Dansie found one more large piece of diamond weaving that turned out to be even older than Spirit Cave's wrap. It was 9,470 years old.[4]

Partial skeletons had also been found at Wizards Beach, on the northeast edge of Pyramid Lake, by avocational archaeologist Peter Ting in 1968. They had been buried in the silt of what was at the time a beach, but the water had risen and covered the beach, then fallen again. Eventually the bones were exposed, and were retrieved. Extinct Ice Age animals, found at the same place, were dated at about 24,500 years old. Erv Taylor dated these human remains too. Some of the bones gave older readings than others. An average age of approximately 9225 BP was produced by two dates taken from amino acids from one set of bones–a male of about forty-five years of age whose remains included a measurable skull. Another group of bones was dated to about 6000 BP.[5]

Since these dates were reported, the museum had stopped relying on any chronologies that had been inferred from the study of stratigraphy. They had stopped doing fieldwork. There is so much in the museum that has to be redated and properly written up, they are overwhelmed.

The museum is the official repository for the U.S. federal government for any remains found on federal lands, and many of the remains in it have come from Bureau of Land Management (BLM) grazing lands scattered throughout Nevada. The Shoshone have been in the courts over those lands for about thirty years, ever since two Shoshone ranchers refused to pay the bureau fees for the right to graze their cattle—on the grounds that the Shoshone never ceded territory and the lands are theirs, not the government's. The museum had inventoried these remains under the NAGPRA, but classified them as unaffiliated. After the extreme antiquity of the Spirit Cave and Wizards Beach remains became known, the Northern Paiute claimed them all as their ancestors. The Bureau of Land Management was still trying to decide whether the Spirit Cave remains were affiliated with any living Native American tribes and would not permit any new destructive tests. However, before the Paiute made their claim, Frederika Kaestle had managed to extract mtDNA from twenty of the twenty-one prehistoric remains found in the Pyramid Lake area (but not on Bureau of Land Management land) and stored at the Museum, including Wizards Beach Man. Kaestle's report had appeared (along with the Owsley and Jantz analysis of Spirit Cave's morphology and other papers about the finds in the museum) in the spring 1997 edition of *Nevada Historical Society Quarterly*. (Kaestle was eventually able to extract mtDNA from more than forty of the remains and this formed the basis of her doctoral thesis.)

Kaestle found all four main Native American lineages to that point identified by the Wallace lab. Wizards Beach was the only one that belonged to lineage C. Her graphs showed that lineage

C was the second most frequent of the Native American lineages found in samples taken from modern Siberians, but that it was found at very low frequencies in the rest of North America, nonexistent in Central America and the third most frequently found in South American samples studied. She had not surveyed for X. At the time of the study, information on Andy Merriwether's two forms of X and Michael Brown's European-related X had not yet been published.[6]

The *Quarterly* also carried reports of what was found in the Spirit Cave Mummy. Spirit Cave was so well preserved that fecal material was found in the mummy's abdominal cavity. Six boli were recovered and screened for both fish bone and pollen. Pollens were found, but at low enough levels they might have just blown into the food being prepared.[7] Spirit Cave ate cyprinids: small minnows, tui-chub, dace, redside and suckers. This finding of fish allowed the reconstruction of a probable environment. "Specific taxa present in the Spirit Cave material and the relatively small size of the elements identified suggest a shallow, moderately swift moving water environment possibly connected to a larger benthic [deep water] system, at least intermittently."[8]

The most important thing that Dansie learned from all of this was to thank God that the Wheelers had never gotten around to having the Spirit Cave Mummy dated back in the 1950s when radiocarbon dating technology was still very primitive. It would have destroyed large amounts of bone and produced only unreliable dates. The other lesson was that the experts who looked at the textiles had seen what they thought they ought to, not what was actually there. Those who had noticed that the Spirit Cave Mummy was wrapped in a woven textile had never imagined that the mummy could be so incredibly old. It was the shock of the unexpected dates that forced Dansie to look at all the other material with fresh eyes.

"Almost all the experts had been here," she said. "Nobody noticed it. They were thinking of what they specialized in. This was a hunter's collection." But most of the sites where spear points had been found were in the open, not in the caves or rock shelters where these bones and textiles were discovered. "Spirit Cave had no diagnostic artifacts," she said. "If there was a stemmed point we would have said 'Bingo.'" Wizards Beach on the other hand was found not far from ancient fishing tools commonly found in Oregon. "He doesn't look like Spirit Cave," she said, looking up at the shelf that held their reconstructed faces. "Wizards Beach and Kennewick look like they could be brothers."

Wizards Beach Man's bones were a great deal more robust than the remains found at Grimes Point, such as the Spirit Cave Mummy. That population was fine-boned, with pointy little chins. Dansie hoped that if the BLM allowed and there were sufficient advances made in mtDNA extraction, someone like Frederika Kaestle would be able to distinguish whether the Grimes Point population was the same as Wizards Beach. But everything was still in limbo. Unlike the Army Corps of Engineers and the Kennewick remains, the Bureau of Land Management had neither accepted nor rejected her view that these remains were culturally unaffiliated to the Paiute. But the Paiute were deadly serious about changing that.

The parallels between Dansie's situation and Chatters' Kennewick story were very interesting. She thought the Paiute had not been terribly concerned about these burials until their extreme age was announced publicly in 1996. Until then, she believed, there had been good cooperation between the Paiute and the museum. In the mid-1980s, for example, after an El Niño winter, a number of ancient graves had washed out in the desert near an area known as the Stillwater Marsh. Some two hundred individuals' bones had been scattered by the flood across the desert. The Native community had asked for help in dealing with them. The U.S. Fish and Wildlife Service and the museum had salvaged those remains, retrieving and measuring them. There was a written agreement between the parties that even allowed some destructive analysis. The one unresolved issue was what to do with the bones after they'd been studied. The Native community was presented with several alternatives and spent about two and a half years trying to pick one. "It was always the last item on the agenda," said Dansie. "They don't want to talk about the dead, it's so unpleasant to them." Eventually, she suggested that an underground crypt could be built that could be reopened in the event that someone needed the remains for an important study. They liked that: they retained the right to say yes or no to reopening the crypt based on their analysis of study proposals. "The tribe didn't want [them] in their own cemetery. They know those might be their enemy."

The Paiute had an oral tradition of having struggled for generations against a people they called the Red-Haired Giants. One of the earliest ethnographers of this area was John Reid, a person Amy Dansie's mother had known. The Paiute had told him they hated the Giants because of their way of life. The Paiute said the Giants built pit traps on the paths through the marshes, and some were cannibals. There was a story of one last battle—the site had even been located by archaeologists—at a place called Lovelock Cave.

But this was where archaeology and oral traditions diverged: the Northern Paiute told this story as if both they and the other people were placed in this area by the Creator, and that the battle had happened eons ago; other tribes told it as if it had happened a few hundred years ago; the archaeological evidence said the last battle took place only 250 years ago, about the time the Paiute appear in the archaeological record of this area of Nevada.

One of the Paiute's elected representatives, Tribal Council Chair Alvin Moyle, had told Dansie that his grandparents told him about those red-haired people they didn't get along with. Not all the legends identified the giants as red-haired, but they all suggested the few survivors from the last battle had fled the area with other Native persons. John Reid had somewhere found a Giant's remains and Amy Dansie's mother had seen him put his own false teeth inside the Giant's immense tooth arch, but physical anthropologists were skeptical about there having once been a population of giants in Nevada. The youngest bones at Stillwater

Marsh had turned out to be 800 years old. Old enough, in Dansie's view, that they might well have been this ancient group the Paiute remembered ousting. She pointed to the Island Man's head on the right side of the shelf. "The Island Man is one of them, he's 890 years old or so, which makes him terminal Lovelock [the name given to the culture of marsh-dwelling basket weavers whose society lasted in this area for some 2,000 years]. They are massively built, much bigger than the Paiute. So how did the Paiute spread out all over the West? They're much more tenacious. These stories say they shot [the Giants] when they left the marsh."

The Lovelock Cave and Humboldt Sink victims looked different from both the Paiutes and the bones found at Stillwater Marsh. And just to further complicate matters, Sheila Brooks, the physical anthropologist who studied the Stillwater Marsh remains, kept saying that none of them were giants. They ranged through the normal scale from big to small. One was the tiniest adult female that Dansie had ever seen. Some of the oldest had massive facial bones. Finally, one last set of remains was found scattered over a tight area of land. Brooks took the bones to measure them. One day she walked into the museum to tell Dansie the news. "I'll never forget the day Brooks walks in and says, 'Amy, call your mother, we've got a giant.'"

"In 1995, when we confirmed the age of the [Spirit Cave] mummy, the first people we got hold of were the Fallon Paiute-Shoshone tribe. If they don't say that," Dansie said with a fierce look, "they're lying through their teeth.... We had a meeting out there with the fish and wildlife service. After talking about that crypt, I told them after, we have important information to discuss. I said we have a very old date on a burial on Grimes Point, the oldest mummy in America. I thought you should know right away. Alvin Moyle said we need a special private meeting of the tribal council. So I drive sixty-five miles at night for this meeting. The same three people [are there]: Alvin, and two women. I wait forty-five minutes for the rest of the council to show up. They were informed, there was an opportunity to discuss it." She was told that they wanted the mummy reburied, and all the other bones in the museum along with them. She explained how the NAGPRA works but she proposed that perhaps the mummy could be put in the protected crypt developed for the Stillwater Marsh remains.

It didn't get "ugly," as Dansie put it, until the time of the press conference announcing Spirit Cave's age. "The Fallon tribe had bulldozed [and exposed] burials on their own land the same week of the press conference. Then the tribal members started saying they were seeing spirits."

Goose bumps rose on my arms as she crossed from the world of science to the world of superstition so seamlessly. She mimicked the high piping voice of a frightened child confronted by a ghost. "Mummy, there's a strange man in the room," she squealed. The Paiute view of these matters is that if you see the ghost, something terrible will happen. "If you see it," said Dansie, "it means someone will die.... [They were] seriously scared." The facial reconstructions the museum had made were also upsetting to the Native community. They were something that drew attention to the remains. Drawing attention to the remains causes the spirits to be upset. Just talking about the remains causes trouble.

"So. We had a huge meeting. Fish and Wildlife people came down from Portland, big officials come all the way...three members of the Fallon tribe, one of them a lawyer.... Alvin [Moyle] officially and formally requested immediate reburials of all the burials. He wanted to solve this problem with spirits. The old ones always said you never disturb the dead. If you do, bad things happen.

"At another meeting the same year," she said, "Alvin came with his tribal manager, just the three of us.... I gave him the entire inventory. I said I don't have to give you this, but this is all the burials.... I have to find all the evidence, all the grave goods, it will take years to do the inventory.... I gave him every bit of factual information we have and told him the truth up front. He didn't seem to be unhappy. He's such a gentle soul, he did not show anger to me. I told

Alvin I had never suffered over anything as much as over these burials. I considered quitting my job. I took the Indian position more seriously as a person. It was tearing me apart. I didn't have time to do the analyses...I was torn between sympathy for their position and my duty as a scientist. I don't think science is the only thing that's important. It took me five years to make the choice. The choice was science."

This choice was helped along when a consultant for the Paiute from Pyramid Lake, near the town of Nixon, also got involved in the dispute. There was a war by Internet. Attacks were made on her spirituality, Dansie said. "They said I was a soulless person on the Internet." She and her boss were accused of being without spirit and causing untold harm to Indian people because of these burials.

Dansie was sick of the whole affair. She knew what she knew—that the Paiute were a thin layer on top of the archaeological record and in her view would not likely be the direct descendants of the Spirit Cave or Wizards Beach population. She had also come to believe that there was more going on here than spiritual concerns about the unquiet dead. She thought she saw evidence that these disputes had to do with land claims.

"I don't think studying human bones," she said, in a burst of outrage, "is any kind of spiritual issue whatsoever. But they can't prove they're right and I can't prove they're wrong."

I told Dansie what Chatters had said to me—about the troubles in what he'd referred to as "Indian country" over Kennewick Man. Even if these fears of ghosts were no part of science, they informed the political process and so their impact was very real.

"By their fruits ye shall know them," Dansie thundered, her voice echoing a little ominously in the basement. "Nothing but good has happened here. Like a miracle. [We] have unprecedented state support [$58,000 more on the budget]. I've heard the Paiute say bad things are happening to them. They're not happening to us. I talked about that to a Washoe lady.... She smiled and said, 'I wouldn't expect this to happen to you. They're *our* ancestors.'"

"That same week, the janitor here brought up at a staff meeting a ghost incident," she continued. "Some guy did die a violent death in the Mint. He was a white guy, of course." The staff began to notice odd things, Dansie explained. A cold draft would flow through the museum when there were no doors open. Something would be seen out of the corner of an eye. Finally, someone took a picture of something hovering. "Then the Polaroid disappeared—it had the ghost in it," said Dansie. "Our Anglo staff, the only ghost experiences they've had are Anglo ghosts. I couldn't help wondering about what the old lady said. Science isn't the only way to answer what's true about the world. It doesn't mean the spirit is not just as real."

In addition to the Anglo ghost, she'd had a peculiar experience with one particular piece of plain woven matting. In her hunt through the museum for more examples of the ancient material, she kept forgetting to search one of the cupboards. It was as if it was hoodooed. She'd remember she hadn't checked it, set out to open it, and something else would come up, or she'd forget what she was doing. It was as if every time she passed that cupboard a veil was drawn over her eyes and she couldn't actually see it. Finally, she had asked her assistant to search it, and when she too forgot to do it, Dansie had marched over and done it herself. In the cupboard she found the largest piece of plain-woven matting in the whole collection. It had lain in the dark untouched for years.

Dansie could understand this stuff about ghosts and spirits. She herself had quit school early to wander as a stranger and a seeker in this desert, in search of God. But she drew a line between scientific explanations of events and this other domain. She thought they could just coexist. In spite of the Internet attacks on her character, in spite of a terrible letter written to the governor about her and her boss, in spite of the allegations made by a man who demanded the state attorney general investigate the museum (which had caused her to spend two weeks going through thousands of documents to answer the complaint), she had decided not to quit. She'd decided she'd be respectful, she'd be careful, but "no one can make me lie." No one could make her say that the Paiute and the Spirit Cave Mummy were one people.

She stood beside her little desk in the basement as I made my way to the stairs, hunched a little, because the ceiling sloped over her head. Like Chatters, she recognized how difficult her life had become since she published on the antiquity of the Spirit Cave and Wizards Beach remains, but she didn't connect one with the other, the bones with the life, not really. "This is the greatest job on the planet," she crowed.

The miracle reversed. The Paiute launched a civil rights action against the museum to get back the Spirit Cave and Wizards Beach remains. The Bureau of Land Management determined that the Spirit Cave remains were culturally unaffiliated but refused to allow any more tests. The word came down from on high that the Nevada State Museum was no longer to do research, but just to concern itself with public outreach, and the museum withdrew its request to do DNA study of the Spirit Cave remains. All the ancient materials Dansie had shown me were locked away. Someone was appointed her superior over her head. She decided it was time to get out. Dansie retired in June 2000 from the Nevada State Museum, a bitter taste in her mouth. The greatest job on the planet was over.

# We were Always Here

## Some Native American Histories

T HE FRIEND WHO PUT me up at his place in Lake Tahoe declared that the roads hereabouts were far too treacherous for strangers to manage. He was absolutely right. He held on to the wheel of his four-wheel-drive monster with both hands as the wind tried to heave us off the highway. The road wound through a wide, terraced valley that cut a path from the toes of the Sierra Nevadas through Reno to Pyramid Lake. There were deep gullies on either side where the water would run in the spring when the mountains shed some of their weight of white. The high terraces are markers of the water level at the end of the Ice Age—this would have been a flat world then, with only the highest hills rising like knobs above the surface of gigantic Lake Lahonton. On the right side of the highway as we drove towards the town of Nixon, the narrow Truckee River chittered and roiled over rocks and stones, its banks bordered by red willows and scrubby cottonwoods, the only trees to be seen. Compared to the Columbia it was a brook. I took pictures as the sun blared down on the bare brown hills. The mountains were ghosts off to my left, and then, as the road turned, straight ahead of us. Below their transparent peaks rose a floating line of extremely bright turquoise blue, the first sight of Pyramid

Lake. As we got closer, the blue pulled itself apart from the dun-colored hills. I could just make out a pyramid rising out of the water like some fabulous Egyptian isle.

The landscape was achingly beautiful in its barren way. But who could live in this wind and this emptiness? What torments would they suffer in the heat of the desert summer? Amy Dansie had spent the first years of her career doing an archaeological survey in the path of hydro towers to be built here. She liked to tell stories of killing rats and lizards and eating them, because she was that thirsty and hungry. She also said the desert north of here was so barren it scared even her. Beside the river, a thick spread of dead tule, all yellowed and bent over, marked a dried-up marsh.

As we drove around in Nixon looking for the Paiute Cultural Center I found myself thinking about the personal troubles these researchers had encountered and how tightly they were linked to each other. Amy Dansie was pulled one way by her professional duty, and another way by her own conscience. She had woken up to the pervasiveness of racism against Native people in Nevada when she was twelve years old. She knew what it was and she hated it. She also knew Chatters, who'd called to ask her what her experience was dealing with the federal government just after he got the date back on Kennewick's bones. And then there was Robson Bonnichsen.

I had stopped to see Bonnichsen at Oregon State University on my way to meet Chatters. He is a tall, thin, large-headed fellow, who received me dressed in academic rumple—a large sweater, chinos, a beard. Like Chatters and Dansie and Owsley and Stanford, he is a Westerner. He was brought up in southern Idaho. He too fell in love with archaeology when he picked up his first artifacts from his backyard. Alan Bryan (who came originally from Alaska) recruited Bonnichsen to archaeology, first at Idaho State University, then to Edmonton to do his doctorate. Later, Bonnichsen had worked on the Old Crow collection at Canada's National Museum after being shown some of the bone artifacts at a conference in Calgary. He was an assistant professor at the University of Maine when his work on ancient tools made by flaking mammoth and caribou bones attracted the interest of the Bingham Trust. The trust offered Bonnichsen money, which he used to set up the Center for the Study of Early Man in the Americas at the University of Maine at Orono.

Like Chatters, Bonnichsen is not exactly Mr. Sensitive. "The femi-Nazis" is what he calls the women who objected to the title of his center (on the reasonable grounds that men could not have inhabited America alone). They graffitied his signs, then complained to the president of the university. Eventually, he'd had enough of what he called "the eastern establishment" and moved the Center out to Oregon in 1991. No less a personage than Jean Auel, bestselling author of *The Clan of the Cave Bear*, has supported it. Bonnichsen publishes a monthly newsletter on Paleo-American research called *Mammoth Trumpet* and an annual peer-reviewed journal.

Bonnichsen first ran afoul of both native sensibilities and the NAGPRA in 1994 when he found long strands of seemingly human hair at a pre-Clovis level on a dig. He wanted to try and date the hair. The local tribe involved objected on the grounds that hair is a human remain. Alan Schneider fought that for him. As Schneider put the plaintiff's argument to me, "You might as well say when you walk into a barber shop, oh, look at all the human remains on the floor."

Bonnichsen had collected hair from caves in France known to have been occupied by people during the Ice Age, and like Dennis Stanford, he wondered about early connections between Europe and the Americas. In other words, when Chatters called him for help, Bonnichsen was a distinguished and inventive scholar with resources and a skeptical view of the Clovis First/ Bering Strait theory. As soon as Bonnichsen put his name on the Kennewick suit, he found himself being attacked by some of his anthropological colleagues. They told him they took the Native American side in this affair. They told him to drop out of the suit. He was ostracized on Oregon State's campus. He told me that he hadn't been invited to a faculty meeting in over a year.

These scientists live in a remarkably small world. They are tied to each other by the architecture of personal history, institutions, mentors, conferences, expectations and by their skepticism concerning the over-arching narrative of who peopled the Americas. They feel a sympathy for Native Americans and a passionate interest in their cultures but they have nevertheless become the enemy of some Native Americans and some anthropologists. Their stories exemplified the way in which anthropology has become a divided house. There are walls between the ethnographers who study cultures and the physical anthropologists and archaeologists who use hard science tools for their investigations. Everybody knows a lot about their tiny area, but the larger structure is expected to take care of itself. Ethnographers are interested in the stories told by Native Americans about themselves, but to archaeologists, who consider themselves hard scientists, Native stories are a curiosity, nothing more, and less useful as evidence than the Bible, which was at least written down.

If there had been a long, long voyage, a walk from the north to the south from a distant homeland, would it not have been told and retold by traditional cultures? It was surprising to me that archaeologists did not often look for such tales and use them as starting points to find evidence to support their migration theories. Israel is full of holes in the ground dug by people guided by the stories in the Bible.

If Native Americans were in the hemisphere before the end of the Ice Age, it seemed reasonable to expect they would have stories about it, specifically flood stories. Geologists know that there were two major flood periods as the Ice Age ended. There was one at the end of the first big warming, around 12,000 BP, when the coasts were inundated and the Bering land bridge was covered by the Pacific and the Arctic oceans. This was followed by a cooling period and a regrowth of glaciers. Then another sudden warming occurred, bringing floods that peaked about 10,000 BP.

In November 1998, the students in archaeology at the University of Calgary organized a large conference on the first peopling of various parts of the globe, including the Americas.[1] They invited Tom Dillehay and Jack Rossen. They invited a Canadian geographer whose work challenged the theory of an ice-free corridor through which ancient Siberians might have walked into the Americas. And they also invited William Asikinack of the Department of Indian Studies at the Saskatchewan Indian Federated College in Regina—to tell stories.

Asikinack told two fascinating tales traditional to the Anishinabe people—the Ojibwa who live now around the Great Lakes and on the Great Plains. He had heard these stories as a child from grandparents. He learned as he grew older that they were layered, highly metaphorical stories, that they packed a great deal of information into a very simple form. "They are as real to us who are aboriginal as the Bible is to those who proclaim Christianity," he told the students. He told them that Glooscapi, a critical figure in both stories, was a culture hero for the people called Mi'kmaq who live in Nova Scotia and New Brunswick. Asikinack also told them that the more times the phrase "long ago" was repeated, the older the story is considered to be.

His first story ostensibly explained the origin of the seasons:

Long ago and long ago and long ago and long ago, the People, as a single nation (nin-wa-windwidji-da-ki-wema, we are of the same land), lived along the eastern shores of the great salt water. At that time the People had a spirit protector called Glooscapi. Glooscapi did many things, and brought many things to the People. Glooscapi brought the plant-beings, the various animal beings, and the swimmers who were placed on the land to help the People survive and live a good life. The People had lived for many generations in this land. Then a strange thing started to happen. The People thought that Glooscapi was the one who had caused this strange thing to happen. Of course the People were right—

Glooscapi and Ki-weyd-de-nonk Mmnid-doo (Spirit of the North) had got into an argument about who was the stronger spirit. Ki-weyd-de-nonk Mmnid-doo to show his strength began to make it cold in the land of the People. The thing we call sook-po (snow) began to come to the land. The snow came and did not stop. As the snow got deeper and deeper (ish-pi-koon-ka) and ice began to walk on the land, the plant-beings stopped returning for each cycle and the animal-beings left the country. The People finally had to leave too. The People went je-wyd-nonk ina-ka-kie-a (southward) along the edge of the salt water with Glooscapi following behind to protect them from the Spirit of the North. The People went far to the south and lived there for many generations. Glooscapi, their friend and spiritual protector, made friends with Je-weyd-nonk Mmnid-doo (Spirit of the South). After a time he convinced Je-weyd-nonk Mmnid-doo to aid him in an attempt to overpower Ki-weyd-de-nonk Mmnid-doo. The three spirits did battle for several generations until finally Glooscapi and Je-weyd-nonk Mmnid-doo began to push Ki-weyd-de-nonk Mmnid-doo from the original lands of the People and back into ki-weyd-de-nonk (the north-lands). As the battle continued, the spirits found that they could only carry on for a certain amount of time because even spirits become tired. So sometimes Je-weyd-nonk Mmnid-doo was the winner and would reign in the land of the People and for almost an equal amount of time Ki-weyd-de-nonk Mmnid-doo would reign over the land of the People. When each of these spirits were coming into their time to reign, there were certain signs that the People learned to under-stand. When it was the turn of Je-weyd-nonk Mmnid-doo to reign, Je-weyd-ni-nod-in (the South Wind) would bring warmth and the return of the plant beings. When Ki-weyd-de-nonk Mmnid-doo had its turn to rule then Ki-weyd-din-nod-in (the North Wind) would come and all the plant beings would go to sleep. Thus it was that the four seasons,

spring, summer, fall, and winter, arrived in the original land
of the People.

Asikinack believes that this story makes it clear his ancestors
were living on the eastern shore of the Atlantic before, as he put
it, the beginning of at least the last ice age. This being the case,
then this particular group of aboriginal people may not have
crossed from Asia as the Bering Strait Theory stipulates and for
certain they were here for much longer than modern science
has suggested.

His second story was in its way even more interesting. It was
about how the Anishinabe came to live in various areas "from
the Great Lakes to the western edge of the woodlands." This
story is about the movements of the Crane clan (which has been
traced by ethnographers through Northern Ontario to Minnesota and Wisconsin):

> After the People had finally returned to their original home-
> land along the shore of the great saltwater, the number of
> families and people began to again grow. As the numbers of
> the People increased, they found that the land might not be
> able to give them enough for them to survive. The People,
> who lived in this land for several generations had begun to
> develop a Dodem (clan) system. The various families identi-
> fied with certain fliers, swimmers, four-leggeds and some
> plant-beings. One group of families, in particular, identified
> themselves with Ot-chi-chak or O-chi-pe-o-ee (the Crane).
>
> It has been told that within this family group there was a
> woman and man with the special ability to transform into
> Crane beings. For these beings, the land had lost its just-
> right-ness and therefore they found that they had to move
> away. The couple who could transform was told by Glooscapi
> that they needed to find a new home for themselves and their
> relations.
>
> Thus, the O-chi-pe-o-ee started to travel toward Ee-ink-

kush-mok (the place where Kee-sis, the Sun, goes to sleep—today called the west). As the O-chi-pe-o-ee couple flew westward, they would choose a place to land. Then at each place where they would stop, they would return to their human form to test the land for its "just right-ness." At each of the places, the O-chi-pe-o-ee found many qualities in the land that were needed for the feeling of "just-right-ness." Thus the People would begin to live at these chosen locations for a period of time. As the family numbers increased, the Anishinabe (the People) would begin to spread out from these locations to other nearby areas.

As the Crane beings traveled ever westward, they transformed seven times. Each time they transformed, some of their relations would join them and would eventually stay behind while the Crane beings travelled further and further west. One of the important places where the Crane beings transformed into human form was place number four. This is near the location where Kit-chi-kumi (the big lake waters) meet. In today's world, this location is called Sault Ste. Marie. To this day, some Anishinabe continue to consider Sault Ste. Marie a sacred meeting place.

The seventh and final stopping spot for the couple was around the area known today as Red Lake, in the state of Minnesota. At this point, when the Crane beings thought that they should again move further west, they realized that they could not transform into their Crane form. If the Anishinabe wished to travel further west, then they would have to do so through o-bam-saa-win (walking) or by chee-maun (canoe). Thus, it was when Wem-tik-kosh-shi (the French) and Jo-o-nosh (the English) arrived in North America they found the Anishinabe occupying the lands from the Great Lakes to the western plains.

Another of the important stopping places is number two. This spot is located just north of Peterborough, Ontario. At this location is what anthropologists call the Peterborough petroglyphs. We call this area the Ki-no-mah-kawh-win a-ji-bik (teaching rocks). In the very center of the site is a very large Crane.[1]

What fascinated me about these stories was that they explained some of the evidence in the ground. The oldest human remains on the eastern side of the Canadian Rockies were found on the Labrador coast in the Canadian northeast, not in the area of the corridor—or the plains. Many of the oldest stone tool sites in North America were found in the U.S. Southeast. Among the people who had a significant percentage of mtDNA of the lineage X, with its middle Ice Age ties to Europe, were the Ojibwa, these same Anishinabe people.

They also echoed the emerging geological description of what the beginning and end of the Ice Age must have been like. There was at first a winter that just kept on going, then the growth of the Laurentide glacier, which radiated out in circles from various centers around Hudson Bay. The end of the Ice Age was very sudden, with rapid, terrifying swings between extreme cold and sudden warming. This seesaw between warm and cold went on for thousands of years, just as the stories suggested.

These stories were also remarkable for what they did not say: there was nothing in them about people trekking from the high Arctic through the center of a continent, between harrowing walls of ice, across vast, sterile, frigid lakes of meltwater.

The Paiute Cultural Center in Nixon, Nevada, about one hundred miles south of the Oregon border, was started in 1976 on a federal grant but not completed until 1998. It is a very odd but beautiful little building, a cross between a hogan and a teepee, but built of stone. It is sunk down into the top of a hill, its back to the wind, with a window slit at one end that runs from top to bottom. Getting from the car to the entrance was like walking on the

Prairie in a blizzard—you had to lean into the wind to make any headway at all. A sign over the door to the display room read "Never to Be Forgotten," in English and in Paiute. On a table inside the entry there was a large branch of sage.

There were glass cases filled with Paiute wicker trays, clothing, and with photographs. One was devoted to the story of a Paiute woman who had not only started the first school, but was also the first Native American to publish a book; she had been blamed (apparently unfairly) for pushing her people into making a dreadful march deep into Oregon during which many died. There were other cases with photos of men dressed in First World War U.S. Army uniforms who had formed the Lost Battalion, and letters of appreciation from President Grover Cleveland. There were buckskin dresses, arrowheads, tools to straighten the shafts of arrows, stones shaped to sink nets to the bottom of a lake or river.

A large poster described the archaeological record of the area and listed the order in which different cultures had lived here. It was the same general chronology as displayed at the Nevada State Museum just sixty miles south at Carson City. The Paiute were shown as the most recent arrivals. Before them were the Ute-Aztecans (usually referred to as the Numic expansion), a group who were thought to have moved into the Great Basin from the southwest and then spread to California. Before them came the basket-maker people called Lovelock.

Another poster showed the different arrow and spear points associated with these cultures. The earliest stone points shown were dated at around 9000 BP. As at the Nevada State Museum, there was no mention here of the finds at Spirit Cave or Wizards Beach. But—and this was different from the Nevada State Museum—there was no mention of the Bering land bridge either.

Wilson Wewa, who was then the cultural center's director, sat very straight in his chair, which he had turned away from his desk so he could face me. His office was in the loft of the building, above the displays set out below. All the sun-warmed air rose up and made me drowsy, in the mood for stories.

He is a plainspoken working man, a bachelor at forty-two. His feet, bulging in his work boots, were placed just so, tight together, toes pointed straight ahead, like a military man sitting at attention. He is very tall, with broad shoulders, long legs, a large chest, a ruddy brown complexion. His head is big, his cheeks very broad. His eyes are bright, with the suggestion of something like an epicanthic fold at the corners, behind his aviator glasses. His hair is black and very thick. His nose spreads wide over his big smile. He wore a multicolored shirt and blue jeans. His hands lay on the chair's arms, his fingers curled under the edges, as if it were a throne.

I looked at him very closely, trying to see him as Hrdlička would have. But he did not look North Asian to me at all. Certainly his eyes suggested North Asian traits, but he was so obviously not a person of Chinese or Japanese ancestry, he was so obviously rooted to this earth here, it was hard to imagine his ancestors walking out of Siberia. Everything about him was American: he wore a wristwatch set in a silver bracelet studded with American turquoise, and around his neck a multi-stranded necklace of rough, unset turquoise stones, all variants of the vibrant, heart-racing blue of Pyramid Lake. In a deep voice, with a careful choice of words, he began to tell me how he became a storyteller.

When he was small, his older cousins were sent to boarding school. In those days, the American government, like the Canadian, still took the view that Native American cultures were the moral equivalent of disease. Bureaucrats, and the churches who acted for them, thought Native people should be forcibly separated from their languages at the tenderest age so as to be more easily molded into simulacra of European immigrants. Effectively, this policy turned every Native child against his parents, turned every native child into an involuntary immigrant immersed in another culture in his own land. With his cousins sent away, Wewa, as a very young boy, had no one to play with. His grandparents felt sorry for him and took him with them when they traveled to their traditional food-gathering place in April and May. They'd go to a site about twenty miles outside Burns, Oregon, to dig roots. There'd be three or four tents full of older people, and after they'd dug for wild onions and potatoes and the like, they'd tell stories and legends. During the day, when someone heard the meadowlark calling, they'd talk about what he said.

"I heard it today," said Wewa with a small smile. "A lot of people forget animals can talk.... Out at the root camp I learned about food, medicines, what the meadowlark says, when animals come out of the ground. Old people talked of that. I remembered it good. And I heard the legends of floods.

"The People," said Wewa, "had experienced two floods. One was when the animals were the people. Before man was put here the animals could talk just like we do today. They were—in the legend, they were like people, they were animals that talked like people. It was that time when they had a common language— bear to fish, fish to meadowlark—they could talk back then. Mostly they ate plant foods, roots, berries.

"One time in the legend Coyote went to the water to drink at a spring. There was no wind. He looked at the water and seeing his reflection for the first time, it scared him. He thought it was a monster, I guess. They didn't know what they looked like. When he found out it was his reflection, he touched his ears, and knew it was himself. He combed his hair, he could make his hair curly or smooth. He got an ego—he got vain. He went to other people, everybody saw how he looked, all slicked back. Other animals got to it, painted feathers blue or yellow, or stripes on that fur. They're still looking like that. They started telling one another, look at how pretty I am, real pretty feathers. Because they were inflated in their thinking, they began to fight over how they looked, calling bad names. The Creator looked down upon them. He was going to wash what they had done off.

"He flooded the world first, to punish the animals. Some got washed off—they're plain now. Some found shelter—blue jays, orioles—they still have color. Coyote became gray. He was painted with white paint and there's white still on his stomach and neck because of that. Anyway, because of that, Creator punished the animal people and took away their language. They can't talk to one another. And because of the enmity during that time, bears eat fish, cougar eat deer and wolf eats deer, because of that, when they became vain.

"Then man. There's a legend of the creation of man. He got placed after the first flood. The same thing, he lived here good, everything is given to him, fish, deer, roots, the bears, are on land for his use. Then man became proud too and started abusing. He could call the animals to him when he wanted to eat. The term now used is shaman. He would sing and pray and the deer would come and he'd kill them. It was easy to get food. But [humans] abused that power. They tried to use that power to make themselves wealthy. The Creator destroyed man the second time with another big flood."

"This history," Wewa said, "has been passed down maybe 500 generations, that a flood was here where we are at Nixon—you can see the terraces on all these mountains. They were all flooded."

This was like the other half of William Asikinack's stories. I remembered Paul Martin's hypothesis that early man had walked into the Americas and found animals that had no fear of humans because they didn't know them as predators. Martin suggested that people were responsible for the extinction of a large number of species of Ice Age animals in a very short span of years after they first entered the Americas.[2] I'd thought it was a ridiculous idea. Yet here was an ancient story that sounded very much like it.

I asked Wewa what he thought the story meant.

He said he'd done a lot of thinking about all of his stories, trying to tie them to the finds of geologists and archaeologists. "My thought is that the people didn't know how big the world was. This basin was our people's world. When it flooded, they thought the whole world flooded. I think it was the same in the Middle

East.... people thinking it was the only world they knew, thought the whole world was flooded.

"It's come to light there were two events in the Northwest that could have caused flooding in the Great Basin. The first is when Mount Hood and Mount Adams and Mount St. Helens all were erupting. All are a few miles from the Columbia River. The Sahaptin-speaking people's legends say the Mountains were people. Two were men and one a lady. The two men were in a fight over the girl mountain—they threw rocks at one another, and blocked the Columbia. The water backed up behind the Cascade range. The geological evidence supports there was at Cascade locks a natural formation [of stone]. When the Columbia broke through, a bridge was formed.... The people here have a legend of crossing that bridge. It was called the Bridge of the Gods. It collapsed. I think that was the basis of the first flood. More recently I heard about a glacier in the Rocky Mountains that blocked up Lake Missoula. It was covering all of Montana, Wyoming and Canada. As the glacier receded, those waters [flowed] onto Idaho, Oregon and here in the Great Basin. I think they said the Snake River flowed backwards for a time and created canyons on the Snake River. To my understanding that was more recent."

He was well acquainted with the theory that people came to America over the Bering land bridge. It seemed to me this Bridge of the Gods he referred to could be a reference to crossing the Bering Strait, not a bridge of rock over the Columbia. He disagreed because of another legend among the Paiute people that also dated back to when the animals were people, before the first flood. He straightened in his chair and began to tell it in his slightly sonorous way.

"A big famine hit the land. All the animal people were starving. The chief was a wolf. He called for his men to go out to check all the land. I get mixed up where they went," Wewa said, shaking his head, "but grizzly bear went north, mouse went to the south, the deer to the west. Another went east to look for food.

They were gone a long time. The one from the east came back first. He went clear to the end of the land and came back. There was a big lake he couldn't get around. It was probably the Atlantic Ocean. The deer from the west said the same thing. The grizzly bear came back. This is where the story talks of big ice. There was a wall, the wall was so high, and so big, he followed it to the east and the west and it went into the water.

"The animals wanted to see. They could see the wall from a long ways. The chief asked the eagle to fly up to see what was on the other side of the wall. He flew out of sight in the sky. He never came back for a long time. Then, someone saw the eagle. He said he went over, and flew across the nothingness—there were no trees, no water, nothing, just snow as far as he could see."

"From that story," said Wewa, still firmly gripping his chair, "I have concluded that man was here in North America before the glacial age made a land bridge of the Bering Strait."

But how did Native Americans get here, from where, and when?

"I've read the Bible," Wewa said. "There are a lot of wonderful things in that book. If it's true, why would God limit himself to creating man on one spot on the world?"

This idea of a multiple creation is anathema to most evolutionary anthropologists: it conflicts with Darwin's theory that a species descends in only one place at one time. Wewa had travelled to Peru, and he'd noted there the stories of cities swallowed by mountains fighting with each other that reminded him of the stories told by Native people throughout Oregon. He was certain that underneath the foot-thick layers of ash and pillars of basalt found all around Oregon, archaeologists would one day discover fire pits and stone tools that would attest to the extreme length of time that Native people have been in North America. How else could his people have stories of walls of ice that stretched from one huge body of water to another?

"So that's why I continue to say our legends have evidence, our legends are a timetable based on fact.... East of Bend, Oregon, there's a pictograph place in a canyon. There's one drawing in there, a circle with a tail, the middle of the red circle painted yellow. It faces northeast. My grandma showed me when I was twelve. She called it, in Paiute, 'patuzo wa chaid'; in essence it means 'a dying star.'" Much later, he said, "We were doing some anthropological assessment south of Dry River Canyon. A Paiute elder there told of caves in that Summer Lake area where the ash is not as thick as it is in outlying areas. The old man said an event had occurred there. In the legends of the Klamath and the Paiute and other tribes there was an event at Summer Lake...a meteorite fall. The dust killed all the people in the area. The Paiute never visited, due to respect for the dead. [There] are a lot of bodies there, choked to death. I put [it] together with the pictograph—the same name [patuzo wa chaid]. [It's] eighty miles south of the pictograph."

Wewa tied the difficulties Native Americans face over the return of bodies and grave goods from looted burial sites to scientists' refusal to believe in the probative value of Native stories. "Because Wilson Wewa doesn't have an MA in anthropology or archaeology or ethnology then I am less than those educated people," he said. "They think our stories are not based on the formula they use to date man's existence or use of places on our land. Their writings say the Paiute have 'legends' or 'myths'—that's the hardest thing for Indian people. The events were important or they wouldn't have been remembered or retold.... They don't consult us. They don't want to recognize people like me. That's why Native Americans don't like to share what we know. We get made fun of or chastised. When evidence comes to light we shake our heads and we say, see? That man who writes it down gets the MA and gets famous. We knew. But we don't get the credit, somebody else does." Strangely enough, Wewa said these bitter things without rancor. He was almost good-humored about how Native reality became unreal in European hands, or how facts became known only when a doctoral student put a stamp of approval on it.

"I came here to work in this place. A local man took me around to look here, it looks like nothing, but within a two-mile radius of the museum are all kinds of wonderful things to see that will be in my mind for the remainder of time. There are writings, pictographs, rock shelters." These were the kinds of things that any archaeologist would salivate over. But he wouldn't be pointing them out to the experts at the Nevada State Museum anytime soon. The Nevada State Museum was locked in battle between educated people and what Wewa called "our Native spirituality."

From the Paiute perspective, it didn't matter whether the remains in the museum were actually direct ancestors of the Paiute or some other Native people. "To our Indian people, all Indian people, a body is a body regardless of what age it comes from. Respect that needs to be paid to a dead person is the same as today.... Just because it's a few thousand years old it [is] still afforded the same protection and respect as in the community cemetery here. If I dug in the local cemetery I'd be punished. But it's okay to dig our burial places and put people on display or treat them like a toy in a drawer. And people handle [the bones] with [their] hands as if [they were] a curiosity. We want to give them the dignity given to them when they lived."

But in the Kennewick case, I said, the man may well have died by accident.

"If he died in a cataclysm he still should be afforded protection as in Oklahoma when that building was bombed," he said. "If in Oklahoma City I crawled over the fence I'd be charged. Why should we study him? Remains have been in lockers for hundreds of years in Europe.... What are they learning from it? It serves no purpose. If it showed us how to have a better or fuller life with some point, maybe Indian people wouldn't feel that way."

The fact is, he explained, the Paiute have specific people who handle remains and there are certain taboos and ritual behaviors regarding death and burial that must be adhered to. As he laid them out, some of these rules sounded distinctly like the restrictions placed on practicing Jews with regard to dealing with the dead. Almost every Jewish community, no matter how tiny, has an organization called the Chevra Kaddisha (the Friends of the

Dead) whose members take charge of washing and wrapping and sitting with the dead until they are interred. Anyone who does these tasks is polluted by their contact with death and must refrain from contact with others until certain cleansing routines have been followed. This is why it is considered a blessed and honorable sacrifice when a person takes on such a task. The Paiute have a similar set of restrictions for those who act for the dead.

"The deceased are dressed in buckskins and wrapped in mats. Our people who do that go into a five-day quarantine. They can't bathe, touch kids, look at another's food. They have to be isolated. On rare occasions I do that when elders request... I don't leave the house to go to work, to go to the sweat house. I don't hunt deer or fish. My brothers do that for me... I keep medicine for both internal and external cleansing. I know the prayers and songs. This community has lost a lot. There are five boys who want to learn what I know. You have to pick the right pupils to teach, who won't abuse the power."

Recently he had gone home to Oregon for the annual winter medicine dance. This is a five-day period when medicine people come together. "We're like the people who wind the clock," he said with a grin. "The next year won't happen if we don't, the roots won't come back, fish won't come back up the river. Lots of sick people come, or those bothered by ghosts. They come and bring gifts. [We] pay a price when we sing. I prepare a whole year buying blankets to give away, to give away every night. People see me when we go to big giveaways. Potlatches some other tribes call them. I get lots of things. Put it away for when I sing. In here," he said, striking his chest, "I'm a wealthy man.... In the old time I'd be taken care of by people. But the belief has gone. I think that's why I was hired here."

Wilson Wewa was obviously someone who would know about the fears the Paiute and other Native communities in Washington and Oregon seemed to have about unearthed bones.

"I believe in ghosts," he said. "I've had the visitations and prayed for people bothered by ghosts. It's a real thing in our world. Almost every culture has it. [The] educated can pass it off as something to scare kids with, but I think the ghost is the essence of life that makes you and I breathe and feel. To be absent from the body is to be present with the Lord. If the Bible is true then God's breath is there, it has to be somewhere. If [it's] not in another body, it's in this world."

His knowledge of ghosts and how to deal with them has been acknowledged by curators who have Native American bones and medicine bags in their museums. He was asked by a museum in Oregon to pray over their collection of medicine bundles; they went to him because the staff had been having problems that could not be explained by scientific means. "All the staff was white. Everyone got sick. Went to physicians, they said nothing's the matter with you—but they couldn't sleep, eat, felt physically drained." Because of stories in the newspaper about his work at a site in Oregon, he was asked to help. "They called me there to bless the collection. I went to the storage room. You could feel like you'd come from the desert to a Louisiana cave, the air was so thick. You could feel it. Had a ceremony. It all went away."

The staff told him the medicine bundles in the collection had always been stored in locked boxes, which he knew was bad for these things. "The Blackfoot take 'em out every year to renew. When they are satiated they put them away till they're needed for healing.... Those things become restless. And they do make things happen." Every year for the last four years, he'd opened the boxes and prayed over the medicine bundles inside. The employees were no longer bothered.

"They believe now. I know this Spirit Cave's bones are being played with. The Elders talked to me. I said they need to bury him but our people are at fault. Different factions want to lead in repatriation and this is causing difficulty too. I've spoken to members of the Nevada State Museum.... The older member of the Nevada State Museum is a dinosaur, not thrilled about repatriating human funerary objects, [while] his subordinates work towards that [proper] end. One day, he'll die. Maybe we'll stuff him and put him in glass here in this museum."

He threw back his head and laughed and laughed, a rich man delighting in his gold.

# Pendejo Cave

## Indiana Jones Digs Down
to the Foundation

T HE PATH TO the oldest human remains in North
America went southeast. I had to fly to El Paso,
Texas, and then drive eighty kilometers north to
get to the winter home of Scotty MacNeish in Orogrande, New
Mexico. MacNeish has the most credible pre-Clovis human remains on the continent. In 1993 he told an assembly of colleagues in Brazil that he'd found ancient hairs and friction skin
imprints at the site he calls Pendejo Cave.[1] The prints had been
made on pieces of clay between 36,000 and 12,150 BP: one
human hair, misidentified at first as bear, had produced radiocarbon dates of 12,240 and 12,370 BP. The Meadowcroft site in
Pennsylvania also has pre-Clovis dates, but James Adovasio, who
dug it, has found no human remains of such great antiquity.[2]
MacNeish's claim regarding friction skin imprints was published
in 1996 in the peer-reviewed journal *American Antiquity*,[3] as evidence that human beings were in America before the end of the
Ice Age. I wanted to look at these remains with my own two eyes.

I don't think I expected MacNeish to pull the equivalent of a
piece of the true cross out of his hat, but I did expect something
tangible at the end of this particular pathway. I had crisscrossed
two countries in search of evidence of the First Americans and
everywhere I went I had been presented only with inferences—

casts, or molds, or models, or databases, or diagrams concerning probabilities of relatedness. Those who have ancient bones didn't want to show me for fear of bringing down the wrath of the politically aroused; those who did want to show me didn't have the real thing in their possession. The Native American stories are fascinating, and suggestive, but they do not answer directly the question of the origins of the First Americans. MacNeish might not have found ancient human bones, but I was willing to settle for a hair or a fingerprint.

And there was something else I wanted from MacNeish. He had lived a long life in American archaeology. I thought he could tell me when and why the Clovis First/Bering Strait theory had taken such a firm grip on the anthropological imagination that for generations it could not be questioned without serious repercussions. He had a wonderful and shaggy reputation for calling things as he saw them. His career spanned the period from the triumph of the Clovis story to its current eclipse. He had dug all over the Americas and in Asia. He was another of those fertile American scholars who've had a hand in shaping other countries' institutions: specifically, he helped invent the archaeology program of the University of Calgary, and he was an archaeologist for Canada's National Museum. His curriculum vitae could be summed up as the archaeology of everything in the Americas, early agriculture in China, plus northwest ethnology and physical anthropology. (In his spare time, he had advised Bill Clinton through a Committee on Cultural Property.) He had a habit of creating new prehistoric narratives. He had boomed his enthusiasm over the phone. "Just back from revolutionizing archaeology in China," he'd roared. "Found the oldest known sites where rice was grown, moved the agriculture chronology back thousands of years." The combination of outrageous statements and his annoying habit of guessing right about where to dig drove MacNeish's colleagues mad.

I found myself, more by good luck than good planning, heading in the right direction on a flat desert, rolling through Wile E.

Coyote country toward the bleak hills south of Almagordo. The road to Roswell was to my right. There were dark and jagged mountains off to my left, so mean, so rough they looked like the sharp back teeth of some junkyard dog. After the road left behind the last monster-home suburb on El Paso's backside and passed through Fort Bliss, it went straight northeast. There were no towns, no gas stations, just miles and miles of creosote and yucca and glittery red sand. Flashes of light on my left showed air force jets squatting in the desert sun, ready to drop the Big One.

Some 200 million years ago this whole landscape was covered by a vast inland sea. A line of cliffs appeared on my right. Straight ahead, small brown mountains popped up out of the sand. Finally, there was a sign that said Orogrande. On my right were two gas stations. On the left, something called the My Place Bar, a false-fronted single-story building that looked as if it hadn't been touched by a paintbrush since 1952.

MacNeish lived in a rented house just a block off the highway, a very odd little house, halfway between a backwoods cottage and something worse. This was the winter home of the Andover Foundation for Archaeological Research, which MacNeish started so he could fund his own work. As I approached, there was a snappy wind. The gate was shut, with a bare electrical wire twined around it, and something made of metal creaked and groaned. A single chair was set out in the barren garden. I was having second thoughts when MacNeish's editor, Jane Libby, came to the door, a smallish woman with silver hair, a shy smile, dangling turquoise earrings. And then there was the legend himself, welcoming me into the tiny living room with its battered, wood-burning heater, its rec-room-from-hell furniture. A door gaped on a bedroom giving a view of an atrocious red-velvet-upholstered headboard. This was not the sort of place one expected to find a scholar honored in the U.S., Canada, Mexico and China.

MacNeish stood in front of me with his legs braced and his head thrown back, like some kind of bantam rooster—or an aged but heterosexual Truman Capote. He was tiny, with a large egg-shaped head, a Fu Manchu goatee, and liver spots and the tremor of age upon his hands. He wore a large Panama hat, which he removed only to scratch his forehead. Straggles of thin gray hair trailed over his collar. His hands were constantly in motion, fingers shooting straight out, then contracting, patting, smoothing. He was dressed in a too-large green checked jacket over a greenish buttoned sweater and baggy brown pants. He smiled a snaggle-toothed grin, then shuffled into the kitchen.

We sat together at the table beside a big window with a view of the bitter yard and the road. Libby disappeared into a back room, but she was ever with us. She was editing MacNeish's forthcoming book on Pendejo Cave, working over the chapters submitted by scholars who had studied particular aspects of the finds. She cursed and fulminated at their footnote errors as MacNeish spun his tale. It was hard to believe, looking at him, that some of his colleagues thought he was the inspiration for Indiana Jones. But the story he told made it plausible.

Richard Stockton MacNeish was born in 1918 in New York City's Presbyterian Hospital, into a rich and social family. His father was a mathematics professor, his mother was educated at Vassar. His mother's eighteenth-century forebear, for whom he was named, had been a member of the first Princeton graduating class and was the first alumnus to be elected a trustee. (He was also a member of the Continental Congress and was one of the signers of the Declaration of Independence.) Right after he was born, MacNeish was written down for Princeton and one of its clubs. His mother died of a brain tumor when he was thirteen, and his father later remarried. MacNeish grew up in the plush suburb of Scarsdale, where he began his revolt against all things bourgeois and bigoted. "My best friends were Jewish, Negro and Italian."

He became interested in archaeology by accident. He went to a private school at White Plains, New York, where he was told to pick a history project from a list the teacher supplied. He chose the Maya, because it started with the letter M, like his name. He did nothing on it till the night before it was due. Then, with the help of his sister and his father, he ransacked the *National Geographic* and a science newsletter. He won first prize. His mother's father, who had made a fortune selling clocks in the U.S., went to Mexico the following year and made his way to Yucatán to see the Mayan ruin at Chichén Itzá. The great archaeologist Alfred Kidder was working on the site: his grandfather talked to Kidder and came home with stories. By the time MacNeish was a teenager, he was saying at dinner parties that he intended to be an archaeologist.

"I wrote to Kidder and asked for a job as a water boy," he said. "He said if I studied hard I could be an archaeologist." All the way through high school MacNeish read everything he could on the Maya, thrilling to new discoveries, but particularly learning about people "that weren't like us."

He was not looking forward, however, to studying at Princeton. It didn't have much of an archaeology department and there was the race problem. He was on a track team in high school, and there was an African-American man on his relay. They went to a meet at Princeton, which wouldn't let his teammate in. "I got teed off at Princeton." So, he deliberately flunked half his college boards and decided he wouldn't go to college at all. His grandfather told him he could make a million dollars selling clocks, as he was doing, and by the time he was thirty he'd have enough money to do all the archaeology he wanted to as a gentleman amateur. But his father wanted him to get a good education. "He intrigued against me," said MacNeish. Through a geologist at Brooklyn College, where he taught, his father heard about a dig going on at Rainbow Bridge on the Navajo reservation in Monument Valley, Arizona. His father told him he could get a job as a mule packer on the expedition for the experience.

MacNeish was eighteen years old. He crossed the country by thumb. "I took no money from my family. It was fifteen dollars a month, never saw a mule before in my life. The agreement was I'd mule-pack three days and do three days of archaeology."

He was the lowest man in the hierarchy. There was a Navajo teenager named Gerry Little Salts who also worked the mules. He pulled on MacNeish all the tricks possible to play on greenhorns. One evening as it was starting to get dark, MacNeish, the track man, suggested they run the last five miles home. "The Navajo was pooped. Now we had peaceful coexistence."

In general the Native Americans he met were treated miserably. The Navajo still lived in hogans and the U.S. government had just begun to hire liberal Indian agents who would provide schools and hospitals. On weekends MacNeish took Kidder's book on the canyons of the southwest and went out in search of sites. On the dig were older men on their way to careers in archaeology at UCLA and Harvard. They decided he had to go to college. So his high school track coach helped him get into Colgate. He arrived that fall with a loan of $150 from his father for tuition, and got himself a job picking up dry cleaning. He also ran track and wrestled and won a boxing championship. "I was a socialist, a Roosevelt Democrat. That was big trouble in a Republican family...I was gonna do it myself and to hell with you. And I did. Eventually."

The enrollment at Colgate was 1,000. His classes were tiny. He learned science method and how it applied to archaeology both in school and by working with a friend on a site under the supervision of William Ritchie, who dug in upper New York State, and later become the state archaeologist of New York. It was at Colgate that MacNeish was taught that the First Americans came to the New World over the Bering Strait. It never occurred to him to question this. "My good professor told me [the way] it was and that's the way it was. I was respectful of early archaeological colleagues."

MacNeish went back to Rainbow Bridge the next summer as a veteran and this time as a driver of a fleet of station wagons provided by the Ford Motor Company. The team left from the

Explorers' Club on New York's Central Park West. They drove to Mesa Verde, Colorado, in a ten-day trip, bringing along sixty boys who'd paid $1,000 for the privilege of being slave labor on an archaeological adventure. They slept in schools and parks along the way. MacNeish was nineteen and a straw boss. Flagstaff was a full day's journey from the camp. When he went into town to buy dry goods, Navajos would hitch a ride. He learned to speak a little Navajo. His nickname was Notiasis, which he said loosely translates as Little Cotton Tail, "cause I could run like hell and [had] a white rear end."

Various experts came to the site. He met Ernst Antevs, a Pleistocene geologist who worked intermittently for the Geological Survey of Canada and had been working out the dates when the last glaciation ended. Antevs proposed that the Mackenzie Valley was the route the First Americans must have used to enter the continent. He believed man arrived in the Americas when the glaciers retreated and couldn't have come earlier because the ice blocked the way. He believed there was nothing in the New World earlier than 10,000, MacNeish said.

What was the proof?

"It was the word of God," MacNeish thundered.

But MacNeish also heard an argument between Antevs and Kirk Bryan of Harvard who had a different view. That was the first time he witnessed conflict between experts on what the evidence was and what it meant.

On that second trip he also learned something of what human remains meant to the Navajo. The traditional practice was to burn a hogan in which a person had died because the spirit would trouble anyone who lived in it afterwards. A road crew working in the area had come across burials. MacNeish was assigned to dig them up. He had Navajo people working with him. The second day on this job he "flipped out an Indian bone." The Navajo took off. "Last time we saw a Navajo," he said. "They had nothing to do with any dead. If you died in a hogan, it would be burned. The spirits were there." This fear had serious consequences. It was well known to the Navajo that people who went into hospital sometimes died there. Hospitals were therefore places filled with restless spirits. Once, the crew decided to salvage the timbers they needed to build a shelter from an abandoned hogan. There was a terrible accident. The hogan's roof collapsed on a Navajo boy and it crushed his chest.

"I had to drive him to hospital in the city. He was in bad shape. My boy said, 'Don't go there, it's full of spirits.'… We drove up to the hospital.… They said get a stretcher. We put him on it. Walked through the door and he died of terror."

As MacNeish understood it, this fear of the spirits of the dead was part of the larger Athabascan tradition. The Najavo and Apache are related to the Athabascan people of the Northwest Territories and Alaska. Anthropologists believe they migrated to the U.S. Southwest within the last thousand years. The languages are very close. "It's clear enough in the speech that when I went to the Mackenzie I could exchange words with the Slaveys of Great Slave Lake. And they have the same beliefs," said MacNeish.[4]

That summer Alfred Kidder, the great man of Mayan archaeology and the same man MacNeish had written to and asked for a job, came to inspect the dig. Kidder by then had turned his attention to the U.S. Southwest and had run an expedition in Pecos that, according to MacNeish, was "the beginning of scientific archaeology in the Southwest." Of course MacNeish had already bragged to everyone on the site that he knew Kidder. As the day grew closer, he became more and more concerned that he would be found out. The whole crew gathered together for Kidder's inspection, as if they were in the army and he was a visiting general. "I must have leaned. He walked back and said, 'Don't I know you?' That was the greatest moment of my life to date."

He returned to Colgate the next fall, but had been told that if he wanted to go to graduate school the best place for archaeology was the University of Chicago. The Oriole Institute there was run by Dr. Fay Cooper-Cole, who had dug at Persepolis for years. The university had a summer field school in southern Illinois. Chicago was a Johnny-come-lately in anthropology and archaeology, "but good dirt archaeology came out of Chicago and the Midwest," according to MacNeish, primarily because of Roosevelt's Works Progress Administration, or WPA. American archaeology was one of the public works done by those thrown out of work by the Depression. These projects were run by graduate students. According to MacNeish, this program was "the birth of great archaeology in the United States." (The physicist Fermi was at Chicago too, building the first nuclear reactor under the football stadium, which would lead both to the Manhattan Project and, in 1949, to the development of radiocarbon dating by W.F. Libby.)

The big thing at Chicago was its summer field school. Students learned archaeology by digging a real site under supervision. The University of Chicago had bought land which harbored Native American burial mounds and had set up housing nearby for students. By 1941, MacNeish had gotten so much practice he was able to run an archaeological project on his own, supervising his own crew of WPA men.

The army called him in 1942. His draft number was twelve. He got a year's leave of absence from the draft to write his doctoral preliminaries. He wrote five exams over a six-day period but had spent at least ten days living "on speed" when he walked in to take his army physical. "They said be there 6 a.m. Monday to take the draft. They said Chicago Commie draft dodgers [are] going in the army. I didn't."

He flunked his army physical. He only passed three out of his five doctoral preliminaries and had to retake two. He figured the army would ask him to retake his physical eventually, so he decided to do WPA field work until the army caught up with him. In May, 1944, on an African-American tenant farmer's field in

Illinois, he found a site close to some burial mounds. The find was bewildering. The mounds were supposed to be Archaic, a period that was thought to have ended at 5000 BP. He had evidence the mounds had been used for more than 2,000 years. But he found the first Folsom fluted points east of the Mississippi on the site nearby. He had been taught that Folsom points were made about 10,000 BP, just after Clovis, but MacNeish concluded the Archaic period started right after Folsom. This was considered heretical.

The popular idea about these Midwestern mounds was that they were extensions of a Mexican culture. The great pyramid at Cahokia (near St. Louis, Missouri) was as big as the Mexican Pyramid of the Sun. On the site in Illinois, pyramid mounds had been built on top of older mounds. "We found feathered serpents, shell gorgets, pipes like in Mexico."

By then evidence of Mexican culture had been found in Arkansas, Texas and Louisiana, including the buzzard cult, tripod vessels, certain bottle shapes and special engravings with feathered serpents. He wanted to find the pathway of that cultural expansion out of northern Mexico. He had a hunch about the Gulf coast and Tamaulipas State. It was about 500 kilometers from the border town of Brownsville, Texas, to Tampico, a Mexican port town on the Gulf coast. This area, mountainous, dry, populated mainly by bandits, was not known to have had "civilized," meaning urbanized, Native Americans. It was southern Mexico that had the pyramids.

He married a Canadian studying at Chicago. She joined him on his first Mexican field expedition. She was a tough field worker, which was good because they took "a Dodge where no Dodge had been before," to Diablo Canyon. "It was tough country full of rattlesnakes," said MacNeish. There were also caves there full of early spear points. This evidence regarding early man in the Americas eventually became so interesting to him that the Mexican cultural pathway to the U.S., his doctoral subject, became almost a side issue.

In 1946 he took up a one-year fellowship at the University of Michigan to work on the origins of Iroquoians. In the course of this research, he went up to the National Museum in Ottawa to look at Iroquoian potsherds in their collection. He found the anthropology department in disarray. Diamond Jenness, its distinguished former head, had resigned and been replaced by Douglas Leishmann, who asked MacNeish what he was doing in Mexico.

"I said, it's like the Mackenzie River. They say [early man] migrated through there, but no one has gone to look. I'm interested in exploring."

Leishmann took him to lunch and told him he'd talked to the head curator of the museum, Dr. Frederick Alcock,[5] about him. "To sponsor a project in Mexico?" MacNeish had asked, hopefully. No, said Leishmann, about MacNeish exploring the Mackenzie River valley for Canada. He informed MacNeish that Alcock would like to have a word with him. MacNeish considered his position: he and his wife had no permanent jobs. On the other hand, he knew nothing about the Mackenzie. He excused himself and ran to the library. He asked for a map of the Mackenzie River region. "Here's the Great Slave, Yellowknife, Fort Simpson. No roads. They had four arrowheads in the National Museum from the Northwest Territories. That was it."

At his meeting with Alcock he was told there was great interest in the north and it would be wonderful to have him there, but there was one little glitch: he was "a bloody American." So MacNeish forgot about it. He went back to Michigan, finished his fellowship, and tried to figure out how to get the money to go back to Mexico and dig those ancient caves. He took on salvage archaeology jobs in the summers in Pennsylvania and in Kentucky, right in the middle of Hatfield and McCoy feud country, for which he was paid the sum of $400 a month for three months. He could go to Tamaulipas for a year on that.

"I handed back my thesis to Chicago and got my Ph.D. I was looking for a job but I wanted to dig Diablo Cave. There is stuff that's 20,000 BP in it. Also Lapera Cave way up Canyon Diablo has baskets, mummies, everything up in the top." There wasn't a lot to choose from in the way of assistants, so he trained the people he could find. "I'm training bandits to be archaeologists."

On his second exploration of the caves of Tamaulipas he found not only Folsom-type points, evidence of early man, but also, underneath that Folsom level, and mixed in with the bones of extinct Ice Age horses, large choppers (rough cutting tools) made out of big pebbles. Tools like these had also been seen on digs in Southeast Asia. In his view, this was obvious evidence of cultures in the Americas before Clovis and Folsom. Alex Kreiger of the University of Texas at Austin had already toured in South America and come back saying that man was there much earlier than in North America and that the major tools of these early cultures were not projectile points. He went to see Kreiger, slept on the floor of his lab.

He ran digs at Diablo Cave and Lapera Cave at the same time. Lapera was fifty kilometers up Diablo Canyon on foot. The money was running out, no one had had a bath for two weeks, nothing interesting was turning up under the top layer at either place, so he decided to close the digs. He walked the fifty kilometers from Diablo Cave down the canyon at night through streams up to his neck to make it into town where he was to meet his assistants from the Lapera dig. They were supposed to have the Jeeps packed ready to go. He found the lead assistant from Lapera waiting for him.

"At the bottom of the Archaic strata they'd found tiny corn cobs, as big as my little finger," said MacNeish, holding his hand up to the light to indicate. This was the earliest known form of domesticated corn: he'd stumbled on one of the earliest sites of agriculture then known in the Americas. Just after he found the corn, he got a letter with a blank application for a job with the Canadian civil service. The National Museum had decided to hire a bloody American after all. The application had to be signed by a Canadian member of parliament, or a notary. He found a Mexican notary—who didn't read English.

"So I'm now looking for early man in the Mackenzie River," MacNeish said with a grin.

Until MacNeish went to the Mackenzie on June 20, 1949, there had been no archaeological survey done to support or disprove the widely held theory that the First Americans entered the continent down this valley.[6] When MacNeish was in high school, the ice-free corridor theory had already been put forward as the only plausible route of entry, yet no archaeologists had toured the Mackenzie and tested it. I had read some of the early work on this subject before I went to see MacNeish and I was amazed at how quickly this early theory and the few observations that supported it had become pseudo facts. In 1933, Diamond Jenness published a book called *The American Aborigines*, a collection of papers given by him and others at the Fifth Pacific Science Congress.[7] The book included W.A. Johnston's survey of what was then known, from the study of the geology, about where the Ice Age glaciers had flowed and when. Much on the shapes and life spans of the glacial ice masses was surmised, but little was known. In this matter of human entry to the continent, archaeology followed on the geology. As W.A. Johnston put it in his paper:

> The geological history of North America during Quaternary time may have an important bearing on the questions of when, and by what route, early man migrated to this continent. The particular phases of the geological history which have a direct bearing on these questions are: the extent of the ice-sheets at different times during the Pleistocene; the climatic and other conditions during inter-glacial time and during the retreat of the last ice-sheets; the possibility of a land bridge connecting Siberia and Alaska; migrations of plants and animals during the Quaternary; and the time that has elapsed since the disappearance of the last ice-sheets....

There appears to be no evidence of the presence of man in North America in interglacial time, as is the case in Europe, so that the main questions are whether conditions favorable for migration existed during the final retreat of the ice-sheets and how long ago migration may have occurred.[8]

It is important to remember that there was no radiocarbon or uranium thorium or any other physical or chemical test known in 1933 (other than estimates made through examining soil deposits) to date the retreat and expansion of the ice. Geological time frames were inferred from the depth of stratigraphic layers of soil in cliff-face cuts, by counting annual layers of sediments in lake bottoms, or counting annually laid down layers of clay. It must also be remembered that at the time Jenness and his colleagues were writing, almost no archaeological surveying had been done anywhere in the Americas by which one could rule out the presence of human beings in the interglacial period. To assume that the lack of evidence of early man or his precursors meant they were never in the Americas was a violation of a basic rule of evidence in science. The same book also carried a paper by Franz Boas who similarly claimed that no evidence of man's precursors in the New World must mean that man originated in the Old World. As Boas put it: "The present status of paleontological knowledge leaves us no doubt that the American race cannot have originated on this continent."[9] This was the same as a man declaring after searching the first few inches of a forty-foot haystack that there could not possibly be a needle below.

Johnston went on to write in his paper that there were great disputes about where and when the edges of glaciers ran. He chose to rely heavily on Ernst Antevs, who had studied annually-laid-down clay layers, or varves, in the Great Lakes region, to establish when the ice retreated. "Probably the best general idea of the time involved is given by Antevs, whose remarkably thorough and outstanding work on the seasonally banded or varved, late-glacial clays has supplied the only reliable data for determining the rate of retreat of the last ice-sheets in North America," Johnston wrote, a method picked up and used in Europe.[10] Antevs had come up with the vague number of 40,000 years, give or take 10,000, for the time when the Laurentide ice sheet was at its maximum. On this very thin base Johnston founded his belief that the Mackenzie River valley was probably open for migration 25,000 to 30,000 years ago.[11]

Such false certainties were now dissolving under the onslaught of better science. Since the 1980s, the Geological Survey of Canada has been producing wonderful work on the surface geology of the Mackenzie Valley and the surrounding mountains, showing exactly where the ice sheets were and when. By the time of my conversation with MacNeish in the late winter of 1999, Alejandra Duk-Rodkin, a geologist with the survey, had already concluded that the Mackenzie River never drained into the Arctic until after the end of the last period of glaciation: for countless millennia it had run instead out of the Mackenzie Mountains and west to Hudson Bay. To use one of MacNeish's favored phrases, this blew a hole in any theory of a Mackenzie Valley migration at the end of the Ice Age—until 10,000 BP there had been no river valley carved through those mountains.[12]

In addition, a Queen's University graduate student in geography had taken sediments out of fifteen lakes in southern and northern Alberta in the theorized ice-free corridor. The sediment cores he pulled out of these closed-in basin lakes forced him to infer that the landscape around them had been extremely unstable even at 10,000 BP, after which everything suddenly changed. Until 10,000 BP the lake bottoms were full of inorganic sediments blown into the water off hills subject to large-scale erosion. He argued that people "could not have entered the ice free corridor until after 10,000 years BP because the game animals upon which they subsist would not have entered a region which did not have enough plant material to support the herd."[13]

But in the 1940s, MacNeish was guided by the generally accepted geological/geographical framework of the day. The narrative, as he understood it, was that man followed beast across the Bering Strait, across the dry and therefore snow-free mountain tops of the Alaskan interior and down the Mackenzie River valley corridor to the plains. It was his job to find the evidence to make it so. On the other hand, he already believed that the Clovis First theory was wrong. He believed human beings had made this trek long before the end of the last ice age.

"I go from Tamaulipas to Ottawa to Edmonton to Yellowknife," laughed MacNeish. "I'm sitting there on the twentieth of June, a Canadian civil servant looking for early man in the Mackenzie River." He was sitting in a bar. A trapper named Sam Otto, in from the Barren Lands, wandered over. He told MacNeish he collected arrowheads and where he found them. MacNeish said, fine, let's go there. After this one trip in a canoe, MacNeish quadrupled the National Museum's collection of Northwest Territories arrowheads. MacNeish had a budget of $1,700 and he managed to go 42,000 miles by hitchhiking plane rides with local bush pilots. "I don't think I paid for more than one."

He worked for the Canadian National Museum for the next twelve years. At Great Bear Lake he found a 10,000 BP site with spear points similar to some from the southwestern U.S. He worked the Yukon and the Arctic coast and found a stratified site at Firth River (a site much disputed). But nothing was earlier than 10,000 BP. He left the museum in 1961.

"I got crucified," he bellowed, "by a senile senator from Saskatchewan."

Who was that?

He searched his memory, smacked his forehead in frustration. "Don't tell me I forgot the son-of-a-bitch's name," he yelled.

Hazen Argue, Liberal MP during the Diefenbaker Conservative majority government, had bombarded the secretary of state and the minister of northern affairs and natural resources with hostile questions about MacNeish, starting with how had MacNeish, an American, become a Canadian civil servant when the law required civil servants to be Canadian or British subjects? (Answer: the privy council set the rule aside so he could be hired.) Argue's questions delved into how much time MacNeish spent in Mexico while on the National Museum's payroll (he continued to dig there for the museum, and for himself when he had vacation), whether he had served in any armed forces during World War II, and how many other Americans he had brought into the National Museum. MacNeish believes that these questions were fed to Argue by a disgruntled Canadian employee of the museum, a man named Tom Lee. Lee had found the old site on Manitoulin island called Sheguiandah, and he claimed to have evidence of a culture that existed there 70,000 years ago. Lee resigned from his position, stating that he would not serve under Dr. MacNeish, "whose professional competence he was not prepared to accept," according to one minister's reply to one of Argue's questions.[14]

"He is my Frankenstein monster," said MacNeish. He had met Lee at Chicago, and taken him along to University of Michigan and then, even though Lee did not get his doctorate, brought him along to the National Museum. Lee blamed MacNeish for refusing to print some of his controversial findings on Sheguiandah, and accused him of suppression when he couldn't get more budget money for further research (Lee had failed to produce sufficient written reports).

Eventually, MacNeish's wife left him and he too resigned from the museum to move to the University of Calgary, where an oil man had funded the establishment of a department devoted to archaeology; MacNeish became the departmental chair. When he left Calgary to get back to doing archaeology he joined the Peabody Foundation in Massachusetts, which supported his search for the beginnings of agriculture in the Americas. He focused on Ayacucho, Peru, and a place called Pikimachay—a cave almost 60 meters across and 20 meters high, with big rocks fallen off the roof. It was at first believed that the roof had collapsed about 10,000 BP.

Underneath the rockfall he found the bones of an extinct giant sloth, fifteen feet high, which had been killed by people. "We had spear points stuck in him," he said. He found three different pre-Clovis layers. These produced radiocarbon dates in the range of 12,000 to 22,000 years BP. The top levels, the youngest ones, had prismatic blades and leaf-shaped spear points. The bottom was mainly big choppers and bone projectile points.

MacNeish toured various South American sites in the 1970s and noted that the French had been enticed to the Lagoa Santa region of Brazil, that a Brazilian was working at rock art sites in a place called Piaui, and that none of them paid much attention to the Clovis First theory. Then he ran into Tom Dillehay at a meeting in 1982 in Vancouver. "He came up with a cigar box and said, 'I dug these associated with mastodon bones. Tell me if they're artifacts.' He brought out flakes. I said, not sure. He brought out a flake stuck in a wooden handle. No doubt about that. I became an early backer of Dillehay." MacNeish became more and more convinced that what he saw in Venezuela and Peru and Chile were real ancient sites of early man. He saw Tom Lynch's site at Guitarrero Cave, which Lynch did not believe was a pre-Clovis site in spite of its ancient dates. MacNeish disagreed, and came away convinced that Lynch had misinterpreted the stratigraphy. Which brought us to MacNeish's own dig, Pendejo Cave.

He found it after he went back to the U.S. Southwest to look for early agriculture. He dug for three or four years at Las Cruces, New Mexico. By then he had put together the Andover Foundation as a means to take in money and spend it on research. He consulted with the archaeologist for the U.S. Army at Fort Bliss. The army had to salvage archaeological sites in the area that it intended to use for troop maneuvers or the firing of live ammunition. One of the army archaeologist's assistants had been in a cave while they were setting up a laser artillery range. MacNeish was told they'd found sandals.

MacNeish pointed out back, beyond the house. "We went across that escarpment over there and found this cave, called

Pintada. It was full of Archaic spear points." There were pic-tographs as well. Around the corner there was a deeper cave, Pendejo. It had corn and baskets on the top. "It looked worth testing. We got permission from the army to salvage before the soldiers looted the cave. The army put in a road from this side to the caves through a Pleistocene lake basin, up through a long canyon."

The digging began in 1990. He worked both caves at once. Two weeks into the dig, he was in Pintada having lunch when his supervisor at Pendejo came bounding over. He had found the toe bones of an extinct horse that turned out to be 25,000 BP. And then they found flint chipped off stone tools, worked bones, and bones of animals that looked as if they'd been butchered by human beings. The site turned out to have twenty layers of extinct animals. In the second season MacNeish began to pull together a multidisciplinary team, as Dillehay had done, to study specific aspects of the evidence. He also asked Paleo-Indian experts to have a look—he called on C. Vance Haynes, Paul Martin, Ervin Taylor and others. He invited Dennis Stanford of the Smith-sonian, too, but he never came.

C. Vance Haynes gave MacNeish a prescription for how to prove the worth of the site. "He said, 'I think the rocks fell off the roof, it's a great paleontological sequence. The burned floors are due to lightning. I don't think the patches are fireplaces. You can test.'"

MacNeish and his colleagues did the tests Haynes suggested. They showed that the rocks were not roof fall but foreign to the cave. Thermoluminescence tests showed the fire had burned from inside the cave out, not the reverse. And then they made their great find: the slab linings of fire pits in the cave had finger-prints burned into the clay.

There were about thirty of these firepits. The ones in the middle of the sequence, which dated to around 30,000 BP, had been lined with clay. Whoever made them had dug a hole and plastered the edge of the fireplace, then built a fire in it, at which point the clay turned to brick. But since they had packed it in with their hands, there were prints of human skin fired into the clay.

"We have four sets of fingerprints," said MacNeish. "We had an article in *American Antiquity* on the fingerprints. We also have human hair."

The direct dates on the human hair were 12,240 and 12,400 BP. He had sent samples of the hairs to the lab of Mark Stoneking at Penn State to have them try to extract mitochondrial DNA. MacNeish said that the mtDNA of the four hairs did not have any of the lineages considered characteristic of Native Americans. "Just like Kennewick," he said. "We have DNA that is not of the four types of American Indians."

"Dr. MacNeish," I said, "there were no results on the mtDNA analysis of Kennewick."

He brushed that off.

I asked if I could see the report by the person who did the extraction and analysis of the mtDNA for him. He didn't have it with him. His colleague Donald Chrisman, who was the first author on the *American Antiquity* paper, had organized that work. Later Chrisman faxed me the report. It had been written on October 21, 1996, by Anne Stone, who was then still at Pennsylvania State's department of anthropology. Her report referred to two hairs. Mitochondrial DNA was successfully precipitated and it was then subjected to primers specific to four sites that defined the four Native American lineages known at that time:

> Neither [hair] possessed any of the characteristic mutations found in the four primary clusters of Native American lineages. This may indicate lineages not included in the four primary clusters or contamination of the samples by non–Native American DNA.

This was not exactly the unambiguous result MacNeish was trumpeting. His colleague, Chrisman, had sent two other hair samples to Merriwether's lab for testing, but Merriwether hadn't got around to doing the work yet.

MacNeish was pressing ahead with a book on Pendejo Cave for University of New Mexico Press. It was going to be huge, almost as big as Dillehay's, with twenty-five chapters and three sections dealing with everything from the geology to the botany—they had taken 25,000 plant remains and 40,000 animal bones out of the cave. The last three or four chapters were to be written by MacNeish on the history of early man.

He was getting tired and so was I. I wanted to see what he had in the way of artifacts and specifically, hair and the fingerprints.

Couldn't show me, he said. The artifacts were mostly in the possession of the U.S. Army and he didn't think they'd haul them out for me. He could show me a few things but it would have to be tomorrow.

The road in front of his house just sort of ran into the desert—petering out into a dirt track that aimed straight toward a gap in an escarpment far in the distance. He'd shown me after lunch at the My Place Bar that Pendejo Cave was off in that direction. I had a strong urge to just drive over and look for myself.

Couldn't I just take a peek? I asked MacNeish.

Well, he didn't think I'd make it very far. Hadn't I noticed the fence? That was a firing range back there.

I drove back to El Paso for the night.

MacNeish and I had argued back and forth over how and when the First Americans got here. He still believed that people had followed herds over the Bering Strait and down into the rest of the Americas, but he thought it had happened way, way back in time, more than 50,000 years ago, when the ice had retracted and the way was open into the heart of the continent. This was why he thought Niéde Guidon's finds in Brazil and Tom Dillehay's extremely early dates at Monte Verde were so important. This was why the long sequence of dates he had at Pendejo Cave was so meaningful.

The problem with this thesis, of course, was that when the glaciers were small on land, the Bering Strait was submerged by the Pacific and the Arctic—much of the water previously locked up as glaciers had sloshed back into the oceans. People and animals would not have been able to walk across. So, I asked him, did they use boats?

MacNeish didn't think that was impossible. He knew that people had found their way to Australia around 50,000 BP, and they must have crossed open water to do so. It was no big thing, he thought, to cross the Bering Strait in a boat. Hell, when he'd flown around up there, you could see across to the Russian side on a good day. Diamond Jenness had done his prime work as an ethnologist on the people who lived on Diomede Island, a little speck of land in the middle of the Strait. The Japanese, and their precursors the Jomon, could well have made it across to the Americas—they were deep-sea fishers. And the physical anthropology sort of leaned that way. The ancient human remains found at Zhoukoudien in China looked more Native American than modern Chinese, there was no doubt about that.

Well, I said, what about the Atlantic side? What about Dennis Stanford's idea that the Clovis people were the descendants of European Solutreans who had somehow made their way across the Atlantic?

"That's all crap," he said forcefully.

I presented myself again at Orogrande the following morning. Same wind. Same sand. Same sun. Same sweater on his back and Panama hat on his head. This time, he had set out on the kitchen table several boxes bulging with files holding the incomplete chapters of his book, and a few white cardboard boxes with all kinds of tidbits wrapped in tinfoil or placed in plastic bags.

He also had a pair of garden gloves that he put on to handle his materials.

"Okay!" he announced, settling himself to the task.

He began to fumble with plastic bags, looking for this specimen and that. I readied my camera, anxious to record the obvious signs of human activity in America during the peak of the Ice Age. He pulled out little dry things that looked like sticks, some with pointy ends, as if they'd been gnawed by something, or possibly, just possibly, whittled. These little objects had been turned over to him by the botanist quite recently. The botanist had been unable to determine their species because the bark had been scraped off. A lot of these items he had just identified as human-altered artifacts. So the critics hadn't even seen this yet.

There were twigs, sticks, various pieces of worked wood. He showed me wood that in his opinion was cut, which meant a back and forth movement, as distinct from incising or chopping. He had graphed these small pieces of wood according to the zone they were found in, and these zones corresponded to dates.

"Zone M is 41,000 to 50,000 BP."

So these little pieces of wood came from those layers? Uh-huh, he said. I clicked my camera, like a tourist visiting another world. Had he dated the wood?

No, he had dated the layers. "They could be dated," he said. "Whether we need that, I don't know."

"These are the ones whittled to a point," he said, and showed me. But to get them out of the bag he took off the garden gloves, and while he was showing me the pieces of wood in his hand, he said he should use the gloves if he wanted to get a date. "Shouldn't put my sweat on it," he said. But it was too late. The sweat was there.

With a magnifying glass he pointed out the features of sticks whittled and found at the Clovis level. He fingered through some more bags. Huh! he said, as if puzzled by something. He turned on the overhead light. This, he said, is a 51,000-year-old piece of whittled wood.

It looked like a gnawed twig to me. Yes, he had considered

rodents as the culprits, but he and his colleagues could tell the difference between gnawed and cut wood. The rodent holes had all been marked so that they took note of any breaks in the strata caused by their burrowing.

We agreed that the light was not good enough to really show these cut marks to advantage.

"Yeah!" he said. "Okay. Here's a doozy. They've shaved this to a point and pointed the point. This is zone H—33,000 B.P."

I snapped a picture. The day was turning all soft and a little muggy. I was not able to see what he saw.

We came to the end of the pieces of wood in the boxes. He had no other artifacts. The clay, the hair, the other things, were all with the army. He had only pictures. He hauled out the pictures of the fingerprints first, and called to his editor for the section of the manuscript dealing with them. It was duly produced. This was going to be chapter nineteen, he said. The authors are Donald Chrisman, R.S. MacNeish, Jamshed Mavalwala (the expert on fingerprints) and, to my surprise, Howard Savage, now deceased, formerly the keeper of the zooarchaeology laboratory at University of Toronto, where the 6,000-year-old Milton-Thomazi skeleton had once resided under the mummified heads.

"The first thing of importance is, are these anthropoid or some other animal? The difference between us and anthropoids is that between each groove [of a fingerprint], we have sweat pores. No other animal has this. Here are the fingerprints blown up." With the help of the little arrows on the photographs I could see the sweat pores.

"It was taken off nodules of clay about two inches long, excavated on the sides of the fireplaces. These tiny pieces came out. They brought them to me in the laboratory. There are sixteen of these."

There were thirty-two fire pits found with clay on the bottom on which fires had been built. The pits yielded charcoal, which had been dated; not all provided fingerprints. Three of the prints came from zone K, which dated between 36,000 and 35,000 BP.

MacNeish pulled up another picture of a strange little puff of clay with marks in it, a could-be-this, could-be-that kind of thing. In the right light it looked like a little bird. He believes it is an effigy. "These lines," he said, pointing, "were incised when the clay was wet. They carried the clay from the arroyo to the cave. Bears and gophers don't drag around lumps of clay, nor do they rock-line fireplaces."

He called to Libby to bring him the chapter on the hair. "We have extinct lion or cat hair, giant sloth hair, short-faced bear hair, rabbit hair and human hair. This human hair dates from the strata coinciding with the period 14,000 BP."

He had another photo, showing a piece of hair fired into a piece of clay. "19,130 years ago," he said. There was a photo of the same thing at higher magnification. He had hairs in cross-section, lateral views, and under magnification sufficient to show the differences between human, bear and sloth hair. I found it hard to tell the difference.

"There's no doubt they are human hairs," he said. "The police in Ontario agree with us." He gave me the name of a person at Ontario's Centre of Forensic Science who had given this opinion. One hair had been dated by University of California, Riverside, at 12,400 BP. It was this authenticated human hair, properly dated, that had then been given to Anne Stone for mtDNA work.

Then there were the textiles. There were almost a thousand pieces of baskets, sandals, cordage, knots, string. He had one knot from zone C2 that corresponded to 14,000 BP. That was the most ancient specimen. He also had a piece of twisted and folded fiber. There was also an interesting study on a "51,000-year-old worked *Bison antiquus* humerus." They found this bone sticking out of zone M. It had broken in half. Another piece was found lying under a rock with charcoal on top dating to 51,000 BP. They took the bones out and found the two pieces fit together. "There are four uses of this buffalo bone by human beings. Lying on top of the bone was a stone chopper."

And finally, there was the geological examination of the area. The caves were in a canyon cut into the escarpment. There were terraces on the rocks, which showed different water levels. There was a wet period around 37,000 BP, then a dry period, then wet again around 18,000. There was a very large lake during the wet periods and a series of little lakes in front of the escarpment during the dry periods. Pine and oak had once covered the mountains. Then it all became very desiccated between 9000 and 7000 BP, just as in the Great Basin in Nevada.

In the closing chapters of his book MacNeish had made a map showing how the First Americans came into the continent and when. A fat arrow came over the Bering Strait, down through the corridor along the Mackenzie River Valley, and stopped right at Pendejo Cave.

He was exhausted. He sat down hard in his chair. I snapped a picture of him. MacNeish in his lair.

Lunch again at the My Place Bar. MacNeish, Libby and me. The cook, Al, had a squared bushy beard. He wore jeans and a jean shirt and a dirty apron. My counter stool tilted sideways. Yesterday the specials had been soggy enchiladas and refried beans or a hamburger with green salsa. Now it was meatloaf and taters, the taters mashed into a milky mound, cratered to receive the sacred brown gravy. The talk was of the way things used to be around these parts, in the days of the cattle wars. This was Billy the Kid country. According to Al, Billy used to steal cows from one rancher and sell them to the rancher's neighbors. No one could handle the Apaches, who dug themselves into a dead end canyon out there, and "suckered in the U.S. Army," according to MacNeish.

Which brought us to the connection between the Apache and the people of Great Slave Lake. Al was a blank screen at the mention of Great Slave, which, when I thought about it, was reasonable.

What would a man in southern New Mexico know about a lake 8,000 thousand kilometers north, a universe away? How could Athabaskan speakers have traveled all the way down here, or was it the other way around? And more to the point, why?

You know, said Al (possibly contemplating such a heroic journey made by people without even a horse to ease their way), the worst of the rustlers had a park named after him, but the Indians, nothing.

MacNeish went home to lie down.

I walked out into the desert with Libby. It seemed so barren, almost as bad as Nevada. What could caribou hunters from the far north ever have seen in it? The hills and mountains, she said, were full of gold, silver, turquoise and iron. In the days of the great cattle ranches, earth dams had been built to hold in the mountain meltwater and there had been a carpet of grass. But now there was a carpet of mesquite, yucca and creosote bushes, the kind that Moses saw burning in the Sinai.

It looked like such a flat landscape from the highway, the growing things so sparse and small, but when I walked out beyond the road, the bushes came up to my shoulders, and some reached as high as the top of my head. The weird yucca, a thick-leaved plant with a tall sprout of seed pods in its center, came up to my waist. What was missed from the highway but apparent at ground level was the deep well of shade under every bush. And there was a wonderful fresh smell.

So what did people eat? I asked Libby.

Mule deer, she said. And just then, right on cue, two roadrunners shot out from under a bush. A rabbit jolted right across my path.

Libby chattered on about how she liked to hike in the hills on the other side of the highway, how she never met anyone, how there was just silence or the sound of birds. I wasn't playing close attention: I was falling in love with the landscape while it was toying with me. The sun browned my winter-white skin, the wind ruffled my hair.

"This is like the Rift Valley in Africa," she said softly.

# Part Two

*T*he Lord God planted a garden in Eden, in the east, and placed there the man whom He had formed. And from the ground the Lord God caused to grow every tree that was pleasing to the sight and good for food, with the tree of life in the middle of the garden, and the tree of knowledge of good and bad.

*A river issues from Eden to water the garden, and it then divides and becomes four branches. The name of the first is Pishon, the one that winds through the whole land of Havilah, where the gold is. (The gold of that land is good; bdellium is there, and lapis lazuli.) The name of the second river is Gihon, the one that winds through the whole land of Cush. The name of the third river is Tigris, the one that flows east of Asshur. And the fourth river is the Euphrates.*

*The Lord God took the man and placed him in the garden of Eden to till it and tend it....*

*The man named his wife Eve, because she was the mother of all the living. And the Lord God made garments of skins for Adam and his wife, and clothed them....*

*And the Lord God said, "Now that the man has become like one of us, knowing good and bad, what if he should stretch* out his hand and take also from the tree of life and eat, and live forever!" So the Lord God banished him from the garden of Eden, to till the soil from which he was taken. He drove the man out, and stationed east of the garden of Eden the cherubim and the fiery ever-turning sword, to guard the way to the tree of life.

— GENESIS: 2, 3

# 11

# Beneath the Southern Cross

The Road Leads Back in Time

T HE MORE I READ, the more scholars I spoke to, the more the archaeological evidence seemed clear. Contrary to the Clovis First/Bering Strait story, the oldest remains of human beings and their works have been found deep in the southern half of the hemisphere, not in the north where they should have been. David Yesner, formerly with McGill University but now at the University of Alaska, had recently reviewed all the archaeological evidence to date for early man in the region. Yesner admitted that after generations of searching, nothing had been found that was definitively man-made anywhere in Alaska older than 11,800 BP.[1] Nothing older than 10,000 BP had been found on the British Columbia coast. Although there was some hope that something might be recovered from now-submerged lands, only a few stone tools had actually been dredged up off the Queen Charlotte Islands.[2] While it was clear that animals found their way over the Bering Strait during the Pleistocene, there was no physical evidence in the north to support MacNeish's view that people came too during the warm interval.

By contrast, in South America the evidence of early human settlement was voluminous. In 1998, Tom Dillehay teamed up with three colleagues to produce a special section on Brazilian archaeology for *Antiquity*, based on an information symposium held at the 1997 annual meeting of the Society for American Archaeology. This showed Brazil to be rich terrain. Many rock shelters had been discovered, their walls covered with paintings and pictographs. Dates at some shelters went back to 12,000 BP.[3]

Brazilian archaeologists were just coming into their own. Until the 1980s, archaeology in Brazil had mainly been done by foreigners, or by the foreign-trained. Americans became active in Brazil in the 1940s, particularly the husband-and-wife team of Clifford Evans (now deceased) and Betty Meggers, who went to Brazil after the Second World War.[4] In 1949, the same year MacNeish was hired by Canada's National Museum to survey the Mackenzie Valley, Meggers and her husband were hired by the Smithsonian. They dug at Marajó and other islands in the mouth of the Amazon. In 1965, they helped direct a broad-based Brazilian archaeological survey of the coast called PRONAPA (Projeto Nacional do Prospecção Arqueológica) and then with a similar survey called PRONABAPA (Programa Nacional de Pesquisas Arqueológicas na Bacia Amazônica) encouraged archaeologists to explore for sites in the Amazon. Meggers and Evans and their Brazilian colleagues' work led to the identification of hundreds of ancient villages.

It also led to a great split in Brazilian archaeology, similar to the fight in North America over Clovis First. Theories about the role played by the Amazon River in the prehistory of human culture in South America echoed some of the ideas about the role of the Mackenzie River Valley. Depending on the scholar, the Amazon was seen either as an unproductive environment into which humans slowly spread from the mountains of the west or as the Garden of Eden, out of which the earliest South American cultures emerged. Donald Lathrap, an American who worked in the Amazon for years, took the latter view and influenced many others, including Anna Roosevelt. Meggers and Evans took the conservative position.[5]

Fairly early on in their careers at the Smithsonian, Meggers and Evans received a visit from a wealthy amateur archaeologist in Ecuador, Emilio Estrada, who invited them to collaborate with him. On one of the sites they excavated together, Valdivia, they found pottery resembling some of the oldest discovered in Peru and Colombia, but more complex. Estrada suggested that it resembled Jomon pottery from Japan. Meggers and Evans looked at the few samples of Jomon pottery in the Smithsonian, and went to Japan to look at the Jomon work for themselves. They came back convinced that the Valdivia pottery was the same as middle Jomon pottery found in southern Japan; there were far too many similarities between the sophisticated decorative styles to be explained away as coincidence. Meggers believed that some Jomon people found their way to Ecuador about 6,000 years ago. She speculated that fishermen were caught out in the Pacific during a catastrophic eruption of a volcano in southern Japan, and were carried across the ocean.[6] Further, Meggers and her husband argued that this immigration of Jomon fisherman brought pottery-making to the Americas, and techniques and decorative styles spread from Valdivia, over the Andes, into the Amazon. Meggers later came to similar conclusions about the Olmec culture in Mexico—she saw many features as a direct extension of the ancient Chinese Shang culture, right down to the use of Shang writing on stone carvings and the use of particular colored stones to represent social status in sculpture.[7]

She and her husband published a huge Smithsonian volume on Valdivia and a shorter version of their claims in *Scientific American* in 1966, which was picked up by television and news magazines. They became instantly famous, but many of their colleagues were outraged. Meggers published at a time when anthropologists knew that they stood on the shoulders of racists, when it was considered unreasonable and demeaning to Native Americans to suggest that they might not have been the inventors of all the complex technologies found on New World sites. It was also anathema to entertain the idea that Jomon deep-sea

fishermen could somehow have made their way by boat across
the Pacific to Ecuador 6,000 years ago.

Nevertheless, Meggers concluded that some American cultures were strongly influenced by Asian cultures, and that the
path of the diffusion into Brazil was along the Amazon system.
She believes that there is evidence of a long period of drought
ending around 7000 BP, during which the closed wall of the
Amazon rain forest opened up, making pathways for people to
move south.

The next generation of American scholars active in Brazil,
particularly Anna Roosevelt, emphatically does not agree with
her. Roosevelt published papers on her own finds in the eastern
Amazon: 8,000-year-old pottery at Taperinha, and a shell midden
and rock art site, at Pedra Pintada, with dates back to 11,000 BP.[8]

While they disagree on the Amazon, Meggers and Roosevelt
are both Clovis First dissenters. Meggers insists that the work
in South America, both by her colleagues and others, is vitally
important, because it demonstrates that human beings were in
South America very early. When I went to see her in Washington, she produced a map for me on which she was keeping track
of South American sites with pre-Clovis radiocarbon dates. It
isn't just Monte Verde that has old dates, she said, there are
numerous dates from many sites ranging from 11,000 to 13,000
BP. Most are in the interior of the continent, and most are
unknown to her North American colleagues, who, she said bitterly, don't read the Portuguese or Spanish literature and have no
idea what is going on down in South America.

She believes that certainty about who came first, how, and
from where will come out of biological studies. It will emerge
from the study of DNA in bones, and from learning the evolutionary history of the viruses and parasites that hooked a ride to
the Americas with human beings. As an example of what she
means by this, she explained that she had been asked to attend an
epidemiology symposium in Chile the previous fall. A certain
cancer-causing retrovirus that is most common in southern

Japan has been identified in prehistoric mummies and surviving indigenous populations in the Andean area of South America, but not in North America. If the human beings carrying that virus had walked around the Pacific Rim, over the Bering Strait and down to Colombia, she thinks they would surely have left traces of this virus in the populations they encountered. But there are no such traces.

In 1993, a conference on the peopling of the Americas was organized by a Brazilian foundation called FUMDHAM.[10] FUMDHAM is an acronym for the Fundação Museu do Homem Americano, established by Brazilian archaeologist Niéde Guidon and her colleague Anne-Marie Pessis in the town of São Raimundo Nonato, in the Brazilian state of Piaui. Guidon and her associates had organized the meeting to share with leading Americanists some of what she had discovered near the rock shelters scattered through Brazil's Serra da Capivara National Park. Stone tool expert Fábio Parenti told the assembly that 50,000 years was the minimum age of the first human occupation of this area, a shocking assertion.

The conference record exposed the sharp differences of opinion within Brazilian anthropological/archaeological circles. While Guidon claimed evidence of human culture going back 50,000 years, and her Brazilian colleague Maria Beltrão made claims for sites more than 295,000 years old, other Brazilian scholars like Marilia Carvalho de Mello e Alvim were firmly orthodox.

Mello e Alvim, of the State University of Rio de Janeiro, was then the senior physical anthropologist in Brazil, known throughout anthropological circles as the Queen of Bones. At the FUMDHAM conference she gave a review of what was known about South American populations and stuck with the standard Hrdličkan framework of how humans came to the Americas and from where. She said Native American populations got their start somewhere between the southern side of Lake Baikal and North China 13,000 years ago. In direct contrast to her colleagues Walter Neves and Hector Pucciarelli, who had published that there was an early population in Brazil different from all the rest, she said that the current population of Native Americans in Brazil was the same as the most ancient remains found in the earliest sites. The terms she used to describe this unchanging Brazilian population were the same terms used to describe modern North American Native people—oblique eyes with epicanthic fold, strong build, high prominent cheekbones, somewhat flat nose, straight thick black hair, shovel-shaped incisors. Skin color was the same as among Native Americans in North America. "On the peopling of the New World," she said, "the only point of general agreement is that the principal route of penetration in the American continent occurred through Beringia by Asian-originated groups. The issues related to when they have come, how many groups they were, as well as their representativity as related to the original populations still remain controversial."[11]

But her colleagues Luiz Ferreira and Adauto Araújo of the Oswaldo Cruz Foundation's National School of Public Health in Rio did not agree. They were both parasitologists who had been working on archaeological sites to learn about the history of the spread of disease. Since the 1920s, parasitologists had been interested in how tropical parasites specific to human beings came to the Americas. Since 1960 it had been widely accepted that the Bering Strait acted as a cold filter to keep out tropical parasites that need to live part of their life cycle in warm soil. While Southern American populations are troubled by tropical parasites, it was believed that all such parasites must have been brought to the Americas after 1492 with the African slaves imported by European colonizers.

"Biologic species do not arise in more than one geographic point, according to the assumption of Charles Darwin's species evolution theory," they told the group. "Parasite infections are thus biologic markers of the hosts' radiation following their occupation of new territories as far as the mesologic conditions allowed."[12] This was a complex way of saying that if tropical parasites were found in archaeological specimens older than the first known arrival of African slaves in South America, one would have some explaining to do about how they got there.

Adauto Araújo told the assembly that he had found the eggs of hookworm, which must cycle in warm soil (ideally between 25 and 30 degrees Celsius), in human coprolites (fossilized feces) found at one of Niéde Guidon's sites in Paiui. These hookworm eggs had been dated to 7,200 BP. Whoever brought the infection to this rock shelter in Piaui hadn't come from the north.

All of this was interesting, even exciting. But what moved me to get on a plane and go see these things in Brazil for myself was a picture that had appeared in *The Peterborough Examiner* in the late spring of 1998. A man and woman in lab coats displayed a human skull of a woman nicknamed Luzia whose remains had just been dated in Brazil.[13] The man was Walter Neves, the same scientist who had published that there was an early population in Brazil unlike those who came after. The *Examiner* said Luzia's bones were 11,500 radiocarbon years old, older than the Clovis First/Bering Strait theory could explain, the oldest known human remains in the Americas.

# 12

# Lunch with Luzia

The Fine African Features of the
Oldest Woman in the Americas

T HE VOYAGE SOUTH began in March 1999, in the
dry, colorless, soulless nowhereness called Pear-
son Airport in Toronto. For our entertainment,
there was a documentary about the migration from Russia to
Saskatchewan of a family of Jews very like my own, one hundred
years ago. Look how far we all traveled to come to the New
World, on boats, trains, wagons, and on foot; look what we built
here! This was a subject suitable for people zipping over the
globe's face like skater bugs speeding across a pond. The plane
flew through snow and wind and landed with a thump at Atlanta.

My seatmate was a physicist and computer architecture specialist, born and trained in Israel, living in Atlanta, who wanted
her daughter to study in Montreal. Her own doctorate was
an attempt to unify the irreducible randomness of quantum
mechanics with the broad calculations of relativity theory. ("If I'd
done it," she said, "you'd have heard of me.") We talked for a
long time about conservatism in science, how it results from the
simple fact that every generation must stand on the shoulders of
those who went before. Who has time to question everything? To
check everyone else's results? All the while, I couldn't stop thinking about my house in Toronto, standing as it does on foundations made by those who were there before me, built on their

postholes, over their broken pottery, their knotted nets, the bones of the animals they killed and most important, over the bones of their dead, buried with care and ceremony in the ancient beach of Glacial Lake Iroquois. Did they make voyages like ours? Some of the archaeological evidence says they did—quarrying chert and copper north of Superior, carrying it to the Rockies or the Mississippi—but very few experts were willing to grant that they traveled in boats back at the dawn of time. The consensus was that people walked—every inch of the way from Beringia to Tierra del Fuego, generation after generation just putting one foot in front of another.

In the airport at Atlanta there was a long run down a ramped corridor, and then another, and another, until, breathless, sweating, there came the grateful slump into a seat with too little leg room. The plane roared up and headed south. It was night, so nothing could be seen outside except wavicles of photons. The mind filled in all the black spaces between—downtown, suburbs, farms, mountains, winding highways. There was a large map displayed in the front of the cabin so those who cared to could take the measure of the outrageous speed with which the plane traversed an impossible distance.

I had become a Crane woman, flying over ocean and forest to a place of just-rightness. I examined the other Crane people flying with me. I had become by then an absolutely shameless people watcher. Everyone's head, the color and texture of their hair, the shape of the bones under their skin, went into the hopper to be analyzed. What could be determined about their origins from the shape of cheekbones, the slant of eye, the twist of a nose? The Israeli-American physicist left behind in Atlanta was a tall, broad woman with graying auburn hair, pale freckled skin and small white teeth. At first glance I had thought she was Russian. There was a little man who had run alongside me to the flight deck. He had a narrow nose, thick straight hair, funny little uplifted eyes, and was a dead ringer for a man I know who is the descendant of many generations of Hungarian nobility. He said he was Portuguese. There were other men sprawled out behind their newspapers, short, blocky men with pale skins (not as pale as mine), thick hands, thick waists, flat heads, and gray hair crinkling back in waves from their foreheads—Iberian hair, just what one would expect of businessmen going home to Brazil, the former Portuguese colony. There were very few women and no Native Americans that I could distinguish from everyone else. I ate and slept.

We flew over Florida, the Caribbean, the Atlantic. A trip that once took many weeks by sailing ship took us about eight hours. I woke up when we hit the equator. The plane broncoed up on the hot, wet air rising up from below, dropped like a stone, then soared over the Amazon's very own rain system. I woke up again when we dropped low over a range of spiky, green-slathered mountains, and swooped down over a huge plain near the south Atlantic coast. The plain was the muted dun color of poured concrete smudged with exhaust fumes. It stretched out, a crazy, highrise-towered mosaic, as far as I could see. This was São Paulo. Some seventeen million people were crowded down there—at least, that was the official count, ten percent of the population of the whole country. And then, finally (after another airport lounge where Shania Twain, formerly of Sudbury but now of the Planet Earth, keened of thwarted northern love), Rio.

Summer in Rio, so hot, so wet, so sensual. Flowers the color of passion swooned over stone fences, rich, unnameable scents flew up my nose, the sea was an opalescent green, the sun blessed my cold winter bones. The taxi honked along the narrow streets above Ipanema Beach, and around the placid lagoon where the rich and merely wealthy jogged with their poodles or punted fast along the glassy surface. There were no Native Americans among them, just a steady flow of tanned Caucasoids. On the other hand, the people I saw sweeping the streets and opening the locked gates of Mediterranean-style villas so their employers' Mercedeses could purr into traffic could have been the descendants of black slaves, or Native Americans, or both. The children of the not-so-rich took their revenge in public: there was graffiti everywhere, marring even the third stories of the glitzy condos. Shania Twain keened again on the taxi radio.

Luzia, the most ancient skeleton in the Americas, was kept at Rio's Museu Naçional, in the care of a senior scientist named Sheila Maria Ferraz Mendonça de Souza. She is both a medical doctor and a physical anthropologist and had been a student of Mello e Alvim, the Queen of Bones, who had died not long after the FUMDHAM conference. I had called de Souza and asked to see Luzia's remains. She arranged it for me. The Brazilians have no qualms about showing Native American bones to anyone. There was no NAGPRA here.

The taxi jolted along in bumper-to-bumper traffic, through a tunnel and into the flat plains of Zona Norte, the very crowded, ugly, industrial part of town. Open apartment windows, cheek to cheek with the freeway, welcomed the grit and the exhaust. The favelas (illegal slum buildings put up by the poor) piled higher and higher up the sides of Rio's Atlantic Mountains, which push straight up from the earth like the tops on brioches. Finally we arrived at the grand district called Quinta da Boa Vista, the former palace of a former emperor of Brazil, Dom Pedro II. He was a man who loved nature and natural history. His former home was turned into the Museu Naçional (or National Museum).

There were hills covered with all kinds of palms and flowering trees and shrubs I couldn't name. The taxi climbed the switch-back road, higher and higher, until we arrived at a cobbled drive. A huge Iberian style palacio—three stories high, with peeling stucco, stone pediments and shuttered windows—commanded the hilltop. One window was open and a woman inside waved me to the corner of the building and a checkpoint for visitors. I walked through a door, into a hall, and out into a courtyard surrounded by the palace on four sides. It was a beautiful, overgrown formal garden, with a gravel path around its square perimeter. There was a round, quiet pool at its center. Palms and flowering bushes grew in each quadrant. A large metal cage housed a silent red parrot. Through the open casement windows I heard laughter, doors slamming, radios. I tried to compare this to the Museum of Civilization in Ottawa, or to the Smithsonian, as my heels crunched the pebbles. There were no points of contact.

Sheila de Souza was in her office, down a long narrow hall lined from top to bottom with gray specimen boxes. I stepped through the louvered swinging door into a tall white room. A French door stood open to a balustraded terrace. Right beside it a child-sized skeleton hung on a metal stand doing a little samba, its tiny bony digits jangling in the breeze from an electric fan. Along one wall a worktable was covered with bubble wrap to protect delicate specimens from their own weight. At the end of the table there was a stone sink. At my back, another skeleton hung from a frame, small, but not quite so small as the one by the door: it was long-headed, with round eye orbits and a slight sagittal keel (a bony ridge like a boat's keel running from front to back across the top of the skull).

De Souza (everyone called her Sheila, pronounced Shayla) sat at a small desk. Her hair is curly brown with gray streaks, falling to her shoulders. She wore a pair of blue jeans, a T-shirt, sandals. She has an interesting face, but there was something like stress or pain pinching around her eyes, which are round, dark and quizzical. She explained that she is a curator of human remains at the museum, as well as a senior researcher at the Oswaldo Cruz Foundation's National School of Public Health, where she studies diseases of the past. She sketched out for me the history of the museum's collection of human bones, which she said comprises about 2,000 individuals. It was a grisly story.

The collection stretches back to the very beginning of natural history in Brazil but also includes new remains recently discovered. The museum has archives full of letters from various important personages who donated special items to the Emperor Dom Pedro II when he still lived in this palace. These included the remains of Native Americans shot by settlers who found them troublesome. Physical anthropology in Brazil had mirrored in its political orientation work done at the same time in the U.S. There was an agenda—to find proof that Native Americans were inferior to Europeans. The first Brazilian anthropologists spent their lives chasing down the ever-elusive perfect representative of each racial type and trying to demonstrate that Native persons' brains are smaller than, and therefore inferior to, Europeans'. As in Canada and the U.S., Native people in Brazil were almost wiped out by diseases that came with the settlers and slaves from Europe and Africa. They were also hunted and shot when their territories were in the path of expansion. In the twentieth century, as Brazil became a nationalist republic and then a dictatorship, the theories concerning a hierarchy among races changed. The new agenda became making Brazil a melting pot where all the races joined together in sexual harmony. A new Brazilian man would be created, stronger than all the rest. This was Aryanism turned on its head.

As in North America, the European settlers were slow to colonize the hinterland to the north. The Amazon rain forest protected the Native people who lived there: as long as they stayed in its darkest reaches, they were hard to contact, hard to infect. But in the 1960s, modern Brazil began to push its way in there too. Just as Canadians and Americans expanded into the Arctic for strategic reasons at the end of the Second World War, the Brazilian military government saw the Amazon as a vital and rich frontier to be defended (from outsiders) and plundered. On de Souza's wall there was a picture of a native Brazilian cacique (chief) with a traditional lipdisk distending his lower mouth. The photo had been taken by a friend of hers who had worked what was called "the attraction front." In the 1970s, Brazil sent anthropologists into the Amazon to contact hidden native tribes and attract them into the light of its civilization (with the army and the road-builders close behind).

The problem with the ancient remains in the museum's collection, de Souza explained, was that the bulk of them had been gathered before the middle of the twentieth century by explorers who did not know how to carry out their work in a scientifically valid way. Most of Brazil's really ancient human remains are no longer in the country at all. They were discovered mixed in with extinct Ice Age animals in the Lagoa Santa region in Minas Gerais by the Danish scientist Peter Lund in the 1840s. The sites he excavated were some of the first places in the world where the bones of early man were found in association with extinct species, well before the first discovery of Neanderthal remains in Europe. Lund sent most of the bones he found to the Museum of Natural History in Copenhagen. "This led to the first idea that man lived with Pleistocene faunas," said de Souza.

At the turn of the last century, some South Americans suggested that early hominids had emerged first in the Americas. An Argentinian named Florentino Ameghino pointed to the cap of a skull discovered by workers digging the port of Buenos Aires, to suggest that the ancestors of modern humans had been in the Americas a great deal earlier than in Europe or northern Asia. The shape of this skullcap was low, heavy and thick, and its stratigraphic position suggested great age. A human skeleton was found later under a glyptodont carapace (a glyptodont is an extinct Ice Age animal) in the Pampas.[2] Hrdlička so successfully ridiculed Ameghino's arguments that these bones slid out of the narrative of the peopling of the Americas almost entirely, as far as North American scholars were concerned. But Lund's finds were not forgotten. In the 1920s, a Czech scientist named Padberg-Drenkpohl, who worked at the National Museum, made the first scientific expedition to the Lagoa Santa region after Lund.

"He brought many bones to the museum in the 1920s," said de Souza. "The way they excavated at that time was not as we would like it. The skulls were from different caves, some got mixed together, some were in mortuary caves, but there was no archaeological context." Padberg-Drenkpohl found nothing that suggested mankind had been in this region during the Ice Age.

The only digs done near Lagoa Santa over the next thirty years were by amateurs. Their attention to stratigraphy was poor to nonexistent and so no one had any idea of the true age of the remains they found, although they did publish monographs about them. In 1955, an American/Brazilian team led by Wesley Hurt of the University of South Dakota also dug in the region. Hurt found few artifacts of interest. He was so disappointed he didn't even try to date his material until the late 1960s. To his surprise, he got dates ranging back to 10,000 BP.

The skeleton called Luzia came to the museum twenty years after Hurt's expedition. In contrast with many other excavations at Lagoa Santa, this one was done to the highest standards. Luzia was found in a very interesting archaeological context. "She was found at Lapa Vermelha," said de Souza, writing the words down in my notebook so that I would spell them properly. "An excavation conducted by Dr. Annette Laming-Emperaire who worked here in the French mission to Brazil.... Laming-Emperaire started excavating about twenty-five years ago to solve the problem of the Lagoa Santa sites, the oldest we knew in Brazil...."

Annette Laming-Emperaire was a French archaeologist. Her husband, Joseph Emperaire, had studied with Paul Rivet of La Musée de l'Homme in Paris. She and her husband had previously dug in Argentina and Chile, looking for signs of early people in the Americas. Rivet believed human beings had populated South America before North America and that they had somehow entered the hemisphere from South Asia. The couple first worked in Brazil in the 1950s. Joseph Emperaire died some years later in an accident on a site in Chile. The wall of an excavation had tumbled on top of him. Annette scrambled into the pit to pull him out, but was too late. In the early 1970s, she came back to Brazil and tried a number of sites around Lagoa Santa, looking for one with suitable structures. Finally she found the rock shelter called Lapa Vermelha. The only human remains found were the bones of Luzia. Shortly after that, Annette Laming-Emperaire too died tragically. She went on a vacation in 1976 to the Brazilian state of Parana, and was asphyxiated in her shower by a defective gas heating element.

The problem with Luzia, explained de Souza, was that her bones were not found in a primary burial. It was a secondary deposition, meaning her bones had rolled down a hill into a crevice in the rock shelter's wall. Held together in a pack of soil, the bones had been transported by water and gently deposited in a pile on top of each other. The stratigraphy suggested there were two thousand years between the soil layer in which the skull was found and the layer in which the mandible was recovered. "Each part of the skeleton fell in a different time," said de Souza. At first there wasn't even any agreement among the scientists who studied the site about whether the bones belonged to one individual or many.

"The physical anthropologist who worked here looked [at the bones] and [saw they were from] the same skeleton," said de Souza. That woman was Marilia Mello e Alvim, the Queen of Bones, de Souza's former professor.

The French archaeological mission to Brazil continued after Annette Laming-Emperaire's death. André Prous found more ancient human remains at a site called Santana do Riacho in the state of Minas Gerais. De Souza had examined those bones and published on them. Prous kept a significant collection of other remains found in the Lagoa Santa region in the natural history museum at the Federal University of Minas Gerais, in the city of Belo Horizonte. But many remains found by explorers other than Lund at sites around Lagoa Santa (most not in association with extinct Ice Age animals) were still in this museum.

Where?

In the glass case behind you, she said.

I turned to look. I saw row on row of stained skulls, the bone mottled in peculiar shades of red, brown, dark blue, yellow. Aside from their color they looked remarkably similar to each other. De Souza's mentor, Mello e Alvim, had studied most of these remains and had been deeply puzzled by them. The dates of the sites where they were found stretched from 12,000 BP (in the case of Luzia) to 6000 BP. While there were differences between skulls and bones found at different sites, by and large they were all very similar. What Mello e Alvim couldn't understand was why there was so little change in the general shape of these skulls over a 6,000-year time span. Why hadn't they been transformed or shown signs of adaptation to a changing environment? The landscape had changed, the vegetation had changed. Why were there no marks of even random mutations over so many millennia?

"For Marilia, this could not happen," said de Souza.

Mello e Alvim assumed the French had made mistakes in their dating due to the incredible complexity of the stratigraphy in which Luzia's bones had been found. But the French archaeologists were very meticulous. They charted the movements of animals, the flow of water, the complex ways in which soils had shifted and moved over the millennia, to be certain that any bone found had always been associated with the particular layer of the charcoal they dated. And de Souza was not certain she agreed with Mello e Alvim that over such a span of time there had to have been significant changes in the shapes of human skulls. The obvious solution was to date the bones directly. Luzia was the first set of Lagoa Santa bones that anyone had tried to date directly, and no one got around to it until 1998.

Dating the protein portion of bone, or even the amino acids, was no longer a difficult task. Good dates could be achieved from even minuscule samples. Why had nothing been done until so recently?

De Souza didn't know. Whatever the reasons, Walter Neves was the first to ask to date Luzia. He did it because he wanted to test his hypothesis that the First Americans found in Brazil were a population that shared a South Asian or African morphology, not North Asian. The ancient date that Neves got on Luzia's bones had not been that surprising. The French had found Luzia's skull at a level that corresponded with a date of around 10,000 BP.

"We had an idea [it] could be that old," said de Souza. But until the time the radiocarbon date came back, no one really believed it. When the remains were first found, the Clovis First theory was the only one widely accepted in the Americas. Rivet's

theories had long since been discredited as far as Brazilian scholars were concerned. "More than twenty-five years ago," de Souza
said, "this was hard to accept. Clovis was the theory. Now we
have many sites in Brazil with [dates of] 30,000 to 20,000, at
Pedra Furada, all over Brazil. At the time [we] thought it was an
error. So Luzia stayed in a box."

Archaeologists in Brazil, she said, no longer have a clear idea
of how people came to the Americas, from where or even when.
Niéde Guidon has talked of a transatlantic arrival. During the Ice
Age, the Atlantic shelf, now under water, would have been dry
land. Niéde Guidon's earliest dates are not accepted, but those
going back to 20,000 BP are accepted in Brazil and France. Even
André Prous, who, de Souza said delicately, "discusses" with
Niéde Guidon, has his own very ancient sites. "The more we
find, the more convinced [we are] that it's not just a mistake,"
she said.

It had long been known that these remains from the Lagoa
Santa region were a distinct population. But it is also known that
these remains are similar to those of Paleo-Indians found in
Argentina and Venezuela. "Marilia Mello e Alvim said they looked
like Negro people," said de Souza softly, nodding to herself as if
pleased to remember her teacher's remarkable insight. (Although,
as Walter Neves later pointed out, Mello e Alvim published that
they were classic Mongoloids.) "Dolichocranic (long-headed),
thin faces, small superorbital ridge, occipital bun, not prog-
nathous very much, but not a flat face. Not wide cheeks. We
know of similar skulls in other countries."

Fifteen years earlier, a researcher working out of the Federal
University of Minas Gerais, in the city of Belo Horizonte, had
found human bones in the state of Bahia (which is on the northeast coast close to Paiui), also mixed with extinct animal bones.
Mello e Alvim had found them to be similar to the Lagoa Santa
remains. These remains had not been dated either. Ancient
remains found recently at Piaui in a dig done by Niéde Guidon
include a skeleton of which the skull has the same morphology.

When Mello e Alvim compared the peculiar features found on the skulls (known as epigenetic traces) of five Lagoa Santa populations with modern remains from the same area, she found them all to be quite similar. Modern, ancient, it all looked like the same genetic stock.

Walter Neves, however, saw things differently: he saw two distinct populations. He had followed a different line of research and a different theory, in his view a broader conception of human evolution. Neves had measured the ancient skulls, and then compared these measurements with those of other modern populations around the world using multivariate analysis, which de Souza and Mello e Alvim had not done. This method, in use since the first half of the century, had become a much more powerful instrument with the introduction of computer databases. De Souza thought Neves had done fine work, but she saw significant problems with this method of analysis, the first being error in measurement. A much more fundamental issue was interpreting the underlying biological significance of what is measured. There is much disagreement about the meaning of such analyses among researchers studying the same populations, she explained, because no one can say how the similarities and differences observed came to be or whether they have any genetic significance.

"Bones," said de Souza, "are affected by environmental pressures." Bones can be affected by what a person eats, for example, and it is hard to distinguish between environmental and genetic influences. "The big problem with any kind of quantitative analysis," she said, "is that it is just math, just numbers. We give them an interpretation.... Even though Marilia could see Negroid traces, even without the cranial measuring methodology, she would never accept this as a proof against the Bering model, and she would choose to understand it as a simple variation of ancient human morphology." Brazilian anthropologist Marta Lahr had pointed out that some modern remains may share certain traits with older ones even though they are not in fact related by direct descent, but share a common ancient ancestor.

So getting a date on Luzia's bone had been vital. Only a good date on bone could settle the issue of whether the Lagoa Santa remains were truly ancient, or indeed whether human bones found with extinct animals meant those humans and animals actually lived side by side during the Ice Age. The date of 11,500 BP that Neves got from Luzia's remains said people who did not look like modern Native Americans were in South America as the Ice Age ended. The date of 11,500 BP said Hrdlička was wrong.

I asked to see Luzia. De Souza stood up and reached above her for a large cardboard box. She placed it on the worktable and opened the lid. She lifted out the skull and placed it gently, gently, on the bubble wrap on the table.

"She was not more than twenty or twenty-two years old," she said. And Luzia was tiny, only 1.5 meters tall. The skull top had a slight bony ridge running from the front to the back like a boat keel, like the skeleton hanging by the door. The forehead was fairly high, the eye sockets square and large, the face and cheekbones narrow. The front teeth were missing. The color of the bone was a light beige with faint veins of pink. De Souza put Luzia's skull on the right, and then put two other skulls beside it so I could compare them. They were a little bit smaller, and the color of the bone was different (one was mottled a furious red), but I could see that their shapes were very similar. The one she placed on the far left of the table from Luzia was from a place called Confins and had been pulled out of a cave by miners a long time ago. The one in the middle was from a place called Cerca Grande. It had been discovered by Wesley Hurt in 1956. All three had the same square eye sockets, the same flatness above the eyes, the same reasonably high foreheads and narrow cheekbones. But their shape was quite different from remains found on the Atlantic coast or in the shell mounds, which date back to about 3000 BP.

She pulled out a skull found in such a mound from the glass

case and set it down in front of Luzia and her Lagoa Santa friends. The top of this skull was similar, the eye sockets were also square, and the nasal opening was a similar triangle. The one striking difference between this skull and the Lagoa Santa remains was the breadth of the face. The skull's cheekbones spread wide below the eyes, just like the Red Giant skull I'd seen in Washington. There were other distinguishing features: the teeth of the Lagoa Santa population were riddled with cavities—not the kind of teeth normally found on hunters. No one knew what they ate, but with teeth like that the Lagoa Santans would have had a hard time eating meat. The shell mound population, on the other hand, had strong teeth without cavities, like those of Archaic skeletons found in Ontario.

We sat and contemplated the four skulls lying before us on the table, picked clean like the remains of a particularly gruesome feast. Mello e Alvim had thought Luzia's skull looked somehow African. Walter Neves had written that when he compared the Lagoa Santa remains to modern populations, they more closely resembled modern Australian Aborigines than anyone else, although his paper had also said the next closest affiliates were African. Marta Lahr, who had studied other South American remains at Cambridge, published in the *Yearbook of Physical Anthropology* for 1995 that they too were likely representative of an early, less specialized form of Mongoloids.

In that paper, Lahr asserted that there had been a single recent origin of modern humans, and that modern Mongoloids had evolved in Asia with various regional differences. The early Asian populations had looked less Mongoloid, she wrote, which "opens the possibility of the earliest Amerindians not being a typical 'Mongoloid' population.... Since a derived, typically Mongoloid morphology cannot be attributed to the early Amerindian and Fuegian-Patagonian populations, it is argued either that the sinodont dental pattern was acquired in parallel in Asia and the Americas or that at least two migratory waves ancestral to Amerinds took place."[3] She reminded her readers that C. Loring Brace had shown there are two populations in Japan: modern Mongoloids, and another people called Ainu who have recognizably different crania and dentition. The Ainu have narrower faces and their teeth are sundadont, not sinodont. It was possible then that this southern, less specialized form of Mongoloidism developed first, and that these early proto-Mongoloids were the first to come to America. Lahr identified the Fuegian-Patagonian remains, from the southern tip of Argentina, as being in this proto-Mongoloid category along with some of the earliest Europeans. Like Neves, she said that all these people tended to look more like modern Australian Aboriginals than anyone else.

De Souza was worried that her mentor's insights had largely disappeared from this discussion. "When Luzia was here twenty-five years [she] was forgotten and people find it now, forgetting people like Marilia Mello e Alvim worked on this as far as they could. They must be remembered."

What about DNA work? I asked.

She thought the inferences drawn from the mtDNA work on modern samples were ludicrous. "All evolution of humans based on three hundred samples all over the world," she scoffed. "It's impossible. You have to laugh. It's not possible to tell us about evolution with a few samples. You can never compare variability in dead populations to living populations where massive extinctions occurred." And massive extinctions had occurred in the Americas after 1492. However, there were people trying to extract ancient mtDNA in Brazil. Lagoa Santa materials had been sampled by a group working at the Federal University of Minas Gerais. There were no results yet. She was waiting to hear from a friend who had taken a sample from teeth: no results there either.

We walked out her French doors to look at Dom Pedro's back garden. I sidled past the little skeleton dangling in the breeze—a child, she said. The one by her office door was a woman who died in the nineteenth century. I thought they both looked a lot like the Lagoa Santa remains. But how could that be? How could Lahr's proto-Mongoloids become something else in Asia while they failed to change at all in South America?

There was a magnificent view beyond the balustrade, a huge forest of flowering tropical trees and beyond that, Rio's mountains. The sky was split down the middle, half terrifying black clouds, half bright blue. We walked around to the front and down the hill. The grass ran on for acres, with large pools of shade provided by spreading, broad-leafed trees covered with flowers as big as my fist. They were the color of blood, the color of sand, the color of oranges, with stamens so thick and rich with pollen they were like small sticks of yellow candy. The flowers plopped down on the pathway in front of my feet, so heavy I could hear them hit the ground. I picked one up to sniff—it was as sweet as a fresh gardenia. De Souza said it came from a monkey tree. There were nuts as big as coconuts hanging in the branches high up. This tree, she said, bore the fruits of last year's flowering cycle, even as it produced the flowers necessary for the next.

I was entranced by the beauty, the scent, the luxury of this landscape. This *was* the Garden of Eden: it was so easy and warm, there was forest, sea, river, flowers and fruit falling at my feet. It made so much sense to me that people lived here while ice covered Canada from Newfoundland to the Rockies, from the Rockies to the Pacific, from the Great Lakes to the Arctic. I began to wonder if the Ojibwa story about travelling far to the south could have meant coming this far. No, I decided. Not possible. They never would have gone home.

The sun burned on my arms and neck as we made our way to a Portuguese Colonial house down below. There were large white tents attached on either side and a patio in front. It was a restaurant and it was jammed with families trying to feed their squirming children. De Souza insisted I try Brazilian specialties and so I feasted on crab wrapped in some kind of warm cheese served on a shell, and a flat fish as wide as a dinner plate. She talked a little about herself. A small boy beside me blasted my ear with his water gun as she told me about becoming a doctor of medicine at a state university, about her three children, and about her husband, who had been an archaeologist. He had written extensively on the history of archaeology in Brazil. When I asked where he was, she had said hurriedly that two years ago he had become depressed, and had died. I told her about Nevada's racist ghosts, the troubles over Kennewick, and the Spirit Cave Mummy, and asked her whether Native people spoke of ghosts in the bones here too.

She brushed the ghost stories aside and focused on her struggle to get the collections into order. For many years, de Souza said, the bones had been piling up unstudied in the museum. Marilia Mello e Alvim used to say that physical anthropologists in Brazil were almost an extinct species. But things had started to turn around: she was teaching three graduate students, Walter Neves was teaching more. In a few years there would be about fifteen in the country with doctorates. And not a moment too soon. "We have big collections," she said. "Archaeologists bring more and more." For many years, the bones had been stored in less than adequate conditions. Three years ago, the museum started to rearrange the collection.

"We had thousands of samples to deal with. We had to open every box, check the number, check against the original list, put it in the computer, to find out where things that disappeared could be and to restore.... Now everything is listed. We have registered the sites. We have started to document each skeleton's skull in forms following standards in the U.S. This is a huge job, apart from the research itself."

She knew all about the flap over Kennewick. She thought demands for the return of bones were made for political reasons, not religious ones, and in any case, there had been no such demands made in Brazil. "Some Indians visit the museum," she said. "They know the bones belong to Indian people. In this museum [we] have never heard of complaints on this. We have a special demand for a sacred axe in the museum in São Paulo University. The Indians asked for it and took it back. It's the only demand I know about."

She was pleased to say she had the right conditions to do proper documentation and research, and to hold on to the information extracted from human remains in the museum's care. And she wasn't just studying Native American remains; she also had "Christians from cemeteries as well. I have slaves, I have everybody. I see these bones like accidents of the time. The process of decay [was] stopped in some way. By some accident they were recovered and brought to my hands to be studied.... I deal with the consequence of human manipulation—the excavation—[and of] nature—worms, trees growing, sand on the burial. It's a long, complex process of change. The last [change] ever is the act of research, when I take a sample for analysis and destroy bone. It doesn't bother me. It bothers me to lose information."

# 13

# Proof Parasite

## A Wormhole in the Bering Strait Theory

IT IS EASY WHEN sitting in some beachside cafe in Rio to be lulled into the belief that Brazil is a First-World country. The traffic thunders by on the normal sort of multi-laned highway, the high-rise hotels are as marbled and teaked and stainless-steeled as any in Manhattan. But Brazil is many countries all sliced up and layered on top of each other. In the biological sciences it is both First World and Third, which oddly enough has given its researchers a leg up on those in scientific establishments to the north. Brazilian scientists in state-run institutions have the wherewithal to do groundbreaking research. That is how two paleoparasitologists at the Oswaldo Cruz Foundation managed to sink another nail into the coffin of the Bering-Strait-only entry theory. Physical anthropologists in North America had not dared to question the dogma that the First Americans entered the New World on foot through the Bering Strait. They had been taught that frigid Beringia blocked the entry of most tropical human pathogens into the New World, which arrived only when Europeans brought in African slaves on ships. Luiz Ferreira and Adauto Araújo, Sheila de Souza's colleagues, have turned this logic upside down. They have quietly shown that early people must have come to Brazil direct from some other tropical area, because they brought hookworm with them.

I had been warned by de Souza that I should give the taxi very precise instructions about which street to use to get to the Oswaldo Cruz Foundation, because otherwise I would find myself in a the middle of a very dangerous favela. I didn't really understand her meaning until the taxi pulled off the freeway on the north side of town. The driver pointed up at a strange, tiled tower billowing like some Kremlin onion dome over a sea of favelas, and said, Oswaldo Cruz. The dome was the roof of the central administration building of a biological sciences campus dedicated to the study of tropical disease, with laboratory buildings, parks, a huge library and clinics for the treatment of the poor, as strange and wonderful a place as I have ever seen. Brazilian stories about Oswaldo Cruz, the man who created it, would soon drop at my feet like the flowers at Quinta da Boa Vista.

De Souza met me this time at the elevator of a tall building with open doors and windows through which cooling breezes were supposed to flow. The backside of the building is close to a river. On the opposite riverbank is one of the roughest favelas in a city with much misery. Drug lords rule; they also make war. In the middle of one such war, journalists climbed up on this building's roof to take pictures: this upset the tenuous diplomatic balance between the favela dwellers and the government employees of Oswaldo Cruz Foundation. Bullets whizzed through the researchers' offices.

De Souza took me to the office of Luiz Fernando Ferreira, the director of the program in paleoparasitology. He is a small man, dark-eyed, dapper, and he sat behind a large desk, surrounded by pictures of the many friends and foreign colleagues he had entertained over the years. There were glass specimen cases loaded with skulls, microscopes, computers and a file cabinet full of little paper reference cards. He waved me to a straight chair and placed Sheila de Souza on his right to help him with his English. He waited impatiently for his younger colleague, Adauto Araújo, to arrive. A young woman student was invited to sit in and observe at the back of the crowded room. Cafezinho made the rounds.

Finally Araújo appeared and plopped down into a striped canvas beach chair that had its own little leg rest: it was Ferreira's favorite perch for a snooze. Araújo is small, with short graying hair and a trimmed beard, and he was dressed like any doctor at any northern hospital. De Souza too had turned herself out in a skirt and silk blouse. Something about Oswaldo Cruz brought out a sense of occasion.

Ferreira explained how he had got into this business of paleoparasitology. He was a doctor specializing in parasite diseases when he read a paper saying that schistosomiasis (a disease caused by a tropical flatworm) came to Brazil from Africa with the slave trade. Other papers he read said this was not true. He reasoned that if he found the worm or its eggs in human coprolites (fossilized feces) on pre-Columbian archaeological sites, that would settle the issue. "That was twenty years ago," he said with a laugh. "I've never seen it in coprolites." But he had seen a lot of other very interesting things and he no longer practiced medicine: he was entirely involved in the study of paleoparasitology.

"One day this boy," he said, waving fondly at Araújo in his deck chair, "he was then a boy, came here. [He said] I'd like to do [my] thesis. I say you do it in paleoparasitology. It was 1978."

Araújo then took up the tale. "In the beginning we started to look for archaeologists who had coprolites," said Araújo. "...We called one friend, the secretary of the Institute of Archaeology. He said, 'We have a lot and we don't know what to do [with them]. Not a lot of people like coprolites.'"

Araújo and Ferreira had to work out many technical problems to study the coprolites offered to them by the archaeologists. They eventually found a workable method to get water back into them so they could be properly studied under a microscope. There were very few papers to help them. In 1978 the field was wide open. Or wide shut, depending on your point of view. The notion that the New World was free of all human-adapted tropical parasites until the 1500s had just begun to be questioned. In 1969, the eggs and larvae of parasites were found in pre-

Columbian mummies in Utah. Two previous reports had been dismissed as errors in identification.[1]

Araújo and Ferreira found parasite eggs almost immediately. "In the first samples we found hookworm eggs and trichuris, an intestinal worm, in human coprolites from a Minas Gerais archaeological site. It was pre-Columbian," said Araújo. They dated the eggs by association with the soil layers on which they were found. The radiocarbon dates from those layers were around 3420 BP.[2]

There are two main species of hookworm that infect man: *Ancylostoma duodenale* and *Necator americanus*, said Araújo. "The eggs and larvae are very similar, the adults are different. Both the species have an African origin—perhaps they both came from an ancestor of man. So, when man migrated from Africa to Europe and Asia, they took the parasite with them. They are in the historical literature, the ancient texts in Egypt and Greece."

While the Egyptians and the Greeks did not identify the worm and its life stages they clearly described the clinical symptoms of hookworm infection—anemia, edema and loss of blood in the feces.

The fact that Araújo and Ferreira found the eggs of hookworm as opposed to another kind of parasite stuck a very large pin in the balloon of the Bering Strait migration theory. Hookworm is a very particular creature. It must spend part of its life cycle in soil and the soil must be of the right temperature. In winter, the temperature of the soil throughout most of Alaska, Canada and Siberia is far too low.

"Hookworm has three larval stages after the hatching of the eggs," explained Araújo. "When the patient is infected, he defecates—and eliminates the eggs. Inside them we find the embryo, but soon after, the larva develops. The eggs hatch in humid soil that is approximately twenty-two degrees centigrade. The range is seventeen to thirty degrees. Then the larvae pass three stages. The last one is the infectious form of the larva. The larva is inside a membrane. It can't eat, or feed in the ground. It can only survive in a host. The infection is by swallowing, or penetration through the skin. They have an obligatory cycle through the lungs to the throat, they are again swallowed and then adults [grow] in the intestine."

So Ferreira and Araújo had found evidence that hookworm was in the Americas more than two thousand years before the accepted date—when Europeans arrived with their slaves. This finding was published in 1980 in *The Transactions of the Royal Society of Tropical Medicine and Hygiene*. It didn't exactly cause an uproar in the paleoparasitology community, and no one in the northern archaeological community seemed to pay the slightest attention. (In fact, no one I asked in North America, other than those who had attended Niéde Guidon's conference in 1993, had heard of these Brazilians and their finds.) Eventually, a well-known paleoparasitologist from Hawaii, Michael M. Kliks, wrote to the journal to explain why Ferreira and Araújo had to be wrong. He argued that the coprolites they studied could well have been the "scat" of a bear or a dog; that they hadn't sufficient evidence to establish the coprolites as human. He also said that even if they did establish that the coprolites were human, they had not established that the eggs were in fact eggs of hookworm. "All of us who work with ancient dung must remember 'all that glisters is not gold,'" wrote Kliks with the heavy-handed humor that seems endemic among parasitologists.[3]

This caused some amusement at Oswaldo Cruz. They replied: "There are no bears or dogs in that part of the continent and dogs were not known by the Indians until the colonization by Europeans. Furthermore in the same coprolites *Trichuris* eggs of the same size as those of *T. trichiura* and smaller than *Trichuris* from dogs were also found. Experimental models with artificial desiccation of faeces in our laboratory have shown that this process does not alter the size of the egg, which thus remains a valid character for identification." They also argued that the site was clearly a site of human occupation, that the hatching of eggs in the fecal mass does happen in tropical settings. Further, they reported, since their first publication they had also found the same eggs and larvae in the intestine of a mummified body. Finally, with a devilish glee, they wrote: "The archaeological site is at Minas Gerais, the Brazilian state where most of our gold mines are found and there, very often 'what glisters is really gold.'"[4]

This discovery of the same kind of eggs in a mummified body was the subject of their next publication. They had found parasitical worm eggs in the mummified body of a child that died about 4000 BP. The mummy had been found in the same cave the coprolites came from. These eggs had been extracted from the child's abdominal cavity using a special instrument that allowed them to penetrate the mummy's side without destroying the fibers in which the mummy had been wrapped. They believed the eggs were of *Trichuris trichiura* and of an ancylostomid, or hookworm. They could not tell which variety of hookworm, *Necator* or *Ancylostoma duodenale*. In this publication they hinted at how they thought the infection had found its way to the Americas. They referred to Betty Meggers' and Clifford Evans' article on how Japanese pottery makers might have come across the Pacific to Ecuador more than five thousand years ago, as published in *Scientific American* in 1966. "One acceptable explanation for such findings is the transpacific migration of Asiatic populations," they wrote.

This paper was published in 1983.[5] Other paleoparasitologists continued to argue that no one could make a diagnosis of hookworm infection from an examination of eggs alone. Araújo and Ferreira wanted to be absolutely certain the eggs they had found in mummies and in coprolites were in fact eggs of hookworm and not something else. Araújo turned to the use of scanning electron microscopes. Working with American paleoparasitologist Karl Reinhard of the University of Nebraska, the team showed that this form of microscopy can be used to clearly identify hookworm in the larval stage, but not in the earlier egg stage.

In 1986 they found larvae of hookworm in human coprolites

taken from an archaeological dig in the state of Piaui at a site called Boqueirão do Sitio da Pedra Furada. The coprolites came from a layer of occupation dated at 7320 years BP. They believed they now had definitive proof that human beings were infected with hookworm long before any known entry to the continent by African slaves brought by European colonizers. The existence of the infection was sufficient to prove a direct link between South America and either South Asia or Africa.[6]

Yet even this extraordinary discovery did not seem to shift the tenor of debate on human origins in the Americas. In fact, it didn't enter the debate at all. This new report got no response. "We have a period of no debate," said Araújo. "Silence. Some years ago, three or four, John Hawdon of the United States published a paper in *Parasitology Today* arguing about a possible migration [of hookworm] through the Aleutian Islands, talking of hypobiosis. We answered in a reply in the same journal."

Hypobiosis is the parasitical equivalent of hibernation. Hawdon argued that the Aleutian Islands were just warm enough that hookworm eggs that fell onto the dirt floors of houses might have lain dormant through the winter and then become actively infectious as the dirt warmed in summer. Human beings moving through the islands would have picked up the infection and somehow carried it to the rest of the hemisphere.

Ferreira and Araújo thought this was most unlikely. Their understanding of the theory of the migration from Siberia over the Beringian land bridge was that it had taken many generations for people to find their way down into the Americas. "This migration means generations crossing this bridge, not one man infected from below Siberia crossing in a year. You can think of hypobiosis in one generation. But think of generations crossing slowly. Even if there is hypobiosis, the next generation would not have the disease."

Furthermore, along with their American colleague Karl Reinhard, they had searched the literature for reports of any remains with hookworm in Siberia, the Aleutians, Alaska or Canada.

They found none. However, there was some sign in the southern region of the United States. "Karl has a coprolite, it is not published yet, with hookworm eggs," said Ferreira.

He was suggesting, in other words, that lack of evidence of hookworm was evidence of its absence, or at least that positive evidence had to be given more weight than no evidence at all. "There are three finds of hookworm eggs of prehistoric coprolites in Minas Gerais and Piaui and Peru. There is a mummy in Peru," said Araújo. He also pointed out that parasites other than hookworm have been shown to have made the passage from Siberia to America. "With pinworm, we can trace all the path of infected people crossing Siberia," said Ferreira. "There are infections there in Alaska and the U.S. and here in South America in the Andean region only. This is an archaeological path." There are mummies with pinworm in Siberia, not extremely old ones, but pre-Columbian. Pinworm was found in the U.S. at Danger Cave in Utah and dated to about 7837 BP. Ruling something out entirely was very difficult, said Ferreira, but so far in northern North America hookworm had not been found.

There had been one more critique of their work published in 1997 by K. Fuller in the journal *Medical Anthropology* under the title "Hookworm: Not a pre-Columbian pathogen."[7] Fuller also accused them of misidentifying the eggs and larvae. Karl Reinhard had written a response. He had not yet submitted it to a journal when I read it. (His long rebuttal and a similar one by another scholar were both rejected by *Medical Anthropology* some time later, but both were asked to prepare short answers to Fuller's arguments.) In his response, Reinhard said that the continuing criticism and doubt based on possible misidentification was really a mask for those who could not let go of an old idea of how people came to the Americas. He wrote:

As late as 1981 parasitologists in general believed that the New World was essentially free of human parasitic disease with the exception of enterobiasis. This notion dates to

Manter's proposition that Beringia acted as a pathogen filter as prehistoric peoples migrated from the Old World to the New World. The "filter effect" was thought to prevent the introduction of the more common human parasites including the hookworm (ancylostomid) genera. This dogma was so strong that early finds of potential ancylostomid larvae were immediately dismissed as impossible by some researchers.... The question today relates to how certain nematod species, especially ancylostomids, reached the prehistoric New World.[8]

Ferreira and Araújo had shown that hookworm infection entered the Americas more than seven thousand years ago. How it came and from where are still open questions. They were moving on in their studies to the use of DNA. Reinhard had spent five months in Brazil the previous year working on protocols for a molecular-biological approach to identifying parasites in archaeological populations. The difficulty they had to solve was the extraction of DNA from paleoparasite eggs or larvae so they could then compare that DNA with that of modern parasites. One of their students had already done this with another tropical parasite, Chagas' disease, which had been found in 2,000-year-old Chilean mummies.

Ferreira wanted me to know the history of the Oswaldo Cruz Foundation, which was in part the personal history of Oswaldo Cruz. There were pictures of him all over the building, dressed in white, wearing a Panama hat, posed formally for the informal tropics. We walked down the hall to the elevator and out into the campus. The foundation, said Ferreira as we marched along, is an extension of the federal ministry of health. All the tropical vaccines are manufactured here; the new library is the best biomedical library in the country.

The day was very hot, very humid. A muddy trail cut from one building to another, through a grove of trees. Giant dieffenbachia

leaves thumped down on the path. This campus was Oswaldo
Cruz's legacy and possibly Brazil's most interesting example of
what can happen when one man's personal extravagance is en-
abled by the public purse. We passed by a strangely designed zoo
with pens and pool made of poured concrete in all kinds of soft,
rounded shapes. This was where Oswaldo Cruz had kept animals
for testing, a kind of cross between a petting zoo and an experimental farm. We walked up to the top of the hill. There was
a magnificent formal garden with steps and urns and flowers and
a vista.

Ferreira's uncle had known Cruz, who died at forty-seven.
"I'm told, of syphilis," he whispered with a wicked grin. Cruz
was a man "who liked French cocottes," said Ferreira, but
many refused to believe in such a dubious ending for the great
man of Brazilian medical science. (Sure enough, de Souza told
me later that Cruz died of renal failure.) Cruz had studied at the
Institut Pasteur in Paris. At the turn of the last century he was
asked by the Brazilian government for help in solving some of
the extreme medical problems that were inhibiting Brazil's development. Rio de Janeiro in those days was a plague zone.
People came and people died, of yellow fever, bubonic plague
and other bizarre diseases that European medicine had not identified. Eventually Chagas' disease was recognized and its insect
vector was identified here. The mysteries of the terrible tropical
disease called leishmaniasis were unraveled here. Rio was a festering pesthole that had to be rebuilt and someone had to take
charge of public health. Oswaldo Cruz, who'd studied in France,
was the man.

We had by this point in the tale arrived at the administration
building, which was unlike anything I had ever seen put to the
purpose of public medicine. It was five or six stories high, made of
brick, with fenestrated stone, stained glass, mahogany and other
tropical woods. There were Casbah-style balconies enclosing the
long windows of the upper floors. There was a gigantic dome sur-
mounting a tower, and in front, a swooping lawn every bit as

beautiful as Dom Pedro II's little spread at Quinta da Boa Vista. And now Ferreira got to his point: Oswaldo Cruz spent the money not on public health, but on this monument.

Where did he get it? I asked.

He got it, said Ferreira, from the government, and no one tried to stop him.

We walked through the cool rooms, paneled in the darkest, densest woods. We crossed over the marble mosaic floors and rode an ornate ironwork elevator to the top of the tower. There was an office there now, and a secretary, but this, said Ferreira, waving his arms, was Oswaldo Cruz's bedroom. In this rounded aerie Cruz had entertained his French women till it killed him. Through a series of doors, I could see a terrace. We went out. The balustrade was Style Moderne, made of stone cut in the shape of ziggurats. We were high enough that the wind whipped my hair, tore at my skirt. There was a view. There was a huge swatch of tropical forest—lush, green, dark, glistening. The whole of the city of Rio was spread at our feet, and beyond that the port with its enormous cranes and bridges, and finally, the brilliant, tossing green sea. Clouds lay down among the mountain peaks like a glamorous woman sprawled on a chaise. It was magnificent, but Ferreira was not finished. I had to be shown the bathroom—the fixtures came from England, he said. The bricks were imported from Portugal and from France—Brazilian bricks were not good enough. Some kind of fever dream had been made real here, a caliph's palace plucked from Baghdad and dropped into this entirely different universe.

I couldn't at first make out why it was so important to Ferreira that I see this. Did he think this monumentalism in the face of abject human need diminished Brazilian science in the eyes of the world? Did he think that Brazilians had spent too long looking for explanations of their southern reality in the universities of other countries?

Cruz put it here, said Ferreira, at the doors to the city, so it could be seen first as you entered—as a sign of the power of science.

# 14

# Revisionist Prehistory

## Bones Beyond the Bounds of Accepted Theory

I HAD AN APPOINTMENT in São Paulo with Walter Neves, the man who had started the biggest shakeup in American physical anthropology since Hrdlička. Neves was the one who had radiocarbon dated Luzia and claimed she was the oldest human in the Americas. He had measured the most ancient Brazilian remains and argued they were not Mongoloid. Neves and his colleague Hector Pucciarelli had published their evidence in 1991, before Gentry Steele and Joe Powell's fresh look at the oldest skeletons in North American museums.[1] Neves had recently entered into a long-distance scholarly association with Powell, who had just been asked by the Department of the Interior to measure the Kennewick remains. Jim Chatters had flown down to show Neves his cast of Kennewick Man's skull. Neves was the man of the hour.

The skies over Rio were black and threatening. The plane flew along the coast all the way to São Paulo, and all the way I worried about the weather. March is the rainy season, known as "the waters"—it comes down as if the sky were a full bathtub that some angry god had abruptly turned upside down. Cars are swept off highways and people drown in the underpasses. Such things had happened only the week before; the newspapers were still full of it. But the sun came out just as the plane turned in from the sea and made its pass over the hills. By the time the taxi hit the freeway it was a glorious, bright day, not too hot, not too cold, just right.

Neves's office was on the sprawling University of São Paulo campus in a spotless bioscience building where everything seemed to be polished or brand new. His name was on a number of doors along the hallway, suggesting that he ran a large laboratory, unusual for an academic physical anthropologist. (In fact he runs the Laboratory for the Study of Human Evolution, in the biology department of the Institute of Biosciences). I found the right door and went into an anteroom with many shelves, desks, computers and some blond young men hovering at their screens. As soon as Neves appeared, I realized I had met him once before, nine years earlier in the office of the director of the Museu Goeldi in Belem, a big city near the mouth of the Amazon River. His circumstances had been much humbler then: he and his colleagues had only allowed me to interview them together, carefully watching their words under the baleful glare of the director, a man with close ties to a government that was just becoming a complete democracy. No one had wanted to stray too far from the government's line. To judge from the anteroom, Neves had now become a man who could draw his lines wherever he wanted to.

He kissed me on both cheeks. He is a small, vigorous fellow, with gray-streaked black hair parted in the middle and falling almost to his chin. His eyes and brows are very dark and his graying beard nicely trimmed. He was dressed in pressed khaki shorts and a dark green Polo golf shirt: casual, but not the least bit rumpled. He waved me into his private office—and there I came to the definite conclusion that Neves's circumstance had changed utterly. The room was lined with new, matching filing cabinets all painted in the same shade of forest green. For the visitor he had a dark green leather French Moderne club chair, with a contrasting green-and-yellow daisy print pillow. I compared this pristine space with the Center for the First Americans at Oregon State University, which had foundation money, plaques with Jean Auel's name on the doors, but offices that were the usual scruffy academic hell. Maybe Neves was personally wealthy?

"I come from a miserable family." (He meant poor; his family was not unhappy.) "Not favelas," he said, "a little bit better. I worked since I was thirteen to survive." He grew up in the Minas Gerais town of Tres Pontas. He did all his undergraduate education in biological sciences at night school at the University of São Paulo. But he'd impressed somebody, because he did graduate work at Stanford and Berkeley while getting his doctorate at São Paulo. How had he gotten into this First Americans business? When we last met, he'd been working in the Amazon on other things.

"It's a very interesting story," he said, settling in his chair and preparing to tell all. He'd joined the Museu Goeldi in 1986. One day the director had called him to his office and said he'd been invited to a large meeting on archaeological salvage work in Sweden, but he couldn't attend. He asked Neves if he'd like to go in his place. Neves was thrilled: he had never thought that he'd have the chance to attend a conference in northern Europe. Since he didn't think he'd ever get back there again, he decided to stop in at the zoological museum in nearby Copenhagen, where most of Peter Lund's collection of human and faunal remains from the Lagoa Santa region of Minas Gerais was stored. "No Brazilian ever saw that collection," said Neves.

When he went to Denmark he was mainly driven by curiosity, but he was also restless and thinking about trying new things. "I am an evolutionary biologist, a biological anthropologist, an archaeologist, and I worked with ecological anthropologists. By that time, in the Amazon I was mostly doing ecological anthropology.... There was not much future in the region for [studying] skeletal remains. I worked with the caboclo population [people of mixed Native American and European descent who live along the rivers of the Amazon]. I had nothing special in mind. This collection is so famous in Brazil, and Lund is a hero for us. I could not resist."

Lund is a hero to Brazilian scientists, according to Neves, because he came alone to a frontier region as one of the first generation of paleontologists in the early part of the nineteenth century. He worked in difficult conditions, without anyone to share his ideas, for many years. He explored more than eight hundred of Lagoa Santa's caves and rock shelters. Neves thinks that what Lund found—the bones of giant animals that became extinct during or just after the end of the Ice Age—must have conflicted with his strong religious views. "He was a creationist. He really could not fit what he found with his beliefs. He could bridge megafauna and modern species, they could have come from others.... But the misery was digging Sumidouro Cave. He found there men associated with [gigantic, extinct Ice Age animals]. He could not agree with that. He sent millions of fossils to Denmark, but then, for unknown reasons, in 1848 [he wrote] his last paper.... I think he was tormented. He was one person alone in the jungle of Minas Gerais and he realized things were not the way we were saying. In my opinion, he was so tormented he couldn't deal with that alone. As far as I know there is no [other] explanation or reason why at forty he stopped working. All of a sudden. He was the father of Brazilian paleontology. If you study the big mammals of the Pleistocene in Brazil, you can't do it without reading Lund. A marvelous man. He died forty years later in Lagoa Santa. There is a statue at his grave there. The people still pay tribute. He was a very special person for Brazilians and a hero in Denmark. If I could convince someone to film his life.... This man, alone, had very important hints of the evolutionary process."

In Neves's opinion, Lund had the material to work out a theory of evolution years before Darwin, but he had stopped short. Regardless of his reasons for not synthesizing his findings,

Lund had at least pulled the evidence out of the ground and saved it for others. The human remains were what interested Neves. "They have seventeen skulls from Lagoa Santa, very well preserved, in the Zoological Museum of Denmark, where they are treated like a treasure, better cared for there than here. I measured them."

There are two standardized methods of measurement that physical anthropologists can use to assess human skulls and bones. The first is called the Monaco Convention—crafted by French and German scientists at the turn of the century. The second was proposed by the American scholar W.W. Howells, who then used these measurements himself for his vast database of populations from around the world. Howells' method was just becoming widely known when Neves went to Denmark, so he used the Monaco Convention to measure the Lagoa Santa skulls. Later, he realized it would have been more useful to use Howells' method, so he could compare his Lagoa Santa population to other populations around the world through Howells' database. Fortunately, seventeen specific measurements are the same in both methods.

When he returned to Brazil, he invited a close friend, the physical anthropologist Hector Pucciarelli, to come to the Goeldi to study its collections of Amazonian primate skulls. He mentioned to him that he had measured the Lund collection in Denmark. Pucciarelli was very enthusiastic and suggested they should do something with his results. "I said since it's probably the oldest in America and there's no one to compare to, [we should] compare to others around the world."

Neves confessed that he had another motive for doing this sort of comparison. By the mid-1980s, Niéde Guidon had begun to publish the results of her excavations at Pedra Furada, asserting that there were clear signs of human occupation in the area more than 30,000 years ago. She was asking questions about where the people could have come from at that time. She had been heard to consider Europe. Her sites, according to Neves, were "fuzzy" and, he thundered, "She is suing André Prous this

week because we are the only voices in this country who are saying, Be careful."

I thought that I'd misheard him at first, but no, he repeated it.
Niéde Guidon was suing archaeologist André Prous. And he,
Neves, expected to be sued as well.

For what? I asked.

Defamation, he said. "This is a shame," he roared. "This is
how science is done in my country."

From his Amazon perch, Neves had read and heard about
what Guidon was doing in Piauí and become increasingly unhappy about it. Her findings challenged fundamental beliefs
about the peopling of the Americas. Neves thought she was de-
luded, and that the truth was obvious: the First Americans had
walked over the Bering Strait from North Asia at the end of the
Ice Age. He thought the bones he'd measured in Copenhagen
could well be a proof of that story. "I said, let's get the samples
from Denmark—the oldest—and compare to the rest and show
they go with North Asians and [there's] no reason to think anything else."

In other words, he set out to refute Niéde Guidon's claims by
demonstrating that the standard theory was correct. The first
analysis he did, with Pucciarelli, compared the Lagoa Santa remains in Denmark to Howells' worldwide modern population
database. To his horror, their results said these Lagoa Santa
remains bore no resemblance to modern Asian peoples. "I wanted
to show there was no reason to believe any other [theory]. The
old model was true. So when we ran the first results of the multivariate analysis in the middle of the jungle, with no one to talk to,
we couldn't deal with it."

Like Lund, his hero, who found the bones of ancient Ice Age
species commingled with those of ancient people, Neves was
appalled by his own results. They did not disprove Niéde Guidon's
thesis at all. This early group of Brazilians pulled out of the
Lagoa Santa caves by Lund were not at all like modern Mongoloids. Neves waved in the direction of his laboratory where

he was working on a different collection of ancient Brazilian skulls. "I will show you skulls where if that is Mongoloid, I am Chinese."

They had to publish, but where? He'd done graduate work in the United States. He knew that if he published in Portuguese it would likely be the equivalent of burying his work in the back yard. No one outside Brazil would read it, or if they did, would take it seriously. "*The Brazilian Journal of Genetics* and *Ciencia e Cultura* are the only ones I would dare.... We published in 1989 in English in the Brazilian journal *Ciencia e Cultura*. The first [paper], we compared [the remains] to Howells. He is a beautiful man. As soon as he completes his data bank, he gave it to everyone. In the middle of nowhere I can compare to the data bank. He covered every continent. For each population he studied fifty males and fifty females. It was a very good sample."

So the results were very persuasive, which disturbed Neves to no end. But then he began to wonder—what did it mean, anyway, to say that an old population was unlike a modern one that might or might not have descended from it? "I told Pucciarelli, I'm not happy. People will say we are comparing the very old with modern material, apples to oranges. I said I want to compare Lagoa Santa with others of the final Pleistocene around the world."

He was not the first to think of trying this. "A man in Australia [P.H. Habgood] had done this. He sent us his data. There were not more than ten or fifteen [remains]." These ancient skeletons were about 20,000 years old.

"I said to Pucciarelli, we have to test if [Lagoa Santa] is similar to the First Australians. There was a clear affinity of Lagoa Santa to the First Australians. I said good, another thing [to test] is the Zhoukoudien Upper Cave." These were the ancient human remains found in eastern China early on in the twentieth century. The skulls found had been measured and studied and cast just before they were carried off by the Japanese during the Second World War. Reports were contradictory, apparently mirroring the minds of their various observers, some of whom thought they were proto-Mongoloids who had not yet developed full Mongo-loid adaptations, while others argued they were representative of the later known types of human beings. The ancient remains ranged in estimated age from 28,000 BP to 11,000 BP.

When Neves had finished with his comparison he realized that there were some affiliations between the remains from the Zhou-koudien Upper Cave and the Lagoa Santa skulls, and that there were also similarities between the Lagoa Santa skulls and the ancient Australians. Neves thought such results were very danger-ous, because they could be misleading. He was afraid to publish them without some kind of theory to explain them. "If we pub-lish without a model Niéde [Guidon] will say Australians came directly to the Americas," said Neves. "I don't believe that.... From Australia and the Americas [there is] no link of standard migration.... We have been very conservative in exploring our unpredicted results. We proposed a very conservative model."

They tried hard to fit their data into the already existing nar-rative of how and when people first came to the Americas. The fact that 25,000-year-old remains from a site in central Europe called Dolni Vestonice and African remains from a site called Taforalt 9 also showed affinities with the Lagoa Santa group was left out of their summary. (In fact, in one graph, Dolni Vestonice was closer to the Brazilians than both ancient and modern Aus-tralians or the ancient Africans.) By not drawing attention to these African/European affinities, and sticking to the old story, they avoided the question of where the ancestors of the Lagoa Santans had come from: everybody "knew" they had come from Asia over the Bering Strait. Neves and Pucciarelli proposed that the First Australians and these First Americans looked most like each other because they shared a common ancestor in Asia. The ancestors of First Americans had moved north, while the ances-tors of the First Australians had moved south. This second paper appeared in *The Journal of Human Evolution*, a well-respected American publication, in 1991.[2]

"But everything was based on a small sample. I knew Brazil

has plenty of collections of early Americans; there were three or four sites with material we could include in our results. I said this is enormous and we should spend lots of time and money on this stuff," said Neves.

These first publications raised sufficient interest that Neves began to have what he calls "visibility" in Brazil. In 1991 he went back to the University of São Paulo to do a postdoctoral study on theoretical cultural anthropology. He'd been looking for an excuse to get out of the Amazon—his lover of many years was dying and needed much better hospital care than was available in Belem. "I was becoming an Amazonist," he said. "I didn't want to be an 'ist.' The region needs so much to be studied, you become that." In 1992, after his lover died, "I was invited to this department, biology, to teach evolution in general, to set up not [only] a laboratory, but one dedicated to paleoanthropological studies. That is what you have now.... My visibility produced money for the best lab in South America," he said with a large grin. "I applied for money for a big project for Lagoa Santa in Brazil and on Colombian material."

A student of his, Danusa Munford, had just finished her thesis on ancient Colombian remains. He found that difficult. When he worked on remains in Brazil, if he was suspicious or worried about a date, he could always speak to the archaeologist and ask that it be checked, but the Colombians would not permit any re-checking: "They are very jealous of their material. I have to accept what my colleagues say." Even in Brazil, material from digs was sometimes hoarded—he could not get access to other materials taken out of Lagoa Santa that were controlled by other researchers. This was a twist on what the plaintiffs in the Kennewick case were dealing with. Replication is essential in science. In physical anthropology, replication means colleagues must have access to all remains, in order to measure and analyze and come to their own conclusions about them. The hoarding of bones makes real replication next to impossible.

He had to make do with what he could get access to. "I

mounted a war operation on the First Americans in Brazil," he said. "My first direction was to go to André Prous [in Minas Gerais] and study one collection of forty individuals he dug in the late 1970s." These remains were not from Lagoa Santa, but from further north in Minas Gerais. The only Lagoa Santa remains Neves had actually measured were those he'd studied in Denmark. "I had no access to any Brazilian collection in Brazil. I wasn't allowed to see these materials."

Well, who owns them? I asked.

"The museum owns, but the professor in charge—! I am a hated person in this country," he cried.

Why are you hated? I asked.

"Big mouth," he said.

"In 1995, when I realized the political climate we worked with … we started going to the museum [in Minas Gerais] to see the old collection that had been gathered since Lund from 1840 to the late 1970s." The problem with this collection was that most of the material had been gathered by amateurs. It was also in terrible condition, the bones all helter-skelter. "So we spent money curating and dating the material. The third vector was to go to the field with Prous and help with the new skeletons found."

His sample size, including the remains in Copenhagen, was now up to forty individuals, most not from the Lagoa Santa region. Very few of the remains in any of the Lagoa Santa collections had been dated. Which brought him to Luzia. He had known of her existence for more than twenty years and he knew she was important. There had been a big "discussion" between the French archaeologists who dug her from the fissure in the rock shelter at Lapa Vermelha and the paleontologists at the National Museum in Rio. The French believed that Luzia (or more properly Lapa Vermelha IV) was extremely old because she had been found twelve meters below the surface and three meters below the bones and coprolite of a giant sloth—a creature that had apparently become extinct at the end of the Ice Age.

"The French had no doubt it was old. But Rio scientists told them [it was] different [for the] skeleton. They thought it was transported [by water] to the bottom of the cave. I believed the French mission. As soon as I had access to the Rio material, it was to date Luzia, to show it was the oldest skeleton in the Americas. We thought it was 11,000 to 11,500 BP. I sent it to Beta Analytic in the United States, the most important commercial [radiocarbon] lab, in Miami.

"No collagen was preserved. They said they couldn't give a precise date, but they could give a minimum date of 9330 BP. This backs up my opinion of the French. So I feel comfortable saying it is probably 11,000 to 11,500 years BP. Thomas Stafford, who was at the University of Colorado at Boulder, is trying to do a new minimum date."

I was crestfallen. I thought of Tom Lynch. No date on collagen? A minimum date? This would not impress Lynch.

So 11,500 BP for Luzia isn't actually a firm date? I asked.

"It's a minimum," Neves said. "I accept the archaeological date of where it was—it was 11,000 to 11,500. We did the same for several skeletons. This gave lots of visibility outside Brazil."

That was an understatement. I couldn't remember the last time an Ontario newspaper had been impressed enough to carry a science story, with a picture, from Brazil. And because his visibility increased outside Brazil, it also expanded inside.

"I will be a full professor," he said, reaching for a huge folder of material, most of which was press clippings. To achieve this new position he has to prove every single line of his curriculum vitae and produce examples of all the public notice taken of his work. Most of the press reports came after he first began to publish in this area in 1989. And it wasn't just the press who took notice. Fundação de Amparo à Pesquisa do Estado de São Paulo (FAPESP), the state of São Paulo's version of the Brazilian National Research Council, funded his "war operation," and he was given about US $100,000 for different projects. He had just applied for US $500,000 for the next four years.

He gave me a (then unpublished) manuscript in which he compared Luzia to Howells' moderns and to measurements of late Pleistocene humans from Europe and South Asia. Working with Joseph Powell, André Prous and Powell's student Erik Ozolins,[3] he first summarized the earlier findings. He and Pucciarelli had shown that the First Americans in South America were closest to South Pacific and African populations. Steele and Powell had shown that the oldest North American remains, when treated with multivariate analytical tools, "seem to occupy an unresolved morphological position between modern South Pacific and European populations." This new paper stated that Luzia, when compared to modern populations, "exhibited an undisputed morphological affinity first with Africans and second with South Pacific populations." When compared with a population of ancient remains, its closest similarities were with early Australians, Zhoukoudien Upper Cave Skull 103 and an African called Taforalt 18. The conclusion: "The results obtained clearly confirm the idea that the Americas were first colonized by a generalized *Homo sapiens* population which inhabited East Asia in the Late Pleistocene before the definition of classic Mongoloid morphology."

He and his students puzzled over the larger meaning of these findings. An interpretation favored by some was that an early, unspecialized population came out of Africa and found its way first to Australia and the Americas, followed by a specifically Mongoloid population that found its way to the Americas later. Others proposed that this nonspecialized population that first entered the Americas evolved in America into Mongoloids, in parallel to the evolution of Mongoloids going on in Asia. Neves doesn't like this idea of parallel evolution. "Why would you get the same morphology in Asia and America?" he asked. "I said, study the evolution of the morphology from the beginning to the last couple of thousand years. We did that in 1995.... Our opinion was, if non-Mongoloids evolved to classic Mongoloids in America, there should be a cline in time."

A cline is a slow change in a species over time: the oldest remains should look like the unspecialized early modern humans, but gradually, as the remains studied get younger, they should show more Mongoloid features. If, on the other hand, Mongoloids came to the Americas after the First Americans, "we should find an abrupt discontinuity and replacement."

"The American Indians today are Mongoloids," Neves said. "We show that everything from 12,000 to 9000 or 8000 BP looks non-Mongoloid. All after 8000 is Mongoloid. There is no gradient."[4] He and his colleagues proposed a four-migration model to account for this. "We say non-Mongoloids entered first. Very soon after Mongoloids entered the continent, we have in South America a major replacement of population, somewhere between 9000 and 7000 BP. At least in central Brazil, the archaeologists detect a different lithic [stone] technology at this time. They interpret this as a result of ecological change. It agrees with my finding of a replacement of the biological population. I have no doubt at all that in South America there was a major replacement of the population between 9000 and 7000. We say what Turner calls the Paleo-Indian is two different migrations: the non-Mongoloid is one and the classic Mongoloid is the other. When did [the first migration] enter? We don't know. I can say that man came to the Americas prior to the domination of Asia by Mongoloids. Soon after [the First Americans' arrival], approximately a couple of thousand years [later] ... the Mongoloids entered the Americas."

I was surprised to hear him say so forcefully that the first population, the Lagoa Santa population represented by Luzia, had been replaced. He meant that their genes were wiped out, that they were overrun, killed off by those who followed, leaving very few descendants or only descendants who looked like the newcomers. In contrast, Mello e Alvim did not find that this early population had been replaced. In her view, the shapes of the 10,000-year-old skulls she examined differed little from those that were 6,000 years old. She had been unable to explain this continuity. And how, I wondered, does his argument fit with what is known about the geology? If he was correct about Luzia's age, and she was indeed 11,500 years old, how on earth had her people come over the Bering Strait? Unless he was willing to accept that Luzia's people had entered around 40,000 to 50,000 years ago, during a time when the glaciers had retracted (which was MacNeish's view), it's hard to see how they could have made their way south to eastern Brazil by 11,500 BP. And of course, when the glaciers retracted, the Bering Strait was under water. So Luzia's ancestors would have had to cross the Strait or follow the current around the top of the North Pacific, by boat.

"I have no problem with boat technology on the north coast," Neves said.

Well, I asked, had he considered Meggers' theories about a voyage from Japan to Ecuador?

"I think straight across needs different navigation technology. One is following the coast and seeing the earth. [It's quite] another [thing] to say you have technology for the open sea. We still favor the idea they came from the north."

Naturally, I thought. What does a Brazilian know about the north? How would a seafaring people, used to living off the marine mammals along the North Pacific coast, find their way and adapt themselves to the climate of central Brazil? And what of Heyerdahl's argument that if a sailor tried to hug the coast coming down from North to South America, his raft or boat could end up dragged out to sea on the major currents or dashed on the shore? According to Heyerdahl, certain kinds of simple vessels are safer on the ocean than the more complex caravels the Europeans used to circumnavigate the globe.[5] For example, the sea-going technology available to the Incas and described by the early Spanish explorers consisted of simple lashed balsa timbers, a thatched hut, a cotton sail and large center boards for navigation. The spaces between the timbers allowed the waves to wash through the boats, which made them extremely stable, even in the worst seas. Such rafts routinely made fishing voyages of over two months' duration beyond sight of land. According to Heyerdahl, there are historical records stating that the Inca Tupac Yupanqui took an army on a flotilla of rafts on a voyage of over a year, and returned with black people in his company. (These stories, told to the early European explorers in South America, are matched by stories told to ethnographers in the South Pacific of a red man, a king named Tupa, who came on a great voyage.) Heyerdahl quotes various historical sources that show that the pre-Columbian Peruvians and Ecuadorians routinely sailed to Easter Island: they told the Spanish precisely how to get there. They may have gone as far as Melanesia. But while it may have been possible for South Americans to move out into the South Pacific, it would not have been so easy for South Asians to make the journey to South America, or for a North American to make a sea voyage south. Several modern sailors intent on proving their various theories of how the Americas were settled have tried to sail in simple vessels from the South Pacific to America, and failed. The only way an Asian in a primitive boat or raft could find his way to the Americas would be by drifting north from Japan on the North Pacific current, which flows south of the Aleutians, and across to the northwest coast of British Columbia. By contrast, logs falling into the sea off the coast of Vancouver Island often drift out to the shores of Hawaii.

I considered ranting about this, but bit my tongue. "Well," I said to Neves, "let's say you're right about that. But how do you explain the different densities of population in north and south, and the fact that so many of the really ancient finds are in South America, and not up in Alaska and the corridor or in Siberia?"

He didn't explain. "I will keep my mouth shut," he said firmly. "I'm a conservative man."

Why would a man who has found "visibility" to be such a useful trait in the gathering in of foundation grants be so conservative about considering alternative methods of entry by early people into the Americas? He was not conservative when he suggested that Paleo-Indians made their way to America earlier than Clovis; nor is he a man who considers it important to be politically correct. "I am known for bitter comments," is how he put it.

I asked what he thinks of the work of Doug Owsley and Richard Jantz, who see European affinities in the ancient North American human remains. "The Smithsonian are Paleo-Indian specialists only for the last two years," he said, sharply. "The only persons in the U.S. I respect are Gentry Steele and Joseph Powell."

It was not clear to me why that would be. Steele and Powell had used simpler methods than Neves and Pucciarelli, what they called "subjective" and bivariate analysis of remains in their 1992 paper in *Human Biology*. That paper, like Neves's conclusions, also suffered from a failure to grapple with the meaning of their findings. On the one hand, they showed that Native American remains between 8,500 and 10,000 years of age have the "closest affinities ... with Asian populations." On the other hand, they said, "where Paleo-Indian specimens differ from modern northern Asians and North American Indians, they tend to resemble southern Asian and European populations ... in this respect our findings resemble the contentions of previous scholars that the earliest recovered samples were proto-Caucasoid or proto-Mongoloid." In other words, they had walked the fence.

In spite of the fact that their views seemed to conflict, Neves and Powell began to work cooperatively in 1997, some months after the Kennewick matter found its way to the U.S. courts. "I asked Powell to come down and analyze tooth variation," said Neves. "Turner was here twenty years ago. I wanted someone fresh."

Powell had made his name by reevaluating Christy Turner's findings that all the teeth found in the Americas were variants of Northeast Asian populations' teeth, or sinodont in character. Powell's paper on this subject had shown that Paleo-Indians' teeth were the most divergent.[6] "The position of Paleo-Indians indicates that they are biologically distinct from their later descendants," he wrote (which was surely a contradiction in terms). Neves and Powell's joint papers showed that the Paleo-Indian populations of both the north and the south are closer to African and Australian populations than they are to any others. Some measures indicated that Paleo-Indians were closer to African populations than Australian populations.[7,8] It seemed to me that if the earliest Americans and Australians diverged from a common African ancestor, the graphs ought to show them to be as close to each other as to African populations.

Not necessarily so, Neves explained. "If you run a multivariate analysis only based on Howells' global populations, you discover that there are two main patterns of cranial morphology on the planet: one relates Australians with Africans, and the other relates Asians, Europeans, and late American Indians with Polynesians floating between these two main groups.... This means only that Australians and Africans are very similar among themselves, and that we cannot clearly discriminate between them."

Three weeks earlier, Jim Chatters had come to Brazil to see Neves. "He brought his cast of Kennewick and also two others, new, not published yet. He taught my students to cast. I allowed him to cast some Lagoa Santa [skulls]." Together, he said, he and Chatters had written a paper on Kennewick.

What a coincidence, I thought. Just after his American partner, Joseph Powell, began his work for the U.S. government studying the affinities of Kennewick Man, Neves went to work with Chatters on the same thing. If Chatters was in the news business, I'd have said he was trying to scoop the government.

"The first one," he said, "shows Kennewick has nothing to do with Europeans; it looks Ainu-Polynesian."

Now that, I thought, was fascinating. When I saw Jim Chatters, only a week before he went to see Neves, he had spoken at length about the Caucasoid-like characteristics of the skull and bones of Kennewick Man, showing me which features had first suggested to him that Kennewick Man could have been a European settler.

He had not suggested that Kennewick shared features with Poly-nesians. And what, after all, did that mean? It is accepted that the Polynesian populations arrived on the chain of islands in the South Pacific only within the last three thousand years. Heyer-dahl put forward the thesis that Polynesia showed evidence of earlier visits from South Americans, who had scattered every-where the botanical evidence of their presence—various plants that had evolved in South America. These plants were discovered growing wild in Polynesia by the first Europeans who sailed there. The Polynesians didn't use them.[9] So what does it say about human migration that Kennewick looks most like Polynes-ians? Are the Polynesians former South Americans who forgot their botany?

I told Neves that the Kennewick cast I saw did not look like other Native Americans to my eye.

"Eye judgement," he laughed. "We stopped using it one hun-dred years ago."

Well, I said, it would certainly be interesting for the man who had used his eye judgement to say Kennewick was possibly a European settler to come forward now and tell the world he looked like a Polynesian.

"I counseled him to set up a press conference in the U.S. to present these new results," Neves said. "This is the first multi-variate analysis comparing Kennewick to human variation in general. He's right, he's not a classic Mongoloid—but he's a generalized Mongoloid. You don't need a fancy model to ex-plain the morphology of Kennewick.... Have you heard about the Buhl burial?"

I had. A human skeleton had been discovered in south central Idaho near the town of Buhl in 1989, in a gravel quarry.[10] This site was not far from the Snake River, which merges with the Columbia near Kennewick. The remains had been studied until just before the time limit allowed under Idaho state law, which requires researchers studying Native American remains to get the nearest tribe's permission for destructive studies and to return the bones for reburial. The Shoshone-Bannock tribe had agreed to dating and isotopic analysis. The skeleton was that of a seventeen- to twenty-one-year-old woman, buried with grave goods that included a stemmed stone point, an eyed needle and a piece of bone that had been incised with a number of lines—approximately seventeen. Isotopic analysis had shown she ate meat and probably fish like salmon. Two bone samples were sent to Beta Analytic. Multiple measurements finally produced a date of about 10,675 BP, which seemed to be verified by where the body was found, buried in the sand just above gravel laid in place by "catastrophic flooding from Lake Bonneville." The remains had been measured and compared to Howells' database, then returned to the Shoshone-Bannock tribe and reburied by the end of 1991. But the article describing her and the site wasn't published until seven years later. It appeared in *American Antiquity* in 1998, right in the middle of the growing controversy about the origins of the First Americans.

The article said the woman was about five foot two and slender, but her craniofacial features fell "within the range of American Indian or East Asian populations." The article reproduced the measurements made. There was also a picture of the skull. It looked like Luzia to me—similar eye sockets, similar nose opening, similar narrow head and cheekbones.

"They arrived at the conclusion it was a typical Mongoloid," Neves said. (The opinion of Richard Jantz, Owsley's colleague, was exactly the opposite.) "I got their data. I ran an analysis of Buhl and Luzia. Even a nonprofessional can see that Luzia is as far as one can get from Buhl. Buhl is Mongoloid. Luzia has nothing to do with [it]. They are extreme opposite positions. If Buhl is 10,500 BP and Luzia is 11,500, the period between the entrances is very short between non-Mongoloids and Mongoloids.... Maybe Kennewick is a result of intermixture of those two.... Maybe these Polynesia–like creatures are a mixture.... I give you my scenario. In my opinion when typical Mongoloids entered South America they squeezed non-

Mongoloids to remote places. Maybe some of them jumped to Easter Island."

I asked to see the paper he'd written with Chatters. Chatters was listed as the first author, Neves the second and Max Blum, a student in Neves's lab, third (this was Chatters' first paper to be published on morphological affinities).[11] The paper assessed the morphological affinities between the Kennewick skull and the modern populations published by Howells in 1989 using principal components analysis. The paper said the skull had been measured in August 1996, following Howells' specifications. It said forty-one variables had been matched between the Kennewick skull and nineteen of Howells' populations, as well as the Ainu. The list of populations Kennewick was measured against included only two Native North American groups, the Arikara and Santa Cruz, and one from South America, referred to as Peru. If looked at from the point of view of the principal measurements responsible for most of the changes in shape, the Kennewick skull displayed a clear association with the Polynesians and the Ainu. If looked at solely on the basis of shape, "the Kennewick skull can be seen as a clear outlier." In other words, from the point of view of shape alone it was like none of the nineteen modern populations it was compared to:

> [T]he Kennewick specimen, featuring a morphology close to the Polynesians when size and shape is considered and being an outlier when shape alone is studied, becomes, among other Paleoindian findings one more clear evidence that a more complex model for the peopling of the Americas is needed. On the other hand, our analysis dismisses the possibility commented by Lahr (1997) of colonization of the continent by European-like individuals since the Kennewick skull does not show any cranial morphological affinities with Europeans, at least when quantitative analysis based on metric variation is performed.

Unlike Neves's previous carefully detailed papers, this one was thin (because, Neves later explained, it was aimed at publication in the journal *Current Research in the Pleistocene*, which accepts only short notes.) There had been no comparison of apples to apples—one couldn't tell from this whether the Kennewick skull was like or unlike the Lagoa Santa remains, or the ancient remains from Australia or Europe, or even the other ancient North American remains studied by Steele and Powell. And as to the conclusion that Lahr was wrong about the Americas having been partly populated by early Europeans, nothing in this paper excluded that possibility. Lahr had not studied the Kennewick remains, and the Kennewick remains had not been compared directly to ancient Europeans.

For all his self-proclaimed conservatism, Neves is convinced that there were human cultures in South America before the Clovis culture developed in the North. Like his colleagues in Rio, he considers it obvious that there are sites at least as old as the date established for Monte Verde.

He also thinks people should stop thinking in terms of migration, and switch instead to the idea of expansions and movement. "We can't know how many times they entered," he said. "It's a movement. There were two main populations in East Asia sampled in the process of occupying America. How many times they entered we will never know."

It was time for a tour of his lab. He was so proud he wanted to show it all. The São Paulo state research foundation had poured $2.5 million into this biosciences unit over the last two years. He threw open a door to a room off his office. "I have the first acclimatized storage room anywhere in Brazil," he said. It was a large space. There were floor-to-ceiling granite shelves, supporting large paper boxes. It was spotless, perfect. We walked through the anteroom to the laboratory, where remains were laid out for study. It was a very large room with glass-fronted shelving, large worktables, microscopes, the works. There were many skulls of many colors and I recognized a cast of Kennewick among them. The other remains had been dug in the 1930s and 1940s by amateurs in Minas Gerais. Neves was about to send them back to André Prous.

He walked to the back of the room and picked up a Lagoa Santa skull. He pointed to the angle formed by the upper jaw. "This prognathism is African," he said.

He showed me another cast to illustrate what he meant by African prognathism. "This is Qafzeh IX," he said. "This is the first modern—100,000 years old, from Israel. They came from Africa. It's amazingly similar."

He showed me the two, side by side. The Lagoa Santa skull was a mineralized black, its teeth white as chalk. He turned it sideways so I could take a picture. "See how gracile," he said. "It makes me nervous. These people in the U.S. say how very robust Lagoa Santa is, but it is the most gracile population I have seen in my life.

"We will spend half a million digging Lagoa Santa. We will dig there for years and years and years. We will have wonderful new collections, well dated... This is my dream since second year [university]. I went there at nineteen. For some reason I always knew I'd be back there."

I wondered if Neves would allow other researchers to come and extract samples of DNA from the skulls under his control. I'd spoken to a woman named Tania Karafet, a Russian now at the University of Arizona at Tucson, who was carving out a specialty in Y-chromosome analysis. This is a relatively new method of studying descent on the male side. Karafet and her colleagues had demonstrated through studies of modern North American and Asian samples that modern Native Americans'

Y-chromosome markers may have originated near Lake Baikal.[12] Another researcher at Stanford had  come to the conclusion that all living Native American males were descended from one man, who lived about 30,000 years ago. But such studies are only as good as the diversity of populations they sample. Karafet had complained that it is very difficult to get South American samples. So, I asked Neves, would he share?

Not a chance, no, said Neves. "When I went to Colombia I had to sign a paper not to remove samples."

But why would you want to perpetuate the wrong?

"If you have the material you have the power," he said. "Paleo-archaeologists won't release it outside Brazil."

But why? I asked. Do you think there is some commercial value to this information?

"It's not commercial," he said. "It's national pride."

# 15

# Brazilian Edens

## The Sheltered Finds of Minas Gerais

I LOOKED AT THE MAP and down at the ground. I was an hour as the plane flies northeast of São Paulo, over the state of Minas Gerais, not far from its capital, Belo Horizonte. Hidden among the green hills, which spread below the wings of the jet like a crumpled velvet bedspread, lay Lagoa Santa and the rock shelter and crevice that had harbored Luzia. Three hundred kilometers to the north at a place called Santana do Riacho was a rock shelter covered with paintings, with dates going back to the end of the Ice Age; 700 kilometers farther to the north and east was Lapa do Boquete, surrounded by sixteen archaeological sites within eleven square kilometers, covered with rock art of every description; and farther northeast still lay the most impressive rock shelter/archaeological site of them all, Boqueirão da Pedra Furada, in the neighboring state of Piaui. I plotted the dots and they formed a line headed northeast (or southwest, depending on point of view). They were all fairly close to the São Francisco River, which begins in the Serra da Canastra range, southwest of Belo Horizonte, and empties into the Atlantic in the northeast, near Recife.

These archaeological sites, hundreds of kilometers inland and a long way south of the equator, made nonsense of the Clovis First theory. To get to Minas Gerais from somewhere in the southern reaches of Siberia on foot would have taken many generations adapting to vast environmental changes as they moved across a huge landscape, yet Luzia had died on the earth below this plane about 11,500 BP. No Crane people flew her there.

I added up the physical barriers: the tundralike or inundated Bering Strait (depending on when people entered); the mountains running down most of the North American coast; the mountains of Mexico and the jungles of Central America; the Andes; the almost continent-wide Amazon system, surrounded by a vast rain forest; a range of southern mountains; and then eventually the São Francisco river. Paddling up such a river was easy compared to walking all that way. Yet archaeologists and physical anthropologists who found, through the use of measurement and statistics, an affinity between the early Lagoa Santa population and people in Africa and Australia, still insisted that their ancestors had come over the Bering Strait.

It seemed to me that they simply refused to shake loose the last constraints of an intellectual prison. The Bering Strait theory did not provide a useful framework, or narrative, to explain the human remains found in the ground. Yet they held on to it the way old prisoners find ways to stay in detention. I knew all the reasons. Everyone wanted to be prudent. No one wanted to fight a battle on more than one front at a time. It was hard enough to stand up in public and declare that the oldest human remains in the Americas were not Mongoloid, were in fact closer in shape to ancient Australians and ancient Africans than to modern Native Americans. So they clung to the rest of the theory as if their lives depended on it.

I found myself parsing carefully the biblical narrative of the creation of the first man and woman and noticing how nicely it organized bits and pieces of new science and how it paralleled the Paiute flood story. Neves had sent me down this path (no doubt unwittingly). He had reminded me that the oldest known modern human beings had been found in Israel at a site called Qafzeh. He had shown me a cast of a Qafzeh skull, an African skull. The original had been dated to about 100,000 BP, just before the start of the last period of glaciation. I knew I was attached to the creation story because it is my own cultural inheritance, but the more carefully I considered it, with the new science fresh in my mind, the more fascinating it became.[1]

In the Bible, the creation story is told twice, and the versions are different. Creation is also directly linked to the narrative of the great flood. The first version tells the story of the whole of creation, which took place in the first six days. In that period, all the animals and creeping things of the sea and the earth and the air were made and then, at the end, God got the idea of making man. "Let us make man in our image, after our likeness. They shall rule the fish of the sea, the birds of the sky, the cattle, the whole earth, and all the creeping things that creep on earth. And God created man in His image, in the image of God He created him; male and female He created them" (Genesis 1: 26–27). When God speaks again, he speaks directly to man. He speaks first of mastery of all living things. Then he says, "See, I give you every seed-bearing plant that is upon all the earth, and every tree that has seed-bearing fruit; they shall be yours for food" (Genesis 1: 29). God makes similar plant provisions for all the other living things, and then takes a rest.

When the story starts again, it's as if the narrator had opened a window to get a closer look at the human portion of creation, or as if there were two kinds of mankind, those who came before (like Wewa's animal people) and those who came after (modern humanity). The narrator goes back over the story of how the first man and the first woman came to be. In this second version the man is formed early on in the process of creation, but not the woman. This man was made even before rain had been set upon the earth. "No grasses of the field had yet sprouted because the Lord God had not sent rain upon the earth and there was no man to till the soil, but a flow would well up from the ground and water the whole surface of the earth—the Lord God formed man from the dust of the earth. He blew into his nostrils the breath of life, and man became a living being" (Genesis 2: 5–7).

The story goes on to say that God "planted a garden in Eden, in the east, and placed there the man whom He had formed. And from the ground the Lord God caused to grow every tree that was pleasing to the site and good for food, with the tree of life in the middle of the garden, and the tree of knowledge of good and bad."

This man is set in this garden to tend and till it. And then the woman is made, as a helper. God puts man to sleep while he pulls out a portion of the man's rib and uses this bone as the basis for creating a living female. The two of them are named. Eve is given her name because she is the mother of all the living. Both Adam and Eve are warned that there are two trees in the garden that are to be avoided. The first is the tree of knowledge, and it is from this forbidden tree that Eve eats and causes Adam to eat: it is this tree that gives them divine knowledge of good and evil, and causes them to make their first rudimentary clothes to cover themselves. God discovers Adam and Eve hiding from Him in the garden. After their confession of what they have done, and the casting of blame, God curses the serpent and curses Eve to bear children in pain and suffering. But Adam and Eve are not expelled from the Garden for eating from this first tree: they are expelled because God became afraid that they would also eat from the second dangerous tree, the tree of life, "and live forever."

The Adam and Eve story conjures up a time when people lived at ease with their surroundings, in a warm garden or forest they farmed, tilled, molded—their relationship to the garden is a good description of the way people lived in the Amazon region until the European colonization. The story suggests that the invention of sewing and the making of clothing is associated with a period of great change in human circumstance, just as the Paiute story about the animals combing themselves and painting themselves is a prelude to a great punishment. The making of clothes is connected to the development of self-consciousness, which is also connected to the knowledge of good and bad. These themes too are echoed in the Paiute flood story told by Wilson Wewa. God thrusts Adam and Eve out into a harsh world beyond the gates of the garden. To prepare them for this transition, he makes for them garments of skin and clothes them, although they had already sewn for themselves loincloths of fig leaves. So it was cold where they were going. The Paiute story ends in the Flood, which wipes out most of the color on the people's furs and feathers and changes their whole relationship to each other and to the rest of nature. In the Paiute story, people go from peaceful coexistence and a diet of berries and fruits to killing each other, as do Adam and Eve's descendants in the biblical account. Depending on how one interprets the very large numbers of years ascribed to Adam and Eve's descendants before they die, God eventually (or quickly) covers the world with a deluge, wiping out all that had become evil and was not worth saving. So, like the Paiute story, which is linked to a great flood, the Adam and Eve story is closely connected to the story of Noah.

The story of this first great change in human circumstance, the expulsion from the life of the garden, is closely followed by the story of another, greater change. First God breaks up the "fountains of the deeps" (as good a phrase as I have ever heard for the deep currents in the ocean that act as sinks for atmospheric carbon dioxide and may therefore affect important aspects of planetary climate). Then the rain pours down. After half a year of rain, all but a small remnant of each species, including mankind, is wiped out. The great plains are inundated, as are the tops of the tallest mountains. The few survivors make their escape in a very large boat.

This was the great narrative framework that Peter Lund lived with when he dug into the caves in Lagoa Santa and found buried in them the bones of Ice Age animals that no longer walked the earth. This was the framework that Neves thought preyed on Lund's mind when he found human remains mixed in with the bones of vanished animals. It must have resonated with Lund as it resonates now. In so many ways, this biblical creation and flood story echoes what geologists and paleontologists and climatologists have begun to say about how the Ice Age came and went, right down to the catastrophic disappearance of large numbers of species of land animals.

The end of the Ice Age changed everything around us, and everything about us. The warming came on very fast, perhaps triggered by a surge of warm currents in the North Atlantic. As the great melt of the glaciers began, there was a rapid change in sea level, which redrew the most basic geography of every continent. Large land masses disappeared under the oceans. All that was left of the plains that once tied what we now call Japan to the Asian mainland were little strings of islands. Much of northern North America, previously covered in glacial ice, was awash with vast icy lakes. It is very meaningful that a boat played an important role at the end of the creation story, in which the few human beings left alive and the very few animals they had managed to save floated over stormy waters to a brand new world.

This was the story Lund found in the Lagoa Santa caves. It was written in the bones and on the shelter walls. It was the story of the end of one creation and the beginning of another.

André Prous is tall and very thin, with wide, schoolboy-frail shoulders and straight thick hair that must once have been jet black. He has straight eyebrows and thick black eyelashes that give him a peculiarly boyish look. But the paleness of his face and the tension around his mouth suggested he was under considerable strain. He did not smile so much as grimace. His fingers, when he shook my hand, were cold.

His archaeological unit at the Federal University of Minas Gerais occupies a series of little stuccoed houses under a canopy of secondary growth, planted to replace what was once a vast, humid forest. His office is in the front room of a charming cottage, with wooden shutters painted a deep Provençal blue. There is no glass in the bottom of his window, under which he has set his desk so he can face into the wall of forest as he works. A small breeze blew in the faint smells of flowering trees and the faint squawks of birds. It had just rained. The creepers and the bushes and the trees glistened in the sun.

He gave me a more detailed version of the Lagoa Santa story. In the eighteenth century, Minas Gerais was one of the more developed parts of Brazil, because it was a storehouse of mineral wealth, gold, diamonds. The scientific exploration of Minas Gerais began with the Napoleonic wars. Until then, foreigners had not been allowed to penetrate the King of Portugal's private treasure-house. But fear of Napoleon sent the King of Portugal in flight to Rio. The English, Portugal's allies, were invited in to trade, and the Portuguese mined saltpeter for the manufacture of gunpowder. Saltpeter is found in limestone caves, and the Lagoa Santa region sits in the middle of a huge limestone triangle pocked with a myriad of caves. In particular, said Prous, a Dane named Peter Clausen came to Lagoa Santa and found, along with the saltpeter, the bony remains of giant mammals, including sloths and armadillos. He bought bones to send back to European museums, which were just becoming interested in the brand new field of learning called paleontology. In 1820, Peter Wilhelm Lund, who had studied with Cuivier, the first paleontologist, followed up on Clausen's work.

"Between 1820 and 1845 he dug in many caves in Lagoa Santa," said Prous. This little "sacred lake" is only a few hours (by car, several days on horseback) from the former capital of the region, Ouro Preto, a town about eighty kilometers south of Belo Horizonte. "The water was supposed to be miraculous," he said. "It was sold in Portugal." It was also supposed to be a region good for the health. Lund had problems with his health, so he stayed in the town of Lagoa Santa until his death at eighty.

One of the places Lund dug was Sumidouro Cave. There was a subterranean lake in the cave where he found the bones of Pleistocene fauna mixed with human skulls all jumbled together.

At that time, explained Prous, there was no such thing as geomorphological studies that could analyze how certain formations were created over time. Lund believed these bones, human and animal, had been laid down together and were of the same age. This was the first evidence found anywhere of mankind that seemed to date back before the Great Flood. "He published this find in 1840," said Prous, "an American antediluvian man."

Lund also noticed that there was art on the walls of rock shelters in the area near Sumidouro Cave. After the 1840s, when he stopped publishing, he continued to correspond with his colleagues in Denmark. Prous believes that Lund was a nephew of Kierkegaard, and, like Neves, that he was religiously troubled by his finds. But in spite of Lund's failure to write anything after 1848, Prous said, "he brought from Denmark an artist to draw the plates of description of the remains and he brought the father of modern ecology, Eugene E. Warming, a botanist, to Lagoa Santa to study the vegetation and landscape, relating soil type and vegetation." This was, according to Prous, the first study of "vegetal ecology" in the world. "Lagoa Santa is a very important place."

By the early part of the twentieth century, no one was much interested in Lund's evidence of an antediluvian man in Brazil. The Creation story was no longer of interest to scientists, and far more ancient examples of early humanity had been found in Europe. Darwin's theory had worked its power on the minds of everyone working in biology, and Hrdlička's writ extended from Alaska to Tierra del Fuego. But in the 1920s, Padberg-Drenkpohl, the Czech scientist who worked for the National Museum in Rio, came to Lagoa Santa to verify or disprove Lund's work. He excavated an ancient cemetery at the hamlet of Confins, near what is now Belo Horizonte's international airport and one kilometer from Lapa Vermelha where Luzia was later found. Padberg-Drenkpohl unearthed many skeletons (now in the National Museum), but no large Ice Age fauna with them. He therefore considered all the skeletons he found to be recent.

Professional scientists lost interest in Lagoa Santa, which was left to the amateurs of the Science Academy of Minas Gerais. This was an organization made up of three people: the British consul, Harold V. Walter; an artist from Belo Horizonte; and a local teacher. Walter went with laborers to a site dug by Padberg-Drenkpohl. Under the layers the professional had excavated there was a layer of hard sediment, a Pleistocene sediment, as Prous described it, which Padberg-Drenkpohl had not bothered to penetrate. Walter paid his workers to dig through it. One day, while none of the Academy members were at the site, the workers found the bones of large mammals, and then another day a skeleton of a man. The Academy published a report that they had found "Pleistocene Man," said Prous. But their claims were not taken very seriously. It was possible whoever had buried this man had dug through the Pleistocene sediment to make his grave. "It was not archaeological," said Prous.

In order to establish some kind of case for their claim, the members of the Academy tried to have the bones dated using a chemical method that involved measuring their fluorine content. These results weren't credible either. Nevertheless, in 1955 the American archaeologist Wesley Hurt agreed to work with a Brazilian from the National Museum to excavate a Lagoa Santa shelter called Cerca Grande. Hurt was interested in Lund's claims and in those of the Academy of Science.

"He excavated for two years," Prous told me. "A big excavation, two shelters. But he found no Pleistocene elements. He hoped to find man with a giant animal. He published almost nothing.... He had taken some charcoal samples, he dated them later to about 10,000 years BP. This was a big surprise. It was the most ancient [then] in South America.... It was very, very unexpected. He had to publish and he published in 1969." This publication of ancient charcoal dates attracted Annette Laming-Emperaire's attention.

"Her father was the French consul in St. Petersburg during the October Revolution." She had previously worked in Patagonia, and then in the 1950s and 1960s had dug with her husband at Brazilian sambaquis (shell mounds). She had been looking for a chance to come back to Brazil. When she read that ancient dates had been taken off a site near Lagoa Santa she made an agreement with the National Museum of Rio de Janeiro. Her project became known as the French "mission to Brazil" and was supported mainly with funds from France's ministry of foreign affairs. She arrived back in Brazil in 1971. Prous came with her.

"I was born in the Pyrenees and studied in Poitiers. After my doctoral dissertation in Paris I got an invitation from the University of São Paulo to come here." Prous taught at São Paulo until 1975, and also worked with Annette Laming-Emperaire in Lagoa Santa. First they made a survey of suitable sites. Then she picked a place to excavate. She began that work in 1973, and continued with it until her death.

Laming-Emperaire searched for and found a site with good stratigraphy that would reflect changes in the climate and wildlife of the region over time. Most of the known sites in Lagoa Santa had been destroyed by the saltpeter mines or by the Science Academy of Minas Gerais. The best site she found was Lapa Vermelha. It was not rich, but there was a rapid rate of sedimentation that had changed in color and structure from dry to humid season, making it almost like a lake varve, a clear annual sequence.

They found hundreds of hearths. But this was not a place where people had lived, it was a place where a few people had taken shelter and then left, a casual place with room for two or three people a night. The amateurs of the Science Academy knew the site but the density of artifacts around it was so low they hadn't bothered digging for its treasures.

The floor of the shelter was excavated by the French mission through eleven meters of sediment. A block had fallen from the overhanging roof more than 15,000 years earlier. There was one sediment that was varved near the wall. At the 10,000-year level there were fallen blocks, then mixed sediments with the bones of a giant sloth above that, then recent levels from around 7000 BP with hundreds of human hearths. They were interested in the levels below 10,000 BP.

"We excavated the human skeleton that Walter nicknames Luzia in the narrow region between 10,000 and 12,000 BP," said Prous. He had found the first bones in the crevice himself in 1974. In 1975, he went to a conference in Mexico City. He'd been away two days when his colleagues back at the site found Luzia's skull. They knew right away that the skull was of the type known as Lagoa Santa man, the same "type" Lund had known from long ago. Prous was not particularly shocked or surprised to find a human remain of such great age in the Americas. For a European such as himself, he explained, it was "no problem to have man 12,000 years ago in America. Clovis doesn't exist here. If I have a date, the stratigraphy and it's all there, 12,000 years ago, why not? I analyze the context of the find. But 20,000 or 12,000 doesn't matter."

The bones had washed into this crevice because every year water ran down beside the shelter and along the wall. They found bones between 10,000 and 12,000 BP. There were intervals between the levels on which they found samples that could be dated, so they had to estimate the dates of the bones from the median rate of accumulation. There were also human coprolites and giant sloth bones found. Complicating things further, in an area adjacent to this crevice, in an interval between a 14,000 BP layer and another 22,000 BP layer, they found one crystal flake and one "instrument" of unknown use.

He showed them to me. They were very crude, very simple. The crystal was absolutely clear, like a piece of glass. The crude stone object had a sharp edge. Prous called it a scraper. "It is between 15,000 and 20,000. But it's completely isolated. As is the flake. A flake of quartz. There is none in the immediate region. Perhaps people threw it [in]. But it is possible there was some perturbation that put it there. It's not like the bones, in good stratigraphy."

If the scraper and the flake had been found in their proper

time sequence, they suggested a human occupation at Lapa Vermelha older than 20,000 years. Prous had nothing against this notion, but nothing to support it either. He considered it important to be prudent. Thus he wanted to be sure I understood that Luzia's bone collagen had not been dated, but rather the humic acids washed off the bone had been dated instead, and produced a minimum date of around 10,000 BP. He believed a date of 11,000 BP was fair.

In 1976, Annette Laming-Emperaire was worried about making certain the excavation had the best controls in order to confirm the dating. That same year, Prous founded this center for archaeology in the Federal University of Minas Gerais. He was not as interested as she was in early humans in the Americas. His interest was the archaeology of the state of Minas Gerais. It was huge, the size of France, and no one had surveyed beyond the Lagoa Santa district.

He and his students surveyed to the east and west. There was very little in the way of good ethnographic material to help him. The people who came to Minas Gerais in the eighteenth century were interested in gold and diamonds, not in Indians, who "were destroyed completely," he said.

The first important site they found was Santana do Riacho. He tested it in July 1976, and then started an excavation. Santana do Riacho was divided in two during its earliest period of occupation. One part was a shelter that was used by people as a quarry and stoneworking area. Another part, higher up the hill, contained a cemetery. There he found no fewer than forty skeletons buried around a very large fallen rock. These people dated back to about 8500 BP: the site itself had produced charcoal dates up to around 11,900 BP. There had not been many changes in the vegetation around the site over time and one of the skeletons seemed to have been wrapped in something suggesting a hammock. They were the same morphology as the Lagoa Santa people.

"We have a few fibers," he said.

I had not read any papers describing textiles found in Santana do Riacho. The age of the skeletons put them in the same general Paleo-Indian category as Spirit Cave and Wizards Beach in Nevada. I asked if I could see what he meant by fibers.

"This is published in Portuguese," he said. "I published a drawing. We have sheets of bark, you mash it, they used this here. And three centimeters of cordage."

He gave me a paperback called *Arquivos do Museu de História Natural*, which recorded the findings of the various digs done by his center since 1976.[2] I flipped quickly through to the section on textiles. It was only seven pages long and its bibliography did not refer to the works of James Adovasio, or any other early textile experts I was familiar with. I couldn't read the Portuguese well enough to be sure I understood the nuances, but what it clearly said was that three pieces of textile had been taken from burials that dated to between 8000 and 10,000 BP. Fragment 1 had been removed from Burial 16, which was an adolescent of about twelve years old, buried in a flexed position. The fragment was large enough to establish how it was made—it was twined using a Z twist. Burial 9 had been recovered with a textile, Fragment 2, described as three dimensional and made from small leaflets of a palm. Fragment 3 was found with Burial 2. This was tied off using an S twist and a Z twist.

An illustration of Fragment 1 showed it had been wrapped around the outside of the first skeleton, and was twined similarly to the rough outer wrap used to cover Spirit Cave: warp and weft were both twisted in Z and S twists. There were three drawings of the three-dimensional Fragment 2: an inside view, an outside view and, finally, an illustration that showed how it had been made. It looked to me as if it was the same plain-weave method that had been used to make the inner mat that covered Spirit Cave, something Amy Dansie thought was unique to the Lahonton Basin.

These human remains found at Santana do Riacho were of a population that was not Mongoloid. Neither was the Spirit Cave Mummy, found so many thousands of miles to the north in

Nevada. And like the people who had buried the Spirit Cave Mummy, they plain-wove a textile that was buried with their dead.

"When I started with Annette," Prous was saying, "the first thing she explained is that the first people of the Americas were not Mongoloid." Paul Rivet had also spent time in São Paulo at the Center for Prehistory there, which had been founded by Paulo Duarte. Duarte sent Joseph Emperaire to the southern tip of South America, to Patagonia, where according to Rivet's theory there had once been a land bridge between Australia and South America, a southern version of the one at Bering Strait. ("We know now there wasn't one recently," said Prous.) For Prous, the more interesting questions had to do with the various industries he found at Santana do Riacho—most particularly the worked crystal points and the art painted all over the shelter walls. "There were some 2,500 figures of art, very nice," he said. "Nicer than in Lagoa Santa."

Some of these paintings have been very well dated. One group was painted in an area out of which a large block fell at 4000 BP. Prous believes that the place was occupied until 2000 BP.

Prous took me out of his office into a larger room where two of his students were hard at work. They were laboriously copying and coloring all the markings made by human beings on the rock face at Santana do Riacho. They unfurled some of their work to let me see. It was alive with color and dancing forms. There were strange geometrics, groups of waves, groups of dots, groups of sticks crossed and single file, groups of stick figures, various very large beasts. There were also all kinds of small animals, fish, and human beings. The geometric forms were tantalizing; did they signify numbers or days, or were they mazes? Some were arranged as if they were nets set up to corral running deer. Prous and his colleagues and students had analyzed these geometric figures every way they could think of. They'd called in astronomers and calendar experts, but none of them had been able to say, yes, this represents a code tied to some aspect of the night sky, or some change in seasons.

Here we were in the presence of the handiwork of ancient human beings, and no one could figure out what it meant.

At the crack of dawn the next morning, I left my mahogany-and-marble-and-glass hotel. Small, tanned, very young people streamed past me on their way to shop or work. I was all tricked out for an expedition in the humid tropics, as ordered. I had my hat, my sandal shoes with socks (to prevent any nasty bugs from crawling over my toes). I wore army pants with pouch pockets deep enough to hold a bottle of water and a camera, and a long-sleeved shirt over my short-sleeved shirt, to avoid being bitten by the insect that carries leishmaniasis. Fernando Costa, Prous's former student, and his son Frederico waited at the curb in the little Fiat I'd rented for this occasion. The driver was a young man named Xexeu (pronounced Shay-shay) Aguimar who spoke no English but was a director of archaeological videos. Costa and Aguimar were to take me to see what was left of the dig at Lapa Vermelha and some of the other sites of the Lagoa Santa region. Prous was not available. He had other things to worry about.

He had finally confessed, under prodding at lunch, that he had been served with papers by Niéde Guidon's lawyers. He'd known her since his days at graduate school in Paris. He was now required to answer her charge that he had morally and actually damaged her reputation with things he had written more than three years earlier. At that time, he had prepared a round-up on the state of archaeology in Brazil for a publication directed by Walter Neves. He had complained in his paper that the young people who worked for Guidon frequently made outlandish claims, particularly on television, about their finds. These claims were never properly published anywhere, but they were never retracted either, leaving confusion in the public's mind as to the truth. He gave an example which I will not repeat here. Now Guidon demanded satisfaction—in a court in Piaui. This meant he had had to hire a lawyer in Belo Horizonte to instruct another lawyer, whom he had also had to hire, in Piaui. His face turning quite white, he said he had no money.

Prous had never gone personally to see Guidon's sites in Piaui (although he had sent an emissary on several occasions), in spite of the fact that one could fly or even make the drive by car in a matter of eight hours. He had tried to go, but when he asked, Guidon's assistant said it wasn't convenient; when she held her international conference in 1993, everyone in the country knew of it before he did, he complained. He received his invitation only one month before the event, and he had no money to go, and besides, he had other plans. So he had contented himself with critiquing what had been published. And that was part of the problem with Guidon—so little had actually been published.

And so Prous had to meet with his lawyer while I drove to the field with Fernando Costa, who explained to me that this modern conflict was as nothing compared to past feuds in Brazilian archaeology. As Xexeu Aguimar drove us through the hills outside of town, Costa, who turned out to be the great-nephew of Harold V. Walter, the man who founded the Science Academy of Minas Gerais, told me all about the bad old days. Costa's thesis topic for his bachelor's degree in the history of science had been the history of the science of archaeology in Minas Gerais, which in large measure was the story of Harold V. Walter. Costa had tracked down all he could of his great-uncle's papers, field notes, and collections; he had learned several unsettling things.

Harold Victor Walter was born in 1896, just south of London. After the First World War, he and his two brothers went to Brazil, and in 1927, Walter was sent to Belo Horizonte by his employer, Unilever. He bought a country house in Confins. He arrived just as the National Museum's expert, Padberg-Drenkpohl, was working at Confins at a rock shelter called Lapa do Confins. "When he finished," said Costa, "my uncle went there and started excavating." After about two months of digging, his uncle's workmen broke through the heavily cemented floor of the cave and, two or three meters beneath it, found a human skull with horse and bear bones—"just fragments," said Costa.

Walter knew the significance. He had read Lund. Along with his two associates, "from 1932 to 1965 he worked at Lagoa Santa at fifty rock shelters to try to prove Lund's hypothesis.... He wrote three books, and twenty-five articles in Portuguese and English," said Costa.

In 1937, Walter became the British consul in Belo Horizonte. In 1940, with the war on, he stopped digging and didn't start up again until 1947. In 1949, Betty Meggers' husband Clifford Evans "worked here for two weeks with my uncle." In 1955, Wesley Hurt arrived. "They knew each other before," said Costa, which may have explained what happened next. "I found two letters from Hurt to my uncle about 1952 or 1953. He [Hurt] worked Cerca Grande. He did not invite my uncle."

It was no accident that Hurt found little of interest at Cerca Grande. Walter knew Hurt was coming six months before he arrived. He was offended that Hurt had not invited him to join his expedition. Walter went to the site with his workmen and dug it before Hurt came, "taking things away," as Costa put it. "They thought Lagoa Santa belonged to them," the great-nephew said, and shrugged. "Nobody in the Museum in São Paulo would come to study. So they took the responsibility. This is typical of Brazil. There is territoriality all over. Meggers and Evans owned the Amazon until the end of the 1980s.

"Before he died in 1976, the French mission [came] with Annette Emperaire and André [Prous]. She found a new site near Lagoa Santa." As he had done to Hurt, Walter sent his laborers to the site the French wanted to excavate before they could begin. "After that, the reputation of my uncle was very bad."

Costa justified him nonetheless. Harold Walter had at least

saved the bones.[3] While Walter took away material, he did publish everything he found and he used his own money to fund his digs. Costa's examination of his field notes suggested that he had tried to do things properly in spite of the fact he had no professional education. "He had a quest. He wanted the oldest human remain. He mixed everything before to get this...but he had Lund's hypothesis and he published all his jobs. And he kept the artifacts. Before he died his son gave it all to the university. André was not there yet. It sat in a wet basement for five years. I found the documents. He gave a hundred arrow points. When André got it, it was thirty, so more than two-thirds of the collection is lost. The human bones are curated by Walter Neves. Lund found fifteen skulls. H.V. Walter's [collection] is thirty skulls. But the notes are lost."

At this point in the story we were far out and away from the center of Belo Horizonte. We had climbed up out of the bowl of hills the city is built on, and had driven through little towns and open, rolling fields. Every farmyard fence seemed to drape itself in billows of bougainvillea. The sky was a brilliant, hot blue, and the flowers and the grass, the sharp yellow-green of young crops in the fields, the tall trees splashed here and there with huge orange flowers, were all utterly beautiful. Then the road had changed. A narrow river chunked along beside it. We had crossed a bridge. Everything above this river, Costa had said, was the Lagoa Santa region. We had moved past the open fields and into an area that was basically one giant hunk of limestone, pitted with deep open-face mines, with trucks zooming down on hairpin roads.

We drove over a hill and down into a bowl—there were trees forming a line across the tops of the distant hills and open fields below, very green. Black-and-white cattle with strange horns (from India, I was told) were scattered here and there. There was a farmhouse, white, with a tiled roof, and beyond that the bowl's rim seemed to rise and become a green-walled cliff. I could make out some streaks of red through the green. We turned off onto a dirt road through the cattle field. We got out of the car in a farmyard full of black-and-white African chickens. A donkey ignored us.

Costa asked the farmer's permission to go up to the rock shelter on the back side of the farmer's fields. I couldn't really make it out. Stone the color of gunmetal peeked out through the field of green. It was like the Niagara Escarpment back home, I thought, clothed entirely in trees. I could see that there was a steep rise because the trees jumped straight up from the fields. Far to the left there was a tiny hint of blue—a little lagoa, a place in the limestone where water welled up and formed a lake. We walked through the field, through the grass, following a fence line, avoiding the large cow pies. I brushed at the grass, which came up to my knees. Costa was telling me about his struggle with leishmaniasis. It had started here with a little bite near his ear, and then it developed into a huge hole that almost took his hearing. The only treatment was to poison the bug with antimony.

I pulled my hat down tight. At the end of the field the trees and underbrush were thick, like a Southern Ontario stand of bush maple. Xexeu laid about him with a machete, while Costa took another route, pulling himself along on a stick. I sweated and steamed and carefully placed my feet on top of roots partially hidden by a layer of soil.

Every now and again, as we climbed up to that flash of rock above our heads—straight up, it seemed to me—I wondered what this landscape had been like in Luzia's time. Wetter, I thought. Probably a large body of water where the fields were.

Finally we pushed through the last wall of bush and there we were, in a little clearing with an overhang of heavy rock. There were several sites here, Costa informed me. There was absolutely nothing to indicate them, no marks, no signs, nothing. The overhang formed a corner. Aguimar disappeared that way, but Costa showed me where Luzia had been found. There was nothing to see really, just the ground sloping away to the back of the shelter, and a deeper crevice, a hole. I took a picture of the hole. There were no paintings on the rocks. Around the corner of the overhang was where the French mission had left the wall of their stratigraphy, "for the generations," Costa said, mockingly. It was supposed to show how they had dug through meters of varved soils to the sterile bedrock, but the years had turned the stratigraphic wall into a kind of muddled sandy hill, and there was little to be seen of what had been done here. In twenty more years it would just be a jumble. There was the faintest mark of red that suggested maybe someone had made a painting. I turned around. Through the screen of brush, there was a breathtaking view of the whole valley, the glint of the little lake below. I could see from hilltop to hilltop. This was the kind of place someone would climb to figure out where to go next: the kind of place one would climb to to have a safe nap out of the heat of the day.

This was where Luzia had been laid to rest.

We drove on to Cerca Grande. We stopped in a little town perched on the top of the limestone hills, right near a huge quarry where giant machines shaved and crushed the stone walls. The houses were large, made of concrete and stucco, with big high fences. There were new cars, but there were also horse- and mule-drawn carts. Children walked barefoot. At an open bar we bought Guaraná (a local soda drink) and Tic Tacs. There were flies on the pastries.

Past the town, the road got narrower. We drove in and out of valleys until we came to one with a large fazenda, a ranch that stretched for miles, with an enclosure for the horses the size of a small hotel. We arrived at a gate and presented our letter of introduction from Prous. There was a brick house behind the fence, surrounded by a garden of very tall corn. We were allowed in, and we followed the dirt road into the fields. Another red-and-gray cliff rose out of the ground like pastry from a flat pan. Great tangled roots of the trees on the mesa above, some as thick as my arm and fifteen meters long, dangled down over the cliff face. As we came closer, large round openings appeared high up in the rock, the kind of places one could imagine stupid boys trying to climb into for the adventure. This was where Costa's great-uncle Harold Walter had dug, and this was where he had taken out remains and artifacts before Wesley Hurt could find them.

You know, said Costa, there's a lot about these people we don't know, like where they lived. We've never found a place of habitation, just these temporary places. They came, took shelter from the rain, and made their graffiti. When the rain stopped, they moved on. Cerca Grande VI and VII, where Hurt dug, had produced between them perhaps twenty skulls, all of the Lagoa Santa morphology.

And they had not found everything by any means. Costa himself had found two shelters here no one else knew about. We arrived, all of a sudden, at the face of the shelter, which turned and twisted in on itself in a series of astonishing and unexpected cuts, one going very deep into a big cave with vast stalagmite formations. At the back, past the giant balancing rocks carved out by the action of water on the soft stone, I could make out a kind of keyhole where light shone through from above and behind. This cut worked its way right through, he said, to a kind of Shangri-la, a little world of grass and trees and water completely surrounded by the high walls of the cliff. The roots from the trees up above dangled right down inside these soft walls. There were bats and spider sacs.

We climbed in over the fallen tumble of giant rocks, made our gingerly way on sandy paths, under the shadow of a truly huge block that seemed to be balancing itself on one small edge. It was cool, much cooler than outside, almost cold, and in the dark upper corners of the cave, who knew what lurked? There was the plaintive sound of water dripping on stone. Everywhere were strange and glorious forms the water had carved out of the limestone, or that the limestone, dissolved in the water, had become. It had dried into puffy mushroom shapes and wizard caps, like soap bubbles turned solid by some magic wand.

Back to the field, the car, the road. We moved around to another side of the limestone mountain. Another farm field, this one bigger, better worked. Another letter of introduction. We drove through the yard and another field of white cattle, parked by a wire fence, and climbed through, and then trudged through the tough, fibrous grass layered over the red, heavy soil. There was a low screen of dried-out looking trees with large roots climbing over sandy ground and somewhere off to the left a dried-up lake. Quite suddenly we came upon a large opening in the wall of stone, heaped with sand—the remains of Hurt's dig. An arrow had been painted on the overhanging rock that reared up over my head. There were some other very faint marks painted on the stone, one in the shape of a fat deer on the run. They were crude, there weren't many.

No one had lived at this shelter. So why did they come? To get water when it was dry? To have a stone wall at their back when they were scared? Perhaps for the adventure, for the challenge of making their mark and telling their story on a high place, like the graffiti in Rio.

We rounded the corner to another site where Hurt had dug. At first the rock face was smooth and forbidding, then one turned a corner and there was an open space with an overhanging roof and a dark crevice at the back. These hidey-holes offered safety, water, vistas, beauty, all combined. They were all places where two ecosystems bumped against each other. There was the dark forest, with its streams and lakes, and the harsh and hot cliff world with its own rules. Pretty as a picture, places made for making pictures.

We walked out and down through the heavily rooted trees. They were like wildly elongated toes, those roots, no, they were like large and misshapen cords. It was remarkable the way they twisted and turned and wrapped themselves in and around each other. They rolled over and under, and without plan or design became passive nets to snare the feet of the unwary. You could invent the basic art of textile making just by looking at them.

Dawn. Hot, damp. My muddy clothes from yesterday, rinsed out
in the hotel bathtub, hadn't dried over the course of eight hours. I
wrung them out again. The sky was soft pink when André Prous
and Xexeu Aguimar arrived to take me out to Santana do Riacho,
a three-hundred-kilometer drive. Prous was in the same shirt, the
same jeans as the first day I met him, but he had a red bandana
and a small old knapsack and sneakers on his feet.

We headed out the same way, to the north, towards the town
of Lagoa Santa. The day before, Costa had offered the opinion
that Lund was an interesting man. He'd had no children, and
never married. In fact, Costa said, he never mentioned women at
all in any of his writings. The first thing he did when he arrived in
Minas Gerais was adopt a young man, twenty years old, who
wrote lovingly to Lund's family in Denmark after he died. This
whole story was delivered with the kind of sexual innuendo only a
young Brazilian man seems capable of.

We drove slowly through the town, beside the sacred lake
itself. It appeared in no way remarkable. The water was school-
room-chalk blue, and there was a grassy verge with small trees
planted here and there, the kind of pond one would linger by,
but not think of swimming in. (I could almost hear the paleoparasitologist Luiz Ferreira warning, "Schistosomiasis!") There
were a number of small villas scattered around the whole of its
perimeter, their front doors facing the lake. At the plaza in the
center of the old part of town, we stopped so I could see the small
bust of Lund in bronze, set upon a plinth.

Xexeu Aguimar gunned the Fiat up and down the steep hills,
and then we rolled out into the countryside. The sun was very
hot, very bright. The country changed, and changed again. First
the rolling fields, then the great limestone cliffs and their mine
pits, with a sickly green scum of water in their deepest basins.
Down there, said Prous, pointing to one particularly huge pit,

Lund made excavations and found megafauna, and the mines have destroyed it all. A narrow river appeared on the right, the Velhas (the Old Ladies), where miners had once panned for gold. When we crossed it, we passed suddenly out of the land of limestone and remnants of forest, and found ourselves in a much stranger country. All at once, with only the river to mark the change, it was dry and treeless, the sandy ground dotted with big shrubs and wild flowers. Over the hills and down into the hollows the road flew up and then down, up and then down, as if we were skimming the surface of a heaving sea.

The wind roared at the window, the humidity was gone, my skin felt hot and prickly dry. Prous sat in the back seat, telling me how he found the site of Santana do Riacho. "We made the survey in 1974," he said. "This place was known." In the 1880s the engineers who had made a survey for the telegraph system had recorded their discovery of a shelter with paintings on the walls. When Prous set out to find it, there was not much in the way of a road—just a dirt donkey path. The site was twenty kilometers from the old road, which was so bad it used to take him a whole day to make one hundred kilometers. There was a village nearby with a population of about nine hundred, but it was the last place in Minas Gerais to get telephone lines, and that was only ten years ago. When he finally found the site, he took Annette Laming-Emperaire to see it. She agreed there was good sedimentation, or at least enough to try and work out a stratigraphy.

Prous went back two weeks later and found the graves right away. He covered them up, went back the next year and excavated a hundred square meters. Because there was not much depth of sediment over the grave sites, he didn't think they were extremely ancient. The first date he got back was 9700 BP.

He published it right away in Brazil, in 1977, and then in France in 1981. He was grateful the site was on private land, or at least not a protected place under Brazilian law. Declaring a site a park or a heritage site was the equivalent of hanging up a sign that said "Treasure here, come and get it." While Brazilian heritage laws are good, reality and the law had few points of contact. There are only four archaeologists employed by the heritage department for the whole country and they are in Rio and Brasilia.

He described the countryside around us as sertão. There were few trees, just bush: all of the vegetation was adapted to a seasonally dry climate. Each tree, he said, had thirty meters of roots, with very thick bark and leaves. The soil was full of aluminum, and therefore toxic. There were various other minerals and plants, which had many uses. The plants were rich in vitamins, the minerals were used by the prehistoric Native peoples for various things, among them the manufacture of paints. Red pigment was derived from a plant called Bixa orelliana, which was used both for food and for body painting; it produced a range of red hues from near-yellow to crimson. Dark lines on the stone walls of the area were drawn with charcoal and geni papo, whose juice is colorless when fresh but darkens to a bluish shade and sets after five days. White was not found, but could have decayed, and could have been derived from a kaolin clay. But all the vegetable products decay after a time, leaving only the lines of the charcoal. So the mystery was, what had the Lagoa Santa people and their descendants used to mark the shelter walls, which had kept true colors for 10,000 years? Prous had invited specialists to study the paintings. He had his own speculations. Minerals don't lose their color over time. At Santana do Riacho he had found plenty of nodules of manganese only a hundred meters from the shelter: it makes a good black line. He thought white might also have been made from calcinated bones, or from burned limestone. He had speculated that since the water is rich in carbonates (like the water at Pyramid Lake) it made a good fixative for pigments. Not all of the paintings had survived: frequently, they were able to make out where a painting had faded out. There were marks like pentimento, a kind of negative image of the painting that had once been there.

As he talked I couldn't take my eyes off the road. We had moved into a vast, empty landscape, rich with color. The soil was pebbly, with bits of crystal stones and a distinctly red tint. The bushes were acid green, and there were wildflowers of white, yellow, mauve. Clouds moved across the sky in great sweeping formations, leaving shadows that moved across the hills in tandem. No camera would ever capture this constant motion and flickering, subtle shift of color. We could see the road winding here and there like a narrow ribbon, unspooling over the tops of the hills and down into the valleys. Every now and again we passed a small house, set out by the road as if hoping for company, without glass in its windows, and with the doors open. Sometimes, there'd be a cow or a donkey. Every now and again a human figure, very dark-skinned, very small, would appear by the side of the road holding up a plastic bag wrapped around indistinct, dark-colored fruits. There were no streams, no lakes.

Prous said there was always a forest lining the banks of the river (which we could no longer see). That was where he fully expected he would find evidence of human habitation, but so far he had found nothing, no evidence of where or how these people lived, no village sites.

Off to the left a range of mountains suddenly appeared, not tall, not small, push-up mountains, he said, the Serra do Cipo range. We finally came over the top of a hill, went down, and there was the river again. It was flanked by tall, red-barked trees with broad spreading arms, dusty green leaves. We passed through a little town, and where rocks had piled up to form a dam and waterfall there was a small hotel, with an azure swimming pool right at the water's edge. We passed through the village, drove up a narrower road. There were no shoulders at all and no guardrails. There were dips bridged with logs, but with nothing to keep the car from tumbling down either side. This is great, Prous kept saying. As we rode up one hill and down another the drops became so sheer I was afraid to look, and they all seemed to be on my side of the car.

Prous said there were shelters all along the edge of the mountains that ran to our left. About every seven kilometers, he had found shelters with paintings. Most of them also had burials. These demonstrations of formerly high human density were completely at odds with the barren emptiness of the landscape now. We drove down into another valley by the river, and we were in a small town. This was Santana do Riacho. There were flowering trees in every yard, and a slender gallery of trees ran on each side of the river. The river and the forest here were protected. There were busloads of Sunday visitors in the town. The dirt road along the river was a bumper-to-bumper line of parked cars, vans, trucks—everyone wanted a place by the water. He waved his hand as if to say, see, this is what happens when you tell people something is special and worth saving—they come and trample it. There was one painting site he knew of, two hundred meters from this road, where there were no sediments to dig, but people ran to see the paintings and used the site as a bathroom. It disgusted him.

We drove and drove. On one hilltop, all by itself, there was a tiny, perfect white stucco church with a brilliant blue door. Its spire caught the sunlight and cast it all around like a vision of hope in a desperate world. The hills rose and fell, the road wound around. We passed through a three-house town. The houses were adobe, the color of damp earth on the bottom with a sharp line midway up, and a lighter shade of yellow above. The insides were dark: the people who sat out in their yards on hard chairs were brown, wrinkled, small, with straight hair, narrow heads, high cheekbones. The mountains were very dark, the foliage of whatever grew on them almost a black green. Prous said the vegetation was extremely varied, depending on where it grew, on hillsides or in the valley, high or low, in sun or shade. The road rolled on and on far into the distance, down, up: it was hypnotic. I felt my head nod, just before it banged into the window.

A town appeared at the top of a hill. It was a small place, not much bigger than Orogrande, New Mexico, and with the same Durango flavor. The houses of adobe or cement had gaping doors, and chickens in the front yards. Dogs slunk away from the sun. We stopped for gas in front of a one-story cement structure with its whole front wide open to the street. It was ten o'clock on a Sunday morning, and this bar was already doing steady business. There was a pitted cement counter, a pool table, a couple of stools, some old men with few teeth, many flies. Aguimar ordered a drink whose name I didn't catch. The bartender grinned, reached under the counter for a large unlabelled plastic bottle filled with a clear liquid. Would I like some, they asked, knocking it back, wiping their lips with the backs of their hands. Cachaça, said Prous. A home brew. Known to blind dogs and lift the hair off the hides of cattle. And my driver had already drunk it.

Finally, the road took a terrible hairpin turn and dipped down, down, round, down, and there was the river, chittering over large, square chunks of stone stained red by ferrous oxide, stained black by manganese. There was an island in the middle, and its arms curved to form a wonderful, cool, still, shady pool, right by the shore. The eucalyptus trees were so tall their boughs met over the river like hands come together in prayer. There was a bridge made up of rotten railroad ties, no rails. I thought the bridge wouldn't hold my weight, let alone the car's. I got out and walked across as Aguimar gunned it over to the other side. Prous disappeared down the shaded lane behind a fence. I sat down on a railroad tie, peered down into the red-stained river. There was a cool breath off the water, the wind was soft, and there was a smell rising from the ground like Jamaican jerk spice. Close to the shore the trees and shrubs bent right down and kissed the water. Small ferns unfurled among the rocks, and spread out near the grass in the lane. There was yellow ladies' purse, and a small bush that looked like lilac. The tall eucalyptus above suddenly shivered and a limb bent down: a black form swung from one branch to another. Oh, I thought, forgetting where I was, a squirrel.

Ha, said Aguimar, monkey.

I wondered if Prous had checked right here for a village. Nothing, he said when he returned, he'd found nothing here, but this was the area where quartzite was found, which was used for side scrapers, and these people had used quartz crystal for spear points. It was all over these mountains.

We drove along the lane and up into a secluded yard. There was a group of small umber stuccoed houses, with blue shutters and broad porches and cement patios belonging to the people who had built a private hydro station here. There was no sign of any shelter site until we drove through a gate and entered a little valley out behind a field. Then I saw it: a broad slash of ocher and black streaking through the bright green wall of trees halfway up the face of a tall cliff. It rose straight up, towering above the flat valley like skyscraper with a flat top. I could hear the faint roar of falling water, which had been channelled through a chute over the top of a mountain back there: the power was harnessed where it fell below. The car could only get us so close. There was a dusty little two-log bridge that even Xexeu Aguimar, fortified by cachaça, didn't dare try. We walked in from there.

We had a long way to climb, but the path wasn't steep. It zig-zagged through a dry, leafless forest with large gnarled roots spreading across the ground. There wasn't much grass or under-brush. Every few meters, Prous stopped and picked up a hunk of black rock that he used to scrawl a line on a stone—manganese—and a piece of something that looked like fired red clay—hematite, or ferrous oxide. It too could make a fine or thick line, or it could be rubbed into the surface of a stone to make a fine, sticky ocher dust just like an oil pastel or a Conté crayon. No more than a few cells of some kind of vegetable matter had been found in any of the paintings they had studied. A group of German scientists, working for NASA on the Mars project, had been here the previous August studying the low iron concentrations in the pigments. What stuck these minerals together and held them fast to the stone shelter walls? There was something deeply funny about rocket science coming to the aid of archaeology to figure out how these primitive people made marks that lasted 10,000 years.

This area, Prous explained, had been glaciated more than 600 million years ago and there were cobbles left all over from the grinding action of that ice. There were tiny slivers of the clearest, glasslike quartz. The ferrous oxide in the earth pushed its way up by osmosis into a tubular grass plant—the locals still use it to paint the outside of their houses.

My legs screamed by the time we climbed through the last screen of leafless trees to the shelter. It was, at first, a complete disappointment. Just an overhang of rock, pockmarked with pieces of quartzite and chalcedony, the limestone eaten away over the eons to leave this oppressive out-thrust. The sandy ground sloped uphill to my left and around a kind of corner. There were pink and black streaks of color all along the exposed stone surface, and every now and again, hidden away from the sun, there were weird black sacs with many openings out of which came a strange buzzing noise.

I stood in the hot, dry sun, gasping for breath. The blacks and reds in front of me began to resolve themselves into images. They were smeary, runny, and they covered over each other. They had not been painted with the grace of those ancient Ice Age cows found on the walls of caves in France: those animals were rendered with a sinuous line that suggested dimension, and they were shaded with an eye to volume and significant detail in a wonderfully integrated style. They were good enough to make anyone who had ever tried to draw weep with joy and frustration. These pictures, on the other hand, were crude. There was very little suggestion of dimension. They were just there, flat in front of the eye. But there was a certain motion, a certain rough energy to the figures. And there were so many pictures, so many marks of the hands of men and women, so many calls from the grave (I was here!) that I didn't know where to look first. The paintings rose from ground level to well over my head, from one end of the exposed surface to another. I'm sure I stood there for a long time with my mouth open.

"There's more than two thousand of them here," said Prous.

My eye finally settled on what looked like a bull's-eye (or a circular maze, or something else?) right in front of me. It was made with a series of circles colored alternately ocher and umber that closed up in the middle. I noticed the animals on either side—armadillos, fish. Then there was a series of sticks with stylized arms and legs, but no heads—stick people, who were much smaller than the animals. Did that signify that the animals these artists drew were creatures much larger than they, or that these people were just a great deal smaller than we are, and saw animals of ordinary size as much more threatening than we would? Luzia was just over five feet high, I remembered, the size of an average ten-year-old today.

These drawings of people were full of motion. It was easy to tell men from women: the men had penises hanging down. They were often depicted with upraised arms and often with dancing legs. There were scenes that looked suspiciously like people copulating. Oh yes, the sex scenes, said Prous. There were scenes of giant deer behind grids with small stick figures all around, as if the deer had been caught in a net or locked in a corral. Then there were grids all by themselves. There was a series of dots, a series of yellow fish. One figure kept calling me back, to look again and again. She had a head, her legs were bent at the knee, and running out from the end of her feet were two crooked lines, as if the artist was showing the time of day by the size of the shadow the person cast on the ground.

I began to talk in a loud voice and wave my hands: look at this, I said pointing at the figure. Look, they've painted her shadow, for God's sake.

Lower your voice, said Prous. The bees don't like it. They are hot, very hot. They are the worst enemy of our work. And there are scorpions and tarantulas.

I looked away from the wall, trying to get a sense of who could have seen these works, how far one could stand away from them and still have them show to advantage. This was the question any artist would have asked when selecting this site: who will come, who will see? The act of painting is the act of trying to communicate with someone else.

From this point in front of the shelter, I could see right across the valley. There were trees marching across the opposite cliff face. Down below was the river: it ran from where two arms of the cliffs met, embracing the waterfall. Anyone following the river would spot this slash of color in the trees, and think about coming here to get out of the sun or the rain. It was an ideal place to record one's stories.

On the trees across the way, there were large sacs, huge, like black balloons filled with water. Termites, Prous said. And at my feet, making a little black trail, there were rows of leafcutter ants, doggedly walking with their little green umbrellas held above their heads. There were so many insects around I didn't focus on what he'd said about the bees. There were some black things, their wings moving so slowly, so lazily, I could see them flutter in the crevices of the rock face. A few of them clustered around what looked like a honeycomb, but a honeycomb stripped of its protective outer cover. I could see into each hexagonal cell. This nest was stuck right to the stone wall, right on top of a painting. I moved along the rock face, pointing out deer copulating, big fish, looking for a sign of a boat, talking loudly, breathing heavily, sweating.

See here, said Prous, this one looks to us like a man reaching into a beehive.

Well, I said, it could just as easily be a man holding up a net. In fact, it looked to me like a ball player straining to make a catch.

The buzz picked up intensity, and all of a sudden, there was something in my hair, buzzing madly, and then a fire needle burned my head behind my ear. I screamed. There was another needle at the nape of my neck, a wild buzzing in my ears. I flung off my hat, beat about me.

Oh no, said Prous, the bees!

There was something black on his brow, right between his eyebrows: he slapped it and it came away in his hand.

My head pounded, and still the heat of the fire built up in my scalp. I wanted to run and shriek but I was afraid that would make me a better target. I moved back carefully, away from the face of the shelter, biting down on my tongue. My hand, where I'd brushed the bees away, was also stung, and it hurt as if I'd stuck it into a pan of boiling water.

I now accepted Prous's interpretation of the painting. It was the record of an act of heroism. This person had stuck his hand into a hive; he was enduring a thousand stings of fire, a triumph of human will over pain. Its meaning would be completely obvious to anyone who spent more than five minutes at this shelter. I was looking at the rock shelter version of the six o'clock news, but all layered up, as if succeeding generations had tried to record over the tapes of those who'd been here before.

We finally turned the corner and climbed up the sandy hill along the cliff face to Level II, the cemetery. There is no way of knowing if the paintings on the wall close to the cemetery were made by the people buried here. Prous had not dated the paint directly, but he was sure the things painted higher up were younger than those closer to ground level. He pointed to a picture of a particular deer with a high rack of antlers, very narrow, completely unlike the wide spreading rack of modern deer I was familiar with, but an accurate rendering, Prous said, of a deer species that was still found in the Pantanal, the swampy wetlands of the west.

We stepped into a sandy area dug out around a large rock. The rock was large but flat on top, like a table or a pedestal. On the wall above it there were pictures of fish, and a giant man with skinny arms held high in the air over his head. He was absolutely huge compared to the other figures. He had knobby knees and a round belly, and he had three digits on his hands and feet, not five. (I later came to think of him as a portrait of a giant sloth— which are known to have been over fifteen feet tall.)

All around this rock, said Prous, was where we found the cemetery.

It was hard to imagine, even with the bodies tightly flexed, how forty people could have been packed in this small space. There was almost no stratigraphy, just loose sand. Prous had brushed away some soil near the big rock and found the bones, then realized that they were all over this level. On the left side of the table rock he found the woman with a newborn baby tied at her waist with a textile he believed was originally a hammock. He found another woman with a fetus in utero. At the very outer edge of this space, close to the little entry path, as if to say this person is not really a part of this community, he had found a woman with a very peculiar skull. When he first examined the bone, Walter Neves had thought it showed evidence of serious pathology. Closer examination revealed that the woman's skull had been burned.

What did it mean that forty people were all buried in the same place? Did it mean this particular group of Lagoa Santa people had lived somewhere near here year round, that (as Dillehay had proposed about the people at Monte Verde) they were sedentary hunter-gatherers? They must have lived close by, surely, or their burials would have been scattered in many locations, not huddled here together. This was not an ossuary, made all at once from the gathering in of bones first laid to rest elsewhere.

Sheila de Souza had done two studies of the population. Her pathology paper described the remains.[4] These bones had not been dated directly, so one could not know how old each remain was, but the age of the pieces of charcoal pulled from the burials varied from 8000 to 9000 BP. They all shared the same Lagoa Santa morphology. Some of the bones showed signs of arthritis in the old (about forty-five years); there were a number of skeletons with bone trauma consistent with violence; many bones showed significant numbers of Harris lines, and yet a significant number of these skeletons had tooth caries, indicating a diet rich in sticky or sweet carbohydrates. A second paper, on paleodemography, plotted their ages at death. This painted a very bleak picture of the life of this community. Some twenty percent of the population of the cemetery had died before the age of three. The next ten years of life were almost as difficult: eighteen percent had died between three and twelve, before they could reproduce. The smallest numbers in the graveyard were teenagers and adults over forty-five. Thirty-four percent of the population had died between twenty-one and thirty five, some of them in childbirth or shortly after. If these people were the painters of these pictures, the energetic, lively, almost jocular stories on the walls belied the truths established by the bones in the ground. On the wall they were heroes recording their triumphant experiences with large animals and with each other. The bones said they made a tenuous living in a world of harsh contingency. Which picture was true? Both. More than 8,500 years ago, they knew how to make textiles, they observed the world around them and had the leisure and the urge to render it in pictures. They were like us. They were like me.

What about ghosts? I asked Prous as we began our descent. While the dead or assimilated Native community gave him no trouble, what about the ghosts in the bones? Did they exact their revenge on these scholars who pulled them from the ground, who handled them in their labs? I was keeping a running count: Annette and Joseph Emperaire had dug many bones, and both had died terrible deaths. Sheila de Souza's husband, the archaeologist, had succumbed to depression, and died. And here was Prous being sued by a powerful colleague.

"Oh, no," he laughed. He stood for a moment with his head cocked to one side, eyeing the shelter wall. More than twenty years after his first discoveries here, he was still enthusiastic. He had tied the red bandana over his head, pirate style. He looked oddly girlish.

"No, there are no English ghosts here," he laughed again. An odd look, a mixture of two parts mischief and one part contempt, crossed his face. (Give the journalist what she wants, he seemed to say to himself. Let her make a fool of herself if she is so inclined.) He stopped at a certain spot along the rock face. He called to me to look. Near his finger was an odd little painting. It was a human form in the same way that Casper the ghost seems vaguely human. It had a rounded and very elongated head, with very large, elongated eyes, and a gestural suggestion of arms and legs. "There," he said. "A little phantom."

We picked our way through sand and stone and grasses beside the little river. It was rushing swiftly by, and the waterfall in a cleft between the two cliff faces made a huge roar. There were little pools of still water trapped by islands formed of fallen logs and mounded sand. I sat under the shade of a low, spreading bush. The air smelled wonderful. I felt wonderful. The very ease of this climate made me rail about my dissatisfaction with the Bering Strait entry theory.

It seemed to me so clear that this was the kind of place human beings without much technology could thrive in. If the Lagoa Santa morphology hadn't changed in 10,000 years, perhaps it was because there was no need, no environmental challenge that rewarded adaptation and punished stability. I couldn't believe that the people who drew pictures of themselves on the walls of the shelter up above our heads were the unchanged descendants of people who'd trekked through thousands of miles of ice and snow. But I could well imagine the reverse—that their descendants had changed as they moved into the north.

All Prous knew of the north was what he'd read as a boy. "I have read of the Franklin expedition," he said. He had often wondered why more people didn't take seriously the idea of a walk down the British Columbia coast. I explained why not. But I was a coward: I didn't ask him what he thought of Alan Bryan's theory that human ancestors were in the Americas long before modern humans evolved. Prous had critiqued Niéde Guidon's work quite thoroughly. And I knew he didn't think highly of Alan Bryan. Bryan had asked to work with Prous in Minas Gerais, but Prous had refused. He'd sent Bryan off to work with Maria Beltrão in the state of Bahia. And Bryan had found nothing in Bahia that was truly old. I asked Prous, instead, why he did not think that people might have come from some southern location, by boat. If people used boats to get to Australia, why not to get to America?

There's a fight about that in Australia, he warned me. It was well known that Rivet had had a theory about Australians walking to South America, but it was also well known that Rivet was wrong. People like to make linkages, like to find patterns of similarity and build theories from them. Prous, a specialist in stone technology, pointed out that some early Australians also made spear points of quartz, just as these Lagoa Santa people had done here in Brazil. But he would never leap to the conclusion that using the same material to make spear points was an expression of a common background between spear-makers in Australia and spear-makers in Minas Gerais. A kind of convergence in style was forced on anyone who used this particular material. There were only so many ways to work with quartz. It's not a shared culture, he said, it's that quartz is quartz.

"Maybe the problem here," he said slowly, as he placed one careful foot before another, "is that archaeology uses the techniques of science, but is not itself a science."

# 16

# Science Contender

Dispatches from the Most
Ancient Trenches

IT WAS A COMPLICATED business to get from André
Prous's lab in Belo Horizonte to Niéde Guidon's
in the state of Piaui. I had to fly first to the city of
Petrolina, which straddles the São Francisco river and the border
between Bahia and Pernambuco states. One of Niéde Guidon's
associates, Rosa Trakalo, was to meet me there and drive me the
three hundred kilometers to Guidon's offices.

Petrolina is about 700 kilometers inland from Recife, a big
city on the Atlantic Ocean where Brazil bulges out towards the
coast of Africa, and about 1,200 kilometers north of Brasilia, the
capital. In short, it's in the middle of nowhere, but even the
middle of nowhere has air service nowadays. The luggage came
into a small room, walled off by glass from the rest of the airport,
through a tiny, square entry port. The passengers jostled fiercely
to see who could get to it first. In the hall outside, a man held a
sign with my name on it. When I approached him, a middle-aged
fellow with a good tan and the blocky body of a very short line-
backer, he thrust a note into my hand. "Very sorry," Rosa Trakalo
had written, "that I can't be there to meet you but this man will
drive you to the park." So I got into a car with a strange man who
spoke no English and who didn't seem to grasp any of the

Portuguese I scrabbled together. How we trust each other in this
modern world! He nosed the car out onto the highway and we
headed west and north to the state of Piaui, the town of São
Raimundo Nonato (Saint Raymond, the Unborn) and the domain
of André Prous's nemesis, Niéde Guidon.

It is a curious thing about traveling in a strange country: the
eye is caught first by the familiar. We rode through mostly dead
flat, big sky country. In the beginning I only saw that this was a
southern version of Saskatchewan, and I felt at home. But slowly
the strangeness seeped in. For one thing, there was no grass. For
another, the bushes that grew everywhere, the scrub trees known
as caatinga, never seemed to reach beyond the height of a small
lilac, but always managed to obscure my view of the fields and
crops and houses set back from the road. They seemed to be all
the same species, with the same mustard-yellow or white flower,
the same bright green leaf. The ground showed itself like a scalp
between the bush rows: it was red, with bright glassy pebbles.
And there were large pools of water stained with mud.

We passed from the state of Pernambuco, through the state of
Bahia, and then into Piaui. There were many signs on the road
warning of undulacãos (bumps), but nothing was written about
the dogs, the pigs, the cows, the goats, the donkeys or, as we
entered Piaui, the children walking or on horseback in the middle
of the highway, all of whom seemed to consider the road their
principal domain. At first, people in the towns and in front of the
farmhouses seemed prosperous. The kids rode on bicycles: there
were satellite dishes on the roofs of even the smallest houses. But
as we drove deeper into Piaui, villages became poorer, smaller,
grimmer. In the richer places, the shoulders of the road were
strewn with garbage and the pigs nosed here and there for dinner.
The truly poor couldn't afford trash. Their houses lined the road
as if it were the main reason for their existence.

Hours drifted by, punctuated by the squeal of brakes and
shuddering stops as the driver went from eighty to zero in sec-
onds, miraculously avoiding splattering the road with a dog, pig,

or child on a horse. The road carried us faster and faster past scenes of poverty and distress: a man walked carrying a large load on his back, no house to be seen for miles; a woman and her children washed clothes in a large rain puddle formed by the dissolving shoulder of the road, the wash water completely red with muck.

The car roared into the town of São Raimundo Nonato just as the sun was going down. There was a river with green reeds at its edges: children were jumping off a dock into the water. There were crowds of people on the sidewalks, walking along the side of the crumbling highway, stepping smartly to avoid deep potholes. Most of them were young, carrying books and wearing what looked like school uniforms. We slowed down to go through a large square: it had an open food market in the middle, a fountain and a clock, and the people who bought and sold or rested there had narrow brown faces and straight dark hair, their cheeks and foreheads grooved by hard work and suffering. We drove past one very large enclosed block: the graveyard. The wall was stucco and more than six feet high, but I could see the grave markers in stone towering over the wall—these people took fine care of their dead.

A little bridge over a stream lush with grass, and then the driver turned up a cobbled drive to a low-slung building stuccoed in a beautiful, smooth peach color. There was a garden dominated by spreading flowering trees. Hibiscus glowed hot pink. A man swept big dry leaves from the stone terrace in front of a dining room whose entire outer wall was glass doors pulled open to the night. This was the official hotel of Serra da Capivara National Park. The hotel and the park were both dependent on interest in the ancient rock art that had been found in scattered shelters, all over the district. There were copies of these ancient works in every room of the hotel. In the restaurant it was on the pottery place settings, and hung as a plaque over the sideboard. The plaque in particular caught my eye: it showed little people, or monkeys, or both, dancing around the base of a spreading tree. My room had a tiled floor, high ceilings, and a shower with a wire attached to the head to warm the water, which made me wonder if this was the sort of shower heater that had killed Annette Laming-Emperaire.

My guide and translator, Elayne Dick, presented herself as I ate breakfast the next morning. I had been closely studying the pottery plaque in the dining room. The characters were very small, very energetic. One appeared to have a tail bent up at the back, like a monkey's, others were definitely people. They raised their arms and they kicked their feet and they danced around the tree. The lines were graceful and strong but the bodies were filled in without shading. The tree was made with a very sophisticated line, drawn by an artist with a strong graphic sense, whose minimal strokes conjured both form and dimension. It reminded me of sumi painting, in which the brush, loaded with ink, in one stroke lays down line and color and volume. But it wasn't just the quality of the art that drew me: the subject matter was somehow reminiscent of both Wilson Wewa's animal people and the story of Adam and Eve.

I pointed out to my guide how well drawn the monkey was. Wrong, she said, that's no monkey. Those are all people, that tail is no tail, it's a penis. Many, many sex scenes here, she added, with a pink lipsticked smile.

Elayne Dick is a tiny woman in her twenties, her skin tanned to the shade of expensive Italian shoe leather, her body as slim and flat as a thirteen-year-old's. What did she know of sex scenes? She comes from the South, from the state of Rio Grande do Sul where the population is mostly German and Italian in origin and where there is sometimes, on the mountains, a dust of snow. Her hair a shining cap of black, she wore tight pink shorts, white sneakers, a white T-shirt. Her English was oddly accented and there were many words she did not know, but I gathered that she was to take me to see Niéde Guidon, who was stuck in meetings with some very important men from the Inter-American Development Bank. They had given money to FUMDHAM, the charitable foundation Guidon and her colleague Anne-Marie Pessis had created to bring money into their projects and this region. I had seen the two IDB men huddled earlier that morning at another table. Their faces had looked very grave.

Robson Bonnichsen had been at pains to tell me to give his best regards to Guidon. She had been publicly ambushed by David Meltzer, Tom Dillehay and James Adovasio, whom she had invited to her conference on the peopling of the Americas in the spring of 1993 along with Bonnichsen, MacNeish and various other colleagues from the U.S. and South America. They had come, discussed, seen her site at Pedra Furada and some of the artifacts studied by Guidon's student, Fábio Parenti.[1] They had returned to the United States and promptly written a critique of Pedra Furada. They had published it in the December 1994 issue of *Antiquity*:

> While we returned from Brazil greatly impressed by the scope of the work at Pedra Furada, we also returned without having been convinced of the site's claims for a Pleistocene human antiquity. This is not, we hasten to add, a final judgement about the site: that must await the appearance of Parenti's unpublished dissertation on the material remains and the summary monographs on the site.... We are also well aware of the potential appearance of bias on our part from two of us having our own pre-Clovis candidates. We will let our paper speak for itself in this regard, but trust the issue of bias will be found to be groundless. After all, we have nothing to gain by showing Pedra Furada is—or is not—as old as it is claimed to be. This is not a competition in which only one site can "win" and others must "lose." Each pre-Clovis claim is independent: the age of one has no bearing on the age of another (Meltzer 1989). It matters not to us whether the first Americans arrived 11,000, 20,000 or 50,000 years ago, or whether one or all of

these sites are accepted. What matters is understanding the virtually unprecedented migration of modern humans across a rich, empty and dynamic Pleistocene landscape, of which solving the question of when it occurred is but the first step toward that understanding...."[2]

Having thus demonstrated their biases while declaring they had none ("pre-Clovis"; "a virtually unprecedented migration of modern humans across a rich, empty, and dynamic Pleistocene landscape"—a phrase their editor should have excised) and wrapped themselves in the words of law ("judgement," "speak for itself," "in this regard"), they proceeded to bash and trash Pedra Furada and the way it was dug. They accepted the hearths and dates of occupation at the site that were clearly after the Ice Age, but they did not accept the claims Guidon made for hearths and tools older than about 12,000 BP. They said the artifacts found, which her student Parenti asserted were worked and had use edges on them, could be explained as geofacts, merely cobbles that had broken from high up on the wall of the shelter and fallen into the site, losing flakes and fracturing when they bounced down into a pile of other cobbles. They argued that these geofacts, especially those found at the back of the site, could have been tumbled there by the action of the waterfall that flowed down the cliff wall when it rained, or by gravity, not just by the agency of human hands as Guidon had argued. Similarly, the early hearths she had found were different from the later ones, and might be just natural arrangements of stones, not hearths at all, as there were no bones or other organic remains associated with them; the charcoal she found and dated could have simply blown into the shelter from the forest fires that must have swept through that tinder-dry caatinga many times over the course of the millennia. And if not caatinga fires, who knew what could have caught on fire during earlier phases? The stratigraphic walls left in place had cobbles in them: the charcoal was too thick to be left by hearths, etc., etc. While Guidon's work on the rock art was interesting, in other words, her work as an archaeologist claiming human occupation as far back as 50,000 years ago was just not proven.

The car pulled up to the corner of a cobbled street. There was a very high wall enclosing what looked from the outside like two houses, but only the tops of two tiled roofs were visible. The wall was in the same color of adobe as the hotel and it was at least eight feet high with razor wire rolled along the top. There was a sign that said FUMDHAM. We entered through a small metal access door into an old, sloping, cobbled courtyard, with lemon trees planted in square plots and a small cement pool full of murky water. Two white geese and two small dogs honked and yapped. There was a long building with a tiled roof on the left, another on the right with French doors. A woman sat behind the glass talking to the two men I'd seen looking grave in the hotel dining room.

Niéde Guidon stumped up to shake my hand. She is no more than five foot two, her hair short and bristly gray. She ran her hands through it habitually, pulling it with her fists. She wore a man's shirt loose over white jeans, and sneakers on her feet. She had two yellow forearm crutches clutched in one hand: she had just returned from France, where she'd had knee surgery. She had caught her feet in between two rocks on a site and fallen down the wrong way. Cartilage had exploded.

Her office is in what looks like a house. The first room, with a view of the courtyard, holds her desk, a large computer, bookshelves and a Botero print (in which a great, fat, pink woman, seen from behind as she unhooks her bra, balloons like a nightmare over the tiny figure of a sleeping man). This picture is placed where Guidon can see it easily from her desk. She hauled out two drawers and stuck her feet on them to elevate her legs and then she briskly, briskly, began to tell her story.

In spite of the mannish style of dress, the blocky upper body, the aggressiveness that rolled from her shoulders, she has about her the air of a woman of the Church. She apparently spends no time whatsoever on her personal appearance; she seems not the least bit interested in being attractive to anyone. Her skin is very pale. Her thick, graying eyebrows form a straight line over light brown eyes. Her nose is short and narrow. There is a mole on her upper lip. As we talked she squinched up her mouth, her nose and her cheeks whenever she laughed or made a particularly vehement point. Her voice was equally without vanity: she did not control its squeaks and its pitch, so it grated and caught at the ear. She spoke with a great deal of energy, or passion: she never troubled to cover up bewilderment and hurt, and there was always a thick current of rage. She is a woman who thinks things through to the end, and so she is a woman who rages.

"I am born in Brazil, my father is of France, my mother is Brazilian," she began. Her grandfather, who was in commerce near Mont Blanc, went to Marseilles on business before the First World War and noticed that many shipments on the docks were going to Brazil. That was in the days when everything was imported from Italy or France, back when Oswaldo Cruz was building his fantastic seraglio in Rio. Her grandfather came to Brazil and moved to an area in São Paulo State where rich coffee planters lived. He opened an import business—he supplied the planters with the best in French cheeses, wines, all the European luxuries their money could buy.

Guidon's inquiring mind likely came from her mother, the first Brazilian woman to earn a diploma to teach. Her mother died when she was six, so she was sent to her grandparents' farm to live and discovered there the joys of nature. When her father remarried and she went back to live with him, dolls were given to her since girls are supposed to like dolls. They gave her one that cried and wet. She cut it open to see how it worked. There was money in the family, but she wanted freedom. Her four brothers were each given everything they needed to set up their families— houses, cars, businesses, the works. All she wanted of her father was that at eighteen she be allowed to live on her own, be allowed to escape from a house where people went to bed at nine o'clock and went to church on Sunday. She had not the slightest intention of escaping through marriage. She had no interest in babies. She thought babies would require all her attention, and she had discovered at sixteen that she was fickle about men—she would always be interested in the next pretty boy who came along.

So she went to the University of São Paulo, lived on her own, bought her own flat, her own car, set herself up in an independent life in the 1950s, at a time when that simply wasn't done, particularly in Brazil. Her first degree in 1959 was from the University of São Paulo in natural history. She took up her first job as a professor of biology in a college in a smaller town in São Paulo State, hired for this task by the ministry of education. But things did not go well. "I was not of the town, didn't go to church and I teach man is not created from God, but came from monkeys." She also was not kind to the laggard children of the local rich. They did not get easy marks from her. The ministry thought it best to send her to work in the Museum of Archaeology and Ethnology of São Paulo.

"I was twenty-six years old. I arrived at the museu and the director said, 'I don't have an archaeologist in Brazil, so you will work with archaeology.' I said, 'What do I have to do?' He gave me a book of Betty Meggers and Clifford Evans, *Archaeology at the Mouth of the Amazon*. He said, 'Read this and you'll be able to do archaeology.' I took the book, read it and said, 'Look, I am not used to make things I am not able, where may I study archaeology?' He said, 'Go to the U.S., or France, but here it is impossible. Here there is no university course on archaeology and only amateurs.'"

So she went to France. She did graduate studies in archaeology at the Sorbonne, in the Université de Paris, in 1960 and came back to Brazil in 1962 with a *certificat*. She began to work again in the museum as an archaeologist but in 1964 there was a military coup and the new government began to root out dangerous leftists. She had never mixed in politics, but nevertheless "someone denounced me and a colleague to say we are inscribed in the Communist Party."

Her aunt, her mother's younger sister, worked for the ministry of education. She arrived at work one day to see Guidon's file and that of her colleague on a table being readied to be sent to the police. "She said, 'You leave Brazil today.' I was furious, [I said it's] not true. She said, 'For you to prove not true, it is too late.' I left Brazil the same day."

Her aunt burned her file (and that of her colleague), which meant that she was not actually in exile. But until her accuser was himself accused, she could not safely return to Brazil. She got a job in Paris with the Centre National de la Recherche Scientifique. She worked at the Musée de l'Homme in the South American collections. In the beginning she studied the collections taken from the shell mounds, as an assistant to Annette Laming-Emperaire. "She asked me to study the collections of Tierra del Fuego and Patagonia."

But Guidon was not really interested in the First Americans' story. She had fallen hard for rock art. Shortly after she had returned to São Paulo in 1962, and had taken up her old position at the museum, she was visited by some mayors from the northeast who brought her pictures of rock art found on shelters near their communities. "They came from Petrolina and São Raimundo Nonato. They asked to talk to the person responsible for collections. They told me in the mountains, near their towns, there were shelters with paintings. They had photos. They showed me. In Brazil, I knew of others in Minas Gerais, but [I could] see these [were] completely different of everything we knew in Brazil. I asked them about the region, took the name. In December, on a holiday, I drove in a car to Casa Nova, which is two hundred kilometers from here. There was a lot of water, the bridge was destroyed at the river, it was impossible to get here. I came back. All the time I had these paintings in my head." Soon after that she had to leave the country. In France, without money or family she was "just a little archaeologist with Professor Emperaire, I was nobody."

But in 1970 her accuser was himself denounced and disgraced, and she returned to Brazil with a friend, a French ethnologist. Her friend had arranged to study among the Kraho who lived in the state of Goiás, not so very far from Piaui. Guidon went to Goiás with her.

When they were finished with that work, Guidon said that now her friend had to come with her to Piaui to see these paintings. "We made a big circuit in a Jeep. We got here in September 1970. I asked people about the shelter. I came by the north, I visited in a little town, and people at the hotel on the road said there were paintings on their brother's property. He took us. I recognized the paintings. We went to seven different sites, made photos. [I] stayed here one week. To come from Floriano today is three hours. It took me two days in a Jeep. São Raimundo had no water, no electricity, nothing. It was incredibly poor. So I went to France with the photos and tried to organize a project in France and money to make a mission here."

It took her three years. In 1973 she got a grant from the Centre National de la Recherche Scientifique (which is similar to the Canadian National Research Council or the U.S. National Science Foundation). Rich friends in São Paulo gave her money to buy a Jeep. "We came here, me and two young functionaries of the museum who were studying with me. I invited the museum in São Paulo to work with me. We worked for three months."

In 1970 she had told everyone she met in the district that she intended to come back. If they found shelters with paintings, they should take a note of their location and when she came back, she would pay them for each one. "They had fifty-two new sites. And I paid in the biggest bank note in Brazil.... We made the photos and recopied the paintings and covered them in plastic...a few months later I came to France and studied all that material. In 1975 I did a doctorate in Paris on the rock paintings of this region with fifty-two sites. I proposed a classification of three different styles. [I had] no chronology, no stratigraphy, only the rock art...." She thought the paintings were likely between five and seven thousand years old, but surely no older than that. "All the teachers said, in America, men came late and painting was very recent," said Guidon. "I didn't have the facts to object. I was taught like this."

So you were taught, I asked, that humans entered across the Bering Strait and then found their way south?

"Yes," she said, nodding vigorously, "they entered in the north of South America around 12,000 years BP. This I was taught."

In 1975, after Guidon was awarded her first doctorate, she returned to Piaui. This time the locals had fifty-five new sites to show her. She paid for them all. She took a job advising UNESCO and then moved up in the academic establishment of France: she was engaged as an assistant *maître*, or lecturer, at the École Haute Études en Sciences Sociales in Paris. Only graduate students attend. She was no longer a nobody from Brazil, but a woman who had a doctorate, and had made an important find; she had a place among the great French scholars of anthropology. In 1977 she managed to organize an official French mission to Piaui through the ministry of foreign affairs. This mission is still running.

"I showed them more than a hundred sites. So they decided to create this mission. In 1978 I went with a French botanist, geomorphologist, topographer and zoologist. We decided then to begin an excavation. We still had no idea about the antiquity.... I stayed here six months in 1978. I began on different sites, test pits.... And we found fifty or sixty more sites.... We worked from the north of what is today the national park about 200 kilometers by 100 kilometers in a rectangle, about 2,000 square kilometers. I think our research area now is about 40,000 square kilometers. It is huge."

In 1981 the laboratory in France tested radiocarbon ages of samples she had brought back. "They called me to say we had a date of 25,000 BP for Pedra Furada. It was charcoal of a hearth we excavated ... to date the paintings. Each year I gave charcoal to date. At the beginning, ten centimeters below the surface, we had 6000, next 7000 and next 12,000 BP. When they told me

25,000 BP in 1981 I said, 'Impossible, you made a mistake, you mixed samples.'"

The director said she should make a larger pit to learn more about the site. So Guidon opened up a 750-square-meter dig at Pedra Furada, which was a very big excavation. "We did not publish the first date. We opened that. We did excavation in the shelter and outside of the shelter to see if there was a difference in sedimentation inside and out of the shelter. Outside there was no charcoal.... So we got a lot of charcoal and began to make [dates] at Beta Analytic in the U.S."

Dating was done free for her at the laboratory in France, but she had to wait years to get results. At Beta Analytic she had to pay but she got results in thirty days. The U.S. lab "confirmed the antiquity of Pedra Furada." In 1986 she published dates back to 32,000 BP in *Nature*.

Specialists began to come to Pedra Furada. They found a lot of stone objects that were also found on other Brazilian sites—quartz tools, crudely made. The critics from the U.S. had focused on them. One of their concerns (first voiced by MacNeish) was that there seemed to be no progress in the quality of toolmaking over the span of 30,000 years. Maybe there was no progress because they weren't tools at all. But Brazilian archaeologists were used to seeing crude tools on relatively recent sites, Guidon argued. In fact Guidon had found them recently on quite modern sites, with pottery, not far from Pedra Furada.

Beta Analytic came back with dates of 28,000 and 29,000 and 30,000 and 35,000 and 39,000. As the dates became older, there were concerns that they were reaching the limits of accuracy for radiocarbon dating. They began to test their findings in a larger accelerator, which measured uranium/thorium decay. "The result they gave us was 50,000 years."

She had a student in Paris, Fábio Parenti, who was working on his doctoral thesis. Parenti came to Pedra Furada and directed the excavation from 1987 to 1989. "When I offered him to make his thesis here, he told me he doesn't believe, and if he comes he will destroy my theories. Then he came and excavated. At the end, he said he 'was sad to say you are right.'"

In 1989 or 1990, she wasn't certain which, she attended a conference of Americanists. Dillehay was there and presented his findings from Monte Verde, including the 33,000 BP dates he'd gotten from the small site beside the main dig. "In France I have no problems," she said, "only with some people in the U.S. And some of the Americans, not all, Alan Bryan and Ruth Gruhn came here—no problem at all." The American critics were convinced that the charcoal she'd dated, which she found in hearths in front of the rock shelter, had just blown in from forest fires. She decided to test that theory, and set one of her students a master's thesis on this problem. If there had been forest fires outside the rock shelters, the burned wood and charcoal would be found in thick layers on the slopes of the hill in front of the shelter. Her student excavated a large trench in front of Pedra Furada. The student dug on the slope and in the valley and dug right down to the bed of the ancient river, now dry, that had once run in front of the shelter. "She found charcoal only twice," said Guidon. "And what she found was inside hearths. One of the camps [was] just on the edge of the river. One gave [a date] of 12,000 BP. The other near the river gave 18,000 BP."

In fact, there was no evidence of forest fires in the Pedra Furada Valley below the shelter.

Look, I said, one of the major criticisms of Pedra Furada is that so little of it has actually been published, particularly Parenti's thesis.

"This is all being published," she countered. Fábio Parenti's thesis was to be published shortly by the French ministry of foreign affairs.[3] The master's thesis was just being finished. She was content to let time and new discoveries deal with the Americans' criticisms. But she was still annoyed that Dillehay and Meltzer and Adovasio came to her conference and then published their critique without following up with her. It had caused her considerable difficulty.

"I think Jacques Cinq-Mars said it was the Inquisition," she said indignantly. "What I didn't like was they came, went to visit and no objections. Then they went back and said things they didn't discuss here.... One of their objections is it's not lithic material made by men because no men. The oldest male fossil is 10,000 years."

She waved her hand as if to dismiss this concern altogether. The climate in Piaui 12,000 years ago was humid tropics, not dry as it is now. The sediment in the shelters was almost entirely acid; bones normally do not survive in such soils. There was little point in looking for human remains of great antiquity in the shelters. It did make sense to hunt for bones in the area's many limestone caves. And she had done so. "We looked for men in the top caves." In one of them, a site called Garrincho Cave, underneath a stalagmite layer, they found Ice Age animal bones, a piece of a human skull, and two human teeth. "This is different from the bones of the human types of 10,000 BP. It is very thick. [We] studied it in France."

She reached into her files and pulled out the paper, published by the Academy of Sciences in Paris.[4] Evelyne Peyre, of the biological anthropology laboratory of the Musée de l'Homme, and her colleagues (including Guidon) described the piece of skull and the two teeth that came out of sediments at the back of the long cave. It had once been inundated and then slowly dried out. Just as H.V. Walter had done at Minas Gerais, they dug underneath the calcite or stalagmite floor, a layer formed when calcium carbonate and other minerals mixed with water and solidified into a hard cap over the sediments below. The hard cap was dated. As with Luzia, none of the bones found in the sediments had yet been dated directly but since they were locked in below the dated stalagmite layer, their minimum age had been established at 10,000 BP.

The fragment of the human skull was much more robust, or thicker, than the average skull seen in modern populations, and it displayed several unique features. The teeth were both like and unlike modern teeth. The incisor was peculiar. When measured and compared to others, modern and ancient, it appeared to be midway between the size and shape of the incisors of European Neanderthals found in caves dating from the middle of the Ice Age, and incisors found in Qafzeh, in Israel, dating from the early part of the last Ice Age. This Garrincho incisor was thus both Neanderthal and modern human in its form and size, and yet it was neither. The other tooth found, a permanent first molar, was more typical of Neanderthal populations than of the Qafzeh remains, and much closer to both than to any later modern populations to which it was compared. But it was also similar to a molar taken from the mandible of a female skeleton found in a site near the cave, dating to 9700 BP. In sum, Peyre and colleagues believed this skull fragment and teeth were consistent with what one would expect from a human being who might have lived in this territory more than 60,000 years ago, though these remains were closer in their form and size to European Neanderthal teeth than to the Middle Eastern Qafzeh remains. This find was rare and important.

Were these people the ancestors of the group now being referred to as Paleo-Indians, the Lagoa Santa population, for example? Guidon had no idea. "By chance," she said, "we found something that is the remains of a very old human group that perhaps disappeared completely."

Why, I asked, was no one trying to date these bones directly?[5] And why was no one using the new techniques to search for plant and animal proteins on stone tools? Surely that would be the best way to settle the debate about whether the objects were geofacts or artifacts—crude tools?

Her answer seemed to boil down to money. "We need a lot of money to finish the excavation," she said. Garrincho Cave was full of water, and was expensive to dig. "Instead of the Americans say[ing] it's not true, why not take a site and excavate? I have sites with layers of the Pleistocene. We need money to make excavations. We have to be here excavating all year. I have another site in a cave. We found lithics—it is possible to find humans. It is full of the fossils of megafauna, so it is possible to find human bones."

What did these finds here, in the middle of nowhere, really mean? Where did these people come from?

She thought there had been many entries into the Americas, not only over the Bering Strait but also through the Aleutian chain of islands, which would have been easier to follow when the sea level was lower. And Neves was right: Guidon did think an entry from the Atlantic Ocean was possible. "Here, in the northeast of Brazil," she explained, "one or two years ago, there was a fishing boat from the Azores. In this boat were three men. There was a very big storm. They drifted. One died. The others arrived here three months later in Brazil. They ate on fish and drank a bit of salt water from the sea. They land I think at Bahia, in the northeast. This was published in all the newspapers."

And she also reminded me that extremely ancient forms of humanity had managed to find their way into the most distant reaches of the globe from Africa. The bones of *Homo erectus*, she said, were found in Australia (actually it was tools associated with *erectus* that were found on an island in Indonesia).[6] "I think it is even possible people came from Africa or the islands nearby Africa."

She said this with great care, as if to put forward such ideas was to invite ridicule. But she thought the current paradigm was way too restricted to explain the facts: she believed that it actually hindered the gathering of facts. For example, she said, the notion that human beings could only have entered the Americas from the Bering Strait at the end of the Ice Age had been so firmly engrained that some of her colleagues simply stopped digging when they came to the layer of soil that represented the Pleistocene period. Very few kept on until they hit bedrock, because everyone believed nothing human would be found in the most ancient layers. She grabbed at both sides of her head and pulled hard at her hair in frustration at how an out-of-date theory effectively cut off the possibility of disproof. "All the paradigms," she said, "were made in an epoch when we thought *Homo sapiens* was only

4000 BP, and Cro-Magnon and Neanderthal only 60,000. We had no idea about *erectus*...in Europe, when I studied, the oldest *sapiens* in Europe was Cro-Magnon at 40,000 BP. Now we know *sapiens* is at least 200,000 BP."

The problem was straightforward: there was a bias against the idea of creatures other than modern human beings having any kind of technology, and there was a bias against the notion that early human beings could have been clever enough to hang on to a log or build a makeshift raft. But Guidon believes that a raft is a simple thing, and many creatures display a problem-solving form of intelligence. She pointed at Chloë, one of her dogs, who was sound asleep on a plastic pillow on the floor of her office. "This little dog, at points she is much more intelligent than a lot of human beings I know...when she has a problem, I see she analyzes, she thinks till she finds solutions. She gets what she wants."

Human societies around the globe at any one time differ in their technological and problem-solving capacities. Piaui was a perfect example. There Guidon sat in her office, with her computers and her learning, and around her was a community that had none of these advantages. It was entirely possible to have modern human beings and their ancestral forms existing in the world at the same time. But the established paradigm didn't allow for such complexities.

Money had become a serious problem for Niéde Guidon. She had tapped every source she could think of to protect the area. It had been declared a national park in 1979, but that was just the beginning. She had to make certain that the people around the park had a stake in its protection. The building she worked in was a donation from the military police; it had formerly been their station. She and her students built the rest of the buildings so they could store their equipment and materials here when they went to France for nine months of the year. There had been complex negotiations in which the state governor gave a building to the University of Piaui, which leased it to her. In exchange, several of the university's students began to study with her on these sites. There was a man in the town who had tried very hard to make a school and a museum to show the finds, but there was never enough money. She got money from the Brazilian National Research Council through the university. Then she decided she needed to create a nongovernmental organization: having worked for UNESCO, she knew that such an organization is necessary in order to receive money from foreign governments or institutions. She sees the archaeological sites as a kind of magnet for development.

Discoveries made here have to stay here, so that people who want to see them or study them will have to come to Piaui.

In 1981, after the ancient dates became known, her colleague Anne-Marie Pessis came from France to make a film on the rock art. She has been in Brazil ever since, and earned the Doctorat d'Etat for her work in Piaui on prehistoric rock shelter and cave art as the first record of culture. In 1986 she and Guidon created the Foundation (the FUMDHAM). Guidon got money from Brazil's ministries of education, culture and environment to establish the park boundaries and build its infrastructure. They got grants from the Inter-American Development Bank and from Embratel (the phone company). By 1991, she and her colleagues had found 320 shelters with rock art and 415 archaeological sites in the region. UNESCO declared this area a World Heritage Site.

The state of Piaui built a hotel and leased it back to the foundation. The people in the community were hired to work in the park, run the hotel and make perfumes and furniture. They also make pottery, which is used in the national park and which the foundation markets wherever it can. Italy helps support schools for the population, which is sixty percent illiterate. There are three schools in the town and there will soon be two more. There are a hundred people working full time at the FUMDHAM and thirty-five researchers of different universities from Brazil, France and Italy studying the sites.

It was altogether a remarkable story. Guidon had started here to get away from the bristling rivalry of those who studied the First Americans. Yet here she was, almost thirty years later, embroiled in the rivalry among scholars studying the First Americans. The community around her was supported by the industry built on ancient charcoal pulled from this ground.

I asked her how much money her operations were chewing through in a year. She said she wasn't sure, but the men from the Inter-American Development Bank would later tell me it was well over a million. They referred to Guidon and Pessis as "the French ladies," and described their work as "a little miracle." The IDB had given a technical infrastructure grant of $2.5 million, and could give no more. The FUMDHAM needed corporate donors, but what corporation would want to help? Worse, Guidon and Pessis didn't have the right connections. They knew the president of the IDB but they had no clout in Brasilia.

Guidon took me across the courtyard to introduce me to Anne-Marie Pessis. A tiny, dangerously thin woman of fifty, she looked utterly exhausted, pasty pale. She stood up at her desk to greet me, with difficulty. She had pneumonia, Guidon said, but she wouldn't go home because she had to explain to the IDB how their money had been spent.

The phone in Guidon's office seemed never to stop ringing. The sun was dying in the courtyard. The sky over the roof of the house across the way was downright theatrical—a wonderful shade of dark, clear, lighting-gel blue. The geese wandered over the paving stones, honking, the dogs lay panting on the cool plastic pillows. The room was warm, the air outside warmer still.

I wanted to know about all the ancient human bones she'd found, what the population here had looked like at the end of the Ice Age. Were they like Luzia?

Guidon began to talk about the Toca dos Coqueiros burial.

One of her doctoral students, Cleonice Vergne, had found the first bone.[7] There were twelve other students, each digging one square. It was July 1997. They were working in a valley of the park known as Baixão das Mulheres, in the municipality of Coronel Jose Dias (named for Colonel Jose Dias, who slaughtered thousands of Indians who refused to be slaves in Piaui in the eighteenth century). There were paintings in what Guidon called the Nordeste (northeast) tradition on this shelter's wall, down to about ten centimeters above ground level. There were sandstone blocks on the shelter floor, which had fallen from the cliff. The digging went slowly through forty centimeters of sediments. They found a hearth, they dated the paintings on a block at 5300 BP, they found a human hair with a flea. And then they found a grave that held a tightly flexed human skeleton.

"It was an intentional burial. We knew because of the position, the artifacts, it was not normal if an accident for the knees to be at the chin. It was very beautiful. First of all they made a cavity in the sand with their hands and covered that with stone slabs. On that they put the body in a fetal position. [They] made fires all around nearby. They made a feast, then covered with the ash and bone and sand on top of the dead man. I think the ash was hot. In the bone of the heel I found a big charcoal that was stuck in the bone. It was attached to the skin and remained stuck. There were two arrowheads near the legs. He was a strong and big man."

His right hand was laid under his head, his left hand was on his left cheek. The man in the grave was thought to have died at 9870 BP, the date of the charcoal stuck to his ankle bone. The human hair with the flea was dated at 10,640 plus or minus 80 BP. The arrowheads were unique, of a type never before seen on a dig in northeast Brazil. One was fishtailed (a style often seen in Archaic sites in Canada and the U.S.). One was made of quartz and the other of chert. Chert in this area is almost as rare as fishtailed arrowheads: there is no flint source and no other flint tools have been found.

Unfortunately, there was no way to know if this man was or

was not a member of the Lagoa Santa population. The skull had
been deformed by the pressure of forty centimeters of sediment
and people walking on top of that. They had carefully wrapped
these remains in toilet paper and then covered them with plaster
until they were able to lift them out of the site intact, carry them
to the museum, and excavate them from the cast. The job had
taken months.

A woman's skeleton and mandible had been found in 1990 at
Toca da Janela da Barra do Antonião, a big shelter near a limestone outcrop.[8] A huge block of stone had fallen on her. "She
slept near a fire. She was on her side with her hand under her
head," explained Guidon, and showed me the position, making
her head tilt to her hand like a sleeping child. "Like a person who
is cold. A block of six tons fell off the cliff. She was in the gap
under the concavity of the block. The skull exploded from the
air—the impact of the wave entered her mouth and nose and exploded. The only thing destroyed was the head.... This one was
dated by charcoal in the fire in front. She was in the big slab of
stone." The age of the charcoal near this female skeleton was
dated at about 9700 BP.

Both these skeletons were older than Kennewick by a thousand years, older than the man found at Prince of Wales, possibly
as old as Luzia. Neither of them would be much help in establishing whether they were like or not like the Lagoa Santa people,
the narrow-headed Paleo-Indians. Why, I asked again, don't you
just date these bones directly, so there can be no argument about
their antiquity and we can know what it really is?

Dating involves the destruction of bone, she said, and she
didn't want to destroy bone until the specialists had finished.
Then she would date them. As for doing protein analysis on the
surfaces of the stone artifacts to see whether they'd been used to
hunt game or crush vegetables, that was a real money problem.
In the first place, that kind of analysis was relatively new. The
practice in Brazil had been to wash stones clean when they were
found on a site, although she preferred to brush them. She was

not certain if plant or animal proteins would still persist on stone after washing, although she did know that someone had found the proteins of boar on a very ancient Mousterian point. The other problem was that someone had to do the work in Brazil of gathering a collection of reference proteins and their anti-sera, so that any proteins found on old stones could be compared to a reasonable array of Brazilian animals and plants. All these new technologies cost money and she didn't have it. At most she had $200,000 a year to spend on excavation. The rest of the money went to the schools, the park, the hotel and feeding the children.

But she had received results of a new method used to date a painting in a cave. She pawed over her desk for the paper she wanted, and found it. The results of the analysis said the painting dates were "between 30,000 and 40,000 years." This was an astonishing result: if it was correct, this cave painting had been made at an earlier time than those found in the Ice Age caves in France and Spain.[9]

"I just got it today," she said. She looked at the paper with her spectacles down on her nose, as if she couldn't quite believe what she was reading. (I couldn't help thinking that this sort of announcement of a result was the very thing that Prous had complained about.) "There are paintings in a cave entrance under calcite," she explained. "[We] can date the calcite." This was the date she had in front of her, done by a physicist at the University of São Paulo. She needed to confirm it with another lab. But this result was going to be presented in Rome in September 1999 at an international conference on thermoluminescence and electron spin resonance dating.

"André Prous," I said," complains you don't publish much." I mentioned his name very carefully, like a soldier sticking his helmet above the foxhole to test for snipers.

"We published a lot," she said. "At least thirty master's and doctoral theses [have been] published here.... We have something like 150 papers in botany, anthropology, paleopathology...."

[But] I think everyone is waiting for the publication on Pedra Furada. Perhaps they will change. An American did Monte Verde. I think Americans don't believe too much in other researchers."

There was an uncomfortable little silence. I asked her why she had chosen to sue André Prous, why she thought academic debate could be helped in this way. What about the importance of freedom of expression?

"Yes," she said with a cranky and emphatic pull at her hair. "I sue Prous because I don't know why he published an article telling that I am so despicable [as] to make Pedra Furada old. [He said] I presented in a meeting in Brasilia a skull, saying it was a skull of a baby and later, I said it was a monkey. First, I was never in [this] meeting in Brasilia. I never talked of a skull of babies. The ones we have are very recent. We don't have a monkey skull. And in Pedra Furada [there are] no skulls. He never visited the site. He never saw the material. This is too much. He is in Brazil, he can't come here?

"I knew him in France when I left in 1964. The University of São Paulo asked Annette to find someone to take my place. She sent Prous." She had never written of his work. She had never seen it, so she didn't feel it appropriate to write about it. She had been told by someone that Prous didn't like her because she had a prestigious job in France, and he, a native of France, did not. But that, she said, was not her fault. She had the correct number of degrees and expertise to earn such a job, he did not. She had no interest whatsoever in competing to see whose paintings and sites were older than whose. "If my paintings [are] only 7,000 years [old], for me [it's] the same pleasure." She came to Piaui because she was fascinated by painting, not because she wanted to find the oldest human site in the Americas.

Nevertheless, she had come to believe that man had been in the Americas a long time: the fact that there was no direct evidence in the north was perhaps due to development, to the building of dams, or to the spread of agriculture, which might have destroyed the evidence. Perhaps there was evidence underwater or on the coast yet to be found. Piauí's sites had been preserved precisely because it was the middle of nowhere, there was no real development, no power, no roads, no mechanized agriculture until after she arrived. It was so poor, so much out of contact with the rest of the world, the sites were so amazingly preserved, it was as if prehistoric man had just left.

I kept seeing André Prous's white and strained face, the effort he made to do his work well, the fear this matter of a lawsuit caused him. He and Guidon were both doing the same thing, unearthing the story of early people in the Americas. I couldn't imagine what she thought could be gained by dragging him through the courts to make him pay for his remarks. Even if they were wrong, so what? Why did it matter?

"I only want him to tell me [of] this meeting in Brasília," she said with gritted teeth, "how he writes that I talked of a baby.... I know how to do science." She calmed herself. She stared at the paper in her hand reporting the results of the dating of the painting in the cave. And then she finally made it clear why these criticisms mattered so much, what they meant in the closed-circuit world of Brazilian archaeology. She had hundreds of people depending on her so their children could study, their families could eat. After Dillehay and Meltzer and Adovasio wrote their critique in *Antiquity*, there were real repercussions. Her funding was attacked.

"An anthropologist of São Paulo wrote to the CNPG and FINEP [both government granting agencies] and told them to cut my money because the Americans proved all my work was fake. My friends told me this."

Her funding was not cut, but it might very well have been. When one has had to run for one's life because one has been denounced by a colleague and the police have been called, one learns to take such matters extremely seriously. She raised again her superior credentials. The first time she did this I thought she was displaying a peculiar kind of arrogance; the second time I thought she had a self-esteem problem; but now I understood:

her credentials are her shield. When her colleagues tried to with-hold the funds she needed to do her work, they had failed—because of the years of effort she'd put in to get those credentials. It was a matter of a person's "formation," as she put it, and hers was top drawer. She had relied on the methods she had learned and on the reputations of those who'd taught them to her. But of course this defense by reputation is also a shroud suffocating the free flow of ideas that good science requires. If one's teachers' reputations become one's own, how can one spurn the teachers' views? The concern for reputation was another reason why the Clovis First/Bering Strait construct had so successfully impris-oned the anthropological imagination.

"I finished in first place in France, me and a Swiss colleague who is director now of the museum in Geneva. They can't say I don't know how to work. This is a big problem. I am a professor in Paris of des Hautes Études en Sciences Sociales. The highest institution in social science in France. Claude Lévi-Strauss, the biggest in social science are there. I'm not a poor guy of a little uni-versity of a little town in Brazil. I am here, they think my education level is the level normal here. Meltzer is Cornell and Southern Methodist University. What is Southern Methodist University, anyway? It is not Harvard. I gave a lecture in Cambridge to that British archaeologist made a lord—Colin Renfrew. No one said it was a fake and no good ... I know how to work."

Her major regret was that the only way to force Prous to jus-tify or retract his comments was to sue him. "No one sues in Brazil," she said. In Brazil, lawsuits take their own sweet time. Complainants and defendants wait for justice until the crack of doom. When the article was first published she asked a lawyer to take it on, to get an explanation. It had taken this long to get papers served. "Perhaps I will die before I have Prous in front of me telling the same history he published," she said.

And, as for Walter Neves, she was not suing him. But he had never come to Piauí either. She knew he didn't think what she found was old and that he had signed on to the critiques made by others. She would have her own form of justice with him. She had six human remains from various sites she'd dug in Piaui. They would be studied in France, or in Rio, not in São Paulo. "I won't give the remains to him," she growled.

She showed me to the gate and the car that was to take me back to the hotel. It had become very dark. The barbed-wire coils on top of the fence glimmered ominously. I could make out the pale forms of the white geese waddling by the pond, totally incongruous in the middle of a research establishment.

"Why do you keep them?"

"Do you know that they saved Rome?" she said with a laugh. Then she leaned closer, and said, seriously, that she kept them because thieves in the town had such nerve they had even cleaned out the belongings of a household of nuns. She had also been told she would be murdered over the matter of the caves. She had run afoul of hunters who killed the endangered animals in the park and were destroying the sites too. There were two ancient caves—one that had produced the extremely ancient date for the painting, and another with a painting of a giant sloth. The cave with the sloth painting had almost been destroyed by those who mine for lime. She had complained to the ministry of the environment, who sent a prosecutor to investigate. He had found the mine workers to be in a condition of virtual slavery.

She was silent for a moment, letting that terrible word, slavery, float out onto the damp night air. Yes, she said, rich people do this. The miners worked only for food, and some of them had lost their fingers, or their hands had been blown off. The investigator had made his report. And this being Brazil, he had been taken off the case. The destruction continued, she said, and I don't know what to do. They threatened to kill me.

She laughed abruptly.

I don't take it seriously, she said. But I keep the geese. I like the noise.

# 17

# Pedra Furada

## Ancient Arts of the Little People

ELAYNE DICK, MY GUIDE, arrived with a brand new car and a driver. She did not trouble to explain the itinerary: no tourist is allowed into the Serra da Capivara park without a guide, so I was at her mercy. I had calculated that I would need a year and a half just to see properly the sites that Guidon had already found here. I was in despair. In two days, how could I even get the flavor of an area of 40,000 square kilometers? I had decided I had to be utterly ruthless. I would only see what I had to see to understand the nature of the claims made about this place. Above all, I had to look at Pedra Furada, and the sites where the human remains had been found.

My guide had plans of her own. And so, in the blinding heat, the air-conditioned car followed a narrow red-dirt road through the outskirts of town, turning this way and that, through thickets of green bushes, beside little yards and farm fields marked off by fences that looked like woven baskets.

One more turn. The Museu do Homem Americano, Dick said, with a broad sweep of her little arm. She stepped out of the car into the sandy parking area. There were two buildings, low-slung, the walls made of that same peach-colored stucco, but with stone detailing. Wooden-beamed rooflines overhung the patio between them in the manner of a Japanese tea house. A beautiful tree with big spreading branches and strange knobby fruits gave fleeting shade. The fruits are called ata, and are very sweet, said Dick. There was a plaque that listed all the important personages from various ministries and international agencies who had been present for the groundbreaking in 1994, and the one who showed up when the place was officially opened in 1998. I tried to figure out why this beautiful little structure sat in the middle of farmers' fields instead of near the highway or in town. Money, said my guide. This was the only big piece of land they could afford to buy.

There was a peculiar box, like an aquarium, right in the middle of the little plaza between the two buildings. Dangling upside down in a purplish liquid were eleven armadillos, looking just like the antiabortionists' displays of bottled fetuses—soft and gray and quite dead. Dick translated the inscription from the Portuguese. It began with an admonition that we must share this earth with everyone. Then it said, "The hunters without hearts who killed these animals don't know they could have Chagas' disease, which is transmitted by a flying insect.... When they prepare the meat to eat, the man can get the disease. Some years later, the hunter will have serious problems in his heart."

We entered through a large wooden door into a black room with brilliantly lighted displays. The first set concerned the botany and zoology of the park. There was a large display map showing how human beings came to the Americas. "Our museum," it said, "is dedicated to prehistoric man and all Indian natives killed by greed—the cruelty of civilization. They were killed, their lands stolen. They were the first people who were despoiled in our history, but not the last."

Another map showed where the precursors of modern human beings had been found at various sites in Africa, Europe and China. Still another showed the most ancient known sites in the Americas, with arrows suggesting origins in Australia and a path over the Bering Strait, or straight across the Pacific from Japan to California. There was no attempt to generate a theory or suggest waves of migration, and absolutely nothing to illustrate Niéde

Guidon's speculation that people might have come from Europe or Africa. Instead there was simply this statement: "At about 12,000 years Before Present, people lived in America from Tierra del Fuego to Alaska. And they came from Asia."

There was a natural history of the area of the park going back 340 million years, a time when this was all under sea. The sea's retreat left behind the strange uplifted cliffs and mesas made of limestone and sandstone that harbored all the caves and shelters in the region. The climate 12,000 years ago was like São Paulo today, hot and very humid—with many rivers meandering through a vast forested plain. Large animals lurked everywhere: armadillos as big as Volkswagens, smilodons (saber-toothed tigers), a now extinct kind of horse, a creature like a llama, and a sloth eight meters high. And there were people.

Some of the paintings found on the shelters' walls were reproduced in the next display. There were two traditions discovered, which Niéde Guidon had named Nordeste (the earlier tradition and the smaller) and Agreste (the much larger style). Agreste, she had decided, came later and was big, sloppy and without a sense of movement or perspective. Some of the Nordeste images appeared over and over—particularly the image of little people dancing around a tree.

My guide marched smartly through the dark hall with its illuminated plastic-covered maps and photographs, telling me what each painting meant. Here was a sex scene, here was a sacrifice, here was a woman giving birth and here a man with a club. This, she said with a flourish and a polite smile, was a gang rape, six on one. I peered and looked and twisted my head. Often, I simply could not see what she insisted so strenuously was there. There were light boxes with artifacts. One was billed as the oldest polished axe in the Americas—the date given on it was 9200 BP, about as old as Spirit Cave. It was very large, shaped like a crescent, a very pale green.

Where, I asked, are the burials?

Upstairs, she said. We climbed. The air thickened noticeably.

At a shelter named Toca dos Coqueiros, said a sign, a burial of a man had been discovered and dated at 9800 BP. Casts of the bones were there, laid on their side, as if sleeping. I peered down at the faux skeleton, trying to discern whether the orbits were square or not: I couldn't decide.

We passed by exact replicas of large burial urns about three hundred years old, discovered two years ago on private land—one holding a small child of about four, with tiny fingers peeking out beside its head, and its blunt haircut quite intact.

There was an arrangement of stone and bones on the floor, the skeleton of a woman. Dick referred to the first skeleton we'd seen, the man, as ZoZo. "[This one is] ZaZa, a woman. They think a big block with six tons fell beside her head and caught her hair and her head blew up. Some bones are missing, maybe an animal ate them, but the hands and mandible are there. It's about 9,700 years old." The woman, she said, had six cavities—two upper incisors were very damaged. She was about one and a half meters tall, small and graceful. She had lived to about thirty.

We moved down to where there were displayed remains of some of the creatures these people may have shared the earth with. There were enormous mastodon bones and a huge piece of tusk found at a limestone site. There was a leg bone from a taxodon, an extinct animal as big as a hippopotamus but with fur. The now vanished glyptodont was like an armadillo but it weighed up to 700 kilograms. The hide was three centimeters thick. There was a meter-long femur from a huge sloth, which would have weighed up to five tons. The hand had claws at least thirty centimeters long. The paleollama was a species previously unknown. It had been named for Niéde Guidon, who had found it at the park.

At nine o'clock the next morning, the FUMDHAM car came again. The son of the previous driver was at the wheel. My guide was again dressed in shorts and a T-shirt and a layer of pink frost lip-stick. I had been ordered to dress in long pants and shirt. Rosa Trakalo, the administrator of the FUMDHAM, had insisted upon it. She had said there was a gigantic flying insect in the bush that was very hard to get rid of, that would attack any bare flesh. Obvi-ously Elayne Dick was not concerned, but the tarantula in the museum display had been as big as my fist and the insect that car-ried Chagas' disease was as big as a finger. I took Rosa's advice.

It was another perfect day. The sky was blue and clear, and at 9 a.m. the temperature hovered at around thirty degrees centi-grade. A woman walked swiftly down the highway; in one hand she carried a bag of fruit, and in the other a stool to sit on while trying to sell it. There was a peppery scent everywhere, with hints of lemon and possibly sage and other herbs I didn't know. It was so delicious, so intriguing, I filled my lungs, over and over, trying to learn this subtle aroma.

The car roared out into the countryside, first taking the high-way that passed in front of the hotel, then veering off to follow another road. We were moving north, I thought, then changed my mind—then changed it again. Yes, it was definitely north. And soon I got a view of Oz—a string of limestone and sandstone mesas in the distance, gray and red, jumping up from the green plain, perpendicular to the road. We drove almost forty kilome-ters from the city, through the flat landscape. Then the car climbed up a rise into a forest at the base of the towering red cliffs.

We were at the park's back gate, said Dick. There was a small but perfect gatehouse at the boundary, made of the same stucco as the museum and the hotel. There was a blue-green tiled patio, with two very deep planters' chairs. The overhanging roof gave shade. Inside was a young man who had books and pamphlets to sell. The washroom was large, bright, tiled and immaculate.

We drove in on a dirt road. Grass grew in the middle and scraped against the tailpipe. The road wound and twisted and there were trees and bushes on both sides, brushing and thump-ing at the windows, and threaded through the trees there were vines with trumpet-shaped pink flowers. The stone cliffs closed in on both sides. There were little signs at the verge of the narrow road with names—Toca da entrada do Pajau and Toca do Pajau. The car stopped. We climbed up stone steps someone had laboriously set into the side of the cliff. We emerged, finally, from the screen of trees beside the upper cliff face where a long boardwalk ran above the sloping floor of the shelter. The site was overhung with a huge curve of sandstone. And on the stone the painters had gone to work, high over the little valley, within easy sight of the cliff on the other side. There were tiny creatures that looked like people with small heads, small arms and legs, sometimes their bodies filled in, sometimes not. In particular there was that image of little dancing people surrounding a tree, much like the image at the hotel. I looked closer. Not all people, I decided. One was a person, the rest were animals, with tails. Elayne Dick said, They're people, of course. No, I said. See? I told her of Wilson Wewa's story about the days of the animal people, and as I told it, I could feel the hair standing up on the back of my neck because it seemed to me this picture, in this place, was like an illustration of it.

Down, back in the car, another site. The pictures were in black and in red. My camera had decided to pack it in so I got Dick, who had hers tied to her neck, to take some for me. The Nordeste-tradition figures, even the animals, were tiny. There was a sequence of long-necked creatures that could have been ostriches or llamas. Their heads faced away from their bodies, as if they were watching someone. Laid on top of these Nordeste paintings were large pictures of animals and people—some with round heads and feathers in crowns, others looking like strange flat figures with an explosion of feathers above, as if a person hid behind a shield.

Down to the car again. Through the narrow road, a turning, another angle, and still the cliffs bulged overhead. Toca do Inferno, she announced. We walked and walked between two very high cliffs, following a narrow pathway that finally came to a dead end. A waterfall trickled down from above. It was beautiful and cool. This was no shelter, really, and no site, she explained, just a place where people had heard weird sounds. I was swimming in my own sweat. Not a single bug had troubled me, but I was sure that these long pants were going to cause me to die from heat prostration. I couldn't breathe from the heat whenever I put one foot out of the shade. The waterfall hadn't been there even two weeks earlier, my guide said, and it would be gone soon.

Back in the car, more thumps along the window. We stopped at a little sign that said Baixão da Vaca. We walked from the road along a forested path. There were yellow flowers, and the pink trumpets, very little in the way of underbrush, dark sand. We climbed up to a small shelter. The paintings were in both styles, Agreste and Nordeste, the Agreste very large and sloppy, laid overtop the small, graceful Nordeste figures. These were painted mostly in black.

There was something curious about the way these paintings were arranged. I puzzled over the strange way in which the creatures had been grouped. There were animals with antennae or feathers protruding directly from their bodies: were they snails without shells? There was one, then two, then three of them, then an image of a man, then two men, and then three. And then there was a line of manlike figures, without heads, just a branching Y at the top to signify arms and another below to signify legs. Abruptly these figures became simple sticks laid out in a horizontal row. It was like looking at the beginning of the abstraction of number, the earliest form of counting. Nearby there was another group of pictures. The men had their arms raised, their knees bent. "A woman giving birth," said Dick, pointing at a group of figures. I peered at it. One pushed on the back and stomach of another. Next to it was the figure of a man with his hand on the shoulder of someone in front. "Sex from behind," she said. Maybe, I thought. Maybe not.

A rest at a picnic table. A drift of pastel-yellow butterflies passed over my head. Back to the car. Toca do Paraguaio was at the end of a mercifully short walk up a flight of steps to a wall of sandstone mixed with great pebbled conglomerate hanging overhead. There were pictures everywhere, in both traditions. The Nordeste were my favorites—these little figures were always dancing or moving with a gleeful grace, even when they appeared to be brandishing sticks and whacking some other figure on the head. The big Agreste figures, by contrast, were ponderous and self-important, not relishing life, imposing themselves on it. The older figures, the Nordeste, were not really well drawn but they had this singing vitality. There were two bent figures, facing in opposite directions, bum to bum, both with a hand on their lower backs, as if complaining in pain and unable to straighten up, one reaching out to touch in curiosity the tail of a giant deer, the other seeming to lean on a stick.

Lunch was across the valley, on the other side of the park, near the main entrance. There was a large parking lot, and then a garden, and a climb up a low hill to a resthouse set below a high cliff red in the sun. There was a large classroom with a lecture hall, a gift shop, and a small terrace served by an outdoor snack bar. We had driven twenty-eight kilometers from the last site to this, across the green plain, through a series of small and grimy villages, the worst I'd seen in a poor place. All the way I'd been thinking about what the pictures meant, and how they hovered between written language and painting, between narration and pure image-making. For images to speak to us we need to know their context, otherwise they just lie there, interesting, curious, but meaningless. The difficulty grows worse when those images are arranged in groups and these groups are meant to convey some larger story. I knew they told a story because they varied in size, in number, in attitude, but what did I know of the context of life so many thousands of years ago? I was moving through this world of theirs in an air-conditioned car, climbing up to their shelters on cut stone steps, stopping for a bottled drink when I was thirsty, eating a bun heated in a microwave when I was hungry, sitting on chairs made with modern tools, my food set before me on pottery decorated with images stolen from these rock faces.

But at the very next shelter, I found something that I could understand. The name was Toca da Fumacaa. It was very small, at the end of a short walk. The figures were in black or a dark red. They were tiny, and they were just above the line where the sediments had been brushed away. I was looking at one thing, then another, and then a crescent-moon-shaped object, with one side higher than the other, caught my eye. There were a few little people set on top. It was clearly a picture of people in a boat. Protruding from the stern on both sides were long oars with very large, square-shaped paddles. There were two smaller ones at the bow, which was a subtly different curve from the stern. The two figures at the stern seemed higher than the rest, as if they were standing on a platform that allowed them to see over the bow. Other than the fact there was no mast and sail, this boat was like a side view of the reed vessels Heyerdahl had built to prove they could cross oceans. He had built the *Tigris* in the manner of the reed boats painted on the walls of Sumerian tombs: he'd used berdi reeds cut for him by the Marsh Arabs of Iraq, who lived on the Tigris river. These salt-resistant reeds were bundled together and wrapped in giant mats knotted for him by the four Aymara Indians he had flown in from Lake Titicaca, Peru, because they still made reed boats in this manner and the Marsh Arabs had forgotten how. Together the Aymara and the Iraqis made mats twenty meters long, wrapped them around the bundles of reeds and then bundled two of these giant sausages together with long ropes wrapped around and around and pulled tight. In other words, these boats (or flow-through rafts, which is what they really were) required the technology of the textile maker more than the arts of the woodworker. What focused my attention on this stone wall in the middle of Brazil were the two square shapes at the bottom of the two stern tiller oars. This particular shape was what was needed to steer such a buoyant reed vessel. Two oars were required, never just one. Heyerdahl's studies had shown that the larger the square, the better the oars performed.

"Look," I said to my guide, "a boat."

No, she said, not a boat, an animal.

There were two large whales beside a small one, a small pod if they were killer whales, although their heads were shaped more like those of right whales. They were laid out as if seen from above: their flukes were clearly visible, and different in each animal. This was observation, not an image meant to signify the general idea of whale, but a rendering of remembered whales. São Raimundo Nonato is almost 1,300 kilometers from the Atlantic coast.

Absolutely, I said, it's a boat, and those are whales.

She agreed with me that the creatures looked like whales, but not boats, no boats.

Finally, we arrived at Toca da Barra do Antonião, the site where a falling rock had killed the woman lying asleep by a fire 9,700 years ago. I had seen the cast of her remains at the museum. This site was close to the snack bar, below the giant towers of red sandstone. There was a huge sandstone overhang. There were very deep squares underneath it, all that was left of the archaeological excavation. The excavation had been very thorough: it went thirty feet down below the lowest line of the drawings. The pictures, according to Dick, were in the early Nordeste tradition.

The light was fading. I wanted to see Pedra Furada. My guide wanted to go back to the snack bar. She had in her mind that I ought to see Pedra Furada after dark, when the sound and light show prepared for the tourists who came to the park could be best appreciated. I wasn't interested in sound and light shows, I wanted to see why some American and Brazilian archaeologists refused to acknowledge the antiquity of this site.

We approached from behind, walking up to the two towers that have become the signature image of the national park, through the gap between them and emerging in front. This was a gigantic shelter, huge in comparison to all the others, and through the screen of trees on the hill in front one could see all across the plain. The top of the mesa towered hundreds of meters above the shelter. There was very little shade because there wasn't much overhang. It was a spectacular setting. There was an excavation left in the ground larger than anything I had seen in Brazil. It had been cut straight down: two giant squares going right down to bedrock and walled off with cement. "I want the truth," Niéde Guidon had said yesterday, "not a fiction." And here was proof of the effort that had been made. Stones had been moved, the former path of the river that had once meandered through the site had been charted, leaving the sand and cobbles as they were found. At one end of the giant mesa that towered over us, set far back from the shelter and the site, there was a dark chute carved into the stone wall by seasonally falling water. The stone glowed green with velvety moss and algae that had bloomed after the last rain, but the waterfall had already dried up. The walls of the shelter area were covered with paintings, which we could see only by walking on the gangway set right beside the stone wall for that purpose. This was also where the excavators had found coprolites, and it was close to the site where Adauto Araújo had found evidence of hookworm in the bowel tract of human remains dated 7300 BP. There were 2,500 paintings on the wall, said my guide. Some 15,000 pieces of stone had been taken from the site, including the "oldest dated human hearths in the hemisphere."

I climbed along the catwalk, dragging her with me, showing her the images I wanted her to shoot. I came by a particular group of marks that was quite stunning. They may have told a story, but not in the usual manner of the other images of dancing men and running beasts (for instance, the picture of a man flipping another off his hands so that the man would land feet first onto the round back of a running beast many times bigger than either of them). This set of markings was a sequence of symbols: they were simple lines divided in groups, and arranged in a particular way. To my eye they looked like a coded form of communication. There was a group of lines formed to look like a square wave. Up above were single strokes of about the same size arranged in groups. In the middle of these marks lay a flat square with interior lines running parallel to the square's perimeter: it looked a little bit like a maze. This was made to convey information to whoever understood the code, as surely as the lines I made in my notebook or the little signs of explanation set out beside the roads throughout the park. These lines were dead straight and only really varied in their length. On reflection, I thought they were like the incised marks Alexander Marshak had found on small stones and ceremonial knives in caves with Ice Age paintings in France. I couldn't bring myself to say any of this out loud.

The next morning I went to see Niéde Guidon again. She was dressed as before in jeans and a man's shirt, and sat as before at her desk, taking calls and visits as they came. People, dogs, geese ran here and there, doing this and that. I had burbled relentlessly to Rosa Trakalo the night before about how I had found a picture of a very interesting boat above some very interesting whales. She had shown me a book written by archaeologist Gabriela Martin who had made a study of recurring images in the rock art of the Brazilian northeast. Boats were recurring themes. So I explained to Guidon that she really ought to be more careful about what her guides were saying about the rock art pictures to people like me.

She looked at me with her head cocked sideways as I went on and on about why I thought this boat was important, why I thought the tree scene with the animals and men gathered round it was interesting, why I disagreed with the guide when she said I was looking only at men and not at animals.

"During six thousand years we have this repeated scene," she said. "At the beginning there is only one tree with two people near the bottom and two near the top. And then it became like this image in the hotel." She believed the men I thought were monkeys were in fact men with erections. There was a site that she would show me herself, and I would see what she meant.

"Several years ago," she said, "we went to the Indian tribe near the São Francisco. They live in town, they lost their language and their culture. But they repeat each year a ceremony with big masks and dancing around a tree. Marie [Anne-Marie Pessis] filmed this. If you stop [the film] you have some of the choreography that is here dated 12,000 years. They lost the meaning, but they keep the gestures. The position of men and women, we have here several times repeated, a man, a woman with hand on shoulder and they dance. We have [pictures] with exactly the same position and number of participants in the scene."

For her thesis, she had started with the paintings and engravings on the first fifty-five shelters she was led to. There were something like 15,000 figures in all. She identified three painting traditions and two different kinds of engravings. After she published, others in Brazil confirmed that they too were identifying different painting traditions. But nobody else had found sites with only geometrical figures like the one I had seen the day before, and which she thought were here from the beginning.

"Nordeste," she said, "seems to originate here.... In the oldest places we have paintings [of that style]. [It's in] some other places in Brazil, but not the same concentration. We have it to the north till seventy kilometers from the sea, and south to Minas Gerais. André Prous dated one site to 2000 years BP. [That was] one of the reasons he said [our sites are] not so old. We have 12,000 BP here. In the northeast it's perhaps to 6000 BP. Then [it] began to spread, perhaps because of Agreste presence. I thought Agreste [was] here at 5000. Then I found one site with paintings dated at 10,000. This begins at 10,000.... An Agreste site at one and a half meters we found paintings on a wall. In front are several hearths. We dated this well. It was Nordeste with Agreste on top of them. Then it goes north near the sea and east to Bahia, and south to Minas Gerais."

And what about the whales?

"Yes, whales," she said. "They are *bothos*." She tried to remember the English word for a sea mammal that enters very large rivers. I thought she might mean manatees, but that was not the animal I had seen on the shelter wall. And as to the representation of the boat, yes, she said, "In the north and east there are several of the representations of the boat. It seems that they represented this because [in the] north there were big rivers about 20,000 years BP. We know it was very rainy till 12,000 BP. We had a moment of tremendous rains at 22,000 BP. After 10,000 the climate dries, I think slowly. I have remnants of megafauna until about 6000 BP. They needed a lot of green leaves and water... This climate now, it was completely in place since 6000 BP. No more humid forest. In Pedra Furada you have [pictures of] crabs, elements of fauna different from today. The capivara [the large rodent, capybara in English, for which the park is named] only lives in the rivers."

So, I asked, what did she think these pictures actually meant?

"Anne-Marie Pessis says the paintings were their way to communicate their history, religion, myths as documents for new generations, as we have our social register." There had been some, she said, who thought that ancient peoples made pictures of the animals they killed or wanted to kill as a form of sympathetic magic. Pessis didn't believe these pictures were about magic and hunting. "This is to keep the memory of their culture," she says. "These paintings are the first graphical register of the American peoples. They are the oldest."

I said I thought there was more going on than the recollection of cultural moments. I told her about an image that seemed to capture the idea of number as represented by specific individuals, and turn them to a more abstract rendition of the same idea, a series of sticks, like a form of counting.

"I don't know if there is counting," she said, "but several sites have this transformation of men to sticks. We have in one site a series of drawings that seem like frogs. You have a frog, the drawing goes, and then a human figure." Some of these images were obvious in their meaning, "but others, no, the keys of the code are lost with these people. They know what they say. For instance, this kind of figure, you have a drawing like this."

She took a piece of paper and made a drawing of a circle surrounded by rays.

"Normally we interpret this as sun. I saw an article on the Guarani Indians. They said [this is] a village and paths to the plantations. For one culture this is sun. But not for them. We have for instance in Pedra Furada a lot of men side by side, each one has a different phallus of size and shape. Why this? A French colleague said this is how girls chose [a] husband.... We have a lot of people with hand on shoulder or on the back of the neck or a bump on the neck. I saw the same in New Mexico and Australia. And also in Colombia. It's like a hump. We don't know what this is. The best thing for guides is not to explain."

Among the oldest paintings at Pedra Furada, at the levels she dated at about 12,000, there were "two people. Then there is another looking, with hands on head or with an exclamation, like 'Oh, my wife!' After, it begins to be collective. At 7000 years we have a lot together making sex. One of these is at Pedra. And who knows what it means."

The traditions had changed and the character of the images definitely changed. "They were totally free at the beginning, each as you want, like Jesus on the Cross, it's as you choose, personal and individual. As this society evolves it has some patterns that set in. They—you see the beginning of violence. At the beginning you have representations of hunting. After that, there are representations of fights, two fighting, or a lot. The bodies begin to be square, all very long, like a rectangle, with geometric drawings—they have cultural attributes like feathers on the head, things on hands. It goes from a free society of hunting to a rigid, stratified society." But these were not even hypotheses, she hastened to say, they were just speculations.

"We never could prove this. You can say what you want, but it's not science—you can't disprove or prove—so this is literature.

I don't know if at 50,000 BP the people are the same as at 12,000 BP, the people who painted."

She wanted to show me the site called Perna where engravings had been found. There was another task she also wanted to do. The day before, in the town, some turtles had been found wandering in the street, as well as a young caiman. One of the veterinarians had asked Guidon if she wanted to come along while she released them back into the park. There was not enough room for three in the truck, and there was no car, so Guidon had one of her staff call a taxi.

She and I climbed into the ancient taxi. Its windows were open, and the taxi driver drove as if his battered car was a wild beast he had barely managed to tame. We flew out of town and across the plain, through the grimy little villages with their strange, basket-weave fences. She yelled into my ear to be heard over the wind, and her hair flapped in her eyes. She looked excited and happy to be going to the park, as if she couldn't wait. We were going toward the eastern gate, where there was a pond that would suit the animals. The truck was ahead of us. The road rose slowly; there was a magnificent view of the whole plain out to the east. I don't know how it happened, exactly, but the talk turned to ghosts, and the strange things that happen to those who study or deal with bones. Ignoring the fact that she had permanently damaged her knees and was suing Prous over her reputation, she said she had had no difficulties. She explained that she had always been very careful about the handling of bones—the dead she had uncovered had been very carefully prepared. They were the remains of people that someone had loved, they were someone's daughter, husband, mother. They had to be treated with respect. She did not allow her students to make jokes in their presence, and she always asked their permission to take them from their resting place and study them.

When she first came here, before there was any electricity or any TV from which the people could pick up strange ideas, the villagers told her that they sometimes saw strange vehicles with lights that came out of the sky and landed nearby. It was like something out of that place, Roswell (New Mexico), she said. She didn't know how they could have acquired these ideas—they didn't read, or go anywhere.

You're talking UFOS? I asked, thinking oh boy, over the top we go.

She then told me what happened when she made an offer to buy, for the park, some land belonging to a farmer in the area. He accepted her offer. They made an appointment for him to sign over the property and for her to give him the money. He missed the appointment. Two more weeks went by and he never came to see her. She thought he must be ill, so she sent someone to find out what had happened to him. He was in his house. He explained he had been unable to leave it: he'd been afraid it would be broken into by whoever was in the ship that had parked next door to him.

She laughed. I laughed.

So, madam scientist, I asked, do you believe in this?

"Some people think Pedra Furada is a place of power," she said. "All kinds of people interested in that come here. The Buddhists send people here to pray."

"Meaning what?"

Well, she said, she was talking about people who were interested in spiritual things, who said there was some sort of feeling there. Once, Globo TV had come to make a documentary about her work here. They had set up the camera and were filming her in front of the Pedra Furada shelter wall, when suddenly the sound man screamed, "Cut." He was picking up some strange machine noise in the background. He took off his head set, listened, heard nothing. Is there any heavy machinery working near here? he asked her. There was nothing, she said. Well, he said, I'm picking up something. He put his head set on, waved around the microphone, nothing. He put it near the ground. Nothing. Stuck it in the ground. There was this sound, she told me, bruuuu-ummba, bruuuuumba, bruuuuuuuumba.

Her words were carried away by the roar of the wind as the taxi gunned up and down over the narrow road. The driver kept reaching down with his hand to lift up his gas pedal when he had to brake: the gas pedal kept jamming on the floor. She told him to turn here, now there, now here again. Finally, we were in a clearing with a small pond. The caiman in his cage was already on the ground. The cage stank of the rotting meat he'd been fed. The turtles didn't want to go in the pond. They clung with their beaks to the pants of the young woman vet as she tried to set them down in the grass. Guidon took pictures of everything, then shooed the caiman towards the water. He wanted nothing to do with any pond either, and scuttled for the bushes behind the truck.

We got back in the taxi, and again Guidon pointed, turn here, now there, until we came, finally, to a place beyond which the taxi could not go. There was a screen of trees. She was out of the cab in a flash, her two yellow crutches under her elbows, hopping along a trail only she could see under the dried-up branches of caatinga. She moved like a grasshopper, up, down, forward, hop, faster than I could jog. I couldn't believe it, a sixty-six-year-old woman on crutches was leaving me gasping in the dust.

In this valley, she yelled over her shoulder, she had excavated the first of eight sites in 1988. In those days, before the road went in, it took her six hours to make her way here from Pedra Furada, across the arid plain. There were two jaguars here, and a tribe of capuchin monkeys.

We walked and hopped over the dry ground. Finally we emerged in front of the sandstone shelter she called Perna. It was on level ground, and chunks of it had fallen down. A cement square marked the edges of the dig. It had been very deep.

"We excavated it all," she said. "We went to rock." The bottom layer of charcoal dated to 9000 BP. They found paintings below that surface, very little figures. At the lowest level there were only two little figures.

She pointed to them. She thought they had to be 10,000 years old because they were so low on the wall in relation to the site and she didn't believe anyone would have painted these figures lying down. (André Prous, of course, disagreed with that notion. Why not? he'd said.) She pointed to other figures higher up, which were very large, painted in the Agreste tradition, and then to another group of figures that were a little like both, but not identical to either, which she had referred to as a tradition midway between. There were no boats, no whales. She pointed to a group of little people painted in the Nordeste style. They were thin, graceful, a group of seven men and women. She thought they held their arms up as if to exclaim, as if they were screaming. They were all individual people, real little portraits: this one had long spidery legs, that one was very short.

Okay, she said, here is the transition to numbering.

A group of stylized people with arms and legs, but no heads, all in a row, turned into a row of sticks. And then she pointed again at the two figures of indeterminate sex at the lowest level of the shelter. They were so tiny, their arms lifted as if to exclaim, just the two of them. They were so touchingly human. One couldn't tell by looking at them if they had square orbits, large jaws, wide noses or narrow heads. They were like cartoon figures, universal. They could have come from Africa, Europe, Asia or right here. Their postures, their gestures, reached out and touched the heart.

By the time I shot the picture, she was halfway back down the trail.

"Don't you think," she said, looking back at me over her shoulder as she rested on her crutches, "that all humans on earth came from the same source?"

# Part Three

Creon: *Tell me, Antigone, do you believe all that flummery about religious burial? Do you really believe that a so-called shade of your brother is condemned to wander for ever homeless if a little earth is not flung on his corpse to the accompaniment of some priestly abracadabra? Have you ever listened to the priests of Thebes when they were mumbling their formula? Have you ever watched those dreary bureaucrats while they were preparing the dead for burial—skipping half the gestures required by the ritual, swallowing half their words, hustling the dead into their graves out of fear that they might be late for lunch?*

Antigone: *Yes, I have seen all that.*

Creon: *And did you never say to yourself as you watched them, that if someone you really loved lay dead under the shuffling, mumbling ministrations of the priests, you would scream aloud and beg the priests to leave the dead in peace?*

Antigone: *Yes, I've thought all that.*

Creon: *And you still insist upon being put to death—merely because I refuse to let your brother go out with that grotesque passport; because I refuse his body the wretched consolation of* that mass-production jibber-jabber, which you would have been the first to be embarrassed by if I had allowed it. The whole thing is absurd!

Antigone: *Yes, it's absurd.*

Creon: *Then why, Antigone, why? For whose sake? For the sake of them that believe in it? To raise them against me?*

Antigone: *No.*

Creon: *For whom then if not for them and not for Polynices either?*

Antigone: *For nobody. For myself.*

Creon: *...this whole business is nothing but politics: the mournful shade of Polynices, the decomposing corpse, the sentimental weeping and the hysteria that you mistake for heroism—nothing but politics...it's stupid, monstrously stupid. But the people of Thebes have got to have their noses rubbed into it a little longer. My God! If it was up to me, I should have had them bury your brother long ago as a mere matter of public hygiene. I admit that what I am doing is childish. But if the featherheaded rabble I govern are to understand what's what, that stench has got to fill the town for a month.*

—JEAN ANOUILH, *Antigone: A Tragedy*

# 18

# Science under Fire

## The Inquisition of Karl Reinhard

PRIL 1999. It was autumn in Brazil, but in Columbus, Ohio, spring was arriving. The leaves were unfurling on all the trees set neatly into the sidewalks. One minute they were buds, the next they were fresh green tongues flapping in the breeze, dappling the streets with broken shafts of light, zebra-striping the homeless man lying across the sidewalk. The earth was awake, birthing herself. The American Association of Physical Anthropologists (AAPA) was holding its annual meeting and the newsstands were full of stories about human origins.

*Science* had new information about the ancient Ice Age art of France.[1] Some of the paintings of animals discovered at Grotte Chauvet in 1994, done with perspective, shading, and brilliantly executed line, had produced a radiocarbon date of 32,000 BP. This was twice as old as the paintings at Lascaux. None of this accorded with the accepted chronology of human development and migration into Europe during the Ice Age. These works had been done when early modern people were supposed to have just entered western Europe (on foot through the Middle East, and then through Greece and Italy, according to the theory). But these paintings of rhinoceroses, lions, mammoths and bears turned the meaning of "early" upside down. These were not the works of primitive minds fumbling to express inchoate feelings and ideas. They were glorious, the end product of a long, complex tradition, and yet there was no evidence of a learning curve. "Who can draw like that?" one of the scientists asked in awe. A second story the following month in *Science* noted that the dangerous animals painted at Grotte Chauvet were similar to paintings recently dated at 28,000 BP, discovered in 1990 in a cave at D'Arcy in the Burgundy region. Forceful style, acute observation, the proper proportions and perspective, the same subtlety of the language of line and shadow were also exhibited in the cave in Burgundy, in the north. This apparent long-distance communication of ideas and culture had to be explained: there was discussion of a north-south corridor.[2]

Chins also wagged about a find made the previous November in Portugal. A Neanderthal burial had been discovered and dated to about 25,000 BP. This was after the time, in the accepted chronology of Europe, that Neanderthals were supposed to have died out and been replaced by modern humans. It was long after the painters of Chauvet had made their magnificent bestiary. The rumor was the Neanderthal bones looked very, very odd.

*Newsweek* ran a big story describing the bubbling ferment over the chronology of the First Americans.[3] The reconstruction of the face of the Spirit Cave Mummy stared out at the world from the cover. Jim Chatters' reconstruction of Kennewick Man was inside, where Owsley's colleague and fellow Kennewick litigant, Richard Jantz, was pictured. Buhl Woman, described as a typical Mongoloid in *American Antiquity*, and confirmed as such by Walter Neves, was described in *Newsweek* as unlike any modern group, but most similar to Polynesians. Who were the First Americans? *Newsweek* asked.

*Newsweek* accepted the worldview of U.S. anthropology, which, in spite of its belated recognition that Clovis might not have been first, continued to pay attention mainly to finds in America (defined as below Canada and above Mexico), or finds made by Americans (such as Dillehay and Roosevelt). *Newsweek* was not much interested in the wider context of the Americas, or in what might have been going on at the end of the Ice Age in Europe or Africa. It made no mention of the rock art finds in France, or the strange Neanderthal bones found in Portugal, or the very interesting concentration of human ingenuity at Pedra Furada in Brazil. While it told a fanciful story about the death of the Spirit Cave Mummy, it did not mention that the textiles found with him were similar to those found in Minas Gerais and (according to American textile experts Olga Soffer and James Adovasio) to textiles whose outlines had been found in the oldest known modern human sites in central Europe (Dolni Vestonice I and II and Pavlov I in the Czech Republic). At the same time that people were painting Grotte Chauvet, these Gravettians, as their culture was called, were making nets, cords, skirts and hats out of twined and woven plant fibers (the same technologies that had been used to make early reed boats). *Newsweek* did grasp that the making of twine had something to do with the sea, and that perhaps France or Spain could have been the source of the culture in America called Clovis: there was a cursory discussion of Stanford's theory about ice-hugging voyages across the North Atlantic. There was an arrow on a map illustrating this possibility and another showing how people might have come into the New World "in canoes" by hugging the Pacific coast. This was progress of a sort, but all the arrows in the Americas pointed in the same direction, from the north to the south, and there were none suggesting a link between North Africa and Brazil. The idea that modern humans might have evolved from an earlier ancestor in the Americas was not entertained. The skull and tooth fragments found near Pedra Furada did not exist for *Newsweek*, nor did the debate over Alan Bryan's calotte. It was surprising in this context that Luzia was even mentioned: she looked Australian and South Asian, according to *Newsweek*. Nothing was said of her African affinities.

Oddly enough, there was no direct mention of the litigation over the right to study Kennewick. But *Newsweek*, which is careful of its facts, must have had what it considered to be a very reliable source on the Kennewick remains because it plowed through the ambiguities of skull measurement with this: "Although early reports described him as Caucasoid or even European (which led the Asatru Folk Assembly, followers of an ancient Nordic religion, to claim him), in fact the 8,000-year-old man most resembles a cross between the Ainu and the Polynesians."

There were only three people I knew of who had actually measured Kennewick's skull: one was Jim Chatters and the other two were Jerome Rose and Joe Powell, hired by the U.S. government to perform this task. Jim Chatters had held no press conference to announce the results of the work he did with Neves. Powell and Rose's conclusions were also still unpublished. So where had *Newsweek* acquired the information it reported here?

It is curious how science gossip transforms itself so quickly into fact. This was particularly true on Capitol Hill, where the Committee on Indian Affairs of the United States Senate had just met in solemn congress to consider certain flaws in the Native American Graves Protection and Repatriation Act. There, just a week before *Newsweek*'s story went to press, facts regarding the application of science to the remains of early Americans had been front and center, along with gossip concerning the work of Karl Reinhard of the University of Nebraska at Lincoln, Araújo and Ferreira's American colleague.

The testimony of Tex Hall, chairman of the Three Affiliated Tribes of the Mandan, Hidatsa and Arikara Nations of the Fort Berthold Reservation was most illuminating.[4] Hall dealt with what he saw as the duplicity and schemes of the Smithsonian and its employee, Doug Owsley, who worked to get his hands on Native American remains. Hall also expressed the fears and worries the Native community had with regard to the motives of Francis P. McManamon, the federal civil servant charged with overseeing the regulations under the NAGPRA for the Department of the Interior's parks service. McManamon had organized for the Army Corps of Engineers the work of the scientific team that had just finished examining Kennewick Man and his context. The Kennewick plaintiffs believed that McManamon's interpretation of the act had to be challenged in the service of science: his view was that any bone that predated 1500 AD was Native American, no matter whether it was a Viking or the remains found in a submerged Chinese junk. For Hall, McManamon was also the enemy: "... He has been working all along to gain for his colleagues unhindered access to Native skeletal remains, bone collagen, DNA and other data that is not provided for in the Act," said Hall. "A consideration of the billions of dollars to be made from the patenting and marketing of Native DNA and DNA by-products fills us with fear," he said, "for we see what we are up against in trying to protect our ancestors' ancient remains."

But the biggest salvos were aimed at Karl Reinhard, a Clovis First dissenter who is tracing the natural history of tropical parasites in the New World:

> Also, senators, we wish to tell you of a situation at the University of Nebraska, Lincoln, where Professor Karl Reinhard conducted, post-NAGPRA, destructive, invasive scientific study of Ponca, Pawnee, Arikara and Wichita ancestors. He extracted DNA from the remains of our relatives and he did this in violation of the law and without our knowledge or permission. We know he did this because he published his speculative findings in a professional paper, in one instance, 'In the Wake of Contact: Biological Responses to Contact,' and openly defied the Ponca tribe's position of no scientific study of their remains in another. Incredibly, Reinhard also lied to promote his illegal, immoral and unethical research agenda to obtain a federal grant by stating that he actually had the Ponca's permission to conduct this type of study on their relatives! You may have read media reports of this professor's exploits, where he put a little Native baby's skull on his hand, and made it "talk" and say inane things to make his students

laugh. He also had sole access to a lab where the remains of an Omaha ancestor were found in a drawer with Taco Bell wrappers and other trash, and he is suspected of removing soft tissue remains from an official NAGPRA inventory and from the boxes themselves, before the rest of the remains were turned over to the Poncas for reburial. The Poncas were led to believe they had received all the remains of their relatives. A coalition of fifteen Great Plains tribes seeks a federal investigation into these allegations, since a state investigation (conducted by colleagues of Reinhard's who hired him to do forensic murder studies) failed to result in charges against him. Moreover, instead of sanctioning Reinhard for his actions, UNL gave him tenure. We are compelled to wonder if acts of this nature are occurring elsewhere, given the pervasiveness of the regrettable attitudes of the science and museum industries we are forced to work with. We fear there are many more tragic stories like this one that just have not come to light yet. The University of Nebraska at Lincoln, however, is a site where a series of acts of professional misconduct, immoral and unethical research and criminal behavior have been carried out without sanctions being brought by any institution or agency. We want you to assist us in opening a federal inquiry into the matter, since no one has acted on our request.

I had spoken with Karl Reinhard on the telephone several times before actually meeting him for breakfast in Columbus. He'd talked of the suppression of ideas in paleoparasitology that followed upon the Clovis-First-Bering-Strait theory becoming an unquestionable orthodoxy. He spoke, in a high, breathy monotone, of how much flak he'd taken for publishing contrary opinions, and I'd formed the mental picture of a very young, small man. He'd said not one word about the trouble he was in over his handling of ancient Native American bones.

He came out of his hotel's elevator, tall, broad-shouldered, with short cropped brown hair and a bushy brown beard. He drifted toward me with his hand outstretched, then realized he'd forgotten the documents he wanted me to read, so he drifted right back into the elevator. Then he sat with me in the restaurant, languidly spooning up some pieces of melon while he spilled out his appalling tale: the study of Native American remains had almost destroyed him.

He had just issued a legal claim against some of his persecutors. He was about to launch a suit against another. There would be more. "So many defendants," he said in that monotone as he handed me one document after another, "so little time."

Start at the beginning, I said, as he gave me the results of a university investigation that exonerated him.

Reinhard was born in Alaska. His father was an epidemiologist and his mother a teacher of nurses. His father spent the latter part of his career looking, through documentary sources, at the history of the spread of diseases in the Arctic, and had sparked his son's interest in the whole question of how human tropical parasites entered the Western hemisphere. "I thought that could also be done with Paleo communities," Reinhard explained. He'd done his bachelor's degree in biology at the University of Arizona and his doctorate at Texas A & M University—he was a physical anthropologist, but his specialty was paleoparasitology. He started work in this area in the early 1980s, two years after Ferreira and Araújo began theirs in Brazil. He too found hookwormlike things in coprolites taken off an archaeological site. "The dogma was that the New World was free of tropical parasites. So I saw these eggs and assumed they had to be something else." His professors had taught that one could not get any parasites out of a coprolite, and that only one parasite with tropical origins, pinworm, was in the New World. The first time Reinhard read Ferreira and Araújo's work he thought it was "interesting but farfetched. But it bugged me."

What bugged him was this: the reason he found it difficult to believe their results was that he *knew* the accepted story of the peopling of the Americas as told by anthropologists. Human beings had walked into the Americas over the Bering Strait. However, those who didn't "know" this theory had no problem with the Brazilians' findings. "I was at Texas A & M," said Reinhard. "I worked with veterinary parasitologists who were quite willing to accept it. No problem."

He arrived at the University of Nebraska's anthropology department in 1989, just as the state's Native remains reburial bill was passed, just as the NAGPRA legislation was about to be passed. He was in favor of NAGPRA. He believed then, and still believes, that no Native American remains should be studied unless the tribe to which they are affiliated wants it done. He believes that science should be of benefit to Native people. The forensic work he was assigned to do at Nebraska, as part of his tenure-required service to the state, reinforced his beliefs. He knew it was more important for the relatives of the dead to have the body buried, than to keep it above ground so scientists could do research and issue publications about what had been learned. He was assigned to work on the repatriation of Omaha tribal remains, and then was asked to find funds for the documentation of skeletons from other tribes. He did that, but the repatriation work was taken over by the newly established NAGPRA committee.

It had also fallen to him to separate the archaeological remains of Native Americans from the mass of other human bones stacked like cordwood in room 109, the osteology teaching laboratory. The Native American bones had been brought to the room by previous members of the anthropology department. The museum associated with the university also had a human remains collection. Remains from both collections were intermingled over the years. Nebraska archaeologists had "excavated burials in the 1940s barely one hundred years dead. I thought it was illegal. This was shocking to me. Nebraska had a collection that was mismanaged, largely thrown away and not really studied. We can't offer repatriation to tribes if we mismanage the collection. I discovered in the early 1990s that thousands of bones were missing." In his effort to explain the ways in which bone collections were mismanaged at Nebraska, Reinhard's words came out in spurts. The museum's collection was 1,300 individuals but there were many more in the department's control. Somehow bones went missing and bones were destroyed. "One of the points of the Indians is they say I deliberately misled the university regarding bones lost to cover my illegal activities. In 1965 [almost twenty years before Reinhard arrived at Nebraska], half a [car] trunk full were incinerated on campus.... They released that information in September [of 1998]. I've been accused of losing bones burned in the 1960s...."

Reinhard was released from his repatriation work in 1994. He thought he knew why. "I'm convinced I was released from the NAGPRA work...after I made it clear many bones were missing and I'd informed the Pawnee and the Omaha tribes. It was very scandalous. We missed in excess of 6,000 or 8,000 from a single site. Some 11,000 out of 18,000 bones were unaccounted for. Since then, some have been found, it's more like 15,000 missing.... I found evidence fifteen sites [were] disturbed. So I couldn't even begin to organize. When I arrived in room 109 it was stacked floor to ceiling with bones, North American, South American, Philippine, but the majority were the museum collection. Many had been transferred from the museum to the department since 1986. Before that, bones dug at archaeological sites were sent to the museum for storage, but brought back to the department as faculty saw fit. The department had used these bones up until I arrived, for teaching, sawing, breaking, as a collection of pathological remains, but out of context of the skeletons. I spent an enormous amount of time just getting bones I could identify back to the museum."

As far as Reinhard was concerned, he was on the side of right. No one was more surprised than he when he was accused, by his colleagues, of major violations under the NAGPRA. Reinhard's troubles with the collections boiled over while he was away in

Brazil in the fall of 1997, but they had been simmering since 1994. In 1996, he ran for the position of chairman of the anthropology department. He lost the election to a man whose specialty is cultural anthropology and issues regarding human rights. There were soon a number of difficulties between Reinhard and the new chairman, Robert Hitchcock. Reinhard applied for a transfer of tenure from anthropology to biological sciences, whose director suggested that the use of room 109 also be transferred as an office for Reinhard, a proposal that was rejected. Just as he was leaving to go down to Brazil to work with Araújo and Ferreira, another man was hired by the department to teach Reinhard's physical anthropology class. Nebraska has a rule that if a married person is hired from somewhere else, the university has to find a job for his or her spouse. The new man in the department was such a spousal hire. He was given access to room 109, where, along with the stored bones, Reinhard kept his work-in-progress. His students were working on slave remains, which were being documented so they could be repatriated to North Carolina. The man promptly got into an argument with one of Reinhard's female graduate students. She called Reinhard in Brazil. On his advice, she launched an affirmative action complaint against the new man. Rumors and allegations began to circulate, including a story that the grad student had been seen carrying a duffel bag full of Native American bones around campus.

A number of the more ancient bones in room 109 had been inventoried, as the NAGPRA required, and left in the lab. A considerable number of other bones in the laboratory were exempt from the law, either because they were not the bones of Native Americans from the United States, or because they were too fragmentary to be identified. The skeletons of the African Americans that were to be repatriated to North Carolina were not NAGPRA bones. There were also remains in Reinhard's laboratory from forensic cases he was working on. He had six such sets of bones locked up in his lab. Reinhard believed that all of these remains and the categories of law under which they fell were known both to the new man, who had been working in the lab since the summer, and to the chairman of the department.

Then Reinhard got a letter in Brazil from the university's vice-chancellor for research who said that bones had been found in his lab that were in violation of NAGPRA. He was told that some of the bones had been moved. Reinhard leaped to the conclusion that these must be remains from his forensic cases, and if they were moved it would break the chain of evidence that the courts require. He e-mailed the university's chancellor, and told him that someone was tampering with the chain of evidence. The university's lawyer then locked down his laboratory. At that point the faculty were called together, and a faculty member made terrible allegations about Reinhard to his peers. "He said I had illegal Omaha remains. I exposed myself in class, I stalked students.... There are thirty-six allegations." The meeting was followed by articles in the university newspaper, *The Journalist*, in February, March and April of 1998.

Later I downloaded one of the articles in question from the Web site maintained by the university's journalism college for its newspaper, *The Journalist*. There were a number of stories in the archive dealing with Native American concerns about the treatment of their ancestors' remains at Nebraska. The story about Reinhard, by Kelly Scott and Kelli Kellogg, was titled "Bones of Contention: UNL's alleged possession of Indian remains would violate federal law."[5] It itemized how bone remains were found in a laboratory in the anthropology department. The story said that a staff member entered the lab in September 1997 to pick up a cast to use in a class and found skeletal remains on a table and bone debris on the floor. He put them away. In October, the same staff member found a graduate student preparing to take some African-American remains from room 109 to work on them as part of her graduate research. He demanded to see documents authorizing the tests. The student, said the newspaper, filed an intimidation complaint and went to the department chair who took her request to study to a faculty meeting. The faculty members at a meeting the next day asked to see the documentation too, but according to the report were shown none. The department chair "reported the presence of the remains and lack of documentation to the NAGPRA committee." (Why he would report on African-American remains to the committee is hard to understand.) According to the story, the committee decided to seal the room and rekey the locks. The graduate student was denied entrance to the room. The story said there had been a study contract signed to authorize the project but the department chair said this contract did not authorize specific tests and he didn't even know there were African-American bones in the school.

The next month, a staff member with a key went into the lab again, looking for another cast, and found fragments of human ribs along with "bags of Taco Bell trash" in a drawer of the main lectern. Masking tape on the ribs said "Omaha," which was taken to mean they were ribs belonging to ancestors of the Omaha tribe, as opposed to what Reinhard said they were—part of a forensic investigation for Omaha law enforcement. Two Omaha police sources were quoted, saying that Reinhard was not known to them as an anthropologist contracted for forensic work. (The problem with this story, as another investigation would later conclude, was that in fact the bones had come to Reinhard from Dr. Mathias Okoye, a Lincoln pathologist, who had been hired by the Douglas County Sheriff's Office in Omaha to identify bones found in the city of Omaha. Reinhard had left them in his lab in an evidence bag marked "Omaha." How they came to be out of the bag and in the lectern drawer beside Taco Bell trash was unknown, but someone, while he was away, had moved these bones. They had nothing to do with the Omaha tribe, and nothing to do with NAGPRA.)

When Reinhard returned, the story continued, he filed a police incident report claiming that two staff members had removed forensic material from room 109. Then, said *The Journalist*, the staff member who found the remains in the room claimed Reinhard had threatened his life. The departmental chairman, Robert Hitchcock, was quoted in the story saying, "There are some serious issues at hand here. First, there is the issue of university responsiveness to Native American concerns and whether or not the university will respond favorably. Are scholarly activities activities that will exploit native peoples? Will the discipline of anthropology exploit native people? . . . I can't be in charge of a department that is breaking federal law."

How had all this come to be in the campus paper? Reinhard had returned to Brazil in the spring of 1998. While he was still away, he'd received an e-mail that the chancellor and president of the university had decided to hire an investigator to look at this whole situation. The university called in another anthropologist to study the remains found in Reinhard's lab and determine if they were Native American. ("He identified a medial fragment as Native American that I couldn't identify as male or female," Reinhard said.) The chairman of the department, according to Reinhard, went to the press alleging the university was covering up Reinhard's illegal activities. Someone complained to the state ombudsman. Someone complained to a state senator. The state senator was given a list of the various allegations made against Reinhard.

"The senator is convinced I'm bad," said Reinhard, "and the university won't dismiss [me]. He calls in the state patrol."

Wait a minute, I said, how does a state senator do that?

"It's Nebraska," said Reinhard, rolling his eyes. "You can do this. He's accused me of crimes on the basis of hearsay—that's a crime in and of itself. Far from implicating me in an illegal act, the state patrol produces a report hundreds of pages long [that's] favorable. Two and a half months, two investigations."

The state patrol investigator went through the various allegations, including one that Reinhard had been disrespectful in his forensic work in the handling of the bones of a murder victim who had been a student on the campus. These allegations were particularly upsetting to Reinhard, who had taken his work on the case very seriously. He worried that the two people who had been found guilty of the murder would, on the basis of this outrageous gossip, come forward on appeal claiming the forensic work had been mishandled. (And sure enough, one of those convicted did ask for a new trial).

Of the thirty-six allegations, the state patrol investigator concerned himself only with those that were criminal and had not been rendered moot by statutes of limitation. Reinhard was cleared of all charges of wrongdoing the police investigated, but not all of the charges raised had been investigated. This gave rise to more gossip, more complaints. The police, it was alleged, gave a favorable report because they had a conflict of interest—they had employed Reinhard in the past and were trying to protect his status as a forensic investigator, so naturally they gave him a clean bill of health. The university's investigation, conducted by a lawyer, thus had to deal not only with the various complaints and allegations made earlier to and about university officials, but also new complaints that arose out of the state patrol report.

By this point in his account, my coffee had grown completely cold. I couldn't eat, I could barely think. How was it possible that a witch hunt like this could take place in an American academic institution, among anthropologists concerned about human rights? Why would his colleagues go after him like this? He had tenure; he was supposed to be protected from attacks—the whole point of tenure is to allow competent people to pursue their work without fear, regardless of how the community at large might see it.

Reinhard met with the university's lawyer, Bob Grimit. Grimit thought his main task was to inquire into the university's compliance with the NAGPRA rules and then to deal with all the other worms rolling on the table. As a result of his investigation, he found in general that the university had done yeoman's work trying to comply with NAGPRA, that its inventory, contrary to the concerns raised, was complete, and that it had beaten larger and better funded universities to the mark. While there might have been errors, there had been no bad faith. Claims had been made that Reinhard illegally retained Native American (Omaha) soft tissue attached to artifacts (for example, rings with small pieces of flesh still clinging to them), but the report stated that the remains in question were not retained by Reinhard; they were in the university's secure facility, with the express permission of the Omaha. In addition, in the matter of the complaints that Reinhard had made destructive tests on Ponca bones in the early 1990s, the lawyer found that these tests had been made by his students, and were not necessarily in violation of either NAGPRA or state law. In the lawyer's view, such testing was permitted if its sole purpose was to determine "cultural affiliation." If done after 1993, and without the express permission of the affiliated tribe, according to the report, such tests would have been in violation of the university's policy. However, for a certain period of time the Ponca were not constituted as a tribe, so there would have been no official body to get approval from. There had been no cover-up or intimidation of UNL officials, said Grimit. As to death threats, the lawyer had advised anyone who said they had been uttered, and believed they had been seriously delivered, to go to the police. Very few, he said in the report, complained to the police.[6]

This report was submitted to the university on April 15, 1999, and made public two weeks before Tex Hall called for a federal investigation of Reinhard. So Reinhard's troubles were far from over. He was still seriously concerned about death threats. A Native activist, Reinhard said, "threatened to kill me. The police [were] concerned...." The man in question had a brother who had called Reinhard the previous summer and suggested that he wouldn't live to see the end of the university's fall semester. "I left town for a while," said Reinhard. Then the activist showed up in his classroom to protest. "The threat to [the] class affected the dean. He moved my class to geosciences, out of anthropology. It's madness." Reinhard was eventually transferred out of the Department of Anthropology and into the School of Natural Resources Science.

In the summer of 1998 one of the faculty charged with NAGPRA responsibilities interviewed a former graduate student who confirmed that sometime between 1965 and 1967, human remains had been destroyed, under the instructions of the chairman of the anthropology department, in an incinerator used to dispose of dead animals. In September 1998, the university publicly apologized to all Native Americans in the U.S. for the destruction of their ancestors' bones (though it could not be verified that all the remains were Native American). The chancellor of the university promised to turn over all the remains in Nebraska's possession, including unaffiliated bones, and to erect a memorial to those persons whose bones had been destroyed.

Reinhard had just filed a complaint for damages against the university newspaper. He showed it to me. It was essentially a claim for damage to his reputation done to him by his employer, the University of Nebraska. The law required him to file this claim with the state's Office of Risk Management before trying to launch a civil suit in the courts. He was asking for $200,000.[7]

"This creates incredible anxiety," said Reinhard. "The state report was great, but [I] was concerned people opposed to me would smarten up and fabricate data.... The people opposed to me sensed that anyone working with bones has a liability and can always be accused of mismanaging the collection."

In spite of the fact that he had been exonerated, he believed that his career was now over. An academic of substance trains great students and often publishes papers jointly with them. Reinhard's students had begun protecting themselves from being contaminated by his notoriety, and being themselves mangled in the small and vicious wars of American anthropology. One of the allegations made was that Reinhard had had an affair with his top graduate student.

"This really pissed her off," he said. "I said, it's just a rumor. She asked if this exists everywhere in anthropology. A week later she asked for a recommendation to law school.... I'll never get out of this—I'll never be able to collect evidence again, my reputation as a forensic anthropologist is destroyed. And my students' too. What is clear as I read this report is how immense these allegations were.... [There'll be] no more forensic work. The pathologist told this investigator he can't use me again. Nor will the county attorney. My evidence will be questionable due to these mad allegations. This was my connection to the private sector."

Nebraska requires tenured professors to fulfill several responsibilities. "We have to do service, teaching and research. My service was all forensically based. Can't do that. I can no longer teach osteology or forensic work. The collections are gone, even [the teaching collections] from India are gone." The atmosphere at work had become so terrifying he had been unable to continue his own research. He had been partway through a book. He'd abandoned it. "I spent a lot of time, until [I was] vindicated, just paralyzed in my office. It's cost me in every aspect of the job. And they'll have to pay me for it, goddammit," he said, making a fist on the table, but with his voice still droning on in that permanent, affectless monotone.

He knew of others investigating him further. And why not? Why wouldn't others believe Reinhard had done something reprehensible, in spite of two reports to the contrary, if his own colleagues pointed fingers and suggested he was a problem?[8] He pulled his chair back and stood up. He had to get over to the convention and pick up some papers and then run to the airport.

And standing up in front of students, I asked him. What about that?

"That was tough," he said. "One of the students ... went to a Hallowe'en party, dressed as me, with a sign that said 'No ethics.'"

We walked together along the wide streets of Columbus. It was a glorious morning. The sky was a brilliant blue. The new leaves cast their shadows everywhere. Reinhard loped along, talking about how his studies of early humans had made him change his diet. He was into fruits and root vegetables now, he tried to eat as they had eaten. I kept thinking, as I hustled to keep up with him, that even if he was wrong about the state of his reputation, he was nonetheless a ruined man.[9]

Ever do any archaeology? I'd asked partway through his grim recitation. He wanted to know why I wanted to know, so I explained that many of the anthropologists I'd spoken to who had pulled bones from the ground had later had problems in life. I felt embarrassed to bring it up. Why, when he'd been so flattened by the awesome power of gossip, should he have to think about superstition as well?

"I dug human remains in Arizona," he said. "At Salmon Run, New Mexico, we excavated a hundred burials there as well." He had no problem at all with most of them. "Then we found a burial, a burial of two children. [They were] laid out on grass mats with tiny pots—in my mind's eye I could see people putting them in the ground."

He had been forced to make a decision. He could look at the burial as a sacred place and leave it alone, or he could look at the bones of these children as actors, and gain insight into the evolution of people of another time, another race, another language. "It seemed a shame to disturb a sacred ground, but we were learning a lot about these people," he said.

He'd pulled them out of the ground.

# The Kennewick Shuffle

## Dancing Around the Hard Questions

THERE WERE THREE meetings going on at the same time at the Greater Columbus Convention Center: the computer people, the undertakers and the physical anthropologists. What better place than an annual convention to observe the lifeways of a population of scientists, to observe them in situ? What better way to slide one's finger along the leading edge of a field than to hear the current arguments from the leading lights? It didn't take long to figure out that the members of the American Association of Physical Anthropologists, at this penultimate annual meeting of the twentieth century, were not exactly a diverse group. Most of the males were past the high-water mark of middle age, while the women were much younger. There were only a few of either gender who looked as if they might be Native American, North or South Asian, or African in origin. By their fruits ye shall know them, Amy Dansie had said. I wanted to listen, learn and decide whether the misery generated by the study of the bones of the dead could at least be justified by the knowledge produced.

The list of papers was about equally divided between the old physical anthropology and the new, between the bone measurers and the gene hunters. There were sessions on everything one could imagine: what the nineteenth-century dead tell us now about poverty and prisons then; the measurements inflicted on children in a New England school from 1935 to 1960; the evolution of scarlet fever; the "fertility of post-menopausal American Indian women." More to the point, there was a full symposium on "New World colonization" during which, at this fin de siècle, representatives of the new and the old technologies would share their views on the peopling of the Americas.[1] Powell, Neves's American associate, was giving a paper. And Chatters was putting up a poster.

A dark room. I peeked in to see what was going on. A woman stood at a lectern talking about bones. The room was very crowded, even though it was large. I recognized some leading scholars, among whom were Richard Jantz, Owsley's colleague and fellow litigant in the Kennewick matter, and C. Loring Brace, whom I'd met in Ann Arbor. The woman speaking had compared the size of bones of Neanderthals and modern humans in what she called the Middle Paleolithic, the period whose end corresponded to the age of the oldest Ice Age painting at Grotte Chauvet. She stumbled through her presentation, so it was difficult to extract any conclusion. I scratched my head. Was she saying there was a change among both Neanderthals and modern humans over time, or not?

No questions.

The room emptied, then filled again. Another speaker took the lectern and began a discourse on modern human pubic bones versus those of Neanderthals. Brace was still there and so was Jantz, and there was Milford Wolpoff standing in the corner of the room, the man who had long argued that there was no simple generation of modern human traits from one great dispersal out of Africa, but diverse evolutionary changes in many parts of the world that had been generously shared through gene flow. He is a bear of a fellow, balding, with a dark fringe of hair around the big dome of his skull, his face defined by thick, square, black glasses. It turned out that pubic bones were larger in Neanderthals than modern humans, and in particular, bigger in Neanderthal males than females, a reverse of the situation among humans.[2]

By now the audience had stuffed the room well beyond capacity. In fact, it was beginning to resemble a theater on a hot opening night. Surely all these people were not here to listen to what I'd just heard? The moderator made an announcement—the new material from Portugal would be discussed at 5 p.m. There was nothing on the schedule about anything from Portugal. The room breathed and rustled with anticipation.

Another man stood at the lectern and slides popped up behind him. Neanderthal bones had long ago been discovered in two caves in northwestern Croatia. In one cave they were 130,000 BP. In the other, the remains dated from 33,000 to 88,000 BP. The younger Neanderthals appeared different from the older ones. Other scholars had suggested these younger Neanderthals were intermediate between modern humans and older Neanderthals. They had been explained by Wolpoff and his colleagues as an example of evolution. This fellow at the lectern proposed an alternative explanation, which he proceeded to disprove through an interesting sort of an algebra of bone.[3]

The next speaker talked about the remains found in the Upper Cave at Zhoukoudien, China, by Weidenreich more than sixty years ago.[4] Weidenreich's findings still obsessed all those who were interested in the origins of modern human shape, who still puzzled over the characteristics that early anthropologists used to define races. Why was it the skulls of people who had been buried in the same place, who were probably related to each other, did not look alike? And why did none of them look like modern Mongoloid Asians? Or did they? Contrary to Lynch's opinion that bones that could no longer be examined were no longer firmly in the science record, the Zhoukoudien casts were studied and published on by everyone. This speaker had examined the casts all over again and compared them to Howells' database of moderns. "These fossils are all over the board. They don't represent any of the populations to which [we] compared [them]," she said. In her view, these results gave some support to the multiregional theory but were far removed from anything that might be predicted by the out-of-Africa hypothesis. She stopped, to great applause.

Wolpoff took the lectern with a certain gravitas, a man radiating his intense interest in these ideas. Where the other speakers had been slow and tentative, he burned confidence like gasoline. He put his finger on what had bothered me about most of the papers I'd been hearing. They measured, they reported, but what question were they seeking to answer? It was vaguely formulated at best. Most did not make sharp, disprovable predictions either. In other words, they didn't advance understanding. He and his colleagues had decided to measure an ancient Australian skull and ask it a precise question—did it have only an African ancestor as the out-of-Africa hypothesis proposed? "If its ancestor is not uniquely African/Levantine, then something is wrong with the theory," he said.[5]

Wolpoff proceeded to describe what was known of the ancient Australian skull called WLH50. It had never been directly dated, but it was assumed to be about 30,000 years old. Its features included a long, flat, low vault, a thick ridge over the orbits of the eyes. He and his colleagues had looked at it in the context of three other old skulls found in Africa and the Levant. One, called Qafzeh 9, Evelyne Peyre had compared with the skull fragment and teeth found at Garrincho Cave near Pedra Furada. Wolpoff had studied them by measurement and by scoring their peculiarities. "Our analysis shows you what the eyeballs can see—which two things are different and which are the same...Qafzeh 9 is not the unique ancestor of WLH50," he said. "The [out-of-Africa] theory doesn't work in this region. Multiregionalism does work—and it means not evolution in all regions, it means evolution in more than one. That is what I've shown you."

Sometimes one has to hear a new idea repeated many times before it sinks in. Wolpoff's study wasn't particularly brilliant, but when he said it showed that evolution in modern humans had occurred in more than one region of the globe, it was as if a light went on for me in a dark room. This was what Niéde Guidon had meant when she said that the American story as told by archaeologists and anthropologists is way too narrow. The narrative assumes change can only happen stepwise from one center. Wolpoff's paper said no, change can happen in many places. There are no rules. In a way, this undercut the certainty in the findings of Ferreira and Araújo, who believe Darwin showed that the same evolutionary change could not occur in two places. Starting from that principle, they argued that since it was known hookworm evolved in Africa and required tropical soil temperatures, it could only have arrived in the Americas by human transport. Yet those studying mtDNA and Y chromosomes had observed that certain kinds of mutations happen more easily and more frequently than others. A creature as simple as hookworm might well have resulted from the same genetic accident in an ancestral species in two or more places. What if similar ecologies encourage similar mutations? What if a stable environment rewards no change at all? How else could one explain the lack of change in human morphology in some places, while change and diversity clearly occurred elsewhere? Perhaps at the end of the Ice Age rapid change was rewarded and stability punished in species living where the climate swings were the greatest. The Lagoa Santa remains showed a lack of diversity over a very long span of time. So did the Australian skulls. Yet in China, much closer to the ice, Weidenreich had found great variation within a seemingly related Ice Age population. Perhaps under similar climatic pressure, certain features seen in North Asians and in Native Americans had emerged in two places at approximately the same time?

I wrote notes furiously in the dark. The last paper was announced. Bob Eckhardt described himself as the warm-up for

Erik Trinkaus, the man who would reveal all about the fascinating new Neanderthal find in Portugal. Eckhardt dumped on the very meaning I had just been trying to extract from the measurements of ancient skulls.[6] He said he was disturbed, no, offended by the use of skull measurement to say anything about evolutionary changes in mankind, because he saw such great change in modern humans. The changes he saw just between lowland and highland South Americans "falsify the argument that Neanderthals can't be the ancestors of humans—the change is so great."

Trinkaus walked to the front of the room with great speed, and spoke with the intensity and urgency of someone reporting on atrocities from a war zone for CNN. He began by setting things straight. He was not, he said, the senior author on the paper that was going to be published soon: that honor belonged to his colleague in Portugal, João Zilhão, the director of Instituto Portugues de Arqueológia (the Portuguese Institute for Archaeology), the man who'd actually found the remains in question.[7] Trinkaus wanted it understood that the site belonged to the Portuguese— he was the invited outsider. He went on and on in an extended preamble, explaining that he knew he should not be speaking to the press, but there were political pressures in Portugal that made it unavoidable, then telling his colleagues in the room to please refrain from taking any notes. By this point I was restless. What in heck was the mystery meat he was about to serve us, anyway? Since I wasn't a colleague, and knew I would not beat him to publication, I kept right on taking notes. The woman beside me jabbed me in the ribs. "Didn't you hear what he said?" she asked, as if God had spoken and all must obey. I ignored her.

Trinkaus wanted us all to understand that he had no previous position on this issue of a Neanderthal/human relationship that would have led him to make a biased finding. The generally accepted theory was that Neanderthals were replaced by modern humans moving in from Africa. He explained that it was believed that modern humans arrived in southwestern Europe about 36,000 BP. The disappearance of Neanderthals from Spain and

Portugal occurred later than elsewhere: in southern Iberia, as he called it, "[it] was complete by 27,000. This burial is around 24,500 BP."

At the end of November 1998, the Portuguese had embarked on a salvage excavation in the Lapedo Valley in north central Portugal, at a limestone rock shelter called Abrigo do Lagar Velho. They excavated carefully and found an animal burrow near the rock face. One of the researchers reached in and pulled out a radius and an ulna, both covered with red ocher—a treatment commonly given by early modern human beings to their dead. Then they pulled out chunks of skull, pieces of the mandible and pieces of the cranial vault about two inches in diameter. When they'd recovered all the bones there were, they realized the skeleton was ninety-five percent complete, and was that of a boy. All the teeth were loose but they were able to see the germs of some of the permanent teeth. The age at death was estimated to be between three-and-a-half and five years. Trinkaus brought the bones to the lab, cleaned them and found almost no signs of pathological lesions. Because the remains had been buried covered in ocher and some small cultural artifacts were found with them, it had not occurred to him that these were anything but the bones of a modern human child. These artifacts were of a kind commonly found in modern human graves of the period. Then he verified length measurements, which came out on the low index.

"I said, oh my God, it's like a Neanderthal, but the other features looked fully modern from Europe." said Trinkaus. "I noticed early, this kid has a chin—rather a large chin for a young child." He put up a slide that showed the mandible, or lower jaw, in profile. There was no doubt about it. Unlike Neanderthal remains, this child's skull did have a chin that jutted forward. He went through the measurements he'd taken, one by one. It was clear that some fell within the Neanderthal range, some the modern human. It was therefore clear to him that this boy was intermediate, with features that represented a mosaic of Neanderthal and modern attributes. When he examined the pelvis and leg bones, it was also clear to him that the way this child must have walked was the way modern humans walk. The tibias were like Neanderthals', but the robustness of the femur was typical of either population.

This finding did not fit with mtDNA results obtained on Neanderthal bones. In 1997 a team of researchers had compared mtDNA extracted from a Neanderthal with samples taken from Europeans. They found important differences between them. They calculated that the age of the closest common ancestor was more than four times as great as the common ancestor of the Europeans.[8] Yet this child, which Trinkaus said lived 24,500 BP, expressed both modern and Neanderthal traits. And here was Trinkaus arguing that this boy had both Neanderthal *and* modern human ancestry. How could the mtDNA results vary so greatly from the evidence of bone shape, if both were reliable methods of discerning ancestry and population affinities?

"What do we have here?" Trinkaus asked his audience. This remain exhibited a mosaic of Neanderthal, modern and intermediate traits. "This mixture is what people who work on interspecies hybrids take for granted. I propose—[I was] correctly quoted—that this is not a lone child, I don't think [the parents] met in the bushes and that was it. [It's] a result of mixed populations. I have no clue what it says of Neanderthal genes in modern Europeans."

The word "mosaic" was also a good description of the ancient teeth and skull fragment Niéde Guidon had found in Garrincho Cave. Guidon would later inform me that she got a radiocarbon date of 12,100 BP from the bone. That person, with teeth that resembled both Neanderthal and modern human teeth, but that were not exactly like either one, had died in Garrincho Cave 12,000 years after this child died in Portugal.

The next morning I attended the symposium on the colonization of the New World. The measurers and the geneticists had been invited, along with a linguist, an archaeologist, and several other outliers to the world of physical anthropology. A Canadian, Emöke Szathmary, who did early work on mtDNA among living Native Americans, had been asked to sum up. She was one of those who'd found a pattern of four founding mitochondrial lineages, which she said required a much longer time in the Americas than the Clovis First theory allowed. "The goal of this symposium," the meeting schedule said, "is to reconcile conflicting points of view by assembling innovative researchers with diverse data and analytical approaches in order to create the broadest possible context for construction of a cohesive theory on New World colonization." I thought it unlikely such a context would be generated by lunchtime, but I was willing to be wrong.

The geneticists went first. Andrew Merriwether, Judy Kidd, Tadd Schurr and Mike Hammer took the audience quickly through the basic findings of mtDNA and Y-chromosome analyses with regard to the origins of Native Americans. Affinities with populations near Lake Baikal was a popular starting point.[9] None of the geneticists mentioned recent findings, described in *Science*, that called into question the basic theory of their work: some researchers now claim there is sexual recombination of the male with the female mitochondria on rare occasions. The morning ran like clockwork. People rolled out their findings as if there would be corporal punishment for running over their allotted time. There was no debate. There were almost no questions.[10] As the speakers droned on, it was apparent researchers used the same samples, from quiescent populations, so the same populations were being looked at over and over again while others weren't examined at all. Few researchers mentioned obtaining permission to do new studies on old samples.

Dennis O'Rourke, from the University of Utah at Salt Lake City, came forward to describe his work looking for modern mtDNA markers in the bones of ancient Americans. He had been able to extract mtDNA from ancient remains taken from an Anasazi burial ground at a site called Grand Gulch. He had used both "soft tissue and bone." He had found four of the major known modern haplotypes, but there were ambiguities. He had also worked on old Aleut material and compared these remains with other known ancient samples. He had a slide that showed the frequency with which the four major haplotypes—A, B, C, D—appeared. There was a color included for Other.

"The Aleut material is distinctive," he said. "It's high in D, low in A, and B and C are absent." He had compared this to the mtDNA extracted by Frederika Kaestle from ancient remains at Pyramid Lake and Stillwater Cave in Nevada. Those remains showed "low or absent A and C. Our material of the eastern basin [in the western U.S.] is high B and little A, with variable C and D. Finally, Anne Stone working on the Oneota [found] C predominant with some A, [and the] others smaller."

In sum, he saw different patterns in old eastern and old western remains. He saw differences between peoples who'd lived in the circumpolar region and those who'd lived on the Pacific Northwest coast. But he also saw regional stability over time in the mtDNA of Native Americans. The ancient Aleut samples could not be distinguished from the current Aleut samples. In fact, he said, when he looked at the ancient versus the modern samples for particular regions, "all the ancient samples are indistinguishable from modern populations." While most of his work was not on the truly old remains, but on bones between two and four thousand years old, he could still say that "the regular patterns are established early."

This was the kind of result that would greatly benefit Native Americans making land claims. But it was hard to understand how it could be true. The extensive movement of Native American populations after the arrival of Europeans was well known. Still, O'Rourke concluded, if one was going to talk about peopling issues, it wasn't enough to study living populations. It was necessary to compare ancient populations of Siberia with ancient populations of the Americas. Apples to apples. Dust to dust.[11]

Jim Chatters had taken a chair in the room. Richard Jantz, Owsley's colleague, was over by the back door. C. Loring Brace had been sitting in the same chair since first thing in the morning.

Johanna Nichols was a breath of fresh air, if only because she spoke about words and sounds instead of flesh and bone. A small woman with a cap of gray hair and large square glasses, she stood in the light shining down on the lectern. I knew that archaeologists and geneticists like to use linguistic analysis to bolster their findings, but up to this point, I had avoided looking at this evidence because I thought it couldn't be tested. Languages leave no mark unless written down, and most of the languages in the Americas appear not to have been written, or have not been deciphered. So how could anything definitive be learned about where particular patterns of speech may have originated?

But as Nichols described her work, it began to make a wacky kind of sense to me. "I'm a multi-wave person," she said. "I track structural features of language on the oldest, deepest languages. We can trace [them back] approximately six thousand years. We call these stocks. For comparison, I break samples into eighteen smaller groups."

She launched into a description of the language equivalent of DNA markers—patterns of usage that can be seen in many different languages. She described, for example, the association of certain kinds of prefixes with subjects and objects. She also referred to a language practice known as "head marking" of verbs—the use of a signifier that tells one what is going on in a sentence. Then there were numeral pacifiers—words that appear between a number and a noun, and link them together. Numeral pacifiers are used in both Mayan and in Mandarin. She was also interested in languages in which the personal pronoun is signified by the sound *n* or *m*. She took all these markers and looked at their geographical distribution around the world—in this case, around the outer rim of the Pacific Ocean.

A map flashed up on the slide screen. Numeral pacifiers followed the coastal Pacific rim. They were used in British Columbia but not in Alaska, and they were not found inland from the coast. A particular word order was another marker that showed itself around the Pacific rim and in Australia. The use of *n* and *m* showed up in Australia and on the western edge of the Americas. She saw suffixes used similarly in western America, Australia and New Guinea that were not frequent elsewhere.

Nichols also found a divide between languages in the eastern and the western Americas. For one thing, the languages on the west side of the continent were younger. There were marked asymmetries in certain kinds of word order in the west, but there was no statistical significance to asymmetries of word order in eastern populations, which she asserted meant the eastern American populations had been around far longer than those on the west coast.

She described another method she uses to compare language ages. She suggested we consider the use of the sound *m* to signify the second person pronoun. She had found twenty-seven stocks that exhibit that usage, primarily in western America. The number of stocks using this feature suggested a time frame for diffusion of about 12,000 years.

I was fascinated. This overview fitted in well with Niéde Guidon's findings—that the oldest communities in Brazil were in the northeast, where no one had thought to look for them. But how could a theory about the time it takes for a language stock to diffuse be tested? Nichols had no time to explain the theoretical underpinnings of her work: she just asserted that the use of radical headmarking on the eastern side of the Americas appeared to be about 18,000 years old. "I infer," she said, "it is pre-Glacial." She concluded that since the languages on the west side of the Americas were younger, they had come into the Americas after the Ice Age was over. She saw eastern languages as having more affinities with Australian and Asian stocks, and the Western languages having ties with western Asia and Siberia. Southeast was older than Northwest.[12]

Joe Powell strode to the microphone, a lanky young man wearing a boxy black suit that swung away from his body, a white shirt, a tie: the kind of clothing one would expect from a middle-ranking civil servant, or a dentist, or an undertaker. His long, straight, thick blond hair was pushed back from his forehead; he held his head up high, and prowled back and forth as he lectured. Powell represents the old physical anthropology made new with digital measuring devices and computer software packages. Chairs that had been empty in this room now filled with people eager to hear what he would say. Powell and his colleague Jerome Rose had completed a study of the Kennewick remains for the U.S. government. The results had not yet been released. Who knew what he might let slip about Kennewick?

Richard Jantz was sitting not far from me. I watched him watching Powell. I couldn't see Chatters' face.

Powell began with a discussion of how, for the last ten years, people had been describing skeletal and dental variation among the remains of Paleo-Indians. He went through the differing models regarding how people came to the Americas through the ice-free corridor. There were, he said, two models to test. One was his colleague Walter Neves's replacement model—Neves believed that the Paleo-Indians who lived from 11,000 to 8,000 years ago were unrelated to modern Indians. The alternative was the continuity model—which proposes that moderns are related to Paleos and differ as a result of genetic diffusion. If Neves was right, he said, one should see that Paleo-Indians are distinct from those called Archaic, who came along after Paleo-Indians, whereas if the continuity model was right, "we should see a similarity to the Old World, and greater within-group variation, and ties to later groups. There would be on any graph of traits nice evidence of a linear trend (as Paleo-Indians morphed into Archaic Indians who in turn became modern Native Americans) rather than a 'distinct break.'" Do the differences among the remains of different periods reflect replacement or repopulation? he asked. And are the Paleo-Indians Europeans?[13]

*Baloney*, muttered the man beside me.

Powell explained that he had measured twenty-four South American and thirteen North American skulls from the Paleo period. He then compared them to Archaic-period samples found across North America and in southeastern Brazil. He compared them all to the modern populations measured by W.W. Howells, and also compared fourteen of their variables to another data set compiled by T. Hanihara. He tested for and found no evidence of observer error. He looked as well at fifteen discrete dental traits from data provided to him by Christy Turner. He corrected for sex and for size. He concentrated on principal components analysis and on typicality probability tests. He also used a statistical approach, which allowed him to study the degree of within-group variation. The slides showed the findings as displayed by several three-dimensional graphs. The first one displayed his finding that "Paleo-Indians clearly [are] differentiated from Archaic, which are intermediate between modern North Americans and Asians."

He also found a consistent pattern. The South American Paleo-Indian measurements clustered more closely together than the North Americans did. When he compared these Paleo samples to Old World populations he got an interesting picture. They aligned with the Ainu and with Europeans; it was, he said, "a mixed signal."

When he compared the Paleo samples to the Archaic samples he got the answer to one of his questions. "They [the Archaic population] have a ninety percent probability of coming from the Paleo sample." He also saw a "linear trend for cranial length and breadth for the Archaic populations to moderns."

In other words, using many of the same tools, examining many of the same remains that Walter Neves investigated, comparing them to many of the same populations, he got the opposite answer. Neves found there had been a replacement of the population. Powell found a continuum.

At this point, a full frontal view of the Kennewick skull flashed up on the screen. I had seen most of the available pictures of the Kennewick skull, at least the ones that had been published. This shot was new to me. I wondered, just for a moment, if this was a picture taken in the course of Powell's examination of the remains. No, I thought, he'd never dare.

"Kennewick Man," said Powell. "Is he European?"

He waited for a moment to let the question sink in, just as any good speaker would. We were on the edges of our seats: here he was, a man sworn by the U.S. government to secrecy in an important lawsuit. Would he strike a blow for freedom of speech and tell us what he found, or not?

"The answer is no," he said.

There was an intake of breath around the room. I glanced at Jantz, the Kennewick litigant. His face remained perfectly blank. He wasn't surprised. That, too, was interesting. I couldn't see Chatters at all.

The next shot was the skull of Neves's Luzia. "Lapa Vermelha," Powell said. "Let's stop talking migration with limited sample sizes and say we have micro-evolution."

Ted Goeble, an archaeologist from the University of Nevada, at Las Vegas, took the microphone. "Do bones and stones and genes tell the same story?" he asked.[14] Aha, I sighed, rubbing my numb writing hand. At last, someone is going to synthesize this for me. "We thought we should concentrate on the archaeology of Siberia, since speakers are searching for Native American origins in Siberia, Lake Baikal and the Amur river basin," he said. "We focused on Lake Baikal." He described this southwestern Siberian region as exhibiting the same general chronology of human occupation as Europe, but he said he had a lot of trouble with the so-called archaeological material that had been found farther to the east, in Beringian Siberia. Lake Baikal is directly north of Ulan Bator and one ancient site had been identified near there. Yet Goeble considered the site dubious—his concern was that the broken rocks previously considered to be artifacts were in fact the result of constant freezing and thawing. This problem appeared in all the most ancient sites identified in eastern Siberia. "Now we wonder if there were *Homo sapiens* there. I think not," he said.

The evidence was better for a Middle Paleolithic occupation in western Siberia. The artifacts found on these sites "are Mousterian," Goeble said. "You could put them in European drawers and it would be hard to tell the difference. [This is] 140,000 to 40,000 years BP." All the sites were found on high ground. "They did not have to move to get a living. And there is absence of sites north of fifty-five degrees north latitude. [Maybe] they were not capable of living on the mammoth steppe."

No sites north of fifty-five degrees north latitude meant that nothing from this period had been found in the region referred to as Beringia. In the south, while no human remains had been discovered, human settlements had been found. These were generally the same as those found throughout Eurasia in the same period. "Same settlement pattern," he said. "Out of caves to the open landscape about 40,000 BP and the use of sites over and over again. This suggests that early modern humans, if they were human, were tethered to their places. [This is] very far to the south. As with the Mousterians, there is no evidence of them spreading north. It was a lateral spread, but not north."

He described the culture called Ma'alta, whose leavings had been found near Lake Baikal and dated to around 25,000 BP. "This is the onset of the last glacial ice sheets expanding in Canada and here," he said. "Siberia [was an] ice-free grassy steppe. Humans here had to rely on animal products in herds. The artifacts are blade technologies...end scrapers, burins and bifacial tools." He reminded us that one of the carved Venus figures had been found at Ma'alta, at a level corresponding to about 21,000 BP. As Dillehay had found at Monte Verde, these people lived in large dwellings and they were not nomadic. People "were at one place, not moving across the landscape." However, exotic stones were found that suggested "an economic network."

At around the same time, he said, blade and biface technology showed up in early sites in Alaska. Goeble said it was easy to assume that these people spread to Beringia, but there was a long gap in the radiocarbon record. "The last glacial maximum closed or gated America from Siberia during this time," he said. "After Ma'alta, we see a decline in archaeological sites [during] the last glacial maximum of 20,000 to 18,000 BP.... So what happened to the people?"

His belief was the cold killed the forests, which were replaced by grasslands. "The bottom line," he said, "is that wood [was] not available [and they] retreated to southern regions. Peopling of Alaska has more to do with the late Upper Paleolithic expansion into Siberia around 17,000 BP. We're left [to conclude] that this event was later than 17,000 or 16,000 BP. That is my take on the evidence now."

This review fitted well with the belief that no one entered this continent over the Bering Strait until the Ice Age was almost over; it also fitted with the linguistic evidence regarding the age of languages on the West Coast, but it didn't seem to fit at all with the mtDNA and Y-chromosome evidence that said people were in the Americas at least 20,000 years ago, and that they shared common ancestors with people now living around Lake Baikal and in Ulan Bator.

It fell to Emöke Szathmary to try and pull all the disparate, clashing views into some kind of order. She appeared at the podium, a tall, gangly, white-haired woman in a maroon business suit. She didn't even try to synthesize. Instead she talked politics. She started on a personal note, with the suggestion that most people in this room were the descendants of recent immigrants to the Americas. "I come from Canada," she said. "I was not born in Canada, my ancestors migrated from Asia."

She also confessed that the issues raised now were similar to those at a symposium she attended back in 1978, except that the sophistication of the work had increased. "I like the studies that reinforce my own prejudice," she said. Thus, she was keen on O'Rourke's findings, which suggested "what is old is new. We have information that shows regionalism existed in the past and there is continuity over time. This issue is really important." So was Joe Powell's work, she said. It showed continuity through the use of statistical analysis, and this, she thought, was particularly important in view of what the public was reading in magazines like *Newsweek*. And while there had been large accumulations of knowledge of Y-chromosome and mtDNA markers, she had a warning about whether those sampled were representative.

"Missing are the samples [of the] difficult-to-work-with aboriginal Americans. [You] need to go through hoops, you need to understand this detail of informed consent, but you must be prepared to modify research designs in order to get consent."

She kept circling back to the notion that physical anthropology as a science had to fit itself into the very real politics concerning Native Americans, that Native Americans, as immigrants to the Americas, were a different order from the rest of us. She told a little story. She had been asked to appear on a radio show ten years earlier and talk about the peopling of the Americas. She had tried to say that migrations are characteristic of the human species.

"That interview was biased. [It] made me look dumb, made it seem I was saying aboriginals are just another bunch of immigrants. This hit a political button.... For Canadians, this caused consternation like you would not believe. I think you ought to be aware [that consternation] exists when you say people came from elsewhere. You have to remember it occurred so long ago....

These were the people who first took dominion over North and South America. It's a biblical word, dominion—five hundred years is but a dot in time. Who cares whether [Native Americans came here] 12,000 years ago or 18,000 years ago? It is their land and we have to acknowledge this. They did take dominion...."

I walked the halls of the convention center trying to sort out what I'd heard, measuring it against the rich story of Adam and Eve and their Garden of Eden, wherever it was, and the Crane people, whoever they were. There are no experts, Anna Roosevelt had said; be your own expert. Sure, I thought, easy for her to say. No one at the symposium had tried to balance one piece of work against another or work out a context. There had been no grappling with fundamental assumptions. There was disagreement on the most basic issue: replacement or continuum. What was not said was as interesting as what was said. No one presented evidence that people walked over the Bering Strait into the Americas before Clovis times. Yet I did hear evidence from many researchers that Americans have been here longer than 20,000 years. There was evidence from mtDNA, Y-chromosome study and bone measurement that microevolution or change took place in the Americas independent of other places in the world. There was linguistic evidence of differences between Native Americans living in the east and those on the Pacific side of the continent. If age and diversity of language go together, as the linguists believe, then the populations in places like east central Brazil have been there a lot longer than populations in western North America. There was genetic evidence that suggested some in the east carried markers similar to those carried by Europeans, and that those in the west came from another stock. That would fit with Walter Neves's observation that all human crania tend to fall in one of two camps—African/Australian or European/ Asian— with the Polynesians midway between. There was not much evidence of human population on the Siberian side of Beringia earlier than on the Alaskan side. But there was evidence of a relationship between Native Americans and Mongolians at some time in the distant past. Which directions they went and which paths they traveled were unknown. In sum, I had heard a great deal of evidence suggesting that Wolpoff and his colleagues were correct: there had been pockets of microevolution in various regions of the globe, and over time these changes had spread widely. But there was also Y-chromosome evidence that some of the mutations that occurred in the Americas were unique.

When the assumptions about migration and methods of travel and points of origin were swept away, when the inferences drawn from the absence of evidence were taken off the table, I found I was still left with interesting observations that could be tested. There was something to this science after all. Slowly, piling one observation after another, these physical anthropologists and linguists had begun to gather the materials to spin a new story of human genesis. There had been more than one Garden of Eden, more than one variety of the tree of life. But the story threads still dangled in the wind; no one here even tried to weave them into a narrative.

It was also appropriate that the New World Colonization Symposium ended with a warning about ethics. Some at this convention seemed oblivious of the fact that they work in a glass house. Science is entirely a public work, a political enterprise in the Greek sense of politics. This is its glory and its bane. Tested and half-tested and untested hypotheses spread out from creative centers and drive public opinion, public policy and behavior even as they are being overturned in the laboratory. How could any physical anthropologist, having read of the battle over access to the remains of Kennewick Man, having heard of the troubles of Karl Reinhard, fail to realize the jeopardy he is in when working on human tissues gathered without informed consent? The use of human tissues without specific permission stirs public opprobrium. It was obvious even to an outsider like me that geneticists need permission to study Native American DNA, and that they need a second informed consent to do studies on old samples put to a new purpose. Blood taken for study from living persons is not the same as a nail clipping left behind in a rock shelter. The bone measurers have to face up to the fact that human bones should not be treated as collectibles. As Szathmary pointed out, this work has a political history and context, from which it cannot be severed.

What should an ethical person do about information dragged unsanctioned from the bones of the dead and the blood of the living? Ignore where it came from? It troubled me that I was trying to build a story out of some of this work. It troubled me, but it didn't stop me. Love of learning is not altruistic.

Jim Chatters sat at a white-draped table in the hallway, writing on a large piece of poster board. His poster was to be exhibited the next morning. He looked like a young boy doing his homework at the last minute. He was all alone—no one tried to speak to him, no one appeared to know or care who he was. I thought about asking whether his display would deal with the Polynesian affinities of Kennewick Man. So far as I knew, Chatters had not widely announced these findings. He looked completely absorbed. No, I thought, I'll just wait for the poster.

Joe Powell drifted by; I asked him whether he had used his own pictures of Kennewick Man for his presentation. There was gossip circulating at the convention that he and his colleagues had already handed in their reports, and his opinions differed from Jim Chatters'. A knowledgeable person had told me that they found the spear point had entered Kennewick's pelvis from the back, not the front as Chatters had asserted.

Yes, Powell said, he had used a 3D computer model generated from the CT scans taken when he examined the remains.

Didn't you sign a paper saying you wouldn't publish until the U.S. government released you? I asked.

He had signed something, he said. When he first agreed to do the study, he thought he would have complete control of his results, but then at the last minute the government forced the researchers to become temporary employees, which gave the government carte blanche about when to release.

So they gave you permission to use the picture? I asked, wanting to be sure he hadn't just slipped the leash.

He nodded. Yes, they had given him permission, but he worried that he'd gone farther than he should have in what he'd said. He wasn't used to this: he hoped the U.S. government would release the report soon because he wanted to publish in a journal by the end of the year.

Curiouser and curiouser. He'd been allowed by the U.S. government to dribble things out. Now, why would that be? And what exactly was the government still trying to keep concealed? I told Powell I thought the government would sit on his report just as long as it could—that it would hold off publishing until the fall, at minimum. I had come to the conclusion that the U.S. Army would do whatever it took to keep the Native community content until after the Umatilla chemical depot was operating. There was an election coming: Vice President Gore was already running for president, and the First Lady was eyeing the New York vacancy in the U.S. Senate. All political constituencies would be carefully served.

November, I said. I bet they won't release till November.

Richard Jantz was waiting just where he'd said he'd be, in the main display hall with the poster exhibit, in front of the poster of one of his students. He was deep in conversation: I waited for him to finish. Cleone Hawkinson, whom I'd last seen in Portland, sidled up to me. The president of Friends of Americas Past (created to educate the public and advocate on the issues raised in the Kennewick suit), she had just come back from Washington, where she had sat in on the hearings on the NAGPRA. She didn't know what to make of the politics displayed there. But she knew she was going to have to learn. She had come to recognize how important politicians were going to be if physical anthropologists in the U.S. wanted to continue studying Native American bones.

Jantz, a professor at the University of Tennessee, has a large head, with thinning, curling brown hair and black-rimmed square glasses with gold earpieces. He was wearing a good-quality tweed jacket and pants, proper brogue shoes. No sandals and slapdash for him. He certainly didn't look like the kind of hard case who would take the U.S. government to court over the right to measure bones. We found a restaurant adjoining the convention complex. Hawkinson and I picked at lunch while Jantz outlined for me how he had come into this debate. It all started for him with the paper by Powell (and Steele) in 1992. "That was the first to address this issue since Hrdlička," he said, "except for a review by Fred Smith in the late 1970s—on the morphology of the issue."

Well, I said, surely Neves and Pucciarelli were first?

"It was the paper by Steele and Powell that got ears perked up," he said. "It conflicted with the tradition that [the] early [remains were the] same as later."

This answer from such a fine scholar surprised me. Many typologists had argued that the early remains were different from the later ones and this idea spread widely. Take for example a book for the general public that appeared first in 1946 and was revised and reissued in 1968, written by Frank C. Hibben.[15] Hibben was the archaeologist who found what he called "Sandia" points in a cave in the U.S. Southwest at a level much older than Clovis (points that Lynch dismissed as unfinished preforms). Writing in 1968, Hibben treated the differences observed between the oldest and the more recent populations in America as if they were so well known as to be old hat. "It has been postulated that the long heads represent the head form of the earliest immigrants to these shores," he wrote. But of course, as Jantz pointed out, insights are not science, and the works of all the typologists had been so thoroughly discredited their opinions were not worth pursuing. For modern biological anthropologists, such as Jantz, such insights were of no value.

Jantz began to tell me about himself. He grew up in the small town of Halstead, Kansas, and had been headed for a chemistry degree at the University of Kansas when he took a course from a leading physical anthropologist, Bill Bass, a major forensic scientist. He was hooked. Jantz switched his major to skeletal biology. "I regard myself as a generalist rather than a specialist," he said, "[a] skeletal biologist also interested in quantification methods." Which was another way of saying statistics, computer modeling and databases. The use of computers in anthropology was just beginning when he was finishing his doctorate in 1971. In the early 1980s, at a meeting of colleagues, he and Clyde Snow heard a paper on how the Terry collection, a group of remains used by forensic anthropologists to decide on the race and gender of unidentified bones, was really not representative of the broad diversity of the American population. The Terry collection comprised "anatomic skeletons of the 1800s to the mid-1900s," Jantz explained. The populations of America had changed a great deal in a hundred years. Jantz put the measurements of modern people, as gathered by forensic anthropologists, into a database with a software package that assigns ethnicity and gender based on bone size and shape. The database is widely used.

As Neves had suggested, Jantz had come late to questions on the origins of Native Americans. "I had a grad student who systematized the Plains database. Pat Key ferreted out Paleo-Indian stuff from the Plains that had never been studied or dated; he found it at the University of Nebraska Museum. Stuff they had there from a number of sources, it was very interesting, all wet gravel specimens.... Mineralized. Weighed a ton. Complete skulls came out of the pit ... at the same level [as] mastodon teeth and Pleistocene fauna."

These finds, in other words, were like the remains found in

the Lagoa Santa region in Minas Gerais. Jantz's student, Key, did his dissertation without remarking on the fact that these ancient remains didn't look quite the way they should have. Jantz didn't connect the dots either—until after the Powell and Steele publication. "I sent Pat's Paleo stuff to Joe and Gentry. They didn't use it. Dates weren't good enough. It wasn't until the early nineties, when we went to Nevada, that I started working on variation of the early population. Then Kennewick popped up."

Did he know what Joe Powell found when he studied Kennewick?

"He said Chatters' cast was basically accurate."

Powell would say, then, that it had Polynesian and Australian affinities. Why was Powell chosen to do this study? I asked. A little theory had been growing in the back of my mind since I heard Powell deliver his paper in the symposium. Unlike his colleague Walter Neves, Powell saw a continuity between North American Paleo-Indians and later American populations. That was the certainly the answer Native Americans would want to hear.

Powell was a friend of McManamon's, Jantz said—the man doing the picking.

I explained that Chatters and Powell's partner Neves had done a study of the Kennewick skull and compared it to other populations and it came out closest to Polynesians.

"[Powell] said to me he anticipated the government will go to phase-two studies," said Hawkinson. Which as she well knew could only mean that he had found the remains were not like any modern Native Americans.

What is your position then? I asked Jantz. Do you think that all unaffiliated remains, like Kennewick, have to be available for study? What about the Native American concerns—they claim these bones as their ancestors (and given what I had heard in the symposium, there was some science on their side). They want to bury their dead.

Jantz wasn't interested in that point of view. While he supported the NAGPRA when affiliation could be demonstrated, it was impossible to project tribal unity (and the NAGPRA only covers officially recognized tribes) nine thousand years into the past. He had dedicated himself to science and knowledge as opposed to superstition and religious belief. He was on the side of right. The fact of these remains being in museum collections was just another product of human warfare, he explained. White, black, Native Americans, it made no difference—all winners behaved like winners and grabbed the spoils of war. Losers just had to take it. "Look," he said, "the Indians were—there was a war, they are a defeated people. That's what people do. That's what they did. I have evidence of violence in the Plains, in the southwest. They push into the next territory, and expand till someone does it to them. Some [of the Native Americans] are expanding now."

Bright and early the next day, before the poster sessions officially opened, I hauled myself over to the poster room at the convention center. Jim Chatters had been given position number one. His poster was right by one of the double doors. When I got there, a man was already peering closely at the photographs Chatters had glued to his display. Chatters stood looking at his own handiwork, explaining his findings to the man.

The man drifted off, and was replaced by Joe Powell, who carefully scrutinized Chatters' pictures of Kennewick Man's remains as if he'd never seen the bones himself. Possibly he was interested in the pictures of the femurs, some portions of which were no longer with the remains. I tried not to eavesdrop on their conversation and concentrated instead on reading what Chatters had written.

"Kennewick Man, a Paleo-American skeleton from the northwest US," was his title.[16] I carefully scanned the prose, looking for a discussion of Kennewick's affinities, looking for the word "Polynesian." I assumed that on this poster Chatters would announce to the world what he'd found, and correct what he'd said previously.

Their heads were close together. At first they spoke to each other very quietly, very carefully, circling, like two lobsters in a tank. Then they began to argue.

"This is going to be fun," said Chatters loudly, like a man putting up his dukes, preparing for a happy war. "That's absolutely flat wrong."

Powell reddened slightly and their heads went back together again. Then Powell walked away.

The first paragraph of Chatters' display spoke of how the skeleton had not been made available to open scientific inquiry, and went on to say that a forensic analysis had been made, along with photographs and casts. The skeleton was described. Kennewick was a middle-aged male, 173 centimeters tall, weighing about seventy-two kilograms and with a gracile build that "bespeaks a subtropical body type which differs markedly from the small, robust stature and short distal limbs of modern Northwestern Amerinds."

There was evidence of numerous injuries to the man before he died. There was a list of some symptoms suffered and their result: "chronic osteomyelitis, acute osteomyelitis of the left sphenoid and a fracture of the left scapula hint at potential cause of death," Chatters had written. (He would give a more complete account in an *American Antiquity* article, which followed in April 2000, on this matter of cause of death.)[17]

There was an attempt to establish whom Kennewick was *not* related to. "Preliminary craniofacial analysis ... sundadont dental characteristics and the subtropical body type distinguish this individual from modern Amerinds. This is consistent with analyses of other early skeletons in North and South America which indicate that the earliest migrants to the Americas were not derived from North Asian stock. The age of the skeleton can be established by the stratigraphy and absolutely by the radiocarbon date on the bone itself. All evidence is consistent with an early Holocene age."

With regard to the geology, he wrote that the remains had

been found "within one meter of the surface of early Holocene alluvium, deposition of which terminates circa 8000 BP." With regard to the archaeology, he said the "spear point in the pelvis is a leaf-shaped serrated-edge point of Cascade type. This point dates between 8000 and 5000 BP. All of this coincides with the radiocarbon date of 8410 plus or minus 60 BP." (In his *American Antiquity* article, published a year later, Chatters referred to Erv Taylor's finding published in 1998 that Kennewick Man may have eaten mostly fish like salmon, which meant he was actually younger than the radiocarbon date suggested by about 530 years.)

"Jim," I asked, "you say the teeth are sundadont. Weren't they too worn to be able to tell? Aren't there supposed to be a bundle of traits that need to be seen?"

"The dentition clearly shows the deep wear," Chatters answered. However, X-rays of the teeth also showed a two-rooted upper first molar and two-rooted first and second lower molars. There was also a lack of any winging on the incisors. The third molar was also the same size as the second. "It's five characteristics, five in a total of eight," he said.

I moved over to the section he'd written on the general health and nutrition of Kennewick Man, and the symptoms of pathology. This was where the first man reading this poster had been standing when I came in. Powell had stood and looked closely at this section too.

On the projectile point and the wound it caused, Chatters had written: "A blade of an atlatl dart entered into or just anterior to the iliac crest from approximately 45 plus or minus 10 degrees above horizontal and 30 plus or minus 10 degrees anterior to the coronal plane. The bone shows extensive lysis (decomposition) and ... remodelling." The wound caused by this entry of the dart into the bone "persisted and drained pus from the man's hip throughout his life.... The condition is chronic osteomyelitis ... [which] would have caused pain when the man walked." He went on to suggest "septicemia" (a broad, system-wide infection) as a "possible cause of death."

I looked again through the whole poster to see whether I had missed any mention of his previous suggestion ("in the forensic venue," as he would so neatly explain it later in *American Antiquity*) that Kennewick was affiliated with "modern Euroamericans," and thus, as he had told *The New Yorker*, would not be noticed on a street in Stockholm. These words did not appear. I looked in vain for his and Neves's recent conclusions that Kennewick Man's affinities lay with Polynesians. The word Polynesian didn't appear either.

While many of the conference papers and posters did not suggest a new narrative framework, some were wonderfully enlivening, even redeeming the worst excesses of the old anthropology. Many of these scientists had found new ways to describe and measure variety, to chart human adaptation to a constantly changing nature. The more I heard and read, the better I understood why the concept of race is utterly useless, why it cannot capture the always moving boundaries between human populations adapting to change. Human beings are best observed as groups, this research said, and as groups, we are shape-shifters. Our bones and skulls bloat and shrink, swell and morph with whatever circumstance brings. Circumstance includes human politics.

An Australian researcher, Patricia Lindsell, had tested a hypothesis accepted in anthropology for a century—that body size and shape change with temperature—following up early observations with proper statistical analysis.[18] Three body shapes had been observed among Australian aboriginals, and researchers had speculated that there must have been three migrations of different populations. If body size and shape really do vary with temperature, Lindsell reasoned, she would see a patterned distribution from large size and shape to small as she compared aboriginal Australians living in different climate zones. She found that size did not vary with temperature, but shape did. She found body shapes became narrower with increasing heat. She found that on the western side of Australia size varied with precipitation—those who lived in rainy climates were bigger than those who lived in arid ones. Yet a mix of both arid and moist was the optimum climate for growth. The tallest individuals lived in "a hot dry climate with a good summer rain" while the shortest lived in rain forest, a finding that mimicked studies in Africa. So far as Lindsell was concerned, these findings had "implications regarding using body shape as a marker." In short, she didn't agree that different body shapes could be used as evidence to support theories of migration. This research made human beings sound like flowers or trees, or colonies of grass.

I stopped for a long time in front of a poster put up by two Italian scholars, neither of whom was around to answer questions.[19] The poster described what they'd learned about how a human population had deteriorated in general health from its earliest days, as hunter-gatherers, to its later years as agriculturalists. Their paper graphically demonstrated how difficult human life became after the expulsion from the Garden, after the beginnings of agriculture.

They had studied human remains found in a cave in the Liguria region in Italy. It had many, many layers of burials, starting in the Gravettian period. These hunter-gatherers had lived at the peak of the last glaciation, when much of northern Europe was bowed down under the weight of ice. They were of the same culture that in Dolni Vestonice developed a complex weaving industry. The bones of these hunter-gatherers were much healthier than the bones of farmers who were buried above them. They had fewer signs of work-related injury, fewer stress lines, no cavities.

Nearby, other posters told the same story: early rural life was miserable. One described the torments written in the bones of the dead found buried among the ruins of an ancient Greek colony near the Black Sea. Another described remains of burials found at Tell Abraq in the United Arab Emirates, the largest burial site in the Arabian peninsula.[20] This cemetery dated back to about 4500 BP (two thousand years after Native people in western Ontario had already learned to make copper tools). These people buried at Tell Abraq, like the early Italian farmers, endured all kinds of disease. Some forty percent of the bones studied showed signs of systemic infection from schistosomiasis, staphylococcus, streptococcus, dysentery and hypnolitic anemia due to malaria. More than half of the bones studied also showed degenerative changes resulting from harsh, repetitive work; there were also pathologies such as bone extrusions from unknown causes, and signs of poliomyelitis. Some forty-six percent of the dead were children.

I walked past Chatters' poster display once more. Powell was there again, peering closely at what Chatters had written about Kennewick Man's wounds, about his fractures, infection and the suffering he endured before his death. This portion of Chatters' work seemed particularly to fascinate Powell, not just the section dealing with the angle of entry of the spear point. It was as if he was checking Chatters' documentation against his own work, to see if he, Powell, could possibly have missed something, as if he could no longer be sure who was right.

# The Reverse Migration

## North, by Boat

A MONTH LATER I was far away from the leading edge, heading due north from Edmonton, Alberta, a part of North America that had not often figured in the papers I heard in Columbus. I was on the trail of ancient people who came this way in boats. The bus whizzed over the wide, groomed plain, the horizon broken only by gray clumps of leafless bush. The sky was clear and bright, and then the wind came up and blew in a new sky, black and ominous and frigid with fat rain aching to be snow. It was the middle of May: the land cried out for mercy. But as we moved up a slight crest and dropped into the bowl carved by a river, a valley folded us in close and warm, its hills swathed in a luminous shawl of new aspen green. Then we climbed up the other side and winter started all over again, nipping at the cold-seared plain—sometimes covered by the leaning corpses of fire-blackened spruce—until the next green-leafed valley. We rode this way, from sorrow to hope, for five hours to Fort McMurray, three hundred kilometers south of Great Slave Lake, where the Mackenzie River Valley begins.

We ran parallel to the water—the Athabasca River, which connects to Lake Athabasca, which connects by river to Great

Slave Lake, which is hooked by the Mackenzie River to Great Bear Lake and the Arctic Ocean. We passed through all kinds of little towns—large and prosperous, blasted and forgotten. The bus stopped longest at Lac La Biche. Native people got on and off, lightly dressed, as if this weather were a warm caress. The bus station was right across the road from the beach. There were whitecaps on the lake, and the wind whipped and wove and tangled the hair of a young girl wrapped around her young man. It billowed their jackets out from their square shoulders, turning them into lively sails straining to be off.

The sight of the open water filled me with joy. It was dark gray, with streaks of pale green, and it heaved and chopped and sprayed white foam. It was a northern lake the way northern lakes are supposed to be—treed, with soft hills gathered around and a stiff, fresh wind out of the northwest.

I'd heard about archaeological finds on land leased by Syncrude, the operators of the world's largest oil sands extraction operation, from Brian (Barney) Reeves, professor emeritus in archaeology at the University of Calgary and the owner of a private company that does archaeological assessment and salvage work. Reeves had made major discoveries on assignment to Syncrude in advance of Syncrude's construction of a new mine and pipeline in the area of the ice-free corridor. One copy of each of his reports was filed in the Alberta government archive; he hadn't published on these finds in any journals. But Reeves had given a talk at the 1998 University of Calgary Chacmool Conference, in which he mentioned that there was a great density of sites around Fort McMurray but that the oldest was only 9700 years old. I phoned for more: he said he'd just figured out the meaning of a series of archaeological finds that represented the "reoccupation" of the northern landscape after a major flood at the end of the Ice Age. In part, his inspiration had come from the geology of a University of Calgary professor, Derald Smith, and his graduate student Timothy Fisher.

In 1993 Smith and Fisher had published the results of their

reevaluation of the geological history of the Athabasca lowlands. It had previously been accepted that as the Ice Age ended, the huge, northern post-glacial lake called Agassiz had emptied into the Gulf of Mexico through the Mississippi. There were some who thought that Glacial Lake Agassiz might have drained to the Northwest, but no one had ever tried to disprove one thesis or the other. Smith and his student looked at the evidence on the ground—the huge valley around Fort McMurray, where the Athabasca, Muskeg and Clearwater rivers meet, and the landscape features left behind by retreating ice and draining water. They concluded that the accepted theory was wrong. Their evidence said that:

> ...a catastrophic flood discharged down the lower Clearwater and Athabasca river valleys 9900 years BP. Geomorphic and chronologic evidence suggests that Glacial Lake Agassiz (Emerson phase) was the probable water source. As the flood incised a drainage divide located near the Alberta-Saskatchewan border, the level of Glacial Lake Agassiz decreased by 46 meters, discharged 2.4 million cubic meters per second for at least 78 days, and stabilized at 438 meters above sea level in the Lake Waskemaio area. At that time, water entered the Arctic Ocean via Glacial Lake McConnell and the Mackenzie River, rather than the Gulf of Mexico via the Mississippi River as previously thought. Such a large influx of fresh water (8.6 thousand cubic kilometers per hour) into the Arctic at the close of the last glaciation may have had an abrupt, major influence on northern climate.[1]

This suggested catastrophic end of gigantic Lake Agassiz qualified as a Great Flood. But did this event put an end to the last Ice Age, as the article implied? I called Smith for clarification. He was no longer so certain of the flood's effects on climate. After the paper's publication he had come to believe that the Arctic Ocean had been buffered from the impact of all that fresh water by Glacial Lake McConnell, which lay to the north of Agassiz and in the path of its drainage. He had not actually checked his dates against the temperature record from the Greenland ice cores, so he couldn't say that the flood had actually abruptly warmed the climate at the end of the last ice age cycle. But the flood had changed this landscape utterly. For one thing, before the flood the Mackenzie River was just a sketch, cutting north across the landscape for the first time in its history. It was mainly a braided delta up in the Arctic, an outlet for McConnell and not much more. It was with this flood that the full stretch of the Mackenzie Valley was carved out, opening the way for people on foot moving north, or south to the heart of the continent. Smith's work badly damaged the theory of any earlier entry through an ice-free corridor into the Americas. There was no Mackenzie Valley corridor until after the flood, which Smith had pinned at about 9889 BP.

Yet most archaeologists and physical anthropologists outside Canada operated as if there had never been anything in peer-reviewed journals that called the ice-free corridor entry into question. It was as if, when one crossed the border, there was an opaque curtain that came down, protecting an outdated theory from contradiction by new findings of fact. Reeves, Smith and the geologist Alejandra Duk-Rodkin had begun to redescribe the prehistory of this northern quarter of the world. But few down south seemed to be paying attention.

Barney Reeves drank his latte, and steered the car with one hand over the nice, two-laned highway leading out of Fort McMurray. I rubbernecked as he drove us north toward the Syncrude mine, which the corporate people had given me permission to visit. I'd imagined Fort McMurray as Sudbury before it was detoxified. At a minimum, I expected the town would stink. Instead, I got off the bus in the late night sun, took a shallow lungful of air and was thrilled. Fort McMurray sits in a valley carved out by the Great Flood, at the junction of two rivers, which are joined by a third, surrounded by escarpments topped with bright, sweet-smelling aspen.

I'd watched Reeves on television in my hotel room the night before. The History Channel had carried a program about Head-Smashed-In Buffalo Jump, a major archaeological landmark in southern Alberta. Reeves had dug at the immense pile of buffalo bones there, to the amazement of many of his colleagues, who thought it a waste of time. What did he think he'd learn from a pile of buffalo bones below a cliff, they'd asked? He'd learned that Native people had used this site for thousands of years to trick the buffalo into falling to their deaths. They had developed ingenious trompe-l'oeil methods to take advantage of the herds' behavior and limited vision. They built small stone cairns at buffalo eye level, which fooled the animals into the conviction that they were walking or running between high hills. The resulting safe kills had produced huge surpluses.

A colleague of Reeves's at the University of Calgary had later analyzed the protein traces left on the used tools found at the site to identify the animals and plants killed or processed. Brian Kooyman was able to confirm that the buffalo had been killed and butchered at the bottom of the cliff. The Alberta government had been slow to recognize the place as a historical site, so Reeves and his colleagues had talked UNESCO into declaring it a World Heritage site.

I'd read the early reports Reeves wrote for Syncrude, which included surveys of others' work. There had been no archaeological explorations anywhere in this midsection of the corridor before the early 1970s. The early studies suggested that most of the sites were less than 7,750 years old. Reeves's work and that of others had moved those dates back: the great majority of sites were now believed to be between 7,750 and 9,500 years old. The older occupations were much more extensive than the younger ones, but they weren't found where the Beaver River sandstone was found (most of the tools were made of this stone). Instead, the sites were scattered on the other side of the Athabasca River, in hinterland areas now queasy with muskeg. Why this odd distribution of sites, Reeves had wondered. Then one of the geologists at Syncrude compared their locations with the edges of the ancient meltwater lakes and rivers that had formed, according to Derald Smith, after Lake Agassiz drained in the Great Flood. There was a "positive correlation" between the former banks of the Athabasca River, the edges of the vanished lakes, and the location of these sites. And further, he'd written, "the sites, we suggest, represent repeated warm weather encampments along the shoreline by native peoples whose primary means of access to this isolated land mass and movement along it was by canoe."[2]

It was this assertion that the first people who came to this area, ten thousand years ago, had arrived by *canoe* that made me get on the bus for Fort McMurray. How many times had I heard Clovis First advocates say there was no evidence of the use of boats by early Americans? A Goshen point, made of the local Beaver River sandstone, had been found near Cold Lake, which suggested that these lowlands had been occupied as soon as Glacial Lake Agassiz began draining to the north. Reeves now expects that the most ancient remains will be found 300 meters above the present shoreline of the Athabasca River, its highwater mark after the flood. The bulk of the tools he'd found were linked by style to the kinds of stone points found at ancient quarries on Lake Superior, and his finds got younger as he moved down toward the present shore. About five thousand years ago the land here had changed to muskeg, no longer good for summer camping. The record dried right up. This was why Reeves thought these sites were so important:

> Such a discoverable record of significant early native reoccupation of the new landscapes at the end of the last ice age, which has not been contaminated by later reoccupation of the landforms, exists in very few locales in North America. The

Lower Athabasca record has outstanding potential to con-
tribute fundamental knowledge to the nature of the early
northern landscapes and their reoccupation by early native
peoples, the nature of these peoples' cultures, their responses
to this landscape and the following initial occupation of the
Western Barren Lands. As such it is of National Significance.[3]

At the time of the flood, Reeves wrote, the ice front was only
eighty kilometers to the east. At about 9500 years BP, the ice
front had shrunk back 180 kilometers to the east, but the "area
[was] only accessible by water craft." Nevertheless, on one ridge
he had found a workshop and points similar to those made at the
same time in Wyoming and Montana. As the water level continued to drop, a lake the Syncrude geologists called Nezu had
formed. From 9400 to about 8800 BP, people had made various
campsites around Lake Nezu. Reeves had found spear points in
the styles called Scotsbluff, Northern Plano and Eastern Plano
and even adzes, which suggested to him that these people were
doing a lot of woodworking. The styles of their tools proved they
had had contact with people as far east as Southern Ontario and
the St. Lawrence.

The Beaver River quarry they made tools from wasn't exposed
by the sinking water level until 7,750 years ago. Until that time,
people used the large boulders of Beaver River sandstone that
had been dragged and dropped along the edges of the rivers and
lakes by the Flood.

Reeves hired Margaret Newman, now at the University of
Calgary, to examine the tools he found for protein traces. She
found the remains of the proteins of bison, deer, moose, black
bear and caribou. This suggested that the area had been a patch-
work of ecozones—a parkland/grassland, suitable for bison, caribou and deer, mixed with the kind of wetland forest area where
moose and black bear are found. "The regional climate was
warmer and dryer than it is now," said Reeves. He hoped to test
for plant and fish antisera although he doubted he would find

much evidence of early fishing since it did not show up in the archaeological record until later on.

The landscape here circa 9500 BP was dotted with ridges, knolls, islands, sand beaches, peninsulas, small ponds and large wetlands, making it an ideal countryside for finding useful plants, shellfish, fish and migratory birds, as well as large game. It was a warm, bountiful garden all summer long. It was an ideal climate for hunter-gatherers who lived much farther south in the winter.

"The people would have had to use watercraft to get across the Athabasca/Muskeg Embayment," wrote Reeves, "which was 2.6 to 6 kilometers wide 9,500 years ago, or across the Athabasca itself west of Cree Burn Lake which was 3.5 kilometers wide 9,500 years ago." Some of the oldest sites where workshop remains had been found were right down where the water once was. To reach these locations, the people would have needed boats.

"The significant components of this record are almost totally contained within and immediately adjacent to the Agassiz Flood Zone," he wrote in a report to Syncrude. "Most lie in areas which will be developed as a surface oil sands mine and related infrastructure on the east side of the Athabasca River north of the Muskeg Escarpment." These sites would either be avoided by Syncrude, or salvaged. He would dig up those to be salvaged and place the artifacts found, for the aid of the public's memory, in the public museum.

In 1977, in advance of digging new mines and building pipelines to carry the slurry away, Syncrude hired Reeves to do an archaeological survey of the western half of its lease. He didn't find much of anything at first. The land was all muskeg and islands, which is typical of the boreal forest. Yet on the east side of the Athabasca River there was a long sequence of sites at a place called Cree Burn Lake. An interesting spear point had been found by other archaeologists, but another consultant said it was okay to obliterate the site by building a highway—which was done. "Turns out it was 8000 BP," said Reeves with a grimace.

In the 1980s Shell Oil came along with a plan to build a mine, and he explored for them as well. Then Syncrude's Aurora Mine plan was developed. Another contractor surveyed the area, applying a so-called random search pattern, which turned up almost nothing. Reeves came along later and did stratified, nonrandom tests, guessing that sites would be found on top of ridges that had aspen and pine growing on them: he had good success. When the highway was built at Cree Burn Lake, thousands of artifacts were exposed, a lot of waste from the making of points, but still no points. Surveying for sites went on for the next decade. Reeves could never figure out why the east side of the river had archaeological sites and the west side had none. "Both sides were the same," he said. "There's grazing there for buffalo. Everything sat pretty much until Aurora. That was 1995. I started by reviewing the literature . . . Derald Smith had published on the Agassiz Flood. . . . He saw evidence of a big catastrophic event. . . . I was looking at an explanation of the difference on the east and west side and the huge density of sites."

By the time Reeves had reached this point in the story we had driven up to a crest of land. There was no forest, but on the left of the highway I could see buffalo grazing, and small, newly planted trees. Syncrude, he explained, had stripped the forest off for its first mines and was now returning the land to something liveable. We topped the rise. Spread below was a gigantic open-face mine—it stretched in all directions to the horizon. Everything was gray or black, or metal. There were blackened hills of mined earth, tracks left in the wake of the dinosaur-machines on caterpillar treads that were working down below, wielding enormous claws for rending and tearing the bituminous ground. Everywhere they'd dug and chewed and eaten they left pits with oily standing water. The sky puffed smoke, and the air smelled like Vaseline.

The contrast between the natural landscape and this was so stark I couldn't speak. Reeves drove on. At Cree Burn Lake, he said, he did a number of test pits and found things that he thought were 8,000 or 9,000 years old. This made him think again about the antiquity of these sites, but it wasn't until the field study he did in 1997 that he realized the points he'd found were not like the others. He uncovered them in the middle of a swamp; they were classic Alberta Scotsbluff or Eastern Plano, but they'd been made out of the local chert. He later found obsidian there, too, which came from Telegraph Creek in British Columbia. The blood residues found on these spear points said that they had been used to kill or butcher buffalo, deer, caribou, bear. But what sense did this site make? Why was this camp here? It was twelve kilometers east of the river.

In the spring of 1998 he and his crew went back to the site, because it was going to be flooded by the mine and there was going to be a pipeline corridor nearby. (They wanted to make sure there was a buffer between any sensitive sites and the pipeline corridor.) The more they thought about it the clearer it seemed that for anyone to have made use of this particular site there would have had to be grassland between it and the river—unless it was beside a lake and they had used boats. But no one had any evidence that people had boats at that time.

"We joked," Reeves said. "Maybe they used boats. Rob Mahood [a Syncrude geologist] had evidence there was a lake. We looked at features there. With the right maps, they looked like shorelines." The sites they found seemed to fit with the ancient lake's former shorelines. "We were getting early points on the north end, later on on the south. We began to say they had boats."

We had by this point passed into a beautiful river valley with aspen forest on its hills. In this area, he said, waving a hand to include both sides of the highway, they had found nothing to speak of. The road surface coincided with the land surface of 8,000 years ago. When he compared the sites with the map he realized they were all related. After he put the township maps together, he could see the pattern of a shoreline where the sites were, and how it fitted with Derald Smith's map of where the great Ice Age lake had been. "It fitted just lovely," Reeves said.

The people who came here in those days were adapted to a big, marshy embayment. They may have hunted buffalo up above the line of the flood, but they had their big camps down along the edge of the water. What had made all of this come together for him was Derald Smith's insight that the flood had been a catastrophic event, not a slow and gradual draining away of water to the south, which is what Reeves had been taught. Of course he'd also been taught that the notion that moving plates underneath the oceans were pushing the continents apart (now geological orthodoxy) was wrong, and its Canadian advocate, J. Tuzo Wilson, "was out of his skull."

Reeves pulled his car off the highway onto a gravel road that passed through a screen of trees. There was a big wide cut through the forest, a pipeline corridor. He parked his car at the place where heavy equipment had gone through, salvaged the trees, and left the ground littered with wood chips. Moving on top of the muskeg was like walking on hillocks of sponge or moss. About a quarter-mile along the corridor there was a little hill where a crew of people were working over a tripod that stood over a big pit. They were in their early twenties mostly, men and women. He introduced the crew leader, Nancy Saxberg, a young woman with reddish-blond hair, a hat, army pants and sweater tied chicly around her neck; she was in charge. The crew were shovelling dirt through quarter-inch mesh screen. My heart sank. This was salvage archaeology, fast and crude, and there wouldn't be any second chances since this site would disappear under a pipeline. They wouldn't be doing any flotation. No systematic hunt for hairs or phytoliths of long-gone plant forms. Reeves explained that no human or plant remains of any size would have survived the acid soil of the boreal forest and muskeg that formed here 5,000 years ago.

Nevertheless, this had turned out to be a very rich site. It was at the 290-meter mark, not the highest point of the flood, but high enough. The stone points Reeves found told him there had been an occupation here 9,500 years ago. The sand on the ridge had sealed it: it had been a campsite, not a quarry, so they had found actual tools instead of just leftover flakes. But the animal bones that people had burned in their campfires had been completely leached of their proteins and so could not be directly dated. No wood or cordage had survived.

"We are on the north shore of the embayment," he said as I scrambled up to the top of the sandy ridge. The ice front at the time of this encampment was 125 kilometers to the east. That's where the people had gone to hunt caribou, the proteinaceous remains of which Reeves had found on the stone tools here.

But where did they come from? I asked.

"I think down near Lac La Biche," he said. "The parklands." A Beaver River sandstone lance-style point and a Beaver River Scotsbluff point, made here, had been found at Lac La Biche. Of course a Beaver River point had also been found on a bison kill site near Kindersley, Saskatchewan, a good eleven hundred kilometers away. And then there were the Eastern Plano points made of the local stone, but in a style normally found in Southern Ontario.

So, I said, who were these people?

He wasn't about to get into a political mess about that. "I don't make inferences with regard to the ethnicity of the people who lived there," he said. He felt comfortable drawing such inferences from sites that were around two thousand years old, but nothing this old. On the other hand, when he saw something that looked like a point from early sites around Cody, Wyoming, Cody Complex is what he called it. "People say it can't be, it's 1,200 miles [from] Cody, Wyoming to here. How can it be?" It wasn't that he assumed individuals were traveling that far, but it showed him there was a very large exchange system. "One of these Beaver River sandstone points is from Fort Assiniboia, northwest of Edmonton. They are obviously going up and down the river. I'd lay money down [that] in the large collections [you'll] find quite a bit of the Beaver River sandstone."

I was curious why he hadn't dated his sites by the normal methods, radiocarbon testing on charcoal taken out of the hearths.

"No hearths," he said. He had not found any arrangements of stones used to contain fires, and he hadn't found any postholes either (marks left behind in the ground by tents or wigwams). Other than the stone points themselves and the waste flakes that fell off the cores as they were manufactured, his crew found nothing but burned animal bones. The forest had churned and uprooted everything else.

"This will be gone by early July," he said, waving his arm over the little hillock of prehistory we stood on. The pipeline would take its place.

We got into a truck to drive over to another site on the former Lake Nezu, this one on the edge of a dike Syncrude was building to hold back a tailing pond from the Aurora Mine. Nancy Saxberg came along with us. We drove back along the highway, then turned onto a gravel road. The trees rapidly thinned out on either side, and then vanished, and we were traveling across a barren, dusty, wheel-marked plain. Gigantic trucks taller than my three-story house roared along in the distance, rolling over the landscape like the Imperial Army's landing vehicles from *Star Wars*. Bill Hunter, a tall, lanky, bearded environmental scientist for Syncrude, met us at the entry gate. He signed us in and handed out hard hats and orange body markers, which we criss-crossed over our chests so the drivers of those immense vehicles could see us before they squashed us like June bugs.

We drove through the mine site to the dike. On the left the muskeg had been packed down and graded: the grade lines had filled with water. Beyond a murky pool, there was a little elevated stand of forest. In there somewhere they'd found another ancient lakeside site. We trudged across the mushy ground, water pooling in my sneakers by the third step. Saxberg disappeared into a rotten stand of lichen-covered spruce. The trees were wet and black underneath their layer of toxic pastel green. The lichen was bright and shiny, as if it got its color from draining the life out of the trees.

There was no path that I could see. I followed the sound of Saxberg crashing over downed spruce ahead. Mosquitoes, too cold to fly and as big as my thumbnail, kept landing on my black sweater as if that would do something for them.

Reeves talked about who came here after the muskeg moved in. First there was a people called the Talthelei, he said. They were followed in historic times by the northern Cree who were forest farmers of the highest order. They used fire as their primary tool to improve the productivity of their Garden of Eden: they set off controlled burns that increased the yields of the berry patches and created openings for the new foliage that grazing animals feast on. Reeves knew of some Native women herbalists in Waterton National Park, where he has a home, who complained that modern park managers, who stamped out fire as if it were the root of all evil, were ruining the whole thing. "The medicinal plants are going to hell," he said. No one was burning and no one was digging roots. One useful root that grew down in Waterton was blue camus, a staple for the Nez Percé and the Paiutes. Lewis and Clark would have starved without it. Slow cooking changes its chemistry into something humans can digest. In the Kamloops area, balsam root was roasted in a similar way.

So where did they come from? I asked again.

"South of the ice sheet is where they came from," Reeves said. "Northern Plano is Lakehead Complex"—meaning from the area around Thunder Bay.

We stood in a clearing, on the edge of a forested hillock. There was water on the right, and a piece of standing forest on the left, a marshy, half-submerged spongy piece of land that rose up out of the standing water. It was cold, and the wind had picked up. A helicopter had dropped Saxberg and a colleague here in the spring of 1997 to test this area. On the maps, this was an ancient shoreline. Saxberg had dug holes in a grid pattern, and pretty soon she came up with calcined bone.

Saxberg pulled a plastic bag out of her pocket with some samples of what she'd found. The bone inside was a whitish blue-gray. She found twelve pieces just by sticking a shovel in the ground. They came back at the end of September to excavate. They trenched and did meter squares in all directions from the trench. They found a scatter of artifacts that petered out along the edge of the former lake. They came back in June of 1998. All told, they dug 130 meters over two years. They found more bones and scraping tools, but no organic remains and not even a hint of a hearth. It was strange how things worked here. They had only had to dig down eight inches to get to the 9,000-year-old surface.

Saxberg opened another plastic bag with some of the spear points they'd recovered. Reeves explained what they were: this, he said, was a point used for stabbing bison. The point had once been lashed to a stick six or eight inches long. The assembly would have included a mainshaft and a foreshaft that could be reloaded. The next was Scotsbluff in style. Reeves laid three of them out on his palm. I shot a picture so I'd remember how they looked. The next point was Eastern Plano. I shot that too. The date of this landform was known to be about 9000 BP. The dates from charcoal found on other sites in the south and east where this style of point had also been found were all about 9000 to 9400 BP—older than Kennewick, but the same age as the mummy in Spirit Cave, Nevada.

We trudged back through the jagged bush and across the water. How did this fit with his ideas about the peopling of the

Americas, I wanted to know. He brushed the question away. The whole thing irritated him. "I lost interest in the debate," he said. "It's a lot of old men getting older. I think people have been here a long time, a quarter of a million years."

He shares that view with Maria Beltrão in Brazil. He said he also agreed with Bill Irving, formerly a professor at the University of Toronto, who said in the 1960s that Clovis was connected to the Solutrean technology in France. He had no problem with the notion that people crossed the Atlantic.

Well, I said, what about these people? What's known about the population they came from?

There were no burials at all that related to the finds he'd made here: the only human remains he knew of associated with spear points of the same style had been found years ago at Renier, Wisconsin (and that was a cremation). He had found the stem of a lance-like spear point here that was like the one found at Renier. Similar spear points had also been found as far south as Texas and as far east as New York, but this style was mainly known from the Missouri River.[4] "It is not people originating west of the Rockies," he said firmly. "Maybe [they came] out of the eastern Woodland."

We all went back to the first site for lunch: Bill Hunter, Nancy Saxberg, Barney Reeves, me. We sat in a circle, watching the sun fight with the clouds for dominion over the earth, talking, telling stories, eating sandwiches, fruit, vegetables, cookies, cheese. The old folks (like me) sat uncomfortably but carefully balanced on overturned buckets. Two Dene women on the crew sat comfortably, their backs against tree stumps, their legs stretched out in front of them on the soft wood-chipped ground. Reeves pulled something made of stone out of a bag and put it in my hand.

"What's this?" he asked me—as if I'd have a clue.

It was a rounded stone object he called a doughnut. It wasn't a doughnut exactly, there was no hole in the center, but it was a stone that someone had carefully shaped and smoothed, flattening the top and bottom, getting rid of ridges and bumps. Right in the center of one flattened surface someone had made a thumb-sized indentation.

"Look," he said. "We have two of them."

He pulled out another, which was the same as the first but had indentations on both sides. I took the second one in my right hand. It was a nice fit, as if it had been made for me to hold between my thumb and fourth or fifth finger. I could make it spin if I held it like that. Or I could flatten things with it. Or I could grind things on it.

I give up, I said. What are they?

Reeves said he didn't know. They had found them both on another site, one he would show me later, in another pipeline corridor like this one only on a larger hillock, with a cut on one side that had been made by the continuous action of waves. Once upon a time it had been a small island completely surrounded by water. There was a place where canoes could have pulled up along its wave-cut north shore. That was where they found these stone doughnuts.

Well, I said, where have you seen things like them?

"Jim Wright called it a hammerstone at Grant Lake," said Reeves, looking at me to see if that rang any bells. Wright is a very senior Canadian archaeologist who worked for many years with the Museum of Civilization, a man who is writing a huge work on the prehistory of Native Canadians. "They put the raw material on there," he said pointing to one of the flattened surfaces, "and hammer on the top. This is totally ground around the edge," he said, showing me what he meant. The whole outer surface of the stone had been rounded and smoothed, not just the top and the bottom. "I've not seen it before."

So where's Grant Lake? I asked.

Directly west of Chesterfield Inlet in the Barren Lands, Reeves explained, "Wright says [he found] a hammerstone with use as an anvil. It's a similar surficial approach. I don't know if it has indentations on both sides. This is granitic. It's not Beaver River. It could occur in glacial till."

Meaning it could have been found anywhere between this site and the edge of the great Canadian Shield, more than three thousand kilometers east. Chesterfield Inlet is on the northwest side of Hudson Bay. How could there have been people up there at a time when the ice front was only a few hundred kilometers from here? One center of the Laurentide ice sheet was supposed to have been somewhere in Hudson Bay, so that would surely have been the last ice to melt. And yet when I called Wright later to confirm, he said yes, he had found such stone platforms or anvils at Grant Lake, just like the ones Reeves had found. The stones at Grant Lake had indentations too, sometimes on both sides, sometimes only on one. He believed that the Grant Lake site was between eight and nine thousand years old.

If Wright had found similar objects used way up in the Barren Lands, did that mean the same people who came to the Athabasca River to work the sandstone had also found their way to Chesterfield Inlet? Did it mean that people had worked their way up the east coast first, and then walked here in winter over frozen lakes covering the Barren Lands? Or vice versa? What would woodworking people want with the Barren Lands, where there were no trees to work? What kind of people could adapt so quickly to such different environments? Rounded stones had also been found in South America—of course they looked more like balls than doughnuts. Dillehay had called the ones he found at Monte Verde bola stones, because they looked like the bolas used by gauchos to hobble cattle. I also remembered reading something about how people in the desert in California used to take small insects and tiny rodents and grind them on small rounded stones to make an edible paste.

Reeves didn't think the California suggestion was right, although he did think the doughnuts were pretty fancy for use as simple anvils.[5] And he didn't like the bola idea either. The only place Reeves knew that bola stones had been found in North America was on the Columbia Plateau, Kennewick Man's locale. They showed up there at around this time, and then disappeared.

I handed them back to Nancy Saxberg, who twirled them slowly in her hands. They looked like fat little dune-buggy wheels.

Last year they had excavated over 900 square meters and found nothing. This year, they came back and found four of these stones, and on the same site they also found obsidian. They laid out the little rectangular black pieces for me to see. They were tiny, only about half an inch long. They hadn't yet done the analysis to be certain where they came from, but they sure didn't come from around here. The closest obsidian mountain is in northern British Columbia: Mount Edziza is about 1,200 kilometers away, up in the Stikine Valley. That trip could be made by canoe.

The fact was, these Paleo people, who seem to have had a shared technology and a vast system of trade, had found their way from Texas to New York to Nebraska and here, all around the edges of the retreating ice. Their remains were disappearing now, under roads and pipelines and mines, faster than consultants like Reeves could find them and make sense of them.

We drove over the highway and hills to Cree Burn Lake. There was a parking place off the highway, and a fence and plaque put up by Syncrude and the provincial government to mark this as a special heritage site. Right inside the fence, in the thigh-high growth of last year's grass, there was a small pile of rounded stones, obviously set there by the hand of man. While it had no arms and legs and was capped with a small pyramid-shaped stone, it looked like a little person. It also reminded me of the buffalo cairns in the film about Head-Smashed-In Buffalo Jump.

It startled both Saxberg and Reeves. It hadn't been here the last time they came and it wasn't supposed to be here at all. Someone in the Native community had lately begun putting these things up. Someone had tried to have this provincial heritage site declared sacred, to keep archaeologists and tourists out, to keep the public away. There had been quite a to-do in town, mostly caused by a few people who, according to Reeves, had lately found their Native spirituality after taking a trip down to the U.S. Southwest. "The cairns appeared here this winter," he said, as we walked fast through open aspen woods, which were just putting out their first fuzz of leaf. "That's all we know."

We were looking out over a round valley. Down below, at the bottom of this sweet bowl, there was a little lake. A shallow hillside made a continuous rim around the whole thing, as if it were a very large stadium. Across the lake, the opposite hillside was covered with tight stands of light aspen and dark spruce, alternating blocks of green and black. The trees shivered in the wind, and their scent perfumed my hair. There were wildflowers showing under last year's leaves, wild strawberries just beginning to take their form. The whole place seemed oddly familiar.

"This is an old sinkhole," Reeves said. "The limestone is right under the water."

Right, I thought, this looks like Lagoa Santa in Brazil. We were on the top of a rock hill that half embraced the lake. We had a spectacular view of the whole countryside. Maybe these trees hid a rock shelter with paintings? Reeves had said there was ocher around here. We walked farther along the path until I could hear a creek gurgling off to the right. It ran at the bottom of a cleft in the stone, covered by trees and grass, down to the lake below. Here Reeves had found a huge workshop and campsite that stretched on for more than a mile. They had worked the Beaver River sandstone.

We walked to the left, back around the rim of the collapsed limestone. There was another little stone man set up just outside the protection of the trees, facing out across the lake.

We walked back to the truck, drove out of the parking lot. Another little stone man, perched high on a hill, watched us peel away onto the highway.

We turned in on a muskeg road to the site where the obsidian and the stone doughnuts had been found. This was an important site, because it provided strong evidence of the huge cultural exchange network that stretched thousands of miles to the northeast, northwest and southeast after the northern version of the Great Flood. Yet there were no signs here to show its significance. There was just the pipeline corridor, miles and miles of muskeg sheared of its tree cover, and a little ridge like an island in the middle of this flattened ground. It rose out of the muskeg like the vertebrae of a thin man. There were piles of dirt at the north end where the stone doughnuts and slivers of obsidian had come from, and boulders at the south end, just as they'd said. Saxberg clambered down the ridge's north face.

Will you publish this? I asked Reeves. If he only wrote reports for Syncrude and filed them with the provincial archives—one copy, no librarian—his colleagues would never know what he'd found. Maybe if he did an article in *American Antiquity*, the doughnuts would be seen by his American colleagues. Maybe someone would make a connection. And maybe his colleagues to the south would finally understand that their theories of an ice-free corridor had nothing to do with the reality of this place, nothing at all.

"We'll put something out in the *Journal of Canadian Archaeology*," replied Reeves abruptly.

Look, Saxberg called, look what's here. She stood on a pile of dirt at the bottom of the ridge. She waved a big, long, lemon-yellow wooden arrow in her hand. We scrambled down the ridge to get a closer look. She had found it sticking out of the dirt right at the northern base of the site, right where the doughnuts had been found, and where they'd uncovered thousands and thousands of flakes left from the making of stone points. Around 8,000 years ago, after the ice had shrunk back sufficiently, the prevailing wind direction had changed and this had become a good, sheltered place to pull up a boat.

The arrow in Saxberg's hand was long, thin and nicely machined. There was a rounded steel cap where there should have been a point. It was a modern arrow, the kind of thing, Reeves said, that people around here used to hunt bear for sport. But who would hunt here at this time of year?

"That's creepy," said Saxberg.

Reeves took it in his hands and turned it over, slowly. Was it here, in this place, by accident, an artifact left by some careless person? Or was it direct-action politics, a physical message to those who would dig in the sands of time and disturb ancient things?

# 21

# The Corridor That Wasn't

## The Cold Facts Behind the Absence of Evidence

SCHIZOID MAY MORNING in Calgary: on one side of the river, blue sky, but to the north clouds black as an iron frying pan, signaling a downpour. This uncertain light fell on Alejandra Duk-Rodkin's hair as she walked gracefully down the lobby staircase of the Geological Survey of Canada's western headquarters. She was a surprising figure, far too small for an overthrower of orthodoxy, almost tiny beside the vast display wall of stone and concrete forms shaped like the fossil animals found throughout the West. She had pixie-cut shiny black hair, huge brown eyes with thick black lashes, a gorgeous smile. She was the only person in this building, as far as I could tell, who'd dressed for the office. Everyone else hustled through in jeans and sweatshirts, hauling backpacks. Here she came in a dark skirt, a coordinated long jacket. A gold necklace. Earrings. She had inferred, as she made her way down, that I must be the person waiting to see her (there was no one else in the lobby but the doorman). She could not quite hide her disappointment. Perhaps she'd expected a chic media person (finally, they've figured out the value of my work!). Instead, she got me—fifty-something, in black jeans and a rain jacket, dog-tired from the bush and the bus.

"She's proven there was no ice-free corridor at the right time," Alan Bryan had told me. "Make her prove it to you," Barney Reeves had said in Fort McMurray. And what, I wondered, would such proof consist of? How could one ever prove a negative? Nevertheless, with two such senior scholars convinced, I had been surprised to see what Alberta's Provincial Museum in Edmonton made of the matter.

I'd gone there the day before meeting Alejandra Duk-Rodkin. It was clear Alberta officials still held tight to the old orthodoxies. Their aboriginal prehistory display had just been redone and renamed the Syncrude Gallery of Aboriginal Culture. Syncrude has made a habit of such philanthropy (and of hiring more Native Canadians and women than most other companies in the West). The very first display was a map, which showed an ice-free corridor open from 12,000 BP on, stretching from the high Arctic to the southern half of the continent. By 11,000, the display copy said, the corridor area was all liveable, and "may have been the route of entry for people coming into North America." A video at the entrance said, "It's 11,000 years since we came here and 500 generations," which artfully implied, but did not claim, a wonderful cultural continuity among the peoples who took dominion over Alberta. Nothing was said about exactly who "we" are. The oldest site was asserted to be at Vermilion Lakes, in the south, near Banff, where charcoal from a hearth had been dated to 10,400 BP. The museum curators had tried to finesse the painful issue of expansions and defeats, but there were displays showing that Missourian Siouans came here and built earthworks and houses, then moved on or were absorbed. There was old copper from north of Superior and shells from the Pacific (both found on the same 2,800-year-old site). One medicine wheel had been laboriously constructed, stone by stone, over a period of 4,500 years.

This presentation made it clear that the brilliant Duk-Rodkin might well be a heroine of geological science, but she was unsung by official Alberta. She was also unknown to most of the anthropologists I'd spoken to. The South American scholars hadn't heard that the ice-free corridor entry theory was in doubt. Many North Americans knew there were problems with it but didn't know what they were, and hadn't heard Duk-Rodkin's name. The avant-garde among them, having heard there was a difficulty, just shifted their proposed route of entry to the Pacific coast and pointed to the work of Harvard's Carole Mandryk, an anthropologist who preferred to be called a paleoecologist. Mandryk knew Duk-Rodkin and the Geological Survey of Canada's maps, but Duk-Rodkin's work was read mainly by her own peers, geologists who were interested in tracking the waxing and waning of ice sheets over the face of the earth and climatologists trying to perfect their models by reference to real data from the past. They knew that Duk-Rodkin and her colleagues had radically rewritten the history of the Mackenzie River, one of the largest river systems on the globe.

The corridor along the way to Duk-Rodkin's office was lined with huge maps and poster displays of her work and that of her colleagues in the terrain sciences division. She sat me down at a large wooden table surrounded by glass-fronted bookshelves and tubes full of maps and began to tell her story—full of political change and migration, reversals and triumphs. She was born in Chile, and finished her undergraduate work at the Catholic University of Valparaiso in 1971. In high school she'd attended careers lectures: a geologist came to speak. "I said, this is it. I loved it. The mystery of rocks.... If you are able to look at the landscape through the eyes of a geologist—it's the best thing you can have. It's just beautiful." There was no graduate education in geology to be had in Chile, then or now. So when she finished her BA in geography she took a scholarship from the Soviet Union and went to Moscow State University.

"The Russians offered the best scholarship in the world—a salary to study," she explained. She also had access to scholars who were just beginning to investigate a huge territory that had been off limits to Western scientists since World War II. She stayed for seven years, finished her doctorate (on Chilean geology), married a Russian geological scientist, and did postdoctoral studies at Moscow State.

Her field of study became the geomorphology of mineral deposits—what one may infer from the surface about mineral formations below—a physical algebra analogous to that of anthropologists using skull measurements to make claims about populations and their relatedness. "I studied the surface expression of mineral fields," she said. This was a cheap way of exploring for mines without a huge investment in exploratory drilling, and was important for a country like Chile which lacked the large capital markets that fund such risky ventures. This was the kind of work generations of geologists had done throughout Canada, pickaxing their way here and there, learning the relationships between the history of rivers, the stains of color on rocks, the placement of certain plant colonies, and minerals like gold, silver, nickel, copper and uranium.

She was offered a job teaching applied geology to civil engineers at the University of Santiago in Chile, which she accepted in 1980. It took her husband another year and a half to get permission to leave the Soviet Union. Soon after he arrived, the director of the university left, and a person from the military was put in charge. Pinochet was then at the height of his power. "So, he decided to clean house," she said, with a wry smile. Those who could be linked to the left were not welcome. She had never been a political activist, but that didn't matter: she'd lived for years in Moscow, she'd taken money from the Soviet state—and look who her husband was. "Canada took us in," was how she put it. In Calgary she studied English and got a three-month contract job with the Geological Survey of Canada, which eventually turned into a permanent position, "which to me was like winning the lottery."

The survey organizes its work into small multidisciplinary teams. Duk-Rodkin applied her specialty to glacial geology and worked with a team lead by Owen Hughes, who passed away, she said, in 1992. Her eyes glazed with tears. "He was my mentor." She pointed out a picture of him that had pride of place, high on the wall of her lab. The Mackenzie Valley and its river were the focus of their work from her first day.

In the early 1970s, when private energy companies were promoting the idea of building a pipeline to bring gas and oil to southern markets from the Beaufort Sea, the preferred route in Canada was the Mackenzie River valley. The crisis created over access to Middle Eastern oil, after the 1973 Yom Kippur War, persuaded the government of Canada that its energy security was at risk. The government had already begun a whole series of studies of the geology, biology and society of the Mackenzie River valley, and launched a commission of inquiry into the advisability of a northern pipeline, under Mr. Justice Berger. What would the impact of such development be on this vast permafrost corridor? What would happen to the Native people and the caribou herds and the slow-growing plants, their life cycles all linked in intricate synchrony? What else might be worth developing along its path? This was the first systematic scientific exploration that had ever been done in the Arctic and the Mackenzie Valley corridor, which included the length of the Mackenzie River from its mouth at the Beaufort Sea to its headwaters at Great Slave Lake. Owen Hughes's team was the first to map the surface geology. It had taken "only two years to cover all that territory."

What had been known of the geology of this territory, the top half of the ice-free corridor, before then? I asked. Prospectors had been moving through the valley for years. Surely many papers had been done by generations of scientists? Her answer stunned me.

Before that, she said, zero. "I came in to do the final compilation of the surficial geology of the Mackenzie corridor. My nature was to go also back, south, to the interior of the mountains...."

In other words, she wasn't content with knowing only what

could be seen in the corridor itself; she also wanted to learn about its formation by studying the adjacent mountains and plains. She gathered together the work of those in her team who had gone through the valley before her, and her own material to confirm their findings and to answer her own questions—"material that told an incredible story," she said.

"I started working on the problem of the Glacial Mackenzie River," she said. It took her ten years to be sure she was right. In 1994 she published a paper in *Quaternary International* that threw out much of what people previously thought they knew about the formation of the Mackenzie River and its valley. Duk-Rodkin and Hughes established that up until the end of the last ice age, the Peel and Porcupine rivers, which drained the mountains in the Yukon, had flowed separately to the Arctic, but that the Richardson and the Mackenzie mountains in the Northwest Territories had drained to the east. Before the last period of glaciation, the old Mackenzie River system, a mighty skein of tributaries, had drained through and past Hudson Bay as the Bell River system. The last and greatest thrust of the Laurentide ice sheet changed what had been unchanged for millions of years. "Late Wisconsinan glaciation deranged these drainage systems," she wrote, "and resulted in the Mackenzie River flowing north parallel to the mountain front. The evidence to support this proposal is based on morphology, provenance of sediments, reconstruction of paleosurfaces and stratigraphy."[1]

Other scientists had considered this possibility with regard to the Yukon River long before Duk-Rodkin went into the field. After all, it fit with the way the rest of the rivers had always run and still run. Most North American rivers flow west to east or north to south. The Mackenzie, flowing south to north, had always been considered an anomaly but no one imagined that it hadn't always run that way. Until Duk-Rodkin and Hughes, no one actually set out to disprove that this was the way things had always been. They walked the river and the adjacent mountains, worked through the samples of rock taken from the river's mouth

and asked fundamental questions. Where did this system originate? The prevailing orthodoxy turned out to have been generated out of thin air. Hughes and then Duk-Rodkin worked back
to the earliest evidence of continent-wide glaciation (around
2.9 million years ago). They pieced the story together from the
study of many exposures, but three stratigraphic cuts found in the
Mackenzie Mountain front provided the most extensive chronology. These cuts recorded change in the region through at least
five different continental montane glaciations, the first dating
back to the Pliocene. The last in the sequence was the Laurentide. "Up until the last continental glaciation maximum, about
30,000 BP, the river drained to Hudson Bay, and only two
drainages, the Porcupine and the Peel rivers, drained into the
Arctic."

She pulled maps from tubes and laid them on her desk so I
could see what she was talking about.

"The Yukon and Koyukuk," she said, tracing their courses
across Alaska with a finger, "go southwest." After the first cordilleran (mountain) glaciation, the drainage system eventually
called the Yukon River was incorporated into the Kwikhpak
(later the Koyukuk) River—the Alaskan portion of the system as
it was more than three million years ago. After the second glaciation, there were more, but minor changes in this drainage caused
by the ice sheet now called the Cordilleran. "In the last one,
major changes to drainage were caused by the continental ice.
The Porcupine river is incorporated into the Yukon, and the
Mackenzie integrates all the rest of the drainage to the Arctic." In
other words, the last glaciation was so huge, with so much weight
of ice, that all the smaller drainage systems were swept together
into the Mackenzie River system, which shifted its course due
north along the edge of the mountains.

The story of how the two ice sheets grew and contracted and
grew again, how the melting ice carved a valley by moving a huge
river perpendicular to its previous course, led Duk-Rodkin to
similarly revolutionary conclusions about the timing of the open-

ing between them. As her various papers laid out, in the last glaciation there were two major ice sheets, the Cordilleran and the Laurentide. They each formed from the coalescence of many independent ice centers that advanced out onto the landscape. The Laurentide sheet had many such domes where the ice built and built and built, and then began to move forward in all directions at once. Glaciers move in two ways: their weight can make their edges deform like plastic, so that they slowly, grindingly, bulge forward; or the huge pressure of ice can create meltwater, which acts as a lubricating surface at the ice sheets' edges, causing them to glide forward.

The Laurentide ice sheet had domes over the Keewatin District of northwest Hudson Bay, on Baffin Island and another over Labrador. But the Cordilleran ice sheet was different. It was created by independent mountain glaciers that were built first in local mountain valleys. The snow fell and the temperature never warmed enough to melt it, until it filled up the valleys. Humid air masses coming in from the Pacific formed an ice sheet first over the Selwyn Mountains. In the much drier conditions of the Mackenzie Mountains, only valley glaciers formed. These independent glaciers finally converged into a mountain-covering carapace of ice, but not at the same time as the Laurentide sheet was at its maximum advance. The Cordilleran valley glaciers coalesced 6,000 years after the Laurentide ice sheet reached its peak at around 30,000 BP. Both these ice sheets grew and shrank as the climate shifted: the climate became colder, then warmer, then damper, then drier, then warmer again. These changes drove and were reflected in the contractions and expansions of ice. The movements of the ice left marks all over the landscape. When the Laurentide retracted, it left behind humps of Shield gravel and crushed rock that it had ground up and transported as it spread out over the prairies and down over the Great Lakes. As the ice withdrew, the newly ice-free areas were repopulated by lichens, sedges, insects, animals and trees. When the ice sheets grew again, and then shrank again, they left behind new moraines of rubble in new places, and huge boulders that were set down helter-skelter wherever the ice carried them, and permanently stranded there as the ice melted away. Just as archaeologists date the charcoal left by human hearths, geologists make a chronology of glaciers' edges by dating the organic remains associated with these moraines. Radiocarbon and other methods of dating allow them to map the ice limits over time.

Alejandra Duk-Rodkin and her colleagues put the story of the rivers and the expanding and contracting ice sheets together. They flew over the Arctic's plains and mountains, photographed the terrain, then searched through acres of aerial photographs looking for interesting features. Then they flew in, walked the ground, took samples and dated them. She had spent every summer for the last fifteen years scouring the ground for evidence.

She and her colleagues had confirmed that the last round of glaciation started in the northeast about 70,000 years ago. The glacial maximum in the western Arctic, the time when the Laurentide ice sheet was at its largest there, was about 30,000 BP. At that time, "the whole northern interior plain is covered in ice right up to the Mackenzie Mountains." These mountains blocked off most of Alaska from the rest of the continent. There was a way through at McDougall Pass, which is near the Arctic Ocean, another through the Middle Peel River–Bonnet Plume Depression, and there was a continuous valley system down the center of the Rocky and Titina mountain trenches, from the Yukon to Kamloops. But these mountain valleys were chock-a-block with smaller glaciers and glacial lakes, making a trip down the trench hard to imagine. At the Laurentide's glacial maximum the ice stretched from the Keewatin all the way across the continent and lapped right up into the Franklin and Richardson mountains further north. The ice sheets flowed uphill.

As the Laurentide retracted, the Cordilleran valley glaciers grew and coalesced and then advanced down the mountains toward the plains. For a while, the two great ice masses actually joined each other. Duk-Rodkin's maps for this period show one large continuous gray ice zone across the mountains and right down over the whole interior of the continent.

"After 12,000 BP," Duk-Rodkin said, "they separate very fast.... At 11,000 BP there are glacial lakes all over. In the interior of the Yukon the ice remained in the valleys. There are geological data only. All I was able to see [of the evidence of man] was the pit houses [houses dug into the ground by ancient Arctic people] in the Arctic. [They are] totally recent. Along the corridor, there was not much to be found except for artifacts from the Tertiary Hills of the Mackenzie Mountains, material that was traded across the continental divide into the Yukon Territory."

Could one have walked through the mountains from Alaska to the south? Could people have walked across these glaciers?

"You can walk on it," she said, "but the lakes interrupt everywhere." These glacial melt lakes were bitterly cold, with practically no life in them. No one could have made their way south from Alaska without some means of crossing the lakes. In other words, in order for ancient people to have walked into the interior by this mountain route, they would have had to have reliable and portable boats, a technology that most proponents of the Bering Strait theory are unwilling to credit to the First Americans.

According to Duk-Rodkin's maps, people either came down into the continent before the glacial maximum of the Laurentide, i.e., before 30,000 years ago, or they didn't come down at all until after 11,000 BP.

I stared at the gray expanse, signifying ice, stretching across the maps on her desk. Since Antevs wrote about the possibility of an ice-free corridor it had been incorporated into wave after wave of anthropological theories about Asian migrations to America. Surely this idea of an ice-free corridor as the pathway for human entry into the Americas had been built on some geological evidence?

Not really, said Duk-Rodkin. While geologists had walked some of the ground, she and her team were the first to go over all of it systematically. She called in her colleague Don Lemmen to help explain their paper on the subject, which was published the same year as her work on the Mackenzie River. Lemmen was the lead author on it.[2]

A tall man in a sweatshirt and jeans, Lemmen perched on a stool as they walked me through the history of ideas they had dealt with. "The ice-free corridor theory," Duk-Rodkin began, "is based on the thought... that cordilleran ice never met the continental ice."

"Never" should have given people pause, of course. "Never" is a word lawyers encourage their clients to avoid. It's impossible to prove by inference (inference only piles up instances, it can't conclude), but it is easy to disprove (one piece of contrary evidence is all it takes). Nevertheless, the notion that the ice sheets never met was what led Antevs in 1937 to suggest there might have been an opening for early man to move over the Bering Strait land bridge and into the continent. There was some evidence to suggest that a corridor had been open between the ice sheets. As late as 1980, a senior glaciologist, Nat Rutter of the University of Alberta in Edmonton, had reviewed the evidence gathered to that point. He also concluded that the two ice systems had not actually met.

Lemmen explained that this misinterpretation had arisen from radiocarbon dates from places where glacial lakes had formed. These radiocarbon dates on plant remains seemed to say that at the height of the last glaciation there had been ice-free lakes, with plants in them, in the area of the corridor. The problem was that these plants had lived in lake water, and the lakes had been full of dead carbon that had leached into them from rocks. The plants sampled had incorporated this old carbon into their tissues: they had given falsely old radiocarbon dates.

Duk-Rodkin and her colleagues showed that the two ice sheets, growing at different rates and times, had repeatedly interacted. The continental ice reached the mountains and then withdrew, and then the mountain glaciers moved down into the plains where the continental ice remained.

"As it retreated, the Cordilleran advanced and met it. You have advancing glaciers in some parts of the world, and retreats in others. In Chile, the maximum advance [of the mountain glaciers] is 12,000 BP. Here the Cordilleran maximum advance is 22,000 BP."

The other evidence that led people to think that the ice fronts had never met was the absence of evidence. It had been assumed that any such a meeting would have left behind spectacular land formations clearly showing the fusion of the two ice sheets. "But it wasn't there," said Lemmen. "In fact, we've discovered that as the ice masses met, they flowed parallel with each other. Glaciers flow, that's how they move. With so much pressure the ice deforms, like a plastic." The evidence of this parallel flow could be seen by those who knew how to look. What Duk-Rodkin and Hughes found was evidence that the ice had transported rocks hundreds to thousands of kilometers away from the center of the Canadian Shield, where the ice domes had formed first, and then retreated, leaving these rocks behind. Similarly, the mountain sheet had also carried different rocks along with it.

Duk-Rodkin got out a slide that illustrated the result. It showed two moraines, all that was left of the two sheets sliding by each other, dropping a pulverized rocky trail under their skirts.

The fact was that not too much time had been spent looking in the north at where or when or how these ice fronts might have met. The bulk of the work on the ice sheets had been done in the U.S., in the lower forty-eight states. "Most of the diagnostic artifacts were sourced from areas from the American Midwest," said Lemmen.

The erroneous plant dates had convinced doubters that the corridor was open when it wasn't. The radiocarbon dates on animal remains told another story but that work wasn't gathered together until recently. Nat Rutter of the University of Alberta had done a review paper in 1996 that looked at all the radiocarbon dates gathered from animal bones found in Alberta—the southern end of the corridor. There was a gap in the record between 11,600 BP and 22,000 BP. No animals found had died in southern Alberta between those two dates. "The faunal remains match the nonexistence of the ice-free corridor," Lemmen explained, by which he meant that the bone dates confirmed that no animals had lived in southern Alberta during the period when their maps said it was covered by ice.

They pulled out more maps. One called "Paleogeography of the Mackenzie River Drainage Basin during the Last Deglaciation" had eight submaps centered on the area of the corridor,[3] representing the chronology of the ice fronts. From 30,000 to 25,000 BP the Laurentide ice stretched right up into the Mackenzie Mountains and right down into southern Alberta. Whatever drainage there was entered ice-dammed glacial lakes way up at Old Crow, or at Nahanni and Hughes lakes. At 21,000 BP there was a little more land and lake exposed at the northern Yukon border, and some water trickling out into the Arctic. At 13,000 BP, the ice still rode all the way into the Mackenzie Mountains and down beside the Rocky Mountains. At 11,500 BP, when the Clovis culture was in New Mexico, Texas and the southeast, the Mackenzie River and its mouth had just begun to form, draining the northern edge of the Laurentide ice into the Arctic. Glacial lakes pooled along the more southerly edges of the western reach of the Laurentide ice sheet. Five hundred years later, there was more open area, and the river had started to drain more of the Mackenzie Mountains. The whole stretch of the river valley did not appear until about 10,500 BP. By 10,000, the huge glacial lakes MacKenzie and McConnell had merged to form the inconceivably enormous Glacial Lake McConnell which covered half the Northwest Territories. By 8500 BP, as the ground bounced back up from the lessening weight of ice, this one lake system rapidly drained and become two smaller ones, Great Bear and Great Slave. The Mackenzie River, by then, stretched its current length, from Great Slave Lake to the Beaufort Sea. These maps made it absolutely clear why Duk-Rodkin had seen no marks of human passage through the

Mackenzie corridor. There wasn't a corridor useful to anyone without a boat until 10,000 BP.

All of this had been explained to the Provincial Museum when they called to consult on what they should say about the ice-free corridor in the new Syncrude Gallery of Aboriginal Culture. Both Lemmen and Duk-Rodkin flushed red when I explained what the curators had chosen to say. They couldn't understand it.

Maybe the curators looked at the work of others, which contradicted theirs, I suggested. Were they aware of any other geologists working on this area?

"There aren't any others," Duk-Rodkin said. "No one else has looked at this."

She was very annoyed. She pointed out photographs taken in the mountains which showed where the mountain ice had flowed out and where the ice of continental origin had flowed in. "I walked all that," she said. "You can see the Shield material, zero here, but it increases as you get to the edge. The ice is melting. The mountain ice pushes into the dead [Laurentide] ice." She had seen the telltale marks, the "loopy hummocky moraines," which mixed Shield with mountain material. She had checked the large boulders left behind by the departing ice from the south Mackenzie Mountains to Fort MacPherson near the Mackenzie Delta, a distance of 800 kilometers. "From 1985 to 1992 or 1993 I was doing surficial mapping—but in my mind a picture was forming. The first time I said to Owen, 'These two ice masses met each other—not at the same time,' he said, 'Oh, no, that can't be.' Then he said, 'Yes.' We looked for more clues."

She did this not only to satisfy curiosity or disprove a theory that had no basis in fact, but because she needed to know the true history of the land and drainage systems to aid those doing mineral exploration. Geologists often find minerals and heavy metals—diamonds, gold, silver—in old river deltas. She gave as an example Lac De Gras, a place where diamonds had been discovered. Diamond pipes up to sixty million years old are the source of the diamonds found recently in the Northwest Territories.

Indicator minerals that predict the presence of diamonds were found in the glacial sediments of the region. "Before, when exploration was going on, they looked for diamonds in the sediments of the Mackenzie River. They found zero of course. The river is new. They have to look east and look for the old tributaries that drained into Hudson Bay."

She'd reviewed all the literature, looked at aerial photos, then done three-dimensional computer modeling of how the ice moved. After that, she went in close to test if she was right. In 1985 she had evidence that the mountain and Laurentide ice sheets met, but she didn't publish until she had all the pieces of the puzzle neatly arrayed. As far as she and her colleagues were concerned, no people came that way until much later.

"A West Coast route is just so much more feasible," said Lemmen. "There's a lot of water and cold winds off ice sheets. There is some lag to a productive environment, probably on the order of hundreds to a thousand years. Look at southern Saskatchewan. We had spruce blasting through there at 10,200 BP. But the ice was gone at 13,000 BP. The trees took a long time to establish. You need to develop a soil. The soil is a biochemical process...."

And without soil, there aren't too many grasses, and without grasses there are few large mammals, so what would there be for early people to eat?

"That's right," said Lemmen.

As far as Alejandra Duk-Rodkin was concerned, the evidence showed that human beings moved up into the north from the south. "South America first," she said. The problem was, "How did early man get there?"

It's amazing how easy it is to find a path in a forest when old deadwood has been cleared away. The Mackenzie River did not drain to the north until after 11,500 BP. There was no Mackenzie Valley along the base of the Mackenzie Mountains until the Mackenzie River began to cut a path for itself there at about 12,000 BP. It was the fact of the two ice masses meeting that created the present path of the Mackenzie River, and its valley. Without the huge volume of water caused by the meltdown of the largest continental glaciation in more than a million years, the Mackenzie would likely have continued to flow to Hudson Bay. The river's present course is testimony to the nonexistence of any ice-free corridor at the right time for Clovis people to wind their way south. The mountains were choked with ice, and the plains surrounding the ice fronts were vast meltwater lakes until 10,000 BP.

Lemmen and Duk-Rodkin had not proved anything, but they had done something much more valuable: they had disproved the theory that there was an ice-free corridor open for human beings between 30,000 BP and 10,500 BP along the Mackenzie Valley. They had pulled another rotten strut out of the old construct.

So what were the alternatives? When Lemmen said he thought they might have followed the Pacific coast, Duk-Rodkin flashed a smile as bright as a hundred-watt light bulb and shook her head. She had reservations about that.

Had the surface along the coast been mapped the way she'd mapped and dated the marks of ice in the Northwest Territories? I asked.

Duk-Rodkin invited me to come back the next day. By then she'd have had a chance to track such maps down.

The next morning, when we walked into the library, Duk-Rodkin asked the young woman on duty for surficial maps showing where the Cordilleran glacier had run along the coast of British Columbia, as tracked by the geologists of the survey. While we waited for them to be pulled up, she explained to me that it was very difficult to do what she had done along the Mackenzie River, on the Pacific coast. She had walked over the ground and tested the surface after spotting interesting features from the air. But the Pacific coast presented many complexities for surficial geologists.

Much of the land that had been exposed by lower sea levels during the glacial maximum was now submerged. The sea level then
had been lower than it is now by more than 120 meters. As the ice
retreated, the meltwaters poured into the sea, which rose very
quickly: huge areas were inundated. Then land that had been
deeply depressed by the weight of the ice rebounded, actually
shooting up fifteen meters higher than it is now by about 9100
BP, and then subsiding after 5000 BP. Charting these changes
was extremely difficult. It was the careful mapping of the ground
that gave her insight into the history of the Mackenzie, the
patient, careful matching of samples to their origins on the earth.
She'd mapped half a million kilometers of Canada's northern
surface—an awesome feat.

The West Coast maps were produced. We spread them out.
They showed that at glacial maximum, the ice ran down the
mountains along the Pacific coast from Alaska to Washington
State, covering all the exposed shelf between the islands and the
mainland, and all the islands and the exposed shelf beyond them
until it dropped right into the sea. Between 18,000 and 13,000
BP the maps showed no ice-free land from the coast of Alaska to
Vancouver Island.

David Yesner, the Alaskan archaeologist, had sent me a paper
he'd given on what had been learned and inferred from various
Alaskan archaeological sites.[4] The earliest sites found along the
edge of the Alaskan peninsula and the southern Alaskan coast
were all younger than 10,000 BP and most sites dated to less than
6000 BP. The earliest sites in Alaska were in the interior mountain valleys along the Tanana River, areas that had warmed for a
time and provided a refuge for a range of animals such as bison,
elk, caribou and a myriad of migratory birds. The land bridge,
according to Yesner, was under water by 12,500 BP, yet these earliest interior mountain sites dated between 11,700 and 11,500
BP. And where would any earlier migrant moving south along the
Alaskan coast from Beringia have found a place to stop, eat, raise
a family? Timothy Heaton had reported in 1996 that he found

ancient bear bones in On Your Knees Cave and Devil's Canopy Cave on Prince of Wales Island, bones that dated back more than 35,000 years. One even dated to 17,565, just about the beginning of the Laurentide retreat and five thousand years after the Cordilleran maximum. Heaton's work showed that at least on this one island in the Alexander Archipelago, and at least for a time, there was refuge from the ice. He had pointed out that mtDNA studies of these bears suggested they had been long isolated from those which later populated the mainland, and that they seemed to be related to polar bears. Heaton had concluded that some parts of the Alexander Archipelago remained ice free.[5]

But these Geological Survey maps showed nothing ice free. Certainly these maps fitted well with what botanists had found. Botanists analyzing core samples dredged from the coastal shelves had said the environment of the now drowned coast was only sufficiently ice free to support human life after about 13,000 BP. Josenhans and Fedje, after dredging and studying with seismic reflection the drowned floor of Hecate Strait between the B.C. coast and the Queen Charlottes, had found rocks that looked like rough human tools in an undersea layer they dated to around 9150 BP.[6]

Well, I asked Duk-Rodkin, how much of this area was surficially mapped the way you mapped the Mackenzie corridor?

"Only the areas shown on the map surrounded by boxes," she said. She pointed to the only two such boxed areas on the map of British Columbia, near Prince Rupert (which is just south of the southern end of the Alexander Archipelago). The boxes covered only a small portion of the mountains to the coastline. In other words, the definitive geological work on the Pacific coast has not yet been done.

Duk-Rodkin insisted I come with her to the laboratory. It was a large room across the hall from her office, with many photographs, microscopes, sample cases. She wanted me to understand what a surficial geologist does, to show me what first led her to suspect that the accepted history of the Mackenzie River was wrong. The idea first occurred to her as she labored over the samples and reports found by others on the Hughes team. She had asked her colleagues what unique type of rock would be required to prove that the pre-Glacial drainage of the Peel river entered the Arctic Ocean, perpendicular to the modern Mackenzie River. Well, one said, you'd need rock that is only found at a site on the eastern side of the continent that could never have been found at the mouth of the Mackenzie if it had always flowed from south to north. Well, what would that be? she'd asked. Jasper, she was told.

So she went to the survey's archive to retrieve the samples of Mackenzie Delta sediment that had been gathered over the years by her colleagues.

She opened the first sample. "I couldn't believe it, there is this piece of jasper."

Similarly, when she was tracing out the history of the Yukon River, she'd plotted the weird terraces found at different elevations in the mountains and looked for materials that could only have been carried there by the Yukon River draining south, and by the edge of the ice. How else to explain the presence of these terraces at all? She thought they were the result of the outwash left by the growing and shrinking Cordilleran ice sheet and the Laurentide glaciation. The proof of this would be finding a Shield rock that had been left behind, something like argillite or chert, which occur only in the mountains on the north side of the Tintina Trench. She was sitting one day with her assistant out in the field, having lunch. There, right beside her was an anthill. In the mouth of the anthill she spied a telltale piece of argillite. She was so excited she screamed out loud. And because one of anything is not enough, she dug under the topsoil to search for more. She found argillite on every terrace she'd marked to search on her aerial maps, proving that the Laurentide ice had spread its fingers right up into the mountains themselves, and that the Yukon River had drained south in pre-Glacial times.

She and her colleagues had searched for and found cuts in the

mountains that laid out the history of the major periods of glaciation as they came and retreated over time. In a paper published in
1996, they detailed the most complete glacial record available
from the North American Cordillera. Five consecutive mountain
glaciations were revealed in a series of stratigraphic sections
they'd found in the foothills and canyons of the Mackenzie
Mountains, exposed by the meltwater of the Laurentide ice
sheet.[7] She hauled out for me samples of what she found as she
chipped away at ancient stone and formerly buried soils. Way
down near the bottom of the stratigraphic cut was a deep layer of
very ancient soil. The soil was made about 1.5 million years ago,
about the time *Homo erectus* lived in Africa.[8] It was so thick, it told
her that for a long time there was no continental glaciation at all.

She put a slide under a microscope for me. It carried some of
the life forms she'd found trapped in that soil. There were tiny,
perfect insects, beetle-like creatures with black, smooth cara-
paces. Another slide carried seeds so small they couldn't be seen
with the naked eye but looked lumpy and rounded, like walnuts,
when magnified. Then she focused the microscope on the vicious
jaws of a group of dust-mote-sized crustaceans. I went through
slide after slide, lost in these leavings of an ancient warm world
that had once flourished in the Arctic.

She did not believe that any early modern human beings came
this way at all, she said, while I feasted my eye on the geologists'
world view. Possibly *H. erectus* came when the sun shone and the
soil was warm. But not in the great long stretches when the ice
held dominion.

I left Duk-Rodkin's office with many more questions. If the
Pacific coast had not been mapped as thoroughly as the Mackenzie corridor, what about the Siberian side of the story? Had any
work been done there to determine whether human beings might
have been able to move into Beringia when the North American

ice sheets were at maximum? I had taken it for granted that when anthropologists said people hunting mammoths followed the beasts across the Beringian land bridge and into Alaska, they knew that Siberia was free of ice at the time.

Duk-Rodkin had taught me to assume nothing. When I thought about it, I realized I had not seen any citations in any papers that referred to ice sheets in Asia. On the other hand, Ted Goeble had mentioned the gap in the archaeological record in Siberia. And the oldest sites in Alaska were around 11,800 BP. In spite of David Yesner's attempts to show a line of descent from the tools found on the oldest Alaskan sites to southern Clovis sites (he was a student of Lynch's, he told me), the animal remains at the oldest level of the oldest site in Alaska were not mammoth but primarily migratory birds.[9] The Siberian archaeological record, according to Yesner, gradually diminished the farther east one moved. The oldest dates of the few sites found in eastern Siberia were between 13,000 and 11,000 BP (the period when the Pacific and the Arctic rose to cover over the land bridge); the best known site was more than 1,500 kilometers southwest of Beringia. On the Alaskan side, most of the mammoths were dead by 12,000 BP. Was it possible that the Siberian side of Beringia had been closed by ice too?

I called around and was directed to Nat Rutter at the University of Alberta in Edmonton. He explained he had been part of a group of scientists who gathered together in the early 1990s to work on global models of climate change. The International Geological Correlation Programme 253 (IGCP 253) had looked at the process of glaciation and deglaciation from a global perspective, trying to tie together ice chronologies from all over the planet. The findings of the first round of consultations and studies and reviews had been published in 1995 by *Quaternary International*. And sure enough, the papers made it clear that all was controversy, particularly the question of whether an ice sheet had covered eastern Siberia during the last glacial maximum as measured in Europe (18,000 BP, as distinct from the Laurentide maximum at 30,000 BP and the Cordilleran at 22,000 BP). This European glacial maximum was when Siberians were supposed to have trudged their way northeast to Beringia, following the trail of migrating mammoths.

The summary of the papers[10] noted that there were several theories about where glaciers ran in Asia and mostly they conflicted. In 1977, a Russian geologist named M.G. Grosswald had proposed that not only was there an ice sheet in Siberia, but that it had formed part of a huge ice system that ran all the way to the Kara Sea, an ice sheet so immense that it circled the whole Arctic. On the other hand, as the summary noted, others questioned whether an east Siberian ice sheet ever existed. There were similar arguments about whether there was a major ice sheet covering all of Tibet. The summary called for more field work to resolve issues.

One of the papers had been written by Andrei Velichko of the Institute of Geography of the Academy of Sciences in Moscow.[11] When I called him to ask what ground proofing had been done in Siberia since his paper was published, he said very little work had been organized after 1995. "You know our problems," he said mournfully over the phone. These were similar to the problems Duk-Rodkin and Lemmen had complained of, only worse—no money was being made available by the Russian government for scientists to do this work, and without money no one could run adequate studies in the field. Nevertheless, Velichko made no bones about his views. After 20,000 BP, he said, Siberia was "absolutely not covered by large sheets. [It was] free of glaciation. Only the mountain areas [had] glaciers."

There was a joint Canadian/Russian expedition to gather data in the Eastern Eurasian Arctic in 1994. Velichko believes it showed that the ice was absent from the eastern side of Siberia during most of the last glacial cycle of 70,000 years. However, this doesn't mean Siberia was a pleasant place during the time of glacial maximum in North America. The evidence suggests that the weather in northeastern Siberia was much more severe than it currently is. It was dry but bitterly cold, with summer lasting about one and a half months, and winter temperatures sinking below minus fifty Celsius. This dry cold is another reason, in Velichko's view, why people would have been able to migrate through Siberia to Beringia. If they wore fur, they would have been warm enough, and there would have been few ice barriers in their way.

But his physical evidence, as published with the rest of the project reports in 1995, came mainly from areas more than 1,500 kilometers to the west of Beringia. His paper focused on Novaya Zemlya, an island in the Kara Sea, 18,000 years ago, where he found there were small glacial caps; he said little about Beringia—the far eastern part of Siberia—other than to note that another scientist had asserted that the mountains of the Chuckchi Peninsula had very large glaciers "due to the Pacific influence." His eastern Siberian evidence seemed to have been generated mainly from his climate model. Nevertheless, the paper concluded that "the amount of data does not confirm the notion of the Panarctic ice cover during the Late Pleistocene. Local glacial systems prevailed over most of Northern Eurasia, the largest ice sheet was the Scandinavian. Ice sheet dimensions decreased steadily eastward, paralleling the regular increase in climate continentality which implied reduction of precipitation in that direction."

Nat Rutter had also looked at the problem of the Siberian ice, and his paper was more neutral than Velichko's.[12] Where Velichko saw no evidence to prove there was an ice sheet, Rutter saw no evidence to prove there wasn't one. Rutter carefully reviewed what little actual evidence from the ground there was, as well as the various theories of where the ice might have been. He was depressingly frank about what was known and what was not: "The debate among scientists centers on the timing and maximum extent of ice over northern Siberia and the Tibetan plateau ... few agree on the presence or absence of ice sheets."

The Siberian issues, as Rutter saw them, fell into two geographic categories. One was the controversy over what occurred in West Siberia, or Eurasia, an area that had been relatively well studied. The second concerned East Siberia toward the end of the Ice Age and the more "remote Laptev Sea area where few investigations have been made and only in the last few years." Rutter found very little published evidence against Grosswald's East Siberian ice sheet theory. The most compelling was the presence of reliably dated mammoth bones "from several sites including the New Siberian Islands that would have been covered by Grosswald's model."

With the Tibetan ice, the story was the same. One researcher favored the notion that the whole plateau was covered by ice. Others disagreed. Dating was either nonexistent or contradictory. However, those who once believed there was no ice sheet over Tibet were starting to consider it possible as more and more evidence was gathered on the ground.

"It ain't easy," Rutter said when I asked what had been learned since 1995. A lot has been done in Scandinavia and in Eurasia on how far the Scandinavian ice spread, but in Rutter's mind it's still an open question whether there was an ice sheet way up in the far east over the New Siberian Islands, as Grosswald suggested, or just a very severe climate in Siberia—cold, but open to man—as Velichko asserted. Rutter thinks the evidence is pointing away from the Grosswald theory. The Siberian mammoths are still the best lead scientists have: radiocarbon dates from the bones of extinct mammals at three sites in Siberia show they were alive between 15,000 and 20,000 BP. Mammoths, extinct everywhere else in the world, continued to live way up on Wrangel Island until 4,000 years ago.

If the sites found in Alaska were homes of the First Americans, and they came from Siberian Beringia to Alaskan Beringia to kill mammoths, they would have done a great deal better to turn around and go right back to Siberia. They certainly could not have headed south: Duk-Rodkin and her colleagues have slammed the ice-free corridor shut, and the coast was not a clear option either. The evidence regarding the existence or nonexistence of ice sheets in northeastern Siberia is just being gathered now. In sum, an ice-free Siberia at the time when people are supposed to have walked over the Beringian land bridge is just an idea, a speculation, a suggestion—nothing less, nothing more. A mountain of papers has been built upon it nonetheless.

Why would well-educated, careful, prudent men and women build their constructs on such a shaky foundation?

Tom Lynch put his finger squarely on the nature of the problem while, at the same time, exemplifying it perfectly. Writing in the Cornell University newsletter about the First Americans in 1993, he said:

> ... [we] know now that they crossed in the vicinity of the present Bering Strait, and that rather than seeing it as a migration, we should consider it an expansion of range of North Eurasian Upper Paleolithic hunters of large herding animals. This "northering" process is well documented in the archaeology of Europe and even Central Eurasia beginning about 15,000 years ago.... If all of this has been known vaguely for hundreds of years and with increasingly great certainty over the last fifty years, why have we seen recently a rash of claims that pre-Paleoindians were the true discoverers of America? Most of the claims have been frivolous, inconsistent, based on the flimsiest of evidence, and quickly disproven. Perhaps part of the answer has to do with the current passion for political correctness. In a reaction to our black legend of the past, some Americans, especially American academics, would prefer to create a "noble savage" rather than discover the true Indian past. It is well known that, at the end of the short Paleoindian florescence, American horses, mammoths, mastodons, giant sloths and other hunted animals suddenly

became extinct. . . . There are as many explanations as professors professing, but virtually all agree that American Indian predation had something—probably an important something—to do with it. If the coincidence of Indian entry and extinctions were not so close, perhaps postglacial climate change could shoulder all the blame. . . . We should not confound the agenda of the environmental movement with advocacy for Indian rights, lands, or philosophies. There is a real American Indian past, one that needs neither sanitizing nor invention. In the interests of truth and dignity, we should restore the American Indian "discovery" and correct the European "discovery," each having its less glorious episodes.[13]

In this article, Lynch displayed amazing certainty about all kinds of things that were not known. When he suggested that the First Americans contributed to the extinction of the major Ice Age animals, he confounded association with cause, a fundamental error in thinking. It was fascinating, too, how he equated the Native American discovery with the entry of Europeans in 1492, as if these were equivalent events instead of processes, as if Native Americans' slow extension of dominion over terrain empty of humankind was comparable to the Europeans' quick displacement and slaughter of long-established peoples. In Lynch's argument (although he would later vehemently deny it) the extinction of the mammoth and the giant sloth by the First Americans seemed to have the same moral weight as the killing of the Caribs and the Beothuks by Europeans. He seemed to be saying that the descendants of the First Americans are as culpable as the descendants of Europeans, since they probably killed all the great Ice Age animals in their greed, just as rapacious Europeans destroyed Native Americans.

But Lynch's basic insight was correct. The retrovirus that has infected every aspect of the accepted story of the First Americans is the politics of replacement. These politics decreed what must be true at the very beginning of European occupation; these politics created the climate for distorted observation, and squeezed out all the contradictions. Native Americans were needed as scapegoats to expiate the sins committed by the Europeans in despoiling them. So, while it was denied that the First Americans could have been technologically adept enough to build ocean-going boats or rafts, they were granted a fine genius for slaughter. The Beringian Walk theory is an artifact of these politics, which is one of the reasons why so many otherwise sensible people seem unable to let it go.

# 22

# Hard Science, Hardball Politics

## Kennewick Reevaluated

S TRONG STORIES sink their hooks into the human imagination. The fight over the right to study Kennewick seemed to have the American press mesmerized. It was like a fine Greek tragedy: everyone knew what the outcome would have to be, everyone had their fated parts to play and yet all waited anxiously for the last scene. The Clovis First/Bering Strait story was more like something from Homer, compelling because it was about heroic struggle. An ancient people had walked, resolute, into the biting teeth of Ice Age storms, over a land bridge at the top of the world, hard on the trail of the gigantic and dangerous mammoth. Armed with nothing but chipped stone points, which they threw from cleverly weighted staves of wood called atlatls, they had quickly dominated a whole hemisphere, laying waste all those gigantic Ice Age animals that lurked by the walls of melting ice. They were the first to enter, and though they were perhaps followed by other Asians who came later, they were human pioneers like no others, braver even than Norman Mailer's astronauts, who relied on the power of American know-how to fly first to the moon. These Clovis folk entered a new hemisphere relying on nothing but their own strength and their way with stone. If we could only find their remains we would know them as the noble savage's noble savage.

Even in the face of Dillehay's dates, Guidon's paintings and bones, Araújo's tropical hookworm eggs and Duk-Rodkin's demonstration that the two gigantic ice sheets met repeatedly, cutting off any possibility that Clovis folk walked from Beringia into the interior of the continent, the story still had allure. Even when a Manchester forensic anthropologist built a model of Luzia's face on the basis of a CT scan, and it came out looking African, it was hard to set the tale aside. The story's simplicity is its best selling point. In science, as in narratives of all kinds, the simplest explanation is considered most likely to be true.

Thus, when a frozen man was discovered at the base of a glacier in Tatshenshini-Alsek Park in northwestern British Columbia, in August 1999, there was a stir of hope. Finally, human remains had been found in the right place to prove the truth of the story. And there was flesh still on them, preserved by the ice. One could sense the gleeful I-told-you-sos fueling the rapid media response. The remains, suggested some stories, could be as much as 12,000 years old.[1]

I felt the excitement myself, a rising surge of that greed to know that had goaded me like a sharp mental stick ever since I sat down with William Finlayson in his office in London, Ontario. Even though I had no intellectual capital invested in the Clovis First story, I nevertheless found myself unnerved by those whose findings tore it apart. They propounded no single counter-story into which new findings could be made to fit. Were the first people in the Americas all one culture? Were they weavers and spinners who groomed the forest, or big game hunters who lived on a diet of meat? Dillehay put forward no claims. Dennis Stanford considered the Clovis technology akin to that of the Solutreans of France and Spain, but there was no Clovis culture in South America. Guidon spoke vaguely of boats crossing the Atlantic, but on the other hand, her colleague Evelyne Peyre had identified tooth remains (which turned out to be only 14,000 years old) as being midway between Neanderthals and modern humans—so who came across on those boats, modern humans or someone who became modern in America? The physical anthropologists pointed every which way; some said there was one expansion out of Africa, others thought many changes occurred in particular settings and were passed around through constant human intermingling. The geneticists spoke of American Adams and Eves with time frames that varied by tens of thousands of years and a point of origin conveniently on the boundary line between Europe and Asia. Compared to this complex discord, the Clovis story had a certain elegance, and more to the point, it was still believed by many serious scholars. Who was I to say which side was right, the conservatives or the proponents of new ideas? All those generations of men expert in flint knapping, and stratigraphy, and the weird workings of the earth, had been telling this story to each other for almost seventy years. Their main remaining argument—absence of evidence is not evidence of absence—was like a foot jammed into a mental door, keeping all options open. Maybe these remains found at Tatshenshini-Alsek Park were what they'd all been waiting for.

I was particularly taken by the illustrations of the artifacts found with the frozen man. They were published in several newspapers. There was a wonderful tight-woven cedar bark hat. There was an object said to be an atlatl. The remains themselves were covered in a fur robe, and there was a leather pouch that had carried fish. Unfortunately, like Gore Creek Man, the body was headless, so no one would be able to establish if this ancient person's skull resembled modern Polynesians or Europeans. A large, frozen moose was found nearby. This gave rise to the theory that the man might have fallen to his death in a confrontation with a big game animal.

The remains were spotted by a group of sheep hunters at the foot of a melting glacier about a thousand miles due north of Kennewick, Washington. The hunters hiked out of the park and reported the body to officials at the Beringia Center in

Whitehorse, who in turn reported it to the Yukon government's Heritage branch, whose officials notified the Champagne and Aishihik First Nations, whose officials flew to the site to view the remains themselves. By August 17 1999, the government of British Columbia had been informed and so had the RCMP. A team was put together to determine how this person had died.

Then the story of the find veered off the narrative line so familiar from the Kennewick affair. For one thing, the Native community, thought to be uniformly opposed to the destructive testing of human remains because of the spiritual implications, agreed that the remains should be studied. This story became both a demonstration of how democratic politics can serve competing interests, and a measuring stick of how far we have come from the racist physical anthropology of Aleš Hrdlička—from the grim demonstrations of power over the defeated through the collection and display and study of the bones of their dead.

Science is unseverable from politics and politics deals with power—who has it, who wants it, how it is organized. Science has often served authority better than truth. In this case, Native Canadians had the power of law on their side. The Tatshenshini-Alsek Park is close to Kluane National Park in the Yukon, and the Glacier Bay and Wrangell–St. Elias national parks in Alaska. It was created by the British Columbia government in 1993, and the four parks of the area were designated a World Heritage site by UNESCO in 1994. A co-management agreement between the province and the Champagne and Aishihik First Nations gave the Native community the sole responsibility for interpreting aboriginal history and traditional land use in the park. They had the sole power to decide what should be done about these remains, whether they should be immediately buried, or studied and buried at a later date. The Native community, whose spokespeople said that they themselves were relative newcomers to this region, agreed with the suggestion made by an archaeologist, a forensic anthropologist, a glaciologist and a conservator that the remains should be removed to the south. The elders thought they recognized some of the artifacts. The hat was of a type worn in the area until after European contact. There was a scraping tool tied to the wrist that looked familiar. They held a ceremony over the remains where they were found. The bones were named by the elders as Kwaday Dan Sinchi, or Long Ago Person Found. The remains were removed to Whitehorse, and from there to the Royal British Columbia Museum in Victoria, the same one that had given back the remains of the 8,500 BP Gore Creek skeleton. A member of the tribe accompanied the body.[2]

The provincial minister and the First Nations jointly announced that a team had been set up to oversee the various studies on the remains and artifacts, three members from the archaeology branch of the ministry, three from the First Nations. They intended to set up a research strategy in consultation with a scientific advisory group that would review all requests and invite many disciplines in—forensics, microbiology, DNA, paleobotany, palynology (pollen studies) and archaeology. There were oral histories that described this glaciated area as a travel route and the community wanted to know what could be learned.

Samples of the hat and the cloak and the moose were sent to Beta Analytic in Florida. At the end of September, the provincial minister in charge called yet another press conference to announce the results. The material in both hat and cloak had been "harvested" at about the same time, somewhere between 1415 and 1445 AD. The moose had died in the 1960s. "The 550 year estimate increases the significance of the find," said the press release. "Human remains in a frozen state dating to pre-contact times are extremely rare, as are the associated well-preserved artifacts made from organic materials."[3]

Well, not exactly. Remains of victims of human sacrifice, even better preserved and with the head attached, had recently been pulled out of a volcano's lip in Peru as glaciers retracted there too. And while all the stops were being pulled to get these relatively recent remains in British Columbia completely studied, fully preserved skin, flesh and even brain tissue were available from burials as much as 8,000 years old found at the Windover site in Florida. These had remained virtually unstudied by scholars outside the University of Florida since their discovery more than a decade earlier. The urgency of the need to know seemed to rise and fall with political winds. What political issues could be resolved by knowledge of early people in Florida?

The Kennewick case continued to ooze its way through the court, with the filing of one quarterly report after another, one plaintiff complaint after another. The U.S. Army and the Department of the Interior's National Park Service did not publish the experts' reports for many months, as I had predicted. Joe Powell and Jerome Rose had examined the bones, the geoarchaeologist Gary Huckleberry and a curator of the Burke Museum, Julie Stein, had studied the soils and compared them to the accretions on the bones, and a contract archaeologist, John L. Fagan, had studied the stone point embedded in the pelvis. They had been finished since April. On September 13, 1999, the plaintiffs went back to the court to ask that the U.S. government be required to state whether it would or would not allow them access to Kennewick Man. Surely three years was long enough, they said. The court, knowing that the government interpreted NAGPRA to mean that any remains older than five hundred years were Native American, and that it had still made no attempt to date the bones, ordered the government to answer the plaintiffs' questions no later than March 24, 2000. Three years after the first radiocarbon date spurred the army to remove the remains from Jim Chatters' lab, the U.S. government announced it would date the bones again to "adequately establish the chronological placement of the remains." Two samples of bone were extracted from the remains, subdivided to ensure unbiased results, and submitted to three radiocarbon laboratories for dating.[4] The government promised that the dates and its determination as to whether the remains were Native American would be finished by the middle of November. But one of the bone samples had insufficient collagen to get a date, and the other two samples produced dates that differed by thousands of years. They had to be done again. It was mid-October before the long-finished experts' reports were finally posted, as promised, on the Internet.

Cleone Hawkinson, president of Friends of America's Past, the nonprofit body associated with the plaintiffs' cause, believed that publication of the scientists' reports had been forced when the plaintiffs complained to the court that the Burke Museum was advertising a lecture series on the Kennewick remains, to begin on October 22, while the reports were still not public. The Burke had invited Joe Powell, and Frank McManamon of the National Park Service (NPS), to give talks. The NPS said that red ocher had been found on the bones, and that Kennewick Man had been ceremonially instead of accidentally buried. The Department of the Interior finally put the experts' reports up on its Web site just before the Kennewick show opened in Seattle.

Francis P. McManamon, the civil servant who oversaw the study process for the Department of Interior and the army, wrote an introductory chapter to the three reports. "By using scientific methods, techniques and interpretations as part of its efforts to resolve this difficult case, the DOI is attempting to demonstrate that NAGPRA is flexible enough to allow good science to go forward at the same time respecting the dignity and recognizing the importance of traditional tribal beliefs."[5]

It might have inspired confidence if McManamon had reported more accurately on the work done, and admitted consistently that the government wasn't even sure where the remains had been found. Instead he wrote, "the remains were found under the water, but close to the river terrace that contains Columbia Park in Kennewick, Washington. It is inferred that erosion caused by boat traffic and variation in pool levels behind

McNary Dam caused the terrace margin that originally contained the remains to 'calve' into the river edge. (Wakely et al. 1998:58). Water action then scattered the remains so that when they were discovered, they were incomplete, disarticulated and distributed over an area of 300 square feet or more, about 10 feet offshore and in about 18 inches of water (Nickens 1998)."

This summary left the erroneous impression that no remains had been found in the soil underneath the river, when in fact the skull itself had been stuck like a rock about twenty feet from shore in the river bottom. McManamon acknowledged that the first-hand documentation of the discovery had been gathered by unnamed others. He did not mention Chatters' name in the report but described his field efforts this way: "Existing first-hand documentation about the recovery actions, items and remains recovered, location of the recoveries, and initial examination of the remains consists of 13 pages of hand-written, difficult to interpret and incomplete field notes. There is no map of the recovery site showing, even approximately, where the various remains were recovered." (Chatters would later complain to me that contrary to McManamon's assertions, he also supplied the army with "sketches, measurements, X-rays, CT scans, a videotape, cast, and four rolls of photographs" and "produced a map," which appeared in his April 2000 article in *American Antiquity*.) Regardless of the dearth of information about where the bones were found, McManamon asserted the federal government's jurisdiction over all the remains, saying "the land where the remains were found is under the management of the U.S. Army Corps of Engineers." But the skull may well have been found in the jurisdiction of the state of Washington, and therefore outside the jurisdiction of the NAGPRA.[6]

McManamon's chapter did make clear that none of the studies done had been sufficient to establish the date at which the man died. This conclusion could have been reached three years earlier: there was no known burial site to date, and the stone point in the pelvis could not prove anything about the date of the man's death. He explained that the government had consulted with the tribes and agreed to hold off doing radiocarbon dating of the bones and other destructive tests until after it had completed these studies of the soil, the bones and the spear point in the pelvis, because the tribes were opposed to such testing. There was no logic to this explanation of the government's process at all: the tribes' interest in the bones seemed to have been established by the first radiocarbon date, which the government now insisted had to be confirmed to be considered a scientific fact. Yet it had been sufficient to cause the army to confiscate the bones, though, as McManamon acknowledged on the last page of his chapter, "If the remains prove to be as ancient as suggested by the radiocarbon date that was obtained on one bone fragment, it would not be possible for any relationship of lineal descent, as defined by NAGPRA, to be made." Translated, this meant the specific tribes involved might have no direct interest in the result. The radiocarbon dates had always been central to the issue: waiting three years to do them again was absurd from the point of view of science and law (but it was good politics).

McManamon's summary also misreported Powell and Rose's findings in particular. McManamon claimed they indicated "that the Kennewick remains are not very similar to any modern ('late Holocene') human populations, although the shape (of the skull) is most similar to Northern Asian populations (e.g. the Ainu)." That was a stretch. In fact, Powell's conclusions were quite different—Powell and Rose's report said Kennewick was unlike any modern human population, but most like modern South Asian or Pacific populations, a crucial difference from the point of view of the NAGPRA.

John Fagan, who studied the stone point found in the pelvis, described what he learned from inspection with a hand lens, X-ray and CT scan, an examination similar to the one done by

Chatters. He concluded that the point was two-sided, pressure-flaked basalt, that it was lanceolate in form, that it had a wide, rounded base and a tapering tip, with no evidence of notches or a stem, that it "resembles a Cascade point in shape and cross section"—but that it was impossible to see whether it was made as true Cascade points were. "The size, shape, raw material and presence of serrations are attributes common to, but not exclusive to, Cascade projectile points," Fagan wrote. "The combination of these attributes, even with the limited ability to see other more definitive characteristics of flake scar patterns, however, supports the identification of the artifact as a possible or probable Cascade projectile point...."[7] He also compared it to other collections and came to the conclusion that it was closest to a Cascade point made and used between seven and five thousand years ago. The point, he wrote, "entered the body from the right side of the back, and with enough force to embed the entire tip deeply in the right ilium. The extensive amount of bone that has grown around the stone point suggests that the point was in place for a considerable amount of time and was not the cause of death."

Huckleberry and Stein did the soil work. They could not take samples from the area that the remains had likely come from, because the Army Corps had moved heaven and earth, and even Washington, to bury it under tons of riprap, rock and planted bushes. Huckleberry and Stein were therefore unable to closely compare the two kinds of soils and accretions stuck to the bones with a soil profile from the presumed site. They could not show conclusively where the bones had come from. They could only conclude it was likely that the bones had come from the area Chatters had identified, and that some of the soil around there was about nine thousand years old. They added one interesting piece of information: a trace element—yttrium—was found in one of the types of sediment on Kennewick Man's skeleton.

The dark sediment from skeletal element A.I.17a (sample HUK-ICP14) has a high yttrium content, more than five times higher than any of the other samples. Yttrium is found in high-level radioactive waste as a byproduct of nuclear fission and although Columbia Park is downstream from the Hanford Nuclear Facility, it is unlikely that this is the source of the elevated yttrium content given the low concentration of other measured radiogenic elements. Also the yttrium content in the dark sediment, although high, is still at a level seen in natural geological materials (Charles Knaack, 1999, personal communication). The relatively high content does suggest, however, that the dark sediment is different from sediments in Lithostratigraphic Units I and II and that it adhered to the skeleton following erosion from the bank, an interpretation supported by the granulometric, TGA, and XRD data. Because Yttrium and other GroupIIB elements are commonly found in high gravity river and beach sands, it is possible that the dark sediment found on the exterior of post-cranial elements are modern beach sediments.[8]

Powell and Rose had examined the bones, made some corrections to Owsley's quickly rendered inventory, and agreed that they belonged to one male individual. Powell then made the craniofacial measurements, before and after reconstruction of the skull, and then compared these measurements to populations in various databases. Powell and Rose were a little kinder to Chatters than McManamon had been: they at least referred to him by name. Powell's reconstruction of the skull produced a sequence of measurements reasonably similar to those Chatters had made from his. The report said this new reconstruction was CT scanned in such a way that other researchers would be able to build a virtual version of the skull and, using computer lithography, create a very accurate plastic model (a suggestion Hawkinson later pooh-poohed).[9]

Contrary to Chatters' characterization of the teeth as sundadont, the report said that since they were studying only one person, it was impossible to assign the remains to either the sinodont or sundadont category since such designations are statistical creations. Any individual drawn from either population could exhibit all to none of the eight variables. The depression on the skull, which Chatters considered a fracture resulting from a blow, they said was obscure in origin but showed no evidence of breakage. Although they agreed there was some sort of lesion in the right collar bone, they saw no sign of the spreading, systemic infection that Chatters had said was a probable cause of death. Since the other clavicle also showed a small injury, they reasoned both were the result of a life of vigorous muscle use. (Paddling a heavy canoe? I asked Rose later. Hadn't considered that, he said.) They also saw no marks of any serious degenerative disease: whatever arthritis he had, particularly in his legs, was minor and caused no difficulty. This man, they said, had died at between forty-five and fifty years of age and had lived a rigorous life, making heavy use of his arms. Many years before his death he had broken two ribs and, possibly at the same time, a humerus (arm bone). The arm healed well and caused no difficulty. And as to the spear point in his pelvis, they concluded this injury had occurred when the man was a teenager, before he completed his full growth. It had caused no major damage. Of the original complete femurs, only a third of the right was with the remains, and only the top half of the left. Using modern Mongoloids as the basis for estimation and the more complete tibia bones rather than the pieces of the femurs, they calculated Kennewick Man stood about five feet nine or ten inches tall. (Chatters had used Mesoamericans and the femurs to estimate and came up with about 173 centimeters, or five feet eight.) They observed a "red ochre-like stain" on the shaft of the right tibia.

They believed the evidence of the bones fitted best with the theory that the remains eroded out of a grave and lay in shallow water for several weeks. The finding of an ocher-like stain on a few of the bones was in their view consistent with other early human burials, although they couldn't be sure it was intentional or even ocher.

When it came to the biological affinities they warned that it was not possible to prove by these means that Kennewick was a Native American related to living Native Americans. The best one could do was use the various databases to make comparisons, which might exclude Kennewick from modern Native American populations. This was interesting, given that Powell had argued in Columbus from the study of ancient and Archaic remains that he could conclude there was a continuum between the earliest Native Americans and those who followed later (while Neves had found a replacement). Such statistics were not sufficient to deal with this problem. As he now wrote, "only a time series analysis of populations from the Plateau region, extending from earliest occupation to the historic period, can provide a statistically valid means of assessing morphometric continuity of populations through time. Data for performing such an analysis are currently unavailable."

Powell and Rose did what they could. When compared with the modern populations measured by Howells, Kennewick—contrary to McManamon's assertions—came out close to none, but closest to "South Japan, the South Pacific Moriori, and then North American Arikara." Using another set of measures, Kennewick turned out to be "closest to South Pacific (Moriori, Easter Island) and the Ainu of Japan." But Kennewick wasn't like any group of people now living, and certainly not like any modern Native Americans. "No modern Native American group is included as a close neighbor in the least conservative approach, which strongly suggests that they bear no morphological resemblance to the Kennewick remains. Furthermore," Powell and Rose wrote, "while the inclusion of the Ainu as a nearest group could be interpreted as a possible 'Caucasoid' morphology for the Kennewick remains if one considers modern Ainu to be 'Caucasoids' (see Jantz and Owsley 1997) we view this as a reflection of the southern Asian/south Pacific morphology of the Kennewick skull given that most researchers tend to associate Ainu groups with earlier populations originating in southern Asia."

The Howells database contains only a few modern Native American groups. So they also compared Kennewick to a database created by T. Hanihara, which has a larger number of Native Americans. This database includes prehistoric groups from Oregon and Washington, Alaska and British Columbia, as well as many other North and South American populations. Thirteen variables were selected, which were measured the same way by both Howells and Hanihara. Again, even in this more extensive Native American context, Kennewick was closest to the Moriori, then to people from Papua New Guinea, then to a group from the Marquesas, and then a California population. When these measurements were geographically grouped, the closest regional groups included Polynesians and Northeast Asians, while the most distant were Africans, Europeans and prehistoric samples from Tennessee.

Powell and Rose took considerable pains to check for observer error and Powell was particularly concerned that their reconstruction of the skull might have been untrue to life. They noted that the differences between their reconstruction and Chatters' cast were statistically significant. Therefore they ran a series of comparisons using only those measurements of the skull that were not affected by either Chatters' or their own reconstruction. Even doing things this way, Kennewick came out unlike any modern group.

However, they did point out that when one did multivariate analysis of these same measurements, something interesting occurred:

One additional point to note is that with the non-reconstructed variables, two so-called 'Caucasoid' groups—Ainu and Zalavar—were indicated as most similar to Kennewick in multivariate space, while none of the American Indian samples were close to the Kennewick skeleton. This is not to say that the Kennewick remains are those of a 'Caucasoid' individual. It does, however, confirm the work of other researchers

(Steele and Powell 1992,1994; Jantz and Owsley 1997 in press) which indicate that early New World populations have some features shared by some modern Polynesian and European groups. The cranial nonmetric and dental data confirm the Polynesian morphology of the Kennewick skeleton, but do not suggest a morphological similarity of this individual to modern populations of Europe.

When only teeth were looked at, some similarity to ancient Native Americans emerged. The few dental features that could be measured showed the teeth were closest to populations buried in Dickson Mound in Ohio, followed by Europeans and South Asians. The discrete tooth and cranial traits could not easily be compared between an individual and populations, but they tried. The most probable group memberships for Kennewick came out sundadont.

Powell and Rose concluded that "The Kennewick skeleton can be excluded, on the basis of dental and cranial morphology, from recent American Indians. More importantly, it can be excluded (on the basis of typicality probabilities) from all late Holocene human groups." This was a terrible result for the U.S. government if it had hoped to show biological affinities between Kennewick and the coalition of tribes from Washington and Oregon, so as to justify repatriation of the bones to them for burial. However, it was in other ways the perfect political result. If the U.S. government got the court to agree that Native American under the NAGPRA means any human remain older than five hundred years, Kennewick would be defined as an unaffiliated Native American remain. That would leave the U.S. government in effective control of Kennewick Man. Repatriation, versus study by the plaintiffs, would be a political decision rather than a matter of law.

Funny that the local press covering the Kennewick affair didn't connect it with the other matter of deep concern to the U.S. Army in the vicinity. The *Tri-City Herald*, which covers Richland, Kennewick, Pasco and the surrounding district, assigned separate reporters to cover the Kennewick story and the plan to incinerate the Umatilla chemical depot's stockpile of nerve gas and mustard gas. Mike Lee wrote about Kennewick Man. Teresa Goffredo wrote about the depot. Both reporters' work was frequently posted on the paper's Web site so it was possible to follow both narrative streams and to note that although the stories involved many of the same actors, neither reporter put the two stories together (at least in print).

But the army's difficulties with the chemical depot explained a great deal about its behavior in the Kennewick affair. The U.S. Army has six installations in the continental U.S. where it stores lethal chemical weapons, including nerve gas. The Umatilla chemical depot holds 11.6 percent of the U.S. stockpile. These agents include the nerve gas GB, commonly known as sarin, and another called VX. They also include a blister agent, mustard gas. All had been stored inside earth-covered concrete "igloos" since the 1960s. The U.S. Congress had ordered the destruction of this entire chemical arsenal in 1986, to be complete by 1994. By 1988 the army had decided that on-site destruction was the safest and most environmentally responsible way to handle the problem. In 1989 it began the process of conducting a local environmental impact assessment and figuring out how to contract out the work. The first public meeting on the Umatilla chemical depot was held at the town of Hermiston, Oregon, in February 1989; the army did numerous reports and held public hearings as required by law over the next six years. It issued its revised draft environmental impact statement and went back for more public comment between December 1995 and March 1996.[10] It had already granted one contract to build such an incinerator, destroy the chemicals and armaments and then remove the incinerator, at Johnston Atoll in the South Pacific, to the engineers and constructors' unit of the Raytheon Demilitarization Company. There had been accidents there, though none had involved the release of nerve gas. The army had also tendered a similar contract to deal with a depot in Utah at the town of Tooele, and had another such storage site at Pine Bluff, Arkansas, less than sixty kilometers from Bill Clinton's former home at Little Rock.[11]

In February 1996, before the environmental impact process was complete, the army signed a contract with Raytheon to build an incinerator, destroy the dangerous and leaky armaments at the Umatilla chemical depot, and then take apart the incinerator, all for the sum of $567 million. The final environmental impact statement wasn't ready until June of 1996. The army may have believed that it had most of the communities nearby onside. Until 1996, when the Umatilla opened their casino, there was high unemployment in the small communities around the depot, and this facility would bring jobs to the area.

U.S. environmental law requires that the federal government be cautious about siting federal installations that could cause environmental problems in poor or minority communities, which might not have the wherewithal to complain or seek redress. The depot stored the same kinds of chemical agents the Israelis were forced to take shelter from in the 1990 Gulf War on Iraq. The emergency planning for a catastrophic leak was to "shelter in place." Eventually, households in the area were issued with some (but not all) of the same kinds of protection devices the Israelis had grown used to—duct tape to seal up the doors and windows of a protected room in the house, and scissors to cut the tape with. There were concerns about where people working at McNary Dam could go for cover in the event of an accident, and people farther away were worried about whether the army and Raytheon had worked out a proper early warning system. The worst-case accident scenarios were very grave—3,700 could be killed within a fifty-kilometer radius of the depot. The largest minority group in the area was Hispanic. But the impact radius also included portions of both the Yakama and Umatilla reservations, and some lands ceded by the Umatilla to the government in 1855 but still used by the Umatilla for traditional activities. The ceded land was within a fifty-kilometer radius of the depot.

During the public consultation process, the Umatilla and the Yakama had stated their concerns in a careful and reasonable way. The tribes' livelihood came mainly from the water and the land, and they had in the past shown themselves concerned enough about water quality and fish stocks to sue federal, state and county governments. The army must have seen that the tribes could cause considerable difficulty if they decided to go to the courts to prevent construction. The public review period for the final environmental impact assessment was to end on July 22, 1996, ten years after the whole process had begun, and one week before the Kennewick remains were found.

That Revised Final Environmental Impact Statement is a document well worth reading. It shows how much the army depended on the good will of the tribes in the area in order to proceed with the Umatilla chemical depot project in a timely fashion. It reproduced all the comments on previous statements by interested parties, including those of the Confederated Tribes of the Umatilla Indian Reservation (CTUIR). The Umatilla had gone through the various publications, processes, procedures and plans for this incinerator with a fine-tooth comb. The Umatilla's concerns, dated March 1996, filled thirty-six dense pages, under a cover letter telling the army its environmental impact statement, processes and plans were inadequate and politically unacceptable. The Umatilla maintained that the Umatilla, Cayuse and Walla Walla tribes, which make up their confederation, could trace their history on the Columbia Plateau "and surrounding regions of the inland Pacific Northwest ... back at least 13,000 years." They warned that unlike other U.S. government departments, the army had not yet recognized it must treat Native American authorities as sovereign powers. While the Umatilla did not directly threaten to derail the Umatilla chemical depot project, the letter made it clear that its trustees had passed a resolution calling for a moratorium on the incinerator until its conditions were met. Unless the army moved quickly to satisfy them, it would have one very unhappy sovereign government to deal with.

The army clearly got the message. Its revised statement devoted a chapter to Native Americans noting their economy, their concern for the environment, their concern that the plants and animals they use not be damaged. The revised statement took careful note that Native Americans on reserves are not like any other minority in the United States, that they are in fact sovereign governments.[12] "Under federal law, federally recognized Indian nations have sovereign status. Both the federal government and the tribal governments are responsible for maintaining government-to-government relationships," said the statement. In 1994, President Clinton set out orders as to how these government-to-government relations were to be conducted. Government agencies were required to consult tribes before taking actions that might affect them, consider tribal rights in drafting any plans, and remove any impediments that might get in the way of dealing directly with tribal governments on any issues that affected their lands or rights. On April 5, 1996, said the statement, "in the interests of establishing a formal government-to- government relationship, Mr. Gilbert F. Decker, Assistant Secretary of the Army for Research, Development and Acquisition for the United States Department of Defense, signed a letter of intent to negotiate a memorandum of agreement (MOA) with Donald G. Sampson, Chairman of the board of Trustees of the CTUIR."

The U.S. Army and the Umatilla were in the middle of this negotiation, with the army under the pressure of a tight deadline to incinerate the gases at the depot, when Kennewick Man's skull was pulled out of the Columbia River. These negotiations continued as Jim Chatters examined the remains, sent samples out to the University of California for radiocarbon dating, and reported the results. Having made, in writing, the claim that they traced their history in the region back 13,000 years, there was no way the Umatilla were going to fail to claim that Kennewick Man was their ancestor. Similarly, while trying to get the Umatilla to agree to let the Umatilla chemical depot project go forward, the army was not about to argue about old bones or allow them to be shipped to the Smithsonian, outside the army's control. The bones of Kennewick Man became a vital bargaining chip for both sides.

The memorandum of agreement between the U.S. Army and the Confederated Tribes of the Umatilla Indian Reservation was not signed until October 17, 1996, after the army had ordered the remains removed from Jim Chatters' lab, and after it formally announced to the world its intention to return the Kennewick remains to the coalition of the Umatilla, the Yakama, the Wanapum, the Colville and the Nez Percé for reburial.

It was hardly a simple commitment to multiculturalism that made the White House intervene to satisfy the demands of the tribes. In the first place, the treaties signed by the Umatilla and the Yakama in 1855 created a special relationship between the tribes and any president of the United States. In the second place, Congress had ratified, and the president had signed, an international chemical weapons convention requiring the U.S. to get rid of its chemical stockpile by 2004. Thus, the army had a great need to stall the plaintiffs' demands to study Kennewick until the incinerator was finished and the chemical incineration had begun. Everything the army did with regard to Kennewick was consistent with holding off the day when the plaintiffs would have to be answered, while pushing forward the incinerator's construction. Building began in 1998. The drop-dead date set by the court for the army to answer the plaintiffs was March 24, 2000. The army won more time by arguing that the radiocarbon dating had to be redone, and more time still by sending samples for mtDNA extraction by Frederika Kaestle, David Glenn Smith and Andrew Merriwether. The new drop-dead date was set back by the court to August 2000. None of the genetics specialists were able to extract mtDNA from the samples. Meanwhile the Umatilla incinerator's scheduled completion date was April

2000. Raytheon hired more than a hundred extra workers to keep things moving on schedule. In spite of a leak of unknown chemicals at the site, which the workers' union later claimed was sarin, resulting in the illness of thirty-four workers and the filing of a statement of claim, the construction barreled ahead. The court ordered the army to reply to the plaintiffs no later than September 24, 2000, right in the middle of the presidential election campaign.

Some scientists, including some of the Kennewick plaintiffs, were not too pleased with some of the things that Joe Powell and Jerome Rose said in their report on the remains. There was uneasiness about how anyone could conclude that the red stain on some bones was ocher (and therefore that the remains had been buried intentionally) without a chemical test. Their unhappiness circulated at Robson Bonnichsen's Clovis symposium at Sante Fe at the end of October 1999.

The Sante Fe conference was very well attended. Bonnichsen had thought that at most three hundred diehards would turn up. Instead, 1,400 people signed on to discuss what is known about the peopling of the Americas. The big dinner was a tribute to one of the retiring deans of the Clovis First epoch, C. Vance Haynes. Dennis Stanford was to be the speaker; the dinner tickets were much sought after. There were twenty scientific poster exhibits on peopling issues on display. Chatters put up one poster. The Friends of America's Past organization put up a scientific poster and a big display in the mezzanine devoted to the chronology of the Kennewick litigation. Cleone Hawkinson was interested to see there a Japanese journalist and a French camera crew who were making a two-hour special on the peopling of the Americas for French national television. The whole area, thanks to Kennewick, thanks to the geneticists, thanks to Stanford, Dillehay and MacNeish, was red hot.

I heard about the event after the fact, from a person I had spoken to several times in the course of gathering research. Powell was there too, my informant said, but he was not well.

Not well? I asked, thinking how unlikely that seemed. Powell had been lively and energetic in April, a young man full of confidence and making his reputation.

Brain cancer, my informant told me. Powell had been diagnosed around the time of his lecture at the Burke. There had been surgery after the conference at Santa Fe. He was working hard to get back the use of his left side.

I counted off the men and women I'd heard about in the last year who'd had terrible things happen to them after studying bones. I'd mentioned this to my informant the last time we'd spoken.

Yes, said my informant. I've been thinking of you.

# 23

# Going Home

## Burying the Bones, Treasuring the Past

I COULD NEVER QUITE explain to myself why I had to be in Saskatoon, Saskatchewan, for the first powwow of the season. There were lots I could have gone to in Ontario, there was even one out in New Brunswick at the Red Bank Reserve that I'd marked on my calendar. As I hauled myself aboard yet another bus I told myself I just wanted to see if the Plains powwows were as I remembered them, if the songs were the same, if the drums still stirred my feet in the dust the way they had when I was small. It was to be held at Wanuskewin, a new Native cultural-center-cum-museum on the north edge of the city, a place my parents had been talking about with the kind of relief that comes when one can see that finally, finally, a wrong is being made right. In order to justify this enterprise I had been trying to think of other things, besides the powwow, that I could cram into the trip. I was curious, for example, about what had been learned from Saskatchewan bones.

It was *beshert*, my mother would say later, which is Yiddish for "It was meant to be."

I knew that some human remains had been found in Saskatchewan: one group of burials associated with what was called the Oxbow culture had been dug up in the late 1970s at the Gray site. Oxbow culture was from the Archaic period. I wondered whether any older remains had ever been found: this was, after all, the southeast end of the no-longer-ice-free corridor. An official at the provincial Department of Heritage in Regina said every last human remain kept by the province at the museum or at the University of Saskatchewan in Saskatoon had been given back for reburial, so there was nothing for me to see. Those remains that could not be tied to any particular culture had been reburied in a central burial ground by the Saskatchewan Indian Cultural Center. Nothing really old, he said, had ever been found.

But if you didn't do radiocarbon dating, how do you know that? I asked, explaining about Spirit Cave and Kennewick Man, which the official had already heard of. Talk to Ernie Walker, he said.

Walker is an archaeologist and physical anthropologist at the University of Saskatchewan in Saskatoon. He agreed to meet me in his lab out at Wanuskewin the first day after the May long weekend. That was opening day of his archaeological field school, and the day before the powwow.

I got into town a few days early. I went straight to see my aunt, who was not well. She had already had her ninety-first birthday, but only the previous May she had danced at a big family party. She had been dressed perfectly in one of her finer sequined dresses, her wrists and fingers laden with significant jewellery. But she hadn't been out of her apartment all winter. In fact, my father said, warning me to control my face so that my shock at how she looked would not frighten her, she was dying.

It wasn't that I believed she'd live forever, just that I'd never imagined a life without her. I loved telling her my stories: I loved measuring my independence against hers. My aunt was a very successful businesswoman who'd dressed most of those who could afford it in the city and on the farms all around. She was my father's second oldest sister: they'd both been born in Canada after their parents came from Yekaterinaslav (now Dnepropetrovsk; then Russia, now Ukraine), to what was then called the Northwest. My grandfather arrived first in 1903, then my grandmother came with their two oldest children. They joined a colony of Jews who had been attracted to the Great Plains by the government of Canada. They came as part of a migration of a million East Europeans to live on grasslands that the buffalo and Native Americans had always used. Canada was so good to them, so cruel to the people they were brought in to replace. The buffalo had by then been virtually destroyed, purposely, by the U.S. Army and hired hunters. The Plains people were being starved into submission: the hope was that stripped of their mobile food supply, settled down on one piece of land, their old superstitions forcibly replaced with the Christian religion, they would eventually dissolve in the strong soup of European culture.

My grandfather was a much better blacksmith than farmer: within two years he had won a job on the Grand Trunk Railway, and after that set up a business in the tent city that was then Saskatoon. My aunt's life spanned the modern history of Saskatchewan from rebellious and uneasy frontier through the great North American socialist experiment to its current state of high-tech FrankenFood bustle. She'd been born in a dugout on the homestead, and now lay in a king-sized bed in a high-rise apartment near the South Saskatchewan River, with an urban view of the whole western side of town. In the same time frame, Native people had gone from dominance to a brutal poverty on the province's margins, and now to a new resurgence. For the first time in many years, Native people made up a sizeable proportion of the population of Saskatchewan.

She lay in her bed, her body barely humping up the covers. Someone was talking to her, the home-care woman I think. I saw her before she saw me. Her head was flat on its pillow. Her hair, gray, but still with a lot of black in it, spread out like a thick brush around her long and wrinkled ears. Her skin was pale as almond paste, and it had wasted loose from her bones. Her left eye seemed to have frozen in its place; it teared along the edge and had taken on a definite slant. Her right eye was the way it was supposed to be, but smaller somehow, shrunk back, beady and birdlike. Her cheekbones, which I'd never noticed before, were in stark relief—broad, high—and her nose, which had once been clothed in a nice layer of flesh, jutted forward like a broken stick. I couldn't help myself: I saw the bones of her skull first, not my aunt. Definitely Eastern European, I thought, wide-headed, high-browed, not at all like Luzia's delicate, narrow African skull, but actually quite a bit like the Plains people's skulls I'd seen in Washington. Death already owned its piece of her. Her face had no expression, like a house with no lights, no one at home.

She saw me at the door. Her hands and arms lay straight out on her gigantic flowered quilt. The puffy, pointed, long fingers that I always remembered first when I thought of her looked so small against the riotous fabric. Instead of being painted as they usually were in some Chinese scarlet, or plum red, her nails were pale and sad. Both hands came up in welcome and I could see her spirit flow back in from wherever it had been hiding, to take charge of her bones again.

"Oh, Elaine," she said, as if to exclaim, Do you see what has taken hold of me, do you see?

The Warman Road passed by a cemetery that had been swallowed by the city. It once resided in isolated splendor outside town, its long rows of headstones shaded majestically by the pines and willows. Now a spreading suburb of big houses had grown up on the opposite side of the road and it seemed to take a long time to get out of town. I could sense the South Saskatchewan River flowing away north and east on my right but I couldn't see it. The prairie ran out on all sides, ahead, around, beyond. The grass was a brilliant spring green, almost emerald with new juices, and everywhere in the shallow depressions there were lakes, the wind riffling their surfaces, which were the most amazing deep sapphire and amethyst. Tall yellowed stalks of last year's bulrushes grew up on the margins. The road curved off to join the highway to the northwest and Lake Waskesiu, but I didn't go that way. At the next corner, beside a huge whitecapped slough, there was a small sign that said Wanuskewin. I followed this road toward the river. I could just make out the top of a new building designed to look like the open peak of a teepee, but made of steel and glass. Then I passed two large gateposts in wood with bison carved on them, and the road curved in to a large parking lot. The building was a cross between a gigantic yurt and a teepee, more than twice the size of the Pyramid Lake Cultural Center at Nixon, Nevada. It was perched right at the edge of a cliff that ran down into a lower valley, with a commanding view of the river. Opamihaw Creek cut through the valley to the river's edge.

The wind whipped at my feet. I scurried across a walkway. Someone had made a series of buffalo sculptures in bronze. Two large ones walked, heads down, grazing on the stone walkway between small stone cairns, the kind used at Head-Smashed-In Buffalo Jump. Behind the two adults, another buffalo seemed to be pulling itself out of a sack or a rock that was attached to the earth, as if it was being born into its own death.

There was a high keening cry and drums, amplified, coming from somewhere. Off to the left of the entryway there was an outdoor amphitheater where people could sit on the poured concrete steps while young men and women demonstrated dances. The song danced my feet, heel and toe, through the glass entry. On the right there was a sign over closed double doors that said the Ernest G. Walker Archaeological Laboratory. Inside, as I walked through the second set of doors, there were two Native people taking tickets. I was supposed to meet someone with expertise on Native Canadian stories and oral history, but no one had seen him, so I wandered through the building instead. Right in front there was a corral, of the kind once used to trap buffalo when there was no suitable hill to run them off. Behind the corral, there was a canvas-covered teepee. At regular intervals during the day, people were shown how this efficient piece of prairie technology is made. Down the hall was a cafeteria with a golf club view of the river and the prairie on the other side. To the right, there was a large museum room. The storyteller never arrived. So I pulled out my notebook and got to work.

Along the entryway there was a series of black-and-white photographs that had been retrieved from the Saskatchewan Archives Board. They showed early European immigrants to Saskatchewan, standing by and on top of gigantic piles of buffalo bones. There were markets in the east for the hooves and the hides and the salted tongues. The bones were shipped out on the railroad; they were ground up and used to refine sugar, and for fertilizer. A researcher had discovered that one company, between 1884 and 1891, had bought up more than five million buffalo skeletons. Regina was the railhead and that's why its early nickname was Pile O'Bones.

I walked into the darkened exhibit hall, set up to simulate a night on the prairies in a Native encampment. On the wall there was a map, the ubiquitous museum map of the Americas, but there were interesting differences between this museum's view of the world and all the others I'd seen. The map had arrows that showed connections between the Subarctic, the Mississippi, the Gulf of Mexico and this spot, Wanuskewin, which was the center of the world. The gallery, said a placard, was set up to reflect the lifestyle on the northern Plains about 1,500 years ago. There was a series of founding stories, one for each of the founding ethnic/ language groups in Saskatchewan. The narratives were different. No curator tried to signify which was true. Not one of them mentioned anything about Asia or the Bering Strait. They all seemed to have a memory of the reconstruction of life after a Great Flood. This was the only museum I had walked through in more than a year that didn't proffer false certainties in the guise of a scientific narrative.

"The eagle saved one girl from the great flood and set her back on earth to found a great nation, Dakota," said one story.

These were the named nations: Dene, Nakota, Nehyawak, Dakota, Anishinabeg, the Blackfoot Confederacy (Sikska, Kainai, Pekuni), the Tsuu-T'ina and the Atsina. They represented the

Siouan, Algonqian and Athabascan language groups (usually said to represent different incursions from Asia). When Europeans arrived, some were allies, some were enemies. Their allegiances tied them into communities down the length and breadth of the continent, across to the eastern Woodlands north of Superior, down the Mississippi and across to the Great Basin.

The displays were of teepees, cured hides, pots, wickerware, and in one glass box, which was actually a window into the laboratory, there was a series of spear points and arrowheads arranged in a chronology. Clovis was there, but it wasn't first. There was a Sandia point too.

There were interactive stations with audio and video, where the viewer was asked which tree, which berry, would be best for a particular application, as in which tree would make the best teepee poles, which berry was good for treating a cough, where would it make sense to look for clay. A video in a room off the gallery described the history of archaeology in Saskatchewan. Wanuskewin had been built on this land which had nineteen known archaeological sites, some of them with more than fifteen levels of culture. Wanuskewin had been a kill site where buffalo were run over the cliffs or herded into corrals and butchered. The oldest material dated to around 6000 BP. They had found here obsidian flakes from the Rocky Mountains, pottery from the middle of the Missouri. And on this property there was a medicine wheel, one of fewer than a hundred known in all of North America.

I went out and walked the marked trails along the riverbank, which started behind the little outdoor auditorium where the music still wailed, but no one danced and no one waited. The trails dipped down the cliff and up the face of another on the other side of the swampy creek. There was a teepee set up at the first curve in the trail, and across from it a small garden of all the useful plants from around here—willow for weaving baskets and back rests, herbs, berries, grasses, all with their characteristics explained.

The trail dipped down below the wind, below the level prairie. Up above was a roiling sea of grass; below it was a willow world, leaves dappling the trail, branches tangling among the white puffs of flowering dogwood and juniper. Aspen rustled down by the swamp and the creek, and a sweet, fresh smell blew up my nose. There was no sight or sound of city, just trail grass, flowering bush, swaying trees and the silvery glint of water. The wind, the strong prairie wind I'd always loved because I could lean into it and it was strong enough to push back, had dropped to nothing. Grasshoppers jumped with every step, and a quick slither of garter snakes made their getaway. There was deer scat.

The sky had separated itself from all these goings-on below. My skin burned and prickled as the sun flashed in and out. There were clouds sliding over the landscape but they took no part in it, their bottoms flattened and dark, all making for the same point on the horizon. I lay in the grass watching them move with awesome speed, like a fish watching a flotilla maneuver above. It was cold up there where they were, and too bright, but warm down here, hidden and cozy, below the level of the prairie.

I looked for the medicine wheel. My map said it was at the very end of the sequence of trails. I walked past a cleft in a grassy hill, littered with great limestone rocks, which was where buffalo had once been corralled. There was a plastic tarp laid over a square patch of earth near the bottom of the hill. It was held down with heavy beams of wood. I walked up the steep slope and emerged on top of the prairie. The wind threw up a veil of dust, the grass was rich and thick on either side of the path. I leaned into the wind and followed the path to a point of land that gave a truly commanding view of the whole river valley. One could see to where the earth curved, hundreds of miles in a great circle. There was a circle fencing something off, and a perimeter walkway. The sign at a circle of stones laid near the edge of the cliff said it was the "Sunburn tipi ring." The plaque read: "For many plains people the circle has a special meaning from the circle of the tipi to the circle of the prairie sky. Life is seen as a circle from childhood to old age, returning to the earth, which brings forth new children. It is for this reason that children and elders grew closer together as they shared in the life of the camp."

The grass covered over entirely the rocks that formed the medicine wheel. All I could see of it was the large rock at its center. There was another plaque showing the shape of this wheel and the shape of one other, for comparison. The pictures were vertical, as they would appear if painted on a wall. They reminded me of some of the strange radiating circles I'd seen painted on the rocks in Brazil, the images that Guidon and her colleagues thought represented suns, but villagers consulted said were the pathways to the village square.

The plaque read:

Of the 70 or more medicine wheels found across the plains, no two are identical. Some have single rings, others double. Some have spokes numbering from three to 28. Many mark star formations. Few medicine wheels are symmetrical but there is an unexpected geometry to the rings. Some are geometrically perfect designs formed by drawing intersecting arcs.

Two other mysteries remain. Two wheels, one in Moose Mountain, Saskatchewan, and another 700 kilometers away in the Bighorn Mountains in Wyoming differ in shape and size. Yet their cairns are identically aligned and oriented to the stars.

Majorville site wheel may have been built at least 5000 BP, 1000 years before Stonehenge, 500 years before the first pyramids.

I looked out over the wheel buried in the grass. Who could say why it was here, just here? Was it a form of art, a way to communicate, another way of telling the news of a people, like those paintings in the south? There was a spectacular view of the river and the prairie. There were large rocks scattered here and there in the grass. Though I had never been out to this spot before, I felt as if I had.

I looked around, trying to put my finger on this sense of familiarity, why this place seemed to fit into a pattern I recognized. I could see the trail like a pale ribbon up the hill across the creek, and I could see the path I'd taken through the green, green grass. The clouds thundered silently overhead, leaving a space for the sun to burn down. Something about the color of the grass and the sky brought other places back in a rush. I was standing on the edge of the desert near Pendejo Cave, I was lost among the nude hills along the ribbon road to Santana do Riacho, I was standing on the red earth plain of Piaui, near Pedra Furada.

My aunt was on my mind while I waited for Ernie Walker to arrive for his class. I busied myself by looking at the stone points and pots set out for students in the large lab. I counted sixteen students waiting in their jeans and sneakers and with their backpacks at the lab tables. There were fifteen young women, only one young man. The pots set out on a counter were dark but well made, almost Iroquoian in style. A placard named the culture as Mortlach.

How interesting, I thought, to stand here as an adult, with a newly learned sense of the complexity and continuities of American prehistory. There was a very large molar of a mammoth set out, and a tusk. My eye kept returning to the pottery. I realized I was surprised to see it: somewhere, since childhood, I'd harbored the ridiculous idea that Plains people did not make pots. Why didn't I know any of the names of the archaeological sites postered on the walls in this room? There was a sign describing the Heron-Eden site, a Paleo-Indian bison processing site outside of town near the Great Sand Hills. I used to go there for Hebrew school picnics when I was a child. There was something about the hills being the remnant of Glacial Lake Saskatoon, a concept new to me. The radiocarbon dates from that site said people were there from 8150 to 10,210 years BP, almost as early as the first site in Alberta.

Ernie Walker stalked in through the lab's back door. He wore blue jeans, a thick leather belt, a short-sleeved shirt. He had rawhide gloves in his belt, and a cell phone. He carried a white Stetson in his hands. He walked tall on cowboy boots, but when he came closer, it was clear he was small; not so small as Chatters, but not much bigger, and slope-shouldered like a bull rider. There was a thickened red scar over his nose. Grizzled gray-brown hair cut short all over. Blue eyes. A pint-size Marlborough Man.

He shooed the class off to the archaeological site they were going to open that morning, under the careful eye of one of his MA students. I could see he was still curious and uncertain about why I'd come. Who had I talked to, he'd asked on the phone, and when I told him, he said, "Well, those are the heavyweights," as if there was no need, then, for me to see the likes of him. He was modest, and had the Saskatchewan habit of seeing himself as an unimportant person living on the edge of things, when in fact, as he would make clear himself, he was dead center.

He began to tell me about how long archaeology had been done in Saskatchewan.

"Relatively recent," he said. Way back in the 1930s there'd been something called the Saskatoon Archaeological Society, which, he said, was one of North America's oldest. It was set up at the University of Saskatchewan by a geologist and a chemist—the chemist was the former president of the university, John Spinks, a man my parents used to speak of with great respect. I could see his grand stone house from my living-room window as I grew up.

"They used to come here," he said, waving his arm to indicate Wanuskewin, "in the thirties, for Sunday afternoon soirées. They came up to the medicine wheel."

You mean you could see it then? I asked.

"In their day, until recently, it was not overgrown. It was grazing land."

Amazing, I thought. And faintly appalling. By the late 1930s the amateurs of Minas Gerais had been hard at their work for years. It was unnerving to think of Saskatchewan as a backwater, even farther from the academic center than Minas Gerais, but it made sense, considering my family had lived in a sod hut only thirty years before that. Until the middle 1950s, the amateurs reigned supreme in Saskatchewan, by which time they were being elbowed aside in Brazil. The Museum of Natural History opened in Regina in 1955, only two years before I went to see it with my public school class.

A department of anthropology and archaeology was set up at the University of Saskatchewan in 1964. It was part of the sociology department and stayed that way for four years. Very few sites were found in the province older than 6000 BP, although individual spear points in the Agate Basin, Cody and even Clovis styles were picked up on the surface. In 1975, Zenon Pohorecky, a professor at Saskatchewan (who had a theory that ancient people had been in Saskatchewan about 37,000 BP) did a test dig out at Wanuskewin. Artifacts had begun to wash out of the creek mouth, but that was long before this area was known as a buffalo jump kill site. Things speeded up with the development of heritage legislation and contract archaeology, the same sort of system that prevailed in Ontario and throughout the U.S., but that didn't happen until the early 1980s. By then, Walker was already digging here.

He had worked on this land as a student at University of Saskatchewan. He did his doctorate at the University of Texas at Austin (where he met Tom Dillehay). When he came back to Saskatchewan the landowner allowed him to wander freely. "It was private at the time. He let me roam. There was no place I didn't find material. It was all over the place. In 1980 he wanted to retire. He asked me to help sell his land to someone who would take care of it. A private developer wanted to buy it. The city wanted to use the creek as a storm sewer. We got a good part

of the property purchased by the Meewasin Valley Authority."
(This is the provincial agency that manages the watershed along
both sides of the South Saskatchewan River in Saskatoon and has
been slowly restoring the native vegetation that was destroyed by
development.)

"We realized the only way to save it was to develop it. So
[there was] the idea of a heritage park." He was thinking they
could do something like Reeves and his colleagues at the University of Calgary had organized at Head-Smashed-In Buffalo
Jump. It took ten years of fundraising.

There was no government money to be had so he and a few
others who'd "caught the vision" set up a nonprofit organization
called Wanuskewin Heritage Incorporated. At first there was a
lot of suspicion from the Native communities. It took years and
years to build up interest; he was repeatedly asked, why should we
help the city white guys? In the end, half the money came from
private sources, the rest in grants from the city and the province.
"This is not a federal park," Walker said proudly. "It's a stand-
alone corporation. It's unique. Wanuskewin Heritage Incorporated owns the property. We wanted to change direction if we
had to, we had to employ First Nations people as best we could. It
works. We call it a bicultural approach, that's the success. The
Navajo, the Haida, the Mi'q-mak people from the Red Bank
reserve in New Brunswick came here asking, how did you do it?
To this day I travel all over, talking of the Wanuskewin model.
But this is the Saskatchewan way.... Most people just do it...if
we'd waited for government money, we still wouldn't have it."

Wanuskewin's money now comes mostly from the gate. And
what did bicultural mean? It meant he, a non-Native scientist,
sat with Native elders on the board of the nonprofit corporation
that owns and runs the place. It meant every single event, every
archaeological dig on the site had to be cleared with the elders
first. He had read personally to the elders every word of what was
written on the plaques throughout the museum and the trails to
make sure they agreed.

Ah, I said. That explains why there are no Bering Strait and Asian references.

"You see the origin stories of all the groups in Saskatchewan," he said. But he was defensive about this, as if he thought I was saying that by avoiding the Bering Strait explanation of Native origins, he was operating this museum on the basis of Native faith instead of hard-headed science.

I explained that I had come to the conclusion the Bering Strait entry theory was not credible. He looked at me oddly, as if he wasn't sure just what he was dealing with here, an irresponsible journalist, or just a kook. "We do talk Bering Strait in lectures," he said. "The interpretative staff knows both stories. I tell them of the scientific explanation for the peopling of the New World.... We once had a time line—you know, Egypt, the Pyramids. We took it out. It was comparing the northern Plains with the Old World stuff. Who needs it? ... Yeah, we are open-minded enough that you hear and see bicultural approaches. They're not in conflict. But a First Nation guide will tell you their teachings, and as an archaeologist I will talk about the scientific explanation, including the so-called ice-free corridor."

He had been working on the sites here for more than twenty years, he said, and then, looking at me sideways, as if he expected me to interject or accuse, "No," he said. "I haven't gone Native."

That had never entered my mind. But it was clearly on the top of his. He kept saying that the two world views were not in conflict, but then he described his work here as a taffy pull, as if he were constantly stretched out between two poles of meaning. But there was no mistaking what he wanted me to understand: if push came to shove, science would rule. "This is a university lab. We do science here."

Biculturalism had not been easy. There were all kinds of tensions when Wanuskewin first opened, only two years after the crisis at Oka. But he believed that from the opening day, Wanuskewin had begun doing its job: to educate, build bridges and learn. He remembered with great pride a man who came up to him after touring the building with a Native elder, to say that he was forty-eight years old, had lived in Saskatchewan all his life and had never before spoken to a Native Canadian. The archaeology was not a problem. In fact, it had become useful to the Native communities. In 1993, Native gaming was a big issue in Saskatchewan. "The Bear Claw Casino was raided by the RCMP. That summer we found gaming pieces in a dig. Became part of their legal battle to defend the casino, and we won. The courts said gaming is part of treaty rights. It's been used to defend illegal hunting cases. This lab was originally taken off the development plans. There was not enough money. The elders wanted it built. [They said archaeology] was like turning the pages of a history book, so put it back on. The elders played a role. We're trying to do things differently."

There are lots of sites in Saskatchewan, but Wanuskewin is unique in its long chronology. Walker likes to think of it as a northern Plains version of Santa Fe. He thinks it can draw people from all over the continent. He'd had to fight to get support from certain councilors at city hall who just didn't get it. One said at a meeting, "Who wants to go and see a few old bones and buffalo chips?" and Walker snapped back, "If I wanted to see that I'd come right to city hall."

"People wanted to develop a huge aquarium in Saskatoon," he said to me, rolling his eyes. "Give me a break."

Was there a distribution pattern to the sites found in Saskatchewan? I asked, thinking of Barney Reeves and his certainty that people had come first from the southeast into northern Alberta, not the other way around. Walker hadn't noticed any. There was a site where a conch shell with holes drilled in it had been found—something that smacked to him of Hopewellian influence reaching all this way, but he couldn't say there was a south-to-north distribution of sites. Saskatoon was full of sites, but they all related to the way the postglacial Saskatchewan River had developed. First, this was all a glacial lake at about 12,000 BP, then as the ice continued to melt away the lake was reduced to a braided series of interconnected rivulets, and finally the rivulets had come together as the Saskatchewan, which had started to cut its current course about 7,500 BP, at the same time as the whole Plains entered a terrific dry spell. Heat and drought hit here at about the same time as in Pedra Furada, the same time as Walter Neves saw evidence of a population replacement in Brazil. This dry heat had lasted for about two thousand years. It was not arid everywhere at the same time, but it was on average two degrees centigrade warmer—the grasslands then stretched all the way up north of Buffalo Narrows. The sites found from that period followed the edge of the river. Walker thought it was possible that people moved up out of the south to get away from even more brutal heat—that had happened in the Dirty Thirties, when people came north out of dust bowls like Nebraska. The river was the key to the sites of that period.

He went off to talk to the elders. He was gone a long time. I stared at the walls. There was a clipping about Scotty MacNeish and how his finds at Pendejo Cave blew "the lid off the Bering Strait theory." There was a map of Saskatchewan marked with sites. Walker might not see a distribution pattern, but as I looked at them I began to think I did. The bulk of them were in the south central part of the province, and they petered out to the north.

Walker came back, and we jumped into his truck to bump across the prairie to the site his students were opening. It was the area covered by plastic I'd seen on my walk. They were scalping it, pulling back the grass cover to get at the soil below. There was a large tripod and a mesh screen. The students sat on the ground with trowels in their hands, sawing and pulling at the tough sod. They could have used one of my grandfather's hand-beaten iron plows.

I watched Walker move decisively among them. He'd told me on the way over that instead of going right away to examine some "floaters," bodies that the RCMP had found in the water and wanted his opinion on, he intended to serve instead at a sweat the elders were holding to prepare for the powwow tomorrow. They were holding one in a secluded area around here. The elders were practicing their religion. "The park plays a role for traditional practices" he'd said, looking straight ahead as he drove, as if he wasn't certain how I would take this. And as to his participation, he acted as a server, bringing in the hot rocks to them, which was, he said, the first step to becoming an elder.

Did he have more than an academic's interest in these things?

Well, he said, it had started out, this business of serving, as a way to show respect. "Haven't gone Native," he said firmly, as if to remind himself. "I've been accused of that before.

"It's a purification," he continued. "It's religious in nature. It's a humbling, [it requires] a certain humility. It's physically demanding. Hot. Totally dark. I used to do it to make a bridge. Now I do it because I like it. They are my friends. This morning I met with elders. One introduced a new elder. He said this *monias* [white man] is unlike the others. When he serves us he's really quick.... It's an honor to serve—just doing that. A traditional elder in Saskatchewan [spends] many years of serving other elders, learning traditional songs. You get a pipe eventually, but it's a long, long apprenticeship. Usually an elder will take some-one under his wing. More often than not, it's not a relative. The function is to lead ceremonies. Most are not healers. Pipe car-riers, blessings, sun dances, conducting sweats, it's like a priest in a way."

So this business of serving at the sweats had evolved into something more than an outward show. I watched him as he swung an axe handle out of the truck and began to parse the site with his graduate student, trying to figure out how to work a new grid pattern around the original test square he'd dug here back in 1982. Yes, I thought, he is a biculturalist in every way, a man stretched between his belief in science and his growing interest in other less quantifiable forms of reality, caught between his duties as a forensic anthropologist and his interest in the ways of people who frown on that sort of thing. At the same time that he was growing more deeply involved in a Native religious society, he was trying hard to serve his best students by having the archaeology program recognized as a degree in natural science. He thought the new biological sciences applied to archaeology were way too complex for arts students to manage. They couldn't get into the advanced courses on DNA and isotope work that they needed. He was tired of losing his best graduate students to science disciplines.

The discipline of anthropology is cutting itself in two; on the one hand, science, on the other, culture. "It's happening all over North America," he said.

Walker conferred with his graduate student. The elders, he told the others, when he'd given his orders, would be sending someone down later to do a sweetgrass ceremony.

I sat and watched my aunt as she lay motionless in her big bed. She had not eaten in a long time. She wouldn't take more than a sip of water. It was too difficult—the straw did not bend and it was hard work even to allow herself to be lifted. I'd said the day before that I'd get her proper straws. I'd offered her treats of everything I could think of. Soup? No good. Fruit? Too sour. Candy? Too sweet. Finally I hit upon what seemed to me a stroke of genius. How about black licorice, I said. A pipe?

Oh, that would be good, she crooned. Her voice had all its usual vigor and if I closed my eyes and merely listened to her, I could see her as she'd always been. Then she clamped her jaws down tight as if talking was also no good. I buffed her nails, but I didn't think she had the patience to have me put polish on them. I contented myself with brushing her hair and trying to maneuver her gently, gently, into a more upright position on a pillow made to resemble an armchair, which reminded me of the woven willow backrests out at Wanuskewin. She allowed me to serve her in this way, the way my favorite cat had once suffered all the pet beds I'd contrived for her. My aunt was being kind: she wanted me to get used to the idea that she could not move herself, that her body hung on her now like a very old dress, heavy enough to trap her helplessly. I was more than a half a foot taller, and much stronger, but I couldn't lift her without help, although her bones felt so small and frail I thought my hug would break her.

I went out shopping for the licorice and the bent straws. I went from store to store on the way to Wanuskewin and on the way back. It was as if bent straws were the best-kept secret in the world; no one but me and my aunt had ever heard of such a thing, and as to licorice pipes, well, not on your life, they went out with the Great Flood. The best substitute I could find was black Twizzlers. The paper bag full of long black twisted licorice now sat beside her bed. She had done a masterly job of faking enthusiasm: she had taken one tiny bite and pretended to chew and to swallow.

She slept. A neighbor came into the living room, a woman I hadn't met before. She had been here the previous night and said that my aunt had been upright and panicky, repeating over and over that she couldn't get out. No one said it, but I knew what this meant: any day now she would break free of her prison. She was waiting for something or someone.

He came the next day. Her oldest nephew, my cousin, her executor. He talked himself hoarse, he said later, because she couldn't talk at all. The call came that night, actually early the next morning, while the light of the sun hovered below the horizon, and the world was split between darkness and light. She found her way out at last.

We went over right away, me, my parents. We had to be there, I wasn't sure why. Something to do with the body not being left alone. It was hard for my parents to face the fact of her death. This was when my mother started to say the word *beshert*, over and over.

I walked into my aunt's bedroom because the home-care people seemed to think that was what needed to be done. Don't you want to say goodbye? said their glances. She lay there in her bed, and her face looked almost as it had the day before, except that someone had shut her eyes and they were sunk down deep in their orbits. Her skin was no longer the tint and texture of almond paste; now it was waxy and without a hint of color, as if it had undergone a change of state, from flesh to something different. I could see that she was out, that her body held her no longer. It wasn't just that she no longer breathed, and the bedclothes no longer rose and fell. It was that whatever it was that had animated her, that had made her my aunt, was utterly not there—it was still in the room somewhere, but not in those covered bones on the bed.

And this, of course, was when I understood completely, from the inside, the nature of the biculturalism afflicting Ernie Walker and every other person of science who deals with the remains of a human life. The animating spirit that made my aunt herself was no longer in charge of her flesh and bones. It had withdrawn, dissipated, dispersed, been replaced. There were no scientific words to describe a truth as plain as the nose on her face. I could try and match the facts to some suitably white-coated and clinical phrase, but that kind of language can't define and measure death. She was dead, a state of nonbeing, but death is also a continuing process that would go on breaking down her blood and bones and tissues for an unknown period of time. I could call that which no longer animated her an organizing principle, or I could say it was a chaotic attractor that had kept all her electrochemical systems in a certain domain. But that was a very poor sort of observation. So what words were left to me to describe what had happened and was happening to my aunt? I could pin these facts on a line among the phrases of the romantics, or the Native pipe carriers, and say that her bones were becoming separate from something more complex and particular, from her spirit, or her soul.

And where exactly was that? And what memory of this chaotic attractor or spirit or soul would reside in her bones until they were no more? Doug Owsley, who measured people's bones, turned their skulls in his hands and stared at them all day long in boxes on his shelves, would think the question ridiculous. But the geneticists, like Merriwether and Frederika Kaestle, had shown that some of the message that made her what she was, that proved her relationship to me, would reside in her bones until they were gone too, and even then, fragments of her message would still be there, broken down and mixed with the soil.

The funeral people came with their gurney and their body bag and took her away.

Later that day, the sun blazed over the prairie and a stiff wind pushed the car in gusts so strong I thought I'd slide off the road. There were big buses full of schoolchildren pulled up in front of Wanuskewin's front door, but they were missing the real action, which was way down past the medicine wheel, out on the prairie. There was a double line of cars parked like horses, noses towards a fence as if at water troughs. The road marked the edge of the farmer's field and Wanuskewin's boundary line. Only two days before there had been nothing but grass, now someone had put up a teepee, a very large white tent, and a circular arbor made of double rows of pine posts with a screen mesh above, overlaid with pine boughs. There were even temporary bleachers.

I had been up since 4:30 in the morning. The whole day had taken on a faintly dreamlike quality: I wasn't sure who moved my feet or turned the wheel of the car. The sound of the drums and the keen of singers attacked and retreated on a rioting wind. I parked and made my way between the rows of cars, through the open gate in the fence. The closer I got to the music, the more people I could see suiting themselves up from the trunks of their cars. A man had pulled on what looked like great clumps of yellowed grass below his knees and above his elbows. On his back there was a full circle of feathers, and also a tall brush that ran over his skull from his forehead to the nape of his neck. When he straightened up, everything swished in the wind, he was both grass and bird man, prancing, but then I came close and I could see the grass was plastic, cut in long strings.

The sun was harsh but the wind was cold. Everybody I saw around me had whips of hair in their eyes or on their shoulders and brightened cheeks.

I saw an empty space in the bleachers and climbed up. I had a good view of the center of the arbor, a grassy circle with a pole in the center. Tied to the pole was a feather headdress, hanging vertically. On the opposite side, people were milling about a group of drummers, who sat in a circle of chairs with round drums on their knees. A group of young boys ran here and there, under the bleachers, laughing at each other.

The arbor made a kind of scimitar of shade around the bright center of the dancing circle. "Ladies," the announcer's voice was saying. There were flags of four nations representing all the countries people had come from. They flapped madly in the wind, Canada, the U.S., what else? My neighbors in the bleachers came and went, small children, adults of all ages, sizes, shapes.

Young women were lining up to enter the dancing circle. The drums began to pound in a certain rhythm. The young women moved forward onto the grass. They were dressed in bright colors, in shocking greens, bright pinks. Their dresses were long, made of shiny cottons and shimmery polyesters. No one wore traditional leathers. The elaborate embroidery I remembered from my childhood was gone. Instead, shoulders and arms and skirts were fringed in different materials. Some had sewn row upon row of shiny silver cartridges on their dresses from shoulder to hem so that they jangled and shivered and tinkled as they moved. They moved one by one into the circle, each dancing alone, each turning round and round, hawks wheeling in their gyres, little tiny steps, stops, starts, heels up and toes down, feathered fans in their hands, hiding their faces.

Modernity had been cut up and laid out and sewn over an ancient pattern. The amplifiers blasted in my ears. A child was crying bitterly at the bottom of the bleachers, as if he'd lost everyone he cared for in the world. His mother wiped his nose.

"Boys' fancy dancing," called the announcer, and he sounded like the master of ceremonies at some arena calling for the next group of skaters or swimmers or divers to come forward, like this was a little Olympics. Little boys, perhaps ten or younger, spilled out onto the grass, their heads covered with strange clumps of upright feathers, their arms, their legs also, even their backs. Some of them held sticks, some were empty-handed, but their arms flew out from their bodies, and they tumbled and rumbled and bumped into each other like sage rolling over the desert in the wind. They had numbers pinned on their backs or their chests so that the judges could remember who was best.

The wind tore at me like a big dog worrying out a buried bone.

And then it was the men's fancy dancing and out they came, each one absolutely himself, each outfit a representation of the man's relationship to something wild and particular, a grouse, a pheasant, something alive. They were feathered everywhere—on their heads, their backs, their arms—and they carried war axes, which turned in huge, wild arcs as they jumped and sprang and cavorted in the air and then sank down, their knees low, surfing on the downbeats. Two teenaged boys grumbled behind me as two young women made their way down in front of the bleachers, carefully not looking up at them or at the men in the circle. They wore their hair in French braids, these girls, and jangled with every step. They took off their numbers as they moved by.

"That your girlfriend," said one boy to the other.

"Sister," said the other, and then the wind carried their words away and their peals of laughter too.

Nothing was the way I remembered it, and yet nothing was unrecognizably different either. The dances were the same, the songs, the drums, but it was all electrified, and the clothes were some kind of amalgam between the new and the traditional. This culture was alive, interacting with others around it; things had been added, subtracted. Like Nashville, I thought, like the way Appalachian country people had been pressed and cleaned up and set before the world on the Grand Ole Opry stage. And the people? They were all sizes, all strengths. There was not one among them I would have ever confused with any modern Asian. It was easy to see, once one stopped trying to cut the facts to fit the theories, to just look, that while we had all come from some common Adam and Eve somewhere, they had become who they are here, on this side of the globe, on these sun-soaked plains. That was what one researcher at Wanuskewin had said when I'd called looking for an oral historian. He'd said his tradition "says the Creator put us in North America. Over thousands of years [we've] changed. I think we were further south and came north.... Our general understanding is people were placed in different spots, the four directions, four colors—red people, blue or black people, white and yellow. Maybe there was a placement in South America. In Canada we say [we were] placed here in North America."

That had a certain resonance, especially in light of the papers read at the AAPA meeting in Columbus. C. Loring Brace had argued that color is an adaptation that changes very slowly, though people move around very quickly. The time scale he estimated was many thousands of years. Body shape reflects the mixture of exposures to sunshine and rainfall. Hot summers and good rain are a recipe for height in Australia. Saskatchewan has its own version of these equations. All of us on these bleachers were as many colors as there were bodies, from pale olive to deep red-bronze, because people had only been in Saskatchewan for the last 10,000 years and they had moved in from the south. They were blond and redheaded, they had black hair and brown hair. The men were mostly tall and broad-shouldered, with deep chests and long legs. They had noses as strong, as interesting as my aunt's. They also had a certain kind of big-shouldered walk I'd never seen anywhere else but in Saskatchewan, a walk that said no matter what, the wind will support me. The young boys were wild-haired and skinny. The older women were like me, heavier than they once were, with shoulders sloping down instead of nicely straight like those of the young, narrow-hipped, straight-backed girls, who ate ice cream and candy and drank pop.

The arbor's shade and the brilliant sky suited them, and me, right down to the ground, this was their ground, and mine too, if one belongs to the ground where one was born and where one's beloved dead leak their messages into the earth. The light played on our faces and on our hands with a harsh love. The drums drove the beat of my heart, moved my immigrant feet through circles in the grass. And took full possession of my bones.

# Epilogue

A BOOK GROWS SLOWLY. The works of many thinkers are read and sifted, the writer calls and asks questions, hops on buses or planes to see things with her own eyes. The struggle to understand and to render it all into a coherent narrative begins. When the manuscript is complete, the process of correction takes over. It must be broken down into its parts and its facts checked. This part of the making of this book went quickly, aided by the wonders of modern technology, specifically the rapid, worldwide reach of the Internet. Whole sections of the manuscript were uploaded and sent to the people whose work was discussed in them. When they replied, it was as if our initial conversations simply continued, but in a much more precise way. Some researchers responded very quickly. Others took their time: they were in the field or overwhelmed with other work of their own (or they were struggling to control their tempers over errors and contrary opinions).

The first requests for comment were sent out in March 2000. By the end of June, almost everyone had answered, except for Alan Bryan and Ruth Gruhn. They had been among the most helpful researchers I'd met in my travels and it was unlike them not to reply. Finally, I broke down and used the telephone. Gruhn answered and explained: they'd been on tenterhooks since the previous fall when they had learned that Bryan's famous calotte had been found in Brazil (something the Brazilians had neglected to tell me). The calotte, Gruhn said, had been CT scanned and had now been proven to be a fake. But they had been reluctant to answer me until they read the forthcoming article that would describe the discovery and tests.

Oh, no, I thought. And then, what will this do to my story? And then, more altruistically, what about the idea I had first picked up from Alan Bryan that modern humans might have evolved in the Americas from an earlier ancestral form? I had grown quite attached to that hypothesis, especially after the human remains found at the foot of the glacier at Tatshenshini-Alsek Park had been shown to be disappointingly recent. As Gruhn talked into my ear, I found myself not wanting to believe her, and grasping instead at the first straw I could think of. Maybe the calotte found was the one discovered by Lund and written on by Poech. Sheila de Souza had mentioned this other calotte to me when I asked her if she knew the whereabouts of Alan Bryan's discovery. I had heard scurrilous gossip that a person in the Brazilian scientific establishment had Bryan's calotte in a private collection. De Souza had been appalled by that suggestion, as I now found myself appalled by this news. I could not believe that Bryan had made a mistake. In a paper he wrote in 1978 for his publication *Early Man in America*, he had firmly countered the hypotheses of his critics who'd argued from the beginning that the calotte he found in Minas Gerais was most probably from H. V. Walter's collection and most probably a fake or a cast: if the calotte was real, they'd said, Walter must have acquired it in England and introduced it into his Lagoa Santa materials. Bryan had argued that if Walter had found it, he'd have known its value, that the calotte did not look at all like that of a Neanderthal. Besides, he wrote "both my wife, Ruth Gruhn, and I have had considerable experience in handling human skeletal material and we are both positive that it was neither a fake nor a cast. It was a human skullcap, the frontal and both parietals, all sutures fused, highly mineralized and stained black, the same color as a minority of fossilized animal bones in the Walter paleontological collection (most are stained red)."

Where and how was the calotte found, I asked Gruhn.

The curators at the National Museum in Rio had located it when they were carefully documenting their collections, said Gruhn. They hadn't told her everything. She'd let me know when she learned more.

I couldn't wait for the slow pace of academic publishing to take its course. I e-mailed Sheila de Souza. Yes, she wrote back, the museum's curator of archaeology had it all in hand. They had indeed found the calotte in the museum's collections. And there was no doubt the calotte found was the one described by Bryan, not the one found by Lund. They had compared it to the photographs Bryan had published: it matched. The curator had then decided to analyze it with a CT scan because of Bryan's belief in its antiquity. The first scan revealed it was "a reconstructed piece of a thing," as de Souza put it. It confirmed, she wrote, that the "calotte had been prepared to have the robust and ancient appearance you have seen in the photos with the add of molded material on the frontal. Last but not least, Marilia Mello e Alvim, Maria Beltrão and others were right." Furthermore, she added that she thought Gruhn and Bryan felt relief that finally, after so many discussions over so many years, there had been the opportunity to examine the calotte properly. De Souza and her colleague Ricardo Santos, a senior researcher in biological anthropology at the museum, had decided to publish an article about this as an example of the kind of error that arises from collections without precise context. "As Ruth herself suggested," she wrote, "we are also sending a note to *Current Anthropology*, where Bryan published his article about the calotte."

Bryan himself sent me his suggested corrections of my manuscript a short time later. He generously included his own story of the calotte denouement. He had attended the conference on the First Americans organized by Robson Bonnichsen at Sante Fe in the fall of 1999. There Erv Taylor had shown him a manuscript he had written with Brazilian archaeologist Maria Beltrão, which they had submitted for publication. "Beltrão said that Ruth and I had been duped by a fake that H.V. Walter had perpetrated on another bone digger at Lagoa Santa, a journalist named Anibal Mattos. According to Beltrão, Walter had glued fake browridges onto a skullcap in order to fool Mattos into believing there really was early man at Lagoa Santa. She added that the calotte was now in the archaeology sector of the Museu Naçional."

Bryan had quickly contacted the museum's curator to ask about the calotte. She had not found it in her sector, according to Bryan, but rather in the human biology section of the museum, and had ordered the CT scan after that.

"We await word that the paper has been accepted for publication," wrote Bryan.

I had to wait until October 2000 for the Kennewick affair to arrive at something like a denoument. I thought the U.S. Department of the Interior would declare that though the remains are Native American, no one could show by any scientific method any proof of cultural affiliation to the tribes claiming them. Having tipped its hat in this way to the scientific community, I thought the government would then bow to those tribes, which could still wreak havoc with the not-quite-complete incinerators at the Umatilla chemical depot, and do what it had already done with the Spirit Cave remains—refuse to allow any further study. This was a cynical prediction, of course, but given the way the government had dealt with such issues in the past, surely cynicism was warranted? Besides, the presidential election campaign was at full throttle. The polls showed that the two major candidates, Vice-President Al Gore and Texas Governor George W. Bush, were running neck and neck. The house and senate races were also tight, especially in the northwestern states: Republican Senator Slade Gorton of Washington, a supporter of the Kennewick plaintiffs' position, was up for reelection; control of the senate was within the Democrats' grasp. The Native American community had put forward candidates and was using its gambling dollars to get political attention. It seemed to me the Department of the Interior had stretched this thing out until the answer to the plaintiffs could deliver the biggest possible political bang for the Democrats' campaign.

Judge Jelderks had ordered the Army to answer whether the plaintiffs would be allowed to study Kennewick Man by September 24, 2000, more than four years after the remains were found. On September 21, Bruce Babbitt, Secretary of the Interior, wrote to Louis Caldera, Secretary of the Army, with his determination of the meaning of the various Kennewick studies. The letter, a press release and relevant studies were posted on the Internet. After explaining the applicable sections of the NAGPRA and its regulations, Babbitt restated the department's previous finding that Kennewick Man was a Native American because radiocarbon studies showed he died before 1492. He asserted that the remains were removed from federal land under the control of the Army Corps of Engineers, not from recognized tribal lands, and that no one could make a successful claim that they were the lineal descendant of Kennewick Man. His department had therefore evaluated whether anyone could successfully claim that these remains were culturally affiliated to any tribe recognized by the United States. To answer this question, all lines of evidence "were deemed equally important and all were accorded equivalent weight."

The Department of the Interior had ordered various new studies to determine this issue. None of these studies had been conclusive or exclusive. Three labs (Merriwether's, Kaestle's and Glenn Smith's) had failed to extract viable mtDNA. Reviews of other archaeological finds, linguistic evidence, bioarchaeological information from other sites in the area (including Gore Creek) and ethnographic material were carried out. None of these scientific studies were able to show a definitive link, or the lack of one, between Kennewick Man and the tribes now living on the plateau. Oral tradition evidence was presented by two of the tribes.

The standard of proof, according to the secretary, was "preponderance of the evidence. This is a threshold that many scholars hesitate to use for interpretations based upon archeological [*sic*], anthropological, and historical evidence. The determination to be made here is informed by, but not controlled by, the evidence as a scholar would weigh it. Instead the determination is for the Secretary of the Interior to make as the one that, on the evidence, would best carry out the purpose of NAGPRA as enacted by Congress."

The secretary, in other words, was forced to rely on his judgment, since science was not helpful. He explained that while the NAGPRA called for the remains to be returned to the closest culturally affiliated tribe and did not specifically mention group claims, he decided the statute permitted finding a cultural affiliation to multiple tribes "where, as here, they submit a joint claim." The secretary recognized that while "some gaps regarding continuity are present, DOI finds that, in this specific case, the geographic and oral tradition evidence establishes a reasonable link between these remains and the present-day Indian tribe claimants." Cultural and historical links could be firmly made between the peoples living on the plateau now, those found in the region by Lewis and Clark, and those whose remains had been found on the plateau by archaeologists. "Consequently," wrote the secretary, "the cultural affiliation determination must focus on whether there is evidence establishing a reasonable cultural connection between the Indian tribes inhabiting the Columbia Plateau approximately 2000–3000 years ago and the cultural group represented by the Kennewick human remains which inhabited the same region 8500–9500 years ago."

Every scientist I had spoken to on this issue had taken it as a given that no such evidence could be found. While Secretary Babbitt acknowledged there seemed to be a discontinuity between 9500 and 8500 years ago, when different artifact types appeared in the archaeological record, and that Kennewick Man does not look like the people now living in the area, "none of the cultural discontinuities suggested by the evidence are inconsistent with a cultural group continuously existing in the region, interacting with other groups migrating through the area and adapting to changing climate conditions." He therefore relied on the only evidence he could get, tribal stories. "The collected oral tradition evidence suggests a continuity between the cultural group represented by the Kennewick human remains and the modern-day claimant Indian tribes. The oral tradition evidence reveals that the claimant Indian tribes possess similar traditional histories that relate to the Columbia Plateau's past landscape. The oral tradition evidence also lacks any reference to a migration of people into or out of the Columbia Plateau." On these grounds, he decided that "the evidence of cultural continuity is sufficient to show by a preponderance of the evidence that the Kennewick remains are culturally affiliated with the present-day Indian tribe claimants."

He put forward a secondary argument, just in case the court found this one hard to swallow. In the 1950s and 1960s, the Umatilla had laid claim to the area where Kennewick Man was found. There had been a series of hearings in which the Indian Claims Commission found against the Umatilla on the grounds that the lands had been used by several tribes in the area, not just the Umatilla. The Umatilla had only relinquished their claim as part of a negotiated settlement. The secretary therefore declared that the proper disposition of the remains "based on cultural affiliation and aboriginal occupation is to the claimants, the Confederated Tribes of the Colville Reservation, Confederated Tribes of the Umatilla Reservation, Confederated Tribes and Bands of the Yakama Indian Nation, the Nez Percé Tribe of Idaho and the Wanapum Band."

Having come to this conclusion, the only answer the army could make to the plaintiffs was no. "Once a disposition decision has been made, NAGPRA does not permit further study prior to the transfer of the remains to the claimants. The claimants have been found to be the legal custodians of the remains and study may only by conducted with their permission."

The secretary had gone well beyond the words of the law to try to grasp its underlying spirit. He had done this knowing that almost every scientist reading the attached reports would find his judgment to be without scientific merit, based as it was on oral tradition, which was treated as less than reliable by his own experts. But after a careful reading of this letter and the reports that accompanied it, it struck me that while September 21, 2000, may have seemed like a bad day for anthropological science, it was a good day for social justice (from which anthropological science will eventually benefit too). I wondered what Judge Jelderks would make of it. On balance, I thought that Judge Jelderks would be hard pressed to place his own judgment ahead of the secretary's, which was balanced and reasonable.

But one should never try to guess what a judge will do. The plaintiffs and the army went back to court on October 25, 2000. The plaintiffs asked that the judge lift the stay of proceedings and let the issues go to trial. The judge asked a number of questions. He focused most closely on the Department of the Interior's definition of Native American as anyone whose remains, found in America, were older than 1492, regardless of what the people may have looked like or where their culture may have originated. Judge Jelderks declared that he would allow a trial to proceed.

The issues were heard on June 19 and 20th, 2001. On June 21, Benton County Coroner, Floyd Johnson, found broken femurs in a cardboard box which he recognized from the Kennewick case, in his lock up at the Sherriff's evidence bunker. Johnson said he was surprised to find them there. Chatters said he too was baffled, but vindicated.

# Acknowledgements

ANNE COLLINS, now vice president and publisher of Random House Canada, was in her former career my editor both at *Toronto Life* and *Saturday Night* magazines. She offered her ear and then her help by asking me to write various articles, and recognized long before I did that they were all connected to each other, that a book-length work lay in wait beyond those stories. When she took on her responsibilities at Random House Canada, she insisted I write it. This book would never have emerged without her.

Stephen Dewar, my husband and colleague, who listens, argues and demands that I get it right, shared his own considerable reading on these subjects and helped me to grasp dense statistical arguments that were well beyond my training, but not his. He also invented and carried out the e-mail fact-check of this book, a huge undertaking that he made seem almost simple. The archaeologist and museum director William Finlayson, whom I met in the course of researching my second published story in this area, was a great source of information and encouragement throughout. He also kindly agreed to read the manuscript and comment on any errors or wrong-headed opinions he spotted, at the cost of considerable time and effort. Similarly, Gordon Dibb, an archaeologist with his own consulting company in Peterborough, Ontario, whom I first contacted when checking into the practices of archaeological inquiry in Ontario, not only quickly located the artifacts I asked him about (in his basement) but from that point on fired at me numerous articles, books, clippings, suggestions and lore from his own library and experience, all of which were wonderfully helpful and instructive.

All the researchers mentioned here (and many whose work is referred to but who are not named) were kind, open and patient with my errors and omissions. They welcomed me into their laboratories, helped me understand their work, led me to their colleagues and then read and commented on my efforts. I thank all of them for their considerable work on my behalf.

I do want to thank by name those who went far beyond what any reporter can expect in the way of cooperation and aid. I have never met more thoughtful or helpful researchers than in Brazil. Sheila Maria Ferraz Mendonça de Souza, Luiz Fernando Ferreira, Adauto Araújo, Walter Neves, André Prous, Fernando Costa and Niéde Guidon not only told me everything they could about what they've found, but also what they think it means. Walter Neves read my report of his work with care and attention, and helped me find a much better expression for my concern about the biological meaning of skull measurement, as did Sheila de Souza. The time they took is much appreciated. André Prous, Xexeu Aguimar and Rosa Trakalo made certain my travels in Brazil were safe and secure.

In North America, Frederika Kaestle and Andy Merriwether tried very hard to get across to me the ideas and hypotheses that underlie their genetic work, and Kaestle spent considerable effort after portions of the manuscript were sent to her making certain I understood the issues she wrestles with, some of which I had misconstrued. Cleone Hawkinson worked most diligently to correct the sections of this work dealing with the Kennewick law suit, as did Alan Schneider. Richard Jantz was similarly generous with his comments and time. James Chatters read the portions of the manuscript dealing with his work very thoroughly and was good enough to offer many useful suggestions. Amy Dansie was similarly thorough. Tom Lynch supplied me with many insights, and much useful reading material. Tom Dillehay and Jack Rossen were also helpful, as were Dennis Stanford and Douglas Owsley. Wilson Wewa listened to every word of his stories as I'd rendered them, and made certain I wrote them exactly as he'd heard them as a boy. William Asikinack wrote his down and sent them to me. Frances Sanderson stood up for me when some of her colleagues wanted me excluded from the meeting she'd organized; she fought for me to be there so I could understand the pain the study of ancestors' bones causes Native people, and why disrespectful behavior must stop. Barney Reeves demonstrated to me that Native Americans had dominion over the continental interior and must also have had boats at the end of the Ice Age. Alan Bryan and Ruth Gruhn shared their work and their ideas most generously, and never flinched at being contradicted by events (while I most certainly did). Scotty MacNeish was a wonderful host and delighted me with the breadth of his experience in archaeology. Unfortunately, he passed away as this book was on the press, as did Margret Milton, a fine physician and respected coroner. Karl Reinhard allowed me to print the awful things that have been said of him so that others might know what can happen to academics studying Native American remains. David Yesner sent me a wealth of material about the archaeology of Alaska and Siberia. Ernie Walker enlightened me about the sweep of the Native American story on my own home turf and made me believe that it is possible to be a fine archaeologist while also serving the demands of the spirit. Alejandra Duk-Rodkin allowed me a glimpse of the joy that comes from doing great science.

Pam Robertson, editorial assistant at Random House Canada, made certain all versions of this manuscript were electronically available in the right order and was most helpful sorting out various practical details. Doris Cowan, my copy editor, untangled my syntactical errors and helped me express myself more accurately and forcefully. My daughter Anna Dewar helped me organize the bibliography, and my daughter Danielle Dewar helped keep the household going during my many absences over the last two years. My friend Charles Greene housed me and drove me all around Nevada. The beautiful design of the book jacket is due to the subtle eye and graceful hand of Carmen Dunjko. The images are adapted from the original works painted on the rock-shelter walls of Pedra Furada by the First Americans, who made them in what Niéde Guidon calls the Nordeste tradition.

None of the above should be blamed for any errors, omissions or misconceptions that have survived the checking and editing process. They are all mine.

# Endnotes

*Part One*

CHAPTER ONE: *Asian Origins?*

1. A.P. Coleman, "The Pleistocene of the Toronto Region Including the Toronto Interglacial Formation," Forty-First Annual Report of the Ontario Department of Mines, 1932, vol. 41, part 7 (Toronto: 1933).
2. The Nisga'a Final Agreement, 13 April 2000.
3. Elaine Dewar, "The Next Ice Age," *Toronto Life*, April 1996.
4. P.F. Karrow and B.G. Warner, "The Geological and Biological Environment for Human Occupation in Southern Ontario," chap. 2 in *The Archaeology of Southern Ontario to A.D. 1650*, ed. Chris J. Ellis and Neal Ferris, Occasional Publication of the London Chapter, Ontario Archaeological Society, no. 5 (1990): 5, 35.
5. R.T. Watson, H. Rodhe, H. Oeschger, U. Siegenthaler, "Greenhouse Gases and Aerosols," *Climate Change: The IPCC Scientific Assessment*, World Meteorological Organization, United Nations Environment Programme (1995).
6. Elaine Dewar, "Behind This Door," *Toronto Life*, May 1997.
7. Chris J. Ellis and D. Brian Deller, "Paleo-Indians," chap. 3 in *The Archaeology of Southern Ontario to A.D. 1650*, ed. Chris J. Ellis and Neal Ferris, Occasional Publications of the London Chapter, *OAS*, no. 5 (1990): 37–63.
8. William D. Finlayson, *Iroquoian Peoples of the Land of Rocks and Water, A.D. 1000 to 1650: A Study in Settlement Archaeology*, vol. 1 of 4 (London, Ont: London Museum of Archaeology, 1998).
9. Darrell Addison Posey, "Ethnoentomology of the Gorotire Kayapo of Central Brazil" (Ph.D. diss., University of Georgia, 1979).
10. Ontario Heritage Act, Revised Statutes of Ontario, 1990, chap. 0.18, September 1992.

11. Dewar, "Behind This Door."

12. Ibid.

13. R.P. Beukens, L.A. Pavlish, R.G.V. Hancock, R.M. Farquhar, G.C. Wilson, P.J. Julig and William Ross, "Radiocarbon Dating of Copper Preserved Organics," *Radiocarbon* 34, no. 3 (1992): 890–97.

14. J.M. Adovasio, O. Soffer and B. Klíma, "Paleolithic Fiber Technology: Data from Pavlov I, Czech Republic, ca. 27,000 B.P.," paper prepared for the 60th Annual Meeting of the Society for American Archaeology.

15. Thomas F. Lynch, "The Discovery of America—Why It Matters," *Arts & Sciences Newsletter* 14, no. 1 (Cornell University: January 1993).

16. C.B. Stringer and P. Andrews, "Genetic and Fossil Evidence for the Origin of Modern Humans," *Science* 239 (11 March 1988): 1263–68.

17. H.P. Schwarcz, R. Grun, B. Vandermeersch, O. Bar-Yosef, H. Valladas and E. Tchernov, "ESR Dates for the Hominid Site of Qafzeh in Israel," *Journal of Human Evolution* 17 (1988): 733–37.

18. Jim Allen, "Radiocarbon Determinations, Luminescence Dating and Australian Archaeology," *Antiquity* 68 (1994): 339–43.

19. T.E.G. Reynolds, "Revolution or Resolution? The Archaeology of Modern Human Origins," *World Archaeology* 23, no. 2 (1991): 155–66.

20. T.D. Stewart, "A Physical Anthropologist's View of the Peopling of the New World," *Southwestern Journal of Anthropology* 16, no. 3 (Autumn 1960): 259–73.

21. C.K. Folland, T.R. Karl and K.Y. Vinnikov, "Observed Climate Variations and Change," chap. 7 of *Climate Change: The IPCC Scientific Assessment*, World Meteorological Organization, United Nations Environment Programme (1995).

22. Frank C. Hibben, *The Lost Americans* (New York: Thomas Y. Crowell, revised and updated 1968), 112.

23. Stewart, "A Physical Anthropologist's View," 259–73.

24. David R. Yesner, "Technological, Chronological and Economic Variability in Paleo-Indian Occupations from Eastern Beringia (Alaska)," "First Things First: Was There 'Pre-Clovis' Occupation of Eastern Beringia?," unpublished manuscripts.

25. Hibben, *Lost Americans*, 28.

26. D.E. Nelson, Richard E. Morlan, J.S. Vogel, J.R. Southon and C.R. Harrington, "New Dates on Northern Yukon Artifacts: Holocene Not Upper Pleistocene," *Science* 232 (1986): 749–51.

27. Jacques Cinq-Mars and Richard E. Morlan, "Blue Fish Caves and Old Crow Basin: A New Rapport," in *Ice Age Peoples of North America: Environment, Origins and Adaptations of the First Americans*, ed. Robson Bonnichsen and Karen L. Turnmire (Corvallis: Oregon State University Press, for the Center for Study of the First Americans, 1999): 212–20.

28. Tom D. Dillehay, *Monte Verde: A Late Pleistocene Settlement in Chile*, vol. 1 (Washington and London: Smithsonian Institution Press, 1989).

29. Nelson et al., "New Dates."
30. Tom D. Dillehay, *Monte Verde: A Late Pleistocene Settlement in Chile*, vol. 2 (Washington and London: Smithsonian Institution Press, 1997).
31. E.F. Greenman, "Comments on the Paleo Indian Tradition in Eastern North America by Ronald J. Mason," *Current Anthropology* 3, no. 3 (June 1962): 252–54.

CHAPTER TWO: *Bones 101*

1. *Native American Graves Protection and Repatriation Act*, Public Law 101-601, 101st Congr., 1st sess., 16 November 1990.
2. Notice of Intent, *Tri-City Herald*, 17 September 1996, D1.
3. Summons in a Civil Case: Complaint, United States District Court, District of Oregon, Case Number CV96-1481-JE, 16 October 1996, point 16, p. 6.
4. R.L. Jantz and Douglas W. Owsley, "Pathology, Taphonomy and Cranial Morphometrics of the Spirit Cave Mummy," *Nevada Historical Society Quarterly* (Spring 1997): 62–84.
5. Order of Judge Jelderks in the United States District Court for the District of Oregon: *Robson Bonnichsen, C. Loring Brace, George W. Gill, C. Vance Haynes, Richard L. Jantz, Douglas W. Owsley, Dennis J. Stanford and D. Gentry Steele, Plaintiffs v. United States of America, Department of the Army, United States Army Corps of Engineers, Bartholomew B. Bohn II, Donald R. Curtis, and Lee Turner, Defendants.* Order Civil Number 96-1481-JE, p. 9.
6. Summons in a Civil Case, 16 October 1996.
7. Douglas Preston, "The Face of Kennewick Man," *The New Yorker*, 9 February 1998.
8. Douglas Preston, "The Lost Man," *The New Yorker*, 16 June 1997.
9. The Cemeteries Act of Ontario, 1 April 1992 (Ontario Regulations 133, 1992, Burial Sites).
10. Analysis of John K. Van De Kamp, Attorney General, State of California, 21 May 1990, as provided to Richard Katz, Member of the State Assembly, State Capitol, Sacramento, California.
11. Results of Freedom of Information request to Municipality of North York: letter of Beth Hanna, manager, Culture Branch, North York Parks and Recreation Department, to Ron Williamson, Archaeological Services, 19 December 1997.
12. David Boyle, *Ontario Archaeological Report* 14, 1901, Being Part of the Appendix to the Report of the Minister of Education, Ontario (Toronto: L.K. Cameron, Printer to the King's Most Excellent Majesty, 1902).
13. Kenneth E. Kidd, "The Excavation and Historical Identification of a Huron Ossuary," *American Antiquity* 18, no. 4 (April 1953): 359–79.
14. Press release, Royal Ontario Museum, 23 August 1999.

15. *Native American Graves Protection and Repatriation Act*, Public Law 101-601, 101st Congr., 1st sess., 16 November 1990, section 5:d (ii).

16. Barbara D. Lynch and Thomas F. Lynch, "The Beginnings of a Scientific Approach to Prehistorical Archaeology in 17th and 18th Century Britain," *Southwestern Journal of Anthropology* 24, no. 1 (Spring 1968): 33–65.

17. Aleš Hrdlička, "Physical Anthropology: Its Scope and Aims; its History and Present Status in America," *American Journal of Physical Anthropology* 1, no. 1 (1918): 3–23.

18. Ibid., 5.

19. Ibid., 18.

20. Ibid., 20.

21. Aleš Hrdlička, "Physical Anthropology: Its Scope and Aims; Its History and Present Status in America," *American Journal of Physical Anthropology* 1, no. 2 (April-June 1918): 133–182.

22. Ibid., 160.

23. Aleš Hrdlička, Bibliography, *American Journal of Physical Anthropology* 1, no. 4 (October-December 1918): 381.

24. Ibid, 3.

25. Ibid., 10.

26. Ibid, 11.

27. *Native American Graves Protection and Repatriation Act*, Public Law 101-601, House Report No. 101-877, 10.

28. Aleš Hrdlička, "Physical Anthropology," *American Journal of Physical Anthropology* 1, no. 1 (1918): 172–74.

29. Franz Boas, "Physical Characteristics of the Indians of the North Pacific Coast," *The American Anthropologist* 4 (January 1891): 25–32.

30. Franz Boas, *Kwakiutl Ethnography*, edited by Helen Codere (Chicago: University of Chicago Press, 1966), 3–6 and 423–32.

31. Ibid.

32. Jack F. Trope and Walter R. Echo-Hawk, "The Native American Graves Protection and Repatriation Act: Background and Legislative History," *Arizona State Law Journal* 24, no. 35 (Spring 1992): 5.

33. Franz Boas, "Changes in the Bodily Form of Descendants of Immigrants," *American Anthropology*, N.S.14 (1912): 530–62.

34. Ibid., 550.

35. Ibid., 562.

36. Ibid., 562.

37. Albert Russell Nelson, "A Craniofacial Perspective on North American Indian Population Affinities and Relations" (Ph.D. diss., University of Michigan, 1998).

38. Mary Margaret Overbey, "AAA Tells Feds to Eliminate 'Race,'" *Anthropology Newsletter* 38, no. 7 (October 1997): 1–5.

CHAPTER THREE: *Found and Lost*

1. D. Gentry Steele and Joseph F. Powell, "Peopling of the Americas: Paleo-biological Evidence," *Human Biology* 64, no. 3 (June 1992): 303–36.
2. Ibid., 329.
3. C.B. Stringer and P. Andrews, "Genetic and Fossil Evidence for the Origin of Modern Humans," *Science* 239 (11 March 1998): 1263–68.
4. Ibid.
5. Jerome S. Cybulski, Donald E. Howes, James C. Haggarty and Morley Eldridge, "An Early Human Skeleton from South-Central British Columbia: Dating and Bioarchaeological Inference," *Canadian Journal of Archaeology*, no. 5 (1981): 49–59.
6. Ibid., 52.
7. Ibid., 52.
8. Scott Hamilton, "Archaeological Investigations at the Wapekeka Burial Site (F1Jj-1)," Cultural Resource Management Report prepared for the Wapekeka First Nation, Ontario Ministry of Transportation, Ontario Ministry of Northern Development and Mines, Federal Department of Indian and Northern Affairs (Canada, 1991). P.J. Julig, "Cummins Paleo-Indian Site and its Paleoenvironment, Thunder Bay, Canada," *Archaeology of Eastern North America* 12 (Fall 1984): 192–209.
9. J. Edson Way, "The Human Osteological Material From the Cloverleaf Bastion of the Fort at Coteau-du-Lac, Quebec," *History and Archaeology/ Histoire et Archéologie* 12, National Historic Parks and Sites Branch, Parks Canada, Department of Indian and Northern Affairs, Minister of Supply and Services (Canada, 1977): 16–20.
10. Robert McGhee, *The Burial at L'Anse-Amour*, Archaeological Survey of Canada, National Museum of Man (Ottawa, 1976).
11. Sonja M. Jerkic, "Description of Skeletal Material," in *An Archaic Sequence from the Strait of Belle Isle, Labrador*, National Museum of Man Mercury Series, Archaeological Survey of Canada, Paper no. 34 (1975): 93–94.
12. Howard Savage, letter to the Hon. Robert Welch, Minister of Culture and Recreation, Province of Ontario (8 March 1978).
13. M. Anne Katzenberg and Norman C. Sullivan, "A Report on the Human Burial from the Milton-Thomazi Site," *Ontario Archaeology*, no. 32 (1979): 27–41.
14. Jim Russell, photograph of Howard Savage and the Milton-Thomazi skull, *Toronto Star*, 12 July 1982, A2.
15. Amy Dansie, "Early Holocene Burials in Nevada, Overview of Localities, Research and Legal Issues," *Nevada Historical Society* 40, no. 1 (Spring 1997): 4–14.
16. Christopher J. Turnbull, "The Augustine Site: A Mound from the Maritimes," *Archaeology of Eastern North America* 4 (Winter 1976): 50–62.
17. Don W. Dragoo, "Adena and the Eastern Burial Cult," *Archaeology of Eastern North America* 4 (Winter 1976): 1–9.

18. Joleen Gordon, *Mi'kmaq Textiles Twining, Rush and Other Fibres, BkCp-1 Site, Pictou, Nova Scotia*, Nova Scotia Department of Education and Culture, Nova Scotia Museum (March 1997): 58.

CHAPTER FOUR: *The Battle for Monte Verde*

1. Rick Gore, "The Most Ancient Americans," *National Geographic* (October 1997): 92–99.
2. Tom D. Dillehay, *Monte Verde: A Late Pleistocene Settlement in Chile*, vol. 1, "Paleoenvironment and Site Context," Smithsonian Institution Press, Washington and London, 1989; and Dillehay, *Monte Verde: A Late Pleistocene Settlement in Chile*, vol. 2, "The Archaeological Context and Interpretation," Smithsonian Institution Press, Washington and London, 1997.
3. Tom D. Dillehay, Complete Curriculum Vitae, 1999.
4. Johanna Nichols, "Linguistic Diversity and the First Settlement of the New World," *Language* 66, no. 3 (1990): 475–521.
5. Dillehay was quite wrong about that. Stuart Fiedel picked through the volumes with a fine-tooth comb and published a lengthy critique, pointing out numerous inconsistencies in the text, in *Discovering Archaeology* in 2000. An interdisciplinary group at the University of Maine spent months analyzing it and decided not to invite Dillehay to speak to them as he would have spent the whole time on the defensive.
6. A.C. Roosevelt, "Paleoindian and Archaic Occupations in the Lower Amazon, Brazil: A Summary and Comparison," chap. 8 in *Explorations in American Archaeology: Essays in Honor of Wesley R. Hurt*, ed. Mark G. Plew (Lanham, New York, Oxford: University of America, Inc., 1998), 165–91.
7. A.C. Roosevelt, "Clovis Clarification: A Follow-Up," *Mammoth Trumpet* 13, no. 1 (January 1998): 14–17.
8. Deborah Tannen, *The Argument Culture* (New York: Random House, 1999).
9. Preston, "Lost Man."
10. Thomas F. Lynch, R. Gillespie, John A.J. Gowlett and R.E.M. Hedges, "Chronology of Guitarrero Cave, Peru," *Science* 229 (30 August 1985): 864–67, and Thomas F. Lynch, "Climate Change and Human Settlement Around the Late-Glacial Laguna De Punta Negra, Northern Chile: The Preliminary Results," *Geoarchaeology: An International Journal* 1, no. 2 (1986): 145–62.
11. E.F. Greenman, "Comments on the Paleo Indian Tradition in Eastern North America by Ronald J. Mason," *Current Anthropology* vol. 3, no. 3 (June 1962): 252–54.
12. Hibben, *Lost Americans*.
13. Lynch et al., "Chronology of Guitarrero Cave."
14. Thomas F. Lynch, "Glacial-Age Man in South America? A Critical Review," *American Antiquity* 55, no. 1 (1990): 12–36.

15. Ibid., 13.
16. Ibid., 26–29.
17. Stuart J. Fiedel, "Older Than We Thought: Implications of Corrected Dates for PaleoIndians," *American Antiquity* 64, no. 1 (1999): 95–115.


CHAPTER FIVE: *The Founding Mothers*

1. Stephen McNallen, personal communication. Also Scott L. Malcomson, "The Color of Bones," *The New York Times Magazine* (2 April 2000): 40–45.
2. Thorz Hammer, request for Kennewick Man remains, 3 January 1996, of the United States Army Corps of Engineers, obtained under a Freedom of Information and Access application of 14 April 1999.
3. Rosemary R. Thomas, request for Kennewick Man remains, 4 October 1996, of the United States Army Corps of Engineers, obtained under a Freedom of Information and Access application of 14 April 1999.
4. Rex Buck Jr. and Robert Tomanawash, on behalf of the Wanapum Band, request 22 October 1996, of the U.S. Army Corps of Engineers for the return of the remains found the weekend of 27 July 1996 and the remains of five individuals found 24 August 1996, obtained under a Freedom of Information and Access application of 14 April 1999. Donald G. Sampson, on behalf of the Confederated Tribes of the Umatilla Indian Reservation, request 2 December 1996, of the U.S. Army Corps of Engineers for the five remains found in July 1996, reiterating the claim in letters regarding Richland Man sent to the Corps on 5 September and 23 October 1996, obtained under a Freedom of Information and Access application of 14 April 1999. Ross Sockzehigh, on behalf of the Confederated Yakama Nation, request 4 October 1996, of the U.S. Army Corps of Engineers, reserving the right to claim at a later date the Kennewick Man remains, obtained under Freedom of Information and Access application of 14 April 1999. Donald G. Sampson, on behalf of the Confederated Tribes of the Umatilla Indian Reservation, request 9 September 1996, of the U.S. Army Corps of Engineers, obtained under a Freedom of Information and Access application of 14 April 1999. Joe Pakootas, on behalf of the Confederated Tribes of the Colville Reservation, request 11 October 1996, of the U.S. Army Corps of Engineers, obtained under Freedom of Information and Access application of 14 April 1999.
5. Federal Defendants' Status Report in Civil No. 96-1481-JE, in the United States District Court for the District of Oregon, Robson Bonnichsen et al., Plaintiffs, vs. United States of America et al., Defendants, 1 October 1997.
6. John Jelderks, Magistrate Judge: Order, in Civil No. 96-1481-JE, 13 May 1998.
7. Native American Graves Protection and Repatriation Act (NAGPRA).
8. Federal Defendants' Response to Plaintiffs' Supplement to Plaintiffs' Second Quarterly Status Report in Civil No. 96-1481-JE, 18 March 1998.

9. Mark Laswell, "The 9,400-Year-Old Man," *Wall Street Journal*, 8 January 1999, W11.

10. Federal Defendants' Third Quarterly Status Report in Civil No. 96-1481-JE, 1 April 1998.

11. Ibid., 4.

12. Federal Defendants' Supplement to Second Quarterly Status Report in Civil No. 96-1481-JE, 10 March 1998.News Release/Walla Walla District U.S. Army Corps of Engineers #98-12, 10 March 1998.

13. *Kennewick Man Chronology to January 21, 1999*, issued by the office of Congressman Doc Hastings.

14. John Jelderks, Magistrate Judge: Order in Civil No. 96-1481-JE, 31 August 1998.

15. Walla Walla District Army Corps of Engineers, Joint Media Advisory, "Ancient human skeleton to be moved from Richland to Seattle," 27 October 1998.

16. Henry C. Harpending, Stephen T. Sherry, Alan R. Rogers and Mark Stoneking, "The Genetic Structure of Ancient Human Populations," *Current Anthropology* 34, no. 4 (August-October 1993): 483–96.

17. Stringer and Andrews, "Genetic and Fossil Evidence," 1263–68 (see chap. 3, n. 3).

18. Theodore G. Schurr, Scott W. Ballinger, Yik-Yuen Gan, Judith A. Hodge, D. Andrew Merriwether, Dale N. Lawrence, William C. Knowler, Kenneth M. Weiss and Douglas C. Wallace, "Amerindian Mitochondrial DNAs Have Rare Asian Mutations at High Frequencies, Suggesting They Derived from Four Primary Maternal Lineages," *American Journal of Human Genetics* 46 (1990): 613–23.

19. D. Andrew Merriwether, "Mitochondrial DNA Variation in South American Indians" (Ph.D. diss., University of Pittsburgh, 1993).

20. Joseph H. Greenberg, Christy G. Turner II and Stephen L. Zegura, "The Settlement of the Americas: A Comparison of the Linguistic, Dental and Genetic Evidence," *Current Anthropology* 27, no. 5 (December 1986): 477–86.

21. D. Andrew Merriwether, William W. Hall, Anders Vahlne and Robert E. Ferrell, "MtDNA Variation Indicates Mongolia May Have Been the Source for the Founding Population for the New World," *American Journal of Human Genetics* 59 (1996): 204–12.

22. Michael D. Brown, Seyed H. Hosseini, Antonio Torroni, Hans-Jurgen Bandelt, Jon C. Allen, Theodore G. Schurr, Rosaria Scozzari, Fulvio Cruciani and Douglas C. Wallace, "MtDNA Haplogroup X: An Ancient Link Between Europe/Western Asia and North America?" *American Journal of Human Genetics* 63 (1998): 1852–61.

CHAPTER SIX: *Virtual Bones*

1. Smithsonian Institution Fact Sheet, April 1999.
2. Statement of Tex Hall, chairman, Three Affiliated Tribes, Forth Berthold Reservation, New Town, North Dakota, to the Hearing before the Committee on Indian Affairs of the United States Senate on U.S. Public Law 101-601 (To Provide for the Protection of Native American Graves), 106th Cong., 1st sess. (20 April 1999): 25.
3. Memorandum of Understanding between Smithsonian Institution and the U.S. Department of the Interior, Great Plains Region of the Bureau of Reclamation, reproduced in Hearings before the Committee on Indian Affairs of the United States Senate on U.S. Public Law 101-601, 106th Cong., 1st sess. (20 April 1999).
4. Letter of Bill Billeck, Repatriation, Department of Anthropology, National Museum of Natural History, Smithsonian Institution, to Tex Hall of the Three Affiliated Tribes, as reproduced in Hearings before the Committee on Indian Affairs of the United States Senate, on U.S. Public Law 101-601, 106th Cong., 1st sess. (22 April 1999): 86–87.
5. Walter A. Neves and Hector M. Pucciarelli, "Morphological Affinities of the First Americans: An Exploratory Analysis Based on Early South American Human Remains," *Journal of Human Evolution* 21 (1991): 261–73.
6. Steele and Powell, "Peopling of the Americas," 303–36 (see chap. 3, n. 1).
7. Jantz and Owsley, "Cranial Morphometrics," 62–84 (see chap. 2, n. 4).
8. Ibid., 68.
9. C. Loring Brace and A. Russell Nelson, "The Peopling of the Americas: Anglo Stereotypes and Native American Realities," in press.
10. Terence E. Fifield, "On Your Knees Cave Update," *The Alaskan Caver* 16, no. 6 (December 1996).
11. Timothy H. Heaton and Frederick Grady, "Fossil Grizzly Bears (*Ursus arctos*) from Prince of Wales Island, Alaska, Offer New Insights into Animal Dispersal, Interspecific Competition, and Age of Deglaciation," *Paleoenvironments: Vertebrates*, CRP 10 (1993): 98–100.
12. E. James Dixon, Timothy Heaton, Terence E. Fifield, Thomas D. Hamilton, David E. Putnam and Frederick Grady, "Late Quaternary Regional Geoarchaeology of Southeast Alaska Karst: A Progress Report," *Geoarchaeology: An International Journal* 12, no. 6 (1997): 689–712.
13. Calvin J. Heusser, *Late-Pleistocene Environments of North Pacific North America: An Elaboration of Late-Glacial and Postglacial Climate, Physiographic and Biotic Changes*. (New York: American Geographical Society, 1960).

CHAPTER SEVEN: *The Kennewick Chronicles*

1. Treaty with the Walla Walla, Cayuse and Umatilla Tribes, 9 June 1855, 12 Stat., 945, ratified 8 March 1859. Proclaimed 11 April 1859. Article 1. (As reproduced in *Disposal of Chemical Agents and Munitions Stored at Umatilla Depot Activity, Oregon*, Revised Final Environmental Impact Statement, November 1996, Appendix H, H2-H7.)

2. *Disposal of Chemical Agents and Munitions Stored at Umatilla Depot Activity, Oregon*. Revised Final Environmental Impact Statement (November 1996): 3–5.

3. Alan Goodman, "Racializing Kennewick Man," *Anthropology Newsletter* (October 1997): 3, 4.

4. James C. Chatters, "Human Biological History, Not Race," *Anthropology Newsletter* (February 1998): 19, 21.

5. George W. Will, "Common Mistakes," *Anthropology Newsletter* (January 1998): 2, 8.

6. George W. Will, "The Beauty of Race and Races," *Anthropology Newsletter* (March 1998): 1, 4.

7. James C. Chatters, "Encounter with an Ancestor," *Anthropology Newsletter* (January 1997): 10.

8. MacMillan published as a forensic anthropologist under the name Catherine J. Sands, and is now deceased.

9. Thomas J. Green, Bruce Cochran, Todd W. Fenton, James C. Woods, Gene L. Titmus, Larry Tieszen, Mary Anne Davis and Susanne J. Miller, "The Buhl Burial: A Paleoindian Woman from Southern Idaho," *American Antiquity* 63, no. 3 (1998): 437–56.

10. Duane Dutch Meier, Department of the Army, the Corps of Engineers press spokesperson in Walla Walla, claimed in his written response of 19 April 1999 to my questions, which he had asked to be faxed to him, that the Corps of Engineers first learned of Chatters' intention to take the remains to the Smithsonian for study on "approximately September 3, 1996. District archaeologist Tracy spoke with Dr. Doug Owsley from the Smithsonian Institution and learned of Owsley's fax to Benton County Coroner Floyd Johnson with discussion of remains movement to the Smithsonian." When this faxed letter was also produced it was clear Meier's assertion was wrong: the letter from Owsley to Floyd Johnson was sent on 31 August, the day after the Corps's counsel had already ordered the remains removed from Chatters' lab after her talk with Floyd Johnson, Benton County coroner. The Corps's counsel, Linda Kirts, later confirmed to me that she had been told by Johnson of the plan in a conversation with him on Friday 30 August.

11. Archaeological Protection Act Permit no. DACW68-4-96-40, issued by the Department of the Army, Corps of Engineers, Walla Walla District, to James C. Chatters, Ph.D., 30 July 1996, for the period beginning 28 July and terminating 3 August, 1996, p. 2.

12. Application of James C. Chatters, Ph.D., 30 July 1996, to Richard Carlton, Real Estate Division, U.S. Army Corps of Engineers, Walla Walla, Washington.

13. Archaeological Permit no. DACW68-96-40, p. 1.

14. Letter to James C. Chatters from Richard Carlton, Chief, Real Estate Division, Army Corps of Engineers, Walla Walla, Washington, 30 July 1996.

15. Letter of extension to James C. Chatters from Richard Carlton, Chief, Real Estate Division, 5 August 1996.

16. According to the documents sent to me by the Department of the Army, Corps of Engineers, in answer to my Freedom of Information and Access request dated 15 June 1999, asking for all claims filed for control of the remains known as Kennewick Man, the earliest claim filed was from the Umatilla—in a letter of 5 September and another of 23 October. Neither of these documents was produced for me by the army. They were referred to in a letter that was produced, dated 2 December 1996, to Lieutenant Colonel Donald R. Curtis, Department of the Army, Corps of Engineers, Walla Walla, Washington, from Donald G. Sampson, Chairman of the Board of Trustees, Confederated Tribes of the Umatilla Indian Reservation.

17. Permit issued to Gary Huckleberry, Ph.D, no. DACW68-4-98-11, dated 5 December 1997. This permit showed that the terms of the permit made Huckleberry "subject to direction by Lillian Wakely, Ph.D., Chief Engineering Geology Branch (Principal Investigator), USACE Waterway Experiment Station."

## CHAPTER EIGHT: *Excavating the Museum Shelves*

1. Gordon, *Mi'kmaq Textiles Twining* (see chap. 3, n. 18).

2. Olga Soffer, James M. Adovasio, David C. Hyland, Bohuslav Klíma and Jiri Svoboda, "Perishable Technologies and the Genesis of the Eastern Gravettian," *Anthropologie* 36, no. 1–2 (1998): 43–68.

3. Amy Dansie, "Early Holocene Burials in Nevada, Overview of Localities, Research and Legal Issues," *Nevada Historical Society Quarterly* (Spring 1997): 5.

4. Donald R. Tuohy and Amy J. Dansie, "New Information Regarding Early Holocene Manifestations in the Western Great Basin," *Nevada Historical Society Quarterly* (Spring 1997): 38.

5. Amy Dansie, "Early Holocene Burials in Nevada, Overview of Localities, Research and Legal Issues," *Nevada Historical Society Quarterly* (Spring 1997): 8.

6. Frederika Kaestle, "Molecular Analysis of Ancient Native American DNA from Western Nevada," *Nevada Historical Society Quarterly* (Spring 1997): 85–96.

7. Peter E. Wigand, "Native American Diet and Environmental Contexts of the Holocene Revealed in the Pollen of Human Fecal Material," *Nevada Historical Society Quarterly* (Spring 1997): 105–16.

8. B. Sunday Eiselt, "Fish Remains from the Spirit Cave Paleofecal Material, 9,400 Year Old Evidence for Great Basin Utilization of Small Fishes," *Nevada Historical Society Quarterly* (Spring 1997): 117–39.

CHAPTER NINE: *We were Always Here*

1. "On Being First: Cultural Innovation and Environmental Consequences of First Peopling" (program and abstracts, 31st Annual Chacmool Conference).

2. Paul S. Martin, "Clovisia the Beautiful!" *Natural History* 10 (October 1987).

CHAPTER TEN: *Pendejo Cave*

1. Richard S. MacNeish, "Pendejo Pre-Clovis Proofs and their Implications," *FUMDHAMentos, Revista da Fundação Museu do Homem Americano*, vol. 1, no. 1, São Raimundo Nonato, Piaui, Brazil (1996), 171–200.

2. James M. Adovasio, "Meadowcroft," *FUMDHAMentos, Revista da Fundação Museu do Homem Americano*, vol. 1, no. 1, São Raimundo Nonato, Piaui, Brazil (1996), 202–19.

3. Donald S. Chrisman, Richard S. MacNeish, Jamshed Mavalwala and Howard Savage, "Late Pleistocene Human Friction Skin Prints from Pendejo Cave, New Mexico," *American Antiquity* 61, no. 2 (1996): 357–76.

4. L. Li, O. Marcaigh, Y. Zhou and M. Cowan, "A New Type of Severe Combined Immunodeficiency Disease Found in Athabascan-Speaking Native Americans," *American Journal of Human Genetics* 63, no. 4 (October 1998): A297. This abstract reported that a recessive T-cell found in high frequency among Athabascan-speaking Apache and Navajo is also found in the children of Athabascan-speaking Dene in the Northwest Territories. The authors suggest this particular disease-causing T-cell found in both populations was the result of a mutation of a novel gene located on a particular chromosome of a shared ancestor.

5. Diamond Jenness resigned from the National Museum staff in 1930 but returned and worked there between 1937 and 1947 as chief anthropologist. Dr. Frederick Alcock was chief curator of the National Museum of Canada from 1947 to 1956.

6. During the Second World War, the Arctic became a region of strategic interest to the governments of Canada and the United States. In the winter of 1946 the Canadian army tried to move men and machines overland in winter across the Barren Grounds for the first time. The expedition made its

way from Churchill to the mouth of the Coppermine River and then south to Edmonton by way of the Mackenzie Valley. The army officers who planned the trip discovered they needed help from those who knew the land best—trappers, bush pilots and Native Canadians. One of the officers on the expedition who recorded geological findings of interest was J. Tuzo Wilson.

7. Diamond Jenness, ed., *The American Aborigines: Their Origin and Antiquity* (Toronto: University of Toronto Press, 1933).
8. W.A. Johnston, "Quaternary Geology of North America in Relation to the Migration of Man," in Jenness, *The American Aborigines*, 12 (see n. 7 above).
9. Franz Boas, "Relationships between North-West America and North-East Asia," in Jenness, *The American Aborigines*, 357 (see n. 7 above).
10. Johnston, "Quaternary Geology," 43.
11. Ibid., 44.
12. Alejandra Duk-Rodkin and Owen L. Hughes, "Tertiary-Quaternary Drainage of the Pre-Glacial Mackenzie Basin," *Quaternary International* 22/23 (1994): 221–41.
13. Brandon Beierle, personal correspondence, 24 November 1998.
14. House of Commons, *Debates*, 1959, Questions 291, 286, 341, 251, 285, 287, 290, 394, 430, 445, 289, 396, and 440.

## Part Two

### CHAPTER ELEVEN: *Beneath the Southern Cross*

1. David R. Yesner, "Human Dispersal into Interior Alaska: Antecedent Conditions, Mode of Colonization and Adaptations," *Quaternary Science Reviews*, in press.
2. Heiner Josenhans, Daryl Fedje, Reinhard Pienitz and John Southon, "Humans and Rapidly Changing Holocene Sea Levels in the Queen Charlotte Islands— Hecate Strait, British Columbia, Canada," *Science* 277 (4 July 1997): 71–74.
3. Renato Kipnis, "Early Hunter-Gatherers in the Americas: Perspectives from Central Brazil," Issues in Brazilian Archaeology, *Antiquity* 72, no. 277 (September 1998): 581–92.
4. Christiana Barreto, "Brazilian archaeology from a Brazilian Perspective," Issues in Brazilian Archaeology, *Antiquity* 72, no. 277 (September 1998): 573–581.
5. Eduardo Goes Neves, "Twenty Years of Amazonian Archaeology in Brazil (1977-1997)," Issues in Brazilian Archaeology, *Antiquity* 72, no. 277 (September 1998): 625–32.
6. Betty J. Meggers and Clifford Evans, "A Transpacific Contact in 3000 B.C.," *Scientific American* 214, no. 1 (January 1966): 28–35.
7. Betty J. Meggers, "The Transpacific Origin of Mesoamerican Civilization:

A Preliminary Review of the Evidence and Its Theoretical Implications," *American Anthropologist* 77, no. 1 (1975).

8. A.C. Roosevelt, R.A. Housely, M. Imazio da Silveira, S. Maranca and R. Johnson, "Eighth Millennium Pottery from a Prehistoric Shell Midden in the Brazilian Amazon," *Science* 254 (1991): 1621–24, and A.C. Roosevelt, M. Limada Costa, C. Lopes Machado, M. Michals, W. Mercier, H. Valladas, J. Feathers, W. Barnett, M. Imazio da Silveira, A. Henderson, J. Silva, B. Chernoff, D.S. Reese, J.A. Holman, N. Toth and K. Schick, "Paleo Indian Cave Dwellers in the Amazon: The Peopling of the Americas," *Science* 272 (1996): 373–84.

9. Neves, "Twenty Years of Amazonian Archaeology," 628 (see n. 5 above).

10. "Proceedings of the International Meeting on the Peopling of the Americas," *FUMDHAMentos, Revista da Fundação Museu do Homem Americano*, vol. 1, no. 1 (1996).

11. Marilia Carvalho Mello e Alvim, "The Peopling of Indian America: Controversial Issues," *FUMDHAMentos, Revista da Fundação Museu do Homem Americano* 1, no. 1 (1996): 140–44.

12. Adauto Araújo and Luiz Fernando Ferreira, "Paleoparasitology and the Peopling of the Americas," *FUMDHAMentos, Revista da Fundação Museu do Homem Americano* 1, no. 1 (1996): 106–11.

13. *The Examiner* (Peterborough, Ont.), Saturday 23 May 1998.

CHAPTER TWELVE: *Lunch with Luzia*

1. Samuel Hearne, *A Journey from Prince of Wales's Fort in Hudson's Bay to the Northern Ocean, Undertaken by Order of the Hudson's Bay Company for the Discovery of Copper Mines, A North West Passage, etc., In the Years 1769, 1770, 1771, & 1772*, (Edmonton: M.G. Hurtig, Booksellers & Publishers, 1971).

2. Gustavo Politis, "A Review of the Late Pleistocene Sites of Argentina," *FUMDHAMentos, Revista da Fundação Museu do Homem Americano* 1, no. 1, (1996): 154.

3. Marta Mirazon Lahr, "Patterns of Modern Human Diversification: Implications for Amerindian Origins," *Yearbook of Physical Anthropology* 38 (1995): 163–98.

CHAPTER THIRTEEN: *Proof Parasite*

1. *Trichuris trichiura* was found in the intestine of a mummy in Chile in 1954 and adult hookworm (*Ancylostoma duodenale*) was found in a mummified body in Tiahuanaco, Peru. This mummy dated from about 900 AD and was reported by M.J. Allison et al. in *The American Journal of Physical Anthropology* 41, no. 6 (1974): 103–06.

2. L.F. Ferreira, A.J.G. de Araújo and U.E.C. Confalonieri, "The Finding of Eggs and Larvae of Parasitic Helminths in Archaeological Material from Unai, Minas Gerais, Brazil," *Transactions of the Royal Society of Tropical Medicine and Hygiene* 74, no. 6 (1980): 798–800.
3. Michael M. Kliks, "Parasites in archaeological material from Brazil," *Transactions of the Royal Society of Tropical Medicine and Hygiene* 76, no. 5 (1982).
4. Luiz Fernando Ferreira, Adauto Jose G. de Araújo and Ulisses E. Confalonieri, "Parasites in Archaeological Material from Brazil: A reply to M. Kliks," *Transactions of the Royal Society of Tropical Medicine and Hygiene* 77, no. 4 (1983): 565–66.
5. L.F. Ferreira, A.J.G. de Araújo and U.E.C. Confalonieri, "The Finding of Helminth Eggs in a Brazilian Mummy," *Transactions of the Royal Society of Tropical Medicine and Hygiene* 77, no. 1 (1983): 65–67.
6. Luiz Fernando Ferreira, Adauto Araújo, Ulisses Confalonieri, Marcia Chame and Benjamim Ribeiro Filho, "Encontro de ovos de Ancilostomideos em Coprolitos Humanos Datados de 7,230+80 Anos, no Estado do Piaui, Brazil" (a presentado no X Congresso da Sociedade Brasileira de Parasitologia, Salvador, Bahia, 2-6, 8/1987).
7. K. Fuller, "Hookworm: Not a pre-Columbian pathogen," *Medical Anthropology* 17 (1997): 297–308.
8. Karl Reinhard, Adauto Araújo, Luiz Fernando Ferreira and Carlos Coimbra, "Hookworms and Prehistoric Migrations," unpublished manuscript.

CHAPTER FOURTEEN: *Revisionist Prehistory*

1. Steele and Powell, "Peopling of the Americas," 303–6 (see chap. 3, n. 1, above).
2. Neves and Pucciarelli, "Morphological Affinities of the First Americans," 261–73 (see chap. 6, n. 5, above).
3. Walter A. Neves, Joseph F. Powell, André Prous and Erik G. Ozolins, "Lapa Vermelha IV Hominid I: Morphological Affinities of the Earliest Known American" (paper presented at the 67th Annual Meeting of the American Association of Physical Anthropologists, Salt Lake City, usa, 1998).
4. Walter A. Neves, Danusa Munford and Maria do Carmo Zanini, "Cranial Morphological Variation and the Colonization of the New World: Towards a Four Migration Model," *American Journal of Physical Anthropology, Supplement* 22 (1996): 176.
5. Thor Heyerdahl, *Early Man and the Ocean* (New York: Vintage Books, Random House, 1980), 208.
6. Joseph F. Powell, "Dental Evidence for the Peopling of the New World: Some Methodological Considerations," *Human Biology* 65, no. 5 (1993): 799–819.
7. Walter A. Neves, Joseph F. Powell and Erik G. Ozolins, "Modern Human Origins as Seen from the Peripheries," unpublished manuscript.

8. Walter A. Neves, Joseph F. Powell and Erik G. Ozolins, "Extra-continental Morphological Affinities of Palli Aike, Southern Chile," *Interciencia* (submitted), 1998.

9. Heyerdahl, *Early Man*.

10. Thomas J. Green, Bruce Cochran, Todd W. Fenton, James C. Woods, Gene L. Titmus, Larry Tieszen, Mary Anne Davis and Susanne J. Miller, "The Buhl Burial: A Paleoindian Woman from Southern Idaho," *American Antiquity* 63, no. 3 (1998): 437–56.

11. James C. Chatters, Walter A. Neves and Max Blum, "The Kennewick Man: A First Multivariate Analysis," unpublished manuscript, 1999.

12. T.M. Karafet, S.L. Zegura, O. Posukh, L. Osipova, A. Bergen, J. Long, D. Goldman, W. Klitz, S. Harihara, P. de Krijff, V. Wiebe, R.C. Griffiths, A.R. Templeton and M.F. Hammer, "Ancestral Asian Source(s) of New World Y Chromosome Founder Haplotypes," *American Journal of Human Genetics* 64 (1999): 817–31.

CHAPTER FIFTEEN: *Brazilian Edens*

1. Genesis, Tanakh, *The Holy Scriptures: The New JPS Translation According to the Traditional Hebrew Text*, (Philadelphia, Jerusalem: Jewish Publication Society, 1985), 3–16.

2. Elayne Granada Lara and Claudina Maria Dutra Moresi, "Material Textil de Santana do Riacho," in *Arquivos do Museu de História Natural, Universidade Federal de Minas Gerais*, vol. 12, Santana do Riacho-Tomo 1, coordenadores André Prous and I.M. Malta (1991), 179–86.

3. Alan Bryan considered Walter to be a poor character, out to enrich himself by collecting and selling artifacts. Bryan believed that the calotte he found in the Belo Horizonte Museum of Natural History (with the Walter collection) and another calotte that was described to him by Marilia Mello e Alvim at the National Museum in Rio (and published on by Poech) must both have been found by Lund. He was sure that if they'd been found by Walter, he'd have known their value and tried to sell them.

4. Sheila Maria Ferraz Mendonça de Souza, "Paleopatologia Humana de Santana do Riacho," in *Arquivos do Museu de História Natural*, Universidade Federal de Minas Gerais, vol. 13, Tomo 2, coordenador André Prous (1992/1993), 129–60; and "Paleodemografia da População do Grande Abrigo de Santana do Riacho, Minas Gerais: Uma Hipótese para Verificação," on pages 161–71 of the same issue.

CHAPTER SIXTEEN: *Science Contender*

1. *FUMDHAMentos, Revista da Fundação Museu do Homem Americano*, vol. 1, no. 1 (1996).

2. David D. Meltzer, James M. Adovasio and Tom D. Dillehay, "On a Pleistocene human occupation at Pedra Furada, Brazil," *Antiquity* 68 (December 1994): 695–714.

3. As this went to press, Fábio Parenti's work was in press with Editions Récherches sur les Civilisations (ERC), a publishing arm of Ministère des Affaires Étrangères Archéologie as "Le gisement quaternaire de la Pedra Furada (Piaui, Brésil)/Stratigraphie, chronologie, evolution culturelle."

4. Evelyne Peyre, Claude Guerin, Niéde Guidon and Yves Coppens, "Des restes humains pleistocenes dans la grotte du Garrincho, Piaui, Brésil," *Paléontologie Humaine/Human Paleontology*, Académie des Sciences, Sciences de la terre et des planetes (1998): 335–60.

5. In fact, in March 2000, Niéde Guidon e-mailed me to say that these teeth from Garrincho Cave were successfully dated by Beta Analytic at a conventional radiocarbon age of 12,170 +/-40 BP.

6. Boris Weintraub, "A Seagoing Human Ancestor?" *National Geographic* (November 1998). A stone flake was found among many other tools discovered on an archaeological site on Flores Island, Indonesia, and dated at about 800,000 or 900,000 years old, just about the time *Homo erectus* is known to have existed in Asia. The only way to reach Flores at that time was by water.

7. Niéde Guidon, Fabio Parenti, Claudia Oliveira and Cleonice Vergne, "Comment on the Grave at Toca dos Coqueiros Serra da Capivara National Park, Brazil," *Clio*, Serie Arqueológia, vol. 1, no. 13 (Recife, Pernambuco, 1998), 199–202.

8. Claude Guerin, Maria Amelia Curvello, Martine Fauré, Marguerite Hugueney and Cecile Mourer-Chauvire, "The Pleistocene Fauna of Piaui (Northeastern Brazil): Paleological and Biochronological Implications," *FUMDHAMMentos, Revista da Fundação Museu do Homem Americano*, vol. 1, no. 1 (1996): 59.

9. Alexander Marshak, "Exploring the Mind of Ice Age Man," *National Geographic* 147, no. 1 (January 1975): 65–89.

*Part Three*

CHAPTER EIGHTEEN: *Science under Fire*

1. Michael Balter, "New Light on the Oldest Art," *Science* 283 (12 February 1999): 920–22.
2. Michael Balter, "Restorers Reveal 28,000-Year-Old Artworks," *Science* 283 (19 March 1999): 1835.
3. Sharon Begley and Andrew Murr, "The First Americans," *Newsweek* (26 April 1999): 50–57.
4. Testimony of Tex Hall at a hearing before the Committee on Indian Affairs, United States Senate, 106th Cong., 1st sess., on Public Law 101-601 to provide for the protection of Native American graves, 20 April 1999, pp. 70–76.
5. Kelly Scott and Kelli Kellogg, "Bones of Contention: UNL's Alleged Possession of Indian Remains Would Violate Federal Law," as downloaded from Web site jet.unl.edu/joe/042198/cover421.html, on 3 May 1999.
6. Report of Robert T. Grimit to Richard R. Wood, vice president and general counsel, University of Nebraska-Lincoln, re Investigation of UNL Compliance with NAGPRA, 15 April 1999.
7. Claim for Injury or Damage under State Tort Claims Act (Section 81–8,209 to 81–8,235) by Karl Reinhard from the State of Nebraska Office of Risk Management, State Claims Board, as sworn on 21 April 1999.
8. The Amended Petition in the District Court of Lancaster County, Nebraska, docket 576, Karl Reinhard, Plaintiff, vs. Stanley Parks, Defendant, served 14 December 1998, read (in part):

> In or about July, 1998, Defendant knowingly made false statements to the media including but not limited to, the *Lincoln Journal Star* and *Omaha World Herald*, on the Internet and to other third persons that:
> A) The Plaintiff ordered inventory records of Native American remains be changed so no one would know about the existence of soft tissue items;
> B) The Plaintiff threatened to terminate the Defendant if he did not change the inventory records;
> C) Bones found in University laboratory, Room 109 of Bessey Hall, were the remains and artifacts from the skeletal and artifact collections the Defendant inventoried and turned over to the Plaintiff;
> D) The Plaintiff did not return the DK2 and DK10 Omaha material;
> E) The Plaintiff is a detriment to the anthropology department, to the science of anthropology and to the University of Nebraska....

Answer in the District Court of Lancaster County, Nebraska, docket 576, Karl Reinhard, Plaintiff, vs. Stanley Parks, Defendant:

> ... While Defendant made truthful certain statements of fact and

also gave his opinions in a memorandum addressed and delivered solely to the chairman of the University Department for which he worked, he did not otherwise publish said statements. Certain news media members obtained that memorandum by means unknown to Defendant and questioned him in regard to it. Defendant acknowledged the memorandum was authored by him and briefly responded to their inquiries.... Defendant expressly denies making any false statements to anyone, as is alleged in Plaintiffs's paragraph 6.... The statements were made in the scope and course of his duties as an employee. They were prepared in memorandum form in response to a request for information by the addressee and were published by Defendant to no one other than the addressee.... Plaintiff's purported cause of action is barred by the doctrine of sovereign immunity for the reason that the defendant at all relevant times was an employee of an agency of the State of Nebraska, performing his duties within the scope of his employment. Neither the Defendant nor the State of Nebraska has consented to this action, the claim is not covered by the State Tort Claims Act, and the Court is without jurisdiction to impose liability upon the Defendant....

9. Karl Reinhard gradually came to feel that teaching and working at Nebraska in order to defend the study of human remains was a better remedy for what had been done to him than filing suits to get money so he could leave academia—not that he intended to cease seeking legal remedies. "I intend to stay at this institution," he wrote, "and further the cause of academic freedom using legal action (while recovering what is owed to me for damage to my health and career). I want to be sure that when this is over, vicious faculty here will think twice before attacking colleagues." He came to this position in part because of the support he got from other colleagues. He was nominated twice for an academic freedom award by the Faculty of Biology, he received a Fulbright Fellowship and had the support of medical and legal communities off the campus.

CHAPTER NINETEEN: *The Kennewick Shuffle*

1. Symposium at the AAPA 1999 annual meeting, "Genetics II and Skeletal Biology II: Population Origins and Evolution in the New World," organized by C. Kolman and J.C. Long.
2. M.T. Black, "Biomechanical Analysis of the Human Superior Pubic Ramus with Implications for Neanderthal Pubic Morphology" (paper given at the AAPA annual meeting in Columbus, Ohio, 29 April 1999).
3. J.C.M. Ahern, "Computational Methods for Addressing Age and Sex Sample Bias: A South-Central European Neanderthal Test Case" (paper given at the AAPA annual meeting in Columbus, Ohio, 29 April 1999).

4. D.L. Cunningham, "Weidenreich Revisited: Morphology of the Upper Cave Crania" (paper given at the AAPA annual meeting in Columbus, Ohio, 29 April 1999).

5. M.H. Wolpoff, J. Hawks, S. Oh, K. Hunley, S. Dobson, G. Cabana and P. Dayalu, "An Australian Test of the Recent African Origin Theory Using the WLH-50 Calvarium" (paper given at the AAPA annual meeting in Columbus, Ohio, 29 April 1999).

6. R.B. Eckhardt, "Evolutionary Morphology: Dynamics of Adaptation in New World Populations Support Continuity in Old World Successions" (paper given at the AAPA annual meeting in Columbus, Ohio, 29 April 1999).

7. Their paper was published in June 1999, in the Proceedings of the National Academy of Sciences.

8. Matthias Krings, Anne Stone, Ralf W. Schmitz, Heike Krainitzki, Mark Stoneking and Svante Paabo, "Neanderthal DNA Sequences and the Origin of Modern Humans," *Cell* 90 (11 July 1997): 19–30.

9. D.A. Merriwether, B. Kemp and J.V. Neel, "Native American Origins and Dispersal: Evidence from Mitochondrial DNA" (paper given at the AAPA annual meeting in Columbus, Ohio, 30 April 1999).

10. Evelyn Strauss, "Can Mitochondrial Clocks Keep Time?" *Science* 283 (5 March 1999): 1435–38. J.R. Kidd and K.K. Kidd, "Autosomal DNA Haplotype Diversity within and among Amerind-speaking populations" (paper given at the AAPA annual meeting in Columbus, Ohio, 30 April 1999). Diego Hurtado de Mendoza and Richard Braginski, "Y Chromosomes Point to Native American Adam," *Science* 283 (5 March 1999): 1439–40. T.G. Schurr, J.T. Lell, R.I. Sukernik, E.B. Starikovskaya and D.C. Wallace, "Reevaluating Siberia As a Source Area for Ancestral Native American Populations" (paper given at the AAPA annual meeting in Columbus, Ohio, 30 April 1999). Michael F. Hammer and Stephen L. Zegura, "The Role of the Y Chromosome in Human Evolutionary Studies," *Evolutionary Anthropology*, 1997. M.F. Hammer, S.L. Zegura, A. Bergen, J.C. Long, W. Klitz, R.C. Griffiths, A.R. Templeton, L.P. Osipova, O.L. Posukh and T.M. Karafet, "New World Y Chromosome Founder Haplotypes and the Peopling of the Americas" (paper given at the AAPA annual meeting in Columbus, Ohio, 30 April 1999).

11. D.H. O'Rourke, S.W. Carlyle and M.G. Hayes, "Ancient DNA patterns and the Peopling of the Americas" (paper given at the AAPA annual meeting in Columbus, Ohio, 30 April 1999).

12. J. Nichols, "The Pleistocene Component of the Native American Population: A Linguistic Perspective" (paper given at the AAPA annual meeting in Columbus, Ohio, 30 April 1999).

13. J.F. Powell, "New Craniofacial and Dental perspectives on Native American origins" (paper given at the AAPA annual meeting in Columbus, Ohio, 30 April 1999).

14. T. Goeble, G.R. Scott, "Archaeology and the Human Colonization of

Siberia, Alaska and New World: Do Stones, Bones and Genes Tell the Same Story?" (paper given at the AAPA annual meeting in Columbus, Ohio, 30 April 1999).

15. Hibben, *Lost Americans* (New York: Thomas Y. Crowell, revised and updated 1968).

16. J. C. Chatters, "Preliminary analysis of 'Kennewick Man,' a Paleoamerican Skeleton from the Northwestern United States" (poster display at the AAPA annual meeting in Columbus, Ohio, 1 May 1999).

17. James C. Chatters, "The Recovery and First Analysis of an Early Holocene Human Skeleton from Kennewick, Washington," *American Antiquity* (April 2000).

18. P.A. Lindsell, "Climate and Body Form in Australian Aborigines" (paper given at the AAPA annual meeting in Columbus, Ohio, 30 April 1999).

19. V. Formicola and A. Canci, "From Hunting to Farming: The Impact on Health Status in Western Liguria (Italy)" (poster display at the AAPA in Columbus, Ohio, 1 May 1999).

20. D.L. Martin, P.K. Stone and N. Parker, "Paleodemography of a Bronze Age Skeletal Population from Tell Abraq, United Arab Emirates" (poster display at the AAPA annual meeting in Columbus, Ohio, 1 May 1999).

CHAPTER TWENTY: *The Reverse Migration*

1. Derald G. Smith and Timothy G. Fisher, "Glacial Lake Agassiz: The Northwestern Outlet and Paleoflood," *Geology* 21 (January 1993): 9–12.

2. Brian Reeves and Nancy Saxberg, "Current Interpretative Status and Implications for Understanding the Early Post Glacial Native Culture, History and Occupation of the Athabasca Lowlands: A Mid-1998 Program Update," report prepared for Aurora Mine Project Historical Resources Management Studies 8 August 1998.

3. Ibid., 3.

4. Ronald J. Mason and Carol Irwin, "An Eden-Scottsbluff Burial in Northeastern Wisconsin," *American Antiquity* 26, no. 1 (1960): 43–57.

5. Later, Reeves told me the results of protein residue analyses made of the surfaces of the doughnuts. Researchers had identified the remains of bear and a plant called chenopodium, which is commonly called goosefoot and is often found in disturbed habitats.

CHAPTER TWENTY-ONE: *The Corridor That Wasn't*

1. Alejandra Duk-Rodkin and Owen L. Hughes, "Tertiary-Quaternary Drainage of the Pre-Glacial Mackenzie Basin," *Quaternary International* 22/23 (1994): 221–41.

2. Donald S. Lemmen, Alejandra Duk-Rodkin and Jan M. Bednarski, "Later Glacial Drainage Systems Along the Northwestern Margin of the Laurentide Ice Sheet," *Quaternary Science Review* 13 (1994): 805–28.

3. D.S. Lemmen, A. Duk-Rodkin, J. Bednarski and T. Robertson, "Paleogeography of the Mackenzie River Drainage Basin during the Last Glaciation," Map of the Terrain Sciences Division, Geological Survey of Canada, 1994.

4. David Yesner, "Human Colonization of Eastern Beringia and the Question of Mammoth Hunting" (paper presented to the International Symposium on Mammoth Site Studies in Eurasia and North America, 1999). Yesner's conclusion in this paper is that the mammoth bones made into tools and found on human sites of occupation in Alaska were likely scavenged from already dead animals: mammoths were already extinct or on the edge of it in Alaska by the time the tools were made.

5. Timothy H. Heaton, "An Ice Age Refugium for Large Mammals in the Alexander Archipelago, Southeastern Alaska," *Quaternary Research* 46 (1996): 186–92.

6. Heiner Josenhans, Daryl Fedje, Reinhard Pienitz and John Southon, "Early Humans and Rapidly Changing Holocene Sea Levels in the Queen Charlotte Islands—Hecate Strait, British Columbia, Canada," *Science* 277 (4 July 1997): 71–74.

7. A. Duk-Rodkin, R.W. Barendregt, C. Tarnocai and F.M. Phillips, "Late Tertiary to Late Quaternary Record in the Mackenzie Mountains, Northwest Territories, Canada: Stratigraphy, Paleosols, Paleomagnetism and Chlorine-36(1)," *Canadian Journal of Earth Sciences* 33, no. 6 (1996): 875–95.

8. Ian Tattersall, "Once We Were Not Alone," *Scientific American* 282, no. 1 (January 2000): 56–62.

9. David R. Yesner, "Human Adaptation at the Pleistocene-Holocene Boundary (circa 13,000 to 8000 BP)," in *Humans at the End of the Ice Age: The Archaeology of the Pleistocene-Holocene Transition*, edited by Lawrence Guy Straus, Berit Valentin Eriksen, Jon M. Erlandson and David R. Yesner (New York: Plenum Press, 1996). In his discussion of the Broken Mammoth site, Yesner explains that different tools and different styles of life are found at the 11,000 BP level, called zone 4, versus the 9000–10,000 BP level, called zone 3. Zone 4 showed a heavy reliance on birds—which Yesner attributed to the fact that with the inundation of the Bering Strait, the normal Pacific migratory bird flyway had been reestablished by 12,000 BP. Zone 3 showed tools somewhat like those found in the south, although there was nothing that looked like a Clovis point. These later sites showed that a broad range of animals were hunted—from the large wapiti to the small Arctic hare and even salmon. The one thing not found was evidence that live mammoths were killed. Although mammoth ivory had been used for making tools, these ivories turned out to be three thousand years older than the sites

themselves. None of this contradicted Duk-Rodkin and Lemmen's geological findings.

10. J. Lundqvist and M. Saarnisto, "Summary of Project IGCP-253," *Quaternary International* 28 (1995): 9–18.

11. A.A. Velichko, "The Pleistocene Termination in Northern Eurasia," *Quaternary International* 28 (1995): 105–11.

12. Nat Rutter, "Problematic Ice Sheets," *Quaternary International* 28 (1995): 19–37.

13. Thomas F. Lynch, "The Discovery of America—Why It Matters," *Arts & Sciences Newsletter* 14, no. 1 (January 1993).

## CHAPTER TWENTY-TWO: *Hard Science, Hardball Politics*

1. Special to *The Toronto Star*, "Hunters Find Frozen Native Man Partially Intact in Mountain Glacier," reprinted from *The Los Angeles Times*, with files from Canadian Press and *The Toronto Star* (25 August 1999), A2.

2. News release, "Tatshenshini Find Moved to Royal B.C. Museum," Ministry of Small Business, Tourism and Culture, British Columbia 13 September 1999.

3. News release, "New Data Indicates Age of Kwaday Dän Sinchi Find," Ministry of Small Business, Tourism and Culture, British Columbia/Champagne and Aishihik First Nations 28 September 1999.

4. Francis P. McManamon, "The Initial Scientific Examination, Description and Analysis of the Kennewick Man Human Remains," *Kennewick Man*, report of United States National Park Service, 1999, as downloaded from the website of Friends of America's Past at http://www.friendsofpast.org.

5. Ibid.

6. United States Department of the Interior, Geological Survey. Kennewick Quadrangle, Washington, 7.5 minute series (topographic) Map, and McNary Lock & Dam, Columbia River, Oregon 8, Washington Segment Q, RE Segment "Q" Map. MNAQQ17.CIT/US Army, Corps of Engineers, 26 July 1951.

7. John L. Fagan, "Analysis of Lithic Artifact Embedded in the Columbia Park Remains," *Kennewick Man*, report of United States National Park Service, 1999, as downloaded from the website of Friends of America's Past at http://www.friendsofpast.org.

8. Gary Huckleberry and Julie K. Stein, "Analysis of Sediments Associated with Human Remains Found at Columbia Park, Kennewick," *Kennewick Man*, report of United States National Park Service, 1999, as downloaded from the website of Friends of America's Past at http://www.friendsofpast.org.

9. Joseph F. Powell and Jerome C. Rose, "Skeletal Reconstruction," *Kennewick*

*Man*, report of United States National Park Service, 1999, as downloaded from the website of Friends of America's Past at http://www.friendsofpast.org.

10. "Purpose of and Need for the Proposed Action," *Disposal of Chemical Agents and Munitions Stored at Umatilla Depot Activity, Oregon*, Revised Final Environmental Impact Statement, Program Manager for Chemical Demilitarization Aberdeen Proving Ground, MD-21010-5401, November 1996, pages 1–13.

11. Press release, "Raytheon Wins $512 Million Army Contract for Chemical Weapons Destruction," Raytheon Engineers & Constructors, Lexington, Mass., 30 July 1997.

12. *Disposal of Chemical Agents and Munitions Stored at Umatilla Depot Activity, Oregon*, Revised Final Environmental Impact Statement, Program Manager for Chemical Demilitarization Aberdeen Proving Ground, MD-21010-5401, November 1996, Appendix H, H5-H6.

# Bibliography

## BOOKS

Anouilh, Jean. *Antigone*. London: Methuen & Co., 1957.

Bandi, Hans-Georg, and Henri Breuil et al. *The Art of the Stone Age: Forty Thousand Years of Rock Art*. Germany: Holle and Co., 1961.

Boas, Franz. *Kwakiutl Ethnography*. Chicago and London: University of Chicago Press, 1966.

Bryan, Alan Lyle, ed. *Early Man in America from a Circum-Pacific Perspective*. Edmonton: Archaeological Researches International, 1978.

Coles, J.M., and E.S. Higgs. *The Archaeology of Early Man*. Harmondsworth, Middlesex, England: Penguin Books, 1975.

Dillehay, Tom D. *Monte Verde: A Late Pleistocene Settlement in Chile.*, vol. 1. Washington and London: Smithsonian Institution Press, 1989.

———. *Monte Verde: A Late Pleistocene Settlement in Chile*, vol. 2. Washington and London: Smithsonian Institution Press, 1997.

———. *The Settlement of the Americas: A New Prehistory*. New York: Basic Books, 2000.

Ellis, Chris J., and Neal Ferris, eds. *The Archaeology of Southern Ontario to A.D. 1650*. London, Ontario: Occasional Publications of the London Chapter, OAS Number 5, 1990.

Ferreira, Luiz Fernando, Adauto Araújo and Ulisses Confalonieri. *Paleoparasitologia No Brasil*. Rio de Janeiro: Fundação Oswaldo Cruz and Escola Nacional de Saúde Publica, 1998.

Finlayson, William D. *Iroquoian Peoples of the Land of Rocks and Water, A.D. 1000-1650: A Study in Settlement Archaeology*, 4 vols. London, Ontario: London Museum of Archaeology, 1998.

Glick, Thomas F., and David Kohn, eds. *Darwin on Evolution: The Development of the Theory of Natural Selection*. Indianapolis and Cambridge: Hackett Publishing Company Inc., 1996.

Granatstein, J.L., and Robert Bothwell. *Pirouette: Pierre Trudeau and Canadian Foreign Policy*. Toronto: University of Toronto Press, 1990.

Hearne, Samuel. *A Journey from Prince of Wales's Fort in Hudson's Bay to the Northern Ocean*. Edmonton: M.G. Hurtig Ltd. Booksellers and Publishers, 1971.

Heusser, Calvin J. *Late-Pleistocene Environments of North Pacific North America*. New York: American Geographical Society, 1960.

Heyerdahl, Thor. *Early Man and the Ocean: A Search for the Beginnings of Navigation and Seaborne Civilizations*. New York: Vintage Books, 1980.

Hibben, Frank C. *The Lost Americans*. New York: Thomas Y. Crowell Company, 1968.

Jenness, Diamond, ed. *The American Aborigines: Their Origin and Antiquity*. Toronto: University of Toronto Press, 1933.

Kennedy, Ian, and Andrew Grubb, eds. *Principles of Medical Law*. Oxford: Oxford University Press, 1998.

Lahr, Marta Mirazon. *The Evolution of Modern Human Diversity: A Study of Cranial Variation*. Cambridge: Cambridge University Press, 1996.

McGhee, Robert. *The Burial at L'Anse-Amour*. Ottawa: National Museum of Man National Museums of Canada, 1976.

Meggers, Betty J. *Amazonia: Man and Culture in a Counterfeit Paradise*. Washington and London: Smithsonian Institution Press, 1996.

Prous, André, and I.M. Malta, eds. *Arquivos Do Museu De História Natural*, vol. 12, *Santana do Riacho*–Tomo I. Belo Horizonte: Universidade Federal De Minas Gerais, 1991.

Prous, André, ed. *Arquivos Do Museu de História Natural*, vol. 13, *Santana do Riacho*–Tomo II. Belo Horizonte: Universidade Federal de Minas Gerais, 1992/1993.

Purdy, Barbara A. *The Art and Archaeology of Florida's Wetlands*. Boca Raton: CRC Press, 1991.

Stanford, Dennis J., and Jane S. Day. *Ice Age Hunters of the Rockies*. Denver: The University Press of Colorado, 1992.

Tanakh: *A New Translation of the Holy Scriptures According to the Traditional Hebrew Text*. Philadelphia and Jerusalem: The Jewish Publication Society, 1985.

Vogel, Virgil J. *American Indian Medicine*. Oklahoma: University of Oklahoma Press, 1977.

Wright, Ronald. *Time Among the Maya*. Markham, Ontario: Penguin Canada, 1990.

## REPORTS AND HEARINGS

Archaeological Services Inc. *A Preliminary Report on the Archaeological Documentation and Exhumation of the Human Remains from the Moatfield Site (AkGu-65)*. City of North York, Ontario, October 1997.

Coleman, A.P. "The Pleistocene of the Toronto Region (including Toronto Inter-glacial Formation)," Forty-First Annual Report of the Ontario Department of Mines, vol. 41, part 7, 1932.

*Disposal of Chemical Agents and Munitions Stored at Umatilla Depot Activity, Oregon.* Revised Final Environmental Impact Statement, Program Manager for Chemical Demilitarization, Aberdeen Proving Ground, November 1996.

Gordon, Joleen. *Mi'kmaq Textiles Twining: Rush and Other Fibres BkCp-1 Site Pictou, Nova Scotia.* Nova Scotia Museum, Curatorial Report no. 82, March 1997.

Grimit, Robert T. "Report of Robert T. Grimit to Richard R. Wood Vice President and General Counsel University of Nebraska-Lincoln re Investigation of UNL Compliance with NAGPRA," 15 April 1999.

Hamilton, Scott. "Archaeological Investigations at the Wapekeka Burial Site (FlJj-1)," Report prepared for the Wapekeka First Nation, Ontario Ministry of Transportation, Ontario Ministry of Northern Development and Mines, Federal Department of Indian and Northern Affairs, 1991.

House of Representatives, Committee on Interior and Insular Affairs. Hearing record of 17 July 1990, regarding protection of Native American graves and the repatriation of human remains and sacred objects.

House of Representatives, a bill, H.R. 1381, 14 March 1989.

House Report No. 101-877. *Native American Graves Protection and Repatriation Act.* Public Law 101-601, Statute 3048, pp. 4367–4392.

Intergovernmental Panel on Climate Change. *Climate Change: The IPCC Scientific Assessment.* World Meteorological Association/United Nations Environment Programme, 1995.

Krueger Enterprises, Inc. Geochron Laboratories Division, Report of Analytical Work, sample number GX-5193-G, 27 January 1978.

*Native American Graves Protection and Repatriation Act*, Hearing before the Committee on Indian Affairs United States Senate, 106th Cong., 1st sess. on Public Law 101-601, to provide for the protection of Native American graves, 20 April 1999.

Reeves, Brian. "Aurora Mine Project Historical Resources Baseline Study, Final Report." Fort McMurray, Alberta: Syncrude Canada Ltd., 1996.

———. "Proposal for Nomination as a Provincial Historical Resource Site, Draft Report." Fort McMurray, Alberta: Syncrude Canada Ltd., 1997.

Reeves, Brian, and Nancy Saxberg. "Aurora Mine Project Historical Resource Management Studies Current Interpretive Status & Implications for Understanding the Early Postglacial Native Culture History and Occupation of the Athabasca Lowlands, a Mid-1998 Program Update," 8 August 1998.

Saxberg, Nancy, Mack W. Shortt and Brian Reeves. "Aurora Mine North Utility and Access Road Corridors, Final Report." Historical Resources Impact Assessment. Fort McMurray, Alberta: Syncrude Canada Ltd., 1998.

Shortt, Mack W., et al. "Aurora Mine North East Pit Opening, Plant Site,

Tailings, and Related Workings HRIA and Mitigation Studies, Final Report."
Fort McMurray, Alberta: Syncrude Canada Ltd., 1998.

U.S. Senate Select Committee on Indian Affairs, Hearing Record Regarding
*Native American Grave and Burial Protection Act (Repatriation): Native American Repatriation of Cultural Patrimony Act*: and the Heard Museum Report,
Monday 14 May 1990.

York North Archaeological Services. "The Flowers Point Site." Report for the
Ontario Provincial Police, Peterborough Detachment.

### DISSERTATIONS

Brace, Ian. "Boulder Monuments of Saskatchewan." Master's thesis, University of
Alberta, Edmonton.

Kaestle, Frederika Ann. "Molecular Evidence for Prehistoric Native American
Population Movement: The Numic Expansion." Submitted in partial satisfaction of the requirements for the degree of Doctor of Philosophy in
Anthropology in the Office of Graduate Studies, University of California,
Davis, 1998.

Posey, Darrell Addison. "Ethnoentomology of the Gorotire Kayapo of Central
Brazil." Ph.D. diss., University of Georgia, 1979.

Nelson, Russell Albert. "A Craniofacial Perspective on North American Indian
Population Affinities and Relations." Ph.D. diss., University of Michigan, 1998.

### ARTICLES

Adovasio, James M. "Meadowcroft." *FUMDHAMentos, Revista da Fundação Museu do
Homem Americano* 1, no. 1 (1996): 201–20.

Adovasio, J.M., J. Donahue, and R. Stuckenrath. "The Meadowcroft Rockshelter
Radiocarbon Chronology 1975-1990." *American Antiquity* 55, no. 2 (1990):
348–54.

Adovasio, J.M., and Thomas F. Lynch. "Preceramic Textiles and Cordage from
Guitarrero Cave, Peru." *American Antiquity* 38, no. 1 (1973): 84–90.

Adovasio, J.M., D.R. Pedler, J. Donahue, and R. Stuckenrath. "Two Decades of
Debate on Meadowcroft Rockshelter." *North American Archaeologist* 19, no. 4
(1998): 317–41.

Adovasio, J.M., Olga Soffer, and Bohuslav Klíma. "Upper Paleolithic Fibre
Technology: Interlaced Woven Finds from Pavlov I, Czech Republic, c.
26,000 Years Ago." *Antiquity* 70 (1996): 526–34.

Allen, Jane, Margaret E. Newman, Mary Riford, and Gavin H. Archer. "Blood
and Plant Residues on Hawaiian Stone Tools from Two Archaeological Sites
in Upland Kane'ohe, Ko'olau Poko District, O'ahu Island." *Asian Perspectives*
34, no. 2 (Fall 1995): 283–302.

Allen, Jim. "Radiocarbon Determinations, Luminescence Dating and Australian Archaeology." *Antiquity* 68 (1994): 339–43.

Alt, Kurt W., Sandra Pichler, Werner Vach, Bohuslav Klíma, Emanuel Vlček and Jürg Sedlmeier, "Twenty-Five Thousand-Year-Old Triple Burial from Dolni Vestonice: An Ice-Age Family?" *American Journal of Physical Anthropology* 102 (1997): 102–23.

Araújo, A.J.G. (Adauto) de, and Luiz Fernando Ferreira. "Paleoparasitology and the Peopling of the Americas." *FUMDHAMentos: Revista da Fundação Museu do Homem Americano* 1, no. 1 (1996): 108–14.

Araújo, A.J.G. de, Karl Reinhard, Otilio M. Bastos, Ligia C. Costa, Claude Pirmez, Alena Iniguez, Ana Carolina Vicente, Carlos M. Morel, and Luiz Fernando Ferreira. "Invited Reply Paleoparasitology: Perspectives with New Techniques." *Revista Instituto Medico Tropical São Paulo* 40, no. 6 (November/December 1998): 371–76.

Astakhov, Valery I. "The Mode of Degradation of Pleistocene Permafrost in West Siberia." *Quaternary International* 28 (1995): 119–21.

Barreto, Christiana. "Brazilian Archaeology from a Brazilian Perspective." *Antiquity* 72 (1998): 573–81.

Beltrão, Maria da Conceição. "Archaeological Region of Central Bahia, Brazil: The Toca da Esperanca (Cave of Hope), a Middle Pleistocene Archaeological Site." *FUMDHAMentos, Revista da Fundação Museu do Homem Americano* 1, no. 1 1996): 115–38.

Beukens, R.P., L.A. Pavlish, R.G.V. Hancock, R.M. Farquhar, G.C. Wilson, P.J. Julig, and William Ross. "Radiocarbon Dating of Copper-Preserved Organics." *Radiocarbon* 34, no. 3 (1992): 890–97.

Bianchi, Nestor O., Cecilia I. Catanesi, Craciela Bailliet, Veronica L. Martinez-Marignac, Claudio M. Bravi, Lidia B. Vidal-Rioja, Rene J. Herrera, and Jorge S. Lopez-Carnelo. "Characterization of Ancestral and Derived Y-Chromosome Haplotypes of New World Native Populations." *American Journal of Human Genetics* 63 (1998): 1862–71.

Bischof, Jens F., and Dennis A. Darby. "Mid- to Late Pleistocene Ice Drift in the Western Arctic Ocean: Evidence for a Different Circulation in the Past." *Science* 277 (4 July 1997): 74–78.

Boas, Franz. "Changes in the Bodily Form of Descendants of Immigrants." *American Anthropologist* 14 (1912): 530–62.

———. "Physical Characteristics of the Indians of the North Pacific Coast." *The American Anthropologist* 4 (January 1891): 25–32.

Borrero, Luis Alberto. "Human and Natural Agency: Some Comments on Pedra Furada." *Antiquity* 69 (1995): 602–3.

Brace, C. Loring, and A. Russell Nelson, "The Peopling of the Americas: Anglo Stereotypes and Native American Realities." in press.

Brace, C. Loring. "Neanderthals 'r' Us?" *Anthropology Newsletter* 38, no. 8 (November 1997).

Brown, Michael D., Seyed H. Hosseini, Antonio Torroni, Hans-Jurgen Bandelt,

Jon C. Allen, Theodore C. Schurr, Rosaria Scozzari, Fulvio Cruciani, and Douglas C. Wallace. "Mtdna Haplogroup X: An Ancient Link between Europe/Western Asia and North America?" *American Journal of Human Genetics* 63 (1998): 1852–61.

Buckmaster, Marla M., and James R. Paquette. "The Gorto Site: Preliminary Report on a Late Paleo-Indian Site in Marquette County, Michigan." *Wisconsin Archaeologist* 69, no. 3: 101–23.

Chatters, James C. "Encounter with an Ancestor." *Anthropology Newsletter* 38, no. 1 (January 1997).

————. "Human Biological History, Not Race." *Anthropology Newsletter* 39, no. 2 (February 1998).

————. "The Recovery and First Analysis of an Early Holocene Human Skeleton from Kennewick, Washington." *American Antiquity* 65, no. 2 (April 2000).

Chen, Tiemei, and Yinyun Zhang. "Paleolithic Chronology and Possible Coexistence of *Homo erectus* and *Homo sapiens* in China." *World Archaeology* 23, no. 2, (1991): 147–54.

Chrisman, Donald, Richard S. MacNeish, Jamshed Mavalwala, and Howard Savage. "Late Pleistocene Human Friction Skin Prints from Pendejo Cave, New Mexico." *American Antiquity* 61, no. 2 (1996): 357–76.

Cinq-Mars, Jacques, C. Richard Harington, E. Erle Nelson, and Richard S. MacNeish. "Engigsteiak Revisited: A Note on Early Holocene AMS Dates from the 'Buffalo Pit.'" *Cahier* no. 1 (1991).

Cinq-Mars, Jacques, and Jean-Luc Pilon, eds. "NOGAP Archaeology Project: An Integrated Archaeological Research and Management Approach." Association Canadienne d'Archéologie, *Cahier* no. 1 (1991).

Cinq-Mars, Jacques, and R.E. Morlan. "Bluefish Caves and Old Crow Basin: A New Rapport." In *Ice Age Peoples of North America: Environment, Origins and Adaptations*, edited by Robson Bonnichsen and Karen L. Turmire. Corvallis: Oregon State University Press, for the Center for Study of the First Americans, 1999, pp. 212–20.

Clapperton, Chalmers M. "Fluctuations of Local Glaciers at the Termination of the Pleistocene: 18-8ka BP." *Quaternary International* 28 (1995): 41–90.

Cockrell, W.A., and Larry Murphy. "Pleistocene Man in Florida." *Archaeology of Eastern North America* 6 (1978): 1–12.

Comas, David, Francesc Clafell, Eva Mateu, Anna Pérez-Lezaun, Elena Bosch, Rosa Martinez-Arias, Jordi Clarimon, Fiorenzo Facchini, Giovanni Fiori, Donata Luiselli, Davide Pettener, and Jaume Bertranpetit. "Trading Genes along the Silk Road: Mtdna Sequences and the Origin of Central Asian Populations." *American Journal of Human Genetics* 63 (1998): 1824–38.

Cybulski, Jerome S., Donald E. Howes, James C. Haggarty, and Morley Eldridge. "An Early Human Skeleton from South-Central British Columbia: Dating and Bioarchaeological Inference." *Canadian Journal of Archaeology* no. 5 (1981): 49–59.

Dansie, Amy. "Early Holocene Burials in Nevada: Overview of Localities, Research and Legal Issues." *Nevada Historical Society Quarterly* 40, no. 1 (Spring 1997): 4–14.

———. "Note on Textiles Associated with the Spirit Cave Burials." *Nevada Historical Society Quarterly* 40, no. 1 (Spring 1997): 17–23.

Dansie, Amy, and Donald R. Tuohy. "What We Can and Can't Know about Great Basin Prehistory," *Anthropology Newsletter* 38, no. 1 (January 1997).

Dickel, D.N., and G.H. Doran. "Severe Neural Tube Defect Syndrome from the Early Archaic of Florida." *American Journal of Physical Anthropology* 80 (1989): 325–34.

Dickel, David N., C. Gregory Aker, Billie R. Barton, and Glen H. Doran. "An Orbital Floor and Ulna Fracture from the Early Archaic of Florida." *Journal of Paleopathology* 2, no. 3 (1989): 165–70.

Dillehay, Tom D. "A Synopsis of the Archaeological Record at Monte Verde." *FUMDHAMentos, Revista da Fundação Museu do Homem Americano* 1, no. 1 (1996): 147–52.

Dixon, E. James, Timothy H. Heaton, Terence E. Fifield, Thomas D. Hamilton, David E. Putnam, and Frederick Grady. "Later Quaternary Regional Geoarchaeology of Southeast Alaska Karst: A Progress Report." *Geoarchaeology: An International Journal* 12, no. 6 (1997): 689–712.

Doran, Glen H. "Problems and Potential of Wet Sites in North America: The Example of Windover." In *The Wetland Revolution in Prehistory*, edited by Bryony Coles. Exeter: University of Exeter, 1992.

Doran, Glen H., and David N. Dickel. "Radiometric Chronology of the Archaic Windover Archaeological Site (8Br246)." *The Florida Anthropologist* 41, no. 3 (September 1988): 365–80.

———. "Multidisciplinary Investigations at the Windover Site." In *Wet Site Archaeology*, edited by Barbara Purdy. Caldwell, New Jersey: Telford Press, 1988, pp. 263–89.

Doran, Glen H., David N. Dickel, and Lee A. Newsom. "A 7,290-Year-Old Bottle-Gourd from the Windover Site, Florida." *American Antiquity* 55, no. 2 (1990): 354–60.

Doyson-Bernard, S.J. "From Twining to Triple Cloth, Experimentation and Innovation in Ancient Peruvian Weaving (ca. 5,000-400 B.C.)." *American Antiquity* 55, no. 1 (1990): 68–47.

Dragoo, Don W. "Adena and the Eastern Burial Cult." *Archaeology of Eastern North America* 4 (Winter 1976): 1–9.

Duk-Rodkin, A., R.W. Barendregt, C. Tarnocai, and F.M. Phillips. "Late Tertiary to Late Quaternary Record in the Mackenzie Mountains, Northwest Territories, Canada: Stratigraphy, Paleosols, Paleomagnetism, and Chlorine-36." *Canadian Journal of Earth Sciences* 33, no. 6 (June 1996): 875–95.

Duk-Rodkin, Alejandra, and Owen L. Hughes. "Quaternary Geology of the Northeastern Part of the Central Mackenzie Valley Corridor, District of Mackenzie, Northwest Territories." *Geological Survey of Canada Bulletin* 458

(1995).

———. "Tertiary-Quaternary Drainage of the Pre-Glacial Mackenzie Basin." *Quaternary International* 22/23 (1994): 221–41.

Easton, Ruth D., D. Andrew Merriwether, Douglas E. Crews, and Robert E. Ferrell. "MtDNA Variation in the Yanomami: Evidence for Additional New World Founding Lineages." *American Journal of Human Genetics* 59 (1996): 213–25.

Edgar, Heather Joy Hecht. "Paleopathology of the Wizards Beach Man (AHUR 2023) and the Spirit Cave Mummy (AHUR 2064)." *Nevada Historical Society Quarterly* 40, no. 1 (Spring 1997): 57–61.

Eiselt, B. Sunday. "Fish Remains from the Spirit Cave Paleofecal Material: 9,400 Year Old Evidence for Great Basin Utilization of Small Fishes." *Nevada Historical Society Quarterly* 40, no. 1 (Spring 1997): 117–39.

Farr, Christine J., and Peter N. Goodfellow. "Hidden Messages in Genetic Maps." *Science* 258 (2 October 1992): 49.

Ferreira, L.F., and A.J.G. de Araújo. "The Finding of Eggs and Larvae of Parasitic Helminths in Archaeological Material from Unai, Minas Gerais, Brazil." *Transactions of the Royal Society of Tropical Medicine and Hygiene* 74, no. 6 (1980): 798–800.

Ferreira, L.F., A.J.G. de Araújo, and U.E.C. Confalonieri. "The Finding of Helminth Eggs in a Brazilian Mummy," *Transactions of the Royal Society of Tropical Medicine and Hygiene* 77, no. 1 (1983): 65–7.

Ferris, Neal. "'I Don't Think We Are in Kansas Anymore': The Rise of the Archaeological Consulting Industry in Ontario." In *Bringing Back the Past: Historical Perspectives on Canadian Archaeology*, edited by P.J. Smith and D. Mitchell. Canadian Museum of Civilization Archaeological Survey of Canada *Mercury Series* 158 (1998): 225–27.

Fiedel, Stuart J. "Older Than We Thought: Implications of Corrected Dates for Paleoindians." *American Antiquity* 64, no. 1 (1999): 95–115.

Fifield, Terence E. "On Your Knees Cave Update." *The Alaskan Caver* 16, no. 6 (1996).

Finlayson, William D. "War and Peace among the Ontario Iroquoians of the Crawford Lake Area, A.D. 1000-1651." In *Leading Edge and The Point Niagara Escarpment and Long Point World Biosphere Reserves*, Conference Proceedings, edited by S. Carty, R. Murzin, S. Powell, and D. Ramsay, 1997, pp. 187–97.

Fischer, Hubertus, Martin Wahlen, Jesse Smith, Derek Mastroianni, and Bruce Deck. "Ice Core Records of Atmospheric $CO_2$ Around the Last Three Glacial Terminations." *Science* 283 (12 March 1999): 1712–14.

Friedlaender, Jonathan. "Commentary: A Perspective on Race in Biology and Medicine." *Anthropology Newsletter* 38, no. 9 (December 1997).

Gaspar, Maria Dulce. "Considerations of the Sambaquis of the Brazilian Coast." *Antiquity* 72 (1998): 592–615.

Gerlach, S. Craig, Margaret Newman, Edward J. Knell, and Edwin S. Hall, Jr. "Blood Protein Residues on Lithic Artifacts from Two Archaeological Sites in the De Long Mountains, Northwestern Alaska." *Arctic* 49, no. 1 (March 1996): 1–10.

Gill, George W. "The Beauty of Race and Races." *Anthropology Newsletter* 39, no. 3 (March 1998).

———. "Common Mistakes." *Anthropology Newsletter* 39, no. 1 (January 1998).

Gnecco, Cristobal, and Santiago Mora. "Late Pleistocene/Early Holocene Tropical Forest Occupations at San Isidro and Pena Roja, Colombia." *Antiquity* 71 (1997): 683–90.

Goodman, Alan. "Racializing Kennewick Man." *Anthropology Newsletter* 38, no. 7 (October 1997).

Green, Thomas J., Bruce Cochran, Todd W. Fenton, James C. Woods, Gene L. Titmus, Larry Tieszen, Mary Anne Davis, and Susanne J. Miller, "The Buhl Burial: A Paleoindian Woman from Southern Idaho." *American Antiquity* 63, no. 3 (1998): 437–56.

Greenberg, Joseph H., Christy G. Turner II, and Stephen L. Zegura, "The Settlement of the Americas: A Comparison of the Linguistic, Dental and Genetic Evidence." *Current Anthropology* 27, no. 5 (December 1986): 477–97.

Greenman, E.F. "Comments on 'The Paleo-Indian Tradition in Eastern North America.'" *Current Anthropology* 3, no. 3 (June 1962): 252–54.

———. "Old Birch Island Cemetery and the Early Historic Trade Route, Georgian Bay, Ontario." In *Occasional Contributions from the Museum of Anthropology of the University of Michigan*, no. 13. Ann Arbor: University of Michigan Press, 1951.

Guerin, Claude, Maria Amelia Curvello, Martine Fauré, Marguerite Hugueney, and Cécile Mourer-Chauvire. "The Pleistocene Fauna of Piaui (Northeastern Brazil): Paleoecological and Biochronological Implications." *FUMDHAMentos, Revista da Fundação Museu do Homem Americano* 1, no. 1 (1996): 56–99.

Guidon, Niéde, Fabio Parenti, Claudia Oliveira, and Cleonice Vergne. "Comment on the Grave at Toca dos Coquerios, Serra da Capivara National Park, Brazil." *Clio* 1, no. 13 (1998): 199–202.

Guidon, Niéde, and Anne-Marie Pessis. "Falsehood or Untruth? A Reply to Meltzer, Adovasio & Dillehay." *FUMDHAMentos, Revista da Fundação Museu do Homem Americano* 1, no. 1 (1996): 379–94.

Guidon, Niéde, Cleonice Vergne, and Irma Ason Vidal. "Toca da Baixa dos Caboclos, a Graveyard Shelter of the Serra da Capivara National Park Archaeological Enclave." *Clio* 1, no. 13 (1998): 145–55.

Guthe, C.E. "Notes on the Cephalic Index of Russian Jews in Boston." *American Journal of Physical Anthropology* 1, no. 2.

Hamilton, Scott, Ron Morrisseau, and Chief Theron McCrady. "New Solitudes: Conflicting World Views in the Context of Contemporary Northern Resource Development." *Canadian Journal of Archaeology/Journal Canadien d'Archéologie* 19 (1995): 3–18.

Hammer, Michael F., T. Karafet, A. Rasanayagam, E.T. Wood, T.K. Altheide, T.

Jenkins, R.C. Griffiths, A.R. Templeton, and S.L. Zegura. "Out of Africa and Back Again: Nested Cladistic Analysis of Human Y Chromosome Variation." *Molecular Biology and Evolution* 15, no. 4 (1998): 427–41.

Hammer, Michael F., and Stephen L. Zegura. "The Role of the Y Chromosome in Human Evolutionary Studies." *Evolutionary Anthropology* (1997): 116–34.

Harpending, Henry C., Stephen T. Sherry, Alan R. Rogers, and Mark Stoneking, "The Genetic Structure of Ancient Human Populations." *Current Anthropology* 34, no. 4 (August-October 1993): 483–96.

Harrison, Faye V., ed. "Contemporary Issues Forum: Race and Racism." *Journal of the American Anthropological Association* 100, no. 3 (September 1988).

Hauswirth, William W., Cynthia D. Dickel, Glen H. Doran, Philip J. Laipis, and David N. Dickel. "8000-year-old Brain Tissue from the Windover Site: Anatomical, Cellular and Molecular Analysis." Zagreb Paleopathology Symposium, 1988.

Heaton, Timothy H. "An Ice Age Refugium for Large Mammals in the Alexander Archipelago, Southeastern Alaska." *Quaternary Research* 46 (1996): 186–92.

Heaton, Timothy H., and Frederick Grady. "Fossil Grizzly Bears (*Ursus arctos*) from Prince of Wales Island, Alaska, Offer New Insights into Animal Dispersal, Interspecific Competition, and Age of Deglaciation. *CRP* 10 (1993): 98–100.

———. "Preliminary Report on the Fossil Bears of El Capitan Cave, Prince of Wales Island, Alaska." *CRP* 9 (1992): 97–99.

Heckenberger, Michael J. "Manioc Agriculture and Sedentism in Amazonia: The Upper Xingu Example." *Antiquity* 72 (1998): 633–48.

Horne, Patrick D. "A Review of the Evidence of Human Endoparasitism in the Pre-Columbian New World through the Study of Coprolites." *Journal of Archaeological Science* 12 (1985): 299–310.

Howell, Neil, Iwona Kubacka, and David A. Mackey. "How Rapidly Does the Human Mitochondrial Genome Evolve?" *American Journal of Human Genetics* 59 (1996): 501–9.

Hrdlička, Aleš. "A Painted Skeleton from Northern Mexico, with Notes on Bone Painting among the American Aborigines." *American Anthropologist* 3 (1901): 701–25.

———. "Physical Anthropology: Its Scope and Aims, Its History and Present Status in America." *American Journal of Physical Anthropology* 1, no. 1 (1918): 3–182.

———. "Physical Anthropology: Its Scope and Aims; Its History and Present Status in America." *American Journal of Physical Anthropology* 1, no. 4 (October-December 1918): 337–414.

Jantz, R.L., and Douglas W. Owsley. "Pathology, Taphonomy, and Cranial Morphometrics of the Spirit Cave Mummy." *Nevada Historical Society Quarterly* 40, no. 1 (Spring 1997): 62–84.

Jenks, A.E. "Minnesota's Brown's Valley Man and Associated Burial Artifacts." *Memoirs, American Anthropological Association* 49.

Jerkic, Sonja M. "Description of Skeletal Material, An Archaic Sequence from the Strait of Belle Isle, Labrador." Archaeological Survey of Canada Paper no. 34, National Museum of Man, *Mercury Series*, Ottawa, 1975.

Josenhans, Heiner, Daryl Fedje, Reinhard Pienitz, and John Southon. "Early Humans and Rapidly Changing Holocene Sea Levels in the Queen Charlotte Islands–Hecate Strait, British Columbia, Canada." *Science* 277 (4 July 1997): 71–74.

Julig, P.J. "Cummins Paleo-Indian Site and Its Paleoenvironment, Thunder Bay, Canada." *Archaeology of Eastern North America* 12 (1984): 192–209.

Kaestle, Frederika. "Molecular Analysis of Ancient Native American DNA from Western Nevada." *Nevada Historical Society Quarterly* 40, no. 1 (Spring 1997): 85–96.

Kamminga, Johan, and R.V.S. Wright. "The Upper Cave at Zhoukoudien and the Origins of the Mongoloids." *Journal of Human Evolution* 17 (1988): 739–67.

Karafet, T.M., S.L. Zegura, O. Posukh, L. Osipova, A. Bergen., J. Long, D. Goldman, W. Klitz, S. Harihara, P. de Knijff, V. Wiebe, R.C. Griffiths, A.R. Templeton, and M.F. Hammer. "Ancestral Asian Source(s) of New World Y-Chromosome Founder Haplotypes." *American Journal of Human Genetics* 64 (1999): 817–31.

Karafet, Tatiana, Stephen L. Zegura, Jennifer Vuturo-Brady, Olga Posukh, Ludmila Osipova, Victor Wiebe, Francine Romero, Jeffrey C. Long, Shinji Harihara, Feng Jin, Bumbein Dashnyam, Tudevdagva Gerelsaikhan, Keiichi Omoto, and Michael F. Hammer. "Y Chromosome Markers and Trans-Bering Strait Dispersals." *American Journal of Physical Anthropology* 102 (1997): 301–14.

Katzenberg, M. Anne, and Norman C. Sullivan. "A Report on the Human Burial From the Milton-Thomazi Site." *Ontario Archaeology* 32: 27–34.

Kidd, Kenneth E. "The Excavation and Historical Identification of a Huron Ossuary." *American Antiquity* 18, no. 4 (1953): 359–79.

Kipnis, Renato. "Early Hunter-Gatherers in the Americas: Perspectives from Central Brazil." *Antiquity* 72 (1998): 581–92.

Kipnis, Renato, Irmhild Wust, Tom Dillehay, and Christopher Chippindale. "Issues in Brazilian Archaeology." *Antiquity* 72 (1998): 571–73.

Kirner, D.L., R. Burky, K. Selsor, D. George, R.E. Taylor, and J.R. Southon. "Dating the Spirit Cave Mummy: The Value of Reexamination." *Nevada Historical Society Quarterly* 40, no. 1 (Spring 1997): 54–56.

Krings, Matthias, Anne Stone, Ralf W. Schmitz, Heike Krainitzki, Mark Stoneking, and Svante Paabo. "Neanderthal DNA Sequences and the Origin of Modern Humans." *Cell* 90 (11 July 1997): 19–29.

Lahr, Marta Mirazon. "Patterns of Modern Human Diversification: Implications for Amerindian Origins." *Yearbook of Physical Anthropology* 38 (1995): 163–98.

Lara, Elayne Granada, and Claudina Maria Dutra Moresi. "Material Textil de Santana do Riacho." In *Arquivos do Museu de História Natural, Universidade*

*Federal de Minas Gerais*, vol. 12, coordenadores André Prous. *Santana do Riacho-Tomo* 1: I.M. Malta, 1991, pp. 179–86.

Lee, Thomas E. "The First Sheguiandah Expedition, Manitoulin Island, Ontario." *American Antiquity* 20, no. 2 (October 1954): 101–12.

Lemmen, Donald S., Alejandra Duk-Rodkin, and Jan M. Bednarski. "Late Glacial Drainage Systems along the Northwestern Margin of the Laurentide Ice Sheet." *Quaternary Science Review* 13 (1994): 805–28.

Lowe, J.J., et al. "Paleoclimate of the North Atlantic Seaboards during the Last Glacial/Interglacial Transition." *Quaternary International* 28 (1995): 51–61.

Loy, Thomas H.E. "Prehistoric Blood Residues: Detection on Tool Surfaces and Identification of Species of Origin." *Science* 220 (17 June 1983): 1269–71.

Loy, Thomas H.E., and James Dixon. "Blood Residues on Fluted Points from Eastern Beringia." *American Antiquity* 63, no. 1 (1998): 21–26.

Lundqvist, J., and M. Saarnisto. "Summary of Project IGCP-253." *Quaternary International* 28 (1995): 9–18.

Lynch, Barbara D., and Thomas F. Lynch. "The Beginnings of a Scientific Approach to Prehistoric Archaeology in 17th and 18th Century Britain." *Southwestern Journal of Anthropology* 14, no. 1 (Spring 1968): 33–65.

Lynch, Thomas F. "The Antiquity of Man in South America." *Quaternary Research* 4 (1974): 356–77.

———. "Chronology of Guitarrero Cave, Peru." *American Association for the Advancement of Science* 229 (1985): 864–67.

———. "Climate Change and Human Settlement Around the Late-Glacial Laguna De Punta Negra, Northern Chile: The Preliminary Results." *Geoarchaeology* 1, no. 2 (1986): 145–61.

———. "The Discovery of America—Why it Matters." *Arts & Sciences Newsletter* (Cornell University) 14, no. 1 (January 1993).

———. "Glacial-Age Man in South America? A Critical Review." *American Antiquity* 55, no. 1 (1990): 12–36.

———. "L'Homme des Glaciations en Amerique du Sud: Une Vision Européenne." *L'Anthropologie* 98, no. 1 (1994): 32–54.

———. "The Nature of the Central Andean Preceramic." *Occasional Papers of the Idaho State University Museum*, no. 21 (1967).

———. "The Peopling of the Americas—A Discussion." In *The First Americans: Search and Research*, edited by Tom D. Dillehay and David J. Meltzer. Boca Raton, Ann Arbor, Boston and London: CRC Press, 1991.

———. "Quishqui Puncu: A Preceramic Site in Highland Peru." *Science* 158, no. 3802 (10 November 1967): 780–83.

Lynch, Thomas F., and Christopher M. Stevenson. "Obsidian Hydration Dating and Temperature Controls in the Punta Negra Region of Northern Chile." *Quaternary Research* 37 (1992): 117–24.

MacNeish, Richard S. "Pendejo Pre-Clovis Proofs and Their Implications." *FUMDHAMentos, Revista da Fundação Museu do Homem Americano* 1, no. 1 (1996): 171–200.

Marlowe, Greg. "Year One: Radiocarbon Dating and American Archaeology, 1947-1948." *American Antiquity* 64, no. 1 (1999): 9–32.

Martin, Gabriela. "The Prehistoric Peopling of the São Francisco Valley (Brazil)." *Clio* 1, no. 13 (1998): 43–69.

Martin, Larry D., R.A. Rogers, and A.M. Neuner. "The Effect of the End of the Pleistocene on Man in North America." In *Environments and Extinctions: Man in Late Glacial North America*, edited by Jim I. Mead and David J. Meltzer. Orono, Maine: Center for the Study of Early Man, 1985.

Martin, Paul. "Paleolithic Players on the American Stage: Man's Impact on the Late Pleistocene Megafauna." In *Arctic and Alpine Environments*, edited by Jack D. Ives and Roger G. Barry. London: Methuen, 1975.

Martin, Paul. "Clovisia the Beautiful!" *Natural History* 10 (1987): 10–13.

Mason, Ronald J. "The Paleo-Indian Tradition in Eastern North America." *Current Anthropology* 3, no. 3 (June 1962): 227–46.

Mason, Ronald J., and Carol Irwin. "An Eden-Scottsbluff Burial in Northeastern Wisconsin." *American Antiquity* 26, no. 1 (1960): 43–57.

Meggers, Betty J. "Amazonia: Real or Counterfeit Paradise?" *Review of Archaeology* 13, no. 2 (Fall 1992): 25–40.

———. "Biogeographical Approaches to Reconstructing the Prehistory of Amazonia." *Biogeographica* 70, no. 3 (1994): 97–110.

———. "Identification and Implications of a Hiatus in the Archaeological Sequence on Marajó Island, Brazil." *Journal of the Washington Academy of Sciences* 78, no. 3 (September 1988): 245–53.

———. "Jomon-Valdivia Similarities: Convergence or Contact?" *New England Antiquities Research Association (NEARA) Journal* 27 (Fall 1992): 23–32.

———. "The Prehistory of Amazonia." In *People of the Tropical Rain Forest*, edited by Julie Sloan Denslow and Christine Padoch. Berkeley, Los Angeles and London: University of California Press, in association with Smithsonian Institution Traveling Exhibition Service, 1987.

———. "The Transpacific Origin of Mesoamerican Civilization: A Preliminary Review of the Evidence and Its Theoretical Implications." *American Anthropologist* 77 (1975): 1–27.

———. "Yes If by Land, No If by Sea: The Double Standard in Interpreting Cultural Similarities." *American Anthropologist* 78 (1976): 637–39.

Meggers, Betty J., and Clifford Evans. "A Transpacific Contact in 3,000 B.C." *Scientific American* 214, no. 1 (January 1966): 28–35.

Mello e Alvim, Marilia Carvalho. "Os Antigos Habitantes da Serra do Cipo, Minas Gerais, Brasil, Estudo Morfologico Preliminar." In *Arquivos do Museu de História Natural, Universidade Federal de Minas Gerais*, vol. 13, coordenatore André Prous, 1992/1993, pp. 107–27.

———. "The Peopling of Indian America: Controversial Issues," *FUMDHAMentos, Revista da Fundação Museu do Homem Americano*, 1996, 139–46.

Mello e Alvim, Marilia Carvalho, and Sheila Maria Ferraz Mendonça de Souza. "Biological Relations between Prehistoric and Present Indian Populations in

Brazil." *Clio* 1, no. 6, Serie Arqueológica (1990): 69–79.

Meltzer, David J., James M. Adovasio, and Tom D. Dillehay. "On a Pleistocene Human Occupation at Pedra Furada, Brazil." *Antiquity* 68 (1994): 695–714.

Mendonça de Souza, Sheila Maria Ferraz. "Paleodemografia da População do Grande Abrigo de Santana do Riacho, Minas Gerais: Uma Hipótese para Verificação." In *Arquivos do Museu de História Natural, Universidade Federal de Minas Gerais*, vol. 13, coordenador André Prous. *Santana do Riacho-Tomo 1*: I.M. Malta, 1992/1993, pp. 161–71.

———. "Paleopatologia Humana de Santana do Riacho." *Arquivos do Museu de História Natural, Universidade Federal do Minas Gerais*, vol. 13, coordenadore André Prous. *Santana do Riacho-Tomo 1*: I.M. Malta, 1992/1993, pp. 129–60.

———. "Variaçoes da Dentogenese em indiviuos do Grupo Pre-Histórico de Santana do Riacho, Lagoa Santa, Minas Gerais." Cad. Saude Publ., Rio de Janeiro, vol. 9, suppl. 1 (1993): 96–98.

Merriwether, D. Andrew, Andrew C. Clark, Scott W. Ballinger, Theodore C. Schurr, Himla Soodyall, Trefor Jenkins, Stephen T. Sherry, and Douglas C. Wallace. "The Structure of Human Mitochondrial DNA Variation." *Journal of Molecular Evolution* 33 (1991): 543–55.

Merriwether, D. Andrew, William W. Hall, Anders Vahlne, and Robert E. Ferrell. "MtDNA Variation Indicates Mongolia May Have Been the Source for the Founding Population for the New World." *American Journal of Human Genetics* 59 (1996): 204–12.

Merriwether, D. Andrew, Sara Houston, Sudha Iyengar, Richard Hamman, Jill M. Norris, Susan M. Shetterly, M. Ilyas Kamboh, and Robert E. Ferrell. "Mitochondrial Versus Nuclear Admixture Estimates Demonstrate a Past History of Directional Mating." *American Journal of Physical Anthropology* 102 (1997): 153–59.

Miller, J.F.V. "The Gray Site: An Early Plains Burial Ground, Volume II." Manuscript Report no. 304, Parks Canada, 1978.

———. "Mortuary Practices of the Oxbow Complex." *Canadian Journal of Archaeology* 5 (1981): 103–17.

Morlan, R.E., and D.E. Nelson. "Accelerator Mass Spectrometry Dates on Bones from Old Crow Basin, Northern Yukon Territory." *Canadian Journal of Archaeology* 14 (1990): 75–92.

Morley, Joseph J., and Linda E. Heusser. "Late Quaternary Atmospheric and Oceanographic Variations in the Western Pacific Inferred from Pollen and Radiolarian Analyses." *Quaternary Science Reviews* 8 (1989): 263–76.

Neel, James V., Robert J. Biggar, and Rem I. Sukernik. "Virologic and Genetic Studies Relate Amerind Origins to the Indigenous People of the Mongolia/Manchuria/Southeastern Siberia Region." *Proceedings of the National Academy of Sciences, USA* 91 (October 1994): 10,737–41.

Nelson, D.E., Richard E. Morlan, J.S. Vogel, J.R. Southon, and C.R. Harington. "New Dates on Northern Yukon Artifacts: Holocene Not Upper Pleistocene."

*Science* 232 (1986): 749–51.

Neves, Eduardo Goes. "Twenty Years of Amazonian Archaeology in Brazil (1977-1997)." *Antiquity* 72 (1998): 625–32.

Neves, Walter A., and Hector M. Pucciarelli. "Morphological Affinities of the First Americans: An Exploratory Analysis Based on Early South American Human Remains." *Journal of Human Evolution* 21 (1991): 261–73.

Neves, Walter A., Joseph F. Powell, and Erik G. Ozolins. "Extra-continental Morphological Affinities of Palli Aike, Southern Chile." *Interciencia*, 24, no. 4 (1999): 258–63.

———. "Modern Human Origins As Seen from the Peripheries." *Journal of Human Evolution* 14 (1999): 53–5.

Newman, Margaret E. "Immunological Analysis of Lithic Artifacts." In *La grotte du Bolis Latterie*, edited by M. Otte and L.G. Straus. Liege: E.R.A.U.L. 80.

———. "Immunological and DNA analysis of Blood Residues from a Surgeon's Kit Used in the American Civil War." *Journal of Archaeological Science* 25 (1998): 553–57.

———. "Organic Residue Analysis of Lithic Artifacts from Le Trou Magrite." In *Le Trou Magrite: Fouilles 1991–1992*. M. Otte and L.G. Straus (dir.). Liege: E.R.A.U.L. 69, 1995.

Newman, Margaret E., Howard Ceri, and Brian Kooyman. "The Use of Immunological Techniques in the Analysis of Archaeological Materials—a Response to Eisele: With Report of Studies at Head-Smashed-In Buffalo Jump." *Antiquity* 70 (1996): 677–82.

Nichols, Johanna. "Linguistic Diversity and the First Settlement of the New World." *Language* 66, no. 3 (1990): 475–521.

———. "Modeling Ancient Population Structures and Movement in Linguistics." *Annual Review of Anthropology* 26 (1997): 359–384.

———. "The Origin and Dispersal of Languages: Linguistic Evidence." *Memoirs of the California Academy of Sciences* 24 (1998): 127–70.

Nichols, Johanna, and David A. Peterson. "The Amerind Personal Pronouns." *Language* 72, no. 2 (1996): 336–71.

Noelli, Francisco Silva. "The Tupi: Explaining Origin and Expansions in Terms of Archaeology and of Historical Linguistics." *Antiquity* 72 (1998): 648–63.

Novick, Gabriel S., Corina C. Novick, Juan Yunis, Emilio Yunis, Pamela Antunez de Mayolo, W. Douglas Scheer, Prescott L. Deininger, Mark Stoneking, Daniel S. York, Mark A. Batzer, and Rene J. Herrera. "Polymorphic Alu Insertions and the Asian Origins of Native American Populations." *Human Biology* 70, no. 1 (February 1998): 23–29.

Ostmo, Einar. "A Local Ship Picture Tradition of the Bronze and Early Iron Ages in Southeast Norway: New Evidence from Rock Carvings at Dalbo." *World Archaeology* 23, no. 2 (1991).

Parenti, Fabio. "Questions about the Upper Pleistocene Prehistory in Northeastern Brazil: Pedra Furada Rock Shelter in Its Regional Context." In *FUMDHAMentos, Revista da Fundação Museu do Homem Americano* 1, no. 1

(1996): 16–53.

Pate, Donald F. "Bone Chemistry and Paleodiet: Reconstructing Prehistoric Subsistence-Settlement Systems in Australia." *Journal of Anthropological Archaeology* 16 (1997): 103–20.

Pavlides, Christina, and Chris Gosden. "35,000-Year-Old Sites in the Rainforests of West New Britain, Papua New Guinea." *Antiquity* 68 (1994): 604–10.

Peyre, Evelyne. "Biometrie du Calvarium et de la Mandible d'une Population Humaine." *Definition et Origines de l'Homme, Table Ronde internationale No. 3*, CNRS, Paris, 5-8 juillet 1983. Paris: Editions du CNRS, 1986.

Peyre, Evelyne, Claude Guerin, Niéde Guidon, and Yves Coppens. "Des restes humains pleistocenes dans la grotte du Garrincho, Piaui, Brésil." Académie des sciences, Paris, *Sciences de la terre et des planetes/Earth & Planetary Sciences* 327 (1998): 335–60.

Pfeiffer, Susan, J.C. Dudar, and S. Austin. "Prospect Hill: Skeletal Remains from a 19th Century Methodist Cemetery, Newmarket, Ontario." *Northeast Historical Archaeology* 18 (1989): 29–48.

Pfeiffer, Susan. "Demographic Parameters of the Uxbridge Ossuary Population." *Ontario Archaeology* 40 (1983): 9–14.

Politis, Gustavo. "A Review of the Late Pleistocene Sites of Argentina." *FUMDHAMentos, Revista da Fundação Museu do Homem Americano* 1, no. 1 (1996): 153–70.

Powell, Joseph F. "Dental Evidence for the Peopling of the New World: Some Methodological Considerations." *Human Biology* 65, no. 5 (October 1993): 799–819.

Prous, André. "Archaeological analysis of the oldest settlements in the Americas." *Brazilian Journal of Genetics* 18, no. 4 (1995): 689–99.

———. "Archaeology of the Pleistocene-Holocene Boundary in Brazil." *Quaternary International* 53/54 (1999): 21–41.

———. "O povamento da America visto do Brasil: Una perspectiva critica." *Revista USP* 34 (Junho/Agosto 1997): 8–21. Sao Paulo.

Reynolds, T.E.G. "Revolution or Resolution? The Archaeology of Modern Human Origins." *World Archaeology* 23, no. 2 (1991): 155–66.

Roebroeks, Wil, and Thijs Van Kolfschoten. "The Earliest Occupation of Europe: A Short Chronology." *Antiquity* 68 (1994): 489–503.

Rogers, R.A., L.A. Rogers, and L.D. Martin. "How the Door Opened: The Peopling of the New World." *Human Biology* 64, no. 3 (June 1992): 281–302.

Rogers, R.A., L.A. Rogers, R.S. Hoffmann, and L.D. Martin. "Native American Biological Diversity and the Biogeographic Influence of Ice Age Refugia." *Journal of Biogeography* 18 (1991): 623–30.

Rogers, R.A., Larry D. Martin, and T. Dale Nicklas. "Ice-Age Geography and the Distribution of Native North American Languages." *Journal of Biogeography* 17 (1990): 131–43.

Roosevelt, A.C. "Clovis Clarification: A Follow Up." *Mammoth Trumpet* 13, no. 1 (January 1998).

———. "Paleoindian and Archaic Occupations in the Lower Amazon, Brazil: A Summary and Comparison." In *Explorations in American Archaeology, Essays in Honor of Wesley R. Hurt,* edited by Mark G. Plew. Lanham, New York and Oxford: University Press of America, Inc., 1998, pp. 165–91.

Rutter, Nat. "Problematic Ice Sheets." *Quaternary International* 28 (1995): 19–37.

Sandweiss, Daniel H., Heather McInnis, Richard L. Burger, Asuncion Cano, Bernardino Ojeda, Rolando Paredes, Maria del Carmen Sandweiss, and Michael D. Glascock. "Quebrada Jaguay: Early South American Maritime Adaptations." *Science* 281 (18 September 1998): 1830–32.

Santos, Fabricio R., Arpita Pandya, Chris Tyler-Smith, Sergio D.J. Pena, Moses Schanfield, William R. Leonard, Ludmila Osipova, Michael H. Crawford, and R. John Mitchell. "The Central Siberian Origin for Native American Y Chromosomes." *American Journal of Human Genetics* 64 (1999): 619–28.

Schneider, Alan L. "Court Rules on Kennewick Man Case." *Anthropology News-letter* 38, no. 6 (September 1997).

———. "Why Kennewick Man is in Court." *Anthropology Newsletter* 38, no. 2 (February 1997).

Schurr, Theodore G., Scott W. Ballinger, Yik-Yuen Gan, Judith A. Hodge, D. Andrew Merriwether, Dale N. Lawrence, William C. Knowler, Kenneth M. Weiss, and Douglas C. Wallace. "Amerindian Mitochondrial DNAs Have Rare Asian Mutations at High Frequencies, Suggesting They Derived from Four Primary Maternal Lineages." *American Journal of Human Genetics* 46 (1990): 613–23.

Schurr, Theodore G., Rem I. Sukernik, Yelena B. Starikovskaya, and Douglas C. Wallace. "Mitochondrial DNA Variation in Koryaks and Itel'men: Population Replacement in the Okhotsk Sea-Bering Sea Region during the Neolithic." *American Journal of Physical Anthropology* 108 (1999): 1–39.

Schurr, Theodore G., and Douglas C. Wallace. "Genetic Prehistory of Paleoasiatic-speaking Populations of Northeastern Siberia and Their Relationships to Native Americans." In *The Anthropological Papers of the American Museum of Natural History,* edited by I. Krupnik, L. Kendall, and M. Balzer. New York: American Museum of Natural History, 1999.

———. "MtDNA Variation in Native Americans and Siberians and Its Impli-cations for the Peopling of the New World." In *Who Were the First Americans?* A Peopling of the Americas Publication, 1999.

Schwarcz, H.P., R. Grun, B. Vandermeersch, O. Bar-Yosef, H. Valladas, and E. Tchernov. "ESR Dates for the Hominid Burial Site of Qafzeh in Israel." *Journal of Human Evolution* 17 (1988): 733–37.

Sher, Andrei. "Is There Any Real Evidence for a Huge Shelf Ice Sheet in East Siberia?" *Quaternary International* 28 (1995): 39–40.

Sims-Williams, Patrick. "Genetics, Linguistics, and Prehistory: Thinking Big and Thinking Straight." *Antiquity* 72 (1998): 505–27.

Smith, Derald G., and Timothy G. Fisher. "Glacial Lake Agassiz: The North-western Outlet and Paleoflood." *Geology* 21 (January 1991): 9–12.

Soffer, Olga, James M. Adovasio, David C. Hyland, Bohuslav Klíma, and Jiri Svoboda. "Perishable Technologies and the Genesis of the Eastern Gravettian." *L'Anthropologie* 36, nos. 1-2 (1998): 43–68.

Starikovskaya, Rem I. Sukernik, Theodore G. Schurr, Andreas M. Kogelnik, and Douglas C. Wallace. "MtDNA Diversity in Chukchi and Siberian Eskimos: Implications for the Genetic History of Ancient Beringia and the Peopling of the New World." *American Journal of Human Genetics* 63 (1998): 1473–91.

Steele, D. Gentry, and Joseph F. Powell. "Peopling of the Americas: Paleobiological Evidence." *Human Biology* 64, no. 3 (June 1992): 303–36.

Steele, James, Jonathan Adams, and Tim Sluckin. "Modelling Paleoindian Dispersals." *World Archaeology* 30, no. 2 (1998): 286–305.

Stewart, T.D. "A Physical Anthropologist's View of the Peopling of the New World." *Southwestern Journal of Anthropology* 16, no. 3 (Autumn 1960): 259–73.

Stone, Tammy T., David N. Dickel, and Glen H. Doran. "The Preservation and Conservation of Waterlogged Bone from the Windover Site, Florida: A Comparison of Methods." *Journal of Field Archaeology* 17 (1990).

Stringer, C.B., and P. Andrews, "Genetic and Fossil Evidence for the Origin of Modern Humans," *Science* 239 (11 March 1988): 1263–68.

Taylor, R.E., C. Vance Haynes Jr., and Minze Stuiver. "Clovis and Folsom Age Estimates: Stratigraphic Context and Radiocarbon Calibration." *Antiquity* 70 (1996): 515–25.

Tuohy, Donald R., and Amy J. Dansie. "New Information Regarding Early Holocene Manifestations in the Western Great Basin." *Nevada Historical Society Quarterly* 40, no. 1 (Spring 1997): 24–53.

Trope, Jack F., and Walter R. Echo-Hawk. "The Native American Graves Protection and Repatriation Act: Background and Legislative History." *Arizona State Law Journal* 24, no. 35 (Spring 1992): 1–35.

Turnbull, Christopher J. "The Augustine Site: A Mound from the Maritimes." *Archaeology of Eastern North America* 4 (1976): 50–62.

Turner II, Christy G. "New World Origins: New Research from the Americas and the Soviet Union." In *Ice Age Hunters of the Rockies*, edited by Dennis J. Stanford and Jane S. Day. Denver: Denver Museum of Natural History and University Press of Colorado, 1992.

Velichko, A.A. "The Pleistocene Termination in Northern Eurasia." *Quaternary International* 28 (1995): 105–11.

Vollrath, Douglas, Simon Foote, Adrienne Hilton, Laura G. Brown, Peggy Beer-Romero, Jonathan S. Bogan, and David C. Page. "The Human Y Chromosome: A 43-Interval Map Based on Naturally Occurring Deletions." *Science* 258 (2 October 1992): 52–59.

Walker, M.J.C. "Climatic Changes in Europe During the Last Glacial/Interglacial Transition." *Quaternary International* 28 (1995): 63–76.

Walthall, John A. "Rockshelters and Hunter-Gatherer Adaptation to the Pleistocene/Holocene Transition." *American Antiquity* 63, no. 2 (1998): 223–38.

Way, J. Edson. "The Human Osteological Material from the Cloverleaf Bastions of the Fort at Coteau-Du-Lac, Quebec." *History and Archaeology/Histoire et Archéologie* 12. National Historic Parks and Sites Branch, Parks Canada, Department of Indian and Northern Affairs, 1977.

Wigand, Peter E. "Native American Diet and Environmental Contexts of the Holocene Revealed in the Pollen of Human Fecal Material." *Nevada Historical Society Quarterly* 40, no. 1 (Spring 1997) 105–15.

Yesner, David R. "Human Adaptation at the Pleistocene-Holocene Boundary (circa 13,000 to 8,000 BP) in Eastern Beringia." In *Humans at the End of the Ice Age: The Archaeology of the Pleistocene-Holocene Transition*, edited by Lawrence Guy Straus, Berit Valentin Eriksen, Jon M. Erlandson, and David R. Yesner. New York: Plenum Press, 1996.

———. "Human Dispersal into Interior Alaska, Antecedent Conditions, Mode of Colonization, and Adaptation." *Quaternary Science Reviews* (in press).

Yohe II, Robert M., Margaret E. Newman, and Joan S. Schneider. "Immunological Identification of Small-Mammal Proteins on Aboriginal Milling Equipment." *American Antiquity* 56, no. 4 (1991): 659–66.

## PAPERS, POSTERS, LETTERS, REVIEWS, ABSTRACTS, STATEMENTS

Adovasio, J.M., D.C. Hyland, and O. Soffer. "Perishable Technology and Early Human Populations in the New World." Paper prepared for the 31st Annual Chacmool Conference, *On Being First: Cultural Innovation and Environmental Consequences of First Peoplings*, Calgary, Alberta, November 1998.

Adovasio, J.M., D.C. Hyland, O. Soffer, and B. Klíma. "Perishable Industries and the Colonization of the East European Plain." Paper prepared for the 15th Annual Visiting Scholar Conference, *Fleeting Identities: Perishable Material Culture in Archaeological Research*. Carbondale, Illinois, April 1998.

Adovasio, J.M., D.C. Hyland, R.L. Andrews, and Nancy Luffman-Yedlowski. "Textiles and Textile Manufacture at Sodom." Paper prepared for the 64th Annual Meeting of the Society for American Archaeology, Chicago, Illinois, March 1999.

Adovasio, J.M., O. Soffer, and B. Klíma. "Paleolithic Fiber Technology: Data from Pavlov I, Czech Republic, ca. 27,000 B.P." Paper prepared for the 60th Annual Meeting of the Society for American Archaeology, Minneapolis, Minnesota, May 1995.

American Anthropological Association. "Statement on 'Race,'" *Anthropology Newsletter*, September, 1998.

Anderson, Duane, Alan Swedlund, and David Breternitz. "Let's Avoid Paleo-Racial Anthropology." *Anthropology Newsletter* 38, no. 9 (December 1997).

Chatters, James J., Walter A. Neves, and Max Blum. "The Kennewick Man: A first Multivariate Analysis," 1999 (a manuscript read before publication).

Dixon, E. James, Timothy H. Heaton, and Terence E. Fifield. "Early Holocene Human Remains and the Paleoenvironment of Prince of Wales Island, Southeast Alaska." Paper presented at the twenty-fourth annual meeting of the Alaska Anthropological Association. Whitehorse, Yukon, Canada, 9–11 April 1997.

Fifield, Terence E., E. James Dixon, Timothy H. Heaton. "Tribal Involvement in Investigations at 49-PET-408 Prince of Wales Island, Southeast Alaska." Paper for the American Anthropological Association *Newsletter*.

Grove, David C. "Olmec Origins and Transpacific Diffusion: Reply to Meggers." *American Anthropologist* 78 (1976): 634–39.

Hagelberg, Erika. "Digging into our Genes." *Antiquity* 69 (1995): 177–79.

Jantz, R.L., and Douglas W. Owsley, "Variation Among Early American Crania." Paper prepared for the annual meeting of the American Association for Physical Anthropologists. Columbus, Ohio, 1999.

Kliks, Michael M. "Parasites in archaeological material from Brazil." *Transactions of the Royal Society of Tropical Medicine and Hygiene* 76, no. 5 (1982): 703.

Lynch, Thomas F. "Lack of Evidence for Glacial-Age Settlement of South America: Reply to Dillehay and Collins and to Gruhn and Bryan." *American Antiquity* 56, no. 2 (1991): 348–55.

———. "Maybe 'Armed Truce.'" *The Sciences*, July/August 1997.

———. "Peopling of the Americas: A Reply to Irving Rouse." *Quaternary Research* 9, no. 1 (1978): 129–31.

McGhee, Robert. "The First Peopling of Arctic North America." Paper prepared for Plenary Session, University of Calgary Archaeology conference. November 1998.

McManamon, Francis P. "Approach to Documentation, Analysis, Interpretation, and Disposition of Human Remains Inadvertently Discovered at Columbia Park, Kennewick, WA." National Park Service, Department of the Interior. November 1998.

McManamon, Francis P. Letter to Donald Curtis Jr., 23 December 1997, regarding the views of the National Park Service, Department of the Interior on certain matters related to the Native American Graves Protection and Repatriation Act (NAGPRA).

Mellars, Paul. "Neanderthals in Perspective." *Antiquity* 68 (1994): 656–58.

Mitchell, R.J., S. Howlett, N.G. White, L. Federle, S.S. Papiha, I. Briceno, J. McComb, M.S. Schenfield, C. Tyler-Smith, L. Osipova, G. Livshitta, and M.H. Crawford. "A Deletion Polymorphism in the Human COL1A2 Gene: Genetic Evidence for a Non-African Population Whose Descendants Spread to All Continents." Paper presented at the annual meeting of the American Association of Physical Anthropologists. Columbus, Ohio, 1999.

Nelson, A. Russell, and C. Loring Brace. "Peopling of the New World: A Comparative Craniofacial View." In preparation, 1999.

Neves, Walter A., Danusa Munford, and Maria do Carmo Zanini. "Cranial Morphological Variation and the Colonization of the New World: Towards a

Four Migration Model." In preparation, 1999.

Neves, Walter A., Joseph F. Powell, André Prous, and Erik G. Ozolins. "Lapa Vermelha IV Hominid I: Morphological Affinities of the Earliest Known American." In preparation, 1999.

Neves, Walter A., Max Blum, and Lyvia Kozameh. "Fuegian Cranial Morphology Revisited: The Haush." In preparation, 1999.

————. "Were the Fuegians Remainders of a Paleoindian Non-Specialized Morphology in the Americas?" In preparation, 1999.

Nichols, Johanna. "The First Four Discoveries of America: Linguistic Evidence." Paper for presentation at the AAAS annual meeting, 16 February 1998.

Ozolins, Erik G. "Are Paleoindians Too Variable to Be From One Population? A Test of a Single Migration Origin." Poster presented at the 68th Annual Meeting of the American Association for Physical Anthropologists. Columbus, Ohio, 1999.

Preston, Douglas. "Kennewick's Message of Unification." *Anthropology Newsletter* 38, no. 9 (December 1997).

Reinhard, Karl, Adauto Araújo, Luiz Fernando Ferreira, and Carlos Coimbra. "Hookworms and Prehistoric Migrations." 1999.

Soffer, O., J.M. Adovasio, and D.C. Hyland. "Perishable Industries from Upper Paleolithic Moravia: New Insights into the Origin and Nature of the Gravettian." Paper presented at the Institute of Archaeology, ASCR, Prague and Masaryk University. Brno, June 1998.

————. "The Well-Dressed 'Venus': Women's Wear ca. 27,000 BV (Before *Vogue*)." Paper prepared for Zamyatnin Conference, Museum of Anthropology and Ethnography, Russian Academy of Sciences. St. Petersburg, Russia, April 1999.

Soto-Heim, Patricia. "Les Hommes de Lagoa Santa (Brésil) Caractères Anthropologiques et Position Parmi d'Autres Populations Paléoindiennes d'Amérique." *L'Anthropologie* 98, no. 1 (1994): 81–109.

Yesner, David R. "Human Colonization of Eastern Beringia and the Question of Mammoth Hunting." Presented to the International Symposium on Mammoth Site Studies in Eurasia and North America, 1999.

Zegura, Stephen L. "Y-Chromosomes and the Trinity." Unpublished manuscript, March 1999.

### INTERNET POSTINGS

Fagan, John L. "Analysis of Lithic Artifact Embedded in the Columbia Park Remains," Chapter 4 in *Kennewick Man*, National Park Service, United States Department of the Interior, October 1999. Downloaded from Friends of America's Past website at http://www.friendsofpast.org.

Huckleberry, Gary, and Julie K. Stein. "Analysis of Sediments Associated with Human Remains Found at Columbia Park, Kennewick, WA." Chapter 3 in

*Kennewick Man*, National Park Service, United States Department of the Interior, October 1999. Downloaded from Friends of America's Past website at http://www.friendsofpast.org.

McManamon, Francis P. "The Initial Scientific Examination, Description and Analysis of the Kennewick Man Human Remains." Chapter 1 in *Kennewick Man*, National Park Service, United States Department of the Interior, October 1999. Downloaded from Friends of America's Past website at http://www.friendsofpast.org.

Merriwether, D. Andrew, Robert E. Ferrell, and Francisco Rothhammer. "MtDNA D-Loop 6-bp Deletion Found in the Chilean Aymara: Not a Unique Marker for Chibcha-Speaking Amerindians." Letters to the Editor, *American Journal of Human Genetics* 56 (1995): 812–13.

Powell, Joseph, and Jerome Rose. "Skeletal Reconstruction." Chapter 2 in *Kennewick Man*, National Park Service, United States Department of the Interior, October 1999. Downloaded from Friends of America's Past website at http://www.friendsofpast.org.

Trinkaus, Erik and Zoão Zilhao. "A Correction to the Commentary of Tattersall and Schwartz Concerning the Interpretation of the Lagar Velho I Child." 24 June 1999. Site LVFAQ-CO.HTM.

POPULAR PRESS

Abraham, Carolyn. "Brilliant minds, but no business savvy." *The Globe and Mail*, 22 December 1998, A16.

———. "World's biggest gene bank proves gold mine for DNA Hunters." *The Globe and Mail*, 26 December 1998, A1 and A7.

———. "Let's make a DNA deal." *The Globe and Mail*, 7 December 1998, A1 and A13.

———. "Genetic trait for diabetes uncovered." *The Globe and Mail*, 8 March 1999, A11.

Angier, Natalie. "Paleo-chic." *The New York Times* Service in *The Globe and Mail*, 15 December 1999, R8.

Avery, Roberta. "Restoring cemetery gives 'rightful place' to black ancestors." *The Toronto Star*, 31 August 1998, B1.

Balter, Michael. "New Light on the Oldest Art." *Science* 283, 12 February 1999, 920–22.

———. "Restorers Reveal 28,000-Year-Old Artworks." *Science* 283, 19 March 1999, 1835.

Barnes, Alan. "DNA tests try to link body to royal remains."*The Toronto Star*, 14 June 2000, A23.

Begley, Sharon, and Andrew Murr. "The First Americans." *Newsweek*, 26 April 1999.

Bowman, Lee. "New data found on origins of ice ages." Scripps Howard News

Service in *The Globe and Mail*, 23 July 1999, A8.

Boyd, Robert. "America's past rewritten by new finds." *The Toronto Star*, 17 February 1998.

Bringhurst, Robert. "Since when has culture been about genetics?" *The Globe and Mail*, 22 November 1999, R3.

Broderick, Diane, and Jason Shallenberger. "Another bone fragment found in Bessey Hall." *The Journalist*, 8 April 1999.

Buhasz, Laszlo. "Rock-solid beauty." *The Globe and Mail*, 8 March 2000, T1.

Calamai, Peter. "B.C. iceman gets new life as science lab specimen." *The Toronto Star*, 27 August 1999, A1.

Chandler, David L. "Guam cave paintings depict stargazers." *The Boston Globe* in *The Globe and Mail*, 12 January 1999, A7.

Contenta, Sandro. "Religious monopoly on death laid to rest." *The Toronto Star*, 4 March 1999.

Dewar, Elaine. "Behind This Door." *Toronto Life*, May 1997.

———. "The Next Ice Age." *Toronto Life*, April 1996.

Dorfman, Andrea. "New Ways to the New World." *Time*, Canadian edition, 17 April 2000, 54.

Edwards, Peter, and Harold Levy. "Ontario Tories ask court to toss Ipperwash lawsuit." *The Toronto Star*, 23 January 1999, A7.

Egan, Timothy. "Tribe Stops Study of Bones That Challenges Its History." *The New York Times*, 30 September 1996, A1 and A10.

Fox, Maggie. "Archaeologist unearths clues to early human diet." Reuters News Agency in *The Globe and Mail*, 11 January 1998.

Ghalwash, Mae. "Cave Drawings in Egypt Could Date to 7000 B.C." *The Toronto Star*, 8 June 2000, A15.

Gibson, Gordon. "Should the Caldwell Indians buy a reserve?" *The Globe and Mail*, 8 June 1999, A17.

Glavin, Terry. "Selectively outraged about land claims." *The Globe and Mail*, 2 April 1999, A13.

*The Globe and Mail*/Agence France-Press. "Tori rowed the boat ashore." 11 December 1999, A28.

*The Globe and Mail*/AP. "Climate changes may have been sudden." 29 October 1999.

*The Globe and Mail*/AP. "Fossil gives clues to evolution of plant life." 27 November 1998.

*The Globe and Mail*/CP. "Natives want own police force." 8 June 1999, A7.

*The Globe and Mail*/CP. "Unique artifact unearthed." 7 June 1999, A5.

*The Globe and Mail*/Reuters. "Big chill of long ago significant for the present, scientists say." 23 July 1999.

*The Globe and Mail*/Reuters. "Half-eaten boat made of flimsy reeds limps to Polynesia." 14 May 1999.

Goffredo, Theresa. "Chemical depot jobs on the rise." *Tri-City Herald*, 7 July 1998.

———. "Umatilla depot workers refuse to return." *Tri-City Herald*, 17 September 1999.

Gore, Rick. "The Most Ancient Americans." *National Geographic*, October 1997.

———. "People Like Us." *National Geographic*, July 2000.

Green, Rick. "Anatomy class brings realism to high school." *The Toronto Star*, 12 November 1998, G10.

Hall, Don Alan. "Database on Humanity's Past." *Mammoth Trumpet* 12, no. 1, January 1997.

Harper, Tim. "Chretien backs treaty for Nisga'a." *The Toronto Star*, 11 November 1998, A7.

———. "Donor law raises ethical questions." *The Toronto Star*, 3 March 1999, A3.

Haskin, Colin. "Did Romans reach Mexico?" *The Globe and Mail*, 1 March 2000, R7.

———. "The ice-man's tattoos." *The Globe and Mail*, 1 March 2000, R7.

Heer, James. "Why Us?" *The Globe and Mail*, 15 March 2000, R7.

Holden, Constance, "Kennewick Man Gets His Day in the Lab." *Science* 283, 26 February 1999, 1239–40.

Howard, Cori. "Nomad's land." *The Globe and Mail*, 5 June 1999, D9.

Hume, Christopher. "The secret museum." *The Toronto Star*, 28 March 1998, M1.

Hurst, Lynda. "Where did we come from?" *The Toronto Star*, 16 May 1999.

Hurtado de Mendoza, Diego, and Ricardo Braginski. "Y Chromosomes Point to Native American Adam." *Science* 283, 5 March 1999, 1439–40.

Infantry, Ashante. "Multiracial balancing act." *The Toronto Star*, 11 March 2000, K6.

Inglis, Joy. "Harry Asu Fought for native fishing rights." *The Globe and Mail*, 12 May 1999, A21.

Ingram, Jay. "Autistic child's art inspires bold theory about cave artists." *The Toronto Star*, 28 February 1999, F8.

———. "Our balmy weather has a chill factor." *The Toronto Star*, 27 February 2000, F8.

Joyce, Greg. "Just how old is Canada's 'iceman'?" Canadian Press in *The Toronto Star*, 26 August 1999, A20.

Kalman, Matthew. "Unearthing history in the Holy Land." *The Globe and Mail*, 2 December 1998, A23.

Kovrig, Michael. "A human ancestor escapes obscurity." *The Globe and Mail*, 20 July 1999, A1.

Kraft, Frances. "Donating organs is 'a noble thing.'" *The Canadian Jewish News*, 16 December 1999, Tevet 7, 5760, 1.

Lasswell, Mark. "The 9,400-Year-Old Man: The White House keeps trying to bury him. Scientists are furious." *The Wall Street Journal*, 8 January 1999, W11.

Lee, Mike. "Asatru asks for DNA test on bones." *Tri-City Herald*, 10 September 1999.

———. "Deadline set for decision on bones," *Tri-City Herald*, 22 September 1999.

———. "Despite tribal objections, Interior still plans to date Kennewick Man bones." *Tri-City Herald*, 29 July 1999.

———. "5 scientists picked to study Kennewick Man." *Tri-City Herald*, 18 February 1999.

———. "Scientists' lawyers renew plea to study ancient bones." *Tri-City Herald*, 4 August 1999.

———. "Seattle museum plans Kennewick Man exhibit." *Tri-City Herald*, 31 August 1999.

———. "U.S. to continue testing ancient bones." *Tri-City Herald*, 2 July 1999.

*The Los Angeles Times*, with files from CP: "Hunters find frozen native man partially intact in mountain glacier." In *The Toronto Star*, 25 August 1999, A2.

Mahoney, Jill. "Glacial melting allowed ancient discovery." *The Globe and Mail*, 25 August 1999, A3.

Malcomson, Scott L. "The color of bones: How a 9,000-year-old skeleton called Kennewick Man sparked the strangest case of racial profiling yet." *The New York Times Magazine*, 2 April 2000.

Marshak, Alexander. "Exploring the Mind of the Ice Age Man." *National Geographic* 147, no. 1, January 1975.

McCoy, Ron. "NAGPRA Repatriation Notices ... And a Book of Note." *American Indian Art Magazine*, Winter 1998.

McIlroy, Anne, and Erin Anderssen. "Ottawa wants natives to accept nuclear waste." *The Globe and Mail*, 9 March 1999, A1 and A2.

Mickelburgh, Rod. "Natives underscore landmark judgement." *The Globe and Mail*, 12 December 1998, A12.

Mittelstaedt, Martin. "The big bad meltdown." *The Globe and Mail*, 9 March 2000, R9.

Morell, Virginia. "Jean Clottes: Rock Art's Jovial Cave Bear." *Science* 283, 12 February 1999, 920–21.

Moseley, Terry. "'Body farm' provides a flesh-and-bones lab." *The Globe and Mail*, 16 March 2000, A11.

*The New York Times*. "Humans' presence in Americas is pushed back a millennium," Science, 11 February 1997.

Ober, Tracey. "Brazilian skull suggests early Americans predated Asian arrival," Reuters, in *The Globe and Mail*, 22 September 1999, A13.

Overbey, Mary Margaret. "The Man behind the Mummy." *Anthropology Newsletter* 38, no. 3, March 1997.

Pennisi, Elizabeth. "Genetic Study Shakes Up Out of Africa Theory." *Science* 283, 19 March 1999, 1828.

Pollack, Andrew. "Buy and cell." *New York Times* Service in *The Globe and Mail*, 8 December 1999, R10.

Preston, Douglas. "The Face of Kennewick Man." *The New Yorker*, 9 February 1998.

———. "The Lost Man." *The New Yorker*, 16 June 1997.

———. "The Mystery of Sandia Cave." *The New Yorker*, 12 June 1995.

Prigg, Mark. "New technique could indicate Iceman's age and death date." *The*

*Toronto Star*, 28 February 1999, F8.

Pringle, Heather. "New Women of the Ice Age." *Discover*, April 1998.

———. "Ice Age Communities May Be Earliest Known Net Hunters." *Science* 277, 29 August 1997.

Quinn, Andrew. "Row erupts over pickled brain of the last of the Yahi nation." Reuters in *The Toronto Star*, 18 April 1999, B8.

Ross, Val. "ROM artifacts to return to Belize." *The Globe and Mail*, 21 September 1999, C1.

Scott, Kelly, and Kelli Kellogg. "Bones of Contention." *The Journalist*, 21 April 1998.

Smith, Dinita, and Nicholas Wade. "Jefferson was father of slave's child, DNA study finds." *The New York Times* Service in *The Globe and Mail*, 2 November 1998.

Stevens, William K. "An ice age is coming—in 10,000 to 20,000 years." *The New York Times* Service in *The Globe and Mail*, 19 February 1999, A11.

———. "Lessons on global warming from ancient hot spots." *The New York Times* Service in *The Globe and Mail*, 25 November 1999, R4.

Stoffman, Judy. "Native history preserved in British Museum." *The Toronto Star*, 12 February 2000, M14.

Strauss, Evelyn. "Can Mitochondrial Clocks Keep Time?" *Science* 283, 5 March 1999, 1435–37.

Tattersall, Ian. "Once We Were Not Alone." *Scientific American*, January 2000.

Thomasson, Emma. "Khoisans' DNA tied to ancient humans." Reuters in *The Toronto Star*, 24 September 1999, A24.

*The Toronto Star*. "Alberta—Indians sue over schools." 2 March 1999, A6.

*The Toronto Star*. "Argentina—last of tribe dies." 4 June 1999, A15.

*The Toronto Star*. "Earth's coldest, longest ice age." 28 August 1998.

*The Toronto Star*. "Petroglyphs may be Nordic." 2 August 1999, A4.

*The Toronto Star*/AP. "How bear poo built MacBlo." 12 December 1998, B6.

*The Toronto Star*/AP-Reuters. "Hominid skeleton called oldest yet." 10 December 1998, A3.

*The Toronto Star*/CP. "Nisga'a await treaty vote tally." 9 November 1998, A2.

*The Toronto Star*/CP. "U of T geologist hits motherlode in the hunt for origins of humans." 9 September 1999, A2.

*The Toronto Star*/Reuters. "Linguist buttresses Bering bridge idea." 15 November 1998, F8.

Toughill, Kelly. "'Dissident' leads N.B. loggers." *The Toronto Star*, 27 April 1998, A2.

———. "Indians take logging fight to court." *The Toronto Star*, 19 April 1999, A6.

———. "Who is an Indian?" *The Toronto Star*, 18 December 1999.

Valpy, Michael. "Toronto: Carrying Place: a country's crossroads." *The Globe and Mail*, 2 August 1999, A1.

Vreeland, James. M. "The Revival of Colored Cotton." *Scientific American*, April 1999.

Weintraub, Boris. "American 'Adam' Left a Genetic Marker." *National Geographic*, October 1999.

———. "A Seagoing Human Ancestor?" *National Geographic*, November 1998.

Werner, Hans. "Canada's war heroes." *The Toronto Star,* Book Review, 20 December 1998, D28.

Wilford, John Noble. "Iodine as the missing link." *The New York Times* Service in *The Globe and Mail*, 5 December 1998, D8.

———. "Mummified Iceman carried medicine." *The New York Times* Service in *The Globe and Mail*, 11 December 1998, A17.

———. "Mystery skull may be crucial piece." *The New York Times* Service in *The Globe and Mail*, 8 September 1999, A9.

———. "So, who did get here first?" *The New York Times* Service in *The Globe and Mail*, 17 November 1999, C7.

Willcocks, Paul. "B.C. kicks off session by welcoming Nisga'a." *The Globe and Mail*, 1 December 1998, A5.

York, Geoffrey. "A way of life is dying with the reindeer." *The Globe and Mail*, 4 March 1999, A19.


STATUTES, REGULATIONS, AGREEMENTS

Native American Graves Protection and Repatriation Act, U.S. Public Law 101-601, 16 November 1990.

Native American Graves Protection and Repatriation Regulations, 43 CER Subtitle A (10-1-96 Edition), Office of the Secretary of the Interior.

Nisga'a Final Agreement. Canada, British Columbia, Nisga'a Nation, as signed for Her Majesty the Queen in Right of Canada, 4 May 1999.

Ontario Heritage Act, Revised Statutes of Ontario, 1990, chapter O.18, printed by the Queen's Printer for Ontario, September, 1992.

Ontario Regulation 133/92, Burial Sites.


COURT DOCUMENTS

Amended Petition. In the District Court of Lancaster County, Nebraska, docket 576. *Karl Reinhard, Plaintiff, v. Stanley Parks, Defendant.*

Answer. In the District Court of Lancaster County, Nebraska, docket 576. *Reinhard, v. Parks.*

Claim for Injury or Damage, State of Nebraska Offices of Risk Management State Claims Board, on behalf of Karl Reinhard, 21 April 1999.

Complaint, in Civil no. 96-1481-JE in the United States District Court for the District of Oregon. *Asatru Folk Assembly, Stephen A. McNallen, William Fox, Plaintiffs, v. United States of America, Department of the Army, U.S. Army Corps of Engineers, Ernest J. Harrell, Donald R. Curtis and Lee Turner, Defendants.*

Federal Defendants' Status Report, in Civil no. 96-1481-JE in the United States District Court for the District of Oregon, *Robson Bonnichsen et al., Plaintiffs, v. United States of America et al., Defendants.*

Federal Defendants' Supplemental Status Report, in Civil no. 96-1481-JE in the United States District Court for the District of Oregon, *Robson Bonnichsen et al., v. United States of America et al.*

Federal Defendants' Response to Plaintiffs' Supplement to Plaintiffs' Second Quarterly Status Report, in Civil no. 96-1481-JE in the United States District Court for the District of Oregon, *Bonnichsen et al., v. United States of America et al.*

Federal Defendants' Second Quarterly Status Report, in Civil no. 96-1481-JE in the United States District Court for the District of Oregon, *Bonnichsen et al., v. United States of America et. al.*

Federal Defendants' Supplement to Second Quarterly Status Report, in Civil no. 96-1481-JE in the United States District Court for the District of Oregon, *Bonnichsen et al., v. United States of America et al.*

Federal Defendants' Third Quarterly Status Report, in Civil no. 96-1481-JE in the United States District Court for the District of Oregon, *Bonnichsen et al., v. United States of America et al.*

Federal Defendants' Supplement to Third Quarterly Status Report, in Civil no. 96-1481-JE in the United States District Court for the District of Oregon, *Bonnichsen et al., v. United States of America et al.*

Federal Defendants' Fourth Quarterly Status Report, in Civil no. 96-1481-JE in the United States District Court for the District of Oregon, *Bonnichsen et al., v. United States of America et al.*

Federal Defendants' Fifth Quarterly Status Report, in Civil no. 96-1481-JE in the United States District Court, District of Oregon, *Bonnichsen et al., v. United States of America et al.*

Federal Defendants' Sixth Quarterly Status Report, in Civil no. 96-1481-JE in the United States District Court, District of Oregon, *Bonnichsen et al., v. United States of America et al.*

Jelderks, Magistrate Judge, in the United States District Court for the District of Oregon.

Opinion in Civil no. 96-1481-JE, *Robson Bonnichsen et al., Plaintiffs, v. United States of America et al., Defendants*, 27 June 1997.

Order in Civil no. 96-1481-JE, *Bonnichsen et al., v. United States of America et al.*, 19 February 1997.

Order in Civil no. 96-1481-JE, *Bonnichsen et al., v. United States of America et al.*, 15 May 1998.

Order in Civil no. 96-1481-JE, *Bonnichsen et al., v. United States of America et al.*, 29 May 1998.

Order in Civil no. 96-1481-JE, 12 June 1998.

Order in Civil no. 96-1481-JE, 31 August 1998.

Plaintiffs' Status Report for 1 October 1997, in Civil no. 96-1481-JE in the

United States District Court for the District of Oregon, *Bonnichsen et al., v. United States of America et al.*

Plaintiffs' Supplemental Status Report, in Civil no. 96-1481-JE in the United States District Court for the District of Oregon, *Bonnichsen et al., v. United States of America et al.*

Supplement to Plaintiffs' Second Quarterly Status Report, in Civil no. 96-1481-JE in the United States District Court for the District of Oregon, *Bonnichsen et al., v. United States of America et al.*

Second Supplement to Plaintiffs' Second Quarterly Status Report, in Civil no. 96-1481-JE in the United States District Court for the District of Oregon, *Bonnichsen et al., v. United States of America et al.*

Plaintiffs' Status Report for 1 January 1998, in Civil no. 96-1481-JE in the United States District Court for the District of Oregon, *Bonnichsen et al., v. United States of America et al.*

Plaintiffs' 1 October 1998 Status Report, in Civil no. 96-1481-JE in the United States District Court for the District of Oregon, *Bonnichsen et al., v. United States of America et al.*

Plaintiffs' Status Report for 1 April 1998, in Civil no. 96-1481-JE in the United States District Court for the District of Oregon, *Bonnichsen et al., v. United States of America et al.*

Plaintiffs' Quarterly Status Report, in Civil. no. 96-1481-JE in the United States District Court for the District of Oregon, *Bonnichsen et al., v. United States of America et al.*, January 1, 1999.

Summons in a Civil Case no. 96-1481-JE in the United States District Court, District of Oregon. *Robson Bonnichsen, C. Loring Brace, George W. Gill, C. Vance Haynes, Richard L. Jantz, Douglas W. Owsley, Dennis J. Stanford, and D. Gentry Steele, v. United States of America, Department of the Army, U.S. Army Corps of Engineers, Ernest J. Harrell, Donald R. Curtis and Lee Turner.*

MAPS

Duk-Rodkin, A., and O.L. Hughes. "Quaternary Geology of the Northeastern Part of the Central Mackenzie Valley Corridor, District of Mackenzie, Northwest Territories," *Geological Survey of Canada Bulletin* 458, 1995.

Duk-Rodkin, A., D.G. Forese, and D.S. Lemmen "Late Pleistocene ice coverage and retreatal stages of the Cordilleran and continental glaciers, N.W., Canada." In *Geological atlas of the northern Canadian mainland sedimentary basin*, in preparation. Geological Survey of Canada.

Lemmen, D.S., A. Duk-Rodkin, J. Bednarski, and T. Robertson. "Paleogeography of the Mackenzie River Drainage Basin During the Last Glaciation." Terrain Sciences Division, Geological Survey of Canada.

"Kennewick Quadrangle, Washington." 7.5 minute series (topographic). United States Department of the Interior, Geological Survey, photorevised 1973.

McNary Lock and Dam, Columbia River, Oregon and Washington. Segment "Q" Map. U.S. Army Corps of Engineers. Audited 27 October 1972.

McNary Lock and Dam, Columbia River, Oregon and Washington. Segment "P" Map. U.S. Army Corps of Engineers. Audited 27 October 1972.

McNary Lock and Dam, Columbia River, Oregon and Washington. Segment "R" Map. U.S. Army Corps of Engineers. Audited 27 October 1972.

Maps of Franklin and Benton County and Columbia River at Columbia Park showing state ownership of aquatic lands. Washington State Department of Natural Resources.

# Index